A MODERN BOOK OF ESTHETICS

A Modern Book of

ESTHETICS

AN ANTHOLOGY
Third Edition

Edited with Introduction and Notes by

MELVIN RADER
University of Washington

Holt, Rinehart and Winston
New York • Chicago • San Francisco
Toronto • London

February, 1966

Library of Congress Catalog Card Number: 60-8597
Copyright © 1935, 1952, 1960 by Holt, Rinehart and Winston, Inc.

27321 - 0510

Printed in the United States of America

ACKNOWLEDGMENTS

Grateful acknowledgment is made to the following persons and publishers who have kindly granted permission to quote from copyrighted works:

Lee and Pembertons, the author's executors, and Macmillan and Company, Ltd.: *Space, Time and Deity,* by Samuel Alexander, 1934.

Charles Scribner's Sons and Sheed and Ward, Ltd.: *Art and Scholasticism,* by Jacques Maritain, 1930.

Charles Scribner's Sons and Constable and Company: *The Sense of Beauty,* by George Santayana, copyright 1896 by Charles Scribner's Sons and 1924 by George Santayana.

Oxford University Press: *What Is Art?* by Leo Tolstoy, in the "World's Classics" series, translated by Aylmer Maude, copyright 1930 by the Oxford University Press. For this version, Tolstoy wrote a Preface saying: "I request all who are interested in my views of art only to judge of them by the work in its present shape."

St. Martin's Press and Macmillan and Company, Ltd.: *The Origins of Art,* by Yrjö Hirn, 1900; and executors of the Estate of S. H. Butcher: *Aristotle's Theory of Poetry and Fine Art,* edited and translated by S. H. Butcher, Third Edition, 1902.

Doubleday and Company: *Laughter,* by Henri Bergson, from the book *Comedy,* copyright 1956 by Wylie Sypher, which contains *Laughter* by Henri Bergson.

The Rice Institute: *The Breviary of Aesthetic,* by Benedetto Croce, 1915.

Mrs. Gladys C. Quinton and Macmillan and Company, Ltd.: *Aesthetic,* by Benedetto Croce, translated by Douglas Ainslee, Second Edition, 1922, reprinted by permission of the owner of the copyright, Mrs. Gladys C. Quinton, Edinburgh, Scotland.

Harper & Brothers and the Syndics of the University Press, Cambridge: *Art and Reality,* by Joyce Cary, copyright © 1958 by Arthur Lucius Michael Cary and David Alexander Ogilvie, executors of the Joyce Cary estate.

The Macmillan Company and George Allen and Unwin, Ltd.: *The Will to Power,* by Friedrich Nietzsche, 1910; *The Interpretation of Dreams,* by Sigmund Freud, Revised Edition, 1937; and *A Study in Aesthetics,* by Louis Arnaud Reid, 1931.

Hogarth Press and Basic Books: "The Relation of the Poet to Day Dreaming," Volume IV of *Collected Papers,* by Sigmund Freud, 1925.

Hogarth Press: *The Artist and Psycho-Analysis* (Hogarth Essays), by Roger Fry, 1924.

Harcourt, Brace and Company and Routledge and Kegan Paul, Ltd.: *Modern Man in Search of a Soul,* by Carl Gustav Jung, 1934; *Practical Criticism,* by I. A. Richards, 1929; and *Technics and Civilization,* by Lewis Mumford, 1934.

Liveright Publishers and George Allen and Unwin, Ltd.: *Introductory Lectures on Psycho-Analysis,* by Sigmund Freud, 1922, Revised Second Edition, 1929.

International Publishers and Lawrence and Wishart, Ltd.: *Illusion and Reality,* by Christopher Caudwell, 1947.

G. P. Putnam's Sons: *Art as Experience,* by John Dewey, copyright 1934 by John Dewey.

The Macmillan Company and Cambridge University Press: *Science and the Modern World*, by Alfred North Whitehead, 1925.

G. E. M. Anscombe and Basil Blackwell and Mott, Ltd.: *Philosophical Investigations*, by Ludwig Wittgenstein, 1953.

Morris Weitz and Thomas Munro, editor of *The Journal of Aesthetics and Art Criticism*: "The Role of Theory in Aesthetics," by Morris Weitz, in *The Journal of Aesthetics and Art Criticism*, Volume 15, September 1956.

A. A. Kassman, Honorary Secretary and Editor of the Aristotelian Society: "Art and Imagination," by Margaret Macdonald, in *Proceedings of the Aristotelian Society*, Volume 53, 1953.

Macmillan and Company, Ltd.: *Three Lectures on Aesthetic*, by Bernard Bosanquet, 1915; and *Oxford Lectures on Poetry*, by Andrew Cecil Bradley, 1909.

Thomas Y. Crowell Company: *Aesthetic Analysis*, by D. W. Prall, 1936.

Charles W. Morris and the editors of the *Kenyon Review*: "Science, Art, and Technology," by Charles Morris, *Kenyon Review*, Volume I (1939).

Charles Scribner's Sons and Routledge and Kegan Paul, Ltd.: *Problems of Art*, by Susanne K. Langer, copyright © 1957 by Susanne K. Langer.

University of California Press: *Art and Visual Perception*, by Rudolf Arnheim, 1954.

I. A. Richards and Routledge and Kegan Paul, Ltd.: *Science and Poetry*, by I. A. Richards, Revised Second Edition, 1935.

Navin Sullivan and Alfred A. Knopf, Inc.: *Beethoven: His Spiritual Development*, copyright 1927 by J. W. N. Sullivan.

Yale University Press: *The Analysis of Art*, by DeWitt H. Parker, 1926.

University of Chicago Press: *Art and the Social Order*, by D. W. Gotshalk, 1947; and "Style," by Meyer Schapiro, in *Anthropology Today*, edited by A. L. Kroeber, 1953.

Cambridge University Press: *The Beautiful*, by Vernon Lee, 1913.

F. C. Bartlett, editor of *British Journal of Psychology*: " 'Psychical Distance' as a Factor in Art and an Aesthetic Principle," by Edward Bullough, *British Journal of Psychology*, Volume V (1913).

José Ortega y Gasset: *La Deshumanización del Arte*, by José Ortega y Gasset, Revista de Occidente, Madrid, 1925.

Bollingen Foundation and John Murray, Ltd.: *The Nude: A Study in Ideal Form*, by Kenneth Clark, copyright 1956 by the Trustees of the National Gallery of Art, Washington, D.C.

The Prang Educational Company: *The Principles of Art Education*, by Hugo Münsterberg, 1905.

International Publishers and George Allen and Unwin, Ltd.: *The Foundations of Aesthetics*, by C. K. Ogden, I. A. Richards, and James Wood, 1922.

Princeton University Press: *The Arts and the Art of Criticism*, by Theodore Meyer Greene, 1940.

Harvard University Press: *The Basis of Criticism in the Arts*, by Stephen Coburn Pepper, copyright 1945 by the President and Fellows of Harvard College.

The editors of *The Journal of Philosophy*: "Isolationist and Contextualist Esthetics: Conflict and Resolution," by Melvin Rader, *Journal of Philosophy*, Volume 44 (1947); and Thomas Munro, editor of *The Journal of Aesthetics and Art Criticism*: "The Artist as Outsider," by Melvin Rader, *Journal of Aesthetics and Art Criticism*, Volume 16 (1958). (A few brief excerpts from these articles are included in the Introduction to the present volume.)

PREFACE

IN PREPARING THIS THIRD EDITION, I have freely interpreted the word "modern" in the title, *A Modern Book of Esthetics*, not limiting the selections to recent writers. In addition, I have included works that have appeared since January 1952, the date of the Revised Edition. A number of the authors quoted—Tolstoy, Croce, Freud, and Richards—are represented by more ample selections than hitherto. The few very brief excerpts—as in the case of Wilde—present an idea no more tersely than in the original source. I have avoided snippity fragments, but I have counted brevity a virtue if the original thought is unmutilated.

The selections are varied to avoid one-sidedness and to present supplementary or conflicting viewpoints. The major arts are discussed: music, architecture, painting, literature, the industrial arts, etc. The book is planned and the selections classified to cover, within the necessary limits of space, almost the entire field of esthetics.

There are many possible ways of classifying the selections, and no classification can be perfectly neat unless the original essays are arbitrarily selected and distorted to fit it. I have found in teaching that the classification I have adopted is very serviceable, but the divisions are not sharp and the selections overlap and interlock in a great variety of ways.

Part One is devoted primarily to the *definition* of art, with emphasis upon the creative process; Part Two discusses the work of art; and Part Three emphasizes the appreciation and criticism of esthetic objects. In the Introduction I have comprehensively discussed the meaning of art, and in Introductory Notes to the chapters I have tried to clarify and interrelate the selections, and to provide a context for their more adequate interpretation.

It has not always been possible to follow the advice that I have received in preparing this edition, but I am none the less grateful. Thanks for generous suggestions and criticism are due to the following individuals: Henry D. Aiken, John Alford, William Barrett, Marvin J. Eisenberg, D. W. Gotshalk, Arnold Isenberg, Harriett Jeffery, Iredell Jenkins, Mortimer J. Kadish, Susanne K. Langer, Ian McGreal, A. I. Melden, Richard M. Millard, Ransom Patrick, Julius Portnoy, Harold R. Smart, Cynthia Schuster, Arthur Smullyan and Glenn Wiprud. I am also indebted to Marion Stanton for her expert assistance as a librarian, to Charlotte Utting for efficient typing of the manuscript, and to my wife, Virginia Rader, for many hours of illuminating conversation about the arts.

University of Washington,　　　　　　　　　　　　　　　　M. R.
January 8, 1960.

CONTENTS

FOUR: ART AS INTUITION, 77

FIVE: ART AS WISH-FULFILLMENT, 116

PART TWO
The Work of Art

PART THREE

Appreciation and Criticism

FIFTEEN: CRITICISM, 447

APPENDIX, 486

BIBLIOGRAPHY, 505

INDEX, 535

INTRODUCTION

The Meaning of Art

I. *The Question of Definition*

A NATURAL OBJECT, such as the song of a meadowlark, has esthetic qualities; and therefore esthetics, which is the theory of esthetic objects and experiences, applies both to natural objects and to works of art. In appreciating the latter, we respond not only to sensuous qualities and forms but to technical, psychological, and cultural values—to the *human* expressiveness of the works. The writers represented in the present anthology have a great deal to say about natural objects, but their main emphasis is upon art; and it is art that I now wish to discuss.

As we turn the pages of this book, we find that art is interpreted in many ways. Among the primary concepts employed are play, illusion, imitation, beauty, emotional expression, imagination, intuition, wish-fulfillment, pleasure, technique, sensuous surface, meaning, form, function, empathy, abstraction, esthetic distance, and isolation. At first glance, these concepts represent a bewildering diversity of opinion; but careful study will reveal that much of this disagreement is merely nominal. Terms such as "imagination," "form," "meaning," and "distance" indicate different facets of a rich and varied subject rather than mutually exclusive definitions. Some of the terms refer primarily to the creation of art, others to the art object, and still others to the act of appreciation. Many unnecessary disputes, as Morris Weitz has suggested, can be avoided if esthetic labels are not pasted in one piece on the whole body of art, but rather are applied separately to the various constituents of the creative process, the esthetic artifact, and the esthetic experience.[1] In his essay "The Role of Theory in Esthetics," Weitz concludes that art is too complex and variable to reduce to a single definition. Each of the classical "definitions" calls attention to an important aspect of art, or recommends some criterion of esthetic excellence—but there is no sharp demarcation or eternal essence that a definition can formulate.

Ludwig Wittgenstein's strain of thought, which underlies Weitz's argument, raises issues too complex and far-reaching for discussion in this brief In-

[1] Cf. *Philosophy of the Arts* (Harvard University Press, Cambridge, 1950), p. 2.

troduction. Let us agree with Wittgenstein that art, like religion and science, cannot be reduced to a simple notion. But there is much more of a consensus among writers on art than appears on the surface. In *An Introduction to Aesthetics* (London, 1950), Professor E. F. Carritt quotes from over forty representative estheticians, ancient and modern, to illustrate the recognition in all ages that art, as a creative process, is the expression of mood, feeling, or spirit. That art is expressive rather than merely formal or descriptive is about as well established as any fact in the whole field of esthetics.

This statement may seem to slight the role that Imitation and Form have played in the history of esthetic theory. But if we look beyond the label to the substance of these theories we find that they do not differ radically from the doctrine of expression. Neither Plato nor Aristotle, for example, favors imitation in the sense of non-expressive copying. Plato refers to the painters and poets that he condemns as mere imitators; but in many passages, he recognizes the existence and value of artistic inspiration, which is non-imitative in any literal sense. According to the *Laws, Phaedrus, Symposium,* and *Ion,* the highest art is inspired by a direct vision of the pure eternal forms of Beauty, Truth, Goodness, and the like. Plato's conclusion, in the *Republic,* is that "the real artist, who knew what he was imitating, would be interested in realities and not in imitations." [2]

In the *Poetics,* Aristotle maintains that poetry has sprung from the mimetic impulse and the instinct for harmony and rhythm. He thus recognizes form as no less fundamental than imitation—indeed, the importance of unity and design is emphasized throughout his essay. The reality imitated, he indicates, is human life and human nature—acts expressive of spirit. An act viewed merely as an external process is not the true object of esthetic imitation. A work of art imitates its original, not as it is in itself but as it *appears* to the senses and imagination. Accordingly the poet ought to prefer "probable impossibilities to possible improbabilities," that is to say, he should aim at convincing semblance. If literal truth is stranger than fiction, then all the worse for truth in the literal sense. Art imitates the *universal;* it expresses the real, rid of irrelevancies and the disturbances of chance; it exhibits the common designs of destiny; it is in this sense more philosophical than history. Tragic characters are "imitated" not as they are but as they "ought to be," displaying a lofty nobility and greatness despite their tragic flaws. In the *Politics,* Aristotle contends that music is, in a sense, the *most* imitative of the arts. "In rhythms and melodies," he declares, "we have the most realistic representations of actual anger and benevolence. . . . Melodies have the power of representing character in themselves. . . . There seems to be a sort of kinship of harmonies and rhythms to our souls." [3]

Such ancient doctrines of imitation and their modern analogues are not

[2] *Republic* (translated by Benjamin Jowett), X, #599.
[3] Translated by E. F. Carritt, *Philosophies of Beauty* (Oxford University Press, New York, 1931), p. 34.

opposed to the expressionist thesis. They recognize, perhaps implicitly, that the artist presents his *evaluative* interpretation of reality, and thereby is expressing his thought and feeling.

Likewise, formalist doctrines should not be regarded as antithetical to the principle of expression. Plato, again to cite his ideas as illustrative, emphasized form as having a profound affinity to spirit and as thus providing a necessary basis for the expression and cultivation of the human soul. He saw that esthetic experience is shot through with formal characteristics—with rhythm, harmony, design—the collaboration of which constitutes the whole. He believed that esthetic education, especially in the early and most formative years of life, would cultivate the habit of seeing things thus in context, in their unity and inward coherence. Little by little, the mind would develop its power of imaginative sympathy, its intuitive sense of order, until the feeling for likeness and fellowship and harmony would become second nature, almost an instinct. The reason that he wanted to censor art is not that he valued it so little but that he valued it so much. He was wrong, I think, in his desire to censor but right in his emphasis upon form and his estimate of art and esthetic education. When thoroughly ingrained and integral to the psyche, esthetic culture impresses the sense of interrelatedness upon the deepest levels of the mind. Without such a deep spontaneous appreciation of vivid qualities, in their mutual relevance and interfusion, there could be little feeling for the unity of life or the spiritual integration of a community.

If we turn from Plato to another great formalist, Immanuel Kant, we find less emphasis upon the moral and political uses of art and greater emphasis upon the isolation and disinterestedness of the esthetic experience. Conceiving fine art as the free creation of beauty for beauty's sake, Kant discovered the essence of beauty in design enjoyed simply for itself. There is an harmonious play of our faculties—a dynamic equilibrium of sense, feeling, imagination, and understanding—which corresponds to, and is stimulated by, the work of art. This harmonious state must be communicable, for one mark of art is its sharability. Thus form is both outward and inward—the design of the work and the harmony of the mind—and the sensuous medium is the vehicle for the communication of form, in this twofold sense. Genius, the talent that creates beautiful works of art, is characterized in addition by *Geist*—"soul" or "spirit"—which is the faculty of conceiving and expressing "esthetical ideas." Such ideas, unlike the concepts of science, have a profundity and connotativeness that can not be put into definite meanings. They provide the elusive and inexhaustible significance that characterizes every great work of art and that gives such mysterious depth to form. Now this theory, although it may be called formalist, is no far cry from the doctrine of expression.

Neither imitation nor form, taken as exclusive, could be considered the defining mark of art, whereas expression comes much closer to the required degree of generality. The expressionist theory, when adequately formulated, incorporates the insights involved in the other two theories, treating the representational and formal elements as the means of expression. Not mere imitation but *expressive* imitation, not mere form but *expressive* form, has artistic point and relevance. The recognition of this fact constitutes the central standpoint of modern esthetics.

Of course, there is some disagreement about what side or aspect of the human mind is expressed in art. In the present book, for example, Maritain emphasizes the intellect; Santayana, pleasure; Croce and Bergson, intuition; Freud, desire and the unconscious; Véron and Tolstoy, emotion; Morris, the sense of values; Bosanquet and Dewey, the mind as an organic whole. But even here it is possible to exaggerate the differences. Freud agrees with Santayana that art is surcharged with pleasure, and with Tolstoy that it expresses emotions and not merely desires. Maritain agrees with Santayana in emphasizing beauty and in defining beauty in terms of pleasure; and he meets Croce and Bergson halfway when he declares that esthetics should recognize both intellectual and intuitive factors in art. So likewise every other writer in the book tends to reach out to embrace the truth represented by other thinkers.

Art, like every creative enterprise, is fluid and "open," and no tight definition will serve. But it is well to try to define what we are concerned with in this book—otherwise our ideas will be too hazy or chaotic. The extent to which estheticians disagree has been exaggerated; their considerable measure of agreement provides a basis for a tentative, working definition. Rather than the advice of Wittgenstein, "Beware of definition," I prefer the guiding principle, "Seek definition *but distrust it.*" This recognizes the virtue of defining while adding the necessary note of caution.

II. *The Expression of Values*

Among the writers represented in this anthology, a number declare that art is expressive of "values" or "appreciations." Alfred North Whitehead maintains that in art "the concrete facts are so arranged as to elicit attention to particular values which are realizable through them. . . . The habit of art is the habit of enjoying vivid values." Louis Arnaud Reid contends that a work of art embodies "value . . . to be savored and enjoyed," and that great art is the means to "appreciation of great values." Charles Morris defines art as "the language for the communication of values." "In works of art," he declares, "men and women have embodied their experience of value, and these experiences are communicable to those who perceive the molded medium." Hugo Münsterberg declares that "the scientist works toward laws where the artist seeks values, the scientist explains where the artist appreciates." Nietzsche asserts: ". . . When a man loves, he is a good liar about himself and to himself: he seems to himself transfigured, stronger, richer, more perfect; he *is* more perfect. . . . *Art* here has an organic function: we find it present in the most angelic instinct "love"; we find it as the great stimulus to life—thus art is sublimely utilitarian, even in the fact that it lies. . . . But we should be wrong to halt at its power to lie: it does more than merely imagine; it actually transposes values. And it not only transposes the *feeling* for values: the lover actually *has* a greater value; he is stronger." I sympathize with these views, and I think that this sort of approach to art is the most illuminating. Art is the expression of values, or—what amounts to the same concept—the expression of appreciations.

All the writers in this book support, in some measure, this point of view. They all maintain that a work of art is not the report of a bare matter of fact, but the projection of the artist's inspiration, his emotions, preferences, appreciations, or sense of values. I do not mean that they all adopt the phrase "expression of values"—other terms are most often employed; but despite the divergences in terminology, there is almost universal agreement that art is a spiritual language, expressing subjective valuations rather than formulating objective descriptions.

The pivot of this doctrine is the distinction between facts and values. Let us therefore carefully examine this distinction. "X is square" is judged a *fact* if a number of competent observers, upon carefully measuring X, find it to be square. Science is the coordination of facts, and the very meaning of a fact, or of a scientific truth as the accurate description of facts, is that it can meet the test of *social* verification. The distinguishing mark of science is its public character, the result of a process of abstraction, generalization, and collective verification; no belief has scientific validity so long as it remains private, the esoteric object of a single individual's perspective. It must be transmitted and interpreted to others and substantiated by them; it must be verified by stubborn and irreducible data, admitted by all qualified observers. It must be consistent with established laws and theories, which in turn have been verified by scientists living and dead. Science is therefore appropriately characterized by Charles Peirce and Josiah Royce as a "community of interpretation."

A *value,* on the other hand, is a quality that excites appreciation. Art, as value-expressive, springs from attitudes of appraisal. It does not reflect existence as merely neutral and colorless; it selects, distorts, and intensifies. What Francis Bacon wrote about poetry applies to all art: ". . . It doth raise and erect the Mind, by submitting the show of things to the desires of the Mind, whereas reason doth buckle and bow the Mind unto the Nature of things." [4] Thus a natural landscape is valued esthetically because it has certain qualities, but some other of its qualities will be quite indifferent or unsatisfactory. An artist intent upon expressing the positive values of the landscape would select the qualities he appreciates and express these, and not the indifferent features. The only way he can do so is to remodel the landscape by means of imagination.

Values, in contrast with facts, are often merely imaginary. "Possibility,"

[4] *The Proficience and Advancement of Learning,* 1605, II, xiii.

as Emily Dickinson has said, "is a fairer house than Prose." [5] Even when values are not possibilities envisaged by the imagination, they are always related to our appreciative attitudes, which *may* be quite private and peculiar. Whereas facts have a uniform character for a community of observers, values have a variable character depending upon the subjective preferences of the individual appreciator. But, as I shall explain in some detail, this variability can be confined within limits; and through art, values attain a kind of social objectivity that is quite different from the objectivity of science.

Values are expressed in the creative activity of the artist whenever he purposefully creates the objective occasions for appreciations. Usually he communicates attitudes of valuation by supplying an appropriate object—namely, a work of art—to another mind; but the object may be created for the artist himself to contemplate as the adequate ground for his own appreciative attitudes. The problem of the artist is to find the objective forms and qualities that will induce the person who contemplates them to discover in the object the values that he wishes to embody. If he succeeds in doing this he has "expressed" the values. This does not mean that the values which the artist expresses need be completely in mind before he starts work: Beethoven in writing a symphony or Michelangelo in decorating the Sistine Chapel must have elaborated his inward vision in the process of objectifying—and it is this inward vision that is expressed.

The problem of the contemplator is somewhat different. The work of art that he beholds consists of an array of signs which he must interpret. It is for him, himself, to supply the sense of values to which these signs correspond. It will depend upon him whether the work awakens to life in his imagination or remains dead and inexpressive. He must evoke from within himself the appropriate attitudes—and thereby intensify his qualitative appreciation of the object—in which he thus discovers the values that the artist has embodied. If he succeeds in doing all this he has "expressed" values in contemplation; since his own activity is, like all interpretative art, essentially creative. From the standpoint of the artist and also from that of the contemplator, art is the expression of values—though we should distinguish between the free expression of the artist and the interpretative expression of the contemplator. Croce, in particular, insists that contemplation is thus expressive, and I think he is right.

III. *The Community of Appreciation*

Science describes facts; art expresses values. It would *seem*, therefore, that science has a collective and impersonal character that art lacks. Science, it may be argued, deals with the more permanent, public, and universal elements of experience; art with the more fleeting, private, and particular elements. Now this contrast has some basis, but I believe that it is a mistake to set up such a sharp

[5] *The Poems of Emily Dickinson* (Little, Brown, Boston, 1932), p. 289.

dichotomy. Gregory Vlastos has pointed out that *both* art and science are essentially communal. "In science," he has written, "one finds truth only insofar as one recasts one's private insight into its most universally sharable form, thus placing it at the disposal of all. Scientific truth is discovered in a community of inquiry in which there is the minimum of hoarding and the maximum of sharing—where each receives the fruit of the labors of others and gives back to the utmost of his ability." Artistic expression is similarly interpersonal: "Beauty is created only in a process of communication wherein the product of individual originality becomes the common possession of mankind. . . . The creator must lose to find himself, lose a subjective intuition to recover it as objective form." [6] Art is man's supreme means of socializing the world of appreciations. By communicating the "incommunicable," art creates a community of appreciation to supplement the community of scientific interpretation. Just as the objectivity of science implies the recognition of a "common world" of describable objects, so the communicability of art implies a "social ego," a common *inner* world of value-appreciation.

A brief discussion of some of the ideas of Josiah Royce, a writer not generally regarded as an esthetician, will help to make clear what we mean by a community of appreciation. A recurrent theme in his books is the contrast between "the world of description" and "the world of appreciation." The world of description is the realm of science—an abstraction from experience of its most communicable aspects. To be describable, the data of experience must be "public"—the same for all qualified observers; and hence the rich, variegated, subjective, fleeting immediacies of experience must be thinned down to pointer readings, or at least to some order and fixity of type, whereby each person's interpretations can be precisely the same as his neighbor's. Such abstract characteristics as number, shape, weight, and spatial and temporal relations, are the most exact and describable. Less so, but still in some measure describable, are such qualities as heat, yellow, or hardness. Comparatively indescribable are the nuances of our inner life. These latter "appreciations," according to Royce, must therefore be excluded from science.

Yet every immediate experience has its appreciative aspect. "That is, it feels to me so or so. I like it or I hate it. Or again, where pleasure and pain aren't marked, still there is an essentially indescribable value that my experience has for me when regarded just as my own feeling. Tastes have one sort of worth for me, colors another. An electric shock from a Leyden jar is appreciated as a peculiar and atrocious interruption of all other trains of feeling, such that its painful value is surely, but inexpressibly, different from that of all other experiences." [7] This appreciative side of life, according to Royce, eludes all our

[6] Gregory Vlastos, "The Religious Foundations of Democracy, Fraternity, and Equality," *Journal of Religion*, Vol. 22 (1942), pp. 152-153.
[7] Josiah Royce, *The Spirit of Modern Philosophy* (Houghton, Mifflin, Boston, 1892), p. 389.

scientific categories and exact measures. Its vivid qualities are too individual, subjective, and personal, too secret and fugitive, too inexpressibly different, to be caught within the web of science. Not the peculiar and private "feel" of things but the observable fact, not the appreciation but the description, give outer truth, and hence a communicable content.

According to Royce, the world of description is, in a sense, real, but superficial. If you are describing a friend, you can indicate his height, his weight, the color of his hair and eyes, even his intelligence quotient; but this leaves out what endears him to you. You can "explain" the sunset according to uniform natural laws, but this leaves out its radiance. All that we value most, Royce believes, falls within the world of appreciation, and yet, he sometimes seems to say, there is no language for this world comparable to the exact language of science. Whereas *facts* are publicly observable and hence describable, *appreciations* are not thus public: we are not mind readers—we cannot *observe* the appreciations within another mind. Yet it is precisely in this realm that there is the greatest need of community: the need of sympathy and understanding and spiritual integration without which life is an arid waste.

Royce tries to secure such a community upon the basis of moral and religious activity: above all, through the virtue of loyalty. Believing that the detached individual is a lost soul, he attempts to transcend the incommunicability of appreciative experiences by "the willing and practical and thoroughgoing devotion of a person to a cause." But this is to put the cart before the horse. Loyalty itself must rest upon social sympathy, and it is therefore dependent upon a community of appreciation. It is easy to say as Royce does, "Live as if thine and thy neighbor's life were one to thee." But how can you do so if there is no way to share your appreciations by means of a vivid and effective language? Although in one of his later works, *The Problem of Christianity*, Royce states that art is a mode of social interpretation, he fails to elaborate his meaning. Hence his account of community remains a bit fragmentary and unconvincing.

In his earlier book, *The Spirit of Modern Philosophy*, he makes the problem unnecessarily difficult by exaggerating the dualism between the world of description and the world of appreciation. Within limits, appreciations *are* describable. Psychologists such as William James, Edward Titchener, Sigmund Freud, and Wolfgang Köhler have acutely described many aspects of the inner life of feeling and volition. Although such descriptions are less exact than the mathematical formulations of modern physics, they are sometimes very illuminating.

There is, however, a profound difference between the scientific account of mental vagaries by a psychologist and the artistic expression of a neurotic's "appreciations" by a novelist such as Dostoevsky. In the former case we are dealing with abstractions; in the latter, with the immediacies of vivid experience as kindled in the mind by imagination. There can be not only *some* description of our appreciations, but also the imaginative expression of the whole world of appreciation by means of art.

Let me sum up what I have been saying. Although art is obviously a mode of self-expression, it also is social. Just as there is a community of scientists engaged in the cooperative search for facts and using the language of description, so there is a community of artists engaged in the cooperative search for values and using the "language" of appreciations. Art is the expression of values, both individual and social.

IV. *The Creative Process*

In the light of the foregoing definition of art, we can characterize art in terms of three standpoints: the creative activity of the artist, the work of art, and the reception of art by the public. Each of these is covered by a Part of the present volume; the divisions are not sharp, yet each Part throws light on all three standpoints. I shall first characterize the creative process.

The activity of the artist, as already stated, is the expression of values. To illustrate, I shall cite the following passage from a letter written by Vincent Van Gogh to his brother: "I should like to paint the portrait of an artist friend, a man who dreams great dreams, who works as the nightingale sings, because it is in his nature. He'll be a fair man. I want to put into my picture my appreciation, the love that I have for him. So I paint him as he is, as faithfully as I can. But the picture is not finished yet. To finish it I am now going to be the arbitrary colorist. I exaggerate the fairness of the hair; I come even to orange tones, chromes, and pale lemon-yellow. Beyond the head, instead of painting the ordinary wall of the mean room, I paint infinity, a plain background of the richest, intensest blue that I can contrive, and by this simple combination of the bright head against the rich blue background I get a mysterious effect, like a star in the depths of an azure sky." [8]

What Van Gogh seeks to communicate through his painting is not a mere factual description; he wishes to paint his "appreciation," his "love," the qualities that excite his preference. He does not literally imitate; faithful reproduction, as he says, is only a point of departure. He imagines the colors and shapes, the contrasts and relationships that will express his sense of values—the mood of appreciation that his friend excites within him.

Yet Van Gogh is not merely expressing his admiration for his friend. He is creating *new* values in the very act of expression. Each color or shape that he paints has a worth of its own. The "rich blue," for example, is beautiful in itself, and it is more beautiful in contrast with the orange shades, the chrome, the pale lemon-yellow. The finished painting can be enjoyed as a pattern of colors and

[8] Irving Stone, *Dear Theo: The Autobiography of Vincent Van Gogh* (Houghton, Mifflin, Boston, 1937), p. 441.

shapes even if it were to be turned upside down so that it is no longer regarded as the representation of a human figure. Many modern pictures, as we all know, do not represent or imitate any natural fact, just as a fugue of Bach does not thus represent or imitate. Since the time of Pythagoras, philosophers have recognized the value-expressiveness of harmonies, rhythms, patterns of color, three-dimensional shapes, and other non-representational elements. One of the merits of certain writers in this anthology, such as Susanne Langer and Rudolf Arnheim, is that they help to explain how such expressiveness occurs.

Many works of art are representational; all works of art have form. Van Gogh, like most artists in the Western tradition, was expressing both representational and formal values. A writer such as Roger Fry, who minimizes representational values, and a writer such as Leo Tolstoy, who minimizes formal values, are both one-sided.

The appreciations expressed by an artist are not separate from their mode of expression. The *what* of art is not separable from the *how*. When James Joyce expresses a shaver's disgust at "the clammy slather of the lather in which the brush was stuck," it is a clammy-slathery disgust that he is expressing. When Picasso expresses serenity with the muted colors and voluminous form of his "Woman in White," it is a color-muted and voluminous serenity that is being expressed. The sadness of music is a peculiarly musical sadness; it is impossible, for instance, to give an adequate verbal phrasing to the majestic sadness of Chopin's Sonata in B Flat Minor. Even in poetry, the values cannot truly be formulated in any other words but that of the poem itself. There is a real creative synthesis, a fusion of mood with sensory configuration. As sensation blends with sensation to create a new quality (for instance, when notes combine to form a chord), so feeling or desire blends with sensation to create the esthetic effect.

To depict the artist as he is sometimes depicted—a kind of spiritual Robinson Crusoe forever marooned within the island of his own subjectivity—is to forget that in art the duality of subject and object disappears. The artist's inner experiences, his appreciative thoughts and moods, are expressed outwardly in the language of sensory qualities. As in dreams, subjective thought and feeling are embodied in sensory images, but in a form communicable to others. The work of art is objective and yet is dyed with emotion and sensibility. It radiates spiritual expressiveness and is thus a link between mind and mind. Art is the only language whereby we can *vividly* transmit our values to others. It breaks down the walls between human beings, and is thus a great solvent of conflict and selfishness. "Love consists in this," the poet Rilke has written, "that two solitudes protect and touch and greet each other." [9] By means of art, the solitudes flow together; love and imaginative understanding become possible.

The artist not only discloses his own moods but transcends his private feelings. He has the singular ability to draw the outer object into his own being—to

[9] Quoted by Walter de la Mare, *Love* (Morrow, New York, 1946), p. 11.

sense its qualities and to feel at one with it. John Keats was reporting more than a personal idiosyncrasy when he wrote: "If a Sparrow come before my Window, I take part in its existence and pick about the gravel." [10] In another letter, Keats described the nature of a poet and cited himself as an example: "A poet is the most unpoetical of anything in existence, because he has no Identity—he is continually in for [sic] and filling some other body. The Sun,—the Moon,—the Sea, and men and women, who are creatures of impulse, are poetical, and have about them an unchangeable attribute; the poet has none, no identity—he is certainly the most unpoetical of all God's creatures. . . . It is a wretched thing to confess; but it is a very fact, that not one word I ever utter can be taken for granted as an opinion growing out of my identical Nature—how can it, when I have no Nature? When I am in a room with people, if I ever am free from speculating on creations of my own brain, then, not myself goes home to myself, but the identity of everyone in the room begins to press upon me, so that I am in a very little time annihilated—not only among men; it would be the same in a nursery of Children." [11] Keats is here describing, in rather paradoxical language, the sensibility that is pre-eminently the artist's but that is shared to a degree by everyone. It is thus that we are "in touch" with other people and things. All of the arts—not simply poetry—cultivate this empathic sensitivity.

V. *The Work of Art*

The work of art conveys the sense of a living presence—it is infused with emotion, instinct with a kind of life. Its beholder reaches out and touches another spirit.

For this reason, idealistic writers such as Croce, Collingwood, and Sartre have maintained that the work of art is spiritual rather than physical. A number of recent philosophers, including Margaret Macdonald in the essay quoted in Chapter VIII, have attacked this position, contending that the work is, at least in many cases, a physical artifact. I am inclined to say that both sides are calling attention to important facts. All parties to the dispute recognize that there is, except in the case of mere imagery, a physical artifact, such as a canvas covered with pigments; but the more idealistic philosophers say that this artifact is only a means to an end, namely, the reproduction of the real work of art in the minds of the beholders, whereas the more materialistic philosophers contend that the physical thing is truly the work of art itself. I think that, as occasions vary, we choose to mean different things by the phrase "work of art," and sometimes our meaning is more akin to Croce's but sometimes more like Miss Macdonald's. A theory such as that of Bosanquet or Alexander, which recognizes both the physical and the mental sides, would seem to be the most adequate.

[10] Letter to Benjamin Bailey, November 22, 1817.
[11] Letter to Richard Woodhouse, October 27, 1818.

The work of art may be defined as an organic unity of value-expressive constituents. The constituents include representations, connotations, and purely sensuous materials, and there is almost no value that cannot be represented, connoted, or sensuously presented. It is therefore impossible to restrict the content of works of art, as Santayana initially and many other writers have tried to do, by limiting it to *beauty*. The content, of course, must be *valued* in concrete terms, and hence must be concretely appreciated. The qualities of the object must be apprehended as, for example, gay, sad, horrible, sublime, or demonic; they must be liked or disliked because of some such concrete value-character; and, I believe, the experience of the work must somehow have intrinsic perceptual worth if it is properly to be called *esthetic*. But no other limitation can be put upon the content of works of art. Not all arts, of course, have the same scope, and it takes all in combination to include, even potentially, every kind of value-content.

Some artists and estheticians agree with Tolstoy and Véron that ugliness may be legitimately introduced into the work of art not merely as a foil to beauty but for the sake of its own independent expressiveness. Others agree with Croce that artistic beauty is simply success in art, or in other words, that the beautiful in art is the completely expressive and the ugly is the inexpressive. Croce's theory would not be seriously transformed if every mention of beauty and ugliness in his pages were deleted: the concepts of expressiveness and inexpressiveness would suffice. Most contemporary artists seem to agree with either Croce or Véron and Tolstoy. Works of art, in the modern mode, have a vast range: they embrace whatever is spiritually expressive, even if the expressiveness is achieved by cacophony in poetry, discords in music, harshness in painting, or unsparing realism in literature.

A work of art, whatever its content, is an organic unity—a concrete structure in which the character of the whole influences the *intrinsic* character of the parts. Every chord in a musical composition, every patch of color in a painting, every sound or image in a poem, attains its meaning and value in its *context*: it is infected through and through by its relations to the other elements and to the whole. This implies that the distinction between form and content is relative: the content is the elements in relation, the form is the relation among the elements, and the total work is both in irrefragable unity. One of the considerable merits of A. C. Bradley's fine essay, "Poetry for Poetry's Sake," is that it vividly describes the work of art in terms of such organic unity.

The question that has most intensely engaged estheticians in the last two decades is not the nature of form or the relation between form and content, but the "meaning" and "truth" of works of art. One of the very lively controversies is concerned with whether art makes "truth claims" and therefore commands belief. On the one hand, we have writers such as I. A. Richards who insist that art is primarily "emotive," and that the work of art does not present verifiable truths. On the other hand, we have writers such as J. W. N. Sullivan and

Theodore M. Greene who believe that much of the great art of the world is distinguished by its truthfulness and profundity in probing the meaning of human existence. I believe that the theory that art is the expression of values provides a basis for answering this question.

If by "truth" one means accurate *description*, Richards is right in maintaining that it falls within the realm of science and not of art. The statement, "The sky is blue," is true in a descriptive sense if it is objectively the case for all qualified observers. But such a truth is quite different from the sentiment expressed in an old hobo song:

> O, why don't you work like other men do?
> How the hell can I work when the sky's so blue?

The *blue* referred to in this song is esthetic, not scientific. It is a value—it has feeling-tone; it is *not* "neutral" for all observers. It is the kind of blue that makes the heart leap up and kick over the traces. Before "blue," as a concept, can become a descriptive term, it must be disinfected of such subjective coloration. Drawn into the sphere of verifiable fact, it has only those features that all can equally acknowledge. These tend to be quantitative, because quantities have a publicly verifiable character. Hence, for exact scientific purposes, "blue" becomes associated with a certain wavelength and frequency. It is scientifically true that an object is blue if it radiates waves of this type. At this level of abstraction, "blue" has completely lost artistic expressiveness; and of course art has nothing to do with "truth" so conceived.

But if by "truth" we mean a value socially communicable, a work of art does indeed contain truths. The "truth" crudely expressed in the hobo song is also social: it has been felt by many hoboes; it appeals to the hobo in all of us. Such a truth can be expressed in a song, a poem, or possibly in a painting. Wordsworth's great sonnet "The world is too much with us," expresses a comparable mood. Such a work of art has a poignancy, a warmth, a vividness, a specificity that withers in a scientific description.

It seems to me that the so-called truths of art can always be so analyzed. They are not abstract formulations; they are concrete evaluations—and consequently no merely prosaic and summary statement can do justice to them. We can say, for example, that Tolstoy, in *War and Peace*, expresses the deterministic interpretation of history that is abstractly formulated in the Appendix to his novel. But surely no one imagines that this Appendix, or any similar abstract formulation, can possibly convey the rich, concrete, warmhearted truth of Tolstoy's story. That truth can be expressed only by the intense *appreciative* visions which the novel itself kindles within the reader's imagination. Whereas scientific truth can usually be translated into quite different language, artistic "truth" cannot thus be translated. In art, as we have already said, *what* is expressed is inseparable from *how* it is expressed.

Noting that a work of art is highly individual and that artists shun mere abstract thought, Benedetto Croce defined art as the knowing of particulars, or intuition, as distinguished from the knowing of universals, or conception. A particular, he supposed, was a unique quality apprehended by an individual mind. His emphasis upon the imaginative inwardness and singularity of art makes it difficult to explain the sharability of the esthetic vision. He failed to note, or at least to emphasize, that qualities may be ever so individualized and still be repeated. The high-fidelity recording of a musical masterpiece by a superb orchestra is a very particularized and unique creation, but it may be issued in thousands of identical copies. Even when the record is played, and the music comes to life in the feeling and imagination of the auditor, its qualities may be essentially the same as in the experience of another listener. In Keats' great *Ode*, the song of the nightingale, which symbolizes the work of art, is no abstract universal, yet it remains the same in the most varied times and places:

> Thou wast not born for death, immortal Bird!
> No hungry generations tread thee down;
> The voice I hear this passing night was heard
> In ancient days by emperor and clown:
> Perhaps the self-same song that found a path
> Through the sad heart of Ruth, when, sick for home,
> She stood in tears amid the alien corn;
> The same that oft-times hath
> Charm'd magic casements, opening on the foam
> Of perilous seas, in faery lands forlorn.[12]

The work of art, like the nightingale's song, is vivid and emotionally toned; but it is as communicable as the most abstract scientific description. When two sensitive beholders contemplate the same work of art, their experiences may not be identical, but they are surely quite similar. The contagiousness of art—its capacity to create a community of appreciation—can be explained upon no other assumption. Art thus involves, even in its uniqueness, a social element: the work of art conveys a *repeatable* particularity.

There is another side to art, the generic, that Croce, with his intuitional theory, tends to deny. Art is both specific and general, intuitional and intellectual: it involves both creative imagination and cognitive insight. What distinguishes an artist from an ordinary person is very largely his ability to imagine some new concrete variation of the old abstract theme. About two-thirds of the poems in the *Oxford Book of English Verse*, for example, deal with love or death, but each one is a unique creation.

The artist *knows*—he does not merely feel—but he knows by sympathetic identification and imaginative insight. He knows as the perspicacious lover

---

[12] In my comment on this passage, I am indebted to Andrew Paul Ushenko, *Dynamics of Art* (Indiana University Press, Bloomington, 1953), pp. 158-159.

knows about the nature of love, by "proving it upon his pulses." He knows by feeling at one with the object, as Keats felt at one with the sparrow. He knows the reality that he suffers when the outer object is drawn into his own being, into the mysterious depths of subjectivity. He knows, not bare facts or abstract laws, but vivid values—he knows things appreciatively, in their immediacy and concreteness. He knows with the totality of his mind-and-body: with sense, mood, instinct, and intelligence, both conscious and subconscious. He knows by descending to the roots of being, which no abstract idea can encompass—to the obscure spring of man's creative intuition—the source alike of dreams and of art.

There, in the deep recesses of his mind, he is in touch with the instinctively common part of man's nature—with the values that are not peculiar to him as an artist nor to one man or a few, but are basic in the emotional experiences and secret longings of most human beings. If it were not so, art could not serve as the language of all humanity—a way of communicating across all the barriers of time and place. The cave-paintings by men of the reindeer age—the paintings at Lascaux and Altamira—would not speak so eloquently to us today; nor would the art of the whole world be a "museum without walls," where any man can find incomparable treasures. The work of all ages and countries—Gothic counterpoint, Egyptian sculpture, Chinese landscape, Mayan temple, Russian ballet, English drama, and American novel—bear alike the spiritual imprint of humanity. In the realm of art, far more than in morals, politics, or religion, the whole world is kin.

The question of whether the communicable content of art properly elicits *belief* is very subtle and complex. In this Introduction I do not have the space to discuss the issue. But my opinion is that the positivistic account of valuation as mere subjective attitude—an account that has strongly influenced Richards—is fraught with insuperable difficulties. One may be truly objective in apprehending values, and an artist sometimes expresses in his work not what he subjectively likes or dislikes, but what he actually finds to be characteristic of the spiritual nature of life. (If some of my readers refuse to call this "truth," I will not quarrel with them. In many works of art there is a kind of value-significance that is faithful to the nature of human existence—call it whatever you will.) A work of art may, in this sense, be as severely subordinated to reality-thinking as a scientific treatise. The tendency of Freud to conceive of art as evasion has only a limited validity. At the same time, the appropriate response to a work of art is *not* belief in abstract factual propositions, but rather a kind of imaginative enactment of value-experience. The imagination must have free play that ordinary literal belief does not permit. In creating or appreciating art—to again quote Keats—the capacity that we need is the "quality . . . which Shakespeare possessed so enormously—I mean *Negative Capability,* that is, when a man is capable of being in uncertainties, mysteries, doubts without any irritable reaching after fact and reason." [13] Only with this freedom of the imagination can the values expressed in works of art be realized in their immediacy and vividness.

VI. *Appreciation and Criticism*

If we turn from the work of art to the audience, we can distinguish between a contemplative and a critical aspect in the audience's reaction. Esthetic contemplation, which is described in the present volume in such terms as "isolation," "psychical distance," "empathy," "abstraction," and "synaesthesis," can be more simply characterized as receptivity to the values expressed by, or embodied in, the esthetic object. It is, so to speak, a "listening" or "looking" or "tasting" with our capacity for value-appreciation. The values are what are to be "tasted" and rolled upon one's appreciative "tongue"; and the attitudes of isolation, distance, empathy, and so forth, are the means of tasting and savoring the values. Of course, "tasting" is a metaphor, but it suggests the nature of contemplation: the throwing oneself open to esthetic values, the development of keenness and breadth of appreciation.

A fundamental issue in Part Three is to be found in the contrast between the writers who emphasize "isolation" and "*high* distance" and the writers who emphasize "context" and "*low* distance." This cleavage between the isolationists and the contextualists appears also in the other Parts of our anthology. Roughly on the side of isolationism are such estheticians as Croce, Fry, Ortega y Gasset, and Münsterberg. Aligned on the other side are such thinkers as Tolstoy, Dewey, Mumford, Clark, and Richards, who emphasize the continuity between esthetic and non-esthetic values rather than their distinctness.

The isolationist type of theory stresses the uniqueness and immediacy of "pure" esthetic experience. Insofar as we concentrate solely upon this component in artistic experience, our senses and concrete imagery *do* fence us off from the world. Insofar as the artist is exclusively absorbed in this phase of art, he concerns himself not with "the why, the whence, or the whither" of things, nor with their general import or ulterior connections, but with "the what" as immediately apprehended. The experience out of which a work of art springs stirs the mind because of no merely ulterior reason, nor because it is a sign or correlate of something absent, but because it is intrinsically moving. The work of art, as the embodiment of such experience, is likewise exciting in its own right, and therefore the beholding of it involves an absorption in certain values as immediately present to sense and imagination. There is truth in such an isolationist theory of art, but we may question whether it is the whole truth.

The conception of art as the expression or appreciation of values lends support to the contextualist view that art is broadly human. Life, in its very essence, is the experience of values; and hence art, which alone can express

[13] Letter to George and Thomas Keats, December 21, 1817.

values concretely, is terribly relevant to life, and is limited in its scope and depth only by its autonomous nature and by the bounds of human life and human genius. Art not only expresses but creates values; for as Nietzsche truly declares: "Valuing is creating: hear it, ye creating ones! Valuation itself is the treasure and jewel of the valued things." [14] Art is thus fundamental to the whole enterprise of living as a means of expression, creation, and appreciation. Art is art, and not morality, religion, technology, or social reform; but neither is it an anodyne or a piddling luxury or an esoteric escape from life. Whether we are speaking of the artist or the contemplator, we should try to reconcile the truth in the isolationist type of theory with the truth in the contextualist type.

The *critical* aspect of esthetic experience consists of *judgment* of the *worth* of the esthetic object. Judgment implies some standard of appraisal; and in Chapter XV we find various standards proposed. But perhaps the basic criterion of art is simply the richness and the fineness of the value-appreciation that it yields. I am using the word "appreciation" not in the superficial sense of amusement or entertainment, but in the deeper sense of a memorable and satisfying experience. We must remember that the worth of any great work of art is not something that can be grasped in a moment. To appreciate and judge an excellent painting, for example, we must do much more than glance at it in a gallery. Ordinarily we must *live* with it until its sensuous qualities, meanings, and forms sink deep into our conscious and subconscious mind. If then, day after day, it works its magic upon us—if its appeal is deep and varied enough to be lasting— we can realize its excellence because our lives are being substantially enriched. The expert critic is one who can sense this amplitude and fineness of value more quickly and surely than the ordinary man.

It should not be overlooked that contemplation and criticism, as Dewey points out, are necessary aspects of the artist's activity and not merely of the public's reaction to his works. No artist can create without appreciating the values that he wishes to express; without contemplating the expressive medium, elements, and forms; and without criticizing the work as it takes shape under his hand. The artist himself is a beholder and judge, and the fineness of his art depends largely upon the quality of his appreciation and judgment. The work of art, on the other hand, comes alive only in imagination, and hence the public must share something of the creative capacity of the artist. There is no absolute distinction between creation and contemplation, between artist and beholder.

VII. *Conclusion*

In my Introduction, I have tried to do justice to the diverse standpoints represented in this anthology, while sketching an inclusive and coherent theory of art. There are many important problems that I have not mentioned, but per-

[14] *Thus Spake Zarathustra* (Macmillan, New York, 1909), p. 74.

haps I have suggested some basis for synthesis and reconciliation of doctrines that might otherwise appear contradictory.

This attempt to resolve conflicts in theory seems to me peculiarly appropriate to esthetics, for art itself is the great reconciler of opposite poles which, in our practical life, ordinarily exclude each other. More than any other form of human experience, it combines such contrasting moments as variety and unity, familiarity and strangeness, repose and stimulation, order and spontaneity, the Appolline and the Dionysian moods. In great tragedy, for example, the extreme intensification of emotions, far from excluding a sense of repose, produces the dynamic calmness which Aristotle terms "catharsis." Likewise, as Freud and Jung point out, art involves the harmonious co-working of the conscious and the subconscious: the dream is inserted into the texture of waking life; the irreal and the real are fused. Or, again as Schiller indicates, art is the reconciliation of law and impulse: the form, the pattern, the "lawfulness" of the experience becomes the expression, not the repression, of impulse. Or, as Lipps and Lee observe, the images of esthetic experience are seemingly objective and yet are colored by the emotion and sensibility of the beholder: the duality of subject and object disappears: the work of art is, in a sense, myself, and I am the object, since I project myself into it. Or, as Aristotle and Maritain understand, the universal essence merges into the specific image; and the more seamless is the unity, the more perfect is the esthetic moment.

Because art, in combining such opposites, is more inclusive than other modes of experience, Schiller, in his *Letters on the Aesthetic Education of Man*, is justified in his contention that it makes man whole, and that man is only whole when he engages in such activity. Likewise John Dewey is right when he declares: "Art is the living and concrete proof that man is capable of restoring consciously, and thus on the plane of meaning, the union of sense, need, impulse, and action characteristic of the live creature." [15]

Art was once at the very center of life's text, but in our scientific and technological age, it tends to be shoved into the margin. No one questions it as a diversion or amusement, but some of us are not satisfied with this conception. We feel that art has a vital function that should be taken seriously even in our colleges and universities. The concept of value-expression helps not only to reconcile conflicts in esthetic theory but to make clear why art is important.

[15] *Art as Experience* (Minton, Balch, New York, 1934), p. 25.

PART ONE

ART AND THE
CREATIVE PROCESS

CHAPTER ONE

Art as Semblance

KONRAD LANGE
Illusion in Play and Art

SAMUEL ALEXANDER
Beauty and Illusion

OSCAR WILDE
Nature's Imitation of Art

Introductory Note

ONE OF THE PERENNIAL THEMES of esthetic theory is the relation of art to nature. In the history of Western thought, the two most influential treatments of this theme are the theory of "imitation," enunciated by Plato and Aristotle, and the theory of "imagination," formulated by Coleridge and other romanticists. The theory of imitation has emphasized the cognitive and realistic elements in art; the theory of imagination has stressed the emotional and purely imaginative factors. These contrasting points of view are synthesized in the interpretations set forth in this chapter. The work of art is conceived as both imitative and imaginative—a convincing semblance that the imagination creates from the data of perception.

As an historian of art at the University of Tübingen, Konrad Lange (1855-1921) elaborated the theory of artistic play that had been suggested by Immanuel Kant and expounded by the great poet, Friedrich Schiller. In his famous *Letters*

3

on the Esthetic Education of Man (1795), Schiller maintained that the source of both play and art is overflowing energy. Even when a lion, for example, is not hungry or mad, it playfully expends its surplus energy through roaring. Similarly the imagination of man enjoys its native power and liberty, although there is perhaps no outward gain to be achieved. Esthetic play, however, requires order and control. Man's esthetic taste directs the spontaneous flow of imagery in which imaginative play consists. Art is thus form imposed by taste upon playful imagistic activity. As in all the higher forms of play, there is a fusion of impulse and law; the rational part of man's nature is united harmoniously with the imaginative and the sensuous. Hence Schiller is able to say, "Man only plays when in the full meaning of the word he is a man, and he is only completely a man when he plays."

In his last two letters on esthetic education, he maintains that the artist is concerned only with appearance, *"Schein,"* as contrasted with literal reality. Taking his cue from this emphasis upon playful illusion, Lange develops an elaborate theory of play and art in his two-volume work, *Das Wesen der Kunst* (1901). Play, he contends, is frequently the "art" of childhood, and art is a mature form of play. Both spring from a surplus of psychic energy and the need for a fuller exercise of human impulses and capacities than actual life permits. Both are essentially forms of "make-believe" or, to use Lange's favorite term, "conscious self-deception," in which the individual escapes from the constriction and humdrum of ordinary existence into a kind of ideal world. The painting, the statue, the poem, or the drama, like the child's doll, lives in the imagination "as if" it were real. Even in the abstract arts, such as music or architecture, art consists of "the illusion of feeling," the sense that these artistic creations palpitate with human emotions and are instinct with a kind of life. In analyzing such conscious self-deception, Lange describes it as a halfway stage between belief and unbelief. This theory, while recognizing the representational function of art, frees the artist from the requirement of literal imitation. It stresses the joy in *creative* activity as fundamental.

Samuel Alexander (1859-1938), the eminent British philosopher, likewise maintains that "the beautiful is illusory," but that "it differs from illusion in that it is not erroneous." One enjoys an appearance while knowing that it is mere appearance. The sadness of a requiem mass, the pride of a statue, or the fearfulness of a tragic drama, exist only for the mind that contemplates them with feeling and imagination. These mind-dependent qualities are called "tertiary" to distinguish them from "primary qualities," such as motions, shapes, and volumes, and "secondary qualities," such as sounds, colors, and textures. As a "realist," Alexander believes that the primary and secondary qualities belong to the real nature of objects independently of the mind that perceives them. Beauty results from "the harmonious blending . . . of these two sets of elements, some existing in reality and some supplied by the mind." But even in imputing tertiary qualities to an object, the beholder is not being whimsical. Esthetic judgment is impersonal or disinterested; it is not, according to Alexander, an expression of mere personal idiosyncrasy.

With his flair for paradox, Oscar Wilde (1856-1900) gave to the theory of illusion an ingenious twist. Instead of maintaining that art imitates nature, he contended that nature imitates art. The artist provides a kind of education of the imagination and the senses, so that we perceive in nature what art has prepared us to see. After the impressionist painters have done their work, we can behold impressionist landscapes that were never discoverable before.

KONRAD LANGE

Illusion in Play and Art

. . . In play as well as in art illusion is involved. There are certain widespread forms of play which can only be called illusion play. We have repeatedly pointed out that a certain kind of illusion is intermixed at times in several games of motion and skill and even in some games of intelligence [such as chess]. But the kinds of play which we shall now consider are directly based upon illusion; the pleasure which they call forth is a pleasure in illusion. The essential feature of them is that the player has the consciousness of playing a role, that is, he imagines himself to be something which he is not, to be doing something which he does not, to be feeling something which he feels not. When children growl or squeak, it is hard to say whether they wish to make a noise which is agreeable to their senses or whether in doing so they pretend to be some animal. When boys run seemingly at random through the woods, it is quite possible that in doing so they play a simple game of motion, but it is also possible that they consider themselves animals or robbers or Hussars. I recollect the time when I read Schwab's *Tales from Classical Antiquity*. I used to throw sedulously with lance-shaped switches at bushes in the garden, and I know I considered this not a simple game of motion but rather a hunting or fighting game. It has even been suggested that the passionate mountain climber thinks of the mountain which he scales, and the gambler thinks of the fate which he challenges, as living beings which he must fight against and which he must overcome.

The favorite illusion game of children is the impersonation of animals. There are cases where the little people quite clearly bark like dogs, moo like cows, neigh like horses, jump like deer, run like hares, etc. Their illusion is so strong that they very much dislike to be called by their names while they are playing. This is plainly a matter of self-deception, for the players certainly know that they are not animals, they only imagine with particular vividness that they are. Naturally, this game would be impossible unless they had a particular interest in animals. And to that extent one can say that the content is important for the vividness of the game. But it is just as certain that the pleasure is not caused by the content in itself, but rather by the play of imagination which is involved. For the idea of being an animal has not the least ethical value for the child; it is no enhancement but rather a degradation of his existence.

A particularly favorite form of the animal game is the hunting game. . . . A perfect play character is found in target shooting and in competitive shooting at wooden birds. And where the child has no opportunity for this it plays "game and hunter" in which one of the players acts as if he were shooting and the other as if he were collapsing under fire. The psychological phase here too consists of conscious self-deception, for both parties know that they are not actually what they pretend to be. And again the content as such is not the decisive factor in arousing enjoyment. For the killed animal finds the same pleasure in the game as the killing hunter. The imaginary experience of wounding, of death, etc., is productive of pleasure only because it is an artistic illusion. The pleasure consists in this case in imagining something which one certainly knows not to be the reality. I do not need to press further the analogy with tragedy.

Also the fighting games are pure illusion games. . . . Even the form of competition in which games of motion and skill generally clothe themselves can be looked at from the standpoint of battle. There are, however, special fighting games which are based on the illusion of a real fight. Among them are, for children, tussling, playing soldier, robber games, and Hussar games, snowball throwing, etc.; for adults boxing, wrestling, tournaments, saber-bouts, etc.

Here, too, it is a matter of conscious self-deception. The emotions of hate and hostility which two tussling boys feel toward one another are not real emotions but only imaginary. This is indicated by the mere fact that after the battle the boys are again the best of friends. And who cannot remember how carefully he tried, during some childhood tussle, not to injure his playfellow. The fist raised to fell the opponent stops in mid-air, the pressure on the throat is not as strong as it might be. For the player knows perfectly well that as soon as the opponent is actually injured the play becomes serious and all the pleasure stops at once. The enjoyment here, too, does not depend at all upon the result. To be sure, the victor has more joy in the play than his defeated opponent. But even the latter enjoys the game. Otherwise weaker boys would never enter a fighting game. The pleasure aroused by the illusion is after all greater than the displeasure over a possible defeat and greater than the displeasurable emotions of hate and rage. This means that the game is dependent upon the condition of conscious self-deception. This is the presupposition for its pleasurable continuation and for the even-tempered and energetic execution of the movement.

One can recognize the fictitious character of fighting games most distinctly in the predetermined saber-bout. The bout occurs, as everybody knows, not as a result of enmity or insult. The fencers are often the best of friends. In the duel enmity is an obvious presupposition and therefore the weapons chosen for it are deadly. In the saber-bout it is not intended to cause serious injury and therefore the contest is carried out with harmless weapons. Whereas in the duel the feeling of offended honor seeks satisfaction, in the saber-bout nobody has been offended at all and the enmity is only a fictitious one entertained for the sake of a lively scrap. This is the only way to explain the much-decried tolerance of the authorities toward it. They do not wish to take seriously something which is only play, even though some blood should be spilt.

The spectator's enjoyment of such fighting games is justly placed parallel to the enjoyment of tragedy. The latter, too, can be enjoyed only if one knows that it is not in earnest. For tragedy, too, it is a question of a conflict, a fictitious battle the vicissitudes of which the spectator follows with expectation, imputing to the players the feelings which are demanded by the plot. A person likes to witness a maneuver or a war game. A real battle, even though one is not participating in it, arouses consternation or displeasure. For this reason the gladiatorial games of the Romans and the bull fights of the Spaniards cannot be called esthetic productions. If art proceeded only from a desire to procure sensations and to experience excitement, these productions would be counted as artistic. Here we have a clear indication that the condition for the esthetic is fictitiousness. And this is exactly the feature in which art and illusion play coincide.

To the illusion games also belong the love games. There are estheticians who are inclined to trace all feeling for beauty to a disguised sexual instinct. This is wrong. Art comprises all emotions which play a role in human life and love is one of these. It is unnecessary to say anything about its importance for man. The same importance which it has in human life it has in art, and also in play.

Sexual traits are intermixed in the fighting games and games of skill. This is to be explained from the standpoint of anthropology. The noblest prize for which primitive man fought was woman. The battle for woman plays a role in the sagas of all peoples. Woman is the spectator and prize-judge in the fighting games of men. The joy in the fighting games is greatest when the participator knows himself to be scrutinized by the eyes of beautiful women. There is a mysterious biological connection between fight and love which in my opinion can only be explained in this way. Most duels are fought for women. At the beginning of puberty the fighting instinct is strongest.

Genuinely erotic games take place only among sexually mature people. For only in them is the sex instinct so strong that it creates in play a fictitious opportunity if a real opportunity is lacking. One must strictly differentiate love play from serious wooing. The former always stops at illusion; the latter is always intended to lead to success. A man who seriously woos a woman, or a woman who seeks to seduce a man, does not play. A man, on the other hand, who without serious intentions courts the wife of another, or a woman who flirts lightly with a stranger, plays a love game. The attractiveness of such a game consists merely in the illusion. Both parties imagine themselves to be in love with each other but they are really not. And either of them incites the other by this fictitious love to a like emotional fiction. . . .

The need for erotic illusion is the fruitful soil of several arts. First, of the dance, whose one element is the play of movement and the other the game of love. On its mimic side the dance is an artistic supplement to wooing. It represents alternate attraction and repulsion, pouting and reconciliation, jealousy, longing, pleasure, and exultant joy. All these emotions, for both the dancer and the spectators, are based on feelings of illusion. To be sure, serious emotions may very easily intermingle with them. But I assume that this is more often the case in man than in woman. Women who in a receptive way are in general more capable of illusion than men, undoubtedly adhere to the illusion of the love game in the dance more closely than men, in whom the illusion easily changes over into sensual indulgence. Woman dances for the sake of the dance, man for the sake of woman. For man the dance is a means to an end, for woman it is an end in itself. Naturally with women, too, the dance has a certain sexual tint. But it seems to be removed into a hazy distance and covered by a delicate veil. . . .

Another predominately erotic art is lyric poetry. Most lyric poems refer to love, longing, renunciation, etc. There is no doubt that the love instinct, when it finds no direct satisfaction, tends to be sublimated into lyrical expression. In all this there is not always present a particular person of the other sex who could be thought of as the object of the poetic enthusiasm. It is psychologically incorrect always to expect to find a real person who functions as the poet's Laura. One can very well conceive of the erotic lyric as a refined love game.

The drama in its erotic aspects is not different from lyric poetry. For also in the drama both the player and the spectator surrender to an illusion of love. Struggle and love, victory and destruction, form the chief content of tragedy. Its origin lies in the need of men to experience great and stirring emotions for which actual life offers no sufficient occasion. If life offered more opportunity for struggle and love, for grappling with danger and death, there would be no tragedy.

Besides the hunting and fighting games and the love games, there are a great number of other illusion games based on the consciousness of playing a role. This can be observed particularly in the activity of children. We shall call these dramatic games. It is characteristic of these games that children perform actions in them which do not agree with their age and which they learn by watching adults.

To these belong, for example, building games, which may be viewed as a preliminary stage of architecture. They appear in two forms. Either the child erects a building of stones, wood, earth, or snow in which he can dwell or he builds from wooden blocks which are given to him small imitations of actual buildings. Each time he imitates an activity of adults he feels himself in the role of a builder. At the same time he knows that the work of his hands is no real house, that no one can really live in it. His enjoyment of this activity must therefore rest upon the play of imagination to which it gives the stimulus. The room or house in which the child actually lives is not half so fascinating as the fictitious house which he has built with his own hands. For he cannot tie up with the former a play of imagination as he can with the latter.

Another type of dramatic game is to be found in the nursery games. They consist in this, that an older child, usually a girl, dresses, undresses, feeds, washes, and cares for a younger child, ordinarily a little brother or sister, as if she were its mother. Here, too, we have an example of conscious self-deception. For the older child knows very well that she is not the mother. Nevertheless she feels herself to be a mother, and in anticipation of a future role, surrenders to the imaginary experience of maternal feelings.

A favorite sequel to the nursery play is playing school. One might think, when children instruct others in the spirit of make-believe, that the enjoyment would consist in an inflated sense of personality, which results from assuming the role of a teacher. But the game is also enjoyed by the children who play at being pupils, even when they are being reproached and punished—another proof that the hedonic value consists not in the content but in the illusion.

Now, besides these, there is a multitude of dramatic illusion games, which one can consider similarly as direct preliminary stages to dramatic art. When a child sitting on his father's knee plays "Hopp, hopp, Reiterlein" ("gallop, gallop, little rider"), or when he leads another trotting child by the bridle, when he acts the businessman, plays bride and bridegroom, when he makes visits or receives visitors, when he cooks, goes to church, etc., he imagines something which he himself does not consider actual. To be more definite, he anticipates in doing so the experiences of the future, since he imitates actions, movements, etc., which he has observed in adults, and thus enjoys the imaginary experience of being something else than he really is. This make-believe may involve the drollest illusions, the strangest degradations, and I have never observed that the child feels such a degrading role as something disagreeable. The same boy who today plays the happy bridegroom or family-man is not ashamed tomorrow to be a watch dog or a sheep. Children are not at all particular in the choice of the content of their illusions, just as the true poet knows how to conquer a seemingly uncongenial subject matter. It is clear that these games, like the drama, originate from the need to experience more than is the lot of the individual to experience. This may explain why the adult does not engage in such dramatic games except perhaps the masquerade; since his need for dramatic illusion is satisfied through histrionic art and dramatic poetry.

That the transition from play to art is quite elastic in this case also, is shown by the Punch and Judy shows and the marionette theater, which approach real art. For the child they serve the same function as the real theater serves for the adult. In the youthful development of most great poets they play a great role. Here, too, the illusion is a very strong one, and small children in beholding them surrender to a real illusion, for example, when they fear the devil. But as they grow older fear disappears and esthetic enjoyment takes its place.

Closely allied to the dramatic games are the plastic games. They arise from a need of the child to have a tangible basis for the illusion. For this purpose it utilizes even the furniture of the nursery. A chair serves as a coach, a row of chairs as a train, a bench as an omnibus, a cradle as a ship. Even living beings are symbolically represented through inanimate objects of the environment. A sofa pillow, an umbrella, a footstool, serves to represent a baby. One is astonished at times at the capacity for illusion which thus manifests itself. There is nothing that children are not able to see in a very insignificant inanimate object. In fact it often seems as if a certain dissimilarity were necessary for enjoyment, because in this way the power of illusion is taxed to the utmost.

To these objects must be added the plastic playthings which the grownup puts in the hands of the child; the doll, the little puppet pulled by a string, the tin soldier, animals made of wood, rubber, or *papier mâché*, doll houses and doll kitchens, horse stables, and tiny department stores with their various content. All these objects are imitations on a very small scale. Their relationship to nature is very similar to that of the plastic picture, only the kind of imitation is mostly a coarser and more conventional one. But this is based on the inaccurate powers of observation of the child which only sees the main features, the persistent traits in the things of nature and of his environment and consequently requires only a general similarity in an imitation.

Again, in looking at these things and playing with them, the child feels a conscious self-deception. For the possibility of a real deception is precluded by the mere fact of their diminutive size. He knows the size of objects from nature and knows that one cannot carry a house away nor move a cow by means of wheels. He sees that the doll bed is not large enough to lie in, and that it can hold nothing bigger than a doll, which in turn is smaller than a living child. . . . The soul of the child engaged in play lives in a world of make-believe which he knows to be unreal. He continually identifies himself with the doll, and the doll becomes his alter ego, his make-believe self, with which he connects all the things he sees, touches, manipulates. The thought of really doing all that he pretends to do, of using all these things in earnest, does not occur to him at all. . . .

The play with the doll belongs likewise to the category of nursery play, only in this case the nursing instinct is directed to an inanimate object instead of a living one. Frequently the various kinds of play blend into one another. The plaything is not only looked upon but also manipulated. The doll is being carried about, dressed and undressed, fed and put to bed; the animal is pulled upon wheels, the houses are built up into cities. In short, the plastic play unites at this stage with the dramatic. Both still form a unity. We must recognize in this respect an essential difference between plastic play and plastic art. A statue stands motionless upon its pedestal; it is not touched by hand, it is only enjoyed esthetically. It serves as an object of disinterested esthetic contemplation. On this level we already notice a separation of plastic and dramatic art. Undoubtedly this should mean for us a higher level, a transition to a further emancipation from the interests of life. . . .

The plastic play of the child is essentially of a receptive nature, but one can already discern the beginnings of a productive activity. The kneading of clay or wax, and the playing in sand or mud have not always just an architectonic, but often also a plastic, significance. . . .

We can likewise distinguish between receptive and productive play among the pictorial pastimes of children. The most important of the receptive ones, in which the adult provides the child with the basis for the activity, is the looking at picture books. To explain this, one must already presuppose complete development of conscious self-deception. It is very improbable that in looking at a picture book the child surrenders to a real illusion. For he himself turns the leaves upon which the pictures are imprinted, he himself points at them with his finger, and he feels in doing so that they are only flat and motionless imitations of real objects. He feels himself while turning the pages the originator of his experience; he is conscious not only of the represented objects but also of his own ego and his voluntary perseverance in artificially producing his perceptions. There is not the slightest reason why this activity should be considered different, psychologically speaking, from the viewing of pictures on the part of adults. The only difference is this, that the higher art of painting has a more significant and deeper content, corresponding to the increased spiritual need of adults, and that the imitation of nature in it is a more exact and intensive one. . . .

The passion for the picture book also arises from an instinctive drive, namely, the impulse to achieve an enlarged view and knowledge of life. The child, particularly, has a pronounced need for this fuller experience because of the narrowness of his existence. And our modern civilized life with its constricting forms can only increase this need. An inquiry conducted recently in the public schools of Berlin showed that fifty-three percent of the pupils had not seen a snail, fifty-nine percent had not seen a wheat field, seventy percent had never seen a sunrise, seventy-five percent had never watched a living rabbit, ninety-eight percent had never beheld a river (except the Spree)! It is easy to understand what the picture book means for the child under these conditions. . . . But esthetically speaking, the pictures most stimulating to the child are those which refer to persons and objects in his environment, which he knows from daily observation. In the presence of them he can evolve a purely esthetic illusion, and there is no doubt that most people gain the faculty for conscious self-deception chiefly through the picture book. For through it is offered the first opportunity of developing the faculty intuitively to add space and motion to the superficial and motionless representations of nature.

It is of interest to note that experiments have been made in this field to remove the illusion-disturbing factors, to produce a real illusion. I mean the so-called movable picture books, in which individual figures or parts of the body may be put in motion by pulling something; or through which a whole picture is separated into different depths, in such a way that the individual objects assume the correct relationship to each other in space. I consider them pedagogically and esthetically unsuitable. For the child is actually barred through them from his own productive illusion. Moreover, once the child has learned to view pictures, he has become accustomed to their lack of motion and to their flatness. From that time on he takes these illusion-disturbing factors for granted. More than that, his pleasure consists precisely in the fact that he seeks to destroy them through the force of his own illusion. How irrational is it to deprive him of this creative activity in which alone his pleasure consists, to build for him a *pons asinorum* which can only hinder real esthetic enjoyment! . . .

The period when children begin to imitate nature by drawing varies with the natural talent. Some children are able to draw quite recognizable pictures in their third or fourth year of life. Drawing with colors is preceded, I think, by a play of mere movement, a playful experimentation with lead and slate pencil. If a child one or two years of age is handed a pencil and paper, he scribbles over the whole surface. The arbitrarily confused lines which result are probably not intended at first to mean anything. They satisfy the child only as visible signs of a movement play which gives him pleasure. He feels himself the author of these black strokes, he enjoys his dominance over matter, the free conscious expression of his will.

At a certain level—naturally it is difficult to say when in every instance—the enjoyment of the illusion is added to this pleasure. The confused lines assume a certain form, they are intended to mean something. From this moment a conscious self-deception is involved. For the child cannot possibly think of the figure of a man which he has drawn as actually living. . . .

With the pictorial play of looking at pictures is often connected the play of telling stories. While the former is a preliminary stage of pictorial enjoyment, the latter is a preparation for the epic. In this case, too, the intensity of the illusion is the condition of enjoyment, but here also conscious self-illusion develops only gradually. It is natural that vivacious children should identify themselves with the heroes of the stories; what the hero experiences they imagine themselves as undergoing. This illusion is at times so intense that they do not entertain the least doubt of the truth of the story which they have heard. Children who hear stories for the first time do not even conceive of the possibility of freely inventing stories for the sake of amusement. They are greatly disappointed when they learn from their meddling brothers and sisters that all is nothing but invention. For this reason the feelings which arise in them while they listen to the story have in part an actual character. By sad happenings they are moved to tears; by joyous ones they are aroused to the greatest pleasure.

But they do not stop very long at this stage. Once they know that the story is not of actual events, they can only listen to it thereafter with an attitude of conscious self-illusion. Despite the initial disappointment which this discovery gives them, they regain the capacity for illusion required to guarantee full enjoyment. And only from this moment on do they feel pure esthetic appreciation.

This transition probably begins with fairy tales, to enjoy which conscious self-deception becomes a necessity from the moment the child has outgrown a fantastic conception of nature and no longer believes in the miraculous. For this very reason, however, the fairy tale is extremely important in the artistic education of the child. Children who do not like fairy tales and wish to hear only true stories will certainly not become poets in their later lives.

The child at the next stage regards not only fairy tales but also apparently true stories as esthetic make-believe. The whole process develops gradually, and this is another indication that the ability to transport one's self into conscious self-deception is the higher stage compared with the confusion of phantom with reality. There is an age-level at which little girls who derive the greatest pleasure from Spyri's *Heidi* cannot read Wildermuth's *Castle and Cabin* because of its sad content. A year later they are fully capable of reading the latter and deriving the greatest pleasure from it. This year is the decisive one for the training of the esthetic emotion. At this point the child has arrived at the stage where he no longer completely identifies his ego with the persons in the story but regards them objectively, in esthetic disinterestedness.

Only conscious self-deception makes it possible for children to be fed so long with lies regarding certain things. The well-known "pious" lies about the Heavenly Father with the flowing beard who sits upon the clouds, about Santa Claus who gives beautiful things to good children, about the stork who brings babies, etc., are believed only by little children. In the case of older children it is often difficult to discover whether they still believe or whether they are beginning to doubt. They hover for years in a sort of intermediary state between belief and unbelief. I surmise that this is the period in which the faculty of conscious self-deception develops in them. They do not now really believe, but they act as if they did; they conceive of these things as real in their imagination.

It is probably a similar matter with whole peoples. The first stage, the springing up of myths, presupposes actual belief. This is followed by a period of conscious self-deception. The common people perhaps still believe, but the leading spirits assume only a poetic attitude toward these things. This is the flowering time of poetry, the period of Homer and the tragic poets. Only later follows the period of unbelief, of knowledge, of criticism. The perfection of artistic illusion represents a transitory stage between belief or superstition, on the one hand, and unbelief or knowledge, research, and criticism, on the other. This period is for peoples, as well as for individuals, wholesome and indispensable. I am convinced that the hatred with which many rational people in later years look back upon the pious lives of their youth is due only to the fact that they, in their youth, were not led by the gentle hand of conscious self-deception to a better knowledge.

When we survey all illusion games so far discussed we can no longer doubt that they are of the same essential nature as art; they are preliminary stages of esthetic activity. There is not a single characteristic of art which does not apply to the illusion games and no single characteristic of the illusion games which could not also be found in art. The only difference is that the latter, corresponding to the more mature view of adults, has as a rule a more significant and profoundly human content. But not even this is universally true, as we can discern from certain still life and flower painting, from ornamentation and certain kinds of music. We have said play is in general the wider concept, art and illusion play the narrower. Not every form of play is art, for not every one of them has the distinguishing feature of illusion. But every art is a form of play, for art has the characteristics of pleasure value, of disinterestedness, etc. The illusion games—excepting a few intelligence games—are the noblest of all; they are those which for any length of time afford the greatest pleasure. And art is an enhanced and refined illusion play adapted to the need of the adult. For every play there is as we have seen an art upon the higher level. The following scheme may visualize this once more:

Acoustic sense-game .... Music
Optic sense-game .... Ornamentation
Motion play .... Dance
Dramatic play .... Histrionic art, dramatics
Looking at picture books .... Painting
Playing with dolls .... Plastic art
Constructive play .... Architecture
Storytelling .... Epic poetry

Lyric poetry is the only art for which I cannot think of an analogy. But we know that children often give expression to their feelings by singing almost meaningless words, and here too the nursery song represents the connecting link.

—*Das Wesen der Kunst* (1901)

SAMUEL ALEXANDER

Beauty and Illusion

Perhaps the simplest way to understand beauty is to contrast the beautiful object on the one hand with a percept and on the other with an illusion. As contrasted with the percept, the beautiful is illusory, but it differs from illusion in that it is not erroneous. Considered from the point of view of cognition, the beautiful object is illusory for it does not as an external reality contain the characters it possesses for the esthetic sense. I perceive the tree in front of me to have a reverse side though I see only the front; but the tree really has a reverse side, and if I change my position the back of it is now seen and the front is supplied in idea. The marble is seen cold, to revert to the trite example, but the cold which is only present in idea really belongs to the marble, and I may in turn feel it cold and with eyes shut represent its whiteness in idea. The painted tree on the other hand looks solid but is not, and no change of my position helps me to see its other side. The Hermes is a marble block of a certain form and is perceived in its real qualities of solidity and hardness, but the block does not possess the repose and playfulness and dignity that I read into it esthetically. The words of a poem are not merely descriptive of their object, but suffused with suggestions of feeling and significance which a mere scientific description would not possess. The more perfect the artistry the more definitely does the work of art present in suggestion features which as a cognized object it has not. Mr. Berenson compares the two Madonnas that stand side by side in the Academy at Florence—the one by Cimabue, the other by Giotto.[1] The Cimabue Madonna is flat and looks flat, though otherwise beautiful. The Giotto is flat but looks three-dimensional, and so far is the more perfectly beautiful.

What is true of works of art is true of natural objects, with the necessary qualifications. In general the natural object is, when its beauty is appreciated, perceived incorrectly, or if it actually has the characters which we add to it, that is for esthetic appreciation an accident, and is the source of a different and additional pleasure. Like the artist in painting a landscape, we select from or add to nature in feeling its beauty. Literal fidelity is, or at least may be, fatal to beauty, for it is the means of securing not beauty but truth and satisfies our scientific rather than our esthetic sense. If this is true for the mere onlooker, it is still more so for the painter or poet who renders the work of nature in an alien material

[1] Bernard Berenson, *Florentine Painters of the Renaissance* (New York and London, third edition), p. 13.

which has its own prescriptions. Or we read our moods into the scene; or endow animate or even inanimate objects with our feelings; see daffodils for instance outdoing in glee the waves which dance beside them, or fancy a straight slender stem as springing from the ground, or liken with it as Odysseus did the youthful grace of a girl.

The cases of natural beauty which most obstinately resist this interpretation are the graceful movements of animals or the beauty of human faces, a large part of which arises from their expressiveness of life and character. You may see a face as majestic as that of the Zeus of Orticoli and the man may perchance possess that character; or the horse's arching of his neck may really proceed from the self-display we read into it in finding it beautiful. But in the first place we read the feeling or the character into these forms before we learn that the creatures in question possess them; and in the next place though a natural form may thus in reality happen to possess the supplement which we add from our minds, and may so far be unlike the work of art, yet the intellectual recognition that it does conform to the esthetic appreciation is not itself esthetic. This is best shown by the truth that the artistic representation may be more beautiful than the original, like the suggested movements of the Winged Victory or of the figures in Botticelli's Spring. But also the knowledge that the natural object possesses the imputed characters—which is esthetically indifferent—may even mar the esthetical effect, for when we learn that a man is really as fine a character as he looks, our appreciation is apt to turn to moral instead of esthetic admiration. In place of esthetic contemplation we may have sympathy or practical respect. We may then safely follow the guidance of the beauty of art and declare that in natural objects beauty, so far as it is appreciated esthetically, involves illusion.

But esthetic semblance is not error, not illusion in the accepted sense, which is cognitive. To express the matter by way of paradox, the esthetic semblance is vital to esthetic truth, or it is an ingredient in a new reality which is esthetic. Cognitive illusion is in fact the transitional stage between reality without value and reality with esthetic value. Illusory appearance, we saw, is the appearance of reality in some of its parts to a mind which for one reason or another is perverse or twisted. It only becomes unreal in the sorting out, insofar as it is believed. As believed in, it is unreal, but it then becomes an element in a new reality which is error. The illusory *thing* in its illusory form, though founded in reality, has as such, in its illusory form, no reality at all, but only as possessed by the mind. But whereas the error is erroneous because it is excluded by the real thing about which it is concerned, the esthetic semblance is not attributed to any real object outside the esthetic experience itself. Watch for a short time a revolving drum, on the paper of which are drawn vertical lines. When the drum is stopped the paper seems to move in the opposite direction. That is an illusory appearance, and is illusion if it is taken to be reality. Contrast this with the esthetic illusion of the figures in the picture of the Spring. It would be cognitive illusion if we thought the figures to be really moving. But they are really in motion in the esthetic reality in which the pictured form and the esthetically imputed motion are indissolubly one. Thus it is because a cognitive illusion is pinned down by the reality which it cognizes, and cognizes falsely, that it is unreal. Insofar as it is a reality, it has become an artificial product of the reality it cognizes and of mind, and was therefore described before as a work of art. When we pass into artistic imagination, whether its object is externalized in stone or words or remains a vision of things, we have a work of art in the proper sense. Illusion is half art, half truth. It fails of being either truth or art for the same reason; it is personal, while both truth and art are impersonal.

Thus in the beautiful object, whether of art or nature, one part is contributed by the mind, and it is relatively a matter of indifference whether the mind in question is that of the person who creates the work of art or that of the mere spectator, who follows in the artist's traces. In the case of natural beauty, the spectator and the creator are one. The element contributed by the mind may vary from the mere addition of external properties, as in seeing the flat picture solid, for example, in the bare esthetic effect of the drawing of a cube or a truncated pyramid, up to distinctively human characters of feeling or character, as in animating a statue with pride, or words or sounds with emotion as in a lyric or in music. Animation with life is intermediate between these extremes, for life though less than mental, and still for us something external which we contemplate, is yet on a higher level of external existence than solidity of form. It is only through what is thus added that the beautiful object has meaning or character or expressiveness.

I add that the expressiveness need not be something characteristic of man. The expressiveness of the work of art is to be itself, to be what it represents, to have the significance appropriate to it; for the painted animal or tree to seem alive and to grow or move according to its kind; for the drawn cube to look solid; for the pillar to seem (and to be) perfectly adjusted to support the weight it bears, and to bear it with ease. An ugly portico with stunted Doric columns gives the impression that the weight which the columns bear is crushing them; the tall columns of the Parthenon suggest that the roof is a light burden; the suggestion in neither case being true in fact. We may naturally enough render these impressions by investing the columns with life—springing up from the ground, and the like—but they belong really to the mechanical order. Thus the imputation of life and character enter into the expressiveness of the beautiful object, only when that object means life or character. They are but one species of expressiveness. Further in every case, no matter how much of mind or character is read into the thing by the mind for which it is beautiful, the expressiveness remains that of the thing and not that of the creating or appreciating mind itself.[2] In choice and treatment of his subject the artist impresses himself indeed upon his work, which so far expresses or reveals him. But to feel Shakespeare in *Hamlet* is not to appreciate *Hamlet* esthetically but to judge it critically. In the expressiveness which he adds to his material from his very personality the artist depersonalizes the work of art. Even in a beautiful lyric the passion ceases to be merely that of the artist. It is the paradox of beauty that its expressiveness belongs to the beautiful thing itself and yet would not be there except for the mind. Under the conditions of the material in which it is expressed, the beautiful owes some part of its meaning to the mind, and so far it owes to the mind not only its *percipi* [being perceived] as every perceived object does, but its *esse* [essence or being]. We have therefore all the greater need of caution in extending what is true of beauty to the objects of knowledge, whose *esse* is not *percipi*, but *esse*, independently of the mind which is compresent with them.

The beauty of the beautiful object lies in the congruence or coherence of its parts. According to the ancient doctrine it is the unity within that variety. Of these elements some are intrinsic to the beautiful thing, and some are imported from the mind and thereby belong to the thing; and it is a condition of the beauty that its external form must be such as to bear and compel that imputation. Disproportion or want of perspective, to take the simplest illustrations, may mar the beauty. Or the material may be inadequate to the effect, as when an architect builds in terra cotta what requires stone for stateliness. In virtue of the harmonious blending within the beautiful of the two sets of elements, some existing in reality and some supplied by the mind, the unity in variety is also expressive or significant. The beautiful satisfies both the ancient and the modern criterion; and a new reality is generated in which mind and the nonmental have become organic to each other, not in the sense that the beautiful necessarily contains mind, though it may do so, for example, in a picture of a man, but that its expressiveness is due to the blending of elements supplied from two sources, and the external beautiful thing is beautiful only through this fitness of the externally real elements to their expressiveness. Like truth and goodness, beauty exists

---

2 I am aware that in the above paragraph I am raising (and evading) several difficult questions. How far may human meaning be read into the esthetic object consistently with beauty? Beyond a certain point the practice of personification may become sentimental. There is, in addition, the question of legitimacy of different effects in different arts. A painter could not paint the flowers dancing with glee as the poem on the daffodils does. It would be interesting to inquire whether Wordsworth always preserves the legitimate limitations of art. These questions illustrate the difficulties raised by Lipps's doctrine of *Einfühlung* or empathy (see his *Aesthetik*, from which as well as from his earlier and well-known *Raumaesthetik* I have learned much). Perhaps in the paragraph I am describing rather an ideal, in urging that the expressiveness of the object belongs to the object itself, and I should rather say that the object is beautiful in proportion as it conforms to this standard. And I quite admit that what is said of beauty in this subchapter applies more easily to the arts of sculpture and painting than to the other arts. Of music I have hardly dared to speak at all, for I do not know whether sounds and their arrangement suggest emotion as sculptured shapes suggest life and character, which I suspect to be the truth; or whether they mean emotion as words mean the things they name.

only as possessed by mind, but whereas in them mind and the external still sit loosely to each other, and in the one case the mind contemplates an external reality which owes to the mind its truth but not its reality, and in the other case the mind alters reality practically but the practical results do not owe their character to mind but only their goodness; in beauty external reality and mind penetrate each other, and the external thing receives its character of coherence from its connection with mind.

Thus when Kant declared that beauty was so judged because it set the understanding at work in harmony with the imagination, he spoke truly, but according to his fashion in subjective terms, and so far inadequately. Truly, because, whereas in perception of an external object the imaginative elements are but a part of the real object which is cognized, in beauty the supplementing imagination is independent of what is perceived and yet is blended with what is perceived into a new esthetic whole. Inadequately, because the beauty or coherence between the elements supplied in sense and in imagination belongs to the esthetic object, and the interplay of cognition and imagination describes only the condition of the mental process involved in the esthetic appreciation and not the beauty of the esthetic thing itself. Such an account considers beauty as a purely subjective character, whereas beauty belongs to the complex of mind and its object, or as I have so often expressed it, to the beautiful object as possessed by the mind. Since the beautiful object owes one part of its constituents to the actual participation of the mind, beauty is in this sense a tertiary "quality" of the beautiful object, thus conceived.

But the analysis of beauty implies something further. The coherence of real external elements with other elements supplied from mind, while constituting beauty, distinguishes beauty from ugliness, and therewith distinguishes the mind which appreciates beauty from that which fails to do so or which sees beauty in ugliness, and unites together the minds which appreciate the beautiful as beautiful. Coherence in the internal constitution of beauty is also coherence among the minds which appreciate it, and exclusion of other minds. The mind for which an object is beautiful is not any mind but one which apprehends or appreciates impersonally or disinterestedly. Beauty in this way involves reference to other minds, and the reason of this or rather the explanation of its possibility is no easy matter. Beauty is not merely something which gives pleasure but which pleases in a certain way, and in a way which can be shared by other minds.

—*Space, Time, and Deity* (1920)

OSCAR WILDE

Nature's Imitation of Art

VIVIAN: . . . Paradox though it may seem—and paradoxes are always dangerous things—it is none the less true that Life imitates art far more than Art imitates life. We have all seen in our own day in England how a certain curious and fascinating type of beauty, invented and emphasized by two imaginative painters, has so influenced Life that whenever one goes to a private view or to an artistic salon one sees, here the mystic eyes of Rossetti's dream, the long ivory throat, the strange square-cut jaw, the loosened shadowy hair that he so ardently loved, there the sweet maidenhood of "The Golden Stair," the blossom-like mouth and weary loveliness of the "Laus Amoris," the passion-pale face of Andromeda, the thin hands and lithe beauty of the Vivien in "Merlin's Dream." And it has always been so. A great artist invents a type, and Life tries to copy it, to reproduce it in a popular form, like an enterprising publisher. Neither Holbein nor Vandyck found in England what they have given us. They brought their types with them, and Life with her keen imitative faculty set herself to supply the master with models. The Greeks, with their quick artistic instinct, understood this, and set in the bride's chamber the statue of Hermes or of Apollo, that she might bear children as lovely as the works of art that she looked at in her rapture or her pain. They knew that Life gains from Art not merely spirituality, depth of thought and feeling, soul-turmoil or soul-peace, but that she can form herself on the very lines and colors of art, and can reproduce the dignity of Phidias as well as the grace of Praxiteles. Hence came their objection to realism. They disliked it on purely social grounds. They felt that it inevitably makes people ugly, and they were perfectly right. We try to improve the conditions of the race by means of good air, free sunlight, wholesome water, and hideous bare buildings for the better housing of the lower orders. But these things merely produce health, they do not produce beauty. For this, Art is required, and the true disciples of the great artist are not his studio-imitators, but those who become like his works of art, be they plastic as in Greek days, or pictorial as in modern times; in a word, Life is Art's best, Art's only pupil. . . .

CYRIL: The theory is certainly a very curious one, but to make it complete you must show that Nature, no less than Life, is an imitation of Art. Are you prepared to prove that?

VIVIAN: My dear fellow, I am prepared to prove anything.

CYRIL: Nature follows the landscape painter then, and takes her effects from him?

VIVIAN: Certainly. Where, if not from the impressionists, do we get those wonderful brown fogs that come creeping down our streets, blurring the gas-lamps and changing the houses into monstrous shadows? To whom, if not to them and their master, do we owe the lovely silver mists that brood over our river, and turn to faint forms of fading grace, curved bridge and swaying barge? The extraordinary change that has taken place in the climate of London during the last ten years is entirely due to this particular school of Art. You smile. Consider the matter from a scientific or a metaphysical point of view, and you will find that I am right. For what is Nature? Nature is no great mother who has borne us. She is our creation. It is in our brain that she quickens to life. Things are because we see them, and what we see, and how we see it, depends on the Arts that have influenced us. To look at a thing is very different from seeing a thing. One does not see anything until one sees its beauty. Then, and then only, does it come into existence. At present, people see fogs, not because there are fogs, but because poets and painters have taught them the mysterious loveliness of such effects. There may have been fogs for centuries in London. I daresay there were. But no one saw them, and so we do not know anything about them. They did not exist till Art had invented them. Now, it must be admitted, fogs are carried to excess. They have become the mere mannerism of a clique, and the exaggerated realism of their method gives dull people bronchitis. Where the cultured catch an effect, the uncultured catch cold. And so, let us be humane, and invite Art to turn her wonderful eyes elsewhere. She has done so already, indeed. That white quivering sunlight that one sees now in France, with its strange blotches of mauve, and its restless violet shadows, is her latest fancy, and, on the whole, Nature reproduces it quite admirably. Where she used to give us Corots and Daubignys, she gives us now exquisite Monets and entrancing Pissaros. Indeed, there are moments, rare, it is true, but still to be observed from time to time, when Nature becomes absolutely modern. Of course she is not always to be relied upon. The fact is that she is in this unfortunate position: Art creates an incomparable and unique effect, and, having done so, passes on to other things. Nature, upon the other hand, forgetting that imitation can be made the sincerest form of insult, keeps on repeating this effect until we all become absolutely wearied of it. Nobody of any real culture, for instance, ever talks nowadays about the beauty of a sunset. Sunsets are quite old-fashioned. They belong to the time when Turner was the last note in art. To admire them is a distinct sign of provincialism of temperament. Upon the other hand they go on. Yesterday evening Mrs. Arundel insisted on my going to the window, and looking at the glorious sky, as she called it. Of course

I had to look at it. She is one of those absurdly pretty Philistines, to whom one can deny nothing. And what was it? It was simply a very second-rate Turner, a Turner of a bad period, with all the painter's worst faults exaggerated and over-emphasized. . . .

—"The Decay of Lying" in *Intentions and the Soul of Man* (1891)

CHAPTER TWO

Art as Beauty

JACQUES MARITAIN
Beauty and Imitation

GEORGE SANTAYANA
The Nature of Beauty

Introductory Note

THE QUESTION CONSIDERED in the preceding chapter is the relation of art to nature. This problem is basic in the scholastic tradition—the tradition of Aristotle, Saint Thomas Aquinas, and modern Catholic philosophers.

Jacques Maritain (1882-   ), the famous French neo-scholastic philosopher, has written in this current of thought. But he has also drawn upon a wide knowledge of art and artists. His many friendships with painters, musicians, and writers include a close association with Rouault, who has greatly inspired and influenced him. He has also learned much from his wife, Raïssa, the poet.

His crowning achievement in esthetics is *Creative Intuition in Art and Poetry,* which grew out of his six A. W. Mellon Lectures in the Fine Arts, given at the National Gallery of Art in Washington in the spring of 1952. But I have chosen a selection from his earlier work, *Art and Scholasticism,* because it tersely sets forth his fundamental ideas and his relation to Saint Thomas and Aristotle

He has classified human activities as follows:

1. *Pure Knowing* (Corresponding to Aristotle's theoretical sciences—metaphysics, mathematics, and physics).

2. *Action,* or doing as distinct from knowing.
   (a) *Practice* (Corresponding to Aristotle's practical sciences—politics, ethics, economics).
   (b) *Making,* or *Art* in the wide sense (Corresponding to Aristotle's productive sciences—poetics, rhetoric, technology in general).
       (1) *Craftsmanship,* or the making of *useful* things—for exam ample, shoemaking, tailoring, carpentry.
       (2) *Fine Art,* or the making of *beautiful* things—for example, painting, poetry, music.

As distinguished from pure knowing, art is not to be confused with science or philosophy, or even with the "intuition" of Croce and Bergson (that is, the knowing of what is individual). As distinguished from practice, art is directed toward the making of some artifact. *Fine* art is closely related to craftsmanship, but it is distinguished by the nature of its function—to make *beautiful* rather than useful things.

Accepting the definition of Saint Thomas, Maritain maintains that beauty is desired, but the desire is appeased on sight, for beauty is what pleases in the mere contemplation. The basis of the enjoyment is not wholly in the mind or wholly in the object, but in a correspondence between the two. The object is fitted, as it were, to be joyfully received by the senses and the intellect; what is intelligible in the object is appreciated by what is intelligent in the subject. Hence beauty, as Santayana has said, is the result of a "conformity between the soul and nature," and thus is a sign of "the supremacy of the good." [1]

The main constituent of beauty is "form," which is not bare abstract design, but a revelation of the specific principle of the thing contemplated (as when the basic meaning of death seems to be revealed in a tragedy). The form may be the essence of a type or species, or of an individual, or of a particular attitude or quality; but in any event it is, in art, a concrete presentment, a vision, appealing simultaneously to the senses and the intelligence. The goal of art is thus delightful meaning which shines out in the unity and design of the sensible constituents. To embody such meaning, the work of art must exhibit clarity, integrity, and right proportion.

With its emphasis upon order and intelligibility, this theory is akin to Aristotle's doctrine of imitation. In the latter part of the selection from Maritain's book, he explains that art may be said to imitate the *forms* of things, but its function is to delight by making something beautiful and not servilely to copy. Again, Aristotle himself conceived of art and imitation in a similar way.

Born in Madrid of Spanish parents but educated largely in America, George Santayana (1863-1952) was familiar with the Greek and Catholic tradition of which Maritain has been a spokesman, but Santayana was a naturalist by convic-

---

[1] George Santayana, *The Sense of Beauty* (Scribner's, New York, 1896), p. 270.

tion and drew his inspiration from diverse sources. While a young professor of philosophy at Harvard, he wrote his first book, *The Sense of Beauty* (1896), in which, like Maritain, he defines beauty in terms of pleasure and conceives art as the making of beautiful things.

In his penetrating analysis, he delimits beauty by a series of exclusions. Since beauty is a value and there is no value apart from conscious preference, the beautiful cannot be the unconscious or the merely indifferent. The purely rational must also be excluded, since value in general and beauty in particular involve feeling rather than reason or knowledge. Moral values, which are mainly negative and extrinsic, must also be distinguished from esthetic values, which are positive and intrinsic. Next Santayana contrasts esthetic and physical pleasures: the former give us the illusion of being relatively free of our bodies, the latter do not. He then criticizes a number of traditional demarcations of the esthetic (playfulness, disinterestedness, universality), and finally defines beauty as *objectified pleasure*.

By "objectification" he means the process of imputing some subjective quality to an object, as when we speak of a *nasty* snow-storm or a *lonely* place. Nothing is more natural and primitive than thus to project our mental states into phenomenal objects. Pleasure is transformed into beauty whenever the value is unconsciously imputed to the object contemplated and not to the body or mind of the person contemplating.

In his later works, Santayana no longer distinguishes sharply between moral and esthetic values. He declares, "I can draw no distinction—save for academic programs—between moral and esthetic values: beauty, being a good, is a moral good; and the practice and enjoyment of art, like all practice and all enjoyment, fall within the sphere of morals—at least if by morals we mean moral economy and not moral superstition. On the other hand, the good, when actually realized and not merely pursued from afar, is a joy in the immediate; it is possessed with wonder and is in that sense esthetic. Such pure joy when blind is called beauty, and when diffused over the thought of ulterior propitious things is called happiness, love, or religious rapture." [2]

[2] George Santayana, "Brief History of My Opinions," in *Contemporary American Philosophy,* edited by G. P. Adams and W. P. Montague (New York, 1930), Volume II, p. 256.

JACQUES MARITAIN

Beauty and Imitation

Editor's Note: To assist the reader in understanding Maritain's discussion, I am prefacing it by the following selections from St. Thomas Aquinas (The *"Summa Theologica"*):

§ 1

Beauty and goodness in a thing are identical fundamentally; for they are based upon the same thing, namely, the form, and consequently goodness is praised as beauty. But they differ logically, for goodness properly relates to the appetite (goodness being what all things desire); and therefore it has the aspect of an end (the appetite being a kind of movement towards a thing). On the other hand, beauty relates to the cognitive faculty; for beautiful things are those which please when seen. Hence beauty consists in due proportion; for the senses delight in things duly proportioned, as in what is after their own kind—because even sense is a sort of reason, just as is every cognitive faculty. Now, since knowledge is by assimilation,[1] and similarity relates to form, beauty properly belongs to the nature of a formal cause.[2] (Part I, question 5, article 4.)

§ 2

For beauty includes three conditions, *integrity* or *perfection,* since those things which are impaired are by the very fact ugly; due *proportion* or *harmony;* and lastly *brightness,* or *clarity,* whence things are called beautiful which have a bright color. . . .

An image is said to be beautiful if it perfectly represents even an ugly thing. (Part I, question 39, article 8.)

§ 3

The beautiful is the same as the good, and they differ in aspect only. For since good is what all seek, the notion of good is that which calms the desire; while the notion of the beautiful is that which calms the desire, by being seen or

---

[1] Assimilation of the knower to the known. Aquinas elsewhere says (I, 27, 1): "It is clear that the more a thing is understood, the more closely is the intellectual conception joined and united to the intelligent agent; since the intellect by the very act of understanding is made one with the object understood."

[2] That is to say, beauty results from the grasp of those characteristics of the object that serve to define its essence or type.

known. Consequently those senses chiefly regard the beautiful, which are the most cognitive, viz., sight and hearing, as ministering to reason; for we speak of beautiful sights and beautiful sounds. But in reference to the other objects of the other senses, we do not use the expression *beautiful*, for we do not speak of beautiful tastes, and beautiful odors. Thus it is evident that beauty adds to goodness a relation to the cognitive faculty: so that *good* means that which simply pleases the appetite; while the beautiful is something pleasant to apprehend. (Part II, [First Part], question 27, article 1.)

I. *Art and Beauty* [3]

1. St. Thomas, who was as simple as he was wise, defined the beautiful as what gives pleasure on sight, *id quod visum placet.* The four words say all that is necessary: a vision, that is to say an *intuitive knowledge,* and a *joy.* The beautiful is what gives joy, not all joy, but joy in knowledge; not the joy peculiar to the act of knowing, but a joy superabounding and overflowing from such an act because of the object known. If a thing exalts and delights the soul by the bare fact of its being given to the intuition of the soul, it is good to apprehend, it is beautiful.

Beauty is essentially the object of *intelligence,* for what *knows* in the full meaning of the word is the mind, which alone is open to the infinity of being. The natural site of beauty is the intelligible world: thence it descends. But it also falls in a way within the grasp of the senses, since the senses in the case of man serve the mind and can themselves rejoice in knowing: "the beautiful relates only to sight and hearing of all the senses, because these two are *maxime cognoscitive.*" [4] The part played by the senses in the perception of beauty becomes in our case enormous and well-nigh indispensable, because our mind is not intuitive like the angelic mind: it can perceive, no doubt, but only on condition of abstracting and discoursing. In man only knowledge derived through the senses possesses fully the intuivity necessary for the perception of the beautiful. So also man can certainly enjoy purely intelligible beauty, but the beautiful which is *connatural* to man is that which comes to delight the mind through the senses and their intuition. Such also is the peculiar beauty of our art, which works upon a sensible matter for the joy of the spirit. It would fain so persuade itself that paradise is not lost. It has the savor of the terrestrial paradise, because it restores for a brief moment the simultaneous peace and delight of the mind and the senses.

If beauty delights the mind, it is because beauty is essentially a certain excellence or perfection in the proportion of things to the mind. Hence the three conditions assigned to it by St. Thomas: integrity, because the mind likes being;

---

[3] Maritain has added many notes, which I omit or abbreviate. (Editor.)
[4] "Most cognoscent." (The translations in these notes are mine.—Editor.)

proportion, because the mind likes order and likes unity; lastly and above all brightness or clarity, because the mind likes light and intelligibility. A certain splendor is indeed according to all the Ancients the essential character of beauty —*claritas est de ratione pulchritudinis*,[5] *lux pulchrificat, quia sine luce omnia sunt turpia*,[6]—but it is a splendor of intelligibility: *splendor veri*,[7] said the Platonists, *splendor ordinis*,[8] said St. Augustine, adding that "unity is the form of all beauty"; [9] *splendor formæ*,[10] said St. Thomas with a metaphysician's precision of language: for *form*, that is to say the principle determining the peculiar perfection of everything which is, constituting and completing things in their essence and their qualities, the ontological secret, so to speak, of their innermost being, their spiritual essence, their operative mystery, is above all the peculiar principle of intelligibility, the peculiar *clarity* of every thing. Every form, moreover, is a remnant or a ray of the creative Mind impressed upon the heart of the being created. All order and proportion, on the other hand, are the work of the mind. So, to say with the Schoolmen that beauty is the *splendor of form shining on the proportioned parts of matter* [11] is to say that it is a lightning of mind on a matter intelligently arranged. The mind rejoices in the beautiful because in the beautiful it finds itself again: recognizes itself, and comes into contact with its very own light. This is so true that they especially perceive and particularly relish the beauty of things who, like St. Francis of Assisi, for example, know that they emanate from a mind and refer them to their Author.

Every sensible beauty, no doubt, implies a certain delight of the eye or the ear or the imagination: but there can be no beauty unless the mind also is in some way rejoiced. A beautiful color "washes the eye" as a powerful scent dilates the nostrils: but of these two "forms" or qualities only color is called "beautiful," because being received, as opposed to the perfume, in a sense capable of disinterested knowledge, it can be, even through its purely sensible brilliance, an object of joy to the mind. Again, the more highly developed a man's culture becomes, the more spiritual grows the brilliance of the form which ravishes him.

It is important, however, to observe that in the beauty which has been termed connatural to man and is peculiar to human art this brilliance of form, however purely intelligible it may be in itself, is apprehended *in the sensible and by the sensible,* and not separately from it. The intuition of artistic beauty so stands at the opposite pole from the abstraction of scientific truth. For in the

[5] "Clarity is of the nature of beauty." St. Thomas, *Comment. in lib. de Divin. Nomin.*, lect. 6.
[6] "Light beautifies, because without light all things are ugly." St. Thomas, *Comment. in Psalm. Ps. xxv. 5.*
[7] "Splendor of truth."
[8] "Splendor of order."
[9] *De Vera Religione*, cap. 41.
[10] "Splendor of form."
[11] *Opusc. de Pulchro et Bono,* attributed to Albertus Magnus and sometimes to St. Thomas.

former case it is precisely through the apprehension of sense that the light of being penetrates to the mind.

The mind then, spared the least effort of abstraction, rejoices without labor and without discussion. It is excused its customary task, it has not to extricate something intelligible from the matter in which it is buried and then step by step go through its various attributes; like the stag at the spring of running water, it has nothing to do but drink, and it drinks the clarity of being. Firmly fixed in the intuition of sense, it is irradiated by an intelligible light granted to it of a sudden in the very sensible in which it glitters; and it apprehends this light not *sub ratione veri*, but rather *sub ratione delectabilis*,[12] by the happy exercise it procures for it and the succeeding joy in appetite, which leaps out to every good of the soul as its own peculiar object. Only afterwards will it more or less successfully analyze in reflection the causes of such joy.[13]

So, although the beautiful is in close dependence upon what is metaphysically true, in the sense that every splendor of intelligibility in things presupposes some degree of conformity with that Intelligence which is the cause of things, the beautiful nevertheless is not a kind of truth, but a kind of good. The perception of the beautiful is related to knowledge, but by way of addition, "as its bloom is an addition to youth"; it is not so much a kind of knowledge as a kind of delight.

The beautiful is essentially delightful. Therefore by its very nature, by its very beauty, it stirs desire and produces love, whereas truth as such only illuminates. "*Omnibus igitur est pulchrum et bonum desiderabile et amabile et diligibile. . . .*"[14]

2. The speculations of the Ancients concerning the nature of the beautiful must be taken in the most formal sense and their thought should not be materialized in any too narrow specification. The idea of *integrity* or perfection or complete execution can be realized not in one way only but in a thousand or ten thousand different ways. The lack of a head or an arm is a considerable defect in a woman but of much less account in a statue—whatever disappointment M. Ravaisson may have felt at being unable to *complete* the Venus of Melos. The slightest sketch of Leonardo's or even Rodin's is nearer to perfection than the

---

[12] "Not according to the mode of truth, but rather according to the mode of delight."

[13] . . . Artistic contemplation affects the heart with a joy which is *before all intellectual*, and it must be admitted with Aristotle (*Poetics*, ix, 3, 1451 b 6) that "poetry is something more philosophic and of graver import than history, since its statements are of the nature rather of universals, whereas those of history are singulars" (Bywater's translation: Aristotle, *On the Art of Poetry*, Oxford, 1909), and yet the apprehension of the universal or the intelligible takes place there without speech or any effort of abstraction. The capital error in Benedetto Croce's neo-Hegelian Esthetics is the failure to perceive that artistic contemplation, however *intuitive* it may be, is none the less above all *intellectual*. Esthetics ought to be *intellectualist* and *intuitivist* at the same time.

[14] "By all, therefore, the beautiful and the good are desired and loved and cherished." Dionysius the Areopagite, *De Divin. Nomin.*, cap. iv.

most finished Bouguereau. And if it pleases a futurist to paint a lady with only one eye, or a quarter of an eye, nobody denies him such a right: all one is entitled to require—and here is the whole problem—is that the quarter eye is all the lady needs *in the given case*.

It is the same with proportion, fitness, and harmony. They differ with the object and the end aimed at. Proportions good in a man are not good in a child. Figures constructed according to the Greek or the Egyptian canon are perfectly proportioned in their kind: but Rouault's yokels are also as perfectly proportioned in their kind. Integrity and proportion have no absolute significance and must be understood solely *in relation* to the end of the work, which is to make a form shine on the matter.

Last and most important: this very brilliance of form, the essence of beauty, shines on matter in an infinite variety of ways.[15]

At one time it is the sensible brilliance of color or tone, at another the intelligible clarity of an arabesque, a rhythm or an harmonious balance, an activity or a movement, or again the reflection upon things of some human or divine thought, but above all it is the profound splendor of the soul shining through, of the soul which is the principle of life and animal energy or the principle of spiritual life, of pain and passion. There is also a more exalted splendor, the splendor of Grace, which the Greeks never knew.

II. *Imitation in Art*

Art, as such, consists not in imitating but in making, in composing or constructing, and that according to the laws of the very thing to be placed in being (ship, house, carpet, colored canvas, or hewn block of stone). This requisite of its generic concept preponderates over everything else in it, and to allot to it for essential end the representation of the real is to destroy it. Plato, with his theory of various degrees of imitation and poetry as an illusion, misconceives, like all extravagant intellectualists, the peculiar nature of art; hence his contempt for poetry. It is clear that if art were a *means of knowledge*, it would be wildly inferior to geometry.

But if art, as such, is far removed from imitation, the Fine Arts, as ordered to Beauty, are related to imitation, in a way difficult enough to define.

"Imitation is natural to mankind from childhood . . . , man is the most imi-

---

15 By *brilliance of form* must be understood an *ontological* splendor which happens to be revealed to our minds, not a *conceptual* clarity. There must be no misunderstanding here: the words *clarity, intelligibility* and *light*, used to characterize the part played by *form* in the heart of things, do not necessarily indicate something clear and intelligible *to us*, but rather something which, although clear and luminous *in itself*, intelligible *in itself*, often remains obscure to our eyes either because of the matter in which the form in question is buried or because of the transcendence of the form itself in the things of the spirit. The more substantial and profound this secret significance, the more concealed from us it is. . . .

tative of animals; through imitation he acquires his first knowledge and from imitations everyone derives pleasure. Works of art prove this, for the very things it gives us pain to see, we enjoy looking at in exact reproductions, the forms, for example, of the most horrible beasts, and corpses. The reason is that to be learning something is the pleasantest thing in the world not only to philosophers but to the rest of men. . . ." [16] When Aristotle wrote this with reference to the first causes of poetry, he was propounding a specific condition imposed upon the Fine Arts, a condition grasped in their earliest origin. But Aristotle is to be understood here in the most *formal* way. If the Philosopher, pursuing his usual method, goes straight to the primitive elementary case, it would be a complete mistake to stop there and to restrict the word "imitation" to its popularly accepted meaning of *exact reproduction or representation of a given reality*. When the man of the reindeer age scrawled the shapes of animals on the walls of caves he was no doubt principally moved by the pleasure of reproducing something exactly.[17] But the *joy of imitation* has since then become remarkably purified. I will try to sharpen the point of this idea of imitation in art.

The Fine Arts aim at producing, by the object they make, joy or delight in the mind through the intuition of the senses: the object of painting, said Poussin, is delight. Such joy is not the joy of the simple act of knowing, the joy of possessing knowledge, of having truth. It is a joy overflowing from such an act, when the object upon which it is brought to bear is well proportioned to the mind.

Such joy, therefore, presupposes knowledge, and the more knowledge there is, the more things given to the mind, the greater will be the possibility of joy. For this reason art, as ordered to beauty, never stops—at all events when its object permits it—at shapes or colors, or at sounds or words, considered in themselves and *as things* (they must be so considered to begin with, that is the first condition), but considers them *also* as making known something other than themselves, that is to say *as symbols*. And the thing symbolized can be in turn a symbol, and the more charged with symbolism the work of art (but spontaneous symbolism intuitively apprehended, not hieroglyphic symbolism), the more immense, the richer and the higher will be the possibility of joy and beauty. The beauty of a picture or a statue is thus incomparably richer than the beauty of a carpet, a Venetian glass, or an amphora.

In this sense, painting, sculpture, poetry, music, even dancing, are imitative arts, that is to say arts realizing the beauty of the work and procuring the joy of the soul by the use of imitation or by producing through the medium of

[16] Aristotle, *Poetics*, iv, 1448 b 5-14.

[17] Or, more probably, from the desire to signify an object by means of an ideogram, with perhaps a magical intention: for such drawings, being necessarily in the dark, could not have been made to be looked at. . . .

certain sensible symbols the spontaneous presence in the mind of something over and above such symbols. Painting *imitates* with colors and plane forms given things outside us, music *imitates* with sound and rhythms—and dancing with rhythm alone, "the character and temperament," in Aristotle's phrase,[18] of the personages represented, and the movements of the soul, the invisible world stirring within us. Making allowance for such a difference in regard to the object symbolized, painting is no more imitative than music, and music no less imitative than painting, if "imitation" be understood exactly in the sense just defined.

But the joy procured by the beautiful does not consist formally in the act of knowing reality or in the act of conformity with what is; it does not depend upon the perfection of the imitation as a reproduction of the real, or the fidelity of the representation. Imitation as reproduction or representation of the real—in other words, imitation *materially considered*—is merely a means, not an end; it relates, along with manual dexterity, to the artistic activity, but no more constitutes it. And the things made present to the soul by the sensible symbols of art— by rhythm, sound, line, color, form, volume, words, meter, rhyme and image, the *proximate matter* of art—are themselves merely a material element of the beauty of the work, just like the symbols in question; they are the *remote matter,* so to speak, at the disposal of the artist, on which he must make the brilliance of a form, the light of being, shine. To set up the perfection of imitation materially considered as an end would therefore involve ordering oneself with a view to what is purely material in the work of art; a servile imitation absolutely foreign to art.[19]

What is required is not that the representation shall conform exactly to a given reality, but that through the material elements of the beauty of the work there shall be transmitted, sovereign and entire, the brilliance of a form—of a form, and therefore of *some truth;* in that sense the great phrase of the Platonists, *splendor veri,* abides for ever. But if the joy produced by a work of beauty proceeds from *some truth,* it does not proceed from the truth of *imitation as a reproduction of things,* it proceeds from the perfection with which the work expresses or manifests form, in the metaphysical sense of the word, it proceeds from the truth *of imitation as manifestation of a form.* There is the *formal element* of imitation in art, the expression or manifestation, in a suitably proportioned work, of some secret principle of intelligibility shining forth. There the *joy of imitation* in art is brought to bear. And it is that which gives art its *universal* value. . . .

. . . If "imitation" were to be understood as meaning *exact reproduction or*

---

[18] *Poetics,* i, 1447 a 28.

[19] "[Cézanne] once asked me what collectors thought of Rosa Bonheur. I told him it was generally agreed that the *Laboureur Nivernaise* was stunning.—'Yes,' replied Cézanne, 'it's *horribly* like the real thing'" (Ambroise Vollard, *Paul Cézanne,* Paris, Crès, 1919).

copy of reality,[20] it would have to be admitted that, apart from the art of the cartographer or the draughtsman of anatomical plates, there is no art of imitation. In that sense, and however deplorable his precepts may be in other respects, Gauguin, in maintaining that painters should give up *painting what they saw*, was formulating an elementary truth which the Masters have never ceased to practice. Cézanne's familiar dictum expressed the same truth: "What we must do is Poussin over again on nature. That's the whole secret." [21] The imitative arts aim neither at copying the appearance of nature nor at depicting "the ideal," but at making something beautiful by the display of a *form* with the help of visible symbols.

The human artist or poet whose mind is not, like the Divine Mind, the cause of things, cannot draw this form complete out of his creative spirit: he goes and gathers it first and foremost in the vast treasure of created things, of sensitive nature as of the world of souls, and of the interior world of his own soul. From this point of view he is first and foremost a man who sees more deeply than other men and discovers in reality spiritual radiations which others are unable to discern. But to make these radiations shine out in his work and so to be truly docile and faithful to the invisible Spirit at play in things, he can, and indeed he must to some extent, deform, reconstruct and transfigure the material appearance of nature. Even in a portrait which is "a speaking likeness" of its subject—in Holbein's drawings, for example—it is always a form conceived in the mind

[20] The truth is, it is difficult to determine in what precisely this imitation-copy consists, the concept of which seems so clear to minds which have their being among the simplified schemata of the popular imagination.

Is it the imitation or the copy of what the thing in itself *is* and its intelligible *type*? But that is an object of conception, not of sensation, a thing invisible and intangible, which art, consequently, cannot directly reproduce. Is it the imitation or the copy of the *sensations* produced in us by the thing? But the sensations attain the consciousness of each one of us only as refracted by an inner atmosphere of memories and emotions, and are, moreover, eternally changing in a flux in which all things become distorted and are continuously intermingled, so that from the point of view of *pure sensation* it must be admitted with the Futurists that "a galloping horse has not four hoofs but twenty, that our bodies sink into the sofas on which we sit and the sofas sink into us, that the motor-bus rushes into the houses it goes past, and that the houses in turn hurl themselves upon the motor-bus and become one with it. . . ."

The reproduction or exact copy of nature thus appears as the object of an impossible pursuit—a concept which vanishes when an attempt is made to define it. In practice it resolves itself into the idea of such a representation of things as photography or casting would give, or rather—for such mechanical processes themselves produce results which are "false" as far as our perception is concerned—into the idea of a representation of things *capable of giving us an illusion and deceiving our senses* (it is then no longer a copy pure and simple but presupposes, on the contrary, an artificial faking). . . .

[21] Ambroise Vollard, *Paul Cézanne*, Paris, Crès, 1919. "On Nature," that is to say, contemplating and deriving inspiration from Nature. If it were to be understood as doing Poussin over again *by painting according to nature*, with nature for a constituent feature, Cézanne's observation would deserve all the criticism it has received. "It is not by sensation you become classical, but by the mind" (Gino Severini, *Du Cubisme au Classicisme*). . . .

of the artist and truly brought to birth in that mind which is expressed by the work, true portraits being merely the "ideal reconstruction of individuals." [22]

Art, then, is fundamentally constructive and creative. It is the faculty of producing, not of course *ex nihilo,* but out of a pre-existing matter, a new creature, an original being capable in its turn of moving a human soul. The new creature is the fruit of a spiritual marriage uniting the activity of the artist to the passivity of a given matter. . . .

Nature is therefore in the first place a stimulus and a check to artists, not a model to be slavishly copied. Ask real painters how they need her. They stand before her in timidity and awe, but with the timidity of modesty, not of servility. They imitate her, in a truly *filial* spirit, and according to the creative agility of the spirit; but their imitation is not literal and servile. As we were coming back after a walk in winter time, Rouault told me that looking at the countryside under the snow in the sunshine he had realized how to paint the white trees of spring. "The model," said Renoir, "is there only to set me alight, to let me dare things I could never imagine without it . . . and it makes me come a cropper, if ever I go too far." [23] Such freedom do the sons of the Creator enjoy.

—*Art and Scholasticism* (1920; translated 1930)

GEORGE SANTAYANA

The Nature of Beauty

The Philosophy of Beauty Is a Theory of Values

It would be easy to find a definition of beauty that should give in a few words a telling paraphrase of the word. We know on excellent authority that beauty is truth, that it is the expression of the ideal, the symbol of divine perfection, and the sensible manifestation of the good. A litany of these titles of honor might easily be compiled, and repeated in praise of our divinity. Such phrases stimulate thought and give us a momentary pleasure, but they hardly bring any permanent enlightenment. A definition that should really define must be nothing less than the exposition of the origin, place, and elements of beauty as an object of human experience. We must learn from it, as far as possible, why, when, and how beauty appears, what conditions an object must fulfill to be beautiful, what

[22] Baudelaire, *Curiosités esthétiques,* Le Musée Bonne-Nouvelle.
[23] Quoted by M. Albert André in his recent book on *Renoir* (Crés).

elements of our nature make us sensible of beauty, and what the relation is between the constitution of the object and the excitement of our susceptibility. Nothing less will really define beauty or make us understand what esthetic appreciation is. The definition of beauty in this sense will be the task of this whole book, a task that can be only very imperfectly accomplished within its limits.

The historical titles of our subject may give us a hint towards the beginning of such a definition. Many writers of the last century called the philosophy of beauty *Criticism,* and the word is still retained as the title for the reasoned appreciation of works of art. We could hardly speak, however, of delight in nature as criticism. A sunset is not criticized; it is felt and enjoyed. The word "criticism," used on such an occasion, would emphasize too much the element of deliberate judgment and of comparison with standards. Beauty, although often so described, is seldom so perceived, and all the greatest excellences of nature and art are so far from being approved of by a rule that they themselves furnish the standard and ideal by which critics measure inferior effects.

This age of science and of nomenclature has accordingly adopted a more learned word, *Esthetics,* that is, the theory of perception or of susceptibility. If criticism is too narrow a word, pointing exclusively to our more artificial judgments, esthetics seems to be too broad and to include within its sphere all pleasures and pains, if not all perceptions whatsoever. Kant used it, as we know, for his theory of time and space as forms of all perception; and it has at times been narrowed into an equivalent for the philosophy of art.

If we combine, however, the etymological meaning of criticism with that of esthetics, we shall unite two essential qualities of the theory of beauty. Criticism implies judgment, and esthetics perception. To get the common ground, that of perceptions which are critical, or judgments which are perceptions, we must widen our notion of deliberate criticism so as to include those judgments of value which are instinctive and immediate, that is, to include pleasures and pains; and at the same time we must narrow our notion of esthetics so as to exclude all perceptions which are not appreciations, which do not find a value in their objects. We thus reach the sphere of critical or appreciative perception, which is, roughly speaking, what we mean to deal with. And retaining the word "esthetics," which is now current, we may therefore say that esthetics is concerned with the perception of values. The meaning and conditions of value are, then, what we must first consider.

Since the days of Descartes it has been a conception familiar to philosophers that every visible event in nature might be explained by previous visible events, and that all the motions, for instance, of the tongue in speech, or of the hand in painting, might have merely physical causes. If consciousness is thus accessory to life and not essential to it, the race of man might have existed upon the earth and acquired all the arts necessary for its subsistence without possessing a single sensation, idea, or emotion. Natural selection might have secured the survival of those automata which made useful reactions upon their environment. An instinct of self-preservation would have been developed, dangers would have been shunned without being feared, and injuries revenged without being felt.

In such a world there might have come to be the most perfect organization. There would have been what we should call the expression of the deepest interests and the apparent pursuit of conceived goods. For there would have been spontaneous and ingrained tendencies to avoid certain contingencies and to produce others; all the dumb show and evidence of thinking would have been patent to the observer. Yet there would surely have been no thinking, no expectation, and no conscious achievement in the whole process.

The onlooker might have feigned ends and objects of forethought, as we do in the case of the water that seeks its own level, or in that of the vacuum which nature abhors. But the particles of matter would have remained unconscious of their collocation, and all nature would have been insensible of their changing arrangement. We only, the possible spectators of that process, by virtue of our own interests and habits, could see any progress or culmination in it. We should see culmination where the result attained satisfied our practical or esthetic demands, and progress wherever such a satisfaction was approached. But apart from ourselves, and our human bias, we can see in such a mechanical world no element of value whatever. In removing consciousness, we have removed the possibility of worth.

But it is not only in the absence of all consciousness that value would be removed from the world; by a less violent abstraction from the totality of human experience, we might conceive beings of a purely intellectual cast, minds in which the transformations of nature were mirrored without any emotion. Every event would then be noted, its relations would be observed, its recurrence might even be expected; but all this would happen without a shadow of desire, of pleasure, or of regret. No event would be repulsive, no situation terrible. We might, in a word, have a world of idea without a world of will. In this case, as completely as if consciousness were absent altogether, all value and excellence would be gone. So that for the existence of good in any form it is not merely consciousness but emotional consciousness that is needed. Observation will not do, appreciation is required.

Preference Is Ultimately Irrational

We may therefore at once assert this axiom, important for all moral philosophy and fatal to certain stubborn incoherences of thought, that there is no value apart from some appreciation of it, and no good apart from some preference of it before its absence or its opposite. In appreciation, in preference, lie the root and essence of all excellence. Or, as Spinoza clearly expresses it, we desire nothing because it is good, but it is good only because we desire it.

It is true that in the absence of an instinctive reaction we can still apply these epithets by an appeal to usage. We may agree that an action is bad or a building good, because we recognize in them a character which we have learned to designate by that adjective; but unless there is in us some trace of passionate reprobation or of sensible delight, there is no moral or esthetic judgment. It is all a question of propriety of speech, and of the empty titles of things. The verbal and mechanical proposition, that passes for judgment of worth, is the great cloak of ineptitude in these matters. Insensibility is very quick in the conventional use of words. If we appealed more often to actual feelings, our judgments would be more diverse, but they would be more legitimate and instructive. Verbal judgments are often useful instruments of thought, but it is not by them that worth can ultimately be determined.

Values spring from the immediate and inexplicable reaction of vital impulse, and from the irrational part of our nature. The rational part is by its essence relative; it leads us from data to conclusions, or from parts to wholes; it never furnishes the data with which it works. If any preference or precept were declared to be ultimate and primitive, it would thereby be declared to be irrational, since mediation, inference, and synthesis are the essence of rationality. The idea of rationality is itself as arbitrary, as much dependent on the needs of a finite organization, as any other ideal. Only as ultimately securing tranquillity of mind, which the philosopher instinctively pursues, has it for him any necessity. In spite of the verbal propriety of saying that reason demands rationality, what really demands rationality, what makes it a good and indispensable thing and gives it all its authority, is not its own nature, but our need of it both in safe and economical action and in the pleasures of comprehension.

It is evident that beauty is a species of value, and what we have said of value in general applies to this particular kind. A first approach to a definition of beauty has therefore been made by the exclusion of all intellectual judgments, all judgments of matter of fact or of relation. To substitute judgments of fact for judgments of value, is a sign of a pedantic and borrowed criticism. If we approach a work of art or nature scientifically, for the sake of its historical connections or proper classification, we do not approach it esthetically. The discovery of its date or of its author may be otherwise interesting; it only remotely affects our esthetic appreciation by adding to the direct effect certain associations. If the direct effect were absent, and the object in itself uninteresting, the circumstances would be immaterial. Molière's *Misanthrope* says to the court poet who commends his sonnet as written in a quarter of an hour,

Voyons, monsieur, le temps ne fait rien à l'affaire,

and so we might say to the critic that sinks into the archaeologist, show us the work, and let the date alone.

In an opposite direction the same substitution of facts for values makes its appearance, whenever the reproduction of fact is made the sole standard of artistic excellence. Many half-trained observers condemn the work of some naïve or fanciful masters with a sneer, because, as they truly say, it is out of drawing. The implication is that to be correctly copied from a model is the prerequisite of all beauty. Correctness is, indeed, an element of effect and one which, in respect to familiar objects, is almost indispensable, because its absence would cause a disappointment and dissatisfaction incompatible with enjoyment. We learn to value truth more and more as our love and knowledge of nature increase. But fidelity is a merit only because it is in this way a factor in our pleasure. It stands on a level with all other ingredients of effect. When a man raises it to a solitary pre-eminence and becomes incapable of appreciating anything else, he betrays the decay of esthetic capacity. The scientific habit in him inhibits the artistic.

That facts have a value of their own, at once complicates and explains this question. We are naturally pleased by every perception, and recognition and surprise are particularly acute sensations. When we see a striking truth in any imitation we are therefore delighted, and this kind of pleasure is very legitimate, and enters into the best effects of all the representative arts. Truth and realism are therefore esthetically good, but they are not all-sufficient, since the representation of everything is not equally pleasing and effective. The fact that resemblance is a source of satisfaction justifies the critic in demanding it, while the esthetic insufficiency of such veracity shows the different value of truth in science and in art. Science is the response to the demand for information, and in it we ask for the whole truth and nothing but the truth. Art is the response to the demand for entertainment, for the stimulation of our senses and imagination, and truth enters into it only as it subserves these ends.

Even the scientific value of truth is not, however, ultimate or absolute. It rests partly on practical, partly on esthetic interests. As our ideas are gradually brought into conformity with the facts by the painful process of selection—for intuition runs equally into truth and into error, and can settle nothing if not controlled by experience—we gain vastly in our command over our environment. This is the fundamental value of natural science, and the fruit it is yielding in our day. We have no better vision of nature and life than some of our predecessors, but we have greater material resources. To know the truth about the composition and history of things is good for this reason. It is also good because of the enlarged horizon it gives us, because the spectacle of nature is a marvelous and fascinating one, full of a serious sadness and large peace, which gives us back our birthright as children of the planet and naturalizes us upon the earth.

This is the poetic value of the scientific *Weltanschauung*. From these two benefits, the practical and the imaginative, all the value of truth is derived.

Esthetic and moral judgments are accordingly to be classed together in contrast to judgments intellectual; they are both judgments of value, while intellectual judgments are judgments of fact. If the latter have any value, it is only derivative, and our whole intellectual life has its only justification in its connection with our pleasures and pains.

Contrast Between Moral and Esthetic Values

The relation between esthetic and moral judgments, between the spheres of the beautiful and the good, is close, but the distinction between them is important. One factor of this distinction is that while esthetic judgments are mainly positive, that is, perceptions of good, moral judgments are mainly and fundamentally negative, or perceptions of evil. Another factor of the distinction is that whereas, in the perception of beauty, our judgment is necessarily intrinsic and based on the character of the immediate experience, and never consciously on the idea of an eventual utility in the object, judgments about moral worth, on the contrary, are always based, when they are positive, upon the consciousness of benefits probably involved. Both these distinctions need some elucidations.

Hedonistic ethics have always had to struggle against the moral sense of mankind. Earnest minds, that feel the weight and dignity of life, rebel against the assertion that the aim of right conduct is enjoyment. Pleasure usually appears to them as a temptation, and they sometimes go so far as to make avoidance of it a virtue. The truth is that morality is not mainly concerned with the attainment of pleasure; it is rather concerned, in all its deeper and more authoritative maxims, with the prevention of suffering. There is something artificial in the deliberate pursuit of pleasure; there is something absurd in the obligation to enjoy oneself. We feel no duty in that direction; we take to enjoyment naturally enough after the work of life is done, and the freedom and spontaneity of our pleasures are what is most essential to them.

The sad business of life is rather to escape certain dreadful evils to which our nature exposes us—death, hunger, disease, weariness, isolation, and contempt. By the awful authority of these things which stand like specters behind every moral injunction, conscience in reality speaks, and a mind which they have duly impressed cannot but feel, by contrast, the hopeless triviality of the search for pleasure. It cannot but feel that a life abandoned to amusement and to changing impulses must run unawares into fatal dangers. The moment, however, that society emerges from the early pressure of the environment and is tolerably secure against primary evils, morality grows lax. The forms that life will further assume are not to be imposed by moral authority, but are determined by the genius of the race, the opportunities of the moment, and the tastes and resources of individual minds. The reign of duty gives place to the reign of freedom, and the law and the covenant to the dispensation of grace.

The appreciation of beauty and its embodiment in the arts are activities which belong to our holiday life, when we are redeemed for the moment from the shadow of evil and the slavery to fear, and are following the bent of our nature where it chooses to lead us. The values, then, with which we here deal are positive; they were negative in the sphere of morality. The ugly is hardly an exception, because it is not the cause of any real pain. In itself it is rather a source of amusement. If its suggestions are vitally repulsive, its presence becomes a real evil towards which we assume a practical and moral attitude. And, correspondingly, the pleasant is never, as we have seen, the object of a truly moral injunction.

Work and Play

We have here, then, an important element of the distinction between esthetic and moral values. It is the same that has been pointed to in the famous contrast between work and play. These terms may be used in different senses and their importance in moral classification differs with the meaning attached to them. We may call everything play which is useless activity, exercise that springs from the physiological impulse to discharge the energy which the exigencies of life have not called out. Work will then be all action that is necessary or useful for life. Evidently if work and play are thus objectively distinguished as useful and useless action, work is a eulogistic term and play a disparaging one. It would be better for us that all our energy should be turned to account, that none of it should be wasted in aimless motion. Play, in this sense, is a sign of imperfect adaptation. It is proper to childhood, when the body and mind are not yet fit to cope with the environment, but it is unseemly in manhood and pitiable in old age, because it marks an atrophy of human nature, and a failure to take hold of the opportunities of life.

Play is thus essentially frivolous. Some persons, understanding the term in this sense, have felt an aversion, which every liberal mind will share, to classifying social pleasures, art, and religion under the head of play, and by that epithet condemning them, as a certain school seems to do, to gradual extinction as the race approaches maturity. But if all the useless ornaments of our life are to be cut off in the process of adaptation, evolution would impoverish instead of enriching our nature. Perhaps that is the tendency of evolution, and our barbarous ancestors amid their toils and wars, with their flaming passions and mythologies, lived better lives than are reserved to our well-adapted descendants.

We may be allowed to hope, however, that some imagination may survive parasitically even in the most serviceable brain. Whatever course history may take—and we are not here concerned with prophecy—the question of what is desirable is not affected. To condemn spontaneous and delightful occupations because they are useless for self-preservation shows an uncritical prizing of life irrespective of its content. For such a system the worthiest function of the universe should be to establish perpetual motion. Uselessness is a fatal accusation to bring against any act which is done for its presumed utility, but those which are done for their own sake are their own justification.

At the same time there is an undeniable propriety in calling all the liberal and imaginative activities of man play, because they are spontaneous, and not carried on under pressure of external necessity or danger. Their utility for self-preservation may be very indirect and accidental, but they are not worthless for that reason. On the contrary, we may measure the degree of happiness and civilization which any race has attained by the proportion of its energy which is devoted to free and generous pursuits, to the adornment of life and the culture of the imagination. For it is in the spontaneous play of his faculties that man finds himself and his happiness. Slavery is the most degrading condition of which he is capable, and he is as often a slave to the niggardliness of the earth and the inclemency of heaven, as to a master or an institution. He is a slave when all his energy is spent in avoiding suffering and death, when all his action is imposed from without, and no breath or strength is left him for free enjoyment.

Work and play here take on a different meaning, and become equivalent to servitude and freedom. The change consists in the subjective point of view from which the distinction is now made. We no longer mean by work all that is done usefully, but only what is done unwillingly and by the spur of necessity. By play we are designating, no longer what is done fruitlessly, but whatever is done spontaneously and for its own sake, whether it have or not an ulterior utility. Play, in this sense, may be our most useful occupation. So far would a gradual adaptation to the environment be from making this play obsolete, that it would tend to abolish work, and to make play universal. For with the elimination of all the conflicts and errors of instinct, the race would do spontaneously whatever conduced to its welfare and we should live safely and prosperously without external stimulus or restraint. . . .

In this second and subjective sense, then, work is the disparaging term and play the eulogistic one. All who feel the dignity and importance of the things of the imagination, need not hesitate to adopt the classification which designates them as play. We point out thereby, not that they have no value, but that their value is intrinsic, that in them is one of the sources of all worth. Evidently all values must be ultimately intrinsic. The useful is good because of the excellence of its consequences; but these must somewhere cease to be merely useful in their turn, or only excellent as means; somewhere we must reach the good that is good in itself and for its own sake, else the whole process is futile, and the utility of our first object illusory. We here reach the second factor in our distinction, between esthetic and moral values, which regards their immediacy. . . .

Esthetic and Physical Pleasure

We have now separated with some care intellectual and moral judgments from the sphere of our subject, and found that we are to deal only with perceptions of value, and with these only when they are positive and immediate. But even with these distinctions the most remarkable characteristic of the sense of beauty remains undefined. All pleasures are intrinsic and positive values, but all pleasures are not perceptions of beauty. Pleasure is indeed the essence of that perception, but there is evidently in this particular pleasure a complication which is not present in others and which is the basis of the distinction made by consciousness and language between it and the rest. It will be instructive to notice the degrees of this difference.

The bodily pleasures are those least resembling perceptions of beauty. By bodily pleasures we mean, of course, more than pleasures with a bodily seat; for that class would include them all, as well as all forms and elements of consciousness. Esthetic pleasures have physical conditions, they depend on the activity of the eye and the ear, of the memory and the other ideational functions of the brain. But we do not connect those pleasures with their seats except in physiological studies; the ideas with which esthetic pleasures are associated are not the ideas of their bodily causes. The pleasures we call physical, and regard as low, on the contrary, are those which call our attention to some part of our own body, and which make no object so conspicuous to us as the organ in which they arise.

There is here, then, a very marked distinction between physical and esthetic pleasure; the organs of the latter must be transparent, they must not intercept our attention, but carry it directly to some external object. The greater dignity and range of esthetic pleasure is thus made very intelligible. The soul is glad, as it were, to forget its connection with the body and to fancy that it can travel over the world with the liberty with which it changes the objects of its thought. The mind passes from China to Peru without any conscious change in the local tensions of the body. This illusion of disembodiment is very exhilarating, while immersion in the flesh and confinement to some organ gives a tone of grossness and selfishness to our consciousness. The generally meaner associations of physical pleasures also help to explain their comparative crudity.

The Differentia of Esthetic Pleasure Not Its Disinterestedness

The distinction between pleasure and the sense of beauty has sometimes been said to consist in the unselfishness of esthetic satisfaction. In other pleasures, it is said, we gratify our senses and passion; in the contemplation of beauty we are raised above ourselves, the passions are silenced and we are happy in the recognition of a good that we do not seek to possess. The painter does not look at a spring of water with the eyes of a thirsty man, nor at a beautiful woman with those of a satyr. The difference lies, it is urged, in the impersonality of the enjoyment. But this distinction is one of intensity and delicacy, not of nature, and it seems satisfactory only to the least esthetic minds.[1]

In the second place, the supposed disinterestedness of esthetic delights is not truly fundamental. Appreciation of a picture is not identical with the desire to buy it, but it is, or ought to be, closely related and preliminary to that desire. The beauties of nature and of the plastic arts are not consumed by being enjoyed; they retain all the efficacy to impress a second beholder. But this circumstance is accidental, and those esthetic objects which depend upon change and are exhausted in time, as are all performances, are things the enjoyment of which is an object of rivalry and is coveted as much as any other pleasure. And even plastic beauties can often not be enjoyed except by a few, on account of the necessity of travel or other difficulties of access, and then this esthetic enjoyment is as selfishly pursued as the rest.

The truth which the theory is trying to state seems rather to be that when we seek esthetic pleasures we have no further pleasure in mind; that we do not mix up the satisfactions of vanity and proprietorship with the delight of contemplation. This is true, but it is true at bottom of all pursuits and enjoyments. Every real pleasure is in one sense disinterested. It is not sought with ulterior motives, and what fills the mind is no calculation, but the image of an object or event, suffused with emotion. A sophisticated consciousness may often take the idea of self as the touchstone of its inclinations; but this self, for the gratification and aggrandizement of which a man may live, is itself only a complex of aims and memories, which once had their direct objects, in which he had taken a spontaneous and unselfish interest. The gratifications which, merged together, make the selfishness are each of them ingenuous, and no more selfish than the most altruistic, impersonal emotion. The content of selfishness is a mass of unselfishness. There is no reference to the nominal essence called oneself either in one's appetites or in one's natural affections; yet a man absorbed in his meat and drink, in his houses and lands, in his children and dogs, is called selfish because these interests, although natural and instinctive in him, are not shared by others. The unselfish man is he whose nature has a more universal direction, whose interests are more widely diffused.

---

[1] Schopenhauer, indeed, who makes much of it, was a good critic, but his psychology suffered much from the pessimistic generalities of his system. It concerned him to show that the will was bad, and, as he felt beauty to be a good if not a holy thing, he hastened to convince himself that it came from the suppression of the will. But even in his system this suppression is only relative. The desire of individual objects, indeed, is absent in the perception of beauty, but there is still present that initial love of the general type and principles of things which is the first illusion of the absolute, and drives it on to the fatal experiment of creation. So that, apart from Schopenhauer's mythology, we have even in him the recognition that beauty gives satisfaction to some dim and underlying demand of our nature, just as particular objects give more special and momentary pleasures to our individualized wills. His psychology was, however, far too vague and general to undertake an analysis of those mysterious feelings.

But as impersonal thoughts are such only in their object, not in their subject or agent, since all thoughts are the thoughts of somebody: so also unselfish interests have to be somebody's interests. If we were not interested in beauty, if it were of no concern to our happiness whether things were beautiful or ugly, we should manifest not the maximum, but the total absence of esthetic faculty. The disinterestedness of this pleasure is, therefore, that of all primitive and intuitive satisfactions, which are in no way conditioned by a reference to an artificial general concept, like that of the self, all the potency of which must itself be derived from the independent energy of its component elements. I care about myself because "myself" is a name for the things I have at heart. To set up the verbal figment of personality and make it an object of concern apart from the interests which were its content and substance, turns the moralist into a pedant, and ethics into a superstition. The self which is the object of *amour propre* is an idol of the tribe, and needs to be disintegrated into the primitive objective interests that underlie it before the cultus of it can be justified by reason.

The Differentia of Esthetic Pleasure Not Its Universality

The supposed disinterestedness of our love of beauty passes into another characteristic of it often regarded as essential—its universality. The pleasures of the senses have, it is said, no dogmatism in them; that anything gives me pleasure involves no assertion about its capacity to give pleasure to another. But when I judge a thing to be beautiful, my judgment means that the thing is beautiful in itself, or (what is the same thing more critically expressed) that it should seem so to everybody. The claim to universality is, according to this doctrine, the essence of the esthetic; what makes the perception of beauty a judgment rather than a sensation. All esthetic precepts would be impossible, and all criticism arbitrary and subjective, unless we admit a paradoxical universality in our judgment, the philosophical implications of which we may then go on to develop. But we are fortunately not required to enter the labyrinth into which this method leads; there is a much simpler and clearer way of studying such questions, which is to challenge and analyze the assertion before us and seek its basis in human nature. Before this is done, we should run the risk of expanding a natural misconception or inaccuracy of thought into an inveterate and pernicious prejudice by making it the center of an elaborate construction.

That the claim of universality is such a natural inaccuracy will not be hard to show. There is notoriously no great agreement upon esthetic matters; and such agreement as there is, is based upon similarity of origin, nature, and circumstance among men, a similarity which, where it exists, tends to bring about identity in all judgments and feelings. It is unmeaning to say that what is beautiful to one man *ought* to be beautiful to another. If their senses are the same, their associations and dispositions similar, then the same thing will certainly be beautiful to both. If their natures are different, the form which to one will be entrancing will be to another even invisible, because his classifications and discriminations in perception will be different, and he may see a hideous detached fragment or a shapeless aggregate of things, in what to another is a perfect whole—so entirely are the unities of objects unities of function and use. It is absurd to say that what is invisible to a given being *ought* to seem beautiful to him. Evidently this obligation of recognizing the same qualities is conditioned by the possession of the same faculties. But no two men have exactly the same faculties, nor can things have for any two exactly the same values.

What is loosely expressed by saying that anyone ought to see this or that beauty is that he would see it if his disposition, training, or attention were what our ideal demands for him; and our ideal of what any one should be has complex but discoverable sources. We take, for instance, a certain pleasure in having our own judgments supported by those of others; we are intolerant, if not of the existence of a nature different from our own, at least of its expression in words and judgments. We are confirmed or made happy in our doubtful opinions by seeing them accepted universally. We are unable to find the basis of our taste in our own experience and therefore refuse to look for it there. If we were sure of our ground, we should be willing to acquiesce in the naturally different feelings and ways of others, as a man who is conscious of speaking his language with the accent of the capital confesses its arbitrariness with gaiety, and is pleased and interested in the variations of it he observes in provincials; but the provincial is always zealous to show that he has reason and ancient authority to justify his oddities. So people who have no sensations, and do not know why they judge, are always trying to show that they judge by universal reason.

Thus the frailty and superficiality of our own judgments cannot brook contradiction. We abhor another man's doubt when we cannot tell him why we ourselves believe. Our ideal of other men tends therefore to include the agreement of their judgments with our own; and although we might acknowledge the fatuity of this demand in regard to natures very different from the human, we may be unreasonable enough to require that all races should admire the same style of architecture, and all ages the same poets.

The great actual unity of human taste within the range of conventional history helps the pretension. But in principle it is untenable. Nothing has less to do with the real merit of a work of imagination than the capacity of all men to appreciate it; the true test is the degree and kind of satisfaction it can give to him who appreciates it most. The symphony would lose nothing if half mankind had always been deaf, as nine-tenths of them actually are to the intricacies of its harmonies; but it would have lost much if no Beethoven had existed. And more: incapacity to appreciate certain types of beauty may be the condition *sine qua non* for the appreciation of another kind; the greatest capacity both for enjoyment and creation is highly specialized and exclusive, and hence the greatest ages of art have often been strangely intolerant.

The invectives of one school against another, perverse as they are philosophically, are artistically often signs of health, because they indicate a vital appreciation of certain kinds of beauty, a love of them that has grown into a jealous passion. The architects that have pieced out the imperfections of ancient buildings with their own thoughts, like Charles V when he raised his massive palace beside the Alhambra, may be condemned from a certain point of view. They marred much by their interference; but they showed a splendid confidence in their own intuitions, a proud assertion of their own taste, which is the greatest evidence of esthetic sincerity. On the contrary, our own gropings, eclecticism, and archaeology are the symptoms of impotence. If we were less learned and less just, we might be more efficient. If our appreciation were less general, it might be more real, and if we trained our imagination into exclusiveness, it might attain to character.

The Differentia of Esthetic Pleasure: Its Objectification

There is, however, something more in the claim to universality in esthetic judgments than the desire to generalize our own opinions. There is the expression of a curious but well-known psychological phenomenon, namely, the transformation of an element of sensation into the quality of a thing. If we say that other men should see the beauties we see, it is because we think those beauties *are in the object,* like its color, proportion, or size. Our judgment appears to us merely the perception and discovery of an external existence, of the real excellence that is without. But this notion is radically absurd and contradictory. Beauty, as we have seen, is a value; it cannot be conceived as an independent existence which affects our senses and which we consequently perceive. It exists in perception, and cannot exist otherwise. A beauty not perceived is a pleasure not felt, and a contradiction. But modern philosophy has taught us to say the same thing of every element of the perceived world; all are sensations; and their grouping into objects imagined to be permanent and external is the work of certain habits of our intelligence. We should be incapable of surveying or retaining the diffused experiences of life, unless we organized and classified them, and out of the chaos of impressions framed the world of conventional and recognizable objects.

How this is done is explained by the current theories of perception. External objects usually affect various senses at once, the impressions of which are thereby associated. Repeated experiences of one object are also associated on account of their similarity; hence a double tendency to merge and unify into a single percept, to which a name is attached, the group of those memories and reactions which in fact had one external thing for their cause. But this percept, once formed, is clearly different from those particular experiences out of which it grew. It is permanent, they are variable. They are but partial views and glimpses of it. The constituted notion therefore comes to be the reality, and the materials of it merely the appearance. The distinction between substance and quality, reality and appearance, matter and mind, has no other origin.

The objects thus conceived and distinguished from our ideas of them, are at first compacted of all the impressions, feelings, and memories, which offer themselves for association and fall within the vortex of the amalgamating imagination. Every sensation we get from a thing is originally treated as one of its qualities. Experiment, however, and the practical need of a simpler conception of the structure of objects lead us gradually to reduce the qualities of the object to a minimum, and to regard most perceptions as an effect of those few qualities upon us. These few primary qualities, like extension which we persist in treating as independently real and as the quality of a substance, are those which suffice to explain the order of our experiences. All the rest, like color, are relegated to the subjective sphere, as merely effects upon our minds, and apparent or secondary qualities of the object.

But this distinction has only a practical justification. Convenience and economy of thought alone determine what combination of our sensations we shall continue to objectify and treat as the cause of the rest. The right and tendency to be objective is equal in all, since they are all prior to the artifice of thought by which we separate the concept from its materials, the thing from our experiences.

The qualities which we now conceive to belong to real objects are for the most part images of sight and touch. One of the first classes of effects to be treated as secondary were naturally pleasures and pains, since it could commonly conduce very little to intelligent and successful action to conceive our pleasures and pains as resident in objects. But emotions are essentially capable of objectification, as well as impressions of sense; and one may well believe that a primitive and inexperienced consciousness would rather people the world with ghosts of its own terrors and passions than with projections of those luminous and mathematical concepts which as yet it could hardly have formed.

This animistic and mythological habit of thought still holds its own at the confines of knowledge, where mechanical explanations are not found. In ourselves, where nearness makes observation difficult, in the intricate chaos of animal and human life, we still appeal to the efficacy of will and ideas, as also in the remote night of cosmic and religious problems. But in all the intermediate realm of vulgar day, where mechanical science has made progress, the inclusion of emotional or passionate elements in the concept of the reality would be now an extravagance. Here our idea of things is composed exclusively of perceptual elements, of the ideas of form and of motion.

The beauty of objects, however, forms an exception to this rule. Beauty is an emotional element, a pleasure of ours, which nevertheless we regard as a quality of things. But we are now prepared to understand the nature of this exception. It is the survival of a tendency originally universal to make every effect of a thing upon us a constituent of its conceived nature. The scientific idea of a thing is a great abstraction from the mass of perceptions and reactions which that thing produces; the esthetic idea is less abstract, since it retains the emotional reaction, the pleasure of the perception, as an integral part of the conceived thing.

Nor is it hard to find the ground of this survival in the sense of beauty of an objectification of feeling elsewhere extinct. Most of the pleasures which objects cause are easily distinguished and separated from the perception of the object: the object has to be applied to a particular organ, like the palate, or swallowed like wine, or used and operated upon in some way before the pleasure arises. The cohesion is therefore slight between the pleasure and the other associated elements of sense; the pleasure is separated in time from the perception, or it is localized in a different organ, and consequently is at once recognized as an effect and not as a quality of the object. But when the process of perception itself is pleasant, as it may easily be, when the intellectual operation, by which the elements of sense are associated and projected, and the concept of the form and substance of the thing produced, is naturally delightful, then we have a pleasure intimately bound up in the thing, inseparable from its character and constitution, the seat of which in us is the same as the seat of the perception. We naturally fail, under these circumstances, to separate the pleasure from the other objectified feelings. It becomes, like them, a quality of the object, which we distinguish from pleasures not so incorporated in the perception of things, by giving it the name of beauty.

The Definition of Beauty

We have now reached our definition of beauty, which, in the terms of our successive analysis and narrowing of the conception, is value positive, intrinsic, and objectified. Or, in less technical language, Beauty is pleasure regarded as the quality of a thing.

This definition is intended to sum up a variety of distinctions and identifications which should perhaps be here more explicitly set down. Beauty is a value, that is, it is not a perception of a matter of fact or of a relation: it is an emotion, an affection of our volitional and appreciative nature. An object cannot be beautiful if it can give pleasure to nobody: a beauty to which all men were forever indifferent is a contradiction in terms.

In the second place, this value is positive, it is the sense of the presence of something good, or (in the case of ugliness) of its absence. It is never the perception of a positive evil, it is never a negative value. That we are endowed with the sense of beauty is a pure gain which brings no evil with it. When the ugly ceases to be amusing or merely uninteresting and becomes disgusting, it becomes indeed a positive evil: but a moral and practical, not an esthetic, one. In esthetics that saying is true—often so disingenuous in ethics—that evil is nothing but the absence of good: for even the tedium and vulgarity of an existence without beauty is not itself ugly so much as lamentable and degrading. The absence of esthetic goods is a moral evil: the esthetic evil is merely relative, and means less of esthetic good than was expected at the place and time. No form in itself gives pain, although some forms give pain by causing a shock of surprise even when they are really beautiful: as if a mother found a fine bull pup in her child's cradle, when her pain would not be esthetic in its nature.

Further, this pleasure must not be in the consequence of the utility of the object or event, but in its immediate perception; in other words, beauty is an ultimate good, something that gives satisfaction to a natural function, to some fundamental need or capacity of our minds. Beauty is therefore a positive value that is intrinsic; it is a pleasure. These two circumstances sufficiently separate the sphere of esthetics from that of ethics. Moral values are generally negative, and always remote. Morality has to do with the avoidance of evil and the pursuit of good: esthetics only with enjoyment.

Finally, the pleasures of sense are distinguished from the perception of beauty, as sensation in general is distinguished from perception; by the objectification of the elements and their appearance as qualities rather of things than of consciousness. The passage from sensation to perception is gradual, and the path may be sometimes retraced: so it is with beauty and the pleasures of sensation. There is no sharp line between them, but it depends upon the degree of objectivity my feeling has attained at the moment whether I say "It pleases me," or "It is beautiful." If I am self-conscious and critical, I shall probably use one phrase; if I am impulsive and susceptible, the other. The more remote, interwoven, and inextricable the pleasure is, the more objective it will appear; and the union of two pleasures often makes one beauty. In Shakespeare's LIVth sonnet are these words:

> O how much more doth beauty beauteous seem
> By that sweet ornament which truth doth give!
> The rose looks fair, but fairer we it deem
> For that sweet odor which doth in it live.
> The canker-blooms have full as deep a dye
> As the perfumèd tincture of the roses,
> Hang on such thorns, and play as wantonly
> When summer's breath their maskèd buds discloses.
> But, for their beauty only is their show,
> They live unwooed and unrespected fade;
> Die to themselves. Sweet roses do not so:
> Of their sweet deaths are sweetest odors made.

One added ornament, we see, turns the deep dye, which was but show and mere sensation before, into an element of beauty and reality; and as truth is here the cooperation of perceptions, so beauty is the cooperation of pleasures. If color, form, and motion are hardly beautiful without the sweetness of the odor, how much more necessary would they be for the sweetness itself to become a beauty! If we had the perfume in a flask, no one would think of calling it beautiful: it would give us too detached and controllable a sensation. There would be no object in which it could be easily incorporated. But let it float from the garden, and it will add another sensuous charm to objects simultaneously recognized, and help to make them beautiful. Thus beauty is constituted by the objectification of pleasure. It is pleasure objectified.

—The Sense of Beauty (1896)

CHAPTER THREE

Art as Emotional Expression

EUGENE VÉRON
Art as the Expression of Emotion

LEO TOLSTOY
The Communication of Emotion

YRJÖ HIRN
Art the Reliever

Introductory Note

ACCORDING TO MARITAIN AND SANTAYANA, whose ideas were presented in Chapter II, art is the creation of beauty, defined in terms of pleasure. The writers to whom we shall now turn reject this view. The function of art, they maintain, is to express the whole gamut of human emotions, even the sad and the terrible; and ugliness may be created for its own expressiveness, not merely as a foil to beauty.

This point of view was first clearly formulated by Eugene Véron (1825-1889) in L'Esthetique (1878), a book much in advance of its time. Véron defines art as the *expression* of emotion. "The merit of a work of art," he declares, "can be finally measured by the power with which it manifests or interprets the emotion that was its determining cause, and that, for a like reason, must constitute its innermost and supreme unity." Some art, he recognizes, is simply decorative: its aim is to create beauty. But other art is broadly expressive: its aim is to express emotions that may be quite unconnected with beauty. We should approach expressive art not with the criterion of beauty or pleasure but with the criterion of expressiveness or significance. The question is not, Does this please me? but, Out of how deep a life does this spring? Great art, to paraphrase Longinus, is the echo of a great soul. But it is the emotional, or subjective, side of the human personality that is expressed; and art is distinguished from science by the predominance of subjectivity over objectivity. Whereas the scientist is one "whose imagination has no modifying influence over the results of his direct observation," the artist is "one whose imagination, impressionability—in a word, whose personality, is so lively and excitable that it spontaneously transforms everything, dyeing them in its own colors, and unconsciously exaggerating them in accordance with its own preferences."

The main contentions of Véron reappear with altered emphasis in the influential pages of Leo Tolstoy (1828-1910). In certain respects they disagree. Tolstoy thinks *communication* is indispensable to art: Véron defines art simply as the *expression* of emotion. Also Tolstoy formulates a more anti-hedonistic and moral interpretation of art. But both maintain that art is the "language" of emotions.

Defining art as the *deliberate* communication of emotions (thus excluding spontaneous yawning, swearing, laughing, or weeping), Tolstoy distinguishes between the *technical adequacy* of the work as a vehicle of emotional communication, and the value and character of the emotions expressed. He thus recognizes that there are two questions to be asked in evaluating a work of art: First, are the emotions of the artist put into effective communicable form? Second, are the emotions worthwhile?

It makes a great difference, he believes, whether the emotions are beneficial or injurious; for art is the great molder of human attitudes—co-equal in importance with science. The only emotions, he thinks, that art should transmit are simple and universal feelings that all men can appreciate, and Christian feelings, particularly of love and human brotherhood. He condemns most of the sophisticated art of Western culture, even such masterpieces as those of Shakespeare and Beethoven and his own *Anna Karenina* and *War and Peace*.

Tolstoy took the extreme stand he did partly because he appreciated so vividly the power of art to mold human character. His book is the most impressive statement in modern esthetics of the view that the value of art lies in its immense social usefulness. The noble ideal to which he wished to dedicate art, the universal brotherhood of man, is the more moving because, in his own life, he tried with such intense conviction to abide by it. There have been others, such as the Marxists, who have insisted upon the social utility of art, but never with a greater compassion or sincerity.

Another contributor to the emotionalist theory was Yrjö Hirn (1870-1952), Professor of Sociology in the University of Helsingfors, Finland, and a leading figure in Scandinavian esthetics. Believing that emotional expression is the essence of all art, he finds the psychological origin of the artist's activity in the need to secure relief from emotional pressure. Art requires critical control in the act of expression and hence the bridling of chaotic passions by intelligence. It impels the artist to embody his emotions in the work of art, and thus to clarify and remove to an objective distance the obscure terrors that bear down upon him. His passions are regularized by the harmonies and measures of esthetic form; and he obtains release from emotional repression in the imaginative overflow of feeling. In these several ways, art purges and calms the emotions. Hirn has thus construed Aristotle's theory of catharsis in the wider context of all artistic expression. He has also strengthened the contention of Nietzsche that art restores mental health through its Dionysiac excitement and its Apollonian serenity. Finally, he has supplied a notable theory of the motivation of the artist and the tranquillizing effect of art upon the spectator.

EUGENE VÉRON

Art as the Expression of Emotion

I. General Definition of Art

Art, far from being the blossom and fruit of civilization, is rather its germ. It began to give evidence of its existence so soon as man became self-conscious, and is to be found clearly defined in his very earliest works.

By its psychologic origin it is bound up with the constituent principles of humanity. The salient and essential characteristic of man is his incessant cerebral activity, which is propagated and developed by countless acts and works of varied kind. The aim and rule of this activity is the search after *the best;* that is to say, the more and more complete satisfaction of physical and moral wants. This instinct, common to all animals, is seconded in man by an exceptionally well-developed faculty to adapt the means to the end.

The effort to satisfy physical wants has given birth to all the industries that defend, preserve, and smooth the path of life; the effort to satisfy the moral wants—of which one of the most important is the gratification of our cerebral activity itself—has created the arts, long before it could give them power sufficient for the conscious elaboration of ideas. The life of sentiment preceded the manifestations of intellectual life by many centuries.

The gratification, *in esse* or *in posse*, of either real or imaginary wants, is the cause of happiness, joy, pleasure, and of all the feelings connected with them; the contrary is marked by grief, sadness, fear, etc.: but in both cases there is emotion to give more or less lively evidence of its existence by means of exterior signs. When expressed by gesture and rhythmic movement, such emotion produces the dance; when by rhythmic notes, music; when by rhythmic words, poetry.

As in another aspect man is essentially sympathetic and his joy or pain is often caused as much by the good or evil fortunes of others as by his own; as, besides, he possesses in a very high degree the faculty of combining series of fictitious facts, and of representing them in colors even more lively than those of reality: it results that the domain of art is of infinite extent for him. For the causes of emotion are multiplied for every man—not only by the number of similar beings who live around him and are attached to him by the more or less closely knit bonds of affection, alliance, similitude of situation or community of ideas and interests; but also, by the never-ending multitude of beings and events that are able to originate or direct the imaginings of poets.

To these elements of emotion and moral enjoyment must be added the combinations of lines, of forms and of colors, the dispositions and opposition of light and shade, etc. The instinctive search after this kind of emotion or pleasure, the special organ of which is the eye, has given birth to what are called the arts of design—sculpture, painting and architecture.

We may say then, by way of general definition, that art is the manifestation of emotion, obtaining external interpretation, now by expressive arrangements of line, form or color, now by a series of gestures, sounds, or words governed by particular rhythmical cadence.

If our definition is exact, we must conclude, from it, that the merit of a work of art, whatever it may be, can be finally measured by the power with which it manifests or interprets the emotion that was its determining cause, and that, for a like reason, must constitute its innermost and supreme unity. . . .

II. *What We Admire in a Work of Art is the Genius of the Artist. Definition of Esthetics*

Imitation is no more the aim of art than a mere collection of letters and syllables is the aim of a writer who wishes to express his thoughts and feelings by the aid of the words which they form. The poet arranging his verses, the musician composing his airs and harmonies, are well aware that their real object lies beyond words and notes. This distinction, as we have here explained it, is perhaps less clear in matters of painting and sculpture. Some artists, and these not the least capable, are quite convinced that when they have a model before them, their one duty is to imitate it. And indeed they do nothing else; and, by virtue of such imitation, they succeed in producing works of incontestable artistic value.

Here we have simply a misunderstanding. If an artist were really able to reduce himself to the condition of a copying machine; if he could so far efface and suppress himself as to confine his work to the servile reproduction of all the features and details of an object or event passing before his eyes: the only value his work would possess would be that of a more or less exact *procès verbal,* and it would perforce remain inferior to reality. Where is the artist who would attempt to depict sunlight without taking refuge in some legerdemain, calling to his aid devices which the true sun would despise? But enough of this. Just because he is endowed with sensibility and imaginative power, the artist, in presence of the facts of nature or the events of history, finds himself, whether he will or not, in a peculiar situation. However thorough a realist he may think himself, he does not leave himself to chance. Now, choice of subject alone is enough to prove that, from the very beginning, some preference has existed, the result of a more or less predeterminate impression, and of a more or less unconscious agreement between the character of the object and that of the artist. This impression and agreement he sets to work to embody in outward form; it is the real aim of his work, and its possession gives him his claim to the name of artist. Without wishing or even knowing it, he molds the features of nature to his dominant impression and to the idea that caused him to take pencil in hand. His work has an accidental stamp, in addition to that of the permanent genius which constitutes his individuality. Poet, musician, sculptor and architect, all pay more or less strict obedience to the same law. To it, point all those rules of artistic composition which pedantic academicism has subtly multiplied until they contradict each other.

The more of this personal character that a work possesses; the more harmonious its details and their combined expression; the more clearly each part communicates the impression of the artist, whether of grandeur, of melancholy or of joy; in fine, the more that expression of human sensation and will predominates over mere imitation, the better will be its chance of obtaining sooner or later the admiration of the world—always supposing that the sentiment expressed be a generous one, and that the execution be not of such a kind as to repel or baffle connoisseurs. It is not of course impossible that an artist endowed with an ill-regulated or morbid imagination may place himself outside all normal conditions and condemn himself to the eternal misapprehension of the public. Impressions that are too particular, eccentric feelings, fantastic execution or processes, which do nothing to raise the intrinsic value or power of inspiration of a work, may give it so strange and ultra-individual a character that it may become impossible for us to arrive at its real merit. The best qualities, when exaggerated, become faults; and that very personality or individuality which, when added to imitative power, results in a work of art, produces when pushed to extravagance nothing but an enigma.

We see, then, if we have succeeded in making ourselves understood, that the beautiful in art springs mainly from the intervention of the genius of man when more or less excited by special emotion.

A work is beautiful when it bears strong marks of the individuality of its author, of the permanent personality of the artist, and of the more or less accidental impression produced upon him by the sight of the object or event rendered.

In a word, it is from the worth of the artist that that of his work is derived. It is the manifestation of the faculties and qualities he possesses which attracts and fascinates us. The more sympathetic power and individuality that these faculties and qualities display, the easier is it for them to obtain our love and admiration. On the other hand, we, for a similar reason, reject and contemn bold and vulgar works that by their shortcomings demonstrate the moral and intellectual mediocrity of their authors, and prove the latter to have mistaken their vocation.

Consequently, then, beauty in art is a purely human creation. Imitation may be its means, as in sculpture and painting; or, on the other hand, it may have nothing to do with it, as in poetry and music. This beauty is of so peculiar a nature that it may exist even in ugliness itself; inasmuch as the exact reproduction of an ugly model may be a beautiful work of art, by the ensemble of qualities which the composition of it may prove are possessed by its author.

The very theory of imitation is but the incomplete and superficial statement of the ideas which we are here advocating. What is it that we admire in imitation? The resemblance? We have that much better in the object itself. But how is it that the similitude of an ugly object can be beautiful? It is obvious that between the object and its counterfeit some new element intervenes. This element is the personality, or, at least, the skill of the artist. This latter, indeed, is what they admire who will have it that beauty consists in imitation. What these applaud, in fact, is the talent of the artist. If we look below the surface and analyze their admiration we shall find that it is so; whether they mean it or not, what they praise in a work is the worker.

This was the opinion of Bürger, who, in his *Salon of 1863*, says: "In works which interest us the authors in a way substitute themselves for nature. However common or vulgar the latter may be, they have some rare and peculiar way of looking at it. It is Chardin himself whom we admire in his representation of a glass of water. We admire the genius of Rembrandt in the profound and individual character which he imparted to every head that posed before him. Thus did they seem to him, and this explains everything simple or fantastic in his expression and execution."

After all this, we need not stop to refute the theory which would found artistic beauty upon the imitation of "beautiful nature." In spite of the brilliant reputation that its triumph in three academies has given to M. Ch. Sevêyne's book upon the science of beauty, it does not seem to us to be founded upon arguments worthy of respect; it has not shown us where "beautiful nature" (*la belle nature*) is to be found in *Le Pouilleux*, in the *Raft of the Medusa*, in the *Battlefield of Eylau*, in the character of *Tartuffe*, or of *La Marneffe*.

The only beauty in a work of art is that placed there by the artist. It is both the result of his efforts and the foundation of his success. As often as he is struck by any vivid impression—whether moral, intellectual, or physical—and expresses that impression by some outward process—by poetry, music, sculpture, painting or architecture—in such a way as to cause its communication with the soul of spectator or auditor; so often does he produce a work of art the beauty of which will be in exact proportion to the intelligence and depth of the sentiment displayed, and the power shown in giving it outward form.

The union of all these conditions constitutes artistic beauty in its most complete expression.

With a few reservations, then, we may preserve the definition of esthetics which usage has sanctified—*The Science of Beauty*. For the sake of clearness, however, and to prevent confusion, we prefer to call it the *Science of Beauty in Art*. Had not the tyranny of formulae by custom become too strong, we would willingly refrain from using the word "beauty" at all, for it has the drawback of being too exclusively connected with the sense of seeing, and of calling up too much the idea of visible form. The employment of this word became general when *the* art *par excellence* was sculpture. To make it apply to the other arts, it was necessary to foist upon it a series of extensions which deprived it of all accuracy. Language possesses no word more vague or less precise. This absence of precision has perhaps contributed more than might at first be supposed to that confusion of ideas which can alone explain the multiplicity and absurdity of current esthetic theories.

All these inconveniences and obscurities may be avoided by simply putting it thus:

Esthetics is the science whose object is the study and elucidation of the manifestations of artistic genius. . . .

III. *Decorative and Expressive Art*

There are two distinct kinds of art. The one, decorative art, we understand to be that whose main object is the gratification of the eye and ear, and whose chief means to perfection of form are harmony and grace of contour, diction, or sound. Such art rests upon the desire for beauty, and has nothing in view beyond the peculiar delight caused by the sight of beautiful objects. It has produced admirable works in the past, and may produce them again now or in the future, on condition that its inspiration be sought in actual and existing life, and not in the imitation of works sanctified by time. We must recognize, however, that modern art has no tendency in this latter direction. Beauty no longer suffices for us. Indeed, for the last two thousand years something more has been required; for even among the *chefs d'œuvre* of the Greeks not a few owe their creation to a different sentiment. Some of the great artists of antiquity were certainly occupied with the interpretation of the moral life; and had not time destroyed their painted works, we should, at the present moment, probably be able to show absolute proofs of this tendency. But we may readily dispense with the confirmation which they would have afforded to our arguments; for we find more than sufficient evidence in the avowed character of the music of the Greeks, in many of the most important works of their sculptors, and in most of their great poems.

The chief characteristic of modern art—of art, that is, left to follow its own inspiration free from academic patronage—is power of expression. Through form this, the second kind of art, traces the moral life, and endeavors to occupy man, body and soul, but with no thought of sacrificing the one to the other. It is ever becoming more imbued with the quite modern idea that the whole being is *one*, metaphysicians notwithstanding, and that its aim can only be complete by refusing to separate the organ from its function. The moral life is but the general result of the conditions of the physical. The one is bound to the other by necessary connections which cannot be broken without destroying both. The first care of the artist should be to seek out and grasp the methods of manifestation so as to comprehend and master their unity.

Art, thus understood, demands from its votary an ensemble of intellectual faculties higher and more robust than if founded solely upon an ideal of beauty. Art founded upon the latter notion would be sufficiently served by one possessing an acute sense of the beautiful—the degree of his sensibility being indicated by the plastic perfection of his work. But expressive art demands a capability of being moved by many varying sentiments, demands the power to penetrate beneath outward appearances and to seize a hidden thought, the power to grasp either the permanent characteristic or the particular and momentary emotion; in a word, it demands that complete eloquence of representation which art might have dispensed with while it confined itself to the investigation or delineation of a single expression, but which became absolutely indispensable from the moment that the interpretation of the entire man became its avowed object.

We may say, too, that modern art is doubly expressive; because, while the artist is indicating by form and sound the sentiments and ideas of the personages whom he introduces, he is also by the power and manner of such manifestation giving an unerring measure of his own sensibility, imagination, and intelligence.

Expressive art is in no way hostile to beauty; it makes use of it as one element in the subjects which require it, but its domain is not enclosed within the narrow bounds of such a conception. It is by no means indifferent to the pleasures of sight and hearing, but it sees something beyond them. Its worth must not be measured only by perfection of form, but also and chiefly, by the double power of expression which we have pointed out, and, as we must not omit to add, by the value of the sentiments and ideas expressed. This latter point is too often and wrongly ignored by artists.

Between two works which give evidence of equal talent—that is to say, of equal facility to grasp the true accents and characteristics of nature, and equal power to bring out both the inner meaning of things and the personality of the artist—we, for our part, would not hesitate to accord the preference to that of which the *Conception* showed the more vigorous intelligence and elevated feeling. The art critics seem to have made it one of their principles to take no account of choice of subject, but only to look at the technical result. Such a principle is plausible rather than true. The individuality of the author can never be excluded from a work, and choice of subject is frequently one of the points by which this individuality is most clearly indicated.

It is true, of course, that elevation of sentiment can never take the place of art talent. On this point we cannot too strongly condemn the practice of academic juries who, on the one hand, reward mere mechanical labor simply because it has been exercised upon what are called classic subjects; and, on the other, persecute more independent artists to punish their obstinacy in deserting the beaten track. Nothing, then, can be further from our thoughts than to require critics to substitute, in every case, consideration of the subject for that of the work itself; or to condemn *a priori* all artists who remain faithful to the traditions, ideas, and sentiments of the past. In these, indeed, some find their only inspiration. We only wish to affirm our conviction that choice of subject is not so indifferent a matter as some say it is, and that it must be taken into account as of considerable weight in determining an opinion of a work of art.

The necessity for this is one consequence of the distinction which we have established between decorative and expressive art. The former, solely devoted to the gratification of eye and ear, affords no measure of its success beyond the pleasure which it gives. The latter, whose chief object is to express the feelings and ideas, and, through them, to manifest the power of conception and expansion possessed by the artist, must obviously be estimated, partly at least, by the moral or other value of the ideas and sentiments in question. And, as the value of a work depends directly upon the capability of its author, and as many artists have been about equal in their technical ability, we must be ready to acknowledge that moral and intellectual superiority is a real superiority, and is naturally marked by the possession of an instinctive and spontaneous power of sympathy.

IV. *Style and Personality*

Style is the man, says Buffon; and he is right. Get some one who *can* read, to read a page of Demosthenes *and* of Cicero, of Bossuet and of Massillon, of Corneille and of Racine, of Lamartine and of Victor Hugo. However slight may be your literary perceptions, you will at once notice that no two of them sound the same. Apart altogether from the subjects or ideas, which may be identical, each one has an air, an accent, which can never either be confounded or replaced. In some of them we find elegance, finesse, grace, the most seductive and soothing harmony; in others, a force and *élan* like the sound of a trumpet, enough to awaken the Seven Sleepers.

Style only exists by virtue of what Bürger calls *the law of separation.* "A being only exists in consequence of his separation from other beings. . . . This law of successive detachment—which alone renders progress possible—may be proved to influence the course of religion, of politics, of literature, and of art. What was the renaissance but a break in the continuity of the middle ages?" It is by style, by the manner of comprehension, of feeling and interpretation, that epochs, races, schools and individuals are separated and distinguished one from the other. In all the arts, analogous differences are to be found; plainly marked, in proportion as a more or less extensive field is offered for the development of artistic personality. Michelangelo and Raphael, Leonardo and Veronese, Titian and Correggio, Rubens and Rembrandt, resembled each other no more and no less than Beethoven resembled Rossini; Weber, Mozart; or Wagner resembles Verdi. Each has his own style, his peculiar mode of thinking and feeling, and of expressing those feelings and thoughts.

Why have mediocre artists no style? For the same reasons that they are mediocrities. The particular characteristic of mediocrity is commonness or vulgarity of thought and feeling. At each moment in the evolution of a social system, there is a general level which marks, for that moment, the average value of the human soul and intellect. Such works as rise above this general level imply an amount of talent or genius in exact proportion to the amount of superior elevation and spontaneity which they display. Mediocrity comes up to the general level, but does not pass it; thus the mediocre artist thinks and feels like the ordinary run of mankind, and has nothing to "separate" him from the crowd. He may have a manner, an ensemble of habits of working peculiar to himself; but he can have no style in the accurate sense of the word. Facility is not style; for the latter is really a product, a reverberation, if we may use the word, from the soul itself, and can no more be artificially acquired than can the sonorousness of bronze or silver be acquired by lead. . . .

Style, which is a simple reflection of the artist's personality, is naturally found in the work of every artist who possesses any personality. The indescribable quality, the *je ne sais quoi* of which Fromentin speaks, is precisely the assemblage of qualities, the condition of being and temperament which caused Rubens to see things differently from Rembrandt. The two extracted from one and the same object or subject emotions widely different though congenial to their respective natures; just as a tightened string in a concert room will vibrate in response to the note which it would itself produce if struck. The one thing needful is the power to vibrate, which is too often wanting.

The question of style has considerable importance. We might even say that it includes the whole of esthetics, which is in fact the question of personality in art. . . .

Truth and personality: these are the alpha and omega of art formulas; *truth* as to facts, and the *personality* of the artist. But, if we look more closely, we shall see that these two terms are in reality but one. Truth as to fact, so far as art is concerned, is above all the truth of our own sensations, of our own sentiments. It is truth as we see it, as it appears modified by our own temperaments, preferences, and physical organs. It is, in fact, our personality itself. Reality, as given by the photographer, reality taken from a point of view without connection with us or our impressions, is the very negation of art. When this kind of truth predominates in a work of art, we cry, "There is realism for you!" Now, realism partakes of the nature of art, only because the most downright of realists must, whether he will or not, put something of his own individuality into his work. When, on the other hand, the dominant quality is what we call human or personal truth, then we at once exclaim, "Here is an artist!"

And the latter is the right meaning of the word. Art consists essentially in the predominance of subjectivity over objectivity; it is the chief distinction between it and science. The man intended for science is he whose imagination has no modifying influence over the results of his direct observation. The artist, on the other hand, is one whose imagination, impressionability—in a word, whose personality is so lively and excitable that it spontaneously transforms everything, dyeing them in its own colors, and unconsciously exaggerating them in accordance with its own preferences.

We think ourselves justified, then, in calling art the direct and spontaneous manifestation of human personality. But we must not omit also to remember the fact that personality—individual and particular as it is from some points of view—is nevertheless exposed to many successive and temporary modifications caused by the various kinds of civilization through which it has had to pass.

—*Æsthetics* (1878; translated 1879)

LEO TOLSTOY

The Communication of Emotion

There is no objective definition of beauty. The existing definitions . . . amount only to one and the same subjective definition, which is (strange as it seems to say so), that art is that which makes beauty manifest, and beauty is that which pleases (without exciting desire). Many estheticians have felt the insufficiency and instability of such a definition, and in order to give it a firm basis have asked themselves why a thing pleases. And they have converted the discussion on beauty into a question of taste, as did Hutcheson, Voltaire, Diderot, and others. But all attempts to define what taste is must lead to nothing, as the reader may see both from the history of esthetics and experimentally. There is and can be no explanation of why one thing pleases one man and displeases another, or *vice versa;* so that the whole existing science of esthetics fails to do what we might expect from it as a mental activity calling itself a science, namely, it does not define the qualities and laws of art, or of the beautiful (if that be the content of art), or the nature of taste (if taste decides the question of art and its merit), and then on the basis of such definitions acknowledge as art those productions which correspond to these laws and reject those which do not come under them. But this science of esthetics consists in first acknowledging a certain set of productions to be art (because they please us), and then framing such a theory of art as all these productions which please a certain circle of people can be fitted into. There exists an art-canon according to which certain productions favored by our circle are acknowledged as being art,—the works of Phidias, Sophocles, Homer, Titian, Raphael, Bach, Beethoven, Dante, Shakespeare, Goethe, and others,—and the esthetic laws must be such as to embrace all these productions. In esthetic literature you will constantly meet with opinions on the merit and importance of art, founded not on any certain laws by which this or that is held to be good or bad, but merely on consideration as to whether this art tallies with the art-canon we have drawn up. . . .

So that the theory of art founded on beauty, expounded by esthetics and in dim outline professed by the public, is nothing but the setting up as good of that which has pleased and pleases us, that is, pleases a certain class of people.

In order to define any human activity, it is necessary to understand its sense and importance; and in order to do this it is primarily necessary to examine that activity in itself, in its dependence on its causes and in connection with its effects, and not merely in relation to the pleasure we can get from it.

If we say that the aim of any activity is merely our pleasure and define it solely by that pleasure, our definition will evidently be a false one. But this is precisely what has occurred in the efforts to define art. . . .

What is art if we put aside the conception of beauty, which confuses the whole matter? The latest and most comprehensible definitions of art, apart from the conception of beauty, are the following:—(1) a, Art is an activity arising even in the animal kingdom, and springing from sexual desire and the propensity to play (Schiller, Darwin, Spencer), and b, accompanied by a pleasurable excitement of the nervous system (Grant Allen). This is the physiological-evolutionary definition. (2) Art is the external manifestation, by means of lines, colors, movements, sounds, or words, of emotions felt by man (Véron). This is the experimental definition. According to the very latest definition (Sully), (3) Art is "the production of some permanent object or passing action which is fitted not only to supply an active enjoyment to the producer, but to convey a pleasurable impression to a number of spectators or listeners, quite apart from any personal advantage to be derived from it."

Notwithstanding the superiority of these definitions to the metaphysical definitions which depended on the conception of beauty, they are yet far from exact. The first, the physiological-evolutionary definition (1), a, is inexact, because instead of speaking about the artistic activity itself, which is the real matter in hand, it treats of the derivation of art. The modification of it, b, based on the physiological effects on the human organism, is inexact because within the limits of such definition many other human activities can be included, as has occurred in the neo-esthetic theories which reckon as art the preparation of handsome clothes, pleasant scents, and even of victuals.

The experimental definition, (2), which makes art consist in the expression of emotions, is inexact because a man may express his emotions by means of lines, colors, sounds, or words and yet may not act on others by such expression—and then the manifestation of his emotions is not art.

The third definition (that of Sully) is inexact because in the production of objects or actions affording pleasure to the producer and a pleasant emotion to the spectators or hearers apart from personal advantage, may be included the showing of conjuring tricks or gymnastic exercises, and other activities which are not art. And further, many things the production of which does not afford pleasure to the producer and the sensation received from which is unpleasant, such as gloomy, heart-rending scenes in a poetic description or a play, may nevertheless be undoubted works of art.

The inaccuracy of all these definitions arises from the fact that in them all (as also in the metaphysical definitions) the object considered is the pleasure art may give, and not the purpose it may serve in the life of man and of humanity.

In order to define art correctly it is necessary first of all to cease to consider it as a means to pleasure, and to consider it as one of the conditions of human life.

Viewing it in this way we cannot fail to observe that art is one of the means of intercourse between man and man.

Every work of art causes the receiver to enter into a certain kind of relationship both with him who produced or is producing the art, and with all those who, simultaneously, previously, or subsequently, receive the same artistic impression.

Speech transmitting the thoughts and experiences of men serves as a means of union among them, and art serves a similar purpose. The peculiarity of this latter means of intercourse, distinguishing it from intercourse by means of words, consists in this, that whereas by words a man transmits his thoughts to another, by art he transmits his feelings.

The activity of art is based on the fact that a man receiving through his sense of hearing or sight another man's expression of feeling, is capable of experiencing the emotion which moved the man who expressed it. To take the simplest example: one man laughs, and another who hears becomes merry, or a man weeps, and another who hears feels sorrow. A man is excited or irritated, and another man seeing him is brought to a similar state of mind. By his movements or by the sounds of his voice a man expresses courage and determination or sadness and calmness, and this state of mind passes on to others. A man suffers, manifesting his sufferings by groans and spasms, and this suffering transmits itself to other people; a man expresses his feelings of admiration, devotion, fear, respect, or love, to certain objects, persons, or phenomena, and others are infected by the same feelings of admiration, devotion, fear, respect, or love, to the same objects, persons, or phenomena.

And it is on this capacity of man to receive another man's expression of feeling and to experience those feelings himself, that the activity of art is based.

If a man infects another or others directly, immediately, by his appearance or by the sounds he gives vent to at the very time he experiences the feeling; if he causes another man to yawn when he himself cannot help yawning, or to laugh or cry when he himself is obliged to laugh or cry, or to suffer when he himself is suffering—that does not amount to art.

Art begins when one person with the object of joining another or others to himself in one and the same feeling, expresses that feeling by certain external indications. To take the simplest example: a boy having experienced, let us say, fear on encountering a wolf, relates that encounter, and in order to evoke in others the feeling he has experienced, describes himself, his condition before the encounter, the surroundings, the wood, his own lightheartedness, and then the wolf's appearance, its movements, the distance between himself and the wolf, and so forth. All this, if only the boy when telling the story again experiences the feelings he had lived through, and infects the hearers and compels them to feel what he had experienced—is art. Even if the boy had not seen a wolf but had frequently been afraid of one, and if wishing to evoke in others the fear he had felt, he invented an encounter with a wolf and recounted it so as to make his hearers share the feelings he experienced when he feared the wolf, that also would be art. And just in the same way it is art if a man, having experienced either the fear of suffering or the attraction of enjoyment (whether in reality or in imagination), expresses these feelings on canvas or in marble so that others are infected by them. And it is also art if a man feels, or imagines to himself, feelings of delight, gladness, sorrow, despair, courage, or despondency, and the transition from one to another of these feelings, and expresses them by sounds so that the hearers are infected by them and experience them as they were experienced by the composer.

The feelings with which the artist infects others may be most various—very strong or very weak, very important or very insignificant, very bad or very good: feelings of love of one's country, self-devotion and submission to fate or to God expressed in a drama, raptures of lovers described in a novel, feelings of voluptuousness expressed in a picture, courage expressed in a triumphal march, merriment evoked by a dance, humor evoked by a funny story, the feeling of quietness transmitted by an evening landscape or by a lullaby, or the feeling of admiration evoked by a beautiful arabesque—it is all art.

If only the spectators or auditors are infected by the feelings which the author has felt, it is art.

To evoke in oneself a feeling one has once experienced and having evoked it in oneself then by means of movements, lines, colors, sounds, or forms expressed in words, so to transmit that feeling that others experience the same feeling—this is the activity of art.

Art is a human activity consisting in this, that one man consciously by means of certain external signs, hands on to others feelings he has lived through, and that others are infected by these feelings and also experience them.

Art is not, as the metaphysicians say, the manifestation of some mysterious Idea of beauty or God; it is not, as the esthetic physiologists say, a game in which man lets off his excess of stored-up energy; it is not the expression of man's emotions by external signs; it is not the production of pleasing objects; and, above all, it is not pleasure; but it is a means of union among men joining them together in the same feelings, and indispensable for the life and progress towards well-being of individuals and of humanity.

As every man, thanks to man's capacity to express thoughts by words, may know all that has been done for him in the realms of thought by all humanity before his day, and can in the present, thanks to this capacity to understand the thoughts of others, become a sharer in their activity and also himself hand on to his contemporaries and descendants the thoughts he has assimilated from others as well as those that have arisen in himself; so, thanks to man's capacity to be infected with the feelings of others by means of art, all that is being lived through by his contemporaries is accessible to him, as well as the feelings experienced by men thousands of years ago, and he has also the possibility of transmitting his own feelings to others.

If people lacked the capacity to receive the thoughts conceived by men who preceded them and to pass on to others their own thoughts, men would be like wild beasts, or like Kasper Hauser.[1]

And if men lacked this other capacity of being infected by art, people might be almost more savage still, and above all more separated from, and more hostile to, one another.

And therefore the activity of art is a most important one, as important as the activity of speech itself and as generally diffused.

As speech does not act on us only in sermons, orations, or books, but in all those remarks by which we interchange thoughts and experiences with one another, so also art in the wide sense of the word permeates our whole life, but it is only to some of its manifestations that we apply the term in the limited sense of the word.

We are accustomed to understand art to be only what we hear and see in theaters, concerts, and exhibitions; together with buildings, statues, poems, and novels. . . . But all this is but the smallest part of the art by which we communicate with one another in life. All human life is filled with works of art of every kind—from cradle-song, jest, mimicry, the ornamentation of houses, dress, and utensils, to church services, buildings, monuments, and triumphal processions. It is all artistic activity. So that by art, in the limited sense of the word, we do not mean all human activity transmitting feelings but only that part which we for some reason select from it and to which we attach special importance. . . .

There is one indubitable sign distinguishing real art from its counterfeit—namely, the infectiousness of art. If a man without exercising effort and without altering his standpoint, on reading, hearing, or seeing another man's work experiences a mental condition which unites him with that man and with others who are also affected by that work, then the object evoking that condition is a work of art. And however poetic, realistic, striking, or interesting, a work may be, it is not a work of art if it does not evoke that feeling (quite distinct from all other feelings) of joy and of spiritual union with another (the author) and with others (those who are also infected by it).

It is true that this indication is an *internal* one and that there are people who, having forgotten what the action of real art is, expect something else from art (in our society the great majority are in this state), and that therefore such people may mistake for this esthetic feeling the feeling of diversion and a certain excitement which they receive from counterfeits of art. But though it is impossi-

[1] "The foundling of Nuremberg," found in the marketplace of that town on 23rd May 1828, apparently some sixteen years old. He spoke little and was almost totally ignorant even of common objects. He subsequently explained that he had been brought up in confinement underground and visited by only one man, whom he saw but seldom.

ble to undeceive these people, just as it may be impossible to convince a man suffering from color-blindness that green is not red, yet for all that, this indication remains perfectly definite to those whose feeling for art is neither perverted nor atrophied, and it clearly distinguishes the feeling produced by art from all other feelings.

The chief peculiarity of this feeling is that the recipient of a truly artistic impression is so united to the artist that he feels as if the work were his own and not some one else's—as if what it expresses were just what he had long been wishing to express. A real work of art destroys in the consciousness of the recipient the separation between himself and the artist, and not that alone, but also between himself and all whose minds receive this work of art. In this freeing of our personality from its separation and isolation, in this uniting of it with others, lies the chief characteristic and the great attractive force of art.

If a man is infected by the author's condition of soul, if he feels this emotion and this union with others, then the object which has effected this is art; but if there be no such infection, if there be not this union with the author and with others who are moved by the same work—then it is not art. And not only is infection a sure sign of art, but the degree of infectiousness is also the sole measure of excellence in art.

The stronger the infection the better is the art, as art, speaking of it now apart from its subject-matter—that is, not considering the value of the feelings it transmits.

And the degree of the infectiousness of art depends on three conditions:

(1) On the greater or lesser individuality of the feeling transmitted; (2) on the greater or lesser clearness with which the feeling is transmitted; (3) on the sincerity of the artist, that is, on the greater or lesser force with which the artist himself feels the emotion he transmits.

The more individual the feeling transmitted the more strongly does it act on the recipient; the more individual the state of soul into which he is transferred the more pleasure does the recipient obtain and therefore the more readily and strongly does he join in it.

Clearness of expression assists infection because the recipient who mingles in consciousness with the author is the better satisfied the more clearly that feeling is transmitted which, as it seems to him, he has long known and felt and for which he has only now found expression.

But most of all is the degree of infectiousness of art increased by the degree of sincerity in the artist. As soon as the spectator, hearer, or reader, feels that the artist is infected by his own production and writes, sings, or plays, for himself, and not merely to act on others, this mental condition of the artist infects the recipient; and, on the contrary, as soon as the spectator, reader, or hearer, feels that the author is not writing, singing, or playing, for his own satisfaction—does not himself feel what he wishes to express, but is doing it for him, the recipient—

resistance immediately springs up, and the most individual and the newest feelings and the cleverest technique not only fail to produce any infection but actually repel.

I have mentioned three conditions of contagion in art, but they may all be summed up into one, the last, sincerity; that is, that the artist should be impelled by an inner need to express his feeling. That condition includes the first; for if the artist is sincere he will express the feeling as he experienced it. And as each man is different from everyone else, his feeling will be individual for everyone else; and the more individual it is—the more the artist has drawn it from the depths of his nature—the more sympathetic and sincere will it be. And this same sincerity will impel the artist to find clear expression for the feeling which he wishes to transmit.

Therefore this third condition—sincerity—is the most important of the three. It is always complied with in peasant art, and this explains why such art always acts so powerfully; but it is a condition almost entirely absent from our upper-class art, which is continually produced by artists actuated by personal aims of covetousness or vanity.

Such are the three conditions which divide art from its counterfeits, and which also decide the quality of every work of art considered apart from its subject matter.

The absence of any one of these conditions excludes a work from the category of art and relegates it to that of art's counterfeits. If the work does not transmit the artist's peculiarity of feeling and is therefore not individual, if it is unintelligibly expressed, or if it has not proceeded from the author's inner need for expression—it is not a work of art. If all these conditions are present even in the smallest degree, then the work even if a weak one is yet a work of art.

The presence in various degrees of these three conditions: individuality, clearness, and sincerity, decides the merit of a work of art as art, apart from subject matter. All works of art take order of merit according to the degree in which they fulfil the first, the second, and the third, of these conditions. In one the individuality of the feeling transmitted may predominate; in another, clearness of expression; in a third, sincerity; while a fourth may have sincerity and individuality but be deficient in clearness; a fifth, individuality and clearness, but less sincerity; and so forth, in all possible degrees and combinations.

Thus is art divided from what is not art, and thus is the quality of art, as art, decided, independently of its subject matter, that is to say, apart from whether the feelings it transmits are good or bad. . . .

How in the subject matter of art are we to decide what is good and what is bad?

Art like speech is a means of communication and therefore of progress, that is, of the movement of humanity forward towards perfection. Speech renders accessible to men of the latest generation all the knowledge discovered by the experience and reflection both of preceding generations and of the best and fore-most men of their own times; art renders accessible to men of the latest genera-tions all the feelings experienced by their predecessors and also those felt by their best and foremost contemporaries. And as the evolution of knowledge proceeds by truer and more necessary knowledge dislodging and replacing what was mis-taken and unnecessary, so the evolution of feeling proceeds by means of art—feelings less kind and less necessary for the well-being of mankind being re-placed by others kinder and more needful for that end. That is the purpose of art. And speaking now of the feelings which are its subject matter, the more art ful-fils that purpose the better the art, and the less it fulfils it the worse the art.

The appraisement of feelings (that is, the recognition of one or other set of feelings as more or less good, more or less necessary for the well-being of mankind) is effected by the religious perception of the age.

In every period of history and in every human society there exists an under-standing of the meaning of life, which represents the highest level to which men of that society have attained—an understanding indicating the highest good at which that society aims. This understanding is the religious perception of the given time and society. And this religious perception is always clearly expressed by a few advanced men and more or less vividly perceived by members of the society generally. Such a religious perception and its corresponding expression always exists in every society. If it appears to us that there is no religious per-ception in our society, this is not because there really is none, but only because we do not wish to see it. And we often wish not to see it because it exposes the fact that our life is inconsistent with that religious perception.

Religious perception in a society is like the direction of a flowing river. If the river flows at all it must have a direction. If a society lives, there must be a religious perception indicating the direction in which, more or less consciously, all its members tend.

And so there always has been, and is, a religious perception in every society. And it is by the standard of this religious perception that the feelings transmitted by art have always been appraised. It has always been only on the basis of this religious perception of their age, that men have chosen from amid the endlessly varied spheres of art that art which transmitted feelings making religious per-ception operative in actual life. And such art has always been highly valued and encouraged, while art transmitting feelings already outlived, flowing from the antiquated religious perceptions of a former age, has always been condemned and despised. All the rest of art transmitting those most diverse feelings by means of which people commune with one another was not condemned and was tolerated if only it did not transmit feelings contrary to religious perception. Thus for instance among the Greeks, art transmitting feelings of beauty, strength, and courage (Hesiod, Homer, Phidias) was chosen, approved, and encouraged, while art transmitting feelings of rude sensuality, despondency, and effeminacy, was condemned and despised. Among the Jews, art transmitting feelings of devotion and submission to the God of the Hebrews and to His will (the epic of Genesis, the prophets, the Psalms) was chosen and encouraged, while art transmitting feelings of idolatry (the Golden Calf) was condemned and despised. All the rest of art—stories, songs, dances, ornamentation of houses, of utensils, and of clothes—which was not contrary to religious perception, was neither distinguished nor discussed. Thus as regards its subject matter has art always and everywhere been appraised and thus it should be appraised, for this attitude towards art proceeds from the fundamental characteristics of human nature, and those characteristics do not change.

I know that according to an opinion current in our times religion is a superstition humanity has outgrown, and it is therefore assumed that no such thing exists as a religious perception common to us all by which art in our time can be appraised. I know that this is the opinion current in the pseudo-cultured circles of today. People who do not acknowledge Christianity in its true meaning because it undermines their social privileges, and who therefore invent all kinds of philosophic and esthetic theories to hide from themselves the meaninglessness and wrongfulness of their lives, cannot think otherwise. These people intentionally, or sometimes unintentionally, confuse the notion of a religious cult with the notion of religious perception, and think that by denying the cult they get rid of the perception. But even the very attacks on religion and the attempts to establish an idea of life contrary to the religious perception of our times, most clearly demonstrate the existence of a religious perception condemning the lives that are not in harmony with it.

If humanity progresses, that is, moves forward, there must inevitably be a guide to the direction of that movement. And religions have always furnished that guide. All history shows that the progress of humanity is accomplished no otherwise than under the guidance of religion. But if the race cannot progress without the guidance of religion—and progress is always going on, and consequently goes on also in our own times—then there must be a religion of our times. So that whether it pleases or displeases the so-called cultured people of today, they must admit the existence of religion—not of a religious cult, Catholic, Protestant, or another, but of religious perception—which even in our times is the guide always present where there is any progress. And if a religious perception exists amongst us, then the feelings dealt with by our art should be appraised on the basis of that religious perception; and as has been the case always and everywhere, art transmitting feelings flowing from the religious perception of our time should be chosen from amid all the indifferent art, should be acknowledged, highly valued, and encouraged, while art running counter to that perception should be condemned and despised, and all the remaining, indifferent, art should neither be distinguished nor encouraged.

The religious perception of our time in its widest and most practical application is the consciousness that our well-being, both material and spiritual, individual and collective, temporal and eternal, lies in the growth of brotherhood among men—in their loving harmony with one another. This perception is not only expressed by Christ and all the best men of past ages, it is not only repeated in most varied forms and from most diverse sides by the best men of our times, but it already serves as a clue to all the complex labor of humanity, consisting as this labor does on the one hand in the destruction of physical and moral obstacles to the union of men, and on the other hand in establishing the principles common to all men which can and should unite them in one universal brotherhood. And it is on the basis of this perception that we should appraise all the phenomena of our life and among the rest our art also: choosing from all its realms and highly prizing and encouraging whatever transmits feelings flowing from this religious perception, rejecting whatever is contrary to it, and not attributing to the rest of art an importance that does not properly belong to it. . . .

Whatever the work may be and however it may have been extolled, we have first to ask whether this work is one of real art, or a counterfeit. Having acknowledged, on the basis of the indication of its infectiousness even to a small class of people, that a certain production belongs to the realm of art, it is necessary on this basis to decide the next question, Does this work belong to the category of bad exclusive art opposed to religious perception, or of Christian art uniting people? And having acknowledged a work to belong to real Christian art, we must then, according to whether it transmits feelings flowing from love of God and man, or merely the simple feelings uniting all men, assign it a place in the ranks of religious art, or in those of universal art.

Only on the basis of such verification shall we find it possible to select from the whole mass of what in our society claims to be art, those works which form real, important, necessary, spiritual food, and to separate them from all the harmful and useless art and from the counterfeits of art which surround us. Only on the basis of such verification shall we be able to rid ourselves of the pernicious results of harmful art and avail ourselves of that beneficent action which is the purpose of true and good art, and which is indispensable for the spiritual life of man and of humanity.

—What Is Art? (1896; translated 1905)

YRJÖ HIRN

Art the Reliever

In the endeavor to secure the transmission and perpetuation of a feeling, the expressional activity gradually loses its purely impulsive character. From an almost reflex outlet for abnormal nervous pressure, it is more and more transformed into deliberate artistic production, which is conscious of its aim as well as of the means for attaining it. The elaboration of a work of art, in which the expression of a feeling-state is to be concentrated, and concentrated in a way which not only facilitates but even enforces in the spectator the assimilation of this state, is a complicated operation which cannot of course take place without the effectual cooperation of intellectual and volitional activities. And their cooperation, on the other hand, must evidently exercise some influence on the primordial feeling.

It is a familiar observation, duly emphasized in all psychological handbooks, that strong feelings make clear thought impossible. Everyday experience, as well as scientific experiment, gives unmistakable evidence of the influence which abnormal excitement or depression exercises, not only on our ideas and their associations, but even on the perceptions. The converse has perhaps not been stated so often. Still, it does not admit of doubt that intensified intellectual activity may, in some cases, even more effectually than motor reaction, overcome the tyranny of a hypernormal feeling. It is true that every mental state becomes more distinct as a phenomenon of consciousness when our thoughts are directed towards it. Feelings of low and moderate intensity may even be enhanced in their purely emotional aspect if we let our intellect play on them. But as soon as a greater intensity of feeling is reached, this relation is reversed. Joy which is so great as to be a burden, "Die Noth der Fülle," [1] and numbing despair, must inevitably decrease when there is an increase of distinctness in their intellectual elements. The more we can compel ourselves to contemplate with cool and clear attention the causes and manifestations of such high-strung states, the more we are also able to master them. It is a familiar experience to every one that strong fear can be vanquished, if only we can succeed in diverting all our attention to its objective source, and "stare the danger in the face." When the attention is concentrated and intensified to the utmost degree, it may even, as in the case of fascination, entirely prevent, to our own danger, the very rise of this self-preserving emotion.

[1] Nietzsche, *Die Geburt der Tragödie*, p. 8.

In artistic creation we are not concerned with an intentional or unintentional effort to overcome feeling. On the contrary the aim is here to keep the strongest possible hold of it in order to give it the most effective embodiment. So irreconcilable, however, is the conflict between emotional excitement and intellectual activity, that the latter, even when it expressly serves the purposes of emotional enhancement, must neutralize the excess of feeling. A state of strong pleasure or pain can never be rendered intelligible to outsiders, unless its expression is bridled and disciplined by thought. By being thus embodied in a fixed form the feeling gains in conceivability as well as in infectious power. But while the effect on spectators and listeners is in this way increased, the artistic form influences the feeling subject himself in a quite different way. Its very clearness and distinctness necessarily brings something of that calm which all excitement seeks as relief.

The immediate reaction which the work of art exercises on its own creator is of course most easily seen and understood in the "higher" art-forms with their pronounced intellectual elements. Literary instances of the "poetic cure" for harassing or oppressing emotion are too numerous to be mentioned. The only point we need dwell on is the question how these instances are to be interpreted. When a poet seeks to give shape and form to his own sufferings by means of fiction, the relief he obtains is no doubt in part an effect of the diversion of activity into the channels of expression. But to a still greater degree it may be a result of the healthful influence exercised by the contemplation of objective reality in the finished work of art. Such an influence is unmistakable in the most illustrious instance of artistic production as a life-preserving expedient: Goethe's *Leiden des jungen Werther*. In his memoirs the old poet frankly and unreservedly describes how, when lacerated by the conflict between hypochondriac, suicidal thoughts and an ineradicable love of life and cheerfulness, he resorted to the old homely remedy of writing down his sufferings. He lays especial stress on his desire to give definite form and body to his vague feelings of distress. And as we read that afterwards, when the work lay finished before him, "bound in boards, as a picture in its frame, so as to prove the more convincingly its individual and concrete existence," he could feel "free and joyful, and entitled to a new life," we cannot but explain this renewed courage to live as a result of the sensation of security and support which the beholding of external form affords.

Thus, to begin with, by its character as a palpable, objective reality, the work of art may diminish the subjective disturbance in which it originates. This influence is supplemented by the retroaction of the esthetic qualities, in the narrowest sense of the term, such as beauty, symmetry, and the like, by which an artist always seeks, intentionally or unintentionally, to arrest the attention of his public. The more therefore the work grows in definiteness in the thought and under the hand of the artist, the more it will repress and subdue the chaotic tumult of emotional excitement. The Dionysiac rapture, as the ancients would have said, gives place to Apollian serenity. In language pruned of mythological symbolism, this only means that art is better able than any of the immediate expressional activities to give complete and effective relief from emotional pressure. And it further implies that however earnestly an artist may strive to communicate to his public the exact feeling he has himself experienced, the emotional content expressed in his work will always be of another and more harmonious character than the mental state by which his production was originally called into existence. To the extent that artistic form appears in a given work or manifestation there will also be present, independently of the subject —cheerful or sad, passionate or calm—a sense of mental liberation, which atones for the excesses of emotional excitement.

In a final and exhaustive treatment of esthetic problems this influence of artistic form would need to be traced through all the departments of art-activity. And it would be one of the most interesting parts of such a research to estimate the relative power with which art in its various branches is able to assuage at the same time as it excites. We need not here undertake such a thorough comparative examination of the different arts. What has been said about literary creation may be applied in substance to formative production as well. And it even remains true with regard to those most lyrical and immediately expressive arts which seem to be altogether destitute of objective form and intellectual content. Although it has often been said that the lowest kinds of music are purely emotional manifestations, we may still discern an element of form in the rhythm which regulates even the simplest songs and dances. And the creation of this form undoubtedly requires a certain amount of conscious intention and intellectual activity. It is therefore natural that the intensest and most abnormally enhanced feeling should exclude the possibility of rhythmical movement. Exalted joy and violent despair are in their external manifestations not only inharmonious and ungraceful, but also unrhythmic. But by subjecting the expression to the yoke of a fixed time order we may succeed in harmonizing it. And while the regular recurrence of intervals facilitates our movements—which thereby gain in ease and gracefulness—the vehemence of our feeling will be abated. Thus it is possible that although rhythm powerfully reinforces musical or dramatic excitement, it may at the same time exercise a restraining influence on hyper-normal feeling. And its effects in music and dance show us, in the simplest and most comprehensive of all examples, the importance of artistic form. The musical catharsis or relief to sensation always involves stimulation, but it may nevertheless affect us as a sedative. The more the form-element and attention to form gain in prominence, the more effectual also is the relieving influence of art. Where the stimulative element is predominant in a work of art, there the relief is less complete. . . .

When trying to summarize our researches on the differences between artistic and non-artistic expression of emotional states in a comprehensive conclusion, we are again led to that eminently illustrative instance—the Bacchantic
condition of the ancient Mænads. We have seen that in their description of
Dionysiac mania the classical authors enumerate almost all the various orgiastic
manifestations which can be found in all periods in different parts of the world.
And if ancient literature affords us an epitome of the various expedients to
which the expressional impulse resorts in its endeavor to enhance and relieve
an emotional state, the force of this craving for expression, on the other hand,
nowhere appears with such convincing clearness as in the Dionysiac monuments of classical art.

The frieze around the Bacchic candelabra in the Louvre proves better than
any psychological analysis to how great a degree the Dionysiac state is alloyed
with pain and the longing for relief. If these Mænads be compared with the
figures on the great vases in the British Museum and with the various Agave
reliefs, it will still more conclusively appear that it is real distress which compels
the dancers to seek in ever-increasing excitement deliverance from the burden
of their feelings. No movement could be more eloquently expressive of the
corresponding psychical state than the peculiar toss of the head and the backward curve of the upper trunk which can always be recognized in the most
violent of the dancers. An approach to this attitude sometimes appears, as
Spencer remarks in his essay on the Physiology of Laughter, in movements of
great joy, which has not been able to find expression by the usual channels of
discharge. But there is no doubt that, however pleasurable the quality of the
original state may have been, its tone must have been radically transformed
before it could produce these strained postures. A feeling which distorts the
body by its efforts to find relief, which is not satisfied with the wild cries, the
dances, and all the madness of the Bacchic intoxication, must in its abnormal
exaggeration be perceived as a pain. The pathological character of this feeling
appears further from the fact that the very same movement may be observed
in Pieter Breughel's paintings of hysteric patients and in M. Charcot's photographs from La Salpétrière.[2] And this same backward toss of the head may be
seen in sculptures of witches, the medieval Bacchantes, where it sometimes gives
an impression of proud and insolent defiance, sometimes one of profound melancholy. But in the reliefs representing Bacchic orgies, side by side with the
dancers whose distorted attitude and violent movements betray the pain underlying the appearance of revel and riot, there may always be seen the figures of
women moving with easy and graceful step. The freedom of their motion shows
that they at least have found deliverance from the oppression of overstrung
feeling. The nervous tension which in their companions manifests itself in

[2] Cf. Charcot and Richer, Les démoniaques dans l'art, Paris, 1887, p. 37; Emmanuel,
La danse grecque antique, Paris, 1896, pp. 102, 196-198, 302, 303.

unrhythmic, inharmonious leapings and writhings, has in their case found relief and given place to a feeling of rest and calm. This expression of peace in their faces, attitudes, and draperies affords an instructive comment on the Greek notion of Dionysus, the god of music, who, with all his wildness is none the less able to still the tempests of overpowering feelings.

This god of music, as conceived by those who gave him a place among the Olympians, was not a symbol of dissolute pleasure. On the contrary, the myths tell us how those who oppose his ritual themselves fall victims to a mania even more violent than the Bacchic frenzy itself. His devotees, on the other hand, receive from the stirring notes of his flute and cymbals a determinate form and mold for their otherwise vehement and irregular expression-movements. Their joy loses its defiant and barbaric character, their black despair is dissolved into gentle sadness. Rightly, therefore, was Dionysus saluted as a deliverer when, with his merry crew, he marched from village to village. Like him art moves among men, ennobling their joy and blunting the edge of their sufferings.

—The Origins of Art (1900)

CHAPTER FOUR

Art as Intuition

HENRI BERGSON

The Individual and the Type

BENEDETTO CROCE

Intuition and Expression

JOYCE CARY

The Gap Between Intuition and Expression

Introductory Note

IN MAINTAINING THAT ART involves a kind of knowing, the intuitionists are like Aristotle, Saint Thomas, and Maritain. But they depart from the Aristotelian-scholastic tradition in being less intellectualist. The objects known, as they conceive them, are particulars, not universals—unique qualities, not general characteristics. Their fundamental doctrine is that art is intuition, which they define as the knowing of what is individual.

The great French philosopher, Henri Bergson (1859-1941), contrasts intellect and intuition, and identifies art with the latter. Ordinary experience, he thinks, is more intellectual than intuitive. The average person's senses give him a greatly conceptualized version of reality. Since he seldom has a clear grasp of the individuality of things, his description of objects will be in general terms. He may say that a certain table is brown. for example, but he is not saying anything that indicates the individuality of the table—there are thousands of things that are brown. Every word that he chooses to describe the table will have this defect—it will not reveal the unique essence of the table, but only, let us say, its rectangularity or smoothness: features that are not at all peculiar to this particular table. This generalized description and awareness of the object is sufficient for practical purposes. If the individuality of the thing eludes him, he nevertheless has distinguished the features that make the object an instrument for his use. Since man's primary need is not knowledge but action, intellect has been slowly developed throughout the course of evolution to deal with things in this way. The concepts employed by the intellect are a kind of mental shorthand to economize effort and expedite action.

To know reality truly, in its uniqueness and novelty, we need to relax the tension of practical effort and teach our minds a new docility to nature. We will then penetrate, by a kind of sympathy, to the real nature of the object, thus discovering for the first time the strangeness and multiplicity of its qualities. Turning our gaze inward, we will discern the continuity and freshness of our inner life. Intuition is this sympathy or direct vision, and the artist is unusually gifted with it. Most works of art are the records of intuition, which alone penetrates to the nature of reality—an ever-changing flux of unique qualities.

One type of art is an exception. In the art of comedy the intellect predominates—what we find laughable is not the individual but the type, not the fresh and creative but the stereotyped and inflexible. This rigidity is comic, and laughter is its corrective. Comedy does not belong to the esthetic sphere alone, since it pursues a utilitarian aim of general improvement and uses the intellect as an instrument of criticism. Incidentally, Bergson's brief remarks about tragedy stand in interesting contrast to Aristotle's emphasis upon the universality of tragic characterization and plot.

Benedetto Croce (1866-1952), the most famous Italian philosopher of this century, has been a very influential proponent of the intuitional interpretation of art. Clinging to idealism, the view that reality consists of minds and their activities, he is intent upon analyzing the stages of mental activity. Apart from sensation, which is relatively passive, these stages may be schematized as follows:

1. *Knowing,* or Theoretic Activity.
   (a) *Art,* the knowing of particulars, or intuition.
       Its value is the *beautiful;* its disvalue, the *ugly.*[1]
   (b) *Pure Science and Philosophy,* the knowing of universals, or conception.
       Value: the *true;* disvalue: the *false.*
2. *Doing,* or Practical Activity.

[1] For Croce, value is tendency-fulfillment. Value results when the activity unfolds freely, and disvalue when the activity is hindered, impeded.

(a) *Economic and Prudential Activity,* the pursuit of individual ends.
Value: the *useful;* disvalue, the *harmful.*

(b) *Morality,* the pursuit of universal ends.
Value: the *morally good;* disvalue, the *morally evil.*

These divisions are not sharp. "The forms of the spirit," declares Croce, "are distinct and not separate, and when the spirit is found in one of its forms, or is *explicit* in it, the other forms are also in it, but *implicit.*" [2] For example, thinking involves doing, and *vice versa.* Also intuition is accompanied by conception, and by the two forms of practical activity. But each stage is marked by its fundamental emphasis, whereby it is defined. Esthetic philosophy, for Croce, consists in explaining the nature of art as intuition, and in contrasting art with sensation and the other stages of human activity.

Sensation is passive; art is active. Art is not mere passive perception or daydreaming; it is inner vision formulated in images. Halfway between the passivity of sensation and the activity of art is fancy. It is art only in the making, because it lacks the unity of genuine intuition. Fancy is too passive; it allows images and sensations to float lazily through the mind, or combines them arbitrarily. Art is complete only when the spirit works upon the relatively formless materials of experience, converting them into expressive and harmonious images.

What gives unity to this imaginative vision is a *lyrical content,* the pervasive expression of "feeling." "Feeling" does not mean merely *emotion,* but rather any subjective mood, including volitional attitudes. "We do not ask the artist for a philosophical system nor for a relation of facts," Croce declares, "but for a dream of his own, for nothing but the expression of a world desired or abhorred, or partly desired and partly abhorred. If he makes us live again in this dream the rapture of joy or the incubus of terror, in solemnity or in humility, in tragedy, or in laughter, that suffices." [3] In thus including both emotion and desire, Croce in effect synthesizes the voluntaristic theory of Schopenhauer, Nietzsche, and Freud and the emotionalist theory of Véron and Tolstoy.

As an imaginative grasp of the unique, art is not concerned with the true and false, real and unreal, useful or harmful, good or bad. Nothing counts in art but the perfection of the imaginative vision in itself, and by its own standard of "expressiveness," which is, for Croce, another word for "beauty."

Intuition, so interpreted, is equivalent to expression. Croce doubts the existence of "mute inglorious Miltons," burdened with inspiration but lacking the gift of expression. If a man truly has Miltonic intuitions, he has no difficulty expressing himself. Indeed, he does not know what he wants to express until he has expressed it, imaginatively, if not overtly.

[2] Benedetto Croce, *The Philosophy of the Practical* (Macmillan, London, 1913) pp. 33-34.
[3] *Ibid.,* p. 268.

Joyce Cary (1888-1957), the great Irish novelist, agrees with Croce in most respects, but disagrees with his identification of expression and intuition. With profound understanding of the creative process, Cary finds that protracted labor is required to close the gap between the original intuition and the final expression. But he notes that most of the minute details are devised during the process of the work; and to this extent, he accepts Croce's doctrine that the intention, or intuition, is elaborated in the very act of expressing. He thinks that the struggle of the artist to express his intuitions is an attempt to come to grips with the nature of things. Like Bergson, he conceives of art as a direct and sympathetic vision of reality.

HENRI BERGSON

The Individual and the Type

What is the object of art? Could reality come into direct contact with sense and consciousness, could we enter into immediate communion with things and with ourselves, probably art would be useless, or rather we should all be artists, for then our soul would continually vibrate in perfect accord with nature. Our eyes, aided by memory, would carve out in space and fix in time the most inimitable of pictures. Hewn in the living marble of the human form, fragments of statues, beautiful as the relics of antique statuary, would strike the passing glance. Deep in our souls we should hear the strains of our inner life's unbroken melody—a music that is ofttimes gay, but more frequently plaintive and always original. All this is around and within us, and yet no whit of it do we distinctly perceive. Between nature and ourselves, nay, between ourselves and our own consciousness a veil is interposed: a veil that is dense and opaque for the common herd—thin, almost transparent, for the artist and the poet. What fairy wove that veil? Was it done in malice or in friendliness? We had to live, and life demands that we grasp things in their relations to our own needs. Life is action. Life implies the acceptance only of the *utilitarian* side of things in order to respond to them by appropriate reactions: all other impressions must be dimmed or else reach us vague and blurred. I look and I think I see, I listen and I think I hear, I examine myself and I think I am reading the very depths of my heart. But what I see and hear of the outer world is purely and simply a selection made by my senses to serve as a light to my conduct; what I know of myself is what comes to the surface, what participates in my actions. My senses and my consciousness, therefore, give me no more than a practical simplification of reality. In the vision they furnish me of myself and of things, the differences that are useless to man are obliterated, the resemblances that are useful to him are emphasized; ways are traced out for me in advance, along which my activity is to travel. These ways are the ways which all mankind has trod before me. Things have been classified with a view to the use I can derive from them. And it is this classification I perceive, far more clearly than the color and the shape of things. Doubtless man is vastly superior to the lower animals in this respect. It is not very likely that the eye of a wolf makes any distinction between a kid and a lamb; both appear to the wolf as the same identical quarry, alike easy to pounce upon, alike good to devour. We, for our part, make a distinction between a goat and a sheep; but can we tell one goat from another, one sheep from another? The *individuality* of things or of beings escapes us, unless it is materially to our advantage to perceive it. Even when we do take note of it—as when we distinguish one man from another—it is not the individuality itself that the eye grasps, that is, an entirely original harmony of forms and colors, but only one or two features that will make practical recognition easier.

[In short, we do not see the actual things themselves; in most cases we confine ourselves to reading the labels affixed to them. This tendency, the result of need, has become even more pronounced under the influence of speech; for words—with the exception of proper nouns—all denote genera. The word, which only takes note of the most ordinary function and commonplace aspect of the thing, intervenes between it and ourselves, and would conceal its form from our eyes, were that form not already masked beneath the necessities that brought the word into existence. Not only external objects, but even our own mental states, are screened from us in their inmost, their personal aspect, in the original life they possess. When we feel love or hatred, when we are gay or sad, is it really the feeling itself that reaches our consciousness with those innumerable fleeting shades of meaning and deep resounding echoes that make it something altogether our own? We should all, were it so, be novelists or poets or musicians. Mostly, however, we perceive nothing but the outward display of our mental state. We catch only the impersonal aspect of our feelings, that aspect which speech has set down once for all because it is almost the same, in the same conditions, for all men. Thus, even in our own individual, individuality escapes our ken. We move amidst generalities and symbols, as within a tilt-yard in which our force is effectively pitted against other forces; and fascinated by action, tempted by it, for our own good, on to the field it has selected, we live in a zone midway between things and ourselves, externally to things, externally also to ourselves. From time to time, however, in a fit of absentmindedness, nature raises up souls that are more detached from life. Not with that intentional, logical systematical detachment—the result of reflection and philosophy—but rather with a natural detachment, one innate in the structure of sense or consciousness, which at once reveals itself by a virginal manner, so to speak, of seeing, hearing or thinking. Were this detachment complete, did the soul no longer cleave to action by any of its perceptions, it would be the soul of an artist such as the world has never yet seen. It would excel alike in every art at the same time; or rather, it would fuse them all into one. It would perceive all things in their native purity: the forms, colors, sounds of the physical world as well as the subtlest movements of the inner life. But this is asking too much of nature. Even for such of us as she has made artists, it is by accident, and on one side only, that she has lifted the veil. In one direction only has she forgotten to rivet the perception to the need. And since each direction corresponds to what we call a *sense*—through one of his senses, and through that sense alone, is the artist usually wedded to art. Hence, originally, the diversity of arts. Hence also the speciality of predispositions. This one applies himself to colors and forms, and since he loves color for color and form for form, since he perceives them for their sake and not for his own, it is the inner life of things that he sees appearing through their forms and colors. Little by little he insinuates it into our own perception, baffled though we may be at the outset. For a few moments at least, he diverts us from the prejudices of form and color that come between ourselves and reality. And thus he realizes the loftiest ambition of art, which here consists in revealing to us nature. Others, again, retire within themselves. Beneath the thousand rudimentary actions which are the outward and visible signs of an emotion, behind the commonplace, conventional expression that both reveals and conceals an individual mental state, it is the emotion, the original mood, to which they attain in its undefiled essence. And then, to induce us to make the same effort ourselves, they contrive to make us see something of what they have seen: by rhythmical arrangement of words, which thus become organized and animated with a life of their own, they tell us—or rather suggest—things that speech was not calculated to express. Others delve yet deeper still. Beneath these joys and sorrows which can, at a pinch, be translated into language, they grasp something that has nothing in common with language, certain rhythms of life and breath that are closer to man than his inmost feelings, being the living law—varying with each individual—of his enthusiasm and despair, his hopes and regrets. By setting free and emphasizing this music, they force it upon our attention; they compel us, willy-nilly, to fall in with it, like passers-by who join in a dance. And thus they impel us to set in motion, in the depths of our being, some secret chord which was only waiting to thrill. So art, whether it be painting or sculpture, poetry or music, has no other object than to brush aside the utilitarian symbols, the conventional and socially accepted generalities, in short, everything that veils reality from us, in order to bring us face to face with reality itself. It is from a misunderstanding on this point that the dispute between realism and idealism in art has arisen. Art is certainly only a more direct vision of reality. But this purity of perception implies a break with utilitarian convention, an innate and specially localized disinterestedness of sense or consciousness, in short, certain immateriality of life, which is what has always been called idealism. So that we might say, without in any way playing upon the meaning of the words, that realism is in the work when idealism is in the soul, and that it is only through ideality that we can resume contact with reality.

Dramatic art forms no exception to this law. What drama goes forth to discover and brings to light, is a deep-seated reality that is veiled from us, often in our own interests, by the necessities of life. What is this reality? What are these necessities? Poetry always expresses inward states. But amongst these states some arise mainly from contact with our fellowmen. They are the most intense as well as the most violent. As contrary electricities attract each other and accumulate between the two plates of the condenser from which the spark will presently flash, so, by simply bringing people together, strong attractions and repulsions take place, followed by an utter loss of balance, in a word, by that electrification of the soul known as passion. Were man to give way to the impulse of his natural feelings, were there neither social nor moral law, these outbursts of violent feeling would be the ordinary rule in life. But utility demands that these outbursts should be foreseen and averted. Man must live in society, and consequently submit to rules. And what interest advises, reason commands: duty calls, and we have to obey the summons. Under this dual influence has perforce been formed an outward layer of feelings and ideas which make for permanence, aim at becoming common to all men, and cover, when they are not strong enough to extinguish it, the inner fire of individual passions. The slow progress of mankind in the direction of an increasingly peaceful social life has gradually consolidated this layer, just as the life of our planet itself has been one long effort to cover over with a cool and solid crust the fiery mass of seething metals. But volcanic eruptions occur. And if the earth were a living being, as mythology has feigned, most likely when in repose it would take delight in dreaming of these sudden explosions, whereby it suddenly resumes possession of its innermost nature. Such is just the kind of pleasure that is provided for us by drama. Beneath the quiet humdrum life that reason and society have fashioned for us, it stirs something within us which luckily does not explode, but which it makes us feel in its inner tension. It offers nature her revenge upon society. Sometimes it makes straight for the goal, summoning up to the surface, from the depths below, passions that produce a general upheaval. Sometimes it effects a flank movement, as is often the case in contemporary drama; with a skill that is frequently sophistical, it shows up the inconsistencies of society; it exaggerates the shams and shibboleths of the social law; and so indirectly, by merely dissolving or corroding the outer crust, it again brings us back to the inner core. But, in both cases, whether it weakens society or strengthens nature, it has the same end in view: that of laying bare a secret portion of ourselves—what might be called the tragic element in our character. This is indeed the impression we get after seeing a stirring drama. What has just interested us is not so much what we have been told about others as the glimpse we have caught of ourselves—a whole host of ghostly feelings, emotions and events that would fain have come into real existence, but, fortunately for us, did not. It also seems as if an appeal had been made within us to certain ancestral memories belonging to a far-away past—memories so deep-seated and so foreign to our present life that this latter, for a moment, seems something unreal and conventional, for which we shall have to serve a fresh apprenticeship. So it is indeed a deeper reality that drama draws up from beneath our superficial and utilitarian attainments, and this art has the same end in view as all the others.

➤ Hence it follows that art always aims at what is *individual*. What the artist fixes on his canvas is something he has seen at a certain spot, on a certain day, at a certain hour, with a coloring that will never be seen again. What the poet sings of is a certain mood which was his, and his alone, and which will never return. What the dramatist unfolds before us is the life-history of a soul, a living tissue of feelings and events—something, in short, which has once happened and can never be repeated. We may, indeed, give general names to these feelings, but they cannot be the same thing in another soul. They are *individualized*. Thereby, and thereby only, do they belong to art; for generalities, symbols or even types, form the current coin of our daily perception. How, then, does a misunderstanding on this point arise?

➤ The reason lies in the fact that two very different things have been mistaken for each other: the generality of things and that of the opinions we come to regarding them. Because a feeling is generally recognized as true, it does not follow that it is a general feeling. Nothing could be more unique than the character of Hamlet. Though he may resemble other men in some respects, it is clearly not on that account that he interests us most. But he is universally accepted and regarded as a living character. In this sense only is he universally true. The same holds good of all the other products of art. Each of them is unique, and yet, if it bear the stamp of genius, it will come to be accepted by everybody. Why will it be accepted? And if it is unique of its kind, by what sign do we know it to be genuine? Evidently, by the very effort it forces us to make against our predispositions in order to see sincerely. Sincerity is contagious. What the artist has seen we shall probably never see again, or at least never see in exactly the same way; but if he has actually seen it, the attempt he has made to lift the veil compels our imitation. His work is an example which we take as a lesson. And the efficacy of the lesson is the exact standard of the genuineness of the work. Consequently, truth bears within itself a power of conviction, nay, of conversion, which is the sign that enables us to recognize it. The greater the work and the more profound the dimly apprehended truth, the longer may the effect be in coming, but, on the other hand, the more universal will that effect tend to become. So the universality here lies in the effect produced, and not in the cause.

Altogether different is the object of comedy. Here it is in the work itself that the generality lies. Comedy depicts characters we have already come across and shall meet with again. It takes note of similarities. It aims at placing types before our eyes. It even creates new types, if necessary. In this respect it forms a contrast to all the other arts.

The very titles of certain classical comedies are significant in themselves. Le Misanthrope, l'Avare, le Joueur, le Distrait, etc., are names of whole classes of people; and even when a character comedy has a proper noun as its title, this proper noun is speedily swept away, by the very weight of its contents, into the stream of common nouns. We say "a Tartuffe," but we should never say "a Phèdre" or "a Polyeucte."

Above all, a tragic poet will never think of grouping around the chief character in his play secondary characters to serve as simplified copies, so to speak, of the former. The hero of a tragedy represents an individuality unique of its kind. It may be possible to imitate him, but then we shall be passing, whether consciously or not, from the tragic to the comic. No one is like him, because he is like no one. But a remarkable instinct, on the contrary, impels the comic poet, once he has elaborated his central character, to cause other characters, displaying the same general traits, to revolve as satellites round him. Many comedies have either a plural noun or some collective term as their title. "Les Femmes savantes," "Les Précieuses ridicules," "Le Monde où l'on s'ennuie," etc., represent so many rallying points on the stage adopted by different groups of characters, all belonging to one identical type. It would be interesting to analyze this tendency in comedy. Maybe dramatists have caught a glimpse of a fact recently brought forward by mental pathology, namely that cranks of the same kind are drawn, by a secret attraction, to seek each other's company. Without precisely coming within the province of medicine, the comic individual, as we have shown, is in some way absentminded, and the transition from absentmindedness to crankiness is continuous. But there is also another reason. If the comic poet's object is to offer us types, that is to say, characters capable of self-repetition, how can he set about it better than by showing us, in each instance, several different copies of the same model? That is just what the naturalist does in order to define a species. He enumerates and describes its main varieties.

➤ This essential difference between tragedy and comedy, the former being concerned with individuals and the latter with classes, is revealed in yet another way. It appears in the first draft of the work. From the outset it is manifested by two radically different methods of observation.

Though the assertion may seem paradoxical, a study of other men is probably not necessary to the tragic poet. We find some of the great poets have lived a retiring, homely sort of life, without having a chance of witnessing around them an outburst of the passions they have so faithfully depicted. But, supposing even they had witnessed such a spectacle, it is doubtful whether they would have found it of much use. For what interests us in the work of the poet is the glimpse we get of certain profound moods or inner struggles. Now, this glimpse cannot be obtained from without. Our souls are impenetrable to one another. Certain signs of passion are all that we ever apperceive externally. These we interpret—though always, by the way, defectively—only by analogy with what we have ourselves experienced. So what we experience is the main point, and we cannot become thoroughly acquainted with anything but our own heart— supposing we ever get so far. Does this mean that the poet has experienced what he depicts, that he has gone through the various situations he makes his characters traverse, and lived the whole of their inner life? Here, too, the biographies of poets would contradict such a supposition. How, indeed, could the same man have been Macbeth, Hamlet, Othello, King Lear, and many others? But then a distinction should perhaps here be made between the personality *we have* and all those we might have had. Our character is the result of a choice that is continually being renewed. There are points—at all events there seem to be—all along the way, where we may branch off, and we perceive many possible directions though we are unable to take more than one. To retrace one's steps, and follow to the end the faintly distinguishable directions, appears to be the essential element in poetic imagination. Of course, Shakespeare was neither Macbeth, nor Hamlet, nor Othello; still, he *might have been* these several characters if the circumstances of the case on the one hand, and the consent of his will on the other, had caused to break out into explosive action what was nothing more than an inner prompting. We are strangely mistaken as to the part played by poetic imagination, if we think it pieces together its heroes out of fragments filched from right and left, as though it were patching together a harlequin's motley. Nothing living would result from that. Life cannot be recomposed; it can only be looked at and reproduced. Poetic imagination is but a fuller view of reality. If the characters created by a poet give us the impression of life, it is only because they are the poet himself—a multiplication or division of the poet —the poet plumbing the depths of his own nature in so powerful an effort of inner observation that he lays hold of the potential in the real, and takes up what nature has left as a mere outline or sketch in his soul in order to make of it a finished work of art.

Altogether different is the kind of observation from which comedy springs.

It is directed outwards. However interested a dramatist may be in the comic features of human nature, he will hardly go, I imagine, to the extent of trying to discover his own. Besides, he would not find them, for we are never ridiculous except in some point that remains hidden from our own consciousness. It is on others, then, that such observation must perforce be practiced. But it will, for this very reason, assume a character of generality that it cannot have when we apply it to ourselves. Settling on the surface, it will not be more than skin-deep, dealing with persons at the point at which they come into contact and become capable of resembling one another. It will go no farther. Even if it could, it would not desire to do so, for it would have nothing to gain in the process. To penetrate too far into the personality, to couple the outer effect with causes that are too deep-seated, would mean to endanger and in the end to sacrifice all that was laughable in the effect. In order that we may be tempted to laugh at it, we must localize its cause in some intermediate region of the soul. Consequently, the effect must appear to us as an average effect, as expressing an average of mankind. And, like all averages, this one is obtained by bringing together scattered data, by comparing analogous cases and extracting their essence, in short by a process of abstraction and generalization similar to that which the physicist brings to bear upon facts with the object of grouping them under laws. In a word, method and object are here of the same nature as in the inductive sciences, in that observation is always external and the result always general.

And so we come back, by a roundabout way, to the double conclusion we reached in the course of our investigations. On the one hand, a person is never ridiculous except through some mental attribute resembling absent-mindedness, through something that lives upon him without forming part of his organism, after the fashion of a parasite; that is the reason this state of mind is observable from without and capable of being corrected. But, on the other hand, just because laughter aims at correcting, it is expedient that the correction should reach as great a number of persons as possible. This is the reason comic observation instinctively proceeds to what is general. It chooses such peculiarities as admit of being reproduced and consequently are not indissolubly bound up with the individuality of a single person—a possibly common sort of uncommonness, so to say—peculiarities that are held in common. By transferring them to the stage, it creates works which doubtless belong to art in that their only visible aim is to please, but which will be found to contrast with other works of art by reason of their generality and also of their scarcely confessed or scarcely conscious intention to correct and instruct. So we were probably right in saying that comedy lies midway between art and life. It is not disinterested, as genuine art is. By organizing laughter, comedy accepts social life as a natural environment, it even obeys an impulse of social life. And in this respect it turns its back upon art, which is a breaking away from society and a return to pure nature.

—*Laughter* (1909; translated 1913)

BENEDETTO CROCE

Intuition and Expression

I. Art as Intuition

. . . As to what is art—I will say at once, in the simplest manner, that art is *vision* or *intuition*. The artist produces an image or a phantasm; and he who enjoys art turns his gaze upon the point to which the artist has pointed, looks through the chink which he has opened, and reproduces that image in himself. "Intuition," "vision," "contemplation," "imagination," "fancy," "figurations," "representations," and so on, are words continually recurring, like synonyms, when discoursing upon art, and they all lead the mind to the same conceptual sphere which indicates general agreement.

But this reply, that art is intuition, obtains its force and meaning from all that it implicitly denies and from which it distinguishes art. What negations are implicit in it? I shall indicate the principal, or at least those that are the most important for us at this present moment of our culture.

It denies, above all, that art is a *physical fact:* for example, certain determined colors, or relations of colors; certain definite forms of bodies; certain definite sounds, or relations of sounds; certain phenomena of heat or of electricity—in short, whatsoever be designed as "physical." The inclination toward this error of physicizing art is already present in ordinary thought, and as children who touch the soap-bubble and would wish to touch the rainbow, so the human spirit, admiring beautiful things, hastens spontaneously to trace out the reasons for them in external nature, and proves that it must think, or believes that it should think, certain colors beautiful and certain other colors ugly, certain forms beautiful and certain other forms ugly. But this attempt has been carried out intentionally and with method on several occasions in the history of thought: from the "canons" which the Greek theoreticians and artists fixed for the beauty of bodies, through the speculations as to the geometrical and numerical relations of figures and sounds, down to the researches of the estheticians of the nineteenth century (Fechner, for example), and to the "communications" presented in our day by the inexpert, at philosophical, psychological, and natural science congresses, concerning the relations of physical phenomena with art. And if it be asked why art cannot be a physical fact, we must reply, in the first place, that physical facts *do not possess reality,* and that art, to which so many devote their whole lives and which fills all with a divine joy, is *supremely real;* thus it cannot be a physical fact, which is something unreal. This sounds at first paradoxical, for nothing seems more solid and secure to the ordinary man than the physical world; but we, in the seat of truth, must not abstain from the good reason and substitute for it one less good, solely because the first should have the appearance of a lie; and besides, in order to surpass what of strange and difficult may be contained in that truth, to become at home with it, we may take into consideration the fact that the demonstration of the unreality of the physical world has not only been proved in an indisputable manner and is admitted by all philosophers (who are not crass materialists and are not involved in the strident contradictions of materialism), but is professed by these same physicists in the spontaneous philosophy which they mingle with their physics, when they conceive physical phenomena as products of principles that are beyond experience, of atoms or of ether, or as the manifestation of an Unknowable: besides, the matter itself of the materialists is a super-material principle. Thus physical facts reveal themselves, by their internal logic and by common consent, not as reality, but as a *construction of our intellect for the purposes of science*. Consequently, the question whether art be a physical fact must rationally assume this different signification: that is to say, *whether it be possible to construct art physically*. And this is certainly possible, for we indeed carry it out always, when, turning from the sense of a poem and ceasing to enjoy it, we set ourselves, for example, to count the words of which the poem is composed and to divide them into syllables and letters; or, disregarding the esthetic effect of a statue, we weigh and measure it: a most useful performance for the packers of statues, as is the other for the typographers who have to "compose" pages of poetry; but most useless for the contemplater and student of art, to whom it is neither useful nor licit to allow himself to be "distracted" from his proper object. Thus art is not a physical fact in this second sense, either; which amounts to saying that when we propose to ourselves to penetrate its nature and mode of action, to construct it physically is of no avail.

Another negation is implied in the definition of art as intuition: if it be intuition, and intuition is equivalent to *theory* in the original sense of contemplation, art cannot be a utilitarian act; and since a utilitarian act aims always at obtaining a pleasure and therefore at keeping off a pain, art, considered in its own nature, has nothing to do with the *useful* and with *pleasure* and *pain,* as such. It will be admitted, indeed, without much difficulty, that a pleasure as a pleasure, any sort of pleasure, is not of itself artistic; the pleasure of a drink of water that slakes thirst, or a walk in the open air that stretches our limbs and makes our blood circulate more lightly, or the obtaining of a longed-for post that settles us in practical life, and so on, is not artistic. Finally, the difference between pleasure and art leaps to the eyes in the relations that are developed between ourselves and works of art, because the figure represented may be dear to us and represent the most delightful memories, and at the same time the picture may be ugly; or, on the other hand, the picture may be beautiful and the figure represented hateful to our hearts, or the picture itself, which we approve as beautiful, may also cause us rage and envy, because it is the work of our enemy or rival, for whom it will procure advantage and on whom it will confer new strength: our practical interests, with their relative pleasures and pains, mingle and sometimes become confused with art and disturb, but are never *identified* with, our esthetic interest. At the most it will be affirmed, with a view to maintaining more effectively the definition of art as the pleasurable, that it is not the pleasurable in general, but a *particular* form of the pleasurable. But such a restriction is no longer a defense, it is indeed an abandonment of that thesis; for given that art is a particular form of pleasure, its distinctive character would be supplied, not by the pleasurable, but by what distinguishes that pleasurable from other pleasurables, and it would be desirable to turn the attention to that distinctive element—more than pleasurable or different from pleasurable. Nevertheless, the doctrine that defines art as the pleasurable has a special denomination (hedonistic esthetic), and a long and complicated development in the history of esthetic doctrines: it showed itself in the Greco-Roman world, prevailed in the eighteenth century, reflowered in the second half of the nineteenth, and still enjoys much favor, being especially well received by beginners in esthetic, who are above all struck by the fact that art causes pleasure. The life of this doctrine has consisted of proposing in turn one or another class of pleasures, or several classes together (the pleasure of the superior senses, the pleasure of play, of consciousness of our own strength, of criticism, etc.), or of adding to it elements differing from the pleasurable, the useful for example (when understood as distinct from the pleasurable), the satisfaction of cognoscitive and moral wants, and the like. And its progress has been caused just by this restlessness, and by its allowing foreign elements to ferment in its bosom, which it introduces through the necessity of somehow bringing itself into agreement with the reality of art, thus attaining to its dissolution as hedonistic doctrine and to the promotion of a new doctrine, or at least to drawing attention to its necessity. And since every error has its element of truth (and that of the physical doctrine has been seen to be the possibility of the physical "construction" of art as of any other fact), the hedonistic doctrine has its eternal element of truth in the placing in relief the hedonistic accompaniment, or pleasure, common to the esthetic activity as to every form of spiritual activity, which it has not at all been intended to deny in absolutely denying the identification of art with the pleasurable, and in distinguishing it from the pleasurable by defining it as intuition.

A third negation, effected by means of the theory of art as intuition, is that art is a *moral act;* that is to say, that form of practical act which, although necessarily uniting with the useful and with pleasure and pain, is not immediately utilitarian and hedonistic, and moves in a superior spiritual sphere. But the intuition, in so far as it is a theoretic act, is opposed to the practical of any sort.

And in truth, art, as has been remarked from the earliest times, does not arise as an act of the will; good will, which constitutes the honest man, does not constitute the artist. And since it is not the result of an act of will, so it escapes all moral discrimination, not because a privilege of exemption is accorded to it, but simply because moral discrimination cannot be applied to art. An artistic image portrays an act morally praiseworthy or blameworthy; but this image, as image, is neither morally praiseworthy nor blameworthy. Not only is there no penal code that can condemn an image to prison or to death, but no moral judgment, uttered by a rational person, can make of it its object: we might just as well judge the square moral or the triangle immoral as the Francesca of Dante immoral or the Cordelia of Shakespeare moral, for these have a purely artistic function, they are like musical notes in the souls of Dante and of Shakespeare. Further, the moralistic theory of art is also represented in the history of esthetic doctrines, though much discredited in the common opinion of our times, not only on account of its intrinsic demerit, but also, in some measure, owing to the moral demerit of certain tendencies of our times, which render possible, owing to psychological dislike, that refutation of it which should be made—and which we here make—solely for logical reasons. The end attributed to art, of directing the good and inspiring horror of evil, of correcting and ameliorating customs, is a derivation of the moralistic doctrine; and so is the demand addressed to artists to collaborate in the education of the lower classes, in the strengthening of the national or bellicose spirit of a people, in the diffusion of the ideals of a modest and laborious life; and so on. These are all things that art cannot do, any more than geometry, which, however, does not lose anything of its importance on account of its inability to do this; and one does not see why art should do so, either. That it cannot do these things was partially perceived by the moralistic estheticians also; who very readily effected a transaction with it, permitting it to provide pleasures that were not moral, provided they were not openly dishonest, or recommending it to employ to a good end the dominion that, owing to its hedonistic power, it possessed over souls, to gild the pill, to sprinkle sweetness upon the rim of the glass containing the bitter draught—in short, to play the courtesan (since it could not get rid of its old and inborn habits), in the service of holy church or of morality: *meretrix ecclesiæ*. On other occasions they have sought to avail themselves of it for purposes of instruction, since not only virtue but also science is a difficult thing, and art could remove this difficulty and render pleasant and attractive the entrance into the ocean of science—indeed, lead them through it as through a garden of Armida, gayly and voluptuously, without their being conscious of the lofty protection they had obtained, or of the crisis of renovation which they were preparing for themselves. We cannot now refrain from a smile when we talk of these theories, but should not forget that they were once a serious matter corresponding to a serious effort to understand the nature of art and to elevate the conception of it; and that among those who believed in it (to limit ourselves to Italian literature) were Dante and Tasso, Parini and Alfieri, Manzoni and Mazzini. And the moralistic doctrine of art was and is and will be perpetually beneficial by its very contradictions; it was and will be an effort, however unhappy, to separate art from the merely pleasing, with which it is sometimes confused, and to assign to it a more worthy post: and it, too, has its true side, because, if art be beyond morality, the artist is neither this side of it nor that, but under its empire, insofar as he is a man who cannot withdraw himself from the duties of man, and must look upon art itself—art, which is not and never will be moral—as a mission to be exercised as a priestly office.

Again (and this is the last and perhaps the most important of all the general negations that it suits me to recall in relation to this matter), with the definition of art as intuition, we deny that it has the character of *conceptual knowledge*. Conceptual knowledge, in its true form, which is the philosophical, is always realistic, aiming at establishing reality against unreality, or at lowering unreality by including it in reality as a subordinate moment of reality itself. But intuition means, precisely, indistinction of reality and unreality, the image with its value as mere image, the pure ideality of the image; and opposing the intuitive or sensible knowledge to the conceptual or intelligible, the esthetic to the noetic, it aims at claiming the autonomy of this more simple and elementary form of knowledge, which has been compared to the dream (the dream, and not the sleep) of the theoretic life, in respect to which philosophy would be the waking. And indeed, whoever should ask, when examining a work of art, whether what the artist has expressed be metaphysically and historically true or false, asks a question that is without meaning, and commits an error analogous to his who should bring the airy images of the fancy before the tribunal of morality: without meaning, because the discrimination of true and false always concerns an affirmation of reality, or a judgment, but it cannot fall under the head of an image or of a pure subject, which is not the subject of a judgment, since it is without qualification or predicate. It is useless to object that the individuality of the image cannot subsist without reference to the universal, of which that image is the individuation, because we do not here deny that the universal, as the spirit of God, is everywhere and animates all things with itself, but we deny that the universal is rendered logically explicit and is thought in the intuition. Useless also is the appeal to the principle of the unity of the spirit, which is not broken, but, on the contrary, strengthened by the clear distinction of fancy from thought, because from the distinction comes opposition, and from opposition concrete unity.

Ideality (as has also been called this character that distinguishes the intuition from the concept, art from philosophy and from history, from the affirmation of the universal and from the perception or narration of what has happened) is the intimate virtue of art; no sooner are reflection and judgment developed from that ideality, than art is dissipated and dies: it dies in the artist, who becomes a critic; it dies in the contemplator, who changes from an entranced enjoyer of art to a meditative observer of life. . . .

And since this vindication of the alogical character of art is, as I have said, the most difficult and important of the negations included in the formula of art-intuition, the theories that attempt to explain art as philosophy, as religion, as history, or as science, and in a lesser degree as mathematics, occupy the greater part of the history of esthetic science and are adorned with the names of the greatest philosophers. Schelling and Hegel afford examples of the identification or confusion of art with religion and philosophy in the eighteenth century; Taine, of its confusion with the natural sciences; the theories of the French verists, of its confusion with historical and documentary observation; the formalism of the Herbartians, of its confusion with mathematics. But it would be vain to seek pure examples of these errors in any of these authors and in the others that might be mentioned, because error is never pure, for if it were so, it would be truth. . . .

But doubt springs up at the feet of truth, "like a young shoot"—as the *terzina* of father Dante has it—doubt, which is what drives the intellect of man "from mount to mount." The doctrine of art as intuition, as fancy, as form, now gives rise to an ulterior (I have not said an "ultimate") problem, which is no longer one of opposition and distinction toward physics, hedonistic, ethic and logic, but the field of images itself, which sets in doubt the capacity of the image to define the character of art and is in reality occupied with the mode of separating the genuine from the spurious image, and of enriching in this way the concept of the image and of art. What function (it is asked) can a world of pure images possess in the spirit of man, without philosophical, historical, religious, or scientific value, and without even moral or hedonistic value? What is more vain than to dream with open eyes in life, which demands, not only open eyes, but an open mind and a nimble spirit? Pure images! But to nourish oneself upon pure images is called by a name of little honor, "to dream," and there is usually added to this the epithet of "idle." It is a very insipid and inconclusive thing; can it ever be art? Certainly, we sometimes amuse ourselves with the reading of some sensational romance of adventure, where images follow images in the most various and unexpected way; but we thus enjoy ourselves in moments of fatigue, when we are obliged to kill time, and with a full consciousness that such stuff is not art. Such instances are of the nature of a pastime, a game; but were art a game or a pastime, it would fall into the wide arms of hedonistic doctrine, ever open to receive it. And it is a utilitarian and hedonistic need that impels us sometimes to relax the bow of the mind and the bow of the will, and to stretch ourselves, allowing images to follow one another in our memory, or combining them in quaint forms with the aid of the imagination, in a sort of waking sleep, from which we rouse ourselves as soon as we are rested; and we sometimes rouse ourselves just to devote ourselves to the work of art, which cannot be produced by a mind relaxed. Thus either art is not pure intuition, and the claims put forward in the doctrines which we believed we had above confuted, are not satisfied, and so the confutation itself of these doctrines is troubled with doubts; or intuition cannot consist in a simple act of imagination. . . .

The intuition is the product of an image, and not of an incoherent mass of images obtained by recalling former images and allowing them to succeed one another capriciously, by combining one image with another in a like capricious manner, joining a horse's neck to a human head, and thus playing a childish game. Old Poetic availed itself above all of the concept of *unity,* in order to express this distinction between the intuition and imagining, insisting that whatever the artistic work, it should be *simplex et unum;* or of the allied concept of *unity in variety*—that is to say, the multiple images were to find their common center unit of union in a comprehensive image: and the esthetic of the nineteenth century created with the same object the distinction, which appears in not a few of its philosophers, between *fancy* (the peculiar artistic faculty) and *imagination* (the extra-artistic faculty).[1] To amass, select, cut up, combine images, presupposes the possession of particular images in the spirit; and fancy produces, whereas imagination is sterile, adapted to extrinsic combinations and not to the generation of organism and life. . . .

The intuition is truly artistic, it is truly intuition, and not a chaotic mass of images, only when it has a vital principle that animates it, making it all one with itself; but what is this principle?

The answer to such a question may be said to result from the examination of the greatest ideal strife that has ever taken place in the field of art (and is not confined to the epoch that took its name from it and in which it was predominant): the strife between *romanticism* and *classicism.* Giving the general definition, here convenient, and setting aside minor and accidental determinations, romanticism asks of art, above all, the spontaneous and violent effusion of the affections, of love and hate, of anguish and jubilation, of desperation and elevation; and is willingly satisfied and pleased with vaporous and indeterminate images, broken and allusive in style, with vague suggestions, with approximate phrases, with powerful and troubled sketches: while classicism loves the peaceful soul, the wise design, figures studied in their characteristics and precise in outline, ponderation, equilibrium, clarity; and resolutely tends toward *representation,* as the other tends toward feeling. And whoever puts himself at one or the other point of view finds crowds of reasons for maintaining it and for confuting the opposite point of view; because (say the romantics), what is the use of an art,

[1] Croce here employs the terms "imagination" and "fancy" in a sense opposite to the modern English usage. The Italian *"fantasia"* corresponds to our word "imagination," and the Italian *"immaginazione"* to our "fancy." The distinction that Croce is making corresponds to Coleridge's contrast between imagination and fancy, except that the terms are interchanged. For Coleridge's account see his *Biographia Literaria,* chapters 4, 12, and 13. Wordsworth has a similar account in his *Preface to the Poems of 1815.* (Editor's note.)

rich in beautiful images, which, nevertheless, does not speak to the heart? And if it do speak to the heart, what is the use if the images be not beautiful? And the others will say, What is the use of the shock of the passions, if the spirit do not rest upon a beautiful image? And if the image be beautiful, if our taste be satisfied, what matters the absence of those emotions which can all of them be obtained outside art, and which life does not fail to provide, sometimes in greater quantity than we desire? But when we begin to feel weary of the fruitless defense of both partial views; above all, when we turn away from the ordinary works of art produced by the romantic and classical schools, from works convulsed with passion or coldly decorous, and fix them on the works, not of the disciples, but of the masters, not of the mediocre, but of the supreme, we see the contest disappear in the distance and find ourselves unable to call the great portions of these works, romantic or classic or representative, because they are both classic and romantic, feelings and representations, a vigorous feeling which has become all most brilliant representation. Such, for example, are the works of Hellenic art, and such those of Italian poetry and art: the transcendentalism of the Middle Ages became fixed in the bronze of the Dantesque *terzina;* melancholy and suave fancy, in the transparency of the songs and sonnets of Petrarch; sage experience of life and badinage with the fables of the past, in the limpid *ottava rima* of Ariosto; heroism and the thought of death, in the perfect blankverse hendecasyllabics of Foscolo; the infinite variety of everything, in the sober and austere songs of Giacomo Leopardi. Finally (be it said in parenthesis and without intending comparison with the other examples adduced), the voluptuous refinements and animal sensuality of international decadentism have received their most perfect expression in the prose and verse of an Italian, D'Annunzio. All these souls were profoundly passionate (all, even the serene Lodovico Ariosto, who was so amorous, so tender, and so often repressed his emotion with a smile); their works of art are the eternal flower that springs from their passions.

These expressions and these critical judgments can be theoretically resumed in the formula, that what gives coherence and unity to the intuition is feeling: the intuition is really such because it represents a feeling, and can only appear from and upon that. Not the idea, but the feeling, is what confers upon art the airy lightness of the symbol: an aspiration enclosed in the circle of a representation—that is art; and in it the aspiration alone stands for the representation, and the representation alone for the aspiration. Epic and lyric, or drama and lyric, are scholastic divisions of the indivisible: art is always lyrical—that is, epic and dramatic in feeling. What we admire in geniune works of art is the perfect fanciful form which a state of the soul assumes; and we call this life, unity, solidity of the work of art. What displeases us in the false and imperfect forms is the struggle of several different states of the soul not yet unified, their stratification, or mixture, their vacillating method, which obtains apparent unity from the will of the author, who for this purpose avails himself of an abstract plan or idea, or of extra-esthetic, passionate emotion. A series of images which seem to be, each in turn, rich in power of conviction, leaves us nevertheless deluded and diffident, because we do not see them generated from a state of the soul, from a "sketch" (as the painters call it), from a motive; and they follow one another and crowd together without that precise intonation, without that accent, which comes from the heart. And what is the figure cut out from the background of the picture or transported and placed against another background, what is the personage of drama or of romance outside his relation with all the other personages and with the general action? And what is the value of this general action if it be not an action of the spirit of the author? The secular disputes concerning dramatic unity are interesting in this connection; they are first applied to the unity of "action" when they have been obtained from an extrinsic determination of time and place, and this finally applied to the unity of "interest," and the interest would have to be in its turn dissolved in the interest of the spirit of the poet—that is, in his intimate aspiration, in his feeling. The negative issue of the great dispute between classicists and romanticists is interesting, for it resulted in the negation both of the art which strives to distract and illude the soul as to the deficiency of the image with mere feeling, with the practical violence of feeling, with feeling that has not become contemplation, and of the art which, by means of the superficial clearness of the image, of drawing correctly false, of the word falsely correct, seeks to deceive as to its lack of inspiration and its lack of an esthetic reason to justify what it has produced. A celebrated sentence uttered by an English critic,[2] and become one of the commonplaces of journalism, states that "all the arts tend to the condition of music"; but it would have been more accurate to say that all the arts are music, if it be thus intended to emphasize the genesis of esthetic images in feeling, excluding from their number those mechanically constructed or realistically ponderous. And another not less celebrated utterance of a Swiss semi-philosopher, which has had the like good or bad fortune of becoming trivial, discovers that "every landscape is a state of the soul":[3] which is indisputable, not because the landscape is landscape, but because the landscape is art.

Artistic intuition, then, is always *lyrical* intuition: this latter being a word that is not present as an adjective or definition of the first, but as a synonym, another of the synonyms that can be united to the several that I have mentioned already, and which, all of them, designate the intuition. And if it be sometimes convenient that instead of appearing as a synonym, it should assume the grammatical form of the adjective, that is only to make clear the difference between the intuition-image, or nexus of images (for what is called image is always a nexus of images, since image-atoms do not exist any more than thought-atoms),

2 Walter Pater, *The Renaissance*, Essay on "The School of Giorgione." (Editor's note.)
    3 Amiel. (Editor's note.)

which constitutes the organism, and, as organism, has its vital principle, which is the organism itself—between this, which is true and proper intuition, and that false intuition which is a heap of images put together in play or intentionally or for some other practical purpose, the connection of which, being practical, shows itself to be not organic, but mechanic, when considered from the esthetic point of view. But the word *lyric* would be redundant save in this explicative or polemical sense; and art is perfectly defined when it is simply defined as intuition.

—The Breviary of Æsthetic (1913; translated 1915)

II. *Intuition and Expression*

➤Knowledge has two forms: it is either *intuitive* knowledge or *logical* knowledge; knowledge obtained through the *imagination* or knowledge obtained through the *intellect;* knowledge of the *individual* or knowledge of the *universal;* of *individual things* or of the *relations* between them: it is, in fact, productive either of *images* or of *concepts.*

In ordinary life, constant appeal is made to intuitive knowledge. It is said that we cannot give definitions of certain truths; that they are not demonstrable by syllogisms; that they must be learnt intuitively. The politician finds fault with the abstract reasoner, who possesses no lively intuition of actual conditions; the educational theorist insists upon the necessity of developing the intuitive faculty in the pupil before everything else; the critic in judging a work of art makes it a point of honor to set aside theory and abstractions, and to judge it by direct intuition; the practical man professes to live rather by intuition than by reason.

But this ample acknowledgment granted to intuitive knowledge in ordinary life, does not correspond to an equal and adequate acknowledgment in the field of theory and of philosophy. There exists a very ancient science of intellectual knowledge, admitted by all without discussion, namely, Logic; but a science of intuitive knowledge is timidly and with difficulty asserted by but a few. Logical knowledge has appropriated the lion's share; and if she does not slay and devour her companion outright, yet yields to her but grudgingly the humble place of maidservant or doorkeeper.—What can intuitive knowledge be without the light of intellectual knowledge? It is a servant without a master; and though a master find a servant useful, the master is a necessity to the servant, since he enables him to gain his livelihood. Intuition is blind; intellect lends her eyes.

Now, the first point to be firmly fixed in the mind is that intuitive knowledge has no need of a master, nor to lean upon any one; she does not need to borrow the eyes of others, for she has excellent eyes of her own. Doubtless it is possible to find concepts mingled with intuitions. But in many other intuitions there is no trace of such a mixture, which proves that it is not necessary. The impression of a moonlight scene by a painter; the outline of a country drawn by a cartographer; a musical motive, tender or energetic; the words of a sighing lyric, or those with which we ask, command and lament in ordinary life, may well all be intuitive facts without a shadow of intellectual relation. But, think what one may of these instances, and admitting further the contention that the greater part of the intuitions of civilized man are impregnated with concepts, there yet remains to be observed something more important and more conclusive. Those concepts which are found mingled and fused with the intuitions are no longer concepts, in so far as they are really mingled and fused, for they have lost all independence and autonomy. They have been concepts, but have now become simple elements of intuition. The philosophical maxims placed in the mouth of a personage of tragedy or of comedy, perform there the function, not of concepts, but of characteristics of such personage; in the same way as the red in a painted face does not there represent the red color of the physicists, but is a characteristic element of the portrait. The whole is that which determines the quality of the parts. A work of art may be full of philosophical concepts; it may contain them in greater abundance and they may there be even more profound than in a philosophical dissertation, which in its turn may be rich to overflowing with descriptions and intuitions. But notwithstanding all these concepts the total effect of the work of art is an intuition; and notwithstanding all those intuitions, the total effect of the philosophical dissertation is a concept. The *Promessi Sposi* contains copious ethical observations and distinctions, but does not for that reason lose as a whole its character of simple story or intuition. In like manner the anecdotes and satirical effusions to be found in the works of a philosopher like Schopenhauer do not deprive those works of their character of intellectual treatises. The difference between a scientific work and a work of art, that is, between an intellectual fact and an intuitive fact, lies in the difference of the total effect aimed at by their respective authors. This it is that determines and rules over the several parts of each, not these parts separated and considered abstractly in themselves.

But to admit the independence of intuition as regards concept does not suffice to give a true and precise idea of intuition. Another error arises among those who recognize this, or who at any rate do not explicitly make intuition dependent upon the intellect, to obscure and confuse the real nature of intuition. By intuition is frequently understood *perception*, or the knowledge of actual reality, the apprehension of something as *real*.

Certainly perception is intuition: the perceptions of the room in which I am writing, of the ink bottle and paper that are before me, of the pen I am using, of the objects that I touch and make use of as instruments of my person, which, if it write, therefore exists; these are all intuitions. But the image that is now passing through my brain of a me writing in another room, in another town, with different paper, pen and ink, is also an intuition. This means that the distinction between reality and non-reality is extraneous, secondary, to the true nature of

intuition. If we imagine a human mind having intuitions for the first time, it
would seem that it could have intuitions of actual reality only, that is to say, that
it could have perceptions of nothing but the real. But since knowledge of reality
is based upon the distinction between real images and unreal images, and since
this distinction does not at the first moment exist, these intuitions would in truth
not be intuitions either of the real or of the unreal, not perceptions, but pure
intuitions. Where all is real, nothing is real. The child, with its difficulty of
distinguishing true from false, history from fable, which are all one to childhood,
can furnish us with a sort of very vague and only remotely approximate idea of
this ingenuous state. Intuition is the undifferentiated unity of the perception of
the real and of the simple image of the possible. In our intuitions we do not oppose ourselves as empirical beings to external reality, but we simply objectify our
impressions, whatever they be.

Those, therefore, who look upon intuition as sensation formed and arranged
simply according to the categories of space and time, would seem to approximate
more nearly to the truth. Space and time (they say) are the forms of intuition;
to have an intuition is to place it in space and in temporal sequence. Intuitive
activity would then consist in this double and concurrent function of spatiality
and temporality. But for these two categories must be repeated what was said of
intellectual distinctions, when found mingled with intuitions. We have intuitions without space and without time: the color of a sky, the color of a feeling,
a cry of pain and an effort of will, objectified in consciousness: these are intuitions which we possess, and with their making space and time have nothing to
do. In some intuitions, spatiality may be found without temporality, in others,
vice versa; and even where both are found, they are perceived by later reflection:
they can be fused with the intuition in like manner with all its other elements:
that is, they are in it *materialiter* and not *formaliter,* as ingredients and not as
arrangement. Who, without an act of reflection which for a moment breaks in
upon his contemplation, can think of space while looking at a drawing or a view?
Who is conscious of temporal sequence while listening to a story or a piece of
music without breaking into it with a similar act of reflection? What intuition
reveals in a work of art is not space and time, but *character, individual physiognomy.* The view here maintained is confirmed in several quarters of modern
philosophy. Space and time, far from being simple and primitive functions, are
nowadays conceived as intellectual constructions of great complexity. And
further, even in some of those who do not altogether deny to space and time the
quality of formative principles, categories and functions, one observes an effort
to unite them and to regard them in a different manner from that in which
these categories are generally conceived. Some limit intuition to the sole category
of spatiality, maintaining that even time can only be intuited in terms of space.
Others abandon the three dimensions of space as not philosophically necessary,
and conceive the function of spatiality as void of all particular spatial determi-

nation. But what could such a spatial function be, a simple arrangement that should arrange even time? It represents, surely, all that criticism and refutation have left standing—the bare demand for the affirmation of some intuitive activity in general. And is not this activity truly determined, when one single function is attributed to it, not spatializing nor temporalizing, but characterizing? Or rather, when it is conceived as itself a category or function which gives us knowledge of things in their concreteness and individuality?

Having thus freed intuitive knowledge from any suggestion of intellectualism and from every later and external addition, we must now explain it and determine its limits from another side and defend it from a different kind of invasion and confusion. On the hither side of the lower limit is sensation, formless matter, which the spirit can never apprehend in itself as simple matter. This it can only possess with form and in form, but postulates the notion of it as a mere limit. Matter, in its abstraction, is mechanism, passivity; it is what the spirit of man suffers, but does not produce. Without it no human knowledge or activity is possible; but mere matter produces animality, whatever is brutal and impulsive in man, not the spiritual dominion, which is humanity. How often we strive to understand clearly what is passing within us! We do catch a glimpse of something, but this does not appear to the mind as objectified and formed. It is in such moments as these that we best perceive the profound difference between matter and form. These are not two acts of ours, opposed to one another; but the one is outside us and assaults and sweeps us off our feet, while the other inside us tends to absorb and identify itself with that which is outside. Matter, clothed and conquered by form, produces concrete form. It is the matter, the content, which differentiates one of our intuitions from another: the form is constant: it is spiritual activity, while matter is changeable. Without matter spiritual activity would not forsake its abstractness to become concrete and real activity, this or that spiritual content, this or that definite intuition.

It is a curious fact, characteristic of our times, that this very form, this very activity of the spirit, which is essentially ourselves, is so often ignored or denied. Some confound the spiritual activity of man with the metaphorical and mythological activity of what is called nature, which is mechanism and has no resemblance to human activity, save when we imagine, with Æsop, that *"arbores loquuntur non tantum ferae."* [1] Some affirm that they have never observed in themselves this "miraculous" activity, as though there were no difference, or only one of quantity, between sweating and thinking, feeling cold and the energy of the will. Others, certainly with greater reason, would unify activity and mechanism in a more general concept, though they are specifically distinct. Let us, however, refrain for the moment from examining if such a final unification be possible, and in what sense, but admitting that the attempt may be made, it is clear that to unify two concepts in a third implies to begin with the

[1] "Talking trees are not so fierce."

admission of a difference between the two first. Here it is this difference that concerns us and we set it in relief.

Intuition has sometimes been confused with simple sensation. But since this confusion ends by being offensive to common sense, it has more frequently been attenuated or concealed with a phraseology apparently designed at once to confuse and to distinguish them. Thus, it has been asserted that intuition is sensation, but not so much simple sensation as *association* of sensations. Here a double meaning is concealed in the word "association." Association is understood, either as memory, mnemonic association, conscious recollection, and in that case the claim to unite in memory elements which are not intuited, distinguished, possessed in some way by the spirit and produced by consciousness, seems inconceivable: or it is understood as association of unconscious elements, in which case we remain in the world of sensation and of nature. But if with certain associationists we speak of an association which is neither memory nor flux of sensations, but a *productive* association (formative, constructive, distinguishing); then our contention is admitted and only its name is denied to it. For productive association is no longer association in the sense of the sensationalists, but *synthesis,* that is to say, spiritual activity. Synthesis may be called association; but with the concept of productivity is already posited the distinction between passivity and activity, between sensation and intuition.

Other psychologists are disposed to distinguish from sensation something which is sensation no longer, but is not yet intellectual concept: the *representation* or *image*. What is the difference between their representation or image and our intuitive knowledge? Everything and nothing: for "representation" is a very equivocal word. If by representation be understood something cut off and standing out from the psychic basis of the sensations, then representation is intuition. If, on the other hand, it be conceived as complex sensation we are back once more in crude sensation, which does not vary in quality according to its richness or poverty, or according to whether the organism in which it appears is rudimentary or highly developed and full of traces of past sensations. Nor is the ambiguity remedied by defining representation as a psychic product of secondary degree in relation to sensation, defined as occupying the first place. What does secondary degree mean here? Does it mean a qualitative, formal difference? If so, representation is an elaboration of sensation and therefore intuition. Or does it mean greater complexity and complication, a quantitative, material difference? In that case intuition is once more confused with simple sensation.

And yet there is a sure method of distinguishing true intuition, true representation, from that which is inferior to it: the spiritual fact from the mechanical, passive, natural fact. Every true intuition or representation is also *expression*. That which does not objectify itself in expression is not intuition or representation, but sensation and mere natural fact. The spirit only intuits in making, forming, expressing. He who separates intuition from expression never succeeds in reuniting them.

Intuitive activity *possesses intuitions to the extent that it expresses them.* Should this proposition sound paradoxical, that is partly because, as a general rule, a too restricted meaning is given to the word "expression." It is generally restricted to what are called verbal expressions alone. But there exist also non-verbal expressions, such as those of line, color and sound, and to all of these must be extended our affirmation, which embraces therefore every sort of manifestation of the man, as orator, musician, painter, or anything else. But be it pictorial, or verbal, or musical, or in whatever other form it appear, to no intuition can expression in one of its forms be wanting; it is, in fact, an inseparable part of intuition. How can we really possess an intuition of a geometrical figure, unless we possess so accurate an image of it as to be able to trace it immediately upon paper or on the blackboard? How can we really have an intuition of the contour of a region, for example of the island of Sicily, if we are not able to draw it as it is in all its meanderings? Everyone can experience the internal illumination which follows upon his success in formulating to himself his impressions and feelings, but only so far as he is able to formulate them. Feelings or impressions, then, pass by means of words from the obscure region of the soul into the clarity of the contemplative spirit. It is impossible to distinguish intuition from expression in this cognitive process. The one appears with the other at the same instant, because they are not two, but one.

The principal reason which makes our view appear paradoxical as we maintain it, is the illusion or prejudice that we possess a more complete intuition of reality than we really do. One often hears people say that they have many great thoughts in their minds, but that they are not able to express them. But if they really had them, they would have coined them into just so many beautiful, sounding words, and thus have expressed them. If these thoughts seem to vanish or to become few and meager in the act of expressing them, the reason is that they did not exist or really were few and meager. People think that all of us ordinary men imagine and intuit countries, figures and scenes like painters, and bodies like sculptors; save that painters and sculptors know how to paint and carve such images, while we bear them unexpressed in our souls. They believe that any one could have imagined a Madonna of Raphael; but that Raphael was Raphael owing to his technical ability in putting the Madonna upon canvas. Nothing can be more false than this view. The world which as a rule we intuit is a small thing. It consists of little expressions, which gradually become greater and wider with the increasing spiritual concentration of certain moments. They are the words we say to ourselves, our silent judgments: "Here is a man, here is a horse, this is heavy, this is sharp, this pleases me," etc. It is a medley of light and color, with no greater pictorial value than would be expressed by a haphazard splash of colors, from among which one could barely make out a few special, distinctive traits. This and nothing else is what we possess in our ordinary life; this is the basis of our ordinary action. It is the index of a book. The labels tied to things (it has been said) take the place of the things themselves. This index and these labels (themselves expressions) suffice for small needs and small actions. From time to time we pass from the index to the book, from the label to the thing, or from the slight to the greater intuitions, and from these to the greatest and most lofty. This passage is sometimes far from easy. It has been observed by those who have best studied the psychology of artists that when, after having given a rapid glance at any one, they attempt to obtain a real intuition of him, in order, for example, to paint his portrait, then this ordinary vision, that seemed so precise, so lively, reveals itself as little better than nothing. What remains is found to be at the most some superficial trait, which would not even suffice for a caricature. The person to be painted stands before the artist like a world to discover. Michaelangelo said, "One paints, not with the hands, but with the brain." Leonardo shocked the prior of the Convent of the Graces by standing for days together gazing at the "Last Supper," without touching it with the brush. He remarked of this attitude: "The minds of men of lofty genius are most active in invention when they are doing the least external work." The painter is a painter, because he sees what others only feel or catch a glimpse of, but do not see. We think we see a smile, but in reality we have only a vague impression of it, we do not perceive all the characteristic traits of which it is the sum, as the painter discovers them after he has worked upon them and is thus able to fix them on the canvas. We do not intuitively possess more even of our intimate friend, who is with us every day and at all hours, than at most certain traits of physiognomy which enable us to distinguish him from others. The illusion is less easy as regards musical expression; because it would seem strange to every one to say that the composer had added or attached notes to a motive which was already in the mind of him who is not the composer; as if Beethoven's Ninth Symphony were not his own intuition and his intuition the Ninth Symphony. Now, just as one who is deluded as to the amount of his material wealth is confuted by arithmetic, which states its exact amount, so he who nourishes delusions as to the wealth of his own thoughts and images is brought back to reality, when he is obliged to cross the *Pons Asinorum* of expression. Let us say to the former, count; to the latter, speak; or, here is a pencil, draw, express yourself.

Each of us, as a matter of fact, has in him a little of the poet, of the sculptor, of the musician, of the painter, of the prose writer: but how little, as compared with those who bear those names, just because they possess the most universal dispositions and energies of human nature in so lofty a degree! How little too does a painter possess of the intuitions of a poet! And how little does one painter possess those of another painter! Nevertheless, that little is all our actual patrimony of intuitions or representations. Beyond these are only impressions, sensations, feelings, impulses, emotions, or whatever else one may term what still falls short of the spirit and is not assimilated by man; something postulated for the convenience of exposition, while actually non-existent, since to exist also is a fact of the spirit.

We may thus add this to the various verbal descriptions of intuition, noted at the beginning: intuitive knowledge is expressive knowledge. Independent and autonomous in respect to intellectual function; indifferent to later empirical discriminations, to reality and to unreality, to formations and apperceptions of space and time, which are also later: intuition or representation is distinguished as *form* from what is felt and suffered, from the flux or wave of sensation, or from psychic matter; and this form, this taking possession, is expression. To intuit is to express; and nothing else (nothing more, but nothing less) than *to express*.

—*Æsthetic* (1901; translation of second edition, 1922)

JOYCE CARY

The Gap Between Intuition and Expression

I. *The Artist and the World*

This is an attempt to examine the relation of the artist with the world as it seems to him, and to see what he does with it. That is to say, on the one side with what is called the artist's intuition, on the other with his production, or the work of art.

My only title to discuss the matter is some practical knowledge of two arts. I know very little about esthetic philosophy, so I shall try, as far as possible, to speak from practical experience.

It is quite true that the artist, painter, writer or composer starts always with an experience that is a kind of discovery. He comes upon it with the sense of a discovery; in fact, it is truer to say that it comes upon *him* as a discovery. It surprises him. This is what is usually called an intuition or an inspiration. It carries with it always the feeling of directness. For instance, you go walking in the fields and all at once they strike you in quite a new aspect: you find it extraordinary that they should be like that. This is what happened to Monet as a young man. He suddenly saw the fields, not as solid flat objects covered with grass or useful crops and dotted with trees, but as color in astonishing variety and subtlety of gradation. And this gave him a delightful and quite new pleasure. It was a most exciting discovery, especially as it was a discovery of something real. I mean, by that, something independent of Monet himself. That, of course, was half the pleasure. Monet had discovered a truth about the actual world.

This delight in discovery of something new in or about the world is a natural and primitive thing. All children have it. And it often continues until the age of twenty or twenty-five, *even* throughout life.

Children's pleasure in exploring the world, long before they can speak, is very obvious. They spend almost all their time at it. We don't speak of their intuition, but it is the same thing as the intuition of the artist. That is to say, it is direct knowledge of the world as it is, direct acquaintance with things, with characters, with appearance, and this is the primary knowledge of the artist and writer. This joy of discovery is his starting point.

Croce, probably the most interesting of the esthetic philosophers, says that art is simply intuition. But he says, too, that intuition and expression are the same thing. His idea is that we can't know what we have intuited until we have named it, or given it a formal character, and this action is essentially the work of art.

But this is not at all the way it seems to an artist or a writer. To him, the intuition is quite a different thing from the work of art. For the essential thing about the work of art is that it is work, and very hard work too. To go back to the painter. He has had his intuition, he has made his discovery, he is eager to explore it, to reveal it, to fix it down. For, at least in a grown, an educated man, intuitions are highly evanescent. This is what Wordsworth meant when he wrote of their fading into the light of common day.

I said the joy of discovery often dies away after twenty years or so. And this is simply a truth of observation; we know it from our own experience. The magic object that started up before our eyes on a spring day in its own individual shape, is apt, in the same instant, to turn into simply another cherry tree, an ordinary specimen of a common class. We have seen it and named it pretty often already. But Housman, as poet, fixed his vision of the cherry tree before it had changed into just another tree in blossom.

Housman fixed it for himself and us, but not by an immediate act, indistinguishable from the intuition. He had to go to work and find words, images, rhyme, which embodied his feeling about the tree, which fixed down its meaning for him, so that he could have it again when he wanted it, and also give it to us. He made a work of art, but he made it by work.

So for the painter, when he has his new, his magic landscape in front of him; he has to fix it down. And at once he is up against enormous difficulties. He has only his paints and brushes, and a flat piece of canvas with which to convey a sensation, a feeling, about a three-dimensional world. He has somehow to translate an intuition from real objects into a formal and ideal arrangement of colors and shapes, which will still, mysteriously, fix and convey his sense of the unique quality, the magic of these objects in their own private existence. That is to say, he has a job that requires thought, skill, and a lot of experience.

As for the novelist, his case is even worse. He starts also with his intuition, his discovery; as when Conrad, in an Eastern port, saw a young officer come out from a trial, in which he had been found guilty of a cowardly desertion of his ship and its passengers after a collision. The young man had lost his honor and Conrad realized all at once what that meant to him, and he wrote *Lord Jim* to fix and communicate that discovery in its full force.

For that he had to invent characters, descriptions, a plot. All these details, as with the painter, had to enforce the impression, the feeling that he wanted to convey. The reader had to *feel,* at the end of the tale, "That is important, that is true." It's no good if he says, "I suppose that is true, but I've heard it before." In that case Conrad has failed, at least with that reader. For his object was to give the reader the same discovery, to make him feel what it meant to that young man to lose his honor, and how important honor is to men.

And to get this sharp and strong feeling, the reader must not be confused by side issues. All the scenes and characters, all the events in the book, must contribute to the total effect, the total meaning. The book must give the sense of an actual world with real characters. Otherwise they won't engage the reader's sympathy, his feelings will never be concerned at all.

But actual life is not like that, it doesn't have a total meaning, it is simply a wild confusion of events from which we have to select what we think significant for ourselves. Look at any morning paper. It makes no sense at all—it means nothing but chaos. We read only what we think important; that is to say, we provide our own sense to the news. We have to do so because otherwise it wouldn't be there. To do this, we have to have some standard of valuation, we have to know whether the political event is more important than a murder, or a divorce than the stock market, or the stock market than who won the Derby.

The writer, in short, has to find some meaning in life before he gives it to us in a book. And his subject matter is much more confused than that of a painter. Of course, in this respect, everyone is in the same boat. Everyone, not only the writer, is presented with the same chaos, and is obliged to form his own idea of the world, of what matters and what doesn't matter. He has to do it, from earliest childhood, for his own safety. And if he gets it wrong, if his idea does not accord with reality, he will suffer for it. A friend of mine, as a child, thought he could fly, and jumped off the roof. Luckily he came down in a flowerbed and only broke a leg.

This seems to contradict what I said just now about the chaos which stands before us every morning. For the boy who failed to fly did not suffer only from bad luck. He affronted a law of gravity, a permanent part of a reality objective to him. As we know very well, underneath the chaos of events, there are laws, or if you like consistencies, both of fact and feeling. What science calls matter, that is to say, certain fixed characteristics of being, presents us with a whole framework of reality which we defy at our peril. Wrong ideas about gravity or the wholesomeness of prussic acid are always fatal.

So, too, human nature and its social relations present certain constants. Asylums and jails are full of people who have forgotten or ignored them. On the other hand, we can still comprehend and enjoy paleolithic art and Homer. Homer's heroes had the same kind of nature as our own.

These human constants are also a part of reality objective to us, that is, a permanent character of the world as we know it. So we have a reality consisting of permanent and highly obstinate facts, and permanent and highly obstinate human nature. And human nature is always in conflict with material facts, although men are themselves most curious combinations of fact and feeling, and actually require the machinery of their organism to realize their emotions, their desires and ambitions. Though the ghost could not exist without the machine which is at once its material form, its servant, its limitation, its perfection and its traitor, it is always trying to get more power over it, to change it.

Men have in fact obtained more power over matter, but to change it is impossible. It may be said that all works of art, all ideas of life, all philosophies are "As if," but I am suggesting that they can be checked with an objective reality. They might be called propositions for truth and their truth can be decided by their correspondence with the real. Man can't change the elemental characters. If you could, the world would probably vanish into nothing. But because of their very permanence, you can assemble them into new forms. You can build new houses with the bricks they used for the oldest Rome, because they are still bricks. For bricks that could stop being bricks at will would be no good to the architect. And a heart that stopped beating at its own will would be no good to the artist. The creative soul needs the machine, as the living world needs a fixed character, or it could not exist at all. It would be merely an idea. But by a paradox we have to accept, part of this fixed character is the free mind, the creative imagination, in everlasting conflict with facts, including its own machinery, its own tools. . . .

II. *Art and Truth*

Art claims to give us truth. According to Croce, in fact, the primary work of art, the expression, must be true, because it is indistinguishable from intuition. This is essential to Croce's esthetic philosophy. He says that if we deny it his system becomes impossible, for at once we place a great gap between reality and our knowledge of it, an unbridgeable gap. To put it in his own words, we "divide the seamless robe of the world."

As I say, Croce's system is probably the most harmonious, the most beautiful of any in its graceful and economical forms. But it is art. And to obtain those harmonies Croce has ignored certain matters of experience, and most notable, the gap between intuition and expression. Every professional artist knows this gap. It is for him a fundamental problem. Tolstoy tells us in his diary how he sat for a long time trying to express his feeling; but he could not find the right words. What is interesting to us is that Tolstoy's feeling—the intuition—remained to be examined, to be compared with the various expressions which were rejected in turn because they failed to be accurate.

What the intuition consisted of here was an impression on the memory, an impression of feeling. It was emotion directly intuited and recorded. Such intuitions are often recorded without our being aware of them. We are asked, "Did you meet So-and-so? What did you think of him?" And remembering So-and-so, we explore our minds, that is to say, some record in the subconscious, to find out what we did think of him. And we are conscious of this effort of exploration; like Tolstoy we look for words to express our feeling, our reaction, and don't find them at once. Tolstoy tells us that he found the task so exasperating he wanted to get up and walk away. There is no short cut across this gap.

The passage from intuition to reflection, from knowledge of the real to expression of that knowledge in viable form is always precarious and difficult. It is, in short, a kind of translation, not from one language into another, but from one state of existence into another, from the receptive into the creative, from the purely sensuous impression into the purely reflective and critical act.

This gap, of course, is simply another representative of the mind-body gap, which all idealist philosophers and mechanists are so eager to get rid of: the first by abolishing the body and the second by abolishing the mind. Unfortunately, though they can contrive this abolition easily enough in words, it remains very definite to our experience. All of us are aware every day of the conflict between our will and bodily machine; no amount of willing, no amount of thinking can compel the body to be completely subservient. On the other hand, we are equally aware of their interdependence; mind needs body to exist and body needs mind for any purposeful activity; that is to say, this gap of which we are so acutely aware occurs within a unity. If we could imagine a motorcar complaining of the gap in its sparkplugs, we should hasten to explain to it that the gap, though certainly existing, is not only an essential part of its construction as a complete unity, but that without this gap it could not work.

In fact, it would be easy to argue that without the gap between body and mind the individual would not exist; he would be merely a part of universal nature, controlled completely by instinct, with all the limitations of creatures whose lives are so controlled. It is the independent reason of man in which his individuality, his freedom, resides. The gap is as necessary to him as the division between his feet and the ground, which enables him, unlike a vegetable, to move about the world by his own volition.

This suggestion itself is merely an attempt in words to suggest an explanation of something which lies beneath and beyond language and its logical systems, and in this essay I am trying to deal with a situation as known to experience; the dilemma of the free individual soul, separated by the very nature of his individuality from the real of which he is nevertheless a part.

It will be seen that this description in words itself falsifies the problem by the mere analysis of an essential unity into the individual on one side and reality on the other; a false dichotomy is introduced and what is highly flexible in practice is given the appearance of rigid and permanent separation. As we should see, the gap itself between body and mind, even to our experience, is not fixed; it varies from individual to individual and continually shifts its place. The gap is not between the individual and the outer world; it is in the man, between his individual mind seeking to know a truth, and the universal consistencies of nature human and material as recorded by his sensibility. That sensibility in a grown man is, of course, individual and particular. His primitive emotions have been given ideal form by his experience and education. But they are still primitive in essence. The child's love for those who tend and feed it has become the mature affection full of judgment and particular appreciation. But it is still love, still within the universal of feeling and objective to the individual mind. That is to say, the educated man is still, in his primitive emotional make-up, part of the universal real. His difference is only ideal and formal, just as a house, however distinctive in itself, is still part of material nature.

In the larger sense, of course, that individual mind is also part of the universal real. All humanity is born with it. And we know it ourselves by experience.

Total reality is given to us in this divided form. Croce's "seamless world" presents itself to us as deeply seamed; the individual mind appears to itself as cut off from the general real except in so far as it can intuit that real. For the artist his intuition always comes to him as from a world of permanent and objective forms. What Tolstoy was looking for was not his own idea of things, but the exact impression they had made on him.

No doubt that intuition contained some elements of choice. It moved Tolstoy in a certain way because he was Tolstoy—with his special sensibility. For no one after the first few months of life retains the primitive emotions as pure general feeling. The moment a child begins to think and record its reflections, judgments begin to attach themselves to its emotions. Its individual mind, so to speak, begins to soak into its emotional make-up. This, in fact, is the process often described as forming a character. But to this character compounded of educated and ideal emotion and a presiding mind, the intuition comes always as a revelation. This is how it appears to the man. It is the very mark and sign of intuition that it does so appear, from outside. It stands over against him, like Housman's cherry tree, a piece of the real whose whole force is in its objectivity and universal truth. And he, as subject, has to use his brains to translate the effect of this real into a symbolic form which gives the same effect to another person.

His problem is to transmit a purely emotional meaning by the same kind of effort that is used to solve a chess problem. In this effort, therefore, there is a direct conflict. A cold thought has to deal with a warm feeling. I said that intuitions are evanescent. Wordsworth's intuitions die not only for the man, they fade very quickly for the child. But conceptual thought cannot only destroy them, it can bar them out.

This is an old tale. The child genius goes to school and becomes a dull man. What we have to ask is why this conflict occurs; if it is inevitable, how anything of the real can pass the gap between the intuition and the expression, the work of art; and, in short, whether art is not, as dictators like to believe, purely subjective and fantastic, the dangerous amusement of a lot of egoistic parasites.

III. *The Realm of Intuition*

Intuition, the recognition of the objective real in its own quality, is, of course, an essential function. The smallest children must have power to know. And they explore the world of things and events, of characters, with intense curiosity and concentration.

I remember one of my children, as a baby of about fourteen months, sitting in its pram watching a newspaper on the grass close by. There was a breeze along the ground and the newspaper was moving. Sometimes the top page swelled up and fluttered; sometimes two or three pages were moved and seemed to struggle together; sometimes the whole paper rose up on one side and flapped awkwardly for a few feet before tumbling down again. The child did not know that this object was a newspaper moved by the wind. It was watching with intense absorbed curiosity a creature entirely new to its experience, and through the child's eyes I had a pure intuition of the newspaper as object, as an individual thing at a specific moment.

The same child, at six, painted a little masterpiece of a tiger in a wood. The wood was practically solid tree trunk—the only indication of branches or leaves was a few minute strokes of brown and spots of green at the extreme top. In fact, a wood intensely seen by a child's eye in its woodiness, and expressed with the highest degree of original force.

A great deal, of course, of that spiritual and perpetual joy that children bring to us is just this power of seeing the world as a new thing, as pure intuition, and so renewing for us the freshness of all life. But they always lose this power of original expression as soon as they begin their education. A small girl of seven once asked me if I would like a drawing. I said yes. She asked, "What shall I draw?"

"Anything you like."

"Shall I draw you a swan?"

"Yes, a swan"; and the child sat down and drew for half an hour. I'd forgotten about the swan until she produced the most original swan I'd ever seen. It was a swimming swan, that is, a creature designed simply to swim. Its feet were enormous and very carefully finished, obviously from life. The whole structure of the feet was shown in heavy black lines. The child was used to seeing swans on a canal at the end of her garden and had taken particular notice of their feet. Below the water the swan was all power. But for body she gave it the faintest, lightest outline, neck and wings included in one round line shaped rather like a cloud—a perfect expression of the cloud-like movement of the swan on the surface.

I was admiring this swan when an older child in the room, aged thirteen, looked at the drawing and said contemptuously, "That's not a bit like a swan. I'll draw you a swan," and produced at once a Christmas-card swan, of the commonest type.

Yet the second child had all the qualities of the first, intelligence, sensibility. A few years before she had had the ability to see for herself, to receive the unique personal impression. She had lost it by the education which emphasizes the fact, measurements, analysis, the concept. Education is, and must be, almost entirely conceptual. And the concept is always the enemy of the intuition. It is said that when you give a child the name of a bird, it loses the bird. It never *sees* the bird again but only a sparrow, a thrush, a swan, and there is a good deal of truth in this. We all know people for whom all nature and art consists of concepts, whose life, therefore, is entirely bound up with objects known only under labels and never seen in their own quality.

This ruin of esthetic intuition by conceptual education has been the theme of teachers for at least fifty years past, and has produced the theory that children should not be taught anything about the arts. They should be assisted, if necessary, only in handling materials. But this is futile. For children want to learn, they are greedy to know, they triumph over each other in knowledge. If you do not teach them they will learn from each other, and probably learn wrong. The attempt to preserve the intuition of the child, in any art, is therefore waste of time. It can be disastrous if it results only in the production of an imitative childishness, a self-conscious *naïveté* which is more stultifying than any mere conventionalism.

Yet Picasso has said, "Give me the mind of a child," and Picasso himself has shown more freshness of intuition and invention, more fertile originality, than any artist in centuries. All the same, Picasso is a product of the schools, he is highly accomplished in technique. He has given immense thought to the problem of artistic expression. And as a young artist he showed all the conventionality of the art student just graduated from years of conceptual teaching in the drawing class. His blue period is the cliché of a student mind attempting originality merely by style and achieving therefore not only the false but the conventional. For nothing is more easy than the novel style invented only to be different.

That is to say, Picasso has passed from the age of true childish inspiration, through years of conceptual and technical training, back to the original vision which is not childish, but has all the originality of the child's eye, combined with the far greater depth and richness of a man's experience.

It may be said—it is sometimes believed—that Picasso's originality is merely a calculated scorn of convention, a deliberate resolution to shock, by what is called willful distortion. That is to say, that it is not founded on intuition at all, but on a conceptual plan. This would be believed only by those without power to appreciate any original art at all. And it can be tested by anyone who should choose to set out, deliberately, to produce an effect of originality simply by a conceptual difference. . . .

IV. *Exploration and Construction*

All symbols fade and die by use. They lose their emotional force and value. Words are gradually deprived of their harmonics. Names take the place of actual events, so that a tourist seeing London gets no reaction from Westminster Abbey except the reflection, "I can now tick that off"; a reaction all the more likely when he has been seeing churches for a week past.

The symbol, in short, like the concept, to which it continually approximates, is also the enemy of the intuition. The moment the artist expresses his intuition in any formal terms, this expression tends to destroy for him the force of his intuition.

I said that, in spite of Croce, the most vivid and continuous experience of all artists is the gap between their intuition and its expression, and all great artists, all great writers, seek continually to overcome it. It's quite easy for any experienced painter or writer to avoid that troublesome problem and use his technical skill to write or paint works which do not attempt to express any intuition at all, but merely imitate some master who has done so. This process, as we saw, is one chief reason for the destruction of each symbolic system in turn, the imitation by hordes of students of what was once an original and expressive creation.

But the great master is perpetually concerned with intuition. It is his primary task to keep in touch with it, that is to say, with the real. Dostoevsky, in *The Brothers Karamazov*, wrecked his whole plan of showing the superiority of the orthodox dogma over Ivan's atheistic attack by giving Ivan the most crushing arguments. That means that when he asked himself how would Ivan see reality, how would he argue about it, he realized with the force of intuition a truth that had been before only the statement of a hypothetic case, and then expressed it, with the utmost power. So that his scheme for that chapter, his concept *a priori* of what that chapter would mean, was completely ruined.

And we saw how Tolstoy sat impatiently trying to find out exactly what his feeling, his intuition, was.

So all great artists are preoccupied, as if by nature, with reality. They assume, from the beginning, that it is their task to reveal a truth about some permanent and fundamental real. The problem of the conflict between the concept and the intuition is always with them. And it is not enough to describe the intuition in words, it has to be given in the work of art.

For the novelist, in fact, there is not only a huge gap between intuition and concept, the first raw statement, but between that statement and its working out in a story, a fable. It is easy for a philosopher, seeking a harmonious whole, to say that the two last processes are the same, that having expressed the situation for himself, the artist has taken the essential step—that he has his work of art and that any further operation is simply recording. This is simply not true in professional experience.

For the truth is that the work of art as completely realized is the result of a long and complex process of exploration, as well as construction. This is true even of a painter. The notion that a painter suddenly imagines a composition expressive of his feeling and straightway puts it down, is untrue. He begins with a general idea, no doubt—if he has a landscape before his eyes, he wants to express his feeling about that landscape in color and form. But he has not yet got color and form on canvas, he has not translated the actual fields and trees into symbols and, however experienced he is, he does not know exactly how to get the effect he wants, or even if it is possible within the limits of his material. He proceeds by trial and error. Watch him at work. He is not only uncertain of the exact effect of separate touches, he is still more uncertain of the result of their contrast and conjunction. And the more experienced he is, the more accomplished and subtle, the more care he will take. Manet would scrape off his paint day after day until, after fifty trials, he could satisfy himself that no further improvement was possible. That is, he was not merely expressing an intuition, he was continually discovering new possibilities in his own work, now become objective to him, and realizing them. The whole process was one of exploration as well as expression.

This is true of all the arts. Poets gradually construct both their verse and their meaning by continued test and alteration; novelists discover new aspects of their theme, and also new limitations of their technique, as they work.

I was once sitting at tea with that great artist and brilliant technician, Miss Compton-Burnett, and she said, "Mr. Cary, I have been wondering when your novel is to be published. I saw it advertised at least a year ago, but it doesn't seem to be out yet." I said that I had run into difficulties; the novel had indeed taken nearly three years. But I thought it was nearly finished because when I changed it for the better in one place, I found I had damaged it in some other. Miss Compton-Burnett answered me at once, "I know exactly what you mean. It happens to me too. At a certain point my novels set. They set just as hard as that jam jar. And then I know they are finished." That is to say, the writing of a novel is not only the exploration of a theme, of character, of possibility, but of technical limits.

When Proust was writing his masterpiece he had a letter from Mme. Schiff to complain that he had made Swann ridiculous. Proust answered that he had had no wish to make Swann ridiculous, far from it. But when he had come to this part of the work, he had found it unavoidable. That is to say, he had been compelled by the logic of the craft to do what he had not intended or imagined himself doing. For if he had not made Swann ridiculous, the whole work would have suffered. I don't know to what passage Mme. Schiff referred, but I have supposed it was to Swann's jealousy. Now without jealousy Swann would lose much of his actuality for us: much, therefore, of our sympathy: and the whole book would lose enormously by this failure in one of its major characters. And jealousy that makes a man ridiculous is all the more authentic, all the more (as we say, truly) real. It belongs to the world of real passions, and, in Swann, conveys us into that world. . . .

This discovery of Proust's that Swann, in spite of Proust's own intention, had got to be ridiculous, is like Dostoevsky's discovery that Ivan Karamazov as a realized character had more powerful arguments than Dostoevsky had allowed for in his plot. It is a form of intuition; it is the immediate recognition of a real truth, a penetration into the realities of character. And it has broken through Proust's first conception of Swann, and immediately deepened his awareness of Swann's possibilities. Swann, as a character created by Proust, here assumes an individual personality, to be intuited by his own author. Of course, this interpretation of Swann is due largely to factors which are beyond Proust's control, I mean the nature of humanity itself. If you invent a man, a person, he has to behave like a person, and, as Tolstoy said, psychology is the one thing an author must not invent.

But the genius of Proust was active both in the realization of Swann's potentiality, in the decision to make him ridiculous, and in the power to adapt the general form of his work to this unforeseen development. For this he required technical invention, experience and dexterity.

Tolstoy said that the difference between great writing and small writing is in the minute details. I think this is true, if by minute details he meant such significant details as Swann's ridiculous conduct in jealousy. And I think he could have added that most of these details are devised during the process of the work, that for the great writer nothing is settled until he has explored all the possibilities of his characters and his theme.

Thus the gap between the writer and his material remains throughout his work. What he has completed becomes at once for him objective, and at once therefore something to be explored. He explores it from two points of view: as artist, to know its possibilities of development; as critic, to know if it has had the effect he intended. For like the painter, he never knows exactly the effect of what he has created, until he has tested it as observer.

—Art and Reality (1958)

CHAPTER FIVE

Art as Wish-Fulfillment

FRIEDRICH NIETZSCHE
The Will to Power in Art

SIGMUND FREUD
Wish-Fulfillment and the Unconscious

CARL GUSTAV JUNG
Psychology of Literature

CHRISTOPHER CAUDWELL
Poetry's Dream-Work

Introductory Note

THE INTUITIONISTS, Bergson, Croce, and Cary, define art as a kind of disinterested vision. Most of the other writers in this volume similarly emphasize the non-practical character of art. Friedrich Nietzsche (1844-1900), like his great contemporary, Leo Tolstoy, challenged this non-utilitarian interpretation. "What does all art do?" he asks. "Does it not praise? Does it not glorify? Does it not select? Does it not bring things into prominence? In all this it *strengthens* or *weakens* certain valuations." [1] Art is thus fundamental to the whole enterprise of living. It is sublimely utilitarian.

[1] Friedrich Nietzsche, *The Twilight of the Idols* (Macmillan, New York, 1924), p. 79.

Paradoxically combining pessimism and optimism, Nietzsche believes that the world, if untransformed by the will and imagination, is a thoroughly nasty place; but that, by means of art and a masterful morality, existence can be made profoundly satisfactory. There are two artistic ways of transforming the values of life—the Apollonian and the Dionysian. Apollonian art is similar to a dream (Apollo is the god of dreams). Man creates in his waking dreams a world of tranquillity and formal beauty, embodied especially in sculpture, architecture, painting, and the more chaste types of literature. The other type of art, symbolized by Dionysus, the god of wine and fertility, is similar to the state of love or intoxication, either of which impels us ecstatically to embrace experience. To explore, by means of Dionysian art, the depths and agonies of life, and imaginatively to cry "Yea," is the supreme triumph of the will to mastery. This type of art is represented above all by music (which for Nietzsche is the most intense of all the arts), but subordinately by dancing, lyric poetry, and tragedy. Nietzsche exhibits a keen insight into the subconscious depths of art, its relation to desire, and its alliance with dreams and love.

The esthetic theory of Sigmund Freud (1856-1939) is a continuation of such voluntaristic esthetics, but deepened and clarified by the knowledge derived from his general theory of psychoanalysis. Like Schopenhauer and Nietzsche, he believes that volition is the most fundamental and dynamic element in the mind. It shows itself in unrest and seeking, leading finally to action that brings the unrest to a close. We might define it broadly as an "impulse toward a goal." If the impulse succeeds, the result is a state of satisfaction. The question arises, Is it possible to separate volition from pleasure and unpleasure? The answer of Freud is *no*. The unrest of desire necessarily involves pain or unpleasure, and the appeasement of desire involves pleasure; these are, in a sense, phases of volition. His theory might be called hedonistic voluntarism.

In his essay, "The Relation of the Poet to Daydreaming," he reveals his indebtedness to the play-theory of Schiller and Lange. Both play and art are described as imaginative expressions and fulfillments of wish. When a person grows up, he must put aside childish play, but he substitutes phantasy, in the form either of day or night dreams, and art. But with profound insight and originality, Freud goes far beyond the play-theory in interpreting both dreams and art as the disguised expression of wishes—repressed but powerfully operative in "the unconscious." The "libido," the deep instinctive force of life, manifests itself in a continual striving for expression. When it is actively repressed by the more critical faculties, it assumes a multitude of disguises in order to circumvent the repressive forces. The chief of these disguises are the imagery of dreams and phantasies, and the symptoms of neurotic disorders. But the artist has an additional resource. By means of what Freud calls "sublimation" he can deflect his psychic energy into channels of creative endeavor. He then learns to control his phantasies, and thus to sublimate his ambition and his sexual impulse in creative art. The dream is consciously inserted into the texture of waking life, and the repressed wishes, which might otherwise lead to neurosis, are fulfilled in imagination.

The shock and disillusionment of the First World War caused Freud to revise his ideas. He thereafter put less emphasis upon "Eros"—the impulse of love —and greater emphasis upon "Thanatos"—the impulse of death and destruction. In addition, he worked out the theory of a three-fold structure of human personality. First, there is the *Id* (Latin for "it")—so-called because we tend to regard its manifestations as foreign to ourselves, as when we say, "That was not what I meant." It is governed by "the pleasure principle," and is the bearer of the primal energies of our deepest instinctive nature. Second, there is the *Ego*. It is our wide-awake "social self," governed by "the reality principle," and concerned with the perception of the environment and the self's adjustment to it. Third, there is the *Super-Ego*. It is the seat of our ideals and moral standards, largely unconscious, and built up in the individual in early childhood. The mind as "Censor" acts frequently at the behest of the Super-Ego, whose demands are more archaic and severe than those of the conscious Ego.

As Herbert Read, the English poet and critic, has written, the work of art derives from all three regions of the mind: "It derives its energy, its irrationality and its mysterious power from the id, which is to be regarded as the source of what we usually call inspiration. It is given formal synthesis and unity by the ego; and finally it may be assimilated to those ideologies or spiritual aspirations which are the peculiar creation of the super-ego." [2] Unfortunately, Freud himself never wrote a sustained exposition of his more mature esthetic theories.

Toward the end of his essay, "The Relation of the Poet to Daydreaming," he remarks that the poet may draw upon the "creations of racial psychology" as expressed in myths, legends, and fairy tales; and in our selection from *The Interpretation of Dreams,* he recognizes universal tragic themes that appear in such literary works as *Oedipus Rex* and *Hamlet.* A number of writers, such as Maud Bodkin and Joseph Campbell, have explored this lead. They have shown that similar symbols, however superficially various, are to be found in the dreams, myths, and imaginative creations of human beings everywhere. This contention has been supported by much data gathered by Frazer and other anthropologists and by the Swiss psychiatrist, Carl Gustav Jung (1875-   ), who, with Freud and Adler, was one of the chief founders of psychoanalysis.

One of Jung's most basic psychological doctrines is the conception of "archetypes," or symbolic constants, which are the common heritage of mankind. The artist draws upon this treasury of unconscious primordial images, the psychological traces left by countless typical experiences of our ancestors. "The essence of art," Jung declares, "does not consist in the fact that it is charged with personal peculiarities—in fact, the more this is the case the less the question of art enters

2 Herbert Read, *Art and Society* (Pantheon Books, New York, 1945), p. 92.

in—but that it rises far above the personal and speaks out of the heart and mind and for the heart and mind of humanity. The personal is a limitation, yes, even a vice of art." [3] This point of view leads Jung to reject Freud's emphasis upon the personal and morbid sources of art, and to maintain that art, being distinctive and autonomous, cannot be wholly explained by psychoanalysis.

A similar collectivist interpretation of art is propounded by Christopher St. John Sprigg, who wrote under the pen name of Christopher Caudwell (1907-1937). An amazingly productive genius (he had published five books on aeronautics, seven detective novels, and both poems and short stories before he reached the age of twenty-five), he attained maturity in the period when fascism and economic crisis were threatening the very existence of civilization; and like many other creative minds—André Gide, Pablo Picasso, Stephen Spender, and Ignazio Silone, to mention only a few—he was greatly attracted by the ideas and prog am of Marxism. Moved to the quick by the Spanish Civil War, he joined the International Brigade, and was killed in action on February 12, 1937. In his brief life, he produced a number of outstanding books: *Illusion and Reality*, *Studies in a Dying Culture* (two volumes), *Poems*, and *The Crisis in Physics*, all published posthumously.

His esthetic doctrines represent primarily a highly original synthesis of Freudian and Marxian ideas, although he also drew upon his wide knowledge of physical science to define the difference between science and art. He believed that Freud had thought too exclusively in terms of individual psychology, and that the Marxian social emphasis is needed to correct this one-sidedness. The dreams and illusions of the neurotic, he maintained, are just peculiar or aberrant in a personal way; the creations of the artist are more social and general—growing out of the funded experiences and traditions of mankind. The artist draws more fully upon the subconscious than does the ordinary normal person; but he differs from the neurotic in being more social, free, and normal. The artist *uses* his subconscious mind, masters it; the neurotic is *used by* it, enslaved to it. The artist plumbs man's universal instinctive nature (which Caudwell terms "the genotype"), but he socializes the visions that arise from these subconscious depths. With profound insight, Caudwell compares poetry with dreams, contrasts it with prose fiction, and defines the nature and function of art in contradistinction to science.

[3] *Psychological Reflections: An Anthology of the Writings of C. G. Jung,* edited by Jolande Jacobi (Pantheon Books, New York, 1953), p. 177.

FRIEDRICH NIETZSCHE

The Will to Power in Art

§ 1

Apollonian, Dionysian. There are two conditions in which art manifests itself in man even as a force of nature, and disposes of him whether he consent or not: it may be as a constraint to visionary states, or it may be an orgiastic impulse. Both conditions are to be seen in normal life, but they are then somewhat weaker: in dreams and in moments of elation or intoxication.

But the same contrast exists between the dream state and the state of intoxication: both of these states let loose all manner of artistic powers within us, but each unfetters powers of a different kind. Dreamland gives us the power of vision, of association, of poetry: intoxication gives us the power of grand attitudes, of passion, of song, and dance.

§ 2

The word *"Dionysian"* expresses: a constraint to unity, a soaring above personality, the commonplace, society, reality, and above the abyss of the *ephemeral;* the passionately painful sensation of superabundance, in darker, fuller, and more fluctuating conditions; an ecstatic saying of yea to the collective character of existence, as that which remains the same, and equally mighty and blissful throughout all change; the great pantheistic sympathy with pleasure and pain, which declares even the most terrible and most questionable qualities of existence good, and sanctifies them; the eternal will to procreation, to fruitfulness, and to recurrence; the feeling of unity in regard to the necessity of creating and annihilating.

The word *"Apollonian"* expresses the constraint to be absolutely isolated, to the typical "individual," to everything that simplifies, distinguishes, and makes strong, salient, definite, and typical: to freedom within the law.

The further development of art is just as necessarily bound up with the antagonism of these two natural art-forces, as the further development of mankind is bound up with the antagonism of the sexes. The plenitude of power and restraint, the highest form of self-affirmation in a cool, noble, and reserved kind of beauty: the Apollonianism of the Hellenic will.

This antagonism of the Dionysian and of the Apollonian in the Greek soul, is one of the great riddles which made me feel drawn to the essence of Hellenism. At bottom, I troubled about nothing save the solution of the question, why precisely Greek Apollonianism should have been forced to grow out of a Dionysian soil: the Dionysian Greek had need of being Apollonian; that is to say in order to break his will to the titanic, to the complex, to the uncertain, to the horrible by a will to measure, to simplicity, and to submission to rule and concept. Extravagance, wildness, and Asiatic tendencies lie at the root of the Greeks. Their courage consists in their struggle with their Asiatic nature: they were not given beauty, any more than they were given logic and moral naturalness: in them these things are victories, they are willed and fought for—they constitute the *triumph* of the Greeks.

§ 3

"Beauty" is, to the artist, something which is above all order of rank, because in beauty contrasts are overcome, the highest sign of power thus manifesting itself in the conquest of opposites; and achieved without a feeling of tension: violence being no longer necessary, everything submitting and obeying so easily, and doing so with good grace; this is what delights the powerful will of the artist.

§ 4

If one should require the most astonishing proof of how far the power of transfiguring, which comes of intoxication, goes, this proof is at hand in the phenomenon of love; or what is called love in all the languages and silences of the world. Intoxication works to such a degree upon reality in this passion that in the consciousness of the lover the cause of his love is quite suppressed, and something else seems to take its place—a vibration and a glitter of all the charm-mirrors of Circe. . . . In this respect to be man or an animal makes no difference: and still less does spirit, goodness, or honesty. If one is astute, one is befooled astutely; if one is thick-headed, one is befooled in a thick-headed way. But love, even the love of God, saintly love, "the love that saves the soul," are at bottom all one; they are nothing but a fever which has reasons to transfigure itself—a state of intoxication which does well to lie about itself. . . . And, at any rate, when a man loves, he is a good liar about himself and to himself: he seems to himself transfigured, stronger, richer, more perfect; he *is* more perfect. . . . *Art* here acts as an organic function: we find it present in the most angelic instinct "love"; we find it as the greatest stimulus of life—thus art is sublimely utilitarian, even in the fact that it lies. . . . But we should be wrong to halt at its power to lie: it does more than merely imagine; it actually transposes values. And it not only transposes the *feeling* for values: the lover actually *has* a greater value; he is stronger. In animals this condition gives rise to new weapons, colors, pigments, and forms, and above all to new movements, new rhythms, new love-calls and seductions. In man it is just the same. His whole economy is richer, mightier, and *more complete* when he is in love than when he is not. The lover becomes a spendthrift; he is rich enough for it. He now dares; he becomes an adventurer, and even a donkey in magnanimity and innocence; his belief in God and in virtue revives, because he believes in love. Moreover, such idiots of happiness acquire wings and new capacities, and even the door to art is opened to them.

If we cancel the suggestion of this intestinal fever from the lyric of tones and words, what is left to poetry and music? . . . *L'art pour l'art* perhaps; the professional cant of frogs shivering outside in the cold, and dying of despair in , their swamp. . . . Everything else was created by love.

§ 5

Pessimism in art?—The artist gradually learns to like for their own sake, those means which bring about the condition of esthetic elation; extreme delicacy and glory of color, definite delineation, quality of tone; distinctness where in normal conditions distinctness is absent. All distinct things, all nuances, in so far as they recall extreme degrees of power which give rise to intoxication, kindle this feeling of intoxication by association;—the effect of works of art is the excitation of the state which creates art, of esthetic intoxication.

The essential feature in art is its power of perfecting existence, its production of perfection and plenitude; art is essentially the affirmation, the blessing, and the deification of existence. . . . What does a pessimistic art signify? Is it not a *contradictio?*—Yes.—Schopenhauer is in error when he makes certain works of art serve the purpose of pessimism. Tragedy does not teach "resignation.". . . To represent terrible and questionable things is, in itself, the sign of an instinct of power and magnificence in the artist; he doesn't fear them. . . . There is no such thing as a pessimistic art. . . . Art affirms. Job affirms. But Zola? and the Goncourts?—the things they show us are ugly; their reason, however, for showing them to us is their love of ugliness. . . . I don't care what you say! You simply deceive yourselves if you think otherwise.—What a relief Dostoevsky is!

§ 6

Romanticism and its opposite. In regard to all esthetic values I now avail myself of this fundamental distinction: in every individual case I ask myself has hunger or has superabundance been creative here? At first another distinction might perhaps seem preferable—it is far more obvious—for example, the distinction which decides whether a desire for stability, for eternity, for Being, or whether a desire for destruction, for change, for Becoming, has been the cause of creation. But both kinds of desire, when examined more closely, prove to be ambiguous, and really susceptible of interpretation only according to that scheme already mentioned and which I think is rightly preferred.

The desire for destruction, for change, for Becoming, may be the expression of an overflowing power pregnant with promises for the future (my term for this, as is well known, is Dionysian); it may, however, also be the hate of the ill-constituted, of the needy and of the physiologically botched, that destroys, and must destroy, because such creatures are indignant at, and annoyed by everything lasting and stable.

The act of immortalizing can, on the other hand, be the outcome of gratitude and love: an art which has this origin is always an apotheosis art; dithyrambic, as perhaps with Rubens; happy, as perhaps with Hafiz; bright and gracious, and shedding a ray of glory over all things, as in Goethe. But it may also, however, be the outcome of the tyrannical will of the great sufferer who would make the most personal, individual, and narrow trait about him, the actual idiosyncrasy of his pain—in fact, into a binding law and imposition, and who thus wreaks his revenge upon all things by stamping, branding, and violating them with the image of his torment. The latter case is romantic pessimism in its highest form, whether this be Schopenhauerian voluntarism or Wagnerian music.

§ 7

What is tragic?—Again and again I have pointed to the great misunderstanding of Aristotle in maintaining that the tragic emotions were the two depressing emotions—fear and pity. Had he been right, tragedy would be an art unfriendly to life: it would have been necessary to caution people against it as against something generally harmful and suspicious. Art, otherwise the great stimulus of life, the great intoxicant of life, the great will to life, here became a tool of decadence, the handmaiden of pessimism and ill-health (for to suppose, as Aristotle supposed, that by exciting these emotions we thereby purged people of them, is simply an error). Something which habitually excites fear or pity, disorganizes, weakens, and discourages: and supposing Schopenhauer were right in thinking that tragedy taught resignation (that is, a meek renunciation of happiness, hope, and of the will to live), this would presuppose an art in which art itself was denied. Tragedy would then constitute a process of dissolution; the instinct of life would destroy itself in the instinct of art. Christianity, Nihilism, tragic art, physiological decadence; these things would then be linked, they would then preponderate together and assist each other onwards—downwards. . . . Tragedy would thus be a symptom of decline.

This theory may be refuted in the most cold-blooded way, namely, by measuring the effect of a tragic emotion by means of a dynamometer. The result would be a fact which only the bottomless falsity of a doctrinaire could misunderstand: that tragedy is a tonic. If Schopenhauer refuses to see the truth here, if he regards general depression as a tragic condition, if he would have informed the Greeks (who to his disgust were not "resigned") that they did not firmly possess the highest principles of life: it is only owing to his *parti pris,* to the need of consistency in his system, to the dishonesty of the doctrinaire—that dreadful dishonesty which step for step corrupted the whole psychology of Schopenhauer (he who had arbitrarily and almost violently misunderstood genius, art itself, morality, pagan religion, beauty, knowledge, and almost everything).

§ 8

The tragic artist.—Whether, and in regard to what, the judgment "beautiful" is established is a question of an individual's or of a people's strength. The feeling of plenitude, of overflowing strength (which gayly and courageously meets many an obstacle before which the weakling shudders)—the feeling of power utters the judgment "beautiful" concerning things and conditions which the instinct of impotence can only value as hateful and ugly. The *flair* which enables us to decide whether the objects we encounter are dangerous, problematic, or alluring, likewise determines our esthetic Yea. ("This is beautiful" is an affirmation.)

From this we see that, generally speaking, a preference for questionable and terrible things is a symptom of strength; whereas the taste for pretty and charming trifles is characteristic of the weak and the delicate. The love of tragedy is typical of strong ages and characters: its *non plus ultra* is perhaps the Divina Commedia. It is the heroic spirits which in tragic cruelty say Yea unto themselves: they are hard enough to feel pain as a pleasure.

On the other hand, supposing weaklings desire to get pleasure from an art which was not designed for them, what interpretation must we suppose they would like to give tragedy in order to make it suit their taste? They would interpret their own feelings of value into it: for example, the "triumph of the moral order of things," or the teaching of the "uselessness of existence," or the incitement to "resignation" (or also half-medicinal and half-moral outpourings, *à la* Aristotle). Finally, the art of terrible natures, insofar as it may excite the nerves, may be regarded by the weak and exhausted as a stimulus: this is now taking place, for instance, in the case of the admiration meted out to Wagner's art. A test of man's well-being and consciousness of power is the extent to which he can acknowledge the terrible and questionable character of things, and whether he is in need of a faith at the end.

This kind of artistic pessimism is precisely the reverse of that religio-moral pessimism which suffers from the corruption of man and the enigmatic character of existence: the latter insists upon deliverance, or at least upon the hope of deliverance. Those who suffer, doubt, and distrust themselves—the sick, in other words—have in all ages required the transporting influence of visions in order to be able to exist at all (the notion "blessedness" arose in this way). A similar case would be that of the artists of decadence, who at bottom maintain a Nihilistic attitude to life, and take refuge in the beauty of form—in those select cases in which Nature is perfect, in which she is indifferently great and indifferently beautiful. (The "love of the beautiful" may thus be something very different from the ability to see or create the beautiful: it may be the expression of impotence in this respect.) The most convincing artists are those who make harmony ring out of every discord, and who benefit all things by the gift of their power and inner harmony: in every work of art they merely reveal the symbol of their inmost experiences—their creation is gratitude for their life.

The depth of the tragic artist consists in the fact that his esthetic instinct surveys the more remote results, that he does not halt shortsightedly at the thing that is nearest, that he says Yea to the whole cosmic economy, which justifies the terrible, the evil, and the questionable; which more than justifies it.

§ 9

Art in the "Birth of Tragedy." A.—The conception of the work which lies right in the background of this book is extraordinarily gloomy and unpleasant: among all the types of pessimism which have ever been known hitherto, none seems to have attained to this degree of malice. The contrast of a true and of an apparent world is entirely absent here: there is but one world, and it is false, cruel, contradictory, seductive, and without sense. . . . A world thus constituted is the true world. We are in need of lies in order to rise superior to this reality, to this truth—that is to say, in order to live. . . . That lies should be necessary to life is part and parcel of the terrible and questionable character of existence.

Metaphysics, morality, religion, science—in this book, all these things are regarded merely as different forms of falsehood: by means of them we are led to believe in life. "Life must inspire confidence": the task which this imposes upon us is enormous. In order to solve this problem man must already be a liar in his heart, but he must above all else be an artist. And he is that. Metaphysics, religion, morality, science—all these things are but the offshoot of his will to art, to falsehood, to a flight from "truth," to a denial of "truth." This ability, this artistic capacity *par excellence* of man—thanks to which he overcomes reality with lies— is a quality which he has in common with all other forms of existence. He himself is indeed a piece of reality, of truth, of nature: how could he help being also a piece of genius in prevarication!

The fact that the character of existence is misunderstood, is the profoundest and the highest secret motive behind everything relating to virtue, science, piety, and art. To be blind to many things, to see many things falsely, to fancy many things: Oh, how clever man has been in those circumstances in which he believed he was anything but clever! Love, enthusiasm, "God"—are but subtle forms of ultimate self-deception; they are but seductions to life and to the belief in life! In those moments when man was deceived, when he had befooled himself and when he believed in life: Oh, how his spirit swelled within him! Oh, what ecstasies he had! What power he felt! And what artistic triumphs in the feeling of power! . . . Man had once more become master of "matter,"—master of truth!

. . . And whenever man rejoices it is always in the same way: he rejoices as an artist, his power is his joy, he enjoys falsehood as his power. . . .

B.–Art and nothing else! Art is the great means of making life possible, the great seducer to life, the great stimulus of life.

Art is the only superior counteragent to all will to the denial of life; it is *par excellence* the anti-Christian, the anti-Buddhistic, the anti-Nihilistic force.

Art is the alleviation of the seeker after knowledge–of him who recognizes the terrible and questionable character of existence, and who *will* recognize it –of the tragic seeker after knowledge.

Art is the alleviation of the man of action–of him who not only sees the terrible and questionable character of existence, but also lives it, will live it–of the tragic and warlike man, the hero.

Art is the alleviation of the sufferer–as the way to states in which pain is willed, is transfigured, is deified, where suffering is a form of great ecstasy.

C.–It is clear that in this book pessimism, or, better still, Nihilism, stands for "truth." But truth is not postulated as the highest measure of value, and still less as the highest power. The will to appearance, to illusion, to deception, to becoming, and to change (to objective deception), is here regarded as more profound, as more primeval, as more metaphysical than the will to truth, to reality, to appearance: the latter is merely a form of the will to illusion. Happiness is likewise conceived as more primeval than pain: and pain is considered as conditioned, as a consequence of the will to happiness (of the will to Becoming, to growth, to forming, that is, to creating; in creating, however, destruction is included). The highest state of Yea-saying to existence is conceived as one from which the greatest pain may not be excluded: the tragico-Dionysian state.

D.–In this way this book is even anti-pessimistic, namely, in the sense that it teaches something which is stronger than pessimism and which is more "divine" than truth: Art. Nobody, it would seem, would be more ready seriously to utter a radical denial of life, an actual denial of action even more than a denial of life, than the author of this book. Except that he knows–for he has experienced it, and perhaps experienced little else!–that art is of more value than truth.

Even in the preface, in which Richard Wagner is, as it were, invited to join with him in conversation, the author expresses this article of faith, this gospel for artists: "Art is the only task of life, art is the metaphysical activity of life. . . ."
                              –*The Will to Power* (1896; translated 1910)

SIGMUND FREUD

Wish-Fulfillment and the Unconscious

I. *Phantasy-Making and Art*

. . . Consider . . . the origin and meaning of that mental activity called "phantasy-making." In general, as you know, it enjoys high esteem, although its place in mental life has not been clearly understood. I can tell you as much as this about it. You know that the ego in man is gradually trained by the influence of external necessity to appreciate reality and to pursue the reality-principle, and that in so doing it must renounce temporarily or permanently various of the objects and aims—not only sexual—of its desire for pleasure. But renunciation of pleasure has always been very hard for man; he cannot accomplish it without some kind of compensation. Accordingly he has evolved for himself a mental activity in which all these relinquished sources of pleasure and abandoned paths of gratification are permitted to continue their existence, a form of existence in which they are free from the demands of reality and from what we call the exercise of "testing reality." Every longing is soon transformed into the idea of its fulfillment; there is no doubt that dwelling upon a wish-fulfillment in phantasy brings satisfaction, although the knowledge that it is not reality remains thereby unobscured. In phantasy, therefore, man can continue to enjoy a freedom from the grip of the external world, one which he has long relinquished in actuality. He has contrived to be alternately a pleasure-seeking animal and a reasonable being; for the meager satisfaction that he can extract from reality leaves him starving. "There is no doing without accessory constructions," said Fontane. The creation of the mental domain of phantasy has a complete counterpart in the establishment of "reservations" and "nature-parks" in places where the inroads of agriculture, traffic, or industry threaten to change the original face of the earth rapidly into something unrecognizable. The "reservation" is to maintain the old condition of things which has been regretfully sacrificed to necessity everywhere else; there everything may grow and spread as it pleases, including what is useless and even what is harmful. The mental realm of phantasy is also such a reservation reclaimed from the encroachments of the reality-principle.

The best-known productions of phantasy have already been met by us; they are called daydreams, and are imaginary gratifications of ambitious, grandiose, erotic wishes, dilating the more extravagantly the more reality admonishes humility and patience. In them is shown unmistakably the essence of imaginary happiness, the return of gratification to a condition in which it is independent of reality's sanction. We know that these daydreams are the kernels and models of night dreams; fundamentally the night dream is nothing but a daydream distorted by the nocturnal form of mental activity and made possible by the nocturnal freedom of instinctual excitations. We are already familiar with the idea that a daydream is not necessarily conscious, that unconscious daydreams also exist; [1] such unconscious daydreams are therefore just as much the source of night dreams as of neurotic symptoms. . . .

The return of the libido [2] . . . to phantasy is an intermediate step on the way to symptom-formation which well deserves a special designation. C. G. Jung has coined for it the very appropriate name of *Introversion,* but inappropriately he uses it also to describe other things. We will adhere to the position that *introversion* describes the deflection of the libido away from the possibilities of real satisfaction and its excessive accumulation upon phantasies previously tolerated as harmless. An introverted person is not yet neurotic, but he is in an unstable condition; the next disturbance of the shifting forces will cause symptoms to develop, unless he can yet find other outlets for his pent-up libido. The unreal character of neurotic satisfaction and the disregard of the difference between phantasy and reality are already determined by the arrest at this stage of introversion. . . .

Before you leave today I should like to direct your attention for a moment to a side of phantasy-life of very general interest. There is, in fact, a path from phantasy back again to reality, and that is—art. The artist has also an introverted disposition and has not far to go to become neurotic. He is one who is urged on by instinctual needs which are too clamorous; he longs to attain to honor, power, riches, fame, and the love of women; but he lacks the means of achieving these gratifications. So, like any other with an unsatisfied longing, he turns away from reality and transfers all his interest, and all his libido too, on to the creation of his wishes in the life of phantasy, from which the way might readily lead to neurosis. There must be many factors in combination to prevent this becoming the whole outcome of his development; it is well known how often artists in particular suffer from partial inhibition of their capacities through neurosis. Probably their constitution is endowed with a powerful capacity for sublimation and with a certain flexibility in the repressions determining the conflict. But the way back to reality is found by the artist thus: He is not the only one who has a life of phantasy; the intermediate world of phantasy is sanctioned by general human consent, and every hungry soul looks to it for comfort and consolation. But to

[1] As Freud earlier explains, a latent dream, the realization of a wish-phantasy, is frequently built up in the unconsciousness. The act of repression creates in the unconscious sphere hidden ideas and impulses isolated from the rest of the personality (Editor's note).

[2] For the meaning of "libido," and an explanation of its artistic sublimation, see the editor's introductory note to this chapter.

those who are not artists the gratification that can be drawn from the springs of phantasy is very limited; their inexorable repressions prevent the enjoyment of all but the meager daydreams which can become conscious. A true artist has more at his disposal. First of all he understands how to elaborate his daydreams, so that they lose that personal note which grates upon strange ears and become enjoyable to others; he knows too how to modify them sufficiently so that their origin in prohibited sources is not easily detected. Further, he possesses the mysterious ability to mold his particular material until it expresses the ideas of his phantasy faithfully; and then he knows how to attach to this reflection of his phantasy-life so strong a stream of pleasure that, for a time at least, the repressions are outbalanced and dispelled by it. When he can do all this, he opens out to others the way back to the comfort and consolation of their own unconscious sources of pleasure, and so reaps their gratitude and admiration; then he has won —through his phantasy—what before he could only win in phantasy: honor, power, and the love of women.

—*Introductory Lectures on Psychoanalysis*
(Lectures delivered 1915-17; translated 1922)

II. *The Relation of the Poet to Daydreaming*

We laymen have always wondered greatly—like the cardinal who put the question to Ariosto—how that strange being, the poet, comes by his material. What makes him able to carry us with him in such a way and to arouse emotions in us of which we thought ourselves perhaps not even capable? Our interest in the problem is only stimulated by the circumstance that if we ask poets themselves they give us no explanation of the matter, or at least no satisfactory explanation. The knowledge that not even the clearest insight into the factors conditioning the choice of imaginative material, or into the nature of the ability to fashion that material, will ever make writers of us does not in any way detract from our interest.

If we could only find some activity in ourselves, or in people like ourselves, which was in any way akin to the writing of imaginative works! If we could do so, then examination of it would give us a hope of obtaining some insight into the creative powers of imaginative writers. And indeed, there is some prospect of achieving this—writers themselves always try to lessen the distance between their kind and ordinary human beings; they so often assure us that every man is at heart a poet, and that the last poet will not die until the last human being does.

We ought surely to look in the child for the first traces of imaginative activity. The child's best-loved and most absorbing occupation is play. Perhaps we may say that every child at play behaves like an imaginative writer, in that he creates a world of his own or, more truly, he rearranges the things of his world and orders it in a new way that pleases him better. It would be incorrect to think that he does not take this world seriously; on the contrary, he takes his play very seriously and expends a great deal of emotion on it. The opposite of play is not serious occupation but—reality. Notwithstanding the large affective cathexis [1] of his play-world, the child distinguishes it perfectly from reality; only he likes to borrow the objects and circumstances that he imagines from the tangible and visible things of the real world. It is only this linking of it to reality that still distinguishes a child's "play" from "daydreaming."

Now the writer does the same as the child at play; he creates a world of phantasy which he takes very seriously; that is, he invests it with a great deal of affect, while separating it sharply from reality. Language has preserved this relationship between children's play and poetic creation. It designates certain kinds of imaginative creation, concerned with tangible objects and capable of representation, as "plays"; the people who present them are called "players." The unreality of this poetical world of imagination, however, has very important consequences for literary technique; for many things which if they happened in real life could produce no pleasure can nevertheless give enjoyment in a play— many emotions which are essentially painful may become a source of enjoyment to the spectators and hearers of a poet's work.

There is another consideration relating to the contrast between reality and play on which we will dwell for a moment. Long after a child has grown up and stopped playing, after he has for decades attempted to grasp the realities of life with all seriousness, he may one day come to a state of mind in which the contrast between play and reality is again abrogated. The adult can remember with what intense seriousness he carried on his childish play; then by comparing his would-be serious occupations with his childhood's play, he manages to throw off the heavy burden of life and obtain the great pleasure of humor.

As they grow up, people cease to play, and appear to give up the pleasure they derived from play. But anyone who knows anything of the mental life of human beings is aware that hardly anything is more difficult to them than to give up a pleasure they have once tasted. Really we never can relinquish anything; we only exchange one thing for something else. When we appear to give something up, all we really do is to adopt a substitute. So when the human being grows up and ceases to play he only gives up the connection with real objects; instead of playing he then begins to create phantasy. He builds castles in the air and creates what are called daydreams. I believe that the greater number of human beings create phantasies at times as long as they live. This is a fact which has been overlooked for a long time, and its importance has therefore not been properly appreciated.

The phantasies of human beings are less easy to observe than the play of children. Children do, it is true, play alone, or form with other children a closed

---

[1] From a Greek word, *Kathexo*, to occupy. "Cathexis" is used here to signify a state of being charged or invested with emotional energy. (Editor's note.)

world in their minds for the purposes of play; but a child does not conceal his play from adults, even though his playing is quite unconcerned with them. The adult, on the other hand, is ashamed of his daydreams and conceals them from other people; he cherishes them as his most intimate possessions and as a rule he would rather confess all his misdeeds than tell his daydreams. For this reason he may believe that he is the only person who makes up such phantasies, without having any idea that everybody else tells themselves stories of the same kind. Daydreaming is a continuation of play, nevertheless, and the motives which lie behind these two activities contain a very good reason for this different behavior in the child at play and in the daydreaming adult.

The play of children is determined by their wishes—really by the child's *one* wish, which is to be grown-up, the wish that helps to "bring him up." He always plays at being grown-up; in play he imitates what is known to him of the lives of adults. Now he has no reason to conceal this wish. With the adult it is otherwise; on the one hand, he knows that he is expected not to play any longer or to daydream, but to be making his way in a real world. On the other hand, some of the wishes from which his phantasies spring are such as to have to be entirely hidden; therefore he is ashamed of his phantasies as being childish and as something prohibited.

If they are concealed with so much secretiveness, you will ask, how do we know so much about the human propensity to create phantasies? Now there is a certain class of human beings upon whom not a god, indeed, but a stern goddess —Necessity—has laid the task of giving an account of what they suffer and what they enjoy. These people are the neurotics; among other things they have to confess their phantasies to the physician to whom they go in the hope of recovering through mental treatment. This is our best source of knowledge, and we have later found good reason to suppose that our patients tell us about themselves nothing that we could not also hear from healthy people.

Let us try to learn some of the characteristics of daydreaming. We can begin by saying that happy people never make phantasies, only unsatisfied ones. Unsatisfied wishes are the driving power behind phantasies; every separate phantasy contains the fulfillment of a wish, and improves on unsatisfactory reality. The impelling wishes vary according to the sex, character, and circumstances of the creator; they may be easily divided, however, into two principal groups. Either they are ambitious wishes, serving to exalt the person creating them, or they are erotic. In young women erotic wishes dominate the phantasies almost exclusively, for their ambition is generally comprised in their erotic longings; in young men egoistic and ambitious wishes assert themselves plainly enough alongside their erotic desires. But we will not lay stress on the distinction between these two trends; we prefer to emphasize the fact that they are often united. In many altarpieces the portrait of the donor is to be found in one corner of the picture; and in the greater number of ambitious daydreams, too, we can discover a woman in some corner, for whom the dreamer performs all his heroic deeds and at whose feet all his triumphs are to be laid. Here you see we have strong enough motives for concealment; a well-brought-up woman is, indeed, credited with only a minimum of erotic desire, while a young man has to learn to suppress the overweening self-regard he acquires in the indulgent atmosphere surrounding his childhood, so that he may find his proper place in a society that is full of other persons making similar claims.

We must not imagine that the various products of this impulse towards phantasy, castles in the air or daydreams, are stereotyped or unchangeable. On the contrary, they fit themselves into the changing impressions of life, alter with the vicissitudes of life; every deep new impression gives them what might be called a "date stamp." The relation of phantasies to time is altogether of great importance. One may say that a phantasy at one and the same moment hovers between three periods of time—the three periods of our ideation. The activity of phantasy in the mind is linked up with some current impression, occasioned by some event in the present, which had the power to rouse an intense desire. From there it wanders back to the memory of an early experience, generally belonging to infancy, in which this wish was fulfilled. Then it creates for itself a situation which is to emerge in the future, representing the fulfillment of the wish—this is the daydream or phantasy, which now carries in it traces both of the occasion which engendered it and of some past memory. So past, present, and future are threaded, as it were, on the string of the wish that runs through them all.

A very ordinary example may serve to make my statement clear. Take the case of a poor orphan lad, to whom you have given the address of some employer where he may perhaps get work. On the way there he falls into a daydream suitable to the situation from which it springs. The content of the phantasy will be somewhat as follows: He is taken on and pleases his new employer, makes himself indispensable in the business, is taken into the family of the employer, and marries the charming daughter of the house. Then he comes to conduct the business, first as a partner, and then as successor to his father-in-law. In this way the dreamer regains what he had in his happy childhood, the protecting house, his loving parents and the first objects of his affection. You will see from such an example how the wish employs some event in the present to plan a future on the pattern of the past.

Much more could be said about phantasies, but I will only allude as briefly as possible to certain points. If phantasies become over-luxuriant and over-powerful, the necessary conditions for an outbreak of neurosis or psychosis are constituted; phantasies are also the first preliminary stage in the mind of the symptoms of illness of which our patients complain. A broad bypath here branches off into pathology.

I cannot pass over the relation of phantasies to dreams. Our nocturnal dreams are nothing but such phantasies, as we can make clear by interpreting them.[2] Language, in its unrivaled wisdom, long ago decided the question of the essential nature of dreams by giving the name of "daydreams" to the airy creations of fantasy. If the meaning of our dreams usually remains obscure in spite of this clue, it is because of the circumstance that at night wishes of which we are ashamed also become active in us, wishes which we have to hide from ourselves, which were consequently repressed and pushed back into the unconscious. Such repressed wishes and their derivatives can therefore achieve expression only when almost completely disguised. When scientific work had succeeded in elucidating the distortion in dreams, it was no longer difficult to recognize that nocturnal dreams are fulfillments of desires in exactly the same way as daydreams are—those phantasies with which we are all so familiar.

So much for daydreaming; now for the poet! Shall we dare really to compare an imaginative writer with "one who dreams in broad daylight," and his creations with daydreams? Here, surely, a first distinction is forced upon us; we must distinguish between poets who, like the bygone creators of epics and tragedies, take over their material ready-made, and those who seem to create their material spontaneously. Let us keep to the latter, and let us also not choose for our comparison those writers who are most highly esteemed by critics. We will choose the less pretentious writers of romances, novels, and stories, who are read all the same by the widest circles of men and women. There is one very marked characteristic in the productions of these writers which must strike us all: they all have a hero who is the center of interest, for whom the author tries to win our sympathy by every possible means, and whom he places under the protection of a special providence. If at the end of one chapter the hero is left unconscious and bleeding from severe wounds, I am sure to find him at the beginning of the next being carefully tended and on the way to recovery; if the first volume ends in the hero being shipwrecked in a storm at sea, I am certain to hear at the beginning of the next of his hair-breadth escape—otherwise, indeed, the story could not continue. The feeling of security with which I follow the hero through his dangerous adventures is the same as that with which a real hero throws himself into the water to save a drowning man, or exposes himself to the fire of the enemy while storming a battery. It is this very feeling of being a hero which one of our best authors has well expressed in the famous phrase, "*Es kann mir nix g'schehen!*" [3] It seems to me, however, that this significant mark of invulnerability very clearly betrays—His Majesty the Ego, the hero of all daydreams and all novels.

The same relationship is hinted at in yet other characteristics of these egocentric stories. When all the women in a novel invariably fall in love with the hero, this can hardly be looked upon as a description of reality, but it is easily understood as an essential constituent of a daydream. The same thing

[2] *Cf.* Freud, *Die Traumdeutung (The Interpretation of Dreams).*
[3] Anzengruber. [The phrase means "Nothing can happen to *me!*"—Translator.]

holds good when the other people in the story are sharply divided into good and bad, with complete disregard of the manifold variety in the traits of real human beings; the "good" ones are those who help the ego in its character of hero, while the "bad" are his enemies and rivals.

We do not in any way fail to recognize that many imaginative productions have traveled far from the original naïve daydream, but I cannot suppress the surmise that even the most extreme variations could be brought into relationship with this model by an uninterrupted series of transitions. It has struck me in many so-called psychological novels, too, that only one person—once again the hero—is described from within; the author dwells in his soul and looks upon the other people from outside. The psychological novel in general probably owes its peculiarities to the tendency of modern writers to split up their ego by self-observation into many component-egos, and in this way to personify the conflicting trends in their own mental life in many heroes. There are certain novels, which might be called "eccentric," that seem to stand in marked contradiction to the typical daydream; in these the person introduced as the hero plays the least active part of anyone, and seems instead to let the actions and sufferings of other people pass him by like a spectator. Many of the later novels of Zola belong to this class. But I must say that the psychological analysis of people who are not writers, and who deviate in many things from the so-called norm, has shown us analogous variations in their daydreams in which the ego contents itself with the role of spectator.

If our comparison of the imaginative writer with the daydreamer, and of poetic production with the daydream, is to be of any value, it must show itself fruitful in some way or other. Let us try, for instance, to examine the works of writers in reference to the idea propounded above, the relation of the phantasy to the wish that runs through it and to the three periods of time; and with its help let us study the connection between the life of the writer and his productions. Hitherto it has not been known what preliminary ideas would constitute an approach to this problem; very often this relation has been regarded as much simpler than it is; but the insight gained from phantasies leads us to expect the following state of things. Some actual experience which made a strong impression on the writer had stirred up a memory of an earlier experience, generally belonging to childhood, which then arouses a wish that finds a fulfillment in the work in question, and in which elements of the recent event and the old memory should be discernible.

Do not be alarmed at the complexity of this formula; I myself expect that in reality it will prove itself to be too schematic, but that possibly it may contain a first means of approach to the true state of affairs. From some attempts I have made I think that this way of approaching works of the imagination might not be unfruitful. You will not forget that the stress laid on the writer's memories of his childhood, which perhaps seems so strange, is ultimately derived from the hypothesis that imaginative creation, like daydreaming, is a continuation of and substitute for the play of childhood.

We will not neglect to refer also to that class of imaginative work which must be recognized not as spontaneous production, but as a refashioning of ready-made material. Here, too, the writer retains a certain amount of independence, which can express itself in the choice of material and in changes in the material chosen, which are often considerable. As far as it goes, this material is derived from the racial treasure-house of myths, legends, and fairy tales. The study of these creations of racial psychology is in no way complete, but it seems extremely probable that myths, for example, are distorted vestiges of the wish-phantasies of whole nations—the age-long dreams of young humanity.

You will say that, although writers came first in the title of this paper, I have told you far less about them than about phantasy. I am aware of that, and will try to excuse myself by pointing to the present state of our knowledge. I could only throw out suggestions and bring up interesting points which arise from the study of phantasies, and which pass beyond them to the problem of the choice of literary material. We have not touched on the other problem at all, that is, what are the means which writers use to achieve those emotional reactions in us that are roused by their productions. But I would at least point out to you the path which leads from our discussion of daydreams to the problems of the effect produced on us by imaginative works.

You will remember that we said the daydreamer hid his phantasies carefully from other people because he had reason to be ashamed of them. I may now add that even if he were to communicate them to us, he would give us no pleasure by his disclosures. When we hear such phantasies they repel us, or at least leave us cold. But when a man of literary talent presents his plays, or relates what we take to be his personal daydreams, we experience great pleasure arising probably from many sources. How the writer accomplishes this is his innermost secret; the essential *ars poetica* lies in the technique by which our feeling of repulsion is overcome, and this has certainly to do with those barriers erected between every individual being and all others. We can guess at two methods used in this technique. The writer softens the egotistical character of the daydream by changes and disguises, and he bribes us by the offer of a purely formal, that is esthetic, pleasure in the presentation of his phantasies. The increment of pleasure which is offered us in order to release yet greater pleasure arising from deeper sources in the mind is called an "incitement premium" or technically, "fore-pleasure." I am of the opinion that all the esthetic pleasure we gain from the works of imaginative writers is of the same type as this "fore-pleasure," and that the true enjoyment of literature proceeds from the release of tensions in our minds. Perhaps much that brings about this result consists in the writer's putting us into a position in which we can enjoy our own daydreams without reproach or shame. Here we reach a path leading into novel, interesting, and complicated researches, but we also, at least for the present, arrive at the end of the present discussion.

—*Neu Revue,* Volume I (1908); translation first published in *Collected Papers,* Volume IV (1925)

III. *Tragic Themes*

According to my already extensive experience, parents play a leading part in the infantile psychology of all persons who subsequently become psychoneurotics. Falling in love with one parent and hating the other forms part of the permanent stock of the psychic impulses which arise in early childhood, and are of such importance as the material of the subsequent neurosis. But I do not believe that psychoneurotics are to be sharply distinguished in this respect from other persons who remain normal—that is, I do not believe that they are capable of creating something absolutely new and peculiar to themselves. It is far more probable—and this is confirmed by incidental observations of normal children—that in their amorous or hostile attitude toward their parents, psychoneurotics do no more than reveal to us, by magnification, something that occurs less markedly and intensively in the minds of the majority of children. Antiquity has furnished us with legendary matter which corroborates this belief, and the profound and universal validity of the old legends is explicable only by an equally universal validity of the above-mentioned hypothesis of infantile psychology.

I am referring to the legend of King Oedipus and the *Oedipus Rex* of Sophocles. Oedipus, the son of Laius, king of Thebes, and Jocasta, is exposed as a suckling, because an oracle had informed the father that his son, who was still unborn, would be his murderer. He is rescued, and grows up as a king's son at a foreign court, until, being uncertain of his origin, he, too, consults the oracle, and is warned to avoid his native place, for he is destined to become the murderer of his father and the husband of his mother. On the road leading away from his supposed home he meets King Laius, and in a sudden quarrel strikes him dead. He comes to Thebes, where he solves the riddle of the Sphinx, who is barring the way to the city, whereupon he is elected king by the grateful Thebans, and is rewarded with the hand of Jocasta. He reigns for many years in peace and honor, and begets two sons and two daughters upon his unknown mother, until at last a plague breaks out—which causes the Thebans to consult the oracle anew. Here Sophocles' tragedy begins. The messengers bring the reply that the plague will stop as soon as the murderer of Laius is driven from the country. But where is he?

"Where shall be found,
Faint, and hard to be known, the trace of the ancient guilt?"

The action of the play consists simply in the disclosure, approached step by step and artistically delayed (and comparable to the work of a psychoanalysis) that Oedipus himself is the murderer of Laius, and that he is the son of the murdered man and Jocasta. Shocked by the abominable crime which he has unwittingly committed, Oedipus blinds himself, and departs from his native city. The prophecy of the oracle has been fulfilled.

The *Oedipus Rex* is a tragedy of fate; its tragic effect depends on the conflict between the all-powerful will of the gods and the vain efforts of human beings threatened with disaster; resignation to the divine will, and the perception of one's own impotence is the lesson which the deeply moved spectator is supposed to learn from the tragedy. Modern authors have therefore sought to achieve a similar tragic effect by expressing the same conflict in stories of their own invention. But the playgoers have looked on unmoved at the unavailing efforts of guiltless men to avert the fulfillment of curse or oracle; the modern tragedies of destiny have failed of their effect.

If the *Oedipus Rex* is capable of moving a modern reader or playgoer no less powerfully than it moved the contemporary Greeks, the only possible explanation is that the effect of the Greek tragedy does not depend upon the conflict between fate and human will, but upon the peculiar nature of the material by which this conflict is revealed. There must be a voice within us which is prepared to acknowledge the compelling power of fate in the *Oedipus,* while we are able to condemn the situations occurring in *Die Ahnfrau* or other tragedies of fate as arbitrary inventions. And there actually is a motive in the story of King Oedipus which explains the verdict of this inner voice. His fate moves us only because it might have been our own, because the oracle laid upon us before our birth the very curse which rested upon him. It may be that we were all destined to direct our first sexual impulses toward our mothers, and our first impulses of hatred and violence toward our fathers; our dreams convince us that we were. King Oedipus, who slew his father Laius and wedded his mother Jocasta, is nothing more or less than a wish-fulfillment—the fulfillment of the wish of our childhood. But we, more fortunate than he, in so far as we have not become psychoneurotics, have since our childhood succeeded in withdrawing our sexual impulses from our mothers, and in forgetting our jealousy of our fathers. We recoil from the person for whom this primitive wish of our childhood has been fulfilled with all the force of the repression which these wishes have undergone in our minds since childhood. As the poet brings the guilt of Oedipus to light by his investigation, he forces us to become aware of our own inner selves, in which the same impulses are still extant, even though they are suppressed. The antithesis with which the chorus departs:—

"... Behold, this is Oedipus,
Who unravelled the great riddle, and was first in power,

Whose fortune all the townsmen praised and envied;
See in what dread adversity he sank!"

—this admonition touches us and our own pride, us who since the years of our childhood have grown so wise and so powerful in our own estimation. Like Oedipus, we live in ignorance of the desires that offend morality, the desires that nature has forced upon us and after their unveiling we may well prefer to avert our gaze from the scenes of our childhood.

In the very text of Sophocles' tragedy there is an unmistakable reference to the fact that the Oedipus legend had its source in dream-material of immemorial antiquity, the content of which was the painful disturbance of the child's relations to its parents caused by the first impulses of sexuality. Jocasta comforts Oedipus—who is not yet enlightened, but is troubled by the recollection of the oracle—by an allusion to a dream which is often dreamed, though it cannot, in her opinion, mean anything:—

"For many a man hath seen himself in dreams
His mother's mate, but he who gives no heed
To suchlike matters bears the easier life."

The dream of having sexual intercourse with one's mother was as common then as it is today with many people, who tell it with indignation and astonishment. As may well be imagined, it is the key to the tragedy and the complement to the dream of the death of the father. The Oedipus fable is the reaction of phantasy to these two typical dreams, and just as such a dream, when occurring to an adult, is experienced with feelings of aversion, so the content of the fable must include terror and self-chastisement. The form which it subsequently assumed was the result of an uncomprehending secondary elaboration of the material, which sought to make it serve a theological intention. The attempt to reconcile divine omnipotence with human responsibility must, of course, fail with this material as with any other.

Another of the great poetic tragedies, Shakespeare's *Hamlet*, is rooted in the same soil as *Oedipus Rex*. But the whole difference in the psychic life of the two widely separated periods of civilization, and the progress, during the course of time, of repression in the emotional life of humanity, is manifested in the differing treatment of the same material. In *Oedipus Rex* the basic wish-phantasy of the child is brought to light and realized as it is in dreams; in *Hamlet* it remains repressed, and we learn of its existence—as we discover the relevant facts in a neurosis—only through the inhibitory effects which proceed from it. In the more modern drama, the curious fact that it is possible to remain in complete uncertainty as to the character of the hero has proved to be quite consistent with the overpowering effect of the tragedy. The play is based upon Hamlet's hesitation in accomplishing the task of revenge assigned to him; the text does not give the cause or the motive of this hesitation, nor have the manifold attempts at interpretation succeeded in doing so. According to the still prevailing conception, a conception for which Goethe was first responsible, Hamlet represents the type of man whose active energy is paralyzed by excessive intellectual activity: "Sicklied o'er with the pale cast of thought." According to another conception, the poet has endeavored to portray a morbid, irresolute character, on the verge of neurasthenia. The plot of the drama, however, shows us that Hamlet is by no means intended to appear as a character wholly incapable of action. On two separate occasions we see him assert himself: once in a sudden outburst of rage, when he stabs the eavesdropper behind the arras, and on the other occasion when he deliberately, and even craftily, with the complete unscrupulousness of a prince of the renaissance, sends the two courtiers to the death which was intended for himself. What is it, then, that inhibits him in accomplishing the task which his father's ghost has laid upon him? Here the explanation offers itself that it is the peculiar nature of this task. Hamlet is able to do anything but take vengeance upon the man who did away with his father and has taken his father's place with his mother—the man who shows him in realization the repressed desires of his own childhood. The loathing which should have driven him to revenge is thus replaced by self-reproach, by conscientious scruples, which tell him that he himself is no better than the murderer whom he is required to punish. I have here translated into consciousness what had to remain unconscious in the mind of the hero; if anyone wishes to call Hamlet an hysterical subject I cannot but admit that this is the deduction to be drawn from my interpretation. The sexual aversion which Hamlet expresses in conversation with Ophelia is perfectly consistent with this deduction—the same sexual aversion which during the next fews years was increasingly to take possession of the poet's soul, until it found its supreme utterance in *Timon of Athens*. It can, of course, be only the poet's own psychology with which we are confronted in *Hamlet;* and in a work on Shakespeare by Georg Brandes (1896) I find the statement that the drama was composed immediately after the death of Shakespeare's father (1601)—that is to say, when he was still mourning his loss, and during a revival, as we may fairly assume, of his own childish feelings in respect of his father. It is known, too, that Shakespeare's son, who died in childhood, bore the name of Hamnet (identical with Hamlet). Just as *Hamlet* treats of the relation of the son to his parents, so *Macbeth,* which was written about the same period, is based upon the theme of childlessness. Just as all neurotic symptoms, like dreams themselves, are capable of hyper-interpretation, and even require such hyper-interpretation before they become perfectly intelligible, so every genuine poetical creation must have proceeded from more than one motive, more than one impulse in the mind of the poet, and must admit of more than one interpretation. I have here attempted to interpret only the deepest stratum of impulses in the mind of the creative poet.

—*The Interpretation of Dreams* (1900; translated 1913; third English edition, 1931)

CARL GUSTAV JUNG

Psychology and Literature

It is obvious enough that psychology, being the study of psychic processes, can be brought to bear upon the study of literature, for the human psyche is the womb of all the sciences and arts. We may expect psychological research, on the one hand, to explain the formation of a work of art, and on the other to reveal the factors that make a person artistically creative. The psychologist is thus faced with two separate and distinct tasks, and must approach them in radically different ways.

In the case of the work of art we have to deal with a product of complicated psychic activities—but a product that is apparently intentional and consciously shaped. In the case of the artist we must deal with the psychic apparatus itself. In the first instance we must attempt the psychological analysis of a definitely circumscribed and concrete artistic achievement, while in the second we must analyze the living and creative human being as a unique personality. Although these two undertakings are closely related and even interdependent, neither of them can yield the explanations that are sought by the other. It is of course possible to draw inferences about the artist from the work of art, and *vice versa,* but these inferences are never conclusive. At best they are probable surmises or lucky guesses. A knowledge of Goethe's particular relation to his mother throws some light upon Faust's exclamation: "The mothers—mothers—how very strange it sounds!" But it does not enable us to see how the attachment to his mother could produce the Faust drama itself, however unmistakably we sense in the man Goethe a deep connection between the two. Nor are we more successful in reasoning in the reverse direction. There is nothing in *The Ring of the Nibelungs* that would enable us to recognize or definitely infer the fact that Wagner occasionally liked to wear womanish clothes, though hidden connections exist between the heroic masculine world of the Nibelungs and a certain pathological effeminacy in the man Wagner.

The present state of development of psychology does not allow us to establish those rigorous causal connections which we expect of a science. It is only in the realm of the psycho-physiological instincts and reflexes that we can confidently operate with the idea of causality. From the point where psychic life begins—that is, at a level of greater complexity—the psychologist must content himself with more or less widely ranging descriptions of happenings and with the vivid portrayal of the warp and weft of the mind in all its amazing intricacy. In doing this, he must refrain from designating any one psychic process, taken by itself, as "necessary." Were this not the state of affairs, and could the psychologist be relied upon to uncover the causal connections within a work of art and in the process of artistic creation, he would leave the study of art no ground to stand on and would reduce it to a special branch of his own science. The psychologist, to be sure, may never abandon his claim to investigate and establish causal relations in complicated psychic events. To do so would be to deny psychology the right to exist. Yet he can never make good this claim in the fullest sense, because the creative aspect of life which finds its clearest expression in art baffles all attempts at rational formulation. Any reaction to stimulus may be causally explained; but the creative act, which is the absolute antithesis of mere reaction, will for ever elude the human understanding. It can only be described in its manifestations; it can be obscurely sensed, but never wholly grasped. Psychology and the study of art will always have to turn to one another for help, and the one will not invalidate the other. It is an important principle of psychology that psychic events are derivable. It is a principle in the study of art that a psychic product is something in and for itself whether the work of art or the artist himself is in question. Both principles are valid in spite of their relativity.

I. *The Work of Art*

There is a fundamental difference of approach between the psychologist's examination of a literary work, and that of the literary critic. What is of decisive importance and value for the latter may be quite irrelevant for the former. Literary products of highly dubious merit are often of the greatest interest to the psychologist. For instance, the so-called "psychological novel" is by no means as rewarding for the psychologist as the literary-minded suppose. Considered as a whole, such a novel explains itself. It has done its own work of psychological interpretation, and the psychologist can at most criticize or enlarge upon this. The important question as to how a particular author came to write a particular novel is of course left unanswered, but I wish to reserve this general problem for the second part of my essay.

The novels which are most fruitful for the psychologist are those in which the author has not already given a psychological interpretation of his characters, and which therefore leave room for analysis and explanation, or even invite it by their mode of presentation. Good examples of this kind of writing are the novels of Benoît, and English fiction in the manner of Rider Haggard, including the vein exploited by Conan Doyle which yields that most cherished article of mass-production, the detective story. Melville's *Moby Dick,* which I consider the greatest American novel, also comes within this class of writings. An exciting narrative that is apparently quite devoid of psychological exposition is just what interests the psychologist most of all. Such a tale is built upon a groundwork of implicit psychological assumptions, and, in the measure that the author is un-conscious of them, they reveal themselves, pure and unalloyed, to the critical discernment. In the psychological novel, on the other hand, the author himself attempts to reshape his material so as to raise it from the level of crude contin-gency to that of psychological exposition and illumination—a procedure which all too often clouds the psychological significance of the work or hides it from view. It is precisely to novels of this sort that the layman goes for "psychology"; while it is novels of the other kind that challenge the psychologist, for he alone can give them deeper meaning.

I have been speaking in terms of the novel, but I am dealing with a psy-chological fact which is not restricted to this particular form of literary art. We meet with it in the works of the poets as well, and are confronted with it when we compare the first and second parts of the Faust drama. The love-tragedy of Gretchen explains itself; there is nothing that the psychologist can add to it that the poet has not already said in better words. The second part, on the other hand, calls for explanation. The prodigious richness of the imaginative material has so overtaxed the poet's formative powers that nothing is self-explanatory and every verse adds to the reader's need of an interpretation. The two parts of *Faust* illustrate by way of extremes this psychological distinction between works of literature.

In order to emphasize the distinction, I will call the one mode of artistic creation *psychological,* and the other *visionary.* The psychological mode deals with materials drawn from the realm of human consciousness—for instance, with the lessons of life, with emotional shocks, the experience of passion and the crises of human destiny in general—all of which go to make up the conscious life of man, and his feeling life in particular. This material is psychically assimi-lated by the poet, raised from the commonplace to the level of poetic experience, and given an expression which forces the reader to greater clarity and depth of human insight by bringing fully into his consciousness what he ordinarily evades and overlooks or senses only with a feeling of dull discomfort. The poet's work is an interpretation and illumination of the contents of consciousness, of the ineluctable experiences of human life with its eternally recurrent sorrow and joy. He leaves nothing over for the psychologist, unless, indeed, we expect the latter to expound the reasons for which Faust falls in love with Gretchen, or which drive Gretchen to murder her child! Such themes go to make up the lot of humankind; they repeat themselves millions of times and are responsible for the monotony of the police court and of the penal code. No obscurity whatever surrounds them, for they fully explain themselves.

Countless literary works belong to this class: the many novels dealing with love, the environment, the family, crime and society, as well as didactic poetry, the larger number of lyrics, and the drama, both tragic and comic. Whatever its particular form may be, the psychological work of art always takes its materials from the vast realm of conscious human experience—from the vivid foreground of life, we might say. I have called this mode of artistic creation psychological because in its activity it nowhere transcends the bounds of psychological intelligibility. Everything that it embraces—the experience as well as its artistic expression—belongs to the realm of the understandable. Even the basic experiences themselves, though non-rational, have nothing strange about them; on the contrary, they are that which has been known from the beginning of time—passion and its fated outcome, man's subjection to the turns of destiny, eternal nature with its beauty and its horror.

The profound difference between the first and second parts of *Faust* marks the difference between the psychological and the visionary modes of artistic creation. The latter reverses all the conditions of the former. The experience that furnishes the material for artistic expression is no longer familiar. It is a strange something that derives its existence from the hinterland of man's mind —that suggests the abyss of time separating us from pre-human ages, or evokes a super-human world of contrasting light and darkness. It is a primordial experience which surpasses man's understanding, and to which he is therefore in danger of succumbing. The value and the force of the experience are given by its enormity. It arises from timeless depths; it is foreign and cold, many-sided, demonic and grotesque. A grimly ridiculous sample of the eternal chaos—a *crimen laesae majestatis humanae* [crime violating human dignity], to use Nietzsche's words—it bursts asunder our human standards of value and of esthetic form. The disturbing vision of monstrous and meaningless happenings that in every way exceed the grasp of human feeling and comprehension makes quite other demands upon the powers of the artist than do the experiences of the foreground of life. These never rend the curtain that veils the cosmos; they never transcend the bounds of the humanly possible, and for this reason are readily shaped to the demands of art, no matter how great a shock to the individual they may be. But the primordial experiences rend from top to bottom the curtain upon which is painted the picture of an ordered world, and allow a glimpse into the unfathomed abyss of what has not yet become. Is it a vision of other worlds, or of the obscuration of the spirit, or of the beginning of things before the age of man, or of the unborn generations of the future? We cannot say that it is any or none of these.

Shaping—re-shaping—
The eternal spirit's eternal pastime.[1]

We find such vision in *The Shepherd of Hermas,* in Dante, in the second part of *Faust,* in Nietzsche's Dionysian exuberance, in Wagner's *Nibelungenring,* in Spitteler's *Olympischer Frühling,* in the poetry of William Blake, in the *Ipnerotomachia* of the monk Francesco Colonna, and in Jacob Boehme's philosophic and poetic stammerings. In a more restricted and specific way, the primordial experience furnishes material for Rider Haggard in the fiction-cycle that turns upon *She,* and it does the same for Benoît, chiefly in *L'Atlantide,* for Kubin in *Die Andere Seite,* for Meyrink in *Das Grüne Gesicht*—a book whose importance we should not undervalue—for Goetz in *Das Reich ohne Raum,* and for Barlach in *Der Tote Tag.* This list might be greatly extended.

In dealing with the psychological mode of artistic creation, we never need ask ourselves what the material consists of or what it means. But this question forces itself upon us as soon as we come to the visionary mode of creation. We are astonished, taken aback, confused, put on our guard or even disgusted—and we demand commentaries and explanations. We are reminded in nothing of everyday, human life, but rather of dreams, night-time fears and the dark recesses of the mind that we sometimes sense with misgiving. The reading public for the most part repudiates this kind of writing—unless, indeed, it is coarsely sensational—and even the literary critic feels embarrassed by it. It is true that Dante and Wagner have smoothed the approach to it. The visionary experience is cloaked, in Dante's case, by the introduction of historical facts, and, in that of Wagner, by mythological events so that history and mythology are sometimes taken to be the materials with which these poets worked. But with neither of them does the moving force and the deeper significance lie there. For both it is contained in the visionary experience. Rider Haggard, pardonably enough, is generally held to be a mere inventor of fiction. Yet even with him the story is primarily a means of giving expression to significant material. However much the tale may seem to overgrow the content, the latter outweighs the former in importance.

The obscurity as to the sources of the material in visionary creation is very strange, and the exact opposite of what we find in the psychological mode of creation. We are even led to suspect that this obscurity is not unintentional. We are naturally inclined to suppose—and Freudian psychology encourages us to do so—that some highly personal experience underlies this grotesque darkness. We hope thus to explain these strange glimpses of chaos and to understand why it sometimes seems as though the poet had intentionally concealed his basic experience from us. It is only a step from this way of looking at the matter to the statement that we are here dealing with a pathological and neurotic art—a

[1] *Gestaltung, Umgestaltung,*
Des ew'gen Sinnes ew'ge Unterhaltung. (Goethe.)

step which is justified in so far as the material of the visionary creator shows certain traits that we find in the fantasies of the insane. The converse also is true; we often discover in the mental output of psychotic persons a wealth of meaning that we should expect rather from the works of a genius. The psychologist who follows Freud will of course be inclined to take the writings in question as a problem in pathology. On the assumption that an intimate, personal experience underlies what I call the "primordial vision"—an experience, that is to say, which cannot be accepted by the conscious outlook—he will try to account for the curious images of the vision by calling them cover-figures and by supposing that they represent an attempted concealment of the basic experience. This, according to his view, might be an experience in love which is morally or esthetically incompatible with the personality as a whole or at least with certain fictions of the conscious mind. In order that the poet, through his ego, might repress this experience and make it unrecognizable (unconscious), the whole arsenal of a pathological fantasy was brought into action. Moreover, this attempt to replace reality by fiction, being unsatisfactory, must be repeated in a long series of creative embodiments. This would explain the proliferation of imaginative forms, all monstrous, demonic, grotesque and perverse. On the one hand they are substitutes for the unacceptable experience, and on the other they help to conceal it.

Although a discussion of the poet's personality and psychic disposition belongs strictly to the second part of my essay, I cannot avoid taking up in the present connection this Freudian view of the visionary work of art. For one thing, it has aroused considerable attention. And then it is the only well-known attempt that has been made to give a "scientific" explanation of the sources of the visionary material or to formulate a theory of the psychic processes that underlie this curious mode of artistic creation. I assume that my own view of the question is not well known or generally understood. With this preliminary remark, I will now try to present it briefly.

If we insist on deriving the vision from a personal experience, we must treat the former as something secondary—as a mere substitute for reality. The result is that we strip the vision of its primordial quality and take it as nothing but a symptom. The pregnant chaos then shrinks to the proportions of a psychic disturbance. With this account of the matter we feel reassured and turn again to our picture of a well-ordered cosmos. Since we are practical and reasonable, we do not expect the cosmos to be perfect; we accept these unavoidable imperfections which we call abnormalities and diseases, and we take it for granted that human nature is not exempt from them. The frightening revelation of abysses that defy the human understanding is dismissed as illusion, and the poet is regarded as a victim and perpetrator of deception. Even to the poet, his primordial experience was "human—all too human," to such a degree that he could not face its meaning but had to conceal it from himself.

We shall do well, I think, to make fully explicit all the implications of that way of accounting for artistic creation which consists in reducing it to personal factors. We should see clearly where it leads. The truth is that it takes us away from the psychological study of the work of art, and confronts us with the psychic disposition of the poet himself. That the latter presents an important problem is not to be denied, but the work of art is something in its own right, and may not be conjured away. The question of the significance to the poet of his own creative work—of his regarding it as a trifle, as a screen, as a source of suffering or as an achievement—does not concern us at the moment, our task being to interpret the work of art psychologically. For this undertaking it is essential that we give serious consideration to the basic experience that underlies it—namely, to the vision. We must take it at least as seriously as we do the experiences that underlie the psychological mode of artistic creation, and no one doubts that they are both real and serious. It looks, indeed, as if the visionary experience were something quite apart from the ordinary lot of man, and for this reason we have difficulty in believing that it is real. It has about it an unfortunate suggestion of obscure metaphysics and of occultism, so that we feel called upon to intervene in the name of a well-intentioned reasonableness. Our conclusion is that it would be better not to take such things too seriously, lest the world revert again to a benighted superstition. We may, of course, have a predilection for the occult; but ordinarily we dismiss the visionary experience as the outcome of a rich fantasy or of a poetic mood—that is to say, as a kind of poetic license psychologically understood. Certain of the poets encourage this interpretation in order to put a wholesome distance between themselves and their work. Spitteler, for example, stoutly maintained that it was one and the same whether the poet sang of an Olympian Spring or to the theme: "May is here!" The truth is that poets are human beings, and that what a poet has to say about his work is often far from being the most illuminating word on the subject. What is required of us, then, is nothing less than to defend the importance of the visionary experience against the poet himself.

It cannot be denied that we catch the reverberations of an initial love-experience in *The Shepherd of Hermas,* in the *Divine Comedy* and in the *Faust* drama—an experience which is completed and fulfilled by the vision. There is no ground for the assumption that the second part of *Faust* repudiates or conceals the normal, human experience of the first part, nor are we justified in supposing that Goethe was normal at the time when he wrote *Part I,* but in a neurotic state of mind when he composed *Part II. Hermas,* Dante, and Goethe can be taken as three steps in a sequence covering nearly two thousand years of human development, and in each of them we find the personal love-episode not only connected with the weightier visionary experience, but frankly subordinated to it. On the strength of this evidence which is furnished by the work of art itself and which throws out of court the question of the poet's particular psychic disposition, we must admit that the vision represents a deeper and more impressive experience than human passion. In works of art of this nature—and we must never confuse them with the artist as a person—we cannot doubt that the vision is a genuine, primordial experience, regardless of what reason-mongers may say. The vision is not something derived or secondary, and it is not a symptom of something else. It is true symbolic expression—that is, the expression of something existent in its own right, but imperfectly known. The love-episode is a real experience really suffered, and the same statement applies to the vision. We need not try to determine whether the content of the vision is of a physical, psychic or metaphysical nature. In itself it has psychic reality, and this is no less real than physical reality. Human passion falls within the sphere of conscious experience, while the subject of the vision lies beyond it. Through our feelings we experience the known, but our intuitions point to things that are unknown and hidden—that by their very nature are secret. If ever they become conscious, they are intentionally kept back and concealed, for which reason they have been regarded from earliest times as mysterious, uncanny, and deceptive. They are hidden from the scrutiny of man, and he also hides himself from them out of *deisidaemonia* [fear of the gods]. He protects himself with the shield of science and the armor of reason. His enlightenment is born of fear; in the daytime he believes in an ordered cosmos, and he tries to maintain this faith against the fear of chaos that besets him by night. What if there were some living force whose sphere of action lies beyond our world of every day? Are there human needs that are dangerous and unavoidable? Is there something more purposeful than electrons? Do we delude ourselves in thinking that we possess and command our own souls? And is that which science calls the "psyche" not merely a question mark arbitrarily confined within the skull, but rather a door that opens upon the human world from a world beyond, now and again allowing strange and unseizable potencies to act upon man and to remove him, as if upon the wings of the night, from the level of common humanity to that of a more than personal vocation? When we consider the visionary mode of artistic creation, it even seems as if the love-episode had served as a mere release—as if the personal experience were nothing but the prelude to the all-important "divine comedy."

It is not alone the creator of this kind of art who is in touch with the night-side of life, but the seers, prophets, leaders and enlighteners also. However dark this nocturnal world may be, it is not wholly unfamiliar. Man has known of it from time immemorial—here, there, and everywhere; for primitive man today it is an unquestionable part of his picture of the cosmos. It is only we who have repudiated it because of our fear of superstition and metaphysics, and because we strive to construct a conscious world that is safe and manageable in that natural law holds in it the place of statute law in a commonwealth. Yet, even in our midst, the poet now and then catches sight of the figures that people the night-world—the spirits, demons and gods. He knows that a purposiveness out-reaching human ends is the life-giving secret for man; he has a presentiment of incomprehensible happenings in the pleroma. In short, he sees something of that psychic world that strikes terror into the savage and the barbarian.

From the very first beginnings of human society onward man's efforts to give his vague intimations a binding form have left their traces. Even in the Rhodesian cliff-drawings of the Old Stone Age there appears, side by side with the most amazingly life-like representations of animals, an abstract pattern—a double cross contained in a circle. This design has turned up in every cultural region, more or less, and we find it today not only in Christian churches, but in Tibetan monasteries as well. It is the so-called sun-wheel, and as it dates from a time when no one had thought of wheels as a mechanical device, it cannot have had its source in any experience of the external world. It is rather a symbol that stands for a psychic happening; it covers an experience of the inner world, and is no doubt as lifelike a representation as the famous rhinoceros with the tick-birds on its back. There has never been a primitive culture that did not possess a system of secret teaching, and in many cultures this system is highly developed. The men's councils and the totem-clans preserve this teaching about hidden things that lie apart from man's daytime existence—things which, from primeval times, have always constituted his most vital experiences. Knowledge about them is handed on to younger men in the rites of initiation. The mysteries of the Greco-Roman world performed the same office, and the rich mythology of antiquity is a relic of such experiences in the earliest stages of human development.

It is therefore to be expected of the poet that he will resort to mythology in order to give his experience its most fitting expression. It would be a serious mistake to suppose that he works with materials received at second hand. The primordial experience is the source of his creativeness; it cannot be fathomed, and therefore requires mythological imagery to give it form. In itself it offers no words or images, for it is a vision seen "as in a glass, darkly." It is merely a deep presentiment that strives to find expression. It is like a whirlwind that seizes everything within reach and, by carrying it aloft, assumes a visible shape. Since the particular expression can never exhaust the possibilities of the vision, but falls far short of it in richness of content, the poet must have at his disposal a huge store of materials if he is to communicate even a few of his intimations. What is more, he must resort to an imagery that is difficult to handle and full of contradictions in order to express the weird paradoxicality of his vision. Dante's presentiments are clothed in images that run the gamut of Heaven and Hell; Goethe must bring in the Blocksberg and the infernal regions of Greek antiquity; Wagner needs the whole body of Nordic myth; Nietzsche returns to the hieratic style and recreates the legendary seer of prehistoric times; Blake invents for himself indescribable figures, and Spitteler borrows old names for new creatures of the imagination. And no intermediate step is missing in the whole range from the ineffably sublime to the perversely grotesque.

Psychology can do nothing towards the elucidation of this colorful imagery except bring together materials for comparison and offer a terminology for its discussion. According to this terminology, that which appears in the vision is the collective unconscious. We mean by collective unconscious, a certain psychic disposition shaped by the forces of heredity; from it consciousness has developed. In the physical structure of the body we find traces of earlier stages of evolution, and we may expect the human psyche also to conform in its make-up to the law of phylogeny. It is a fact that in eclipses of consciousness—in dreams, narcotic states and cases of insanity—there come to the surface psychic products or contents that show all the traits of primitive levels of psychic development. The images themselves are sometimes of such a primitive character that we might suppose them derived from ancient, esoteric teaching. Mythological themes clothed in modern dress also frequently appear. What is of particular importance for the study of literature in these manifestations of the collective unconscious is that they are compensatory to the conscious attitude. This is to say that they can bring a one-sided, abnormal, or dangerous state of consciousness into equilibrium in an apparently purposive way. In dreams we can see this process very clearly in its positive aspect. In cases of insanity the compensatory process is often perfectly obvious, but takes a negative form. There are persons, for instance, who have anxiously shut themselves off from all the world only to discover one day that their most intimate secrets are known and talked about by everyone.[2]

If we consider Goethe's *Faust,* and leave aside the possibility that it is compensatory to his own conscious attitude, the question that we must answer is this: In what relation does it stand to the conscious outlook of his time? Great poetry draws its strength from the life of mankind, and we completely miss its meaning if we try to derive it from personal factors. Whenever the collective unconscious becomes a living experience and is brought to bear upon the conscious outlook of an age, this event is a creative act which is of importance to everyone living in that age. A work of art is produced that contains what may truthfully be called a message to generations of men. So *Faust* touches something in the soul of every German. So also Dante's fame is immortal, while *The Shepherd of Hermas* just failed of inclusion in the New Testament canon. Every period has its bias, its particular prejudice and its psychic ailment. An epoch is like an individual; it has its own limitations of conscious outlook, and therefore requires a compensatory adjustment. This is effected by the collective unconscious in that a poet, a seer or a leader allows himself to be guided by the unexpressed desire of his times and shows the way, by word or deed, to the

[2] See my article: "Mind and the Earth," in *Contributions to Analytical Psychology* (Harcourt, Brace, New York, 1928).

attainment of that which everyone blindly craves and expects—whether this attainment results in good or evil, the healing of an epoch or its destruction.

It is always dangerous to speak of one's own times, because what is at stake in the present is too vast for comprehension. A few hints must therefore suffice. Francesco Colonna's book is cast in the form of a dream, and is the apotheosis of natural love taken as a human relation; without countenancing a wild indulgence of the senses, he leaves completely aside the Christian sacrament of marriage. The book was written in 1453. Rider Haggard, whose life coincides with the flowering-time of the Victorian era, takes up this subject and deals with it in his own way; he does not cast it in the form of a dream, but allows us to feel the tension of moral conflict. Goethe weaves the theme of Gretchen-Helen-Mater-Gloriosa like a red thread into the colorful tapestry of Faust. Nietzsche proclaims the death of God, and Spitteler transforms the waxing and waning of the gods into a myth of the seasons. Whatever his importance, each of these poets speaks with the voice of thousands and ten thousands, foretelling changes in the conscious outlook of his time.

II. *The Poet*

Creativeness, like the freedom of the will, contains a secret. The psychologist can describe both these manifestations as processes, but he can find no solution of the philosophical problems they offer. Creative man is a riddle that we may try to answer in various ways, but always in vain, a truth that has not prevented modern psychology from turning now and again to the question of the artist and his art. Freud thought that he had found a key in his procedure of deriving the work of art from the personal experiences of the artist.[3] It is true that certain possibilities lay in this direction, for it was conceivable that a work of art, no no less than a neurosis, might be traced back to those knots in psychic life that we call the complexes. It was Freud's great discovery that neuroses have a causal origin in the psychic realm—that they take their rise from emotional states and from real or imagined childhood experiences. Certain of his followers, like Rank and Stekel, have taken up related lines of inquiry and have achieved important results. It is undeniable that the poet's psychic disposition permeates his work root and branch. Nor is there anything new in the statement that personal factors largely influence the poet's choice and use of his materials. Credit, however, must certainly be given to the Freudian school for showing how far-reaching this influence is and in what curious ways it comes to expression.

Freud takes the neurosis as a substitute for a direct means of gratification. He therefore regards it as something inappropriate—a mistake, a dodge, an excuse, a voluntary blindness. To him it is essentially a shortcoming that should never have been. Since a neurosis, to all appearances, is nothing but a disturbance

[3] See Freud's essay on Jensen's *Gradiva* and on Leonardo da Vinci.

that is all the more irritating because it is without sense or meaning, few people will venture to say a good word for it. And a work of art is brought into questionable proximity with the neurosis when it is taken as something which can be analyzed in terms of the poet's repressions. In a sense it finds itself in good company, for religion and philosophy are regarded in the same light by Freudian psychology. No objection can be raised if it is admitted that this approach amounts to nothing more than the elucidation of those personal determinants without which a work of art is unthinkable. But should the claim be made that such an analysis accounts for the work of art itself, then a categorical denial is called for. The personal idiosyncrasies that creep into a work of art are not essential; in fact, the more we have to cope with these peculiarities, the less is it a question of art. What is essential in a work of art is that it should rise far above the realm of personal life and speak from the spirit and heart of the poet as man to the spirit and heart of mankind. The personal aspect is a limitation— and even a sin—in the realm of art. When a form of "art" is primarily personal it deserves to be treated as if it were a neurosis. There may be some validity in the idea held by the Freudian school that artists without exception are narcissistic —by which is meant that they are undeveloped persons with infantile and auto-erotic traits. The statement is only valid, however, for the artist as a person, and has nothing to do with the man as an artist. In his capacity of artist he is neither auto-erotic, nor hetero-erotic, nor erotic in any sense. He is objective and impersonal—even inhuman—for as an artist he is his work, and not a human being.

Every creative person is a duality or a synthesis of contradictory aptitudes. On the one side he is a human being with a personal life, while on the other side he is an impersonal, creative process. Since as a human being he may be sound or morbid, we must look at his psychic make-up to find the determinants of his personality. But we can only understand him in his capacity of artist by looking at his creative achievement. We should make a sad mistake if we tried to explain the mode of life of an English gentleman, a Prussian officer, or a cardinal in terms of personal factors. The gentleman, the officer and the cleric function as such in an impersonal rôle, and their psychic make-up is qualified by a peculiar objectivity. We must grant that the artist does not function in an official capacity—the very opposite is nearer the truth. He nevertheless resembles the types I have named in one respect, for the specifically artistic disposition involves an overweight of collective psychic life as against the personal. Art is a kind of innate drive that seizes a human being and makes him its instrument. The artist is not a person endowed with free will who seeks his own ends, but one who allows art to realize its purposes through him. As a human being he may have moods and a will and personal aims, but as an artist he is "man" in a higher sense—he is "collective man"—one who carries and shapes the unconscious, psychic life of mankind. To perform this difficult office it is sometimes necessary for him to sacrifice happiness and everything that makes life worth living for the ordinary human being.

All this being so, it is not strange that the artist is an especially interesting case for the psychologist who uses an analytical method. The artist's life cannot be otherwise than full of conflicts, for two forces are at war within him—on the one hand the common human longing for happiness, satisfaction, and security in life, and on the other a ruthless passion for creation which may go so far as to override every personal desire. The lives of artists are as a rule so highly unsatisfactory—not to say tragic—because of their inferiority on the human and personal side, and not because of a sinister dispensation. There are hardly any exceptions to the rule that a person must pay dearly for the divine gift of the creative fire. It is as though each of us were endowed at birth with a certain capital of energy. The strongest force in our make-up will seize and all but monopolize this energy, leaving so little over that nothing of value can come of it. In this way the creative force can drain the human impulses to such a degree that the personal ego must develop all sorts of bad qualities—ruthlessness, selfishness and vanity (so-called "auto-erotism")—and even every kind of vice, in order to maintain the spark of life and to keep itself from being wholly bereft. The auto-erotism of artists resembles that of illegitimate or neglected children who from their tenderest years must protect themselves from the destructive influence of people who have no love to give them—who develop bad qualities for that very purpose and later maintain an invincible egocentrism by remaining all their lives infantile and helpless or by actively offending against the moral code or the law. How can we doubt that it is his art that explains the artist, and not the insufficiencies and conflicts of his personal life? These are nothing but the regrettable results of the fact that he is an artist—that is to say, a man who from his very birth has been called to a greater task than the ordinary mortal. A special ability means a heavy expenditure of energy in a particular direction, with a consequent drain from some other side of life.

It makes no difference whether the poet knows that his work is begotten, grows and matures with him, or whether he supposes that by taking thought he produces it out of the void. His opinion of the matter does not change the fact that his own work outgrows him as a child its mother. The creative process has feminine quality, and the creative work arises from unconscious depths—we might say, from the realm of the mothers. Whenever the creative force predominates, human life is ruled and molded by the unconscious as against the active will, and the conscious ego is swept along on a subterranean current, being nothing more than a helpless observer of events. The work in process becomes the poet's fate and determines his psychic development. It is not Goethe who creates *Faust,* but *Faust* which creates Goethe. And what is *Faust* but a symbol? By this I do not mean an allegory that points to something all too familiar, but an expression that stands for something not clearly known and yet profoundly alive. Here it is something that lives in the soul of every German, and that Goethe has helped to bring to birth. Could we conceive of anyone but a German writing *Faust* or *Also sprach Zarathustra?* Both play upon something that reverberates in the German soul—a "primordial image," as Jacob Burckhardt once called it—the figure of a physician or teacher of mankind. The archetypal image of the wise man, the saviour or redeemer, lies buried and dormant in man's unconscious since the dawn of culture; it is awakened whenever the times are out of joint and a human society is committed to a serious error. When people go astray they feel the need of a guide or teacher or even of the physician. These primordial images are numerous, but do not appear in the dreams of individuals or in works of art until they are called into being by the waywardness of the general outlook. When conscious life is characterized by one-sidedness and by a false attitude, then they are activated—one might say, "instinctively"—and come to light in the dreams of individuals and the visions of artists and seers, thus restoring the psychic equilibrium of the epoch.

In this way the work of the poet comes to meet the spiritual need of the society in which he lives, and for this reason his work means more to him than his personal fate, whether he is aware of this or not. Being essentially the instrument for his work, he is subordinate to it, and we have no reason for expecting him to interpret it for us. He has done the best that in him lies in giving it form, and he must leave the interpretation to others and to the future. A great work of art is like a dream; for all its apparent obviousness it does not explain itself and is never unequivocal. A dream never says: "You ought," or: "This is the truth." It presents an image in much the same way as nature allows a plant to grow, and we must draw our own conclusions. If a person has a nightmare, it means either that he is too much given to fear, or else that he is too exempt from it; and if he dreams of the old wise man it may mean that he is too pedagogical, as also that he stands in need of a teacher. In a subtle way both meanings come to the same thing, as we perceive when we are able to let the work of art act upon us as it acted upon the artist. To grasp its meaning, we must allow it to shape us as it once shaped him. Then we understand the nature of his experience. We see that he has drawn upon the healing and redeeming forces of the collective psyche that underlies consciousness with its isolation and its painful errors; that he has penetrated to that matrix of life in which all men are embedded, which imparts a common rhythm to all human existence, and allows the individual to communicate his feeling and his striving to mankind as a whole.

The secret of artistic creation and of the effectiveness of art is to be found in a return to the state of *participation mystique*—to that level of experience at which it is man who lives, and not the individual, and at which the weal or woe of the single human being does not count, but only human existence. This is why every great work of art is objective and impersonal, but none the less profoundly moves us each and all. And this is also why the personal life of the poet cannot be held essential to his art—but at most a help or a hindrance to his creative task. He may go the way of a Philistine, a good citizen, a neurotic, a fool or a criminal. His personal career may be inevitable and interesting, but it does not explain the poet.

—German text, 1929; translation in
Modern Man in Search of a Soul (1933)

CHRISTOPHER CAUDWELL

Poetry's Dream-Work

§ 1

Dream is neither directed thinking nor directed feeling, but free—that is non-social—association. Hence the associations of dream are personal and can only be understood by reference to the dreamer's personal life. The secret law of dream's structure is the "dream-work."

Poetic irrationality bears this resemblance to dream, that its flow of images is explained by affective laws; but it is not "free" association as in dream. Poetic feeling is directed feeling—feeling controlled by the social ego. Poetic associations are social.

As the dreamer lives entirely in the images of his dream, without reference to another reality, so the reader of poetry lives in the words of the poetry, without reference to the external world. The poet's world is *his* world. As he reads the poem he feels the emotions of the poet. Just as the pythoness or bacchante speaks for the god in the first person, so the reader under the influence of poetic illusion feels for the poet in the first person.

The images of dream, like the ideas of poetry, are concrete. In each dream, and in each poem, the memory-image and the word play a different part, and therefore have different meanings. Dreams and poems are inconsistent among themselves. Each dream and each poem is a world of its own.

Poetry is rhythmical. Rhythm secures the heightening of physiological consciousness so as to shut out sensory perception of the environment. In the rhythm of dance, music or song we become *self*-conscious instead of conscious. The rhythm of heart-beat and breathing and physiological periodicity negates the physical rhythm of the environment. In this sense sleep too is rhythmical. The dreamer retires into the citadel of the body and closes the doors.

Why is "physiological" introversion more necessary in poetry than in story, so that the poet accepts the difficulties of meter and rhyme? The answer is that introversion must be stronger in poetry. By introversion is not meant merely a turning-away from immediate environment—that could be secured by sitting in a quiet study, without disturbance. Such introversion is equally desirable for all kinds of thought, for scientific thinking and novel-reading as well as poetry, and it is not secured by the order of the words but by an effort of concentration. Some people can "concentrate" on a difficult scientific book or a book of poetry in conditions where others cannot. This kind of introversion does not therefore depend upon the order of the words. No one has suggested facilitating scientific writing by making it metrical.

But there is another aspect of introversion. In introversion for scientific phantasy it is true that we turn away from immediate environment, yet none the less we turn towards those parts of external reality of which the words are symbols. Ordinarily we see, hovering behind language, the world of external reality it describes. But in poetry the thoughts are to be directed on to the feeling-tone of the words themselves. Attention must sink below the pieces of external reality symbolized by the poetry, down into the emotional underworld adhering to those pieces. In poetry we must penetrate behind the dome of many-colored glass into the white radiance of the self. Hence the need for a physiological introversion, which is a turning-away not from the immediate environment of the reader *but from the environment (or external reality) depicted in the poem.* Hence poetry in its use of language continually distorts and denies the structure of reality to exalt the structure of the self. By means of rhyme, assonance or alliteration it couples together words which have no rational connection, that is, no nexus through the world of external reality. It breaks the words up into lines of arbitrary length, cutting across their logical construction. It breaks down their associations, derived from the world of external reality, by means of inversion and every variety of artificial stressing and counterpoint.

Thus the world of external reality recedes, and the world of instinct, the affective emotional linkage behind the words, rises to the view and becomes the world of reality. The subject emerges from the object: the social ego from the social world. Wordsworth said correctly: "The tendency of meter is to divest language, in a certain degree, of its reality, and thus to throw a sort of half-consciousness of unsubstantial existence over the whole composition." In the same way Coleridge reached out after a like conception to ours: "Meter is simply a stimulant of attention"—not of any attention but a special kind of attention —attention to the affective associations of the words themselves.

We have here a distinction between poetry and the novel which it is vital to grasp. In the novel too the subjective elements are valued for themselves and rise to view, but in a different way. The novel blots out external reality by substituting a more or less consistent mock reality which has sufficient "stuff" to stand between reader and reality. This means that in the novel the emotional associations attach not to the words but to the moving current of mock reality symbolized by the words. That is why rhythm, "preciousness," and style are alien to the novel; why the novel translates so well; why novels are not composed of words. They are composed of scenes, actions, *stuff*, people, just as plays are. A "jeweled" style is a disadvantage to the novel because it distracts the eye from the things and people to the words—not as words, as black outlines, but as symbols to which a variety of feeling-tone is directly attached. For example when someone exclaims "Brute!" we do not think of animals and then of brutish qualities, but have a powerful subjective reaction suggesting cruelty and clumsiness. This is a poetic reaction to a word; the other is a story reaction.

Because words are few they are what Freud called "over-determined." One word has many affective associations because it has many "meanings" (for example, the word "brute" can mean a foolish person, a cruel person, the order of animals, etc.). In novel-writing the words are arranged so that all other pieces of reality are excluded except the piece required, and the emotional association is to the resulting structure. Poetic writing is concerned with making the emotional associations either exclude or reinforce each other, without a prior reference to a coherent piece of reality; for example, in novel-writing, in the phrase "the Indian Ocean" the word "ocean" has been restricted to a specific geographical ocean, which *then* has emotional associations for the reader. In poetry "the Indian sea" has a different meaning, for the emotional associations are, not to a particular sea but to the word "Indian" and the word "sea," which affect each other and blend to produce a glowing cloudy "feeling" quite different from the novel-writer's phrase.

Of course there may be stretches of poetic writing in a novel (for example in Proust, Malraux, Lawrence, and Melville) or of novel-writing in poetry (the purely explanatory patches in Shakespeare's plays), but this does not affect the general characteristics. The difference is so marked that it explains the strange insensitivity to poetry displayed by so many great novelists, and a similar fondness for bad novels on the part of so many great poets. This difference between the technique of poetry and the novel determines the difference between the spheres of the two arts.

§ 2

What is the basis of literary art? What is the inner contradiction which produces its onward movement? Evidently it can only be a special form of the contradiction which produces the whole movement of society, the contradiction between the instincts and the environment, the endless struggle between man and Nature which is life.

I, the artist, have a certain consciousness, molded by my social world. As artist I am concerned with my artistic consciousness, represented by the direct and indirect effect on me of all the art I have felt, and all the emotional organization which has produced in me a conscious subject. This consciousness is contradicted by my experience—that is, I have a *new* personal experience, something not given in the social world of poetry. Therefore I desire what is called self-expression but is really self-socialization, the casting of my private experience in such a form that it will be incorporated in the social world of art and appear as an art-work. The art-work represents the negation of the negation—the synthesis between the existing world of art (existing consciousness of theory) and my experience (life or practice).[1]

Therefore at the finish the world of art will be changed by the incursion of my art-work. That is the revolutionary aspect of my role as artist. But also my consciousness will be changed because I have, through the medium of the art world, forced my life experience, new, dumb, and unformulated, to become conscious, to enter my conscious sphere. That is the adaptative aspect of my role as artist. In the same way with the appreciator of art, his consciousness will be revolutionized by the incursion into it of a new art-work; but his appreciation of it will only be possible to the extent that he has had some similar experience in life. The former process will be revolutionary; the latter adaptative.

Rather than use the word revolutionary, however, it would be better to use the word evolutionary, restricting the other to cases where the new content of experience is so opposed to the existing consciousness that it requires a wholesale change, a complete revision of existing categories (conventions, traditions, artistic standards) for its inclusion, a revision which is only possible because concrete life itself has undergone a similar change in the period. The Elizabethan age was one of such periods. We are at the beginning of another such now.

It is plain that it is the emotional consciousness—that consciousness which springs directly from the instincts—with which the artist is concerned. Yet exactly the same relation holds between the scientist and his hypothesis (equivalent of the art-work) and the rational consciousness, that consciousness which springs directly from the perception.

Since the mediating factor in art processes is the social ego in its relation to the experience of individuals, it is plain that the integration performed by the art-work can only be achieved on condition that the item of private experience which is integrated (*a*) is *important,* concerned with deep emotional drives, with the unchanging instincts which, because they remain the same beneath the changing adaptations of culture, act as the skeleton, the main organizing force in the social ego which ages of art have built up; (*b*) is *general,* is not a con-

---

[1] According to Hegel and Marx, development generally takes the form of a threefold movement: first, an active force or tendency (the thesis); second, a counterforce or conflicting tendency (the antithesis, or *negation*); and third, a reconciliation of the conflicting forces or tendencies in a new synthesis (the synthesis, or *negation of the negation*). Caudwell is here maintaining that the art-work represents a creative synthesis which reconciles the *personal* consciousness and self-expression of the artist with the *social* traditions and demands of art. (Editor's note.)

tradictory item of experience peculiar to the artist or one or two men, but is encountered in a dumb unconscious way in the experiences of most men—otherwise how could the art-work be meaningful to them, how could it integrate and give expression to their hitherto anarchic experience as it gave expression to the artist's?

Condition (a) secures that great art—art which performs a wide and deep feat of integration—has something universal, something timeless and enduring from age to age. This timelessness we now see to be the timelessness of the instincts, the unchanging secret face of the genotype which persists beneath all the rich superstructure of civilization. Condition (b) explains why contemporary art has a special and striking meaning for us, why we find in even minor contemporary poets something vital and immediate not to be found in Homer, Dante, or Shakespeare. They live in the same world and meet the same bodiless forces whose power they experience.

This also explains why it is correct to have a materialist approach to art, to look in the art-works of any age for a reflection of the social relations of that age. For the experience of men in general is determined in general by the social relations of that age or, to be more accurate, the social relations of that age are simply man's individual experiences averaged out, just as a species is a group of animals' physical peculiarities averaged out. Since art lives in the social world, and can only be of value in integrating experiences general to men, it is plain that the art of any age can only express the general experiences of men in that age. So far from the artist's being a lone wolf, he is the normal man of that age—insofar as he is an artist. Of course normality in consciousness is as rare as normality in vision, and, unlike the latter, it is not a fixed physical standard but one which varies from year to year. Moreover his normality is, so to speak, the norm of abnormal experiences. It is the norm of the queerness and newness and accident in contemporary men's lives: all the incursions of the unexpected which shake their inherited consciousness. Hence the apparent abnormality of the artist.

This, finally, explains why in a class society art is class art. For a class, in the Marxian sense, is simply a group of men whose life-experiences are substantially similar, that is, with less internal differences on the average than they have external differences from the life-experiences of men in other classes. This difference of course has an economic basis, a material cause arising from the inevitable conditions of economic production. Therefore the artist will necessarily integrate the new experience and voice the consciousness of that group whose experience in general resembles his own—his own class. This will be the class which practices art—the class at whose pole gathers the freedom and consciousness of society, in all ages the ruling class.

This is the most general movement of literary art, reflecting the most general law of society. Because of the different techniques of poetry and the novel—

already explained—this movement is expressed in different ways in poetry and in the novel.

Poetry concentrates on the immediate affective associations of the word, instead of going first to the object or entity symbolized by the word and then drawing the affective association from that. Since words are fewer than the objects they symbolize, the affects of poetry are correspondingly condensed, but poetry itself is correspondingly cloudy and ambiguous. This ambiguity, which Empson takes to be the essence of poetry, is in fact a by-product.[2] Now this concentration upon the affective tones of words, instead of going first to the symbolized reality and then to the feeling-tone of that reality, is—because of the nature of language—a concentration on the more dumb and instinctive part of man's consciousness. It is an approach to the more instinctively common part of man's consciousness. It is an approach to the secret unchanging core of the genotype in adapted man. Hence the importance of physiological introversion in poetry.

This genotype is undifferentiated because it is relatively unchanging. Hence the timelessness of poetry as compared to the importance of time sequence in the novel. Poetry speaks timelessly for one common "I" round which all experience is orientated. In poetry all the emotional experiences of men are arranged round the instincts, round the "I." Poetry is a bundle of instinctive perspectives of reality taken from one spot. Precisely because it is cloudy and ambiguous, its view is far-reaching; its horizon seems to open and expand and stretch out to dim infinity. Because it is instinctive, it is enduring. In it the instincts give one loud cry, a cry which expresses what is common in the general relation of every man to contemporary life as a whole.

But the novel goes out first to reality to draw its subjective associations from it. Hence we do not seem to feel the novel "in us," we do not identify our feelings with the feeling-tones of the novel. We stand inside the mock world of the novel and survey it; at the most we identify ourselves with the hero and look round with him at the "otherness" of his environment. The novel does not express the general tension between the instincts and the surroundings, but the changes of tension which take place as a result of change in the surroundings (life-experience). This incursion of the time element (reality as a process) so necessary in a differentiated society where men's time-experiences differ markedly among themselves, means that the novel must particularize and have characters whose actions and feelings are surveyed from without. Poetry is internal—a bundle of "I" perspectives of the world taken from one point, the poet. The story is external—a bundle of perspectives of one "I" (the character) taken from different parts of the world.

Obviously the novel can only evolve in a society where men's experiences

[2] Cf. William Empson's discussion of poetic ambiguity in his *Seven Types of Ambiguity* (Chatto and Windus, London, 1930). (Editor's note.)

do differ so markedly among themselves as to make this objective approach necessary, and this difference of experience is itself the result of rapid change in society, of an increased differentiation of functions, of an increased realization of
life as process, as dialectic. Poetry is the product of a tribe, where life flows on
without much change between youth and age; the novel belongs to a restless age
where things are always happening to people and people therefore are always
altering.

§ 3

Yet all art is subjective. All art is emotional and therefore concerned with
the instincts whose adaptation to social life produces emotional consciousness.
Hence art cannot escape its close relation with the genotype whose secret desires
link in one endless series all human culture.

Now this genotype can be considered from two aspects: the timeless and the
timeful, the changeless and changeful, the general and the particular.

(a) Timeless, changeless, general in that on the whole the genotype is
substantially constant in all societies and all men. There is a substratum of likeness. Man does not change from Athenian to Ancient Briton and then to Lon-
doner by innate differences stamped in by natural selection, but by acquired
changes derived from social evolution. Poetry expresses this constant instinctive
factor.

(b) Yet beneath this likeness the genotypes, because they are bundles
of genes, reveal individual differences. These genes are perpetually shuffled to
reveal new personalities. Because men differ in this way among themselves they
cannot be satisfied with the simple tribal life of collective civilization. They demand "luxuries," freedom, special products which cannot be satisfied within the
ambit of such a primitive economy. This leads to an economic differentiation of
society which . . . is not the means of suppressing individuality but of realizing it.
Hence these individual genetic differences produce change in time and also the
realization of *characters,* of man's deviation from the social "norm." Thus the
very technique of the novel makes it interested in the way characters strive to
realize in existing society their individual differences.

Poetry expresses the freedom which inheres in man's general timeless unity
in society; it is interested in society as the sum and guardian of common instinctive tendencies; it speaks of death, love, hope, sorrow, and despair as all men
experience them. The novel is the expression of that freedom which men seek,
not in their unity in society but in their differences, of their search for freedom
in the pores of society, and therefore of their repulsions from, clashes with, and
concrete motions against *other* individuals different from themselves.

The novel was bound to develop therefore under capitalism, whose increase
in the productive forces brought about by the division of labor not only vastly
increased the differentiation of society but also, by continually revolutionizing

its own basis, produced an endless flux and change in life. Equally, as capitalism decayed, the novel was bound to voice the experience of men that economic differentiation had changed from a means of freedom to a rubber-stamp crushing individuality (the ossification of classes), and that the productive forces, by being held back from developing further, had choked the free movement of life (the general economic crisis). Necessarily therefore in such a period the decay of the novel occurs together with a general revolutionary turmoil.

Thus we see in the technical differences of poetry and the novel the difference between changelessness and change, space and time, and it is clear that these are not mutually exclusive opposites but are opposites which interpenetrate, and, as they fly apart, continually generate an enrichening reality.

This was the same kind of difference as that between the evolutionary and classificatory sciences.[3] And just as the technique of poetry demands an immediate concentration on the word, so the classificatory sciences, such as geometry and mathematics, demand an immediate concentration on the symbol. The novel demands that we pass from the symbol to reality, and only then to the affective organization; biology demands that we go first to the concrete objects, and only then to their rational organization. Poetry passes straight from the word to the affective organization, careless of the reality whose relation it accepts as already given in the word. Mathematics passes straight from the symbol to the perceptual organization, careless of the concrete object, whose important qualities (to it) are already accepted as crystallized in the symbol. Hence the vital importance of precise speech—of the absolutely correct word or correct symbol—both to poet and mathematician, contrasted with the looser speech permitted to the biologist or novelist.

We have seen that music is an extreme kind of poetry, that just as mathematics escapes almost altogether from the subjective qualities of matter, so music (unlike poetry) escapes almost altogether from the objective references of sounds. Therefore the musician is even preciser in his language than the poet, and the affective laws of music's symbols are as careful and minute as are the perceptual laws of mathematical symbols.

We can now understand more clearly why poetry resembles dream in its technique. The characteristic of dreams is that the dreamer always plays the leading part in it. He is always present in it, sometimes (as analysis shows) in

[3] Caudwell refers to this distinction in an earlier passage (pp. 184-5): "The classificatory sciences, of which mathematics is the queen and physics an important sphere, deal with space-like orderings which are independent of time. . . . The evolutionary sciences . . . are historical in their approach. They deal with reality as a process, as the emergence of new qualities. Sociology, biology, geology, psychology, astronomy, and physiology are all sciences which are interested in time. . . . The same division in the field of art gives rise to a similar distinction. In literary art the novel is evolutionary and the poem is classificatory." Music, architecture, and the static plastic arts are "classificatory" like poetry; prose drama film, and ballet are "evolutionary" like the novel. (Editor's note.)

many disguises. The same egocentricity is characteristic of poetry. Quite naïvely the poet records directly all his impressions, experiences, thoughts, images. Hence the apparent egoism of poetry, for everything is seen and experienced directly. Poetry is a relationship of memory-images mediated by only two words—"I" and "like."

But this is not the egoism of dream; it is a social egoism. The particular emotional organization of the poet is condensed into words, and the words are read, and the psyche of the reader experiences the same emotional reorganization. The reader puts himself, for the duration of the poem, in the place of the poet, and sees with his eyes. He *is* the poet.

In a poem by Shelley, we are Shelley. As we read Shakespeare, we see with his profound shimmering vision. Hence the unexpected individuality of the poet. Though it is the common human creature, the genotype, and not the "character" who looks out in poetry on the common contemporary scene, she looks at it through the eyes of one man, through the windows of the poet's psyche.

How is this done? That is the peculiar secret of poetic technique. Just as poetry can be equated with dream, poetic technique is similar to dream technique. The nature of dream technique has been explored by analysts under the general name of "the dream-work."

A dream consists of two layers. Obvious is the *manifest* content. We are walking by the seaside, a ship comes alongside, we step on it, we land in France, certain adventures befall us, and so on. This is the manifest content of the dream as we tell it at breakfast next morning to our bored family, who cannot understand our interest in it. But our interest in it was due to the fact that the illusion was perfect. While they lasted, these things really seemed to be happening to us. And this vividness must spring from some affective cause. But we felt little real emotion in the dream, however surprising the adventures that befell us. If we felt emotion, it was out of all real proportion to our adventures. Surprising things happened and we were not surprised. Trifling things happened and we were appalled. The affects were displayed in relation to reality. If we are asked to give our associations to these various component images just as they spring to our mind, a whole undergrowth of displaced affective life is revealed. Each symbol is associated with memories in our life, not by association of ideas but by affective associations.

The characteristic of "dream-work" is that every dream-symbol is over-determined and has a multitude of different emotional significances. This we also saw was the characteristic of poetic words, and springs from the same cause, that dream-symbols are valued directly for their affective content and not as symbols of a consistent mock world in which we first orientate ourselves. Hence the inconsequence of dream matches the "illogical" rhythm and assonance of poetry.

The organization of the psyche is such that in sleep all the conscious wishes, hopes, fears and love of the instinctive are replaced by apparently arbitrary memory-images, but which really are associated by the affective ties of simple unconscious wishes. They are organized by the appetitive activity of the instinctive and therefore unsleeping part of the psyche which, because it is archaic phylogenetically, is unmodified and therefore anti-social, or rather non-social. This affective substratum does not normally appear in dream. It is "repressed." Only the arbitrary symbols, apparently unconnected, appear in the consciousness. But this affective basis is the "reasoning" of the dream, and directs its course. It is the latent content. . . . Dreams, then, contain a manifest and a latent content. The manifest content is imagic phantasy, the latent content is affective reality. . . .

§ 4

. . . Poetry, like dream, contains *manifest* and *latent* contents. The manifest content can be roughly arrived at by paraphrasing the poem. It is the imagery or the "ideas." In a paraphrase the latent content, that is, the emotional content, has almost entirely vanished. It was contained, then, not in the external reality symbolized by the words (for this has been preserved) but in the words themselves. The manifest content is the poetry interpreted "rationally." It is the external reality in the poem. It can be expressed in other ways and other languages. But the latent content of poetry is in that particular form of wording, and in no other.

How is the latent content contained in the original words and not contained in the *sense* of the words—that is, in the portions of external reality which the words symbolize? The emotions are not associated affectively with the portion of external reality symbolized by the manifest content, for another language can be made to symbolize the same portion of external reality, and still it is not the poem. How then did the original words contain the emotional content "in themselves" and not in the things they symbolized? Dream analysis gives us the answer, by *affective* association of ideas. In any association of ideas two images are tied to each other by something different, like sticks by a cord. In poetry they are tied by affects.

If a word is abstracted from its surroundings and concentrated on in the same way as an analyst asked his patient to concentrate on any particular image of a dream, a number of associations will rise vaguely to the mind. In a simple word like "spring" there are hundreds of them; of greenness, of youth, of fountains, of jumping; every word drags behind it a vast bag and baggage of emotional associations, picked up in the thousands of different circumstances in which the word was used. It is these associations that provided the latent content of affect which is the poem. Not the ideas of "greenness," "youth," but the affective cord linking the ideas of "greenness" and "youth" to the word "spring," constitutes the raw material of poetry.

Of course the *thing* "spring" (the season) denoted by the word "spring" also has many affective associations. These are used by the novel. Poetry is concerned with the more general, subtle and instinctive affects which are immediately associated with the word "spring" and therefore include such almost punning associations as those connected with spring (a fountain) and spring (to jump). Hence the tendency of poetry to play with words, to pun openly or secretly, to delight in the texture of words. This is part of the technique of poetry which treats words anti-grammatically to realize their immediate and even contradictory affective tones. The novel uses words grammatically so as sharply to exclude all meanings and therefore all affective tones, except one clear piece of reality, and then derives the emotional content from this piece of reality and its active relation with the other pieces of reality in the story as part of a perceptual life-experience.

When we read a line of poetry these other ideas to which the affects are associated do not rise to the mind. We get the leaping and gushiness of "spring" in poetry's use of it as a word for the idea "season," but we do not get the fountain or the jump except in an open poetic pun. They remain unconscious. *Poetry is a kind of inverted dream.* Whereas in dream the real affects are partly suppressed and the blended images rise into the conscious, in poetry the associated images are partly suppressed and it is the blended affects that are present in the consciousness, in the form of affective organization.

Why is there a manifest content at all? Why are not all images suppressed? Why is not great poetry like the poetry of the extreme symbolists, a mere collection of words, meaning nothing, but words themselves full of affective association? Why should poetry state, explain, narrate, obey grammar, have syntax, be capable of paraphrase, since if paraphrased it loses its affective value?

The answer is, because poetry is an adaptation to external reality. It is an emotional attitude towards the world. It is made of language and language was created to signify otherness, to indicate portions of objective reality shared socially. It lives in the same language as scientific thought. The manifest content represents a statement of external reality. The manifest content is symbolic of a certain *piece* of external reality—be it scene, problem, thought, event. And the emotional content is *attached* to this statement of reality, not in actual experience but in the poem. The emotional content sweats out of the piece of external reality. In life this piece of external reality is devoid of emotional tone, but described in those particular words, and no others, it suddenly and magically shimmers with affective coloring. That affective coloring represents an emotional organization similar to that which the poet himself felt when faced (in phantasy or actuality) with that piece of external reality. When the poet says,

> Sleep, that knits up the ravelled sleave of care,

he is making a manifest statement. The paraphrase

> Slumber, that unties worry, which is like a piece of tangled knitting,

carries over most of the manifest content, but the affectives tones which lurked in the associations of the words used have vanished. It is like a conjuring trick. The poet holds up a piece of the world and we see it glowing with a strange emotional fire. If we analyze it "rationally," we find no fire. Yet none the less, for ever afterwards, that piece of reality still keeps an afterglow about it, is still fragrant with emotional life. So poetry enriches external reality for us.

The affective associations used by poetry are of many forms. Sometimes they are sound associations, and then we call the line "musical"—not that the language is specially harmonious; to a foreigner it would probably have no particular verbal melody:

> Thick as autumnal leaves that strow the brooks
> In Vallambrosa

is not musical to someone who knows no English. But to an English ear the emotive associations wakened are aroused through sound rather than sense link-ages, and hence we call the line musical. So, too, with Verlaine's line, musical only to ears attuned to the emotive associations of French nasals:

> *Et O—ces voix d'enfants chantant dans la coupole,*

or the old fairy-tale title, "La Belle aux bois dormant."

It is impossible to have affects in poetry without their adherence to symbols of external reality, for poetry's affects (insofar as they are poetic) are social, and it is impossible for different subjects to be linked except by a common object (by "matter"). The logical conclusion of symbolism is not poetry but music. And here it may be objected—music consists of sounds which refer to no external reality and yet music is an art and has a social content. Exactly—because in music the symbols have ceased to "refer" to external reality and have become portions of external reality themselves and, in doing so, have necessarily gen-erated a formal structure (the scale, "rules" of harmony, etc.) which gives them the rigidity and social status of external reality. The notes of music themselves are the manifest content of music, and they therefore obey not grammatical (subjective) but pseudo-mathematical (objective) laws: of course they are neces-sarily distorted or organized within the compass of those rules. In the same way architecture becomes external reality and is distorted or organized within the compass of the rules of use-function.

The technique of the poet consists in this, that not all the affects associated with any particular words rise up into the consciousness, but only those that are required. This is done by the arrangement of the words in such a way that their clusters of associations, impinging on each other heighten some affective associa-tions and inhibit the others, and so form an organized mass of emotion. The affective coloring of one word takes reflected shadow and light from the colors of the other words. It does this partly through their contiguity, particularly in synthetic languages (Latin and Greek), and partly through their grammatical connection, particularly in analytic languages (English, Chinese); but chiefly through the "meaning" as a whole. The manifest content, the literal meaning, the paraphrasable sense, is a kind of bridge, or electrical conductor, which puts all the affective currents of each word into contact. It is like a switchboard; some of the affective associations fade away directly they enter it, others run down into other words and alter their color; others blend together and heighten a particular word. The whole forms the specific fused glow which is that poem's affective organization or emotional attitude to its meaning. Hence the same word has a different affective coloration in one poem from what it has in another, and it is for this reason that a poem is concrete. It is affectively concrete; each word has a special affective significance in that poem different from what it has in another. In this way the emotional content does not float about fluidly in the mind; it is firmly attached, by a hundred interweaving strands, to the manifest content—a piece of external reality. A poem's content is not just emotion, it is *organized* emotion, an organized emotional attitude to a piece of external reality. Hence its value—and difficulty—as compared with other emotions, however strong, but un-organized—a sudden inexplicable fit of sorrow, a gust of blind rage, a blank despair. Such emotions are unesthetic because unorganized. They are unor-ganized socially because they are not organized in relation to a socially accepted external reality. They are unconscious of outer necessity. The emotions of poetry are *part* of the manifest content. They seem to be in the external reality as it appears in the poem. We do not appear to take up an emotional attitude to a piece of reality; it is there, given in the reality: that is the way of emotional cognition. In poetic cognition, objects are presented already stamped with feeling-judg-ments. Hence the adaptive value of poetry. It is like a real emotional experience.

It is plain that poetry may be judged in different ways; either by the im-portance of the manifest content, or by the vividness of the affective coloring. To a poet who brings a new portion of external reality into the ambit of poetry, we feel more gratitude than to one who brings the old stale manifest contents. But the first poet may be poor in the affective coloring with which he soaks his piece of reality. It may be the old stale coloring, whereas our other poet, in spite of his conventional piece of reality, may achieve a new affective tone. Old poets we shall judge almost entirely by their affective tone; their manifest contents have long belonged to our world of thought. Hence the apparent triteness of old poetry which yet is a *great* triteness. From new poets we demand new manifest contents and new affective coloring, for it is their function to give us new emo-tional attitudes to a new social environment. A poet who provides both to a high degree will be a good poet. A poet who brings into his net a vast amount of new reality to which he attaches a wide-ranging affective coloring we shall call a *great* poet, giving Shakespeare as an instance. Hence great poems are always long poems, just because of the quantity of reality they must include as manifest content. But the manifest content, whatever it is, is not the *purpose* of the poem. The purpose is the specific emotional organization directed towards the manifest content and provided by the released affects. The affects are not "latent," as in dream; it is the associated ideas which are suppressed to form the latent content. Just as the key to dream is a series of instinctive attitudes which provide the mechanism of dream-work, so the key to poetry is a cluster of suppressed pieces of external reality—a vague unconscious world of life-experience.

Poetry colors the world of reality with affective tones. These affective colors are not "pretty-pretty," for it is still the real world of necessity, and great poetry will not disguise the nakedness of outer necessity, only cause it to shine with the glow of interest. Poetry soaks external reality—nature and society—with emotional significance. This significance, because it gives the organism an appetitive interest in external reality, enables the organism to deal with it more resolutely, whether in the world of reality or of phantasy. The primitive who would lose interest in the exhausting labor necessary to plow an arid abstract collection of soil, will find heart when the earth is charged with the affective coloring of "Mother Nature," for now, by the magic of poetry, it glows with the appetitive tints of sexuality or filial love. These affective colors are not unreal because they are not scientific, for they are the coloring of the genotype's own instincts, and these instincts are as real as the earth is real. The significant expression projected by poetry on to the face of external reality is simply this, a prophecy of the endless attempt of the genotype to mold necessity to its own likeness, in which it obtains a continually increasing success. "Matter, surrounded by a sensuous poetic glamour, seems to attract man's whole entity by winning smiles." So said Marx and Engels of materialism before it became one-sided mechanical materialism, when it was still bathed in the artistic splendor of the Renaissance. That sensuous glamour is given by poetry; and materialism became one-sided when, afraid of feeling the self, it became aridly scientific, and matter vanishes in a logical but empty wave-system. Poetry restores life and value to matter. and puts back the genotype into the world from which it was banished. . . .

§ 5

If we are asked the purpose of art, we can make an answer—the precise nature of it depending on what we mean by *purpose*. Art has "survived"; cultures containing art have outlived and replaced those that have not, because art adapts the psyche to the environment, and is therefore one of the conditions of the development of society. But we get another answer if we ask *how* art performs its task, for it does this by taking a piece of environment and distorting it, giving it a non-likeness to external reality which is also a likeness to the genotype. It remolds external reality nearer to the likeness of the genotype's instincts, but since the instinctive genotype is nothing but an unconscious and dynamic desire it remolds external reality nearer to the heart's desire. Art becomes more socially and biologically valuable and greater art the more that remolding is comprehensive and true to the nature of reality, using as its material the sadness, the catastrophes, the blind necessities, as well as the delights and pleasures of life. An organism which thinks life is all "for the best in the best possible of worlds" will have little survival value. Great art can thus be great tragedy, for here, reality at its bitterest—death, despair, eternal failure—is yet given an organization, a shape, an affective arrangement which expresses a deeper and more social view of fate. By giving external reality an affective organization drawn from its heart, the genotype makes all reality, even death, more interesting because more true. The world glows with interest; our hearts go out to it with appetite to encounter it, to live in it, to get to grips with it. A great novel is how we should like our own lives to be, not petty or dull, but full of great issues, turning even death to a noble sound:

> Notre vie est noble et tragique
> Comme le masque d'un tyran
> Nul drame hazardeux et magique
> Aucun détail indifférent
> Ne rend notre amour pathetique.[4]

A great picture is how we should like the world to look to us—brighter, full of affective color. Great music is how we should like our emotions to run on, full of strenuous purpose and deep aims. And because, for a moment, we saw how it might be, were given the remade object into our hands, forever after we tend to make our lives less petty, tend to look around us with a more-seeing eye, tend to feel richly and strenuously.

If we ask why art, by making the environment wear the expression of the genotype, comes to us with the nearness and significance it does, we must say still more about art's essence. In making external reality glow with our expression, art tells us about ourselves. No man can look directly at himself, but art makes of the Universe a mirror in which we catch glimpses of ourselves, not as we are, but as we are in active potentiality of becoming in relation to reality through society. The genotype we see is the genotype stamped with all the possibilities and grandeur of mankind—an elaboration which in its turn is extracted by society from the rest of reality. Art gives us so many glimpses of the inner heart of life; and that is its significance, different from and yet arising out of its purpose. It is like a magic lantern which projects our real selves on the Universe and promises us that we, as we desire, can alter the Universe, alter it to the measure of our needs. But to do so, we must know more deeply our real needs, must make ourselves yet more conscious of ourselves. The more we grip external reality, the more our art develops and grows increasingly subtle, the more the magic lantern show takes on new subtleties and fresh richnesses. Art tells us

[4] Apollinaire.

what science cannot tell us, and what religion only feigns to tell us—what we are and why we are, why we hope and suffer and love and die. It does not tell us this in the language of science, as theology and dogma attempt to do, but in the only language that can express these truths, the language of inner reality itself, the language of affect and emotion. And its message is generated by our attempt to realize its essence in an active struggle with Nature, the struggle called life.

—*Illusion and Reality* (1937)

CHAPTER SIX

Art as Vivid Experience

JOHN DEWEY
Having an Experience

ALFRED NORTH WHITEHEAD
The Habit of Art

Introductory Note

SIDING WITH WRITERS SUCH AS Nietzsche and Caudwell in opposing an isolationist interpretation of art, the great American pragmatist, John Dewey (1859-1952), reacts strongly against the idea that esthetic and practical activity are quite separate. Instead of emphasizing the difference between art and nature or between art and actual experience, he maintains that the function of art is to organize experience more meaningfully, more coherently, more vividly, than ordinary life permits. Art is experience in its most articulate and adequate form: "the union of sense, mood, impulse, and action characteristic of the live creature." It is not differentiated by the predominance of any one mental faculty, such as emotion or imagination, but by a greater inclusiveness of psychological factors. It has no highly restricted subject matter: anything vividly and imaginatively realized, indeed, may be the source of "an experience that is *an* experience"—the kind of experience that is art.

Underlying this doctrine of the oneness of art and life is the conviction that means and ends should not be sharply separated. Experience is most satisfactory when means and ends interpenetrate, and art is experience when it reaches this peak. For art is not a mere anodyne, an escape, an isolated pastime, nor is it a grim discipline undertaken simply for the sake of its consequences. It is full of enjoyed meanings and yet it is instrumental to new satisfying events. The frequent tendency to separate means and ends leads to some of the worst evils of our civilization. As Irwin Edman, a follower of Dewey, has said, "It produces, on the one hand, a practical civilization in which there is no interest in sensuous charm or imaginative grace, the Land of Smoke-Over celebrated in the legends of L. P. Jacks. It produces, on the other hand, the soft luxuriance of the esthete whose dainty creations and enjoyments have no connection with the rest of life." [1] Against such dualism Dewey's philosophy has been a powerful protest.

The effort to re-integrate art and life finds another contemporary spokesman in Alfred North Whitehead (1861-1947). When his *Science and the Modern World* was published, John Dewey greeted the book with the exclamation, "There is news in the realm of the mind. The intellectual climate, the mentality, which has prevailed for three centuries is changing." [2] As a leader in this fundamental intellectual reorientation, Whitehead maintains that reality is organic in structure, and interprets the laws of the mechanical sciences as expressing certain abstract relations between organisms—not as summing up mechanistically the whole content and limits of nature. He endeavors to bridge the chasm between external nature and concrete experience, and interprets the values of the latter as not irrelevant to the former. He thinks the opposite tendency of science, to emphasize *things* to the exclusion of *values,* has often played a mischievous role. For example, the abstractions of economics have "been disastrous in their influence on modern mentality." The remedy is partly to cultivate the esthetic capacity to perceive vivid values, and to foster the initiative toward the practice and appreciation of art, broadly interpreted. "The habit of art," he declares, "is the habit of enjoying vivid values."

JOHN DEWEY

Having an Experience

Experience occurs continuously, because the interaction of live creature and environing conditions is involved in the very process of living. Under conditions of resistance and conflict, aspects and elements of the self and the world

[1] Irwin Edman, *The World, the Arts, and the Artist* (Norton, New York, 1928), pp. 34-35.
[2] *The New Republic*, February 17, 1926, p. 360.

that are implicated in this interaction qualify experience with emotions and ideas so that conscious intent emerges. Oftentimes, however, the experience had is inchoate. Things are experienced but not in such a way that they are composed into *an* experience. There is distraction and dispersion; what we observe and what we think, what we desire and what we get, are at odds with each other. We put our hands to the plow and turn back; we start and then we stop, not because the experience has reached the end for the sake of which it was initiated but because of extraneous interruptions or of inner lethargy.

In contrast with such experience, we have *an* experience when the material experienced runs its course to fulfillment. Then and then only is it integrated within and demarcated in the general stream of experience from other experiences. A piece of work is finished in a way that is satisfactory; a problem receives its solution; a game is played through; a situation, whether that of eating a meal, playing a game of chess, carrying on a conversation, writing a book, or taking part in a political campaign, is so rounded out that its close is a consummation and not a cessation. Such an experience is a whole and carries with it its own individualizing quality and self-sufficiency. It is *an* experience.

Philosophers, even empirical philosophers, have spoken for the most part of experience at large. Idiomatic speech, however, refers to experiences each of which is singular, having its own beginning and end. For life is no uniform uninterrupted march or flow. It is a thing of histories, each with its own plot, its own inception and movement toward its close, each having its own particular rhythmic movement; each with its own unrepeated quality pervading it throughout. A flight of stairs, mechanical as it is, proceeds by individualized steps, not by undifferentiated progression, and an inclined plane is at least marked off from other things by abrupt discreteness.

Experience in this vital sense is defined by those situations and episodes that we spontaneously refer to as being "real experiences"; those things of which we say in recalling them, "that *was* an experience." It may have been something of tremendous importance—a quarrel with one who was once an intimate, a catastrophe finally averted by a hair's breadth. Or it may have been something that in comparison was slight—and which perhaps because of its very slightness illustrates all the better what it is to be an experience. There is that meal in a Paris restaurant of which one says "that *was* an experience." It stands out as an enduring memorial of what food may be. Then there is that storm one went through in crossing the Atlantic—the storm that seemed in its fury, as it was experienced, to sum up in itself all that a storm can be, complete in itself, standing out because marked out from what went before and what came after.

In such experiences, every successive part flows freely, without seam and without unfilled blanks, into what ensues. At the same time there is no sacrifice of the self-identity of the parts. A river, as distinct from a pond, flows. But its flow gives a definiteness and interest to its successive portions greater than exist in the homogenous portions of a pond. In an experience, flow is from something to something. As one part leads into another and as one part carries on what went before, each gains distinctness in itself. The enduring whole is diversified by successive phases that are emphases of its varied colors.

Because of continuous merging, there are no holes, mechanical junctions, and dead centers when we have *an* experience. There are pauses, places of rest, but they punctuate and define the quality of movement. They sum up what has been undergone and prevent its dissipation and idle evaporation. Continued acceleration is breathless and prevents parts from gaining distinction. In a work of art, different acts, episodes, occurrences melt and fuse into unity, and yet do not disappear and lose their own character as they do so—just as in a genial conversation there is a continuous interchange and blending, and yet each speaker not only retains his own character but manifests it more clearly than is his wont.

An experience has a unity that gives it its name, that meal, that storm, that rupture of friendship. The existence of this unity is constituted by a single *quality* that pervades the entire experience in spite of the variation of its constituent parts. This unity is neither emotional, practical, nor intellectual, for these terms name distinctions that reflection can make within it. In discourse *about* an experience, we must make use of these adjectives of interpretation. In going over an experience in mind *after* its occurrence, we may find that one property rather than another was sufficiently dominant so that it characterizes the experience as a whole. There are absorbing inquiries and speculations which a scientific man and philosopher will recall as "experiences" in the emphatic sense. In final import they are intellectual. But in their actual occurrence they were emotional as well; they were purposive and volitional. Yet the experience was not a sum of these different characters; they were lost in it as distinctive traits. No thinker can ply his occupation save as he is lured and rewarded by total integral experiences that are intrinsically worthwhile. Without them he would never know what it is really to think and would be completely at a loss in distinguishing real thought from the spurious article. Thinking goes on in trains of ideas, but the ideas form a train only because they are much more than what an analytic psychology calls ideas. They are phases, emotionally and practically distinguished, of a developing underlying quality; they are its moving variations, not separate and independent like Locke's and Hume's so-called ideas and impressions, but are subtle shadings of a pervading and developing hue.

We say of an experience of thinking that we reach or draw a conclusion. Theoretical formulation of the process is often made in such terms as to conceal effectually the similarity of "conclusion" to the consummating phase of every developing integral experience. These formulations apparently take their cue from the separate propositions that are premises and the proposition that is the conclusion as they appear on the printed page. The impression is derived that there are first two independent and ready-made entities that are then manipulated so as to give rise to a third. In fact, in an experience of thinking, premises emerge only as a conclusion becomes manifest. The experience, like that of watching a storm reach its height and gradually subside, is one of continuous movement of subject-matters. Like the ocean in the storm, there are a series of waves; suggestions reaching out and being broken in a clash, or being carried onwards by a cooperative wave. If a conclusion is reached, it is that of a movement of anticipation and cumulation, one that finally comes to completion. A "conclusion" is no separate and independent thing; it is the consummation of a movement.

Hence *an* experience of thinking has its own esthetic quality. It differs from those experiences that are acknowledged to be esthetic, but only in its materials. The material of the fine arts consists of qualities; that of experience having intellectual conclusion are signs or symbols having no intrinsic quality of their own, but standing for things that may in another experience be qualitatively experienced. The difference is enormous. It is one reason why the strictly intellectual art will never be popular as music is popular. Nevertheless, the experience itself has a satisfying emotional quality because it possesses internal integration and fulfillment reached through ordered and organized movement. This artistic structure may be immediately felt. Insofar, it is esthetic. What is even more important is that not only is this quality a significant motive in undertaking intellectual inquiry and in keeping it honest, but that no intellectual activity is an integral event (is *an* experience), unless it is rounded out with this quality. Without it, thinking is inconclusive. In short, esthetic cannot be sharply marked off from intellectual experience since the latter must bear an esthetic stamp to be itself complete.

The same statement holds good of a course of action that is dominantly practical, that is, one that consists of overt doings. It is possible to be efficient in action and yet not have a conscious experience. The activity is too automatic to permit of a sense of what it is about and where it is going. It comes to an end but not to a close or consummation in consciousness. Obstacles are overcome by shrewd skill, but they do not feed experience. There are also those who are wavering in action, uncertain, and inconclusive like the shades in classic literature. Between the poles of aimlessness and mechanical efficiency, there lie those courses of action in which through successive deeds there runs a sense of growing meaning conserved and accumulating toward an end that is felt as accomplishment of a process. Successful politicians and generals who turn statesmen like Caesar and Napoleon have something of the showman about them. This of itself is not art, but it is, I think, a sign that interest is not exclusively, perhaps not mainly, held by the result taken by itself (as it is in the case of mere efficiency), but by it as the outcome of a process. There is interest in completing an experience. The experience may be one that is harmful to the world and its consummation undesirable. But it has esthetic quality.

The Greek identification of good conduct with conduct having proportion, grace, and harmony, the *kalon-agathon,* is a more obvious example of distinctive esthetic quality in moral action. One great defect in what passes as morality is its anesthetic quality. Instead of exemplifying wholehearted action, it takes the form of grudging piecemeal concessions to the demands of duty. But illustrations may only obscure the fact that any practical activity will, provided that it is integrated and moves by its own urge to fulfillment, have esthetic quality.

A generalized illustration may be had if we imagine a stone, which is rolling downhill, to have an experience. The activity is surely sufficiently "practical." The stone starts from somewhere, and moves, as consistently as conditions permit, toward a place and state where it will be at rest—toward an end. Let us add, by imagination, to these external facts, the ideas that it looks forward with desire to the final outcome; that it is interested in the things it meets on its way, conditions that accelerate and retard its movement with respect to their bearing on the end; that it acts and feels toward them according to the hindering or helping funcion it attributes to them; and that the final coming to rest is related to all that went before as the culmination of a continuous movement. Then the stone would have an experience, and one with esthetic quality.

If we turn from this imaginary case to our own experience we shall find much of it is nearer to what happens to the actual stone than it is to anything that fulfills the conditions fancy just laid down. For in much of our experience we are not concerned with the connection of one incident with what went before and what comes after. There is no interest that controls attentive rejection or selection of what shall be organized into the developing experience. Things happen, but they are neither definitely included nor decisively excluded; we drift. We yield according to external pressure, or evade and compromise. There are beginnings and cessations, but no genuine initiations and concludings. One thing replaces another, but does not absorb it and carry it on. There is experience, but so slack and discursive that it is not *an* experience. Needless to say, such experiences are anesthetic.

Thus the non-esthetic lies within two limits. At one pole is the loose succession that does not begin at any particular place and that ends—in the sense of ceasing—at no particular place. At the other pole is arrest, constriction, proceeding from parts having only a mechanical connection with one another. There exists so much of one and the other of these two kinds of experience that unconsciously they come to be taken as norms of all experience. Then, when the esthetic appears, it so sharply contrasts with the picture that has been formed of experience, that it is impossible to combine its special qualities with the features of the picture and the esthetic is given an outside place and status. The account that has been given of experience dominantly intellectual and practical is intended to show that there is no such contrast involved in having an experience; that, on the contrary, no experience of whatever sort is a unity unless it has esthetic quality.

The enemies of the esthetic are neither the practical nor the intellectual. They are the humdrum; slackness of loose ends; submission to convention in practice and intellectual procedure. Rigid abstinence, coerced submission, tightness on one side and dissipation, incoherence and aimless indulgence on the other, are deviations in opposite directions from the unity of an experience. Some such considerations perhaps induced Aristotle to invoke the "mean proportional" as the proper designation of what is distinctive of both virtue and the esthetic. He was formally correct. "Mean" and "proportion" are, however, not self-explanatory, nor to be taken over in a prior mathematical sense, but are properties belonging to an experience that has a developing movement toward its own consummation.

I have emphasized the fact that every integral experience moves toward a close, an ending, since it ceases only when the energies active in it have done their proper work. This closure of a circuit of energy is the opposite of arrest, of *stasis*. Maturation and fixation are polar opposites. Struggle and conflict may be themselves enjoyed, although they are painful, when they are experienced as means of developing an experience; members in that they carry it forward, not just because they are there. There is, as will appear later, an element of undergoing, of suffering in its large sense, in every experience. Otherwise there would be no taking in of what preceded. For "taking in" in any vital experience is something more than placing something on the top of consciousness over what was previously known. It involves reconstruction which may be painful. Whether the necessary undergoing phase is by itself pleasurable or painful is a matter of particular conditions. It is indifferent to the total esthetic quality, save that there are few intense esthetic experiences that are wholly gleeful. They are certainly not to be characterized as amusing, and as they bear down upon us they involve a suffering that is none the less consistent with, indeed a part of, the complete perception that is enjoyed.

I have spoken of the esthetic quality that rounds out an experience into completeness and unity as emotional. The reference may cause difficulty. We are given to thinking of emotions as things as simple and compact as are the words by which we name them. Joy, sorrow, hope, fear, anger, curiosity, are treated as if each in itself were a sort of entity that enters full-made upon the scene, an entity that may last a long time or a short time, but whose duration, whose growth and career, is irrelevant to its nature. In fact emotions are qualities, when they are significant, of a complex experience that moves and changes. I say, when they are *significant*, for otherwise they are but the outbreaks and eruptions of a disturbed infant. All emotions are qualifications of a drama and they change as the drama develops. Persons are sometimes said to fall in love at first sight. But what they fall into is not a thing of that instant. What would love be were it compressed into a moment in which there is no room for cherishing and for solicitude? The intimate nature of emotion is manifested in the experience of one watching a play on the stage or reading a novel. It attends the development of a plot; and a plot requires a stage, a space, wherein to develop and time in which to unfold. Experience is emotional but there are no separate things called emotions in it.

By the same token, emotions are attached to events and objects in their movement. They are not, save in pathological instances, private. And even an "objectless" emotion demands something beyond itself to which to attach itself, and thus it soon generates a delusion in lack of something real. Emotion belongs of a certainty to the self. But it belongs to the self that is concerned in the movement of events toward an issue that is desired or disliked. We jump instantaneously when we are scared, as we blush on the instant when we are ashamed. But fright and shamed modesty are not in this case emotional states. Of themselves they are but automatic reflexes. In order to become emotional they must become parts of an inclusive and enduring situation that involves concern for objects and their issues. The jump of fright becomes emotional fear when there is found or thought to exist a threatening object that must be dealt with or escaped from. The blush becomes the emotion of shame when a person connects, in thought, an action he has performed with an unfavorable reaction to himself of some other person.

Physical things from far ends of the earth are physically transported and physically caused to act and react upon one another in the construction of a new object. The miracle of mind is that something similar takes place in experience without physical transport and assembling. Emotion is the moving and cementing force. It selects what is congruous and dyes what is selected with its color, thereby giving qualitative unity to materials externally disparate and dissimilar. It thus provides unity in and through the varied parts of an experience. When the unity is of the sort already described, the experience has esthetic character even though it is not, dominantly, an esthetic experience.

Two men meet; one is the applicant for a position, while the other has the disposition of the matter in his hands. The interview may be mechanical, consisting of set questions, the replies to which perfunctorily settle the matter. There is no experience in which the two men meet, nothing that is not a repetition, by way of acceptance or dismissal, of something which has happened a score of times. The situation is disposed of as if it were an exercise in bookkeeping. But an interplay may take place in which a new experience develops. Where should we look for an account of such an experience? Not to ledger-entries nor yet to a treatise on economics or sociology or personnel-psychology, but to drama or fiction. Its nature and import can be expressed only by art, because there is a unity of experience that can be expressed only as an experience. The *experience* is of material fraught with suspense and moving toward its own consummation through a connected series of varied incidents. The primary emotions on the part of the applicant may be at the beginning hope or despair, and elation or disappointment at the close. These emotions qualify the experience as a unity. But as the interview proceeds, secondary emotions are evolved as variations of the primary underlying one. It is even possible for each attitude and gesture, each sentence, almost every word, to produce more than a fluctuation in the intensity of the basic emotion; to produce, that is, a change of shade and tint in its quality. The employer sees by means of his own emotional reactions the character of the one applying. He projects him imaginatively into the work to be done and judges his fitness by the way in which the elements of the scene assemble and either clash or fit together. The presence and behavior of the applicant either harmonize with his own attitudes and desires or they conflict and jar. Such factors as these, inherently esthetic in quality, are the forces that carry the varied elements of the interview to a decisive issue. They enter into the settlement of every situation, whatever its dominant nature, in which there are uncertainty and suspense.

There are, therefore, common patterns in various experiences, no matter how unlike they are to one another in the details of their subject matter. There are conditions to be met without which an experience cannot come to be. The outline of the common pattern is set by the fact that every experience is the result of interaction between a live creature and some aspect of the world in which he lives. A man does something; he lifts, let us say, a stone. In consequence he undergoes, suffers, something: the weight, strain, texture of the surface of the thing lifted. The properties thus undergone determine further doing. The stone is too heavy or too angular, not solid enough; or else the properties undergone show it is fit for the use for which it is intended. The process continues until a mutual adaptation of the self and the object emerges and that particular experience comes to a close. What is true of this simple instance is true, as to form, of every experience. The creature operating may be a thinker in his study and the environment with which he interacts may consist of ideas instead of a stone. But interaction of the two constitutes the total experience that is had, and the close which completes it is the institution of a felt harmony.

An experience has pattern and structure, because it is not just doing and undergoing in alternation, but consists of them in relationship. To put one's hand in the fire that consumes it is not necessarily to have an experience. The action and its consequence must be joined in perception. This relationship is what gives meaning; to grasp it is the objective of all intelligence. The scope and content of the relations measure the significant content of an experience. A child's experience may be intense, but, because of lack of background from past experience, relations between undergoing and doing are slightly grasped, and the experience does not have great depth or breadth. No one ever arrives at such maturity that he perceives all the connections that are involved. There was once written (by Mr. Hinton) a romance called "The Unlearner." It portrayed the whole endless duration of life after death as a living over the incidents that happened in a short life on earth, in continued discovery of the relationships involved among them.

Experience is limited by all the causes which interfere with perception of the relations between undergoing and doing. There may be interference because of excess on the side of doing or of excess on the side of receptivity, of undergoing. Unbalance on either side blurs the perception of relations and leaves the experience partial and distorted, with scant or false meaning. Zeal for doing, lust for action, leaves many a person, especially in this hurried and impatient human environment in which we live, with experience of an almost incredible paucity, all on the surface. No one experience has a chance to complete itself because something else is entered upon so speedily. What is called experience becomes so dispersed and miscellaneous as hardly to deserve the name. Resistance is treated as an obstruction to be beaten down, not as an invitation to reflection. An individual comes to seek, unconsciously even more than by deliberate choice, situations in which he can do the most things in the shortest time.

Experiences are also cut short from maturing by excess of receptivity. What is prized is then the mere undergoing of this and that, irrespective of perception of any meaning. The crowding together of as many impressions as possible is thought to be "life," even though no one of them is more than a flitting and a sipping. The sentimentalist and the daydreamer may have more fancies and impressions pass through their consciousness than has the man who is animated by lust for action. But his experience is equally distorted, because nothing takes root in mind when there is no balance between doing and receiving. Some decisive action is needed in order to establish contact with the realities of the world and in order that impressions may be so related to facts that their value is tested and organized.

Because perception of relationship between what is done and what is undergone constitutes the work of intelligence, and because the artist is controlled in the process of his work by his grasp of the connection between what he has already done and what he is to do next, the idea that the artist does not think as intently and penetratingly as a scientific inquirer is absurd. A painter must consciously undergo the effect of his every brush stroke or he will not be aware of what he is doing and where his work is going. Moreover, he has to see each particular connection of doing and undergoing in relation to the whole that he desires to produce. To apprehend such relations is to think, and is one of the most exacting modes of thought. The difference between the pictures of different painters is due quite as much to differences of capacity to carry on this thought as it is to differences of sensitivity to bare color and to differences in dexterity of execution. As respects the basic quality of pictures, difference depends, indeed, more upon the quality of intelligence brought to bear upon perception of relations than upon anything else—though of course intelligence cannot be separated from direct sensitivity and is connected, though in a more external manner, with skill.

Any idea that ignores the necessary role of intelligence in production of works of art is based upon identification of thinking with use of one special kind of material, verbal signs and words. To think effectively in terms of relations of qualities is as severe a demand upon thought as to think in terms of symbols, verbal and mathematical. Indeed, since words are easily manipulated in mechanical ways, the production of a work of genuine art probably demands more intelligence than does most of the so-called thinking that goes on among those who pride themselves on being "intellectuals."

I have tried to show . . . that the esthetic is no intruder in experience from without, whether by way of idle luxury or transcendent ideality, but that it is the clarified and intensified development of traits that belong to every normally complete experience. This fact I take to be the only secure basis upon which esthetic theory can build. It remains to suggest some of the implications of the underlying fact.

We have no word in the English language that unambiguously includes what is signified by the two words "artistic" and "esthetic." Since "artistic" refers primarily to the act of production and "esthetic" to that of perception and enjoyment, the absence of a term designating the two processes taken together is unfortunate. Sometimes, the effect is to separate the two from each other, to regard art as something superimposed upon esthetic material, or, upon the other side, to an assumption that, since art is a process of creation, perception and enjoyment of it have nothing in common with the creative act. In any case, there is a certain verbal awkwardness in that we are compelled sometimes to use the term "esthetic" to cover the entire field and sometimes to limit it to the receiving perceptual aspect of the whole operation. I refer to these obvious facts as preliminary to an attempt to show how the conception of conscious experience as a perceived relation between doing and undergoing enables us to understand the connection that art as production and perception and appreciation as enjoyment sustain to each other.

Art denotes a process of doing or making. This is as true of fine as of technological art. Art involves molding of clay, chipping of marble, casting of bronze, laying on of pigments, construction of buildings, singing of songs, playing of instruments, enacting roles on the stage, going through rhythmic movements in the dance. Every art does something with some physical material, the body or something outside the body, with or without the use of intervening tools, and with a view to production of something visible, audible, or tangible. So marked is the active or "doing" phase of art, that the dictionaries usually define it in terms of skilled action, ability in execution. The Oxford Dictionary illustrates by a quotation from John Stuart Mill: "Art is an endeavor after perfection in execution" while Matthew Arnold calls it "pure and flawless workmanship."

The word "esthetic" refers, as we have already noted, to experience as appreciative, perceiving, and enjoying. It denotes the consumer's rather than the producer's standpoint. It is Gusto, taste; and, as with cooking, overt skillful action is on the side of the cook who prepares, while taste is on the side of the consumer, as in gardening there is a distinction between the gardener who plants and tills and the householder who enjoys the finished product.

These very illustrations, however, as well as the relation that exists in having an experience between doing and undergoing, indicate that the distinction between esthetic and artistic cannot be pressed so far as to become a separation. Perfection in execution cannot be measured or defined in terms of execution; it implies those who perceive and enjoy the product that is executed. The cook prepares food for the consumer and the measure of the value of what is prepared is found in consumption. Mere perfection in execution, judged in its own terms in isolation, can probably be attained better by a machine than by human art. By itself, it is at most technique, and there are great artists who are not in the first ranks as technicians (witness Cézanne), just as there are great performers on the piano who are not great esthetically, and as Sargent is not a great painter.

Craftsmanship to be artistic in the final sense must be "loving"; it must care deeply for the subject matter upon which skill is exercised. A sculptor comes to mind whose busts are marvelously exact. It might be difficult to tell in the presence of a photograph of one of them and of a photograph of the original which was of the person himself. For virtuosity they are remarkable. But one doubts whether the maker of the busts had an experience of his own that he was concerned to have those share who look at his products. To be truly artistic, a work must also be esthetic—that is, framed for enjoyed receptive perception. Constant observation is, of course, necessary for the maker while he is producing. But if his perception is not also esthetic in nature, it is a colorless and cold recognition of what has been done, used as a stimulus to the next step in a process that is essentially mechanical.

In short, art, in its form, unites the very same relation of doing and undergoing, outgoing and incoming energy, that makes an experience to be an experience. Because of elimination of all that does not contribute to mutual organization of the factors of both action and reception into one another, and because of selection of just the aspects and traits that contribute to their interpenetration of each other, the product is a work of esthetic art. Man whittles, carves, sings, dances, gestures, molds, draws and paints. The doing or making is artistic when the perceived results is of such a nature that *its* qualities *as perceived* have con-trolled the question of production. The act of producing that is directed by in-tent to produce something that is enjoyed in the immediate experience of perceiving has qualities that a spontaneous or uncontrolled activity does not have. The artist embodies in himself the attitude of the perceiver while he works.

Suppose, for the sake of illustration, that a finely wrought object, one whose texture and proportions are highly pleasing in perception, has been be-lieved to be a product of some primitive people. Then there is discovered evi-dence that proves it to be an accidental natural product. As an external thing, it is now precisely what it was before. Yet at once it ceases to be a work of art and becomes a natural "curiosity." It now belongs in a museum of natural his-tory, not in a museum of art. And the extraordinary thing is that the difference that is thus made is not one of just intellectual classification. A difference is made in appreciative perception and in a direct way. The esthetic experience—in its limited sense—is thus seen to be inherently connected with the experience of making.

The sensory satisfaction of eye and ear, when esthetic, is so because it does not stand by itself but is linked to the activity of which it is the consequence. Even the pleasures of the palate are different in quality to an epicure than in one who merely "likes" his food as he eats it. The difference is not of mere in-tensity. The epicure is conscious of much more than the taste of the food. Rather, there enter into the taste, as directly experienced, qualities that depend upon reference to its source and its manner of production in connection with criteria of excellence. As production must absorb into itself qualities of the product as perceived and be regulated by them, so, on the other side, seeing, hearing, tasting, become esthetic when relation to a distinct manner of activity qualifies what is perceived.

There is an element of passion in all esthetic perception. Yet when we are overwhelmed by passion, as in extreme rage, fear, jealousy, the experience is definitely non-esthetic. There is no relationship felt to the qualities of the activity that has generated the passion. Consequently, the material of the ex-perience lacks elements of balance and proportion. For these can be present only when, as in the conduct that has grace or dignity, the act is controlled by an exquisite sense of the relations which the act sustains—its fitness to the occasion and to the situation.

The process of art in production is related to the esthetic in perception organically—as the Lord God in creation surveyed his work and found it good. Until the artist is satisfied in perception with what he is doing, he continues shaping and reshaping. The making comes to an end when its result is experi-enced as good—and that experience comes not by mere intellectual and outside judgment but in direct perception. An artist, in comparison with his fellows, is one who is not only especially gifted in powers of execution but in unusual sensitivity to the qualities of things. This sensitivity also directs his doings and makings.

As we manipulate, we touch and feel, as we look, we see; as we listen, we hear. The hand moves with etching needle or with brush. The eye attends and reports the consequence of what is done. Because of this intimate connection, subsequent doing is cumulative and not a matter of caprice nor yet of routine. In an emphatic artistic-esthetic experience, the relation is so close that it controls simultaneously both the doing and the perception. Such vital intimacy of connection cannot be had if only hand and eye are engaged. When they do not, both of them, act as organs of the whole being, there is but a mechanical sequence of sense and movement, as in walking that is automatic. Hand and eye, when the experience is esthetic, are but instruments through which the entire live creature, moved and active throughout, operates. Hence the expression is emotional and guided by purpose.

Because of the relation between what is done and what is undergone, there is an immediate sense of things in perception as belonging together or as jarring; as reinforcing or as interfering. The consequences of the act of making as reported in sense show whether what is done carries forward the idea being executed or marks a deviation and break. In as far as the development of an experience is *controlled* through reference to these immediately felt relations of order and fulfillment, that experience becomes dominantly esthetic in nature. The urge to action becomes an urge to that kind of action which will result in an object satisfying in direct perception. The potter shapes his clay to make a bowl useful for holding grain; but he makes it in a way so regulated by the series of perceptions that sum up the serial acts of making, that the bowl is marked by enduring grace and charm. The general situation remains the same in painting a picture or molding a bust. Moreover, at each stage there is anticipation of what is to come. This anticipation is the connecting link between the next doing and its outcome for sense. What is done and what is undergone are thus reciprocally, cumulatively, and continuously instrumental to each other.

The doing may be energetic, and the undergoing may be acute and intense. But unless they are related to each other to form a whole in perception, the thing done is not fully esthetic. The making, for example, may be a display of technical virtuosity, and the undergoing a gush of sentiment or a revery. If the artist does not perfect a new vision in his process of doing, he acts mechanically and repeats some old model fixed like a blueprint in his mind. An incredible amount of observation and of the kind of intelligence that is exercised in perception of qualitative relations characterizes creative work in art. The relations must be noted not only with respect to one another, two by two, but in connection with the whole under construction; they are exercised in imagination as well as in observation. Irrelevancies arise that are tempting distractions; digressions suggest themselves in the guise of enrichments. There are occasions when the grasp of the dominant idea grows faint, and then the artist is moved uncon-sciously to fill in until his thought grows strong again. The real work of an artist is to build up an experience that is coherent in perception while moving with constant change in its development.

When an author puts on paper ideas that are already clearly conceived and consistently ordered, the real work has been previously done. Or, he may depend upon the greater perceptibility induced by the activity and its sensible report to direct his completion of the work. The mere act of transcription is esthetically irrelevant save as it enters integrally into the formation of an experience moving to completeness. Even the composition conceived in the head and, therefore, physically private, is public in its significant content, since it is conceived with reference to execution in a product that is perceptible and hence belongs to the common world. Otherwise it would be an aberration or a passing dream. The urge to express through painting the perceived qualities of a landscape is contin-uous with demand for pencil or brush. Without external embodiment, an experi-ence remains incomplete; physiologically and functionally, sense organs are motor organs and are connected, by means of distribution of energies in the human body and not merely anatomically, with other motor organs. It is no linguistic accident that "building," "construction," "work," designate both a process and its finished product. Without the meaning of the verb that of the noun remains blank.

Writer, composer of music, sculptor, or painter can retrace, during the process of production, what they have previously done. When it is not satisfac-tory in the undergoing or perceptual phase of experience, they can to some degree start afresh. This retracing is not readily accomplished in the case of architecture—which is perhaps one reason why there are so many ugly buildings. Architects are obliged to complete their idea before its translation into a complete object of perception takes place. Inability to build up simultaneously the idea and its objective embodiment imposes a handicap. Nevertheless, they too are obliged to think out their ideas in terms of the medium of embodiment and the object of ultimate perception unless they work mechanically and by rote. Prob-ably the esthetic quality of medieval cathedrals is due in some measure to the fact that their constructions were not so much controlled by plans and specifica-tions made in advance as is now the case. Plans grew as the building grew. But even a Minerva-like product, if it is artistic, presupposes a prior period of gestation in which doings and perceptions projected in imagination interact and mutually modify one another. Every work of art follows the plan of, and pattern of, a complete experience, rendering it more intensely and concentratedly felt.

It is not so easy in the case of the perceiver and appreciator to understand the intimate union of doing and undergoing as it is in the case of the maker. We are given to supposing that the former merely takes in what is there in finished form, instead of realizing that this taking in involves activities that are comparable to those of the creator. But receptivity is not passivity. It, too, is a process consisting of a series of responsive acts that accumulate toward objective fulfillment. Otherwise, there is not perception but recognition. The difference between the two is immense. Recognition is perception arrested before it has a chance to develop freely. In recognition there is a beginning of an act of perception. But this beginning is not allowed to serve the development of a full perception of the thing recognized. It is arrested at the point where it will serve some *other* purpose, as we recognize a man on the street in order to greet or to avoid him, not so as to see him for the sake of seeing what is there.

In recognition we fall back, as upon a stereotype, upon some previously formed scheme. Some detail or arrangement of details serves as cue for bare identification. It suffices in recognition to apply this bare outline as a stencil to the present object. Sometimes in contact with a human being we are struck with traits, perhaps of only physical characteristics, of which we were not previously aware. We realize that we never knew the person before; we had not seen him in any pregnant sense. We now begin to study and to "take in." Perception replaces bare recognition. There is an act of reconstructive doing, and consciousness becomes fresh and alive. *This* act of seeing involves the cooperation of motor elements even though they remain implicit and do not become overt, as well as cooperation of all funded ideas that may serve to complete the new picture that is forming. Recognition is too easy to arouse vivid consciousness. There is not enough resistance between new and old to secure consciousness of the experience that is had. Even a dog that barks and wags his tail joyously on seeing his master return is more fully alive in his reception of his friend than is a human being who is content with mere recognition.

Bare recognition is satisfied when a proper tag or label is attached, "proper" signifying one that serves a purpose outside the act of recognition—as a salesman identifies wares by a sample. It involves no stir of the organism, no inner commotion. But an act of perception proceeds by waves that extend serially throughout the entire organism. There is, therefore, no such thing in perception as seeing or hearing *plus* emotion. The perceived object or scene is emotionally pervaded throughout. When an aroused emotion does not permeate the material that is perceived or thought of, it is either preliminary or pathological.

The esthetic or undergoing phase of experience is receptive. It involves surrender. But adequate yielding of the self is possible only through a controlled activity that may well be intense. In much of our intercourse with our surroundings we withdraw; sometimes from fear, if only of expending unduly our store of energy; sometimes from preoccupation with other matters, as in the case of recognition. Perception is an act of the going-out of energy in order to receive, not a withholding of energy. To steep ourselves in a subject matter we have first to plunge into it. When we are only passive to a scene, it overwhelms us and, for lack of answering activity, we do not perceive that which bears us down. We must summon energy and pitch it at a responsive key in order to *take* in.

Every one knows that it requires apprenticeship to see through a microscope or telescope, and to see a landscape as the geologist sees it. The idea that esthetic perception is an affair for odd moments is one reason for the backwardness of the arts among us. The eye and the visual apparatus may be intact; the object may be physically there, the cathedral of Notre Dame, or Rubens' portrait of Hendrik Stoeffel. In some bald sense, the latter may be "seen." They may be looked at, possibly recognized, and have their correct names attached. But for lack of continuous interaction between the total organism and the objects, they are not perceived, certainly not esthetically. A crowd of visitors steered through a picture-gallery, by a guide, with attention called here and there to some high point, does not perceive; only by accident is there even interest in seeing a picture for the sake of subject matter vividly realized.

For to perceive, a beholder must *create* his own experience. And his creation must include relations comparable to those which the original producer underwent. They are not the same in any literal sense. But with the perceiver, as with the artist, there must be an ordering of the elements of the whole that is in form, although not in details, the same as the process of organization the creator of the work consciously experienced. Without an act of re-creation the object is not perceived as a work of art. The artist selected, simplified, clarified, abridged and condensed according to his interest. The beholder must go through these operations according to his point of view and interest. In both, an act of abstraction, that is of extraction of what is significant, takes place. In both, there is comprehension in its literal signification—that is, a gathering together of details and particulars physically scattered into an experienced whole. There is work done on the part of the percipient as there is on the part of the artist. The one who is too lazy, idle, or indurated in convention to perform this work will not see or hear. His "appreciation" will be a mixture of scraps of learning with conformity to norms of conventional admiration and with a confused, even if genuine, emotional excitation.

The considerations that have been presented imply both the community and the unlikeness, because of specific emphasis, of *an* experience, in its pregnant sense, and esthetic experience. The former has esthetic quality; otherwise its materials would not be rounded out into a single coherent experience. It is not possible to divide in a vital experience the practical, emotional, and intellectual from one another and to set the properties of one over against the characteristics of the others. The emotional phase binds parts together into a single whole; "intellectual" simply names the fact that the experience has meaning; "practical" indicates that the organism is interacting with events and objects which surround it. The most elaborate philosophic or scientific inquiry and the most ambitious industrial or political enterprise has, when its different ingredients constitute an integral experience, esthetic quality. For then its varied parts are linked to one another, and do not merely succeed one another. And the parts through their experienced linkage move toward a consummation and close, not merely to cessation in time. This consummation, moreover, does not wait in consciousness for the whole undertaking to be finished. It is anticipated throughout and is recurrently savored with special intensity.

Nevertheless, the experiences in question are dominantly intellectual or practical, rather than *distinctly* esthetic, because of the interest and purpose that initiate and control them. In an intellectual experience, the conclusion has value on its own account. It can be extracted as a formula or as a "truth," and can be used in its independent entirety as factor and guide in other inquiries. In a work of art there is no such single self-sufficient deposit. The end, the terminus, is significant not by itself but as the integration of the parts. It has no other existence. A drama or novel is not the final sentence, even if the characters are disposed of as living happily ever after. In a distinctly esthetic experience, characteristics that are subdued in other experiences are dominant; those that are subordinate are controlling—namely, the characteristics in virtue of which the experience is an integrated complete experience on its own account.

In every integral experience there is form because there is dynamic organization. I call the organization dynamic because it takes time to complete it, because it is a growth. There are inception, development, fulfillment. Material is ingested and digested through interaction with that vital organization of the results of prior experience that constitutes the mind of the worker. Incubation goes on until what is conceived is brought forth and is rendered perceptible as part of the common world. An esthetic experience can be crowded into a moment only in the sense that a climax of prior long enduring processes may arrive in an outstanding movement which so sweeps everything else into it that all else is forgotten. That which distinguishes an experience as esthetic is conversion of resistance and tensions, of excitations that in themselves are temptations to diversion, into a movement toward an inclusive and fulfilling close.

Experiencing like breathing is a rhythm of intakings and outgivings. Their succession is punctuated and made a rhythm by the existence of intervals, periods in which one phase is ceasing and the other is inchoate and preparing. William James aptly compared the course of a conscious experience to the alternate flights and perchings of a bird. The flights and perchings are intimately connected with one another; they are not so many unrelated lightings succeeded by a number of equally unrelated hoppings. Each resting place in experience is an undergoing in which is absorbed and taken home the consequences of prior doing, and, unless the doing is that of utter caprice or sheer routine, each doing carries in itself meaning that has been extracted and conserved. As with the advance of an army, all gains from what has been already effected are periodically consolidated, and always with a view to what is to be done next. If we move too rapidly, we get away from the base of supplies—of accrued meanings—and the experience is flustered, thin, and confused. If we dawdle too long after having extracted a net value, experience perishes of inanition.

The *form* of the whole is therefore present in every member. Fulfilling, consummating, are continuous functions, not mere ends, located at one place only. An engraver, painter, or writer is in process of completing at every stage of his work. He must at each point retain and sum up what has gone before as a whole and with reference to a whole to come. Otherwise there is no consistency and no security in his successive acts. The series of doings in the rhythm of experience give variety and movement; they save the work from monotony and useless repetitions. The undergoings are the corresponding elements in the rhythm, and they supply unity; they save the work from the aimlessness of a mere succession of excitations. An object is peculiarly and dominantly esthetic, yielding the enjoyment characteristic of esthetic perception, when the factors that determine anything which can be called *an* experience are lifted high above the threshold of perception and are made manifest for their own sake.

—*Art as Experience* (1934)

ALFRED NORTH WHITEHEAD

The Habit of Art

There is no easy single solution of the practical difficulties of education. We can, however, guide ourselves by a certain simplicity in its general theory. The student should concentrate within a limited field. Such concentration should include all practical and intellectual acquirements requisite for that concentration. This is the ordinary procedure; and, in respect to it, I should be inclined even to increase the facilities for concentration rather than to diminish them. With the concentration there are associated certain subsidiary studies, such as languages for science. Such a scheme of professional training should be directed to a clear end congenial to the student. It is not necessary to elaborate the qualifications of these statements. Such a training must, of course, have the width requisite for its end. But its design should not be complicated by the consideration of other ends. This professional training can only touch one side of education. Its center of gravity lies in the intellect, and its chief tool is the printed book. The center of gravity of the other side of training should lie in intuition without an ana-

lytical divorce from the total environment. Its object is immediate apprehension
with the minimum of eviscerating analysis. The type of generality, which above
all is wanted, is the appreciation of variety of value. I mean an esthetic growth.
There is something between the gross specialized values of the mere practical
man, and the thin specialized values of the mere scholar. Both types have missed
something; and if you add together the two sets of values, you do not obtain the
missing elements. What is wanted is an appreciation of the infinite variety of
vivid values achieved by an organism in its proper environment. When you
understand all about the sun and all about the atmosphere and all about the rota-
tion of the earth, you may still miss the radiance of the sunset. There is no substitute for the direct perception of the concrete fact with a high light thrown
on what is relevant to its preciousness.

What I mean is art (and esthetic education). It is, however, art in such a
general sense of the term that I hardly like to call it by that name. Art is a special
example. What we want is to draw out habits of esthetic apprehension. According to the metaphysical doctrine which I have been developing, to do so is to increase the depth of individuality. The analysis of reality indicates the two
factors, activity emerging into individualized esthetic value. Also the emergent
value is the measure of the individualization of the activity. We must foster the
creative initiative towards the maintenance of objective values. You will not
obtain the apprehension without the initiative, or the initiative without the
apprehension. As soon as you get towards the concrete, you cannot exclude action. Sensitiveness without impulse spells decadence, and impulse without
sensitiveness spells brutality. I am using the word "sensitiveness" in its most
general significance, so as to include apprehension of what lies beyond oneself;
that is to say, sensitiveness to all the facts of the case. Thus "art" in the general
sense which I require is any selection by which the concrete facts are so arranged
as to elicit attention to particular values which are realizable by them. For example, the mere disposing of the human body and the eyesight so as to get a
good view of a sunset is a simple form of artistic selection. The habit of art is the
habit of enjoying vivid values.

But, in this sense, art concerns more than sunsets. A factory, with its
machinery, its community of operatives, its social service to the general population, its dependence upon organizing and designing genius, its potentialities as a
source of wealth to the holders of its stock is an organism exhibiting a variety of
vivid values. What we want to train is the habit of apprehending such an organism in its completeness. It is very arguable that the science of political economy,
as studied in its first period after the death of Adam Smith (1790), did more
harm than good. It destroyed many economic fallacies, and taught how to think
about the economic revolution then in progress. But it riveted on men a certain
set of abstractions which were disastrous in their influence on modern mentality.
It de-humanized industry. This is only one example of a general danger inherent

in modern science. Its methodological procedure is exclusive and intolerant, and rightly so. It fixes attention on a definite group of abstractions, neglects everything else, and elicits every scrap of information and theory which is relevant to what it has retained. This method is triumphant, provided that the abstractions are judicious. But, however triumphant, the triumph is within limits. The neglect of these limits leads to disastrous oversights. The anti-rationalism of science is partly justified, as a preservation of its useful methodology; it is partly mere irrational prejudice. Modern professionalism is the training of minds to conform to the methodology. The historical revolt of the seventeenth century, and the earlier reaction towards naturalism, were examples of transcending the abstractions which fascinated educated society in the Middle Ages. These early ages had an ideal of rationalism, but they failed in its pursuit. For they neglected to note that the methodology of reasoning requires the limitations involved in the abstract. Accordingly, the true rationalism must always transcend itself by recurrence to the concrete in search of inspiration. A self-satisfied rationalism is in effect a form of anti-rationalism. It means an arbitrary halt at a particular set of abstractions. This was the case with science.

There are two principles inherent in the very nature of things, recurring in some particular embodiments whatever field we explore—the spirit of change, and the spirit of conservation. There can be nothing real without both. Mere change without conservation is a passage from nothing to nothing. Its final integration yields mere transient nonentity. Mere conservation without change cannot conserve. For after all, there is a flux of circumstance, and the freshness of being evaporates under mere repetition. The character of existent reality is composed of organisms enduring through the flux of things. The low type of organisms have achieved a self-identity dominating their whole physical life. Electrons, molecules, crystals, belong to this type. They exhibit a massive and complete sameness. In the higher types, where life appears, there is greater complexity. Thus, though there is a complex, enduring pattern, it has retreated into deeper recesses of the total fact. In a sense, the self-identity of a human being is more abstract than that of a crystal. It is the life of the spirit. It relates rather to the individualization of the creative activity; so that the changing circumstances received from the environment, are differentiated from the living personality, and are thought of as forming its perceived field. In truth, the field of perception and the perceiving mind are abstractions which, in the concrete, combine into the successive bodily events. The psychological field, as restricted to sense-objects and passing emotions, is the minor permanence, barely rescued from the nonentity of mere change; and the mind is the major permanence, permeating that complete field, whose endurance is the living soul. But the soul would wither without fertilization from its transient experiences. The secret of the higher organisms lies in their two grades of permanences. By this means the freshness of the environment is absorbed into the permanence of the soul. The changing environment is no longer, by reason of its variety, an enemy to the endurance of the organism. The pattern of the higher organism has retreated into the recesses of the individualized activity. It has become a uniform way of dealing with circumstances; and this way is only strengthened by having a proper variety of circumstances to deal with.

This fertilization of the soul is the reason for the necessity of art. A static value, however serious and important, becomes unendurable by its appalling monotony of endurance. The soul cries aloud for release into change. It suffers the agonies of claustrophobia. The transitions of humor, wit, irreverence, play, sleep, and—above all—of art are necessary for it. Great art is the arrangement of the environment so as to provide for the soul vivid, but transient, values. Human beings require something which absorbs them for a time, something out of the routine which they can stare at. But you cannot subdivide life, except in the abstract analysis of thought. Accordingly, the great art is more than a transient refreshment. It is something which adds to the permanent richness of the soul's self-attainment. It justifies itself both by its immediate enjoyment, and also by its discipline of the inmost being. Its discipline is not distinct from enjoyment, but by reason of it. It transforms the soul into the permanent realization of values extending beyond its former self. This element of transition in art is shown by the restlessness exhibited in its history. An epoch gets saturated by the master-pieces of any one style. Something new must be discovered. The human being wanders on. Yet there is a balance in things. Mere change before the attainment of adequacy of achievement, either in quality or output, is destructive of great-ness. But the importance of a living art, which moves on and yet leaves its permanent mark, can hardly be exaggerated.

In regard to the esthetic needs of civilized society the reactions of science have so far been unfortunate. Its materialistic basis has directed attention to *things,* as opposed to *values.* The antithesis is a false one, if taken in a concrete sense. But it is valid at the abstract level of ordinary thought. This misplaced emphasis coalesced with the abstractions of political economy, which are in fact the abstractions in terms of which commercial affairs are carried on. Thus all thought concerned with social organization expressed itself in terms of material things and of capital. Ultimate values were excluded. They were politely bowed to, and then handed over to the clergy to be kept for Sundays. A creed of com-petitive business morality was evolved, in some respects curiously high; but en-tirely devoid of consideration for the value of human life. The workmen were conceived as mere hands, drawn from the pool of labor. To God's question, men gave the answer of Cain—"Am I my brother's keeper?"; and they incurred Cain's guilt. This was the atmosphere in which the industrial revolution was accom-plished in England, and to a large extent elsewhere. The internal history of England during the last half century has been an endeavor slowly and painfully to undo the evils wrought in the first stage of the new epoch. It may be that civilization will never recover from the bad climate which enveloped the intro-duction of machinery. This climate pervaded the whole commercial system of the progressive northern European races. It was partly the result of the esthetic errors of Protestantism and partly the result of scientific materialism, and partly the result of the abstractions of political economy. An illustration of my point is to be found in Macaulay's essay criticizing Southey's *Colloquies on Society*. It was written in 1830. Now Macaulay was a very favorable example of men liv-ing at that date, or at any date. He had genius; he was kind-hearted, honorable, and a reformer. This is the extract: "We are told, that our age has invented atrocities beyond the imagination of our fathers; that society has been brought into a state compared with which extermination would be a blessing; and all be-cause the dwellings of cotton-spinners are naked and rectangular. Mr. Southey has found out a way he tells us, in which the effects of manufacturers and agri-culture may be compared. And what is this way? To stand on a hill, to look at a cottage and a factory, and to see which is the prettier."

Southey seems to have said many silly things in his book; but, so far as this extract is concerned, he could make a good case for himself if he returned to earth after the lapse of nearly a century. The evils of the early industrial system are now a commonplace of knowledge. The point which I am insisting on is the stone-blind eye with which even the best men of that time regarded the im-portance of esthetics in a nation's life. I do not believe that we have as yet nearly achieved the right estimate.

—Science and the Modern World (1925)

CHAPTER SEVEN

Can "Art" Be Defined?

LUDWIG WITTGENSTEIN
Games and Definitions

MORRIS WEITZ
The Role of Theory in Esthetics

Introductory Note

IN THE PRECEDING CHAPTERS we have been reviewing different conceptions of art. Various writers have informed us that art is playful illusion, semblance or imitation, creation of beauty, expression of emotion, intuition, unconscious wish-fulfillment, or enjoyment of vivid values. In later chapters we shall find an emphasis upon form, empathy, abstraction, or some other "differentia" of art.

We shall now turn to a theory that criticizes all such definitions and denies the conception of philosophy that underlies them. This challenge stems from Ludwig Wittgenstein (1889-1951). Although he was born and reared in Austria, he spent much of his lifetime in England, as a student and later as a professor at Cambridge University. His immense influence has been exerted through the spell of his powerful personality and his two remarkable books, *Tractatus Logico-Philosophicus* (1921) and *Philosophical Investigations* (1953).

Richly endowed with artistic ability, he could design a house, mold a statue, play a clarinet, conduct an orchestra, or write an imaginary dialogue. "Topics in esthetics," declares his former student Norman Malcolm, "were perhaps the most frequent at [his] at-homes, and the depth and richness of

Wittgenstein's thinking about art were very exciting." [1] Nevertheless, his published writings contain only casual references to art, and his influence is to be found mainly in his general ideas and method. As the reader peruses Wittgenstein's remarks on "games and definitions," he should consider just how the ideas apply to esthetics.

One of his remarks, as quoted by Malcolm, sums up a good deal of his philosophy: "An expression has meaning only in the stream of life." [2] The meanings of a concept, such as "beauty" or "art," can best be determined by studying its actual use by ordinary human beings as they go about the business of living. When we lay aside preconceptions and study words in their vital employment we discover that they have no fixed meanings and no sharp edges. An example discussed in the following selection is the word "game." We can find no mark or characteristic, no "essence," that is common to all games—nothing that would permit us to encompass all the games in a formula or definition.

"The meaning is the use" is Wittgenstein's famous slogan—and the uses are various and unpredictable. In actual life, words are like tools that can be employed for many different purposes: "Think of the tools in a tool-box; there is a hammer, pliers, a saw, a screwdriver, a rule, a glue-pot, glue, nails and screws. —The functions of words are as diverse as the functions of these objects." [3] Even a single word, such as "beauty," has a multiplicity of uses, and this multiplicity is not predetermined or fixed. We should therefore respect the "open texture" of language, recognizing that a word has an indefinite variety of meanings and that new and unprecedented meanings will arise as the contexts of life alter. The appropriate uses of a word in such a vital context Wittgenstein calls a "language-game," and such "games" vary from one "form of life" to another.

These and other implications of Wittgenstein's philosophy are pointed out by Morris Weitz (1916-   ), Professor of Philosophy at Ohio State University and author of several important books and articles in esthetics. His essay is an example of the very considerable influence that Wittgenstein's ideas, now at the height of their power, are exercising upon the philosophy of art.

[1] Norman Malcolm, *Ludwig Wittgenstein: A Memoir* (London, Oxford University Press. 1958), p. 53.
[2] *Ibid.*, p. 93.
[3] *Philosophical Investigations*, Section 11.

LUDWIG WITTGENSTEIN
Games and Definitions [1]

65. Here we come up against the great question that lies behind all these considerations.—For someone might object against me: "You take the easy way out! You talk about all sorts of language-games, but have nowhere said what the essence of a language-game, and hence of language, is: what is common to all these activities, and what makes them into language or parts of language. So you let yourself off the very part of the investigation that once gave you yourself most headache, the part about the *general form of propositions* and of language."

And this is true.—Instead of producing something common to all that we call language, I am saying that these phenomena have no one thing in common which makes us use the same word for all,—but that they are *related* to one another in many different ways. And it is because of this relationship, or these relationships, that we call them all "language." I will try to explain this.

66. Consider for example the proceedings that we call "games." I mean board games, card games, ball games, Olympic games, and so on. What is common to them all?—Don't say: "There *must* be something common, or they would not be called 'games' "—but *look and see* whether there is anything common to all.—For if you look at them you will not see something that is common to *all*, but similarities, relationships, and a whole series of them at that. To repeat: don't think, but look!—Look for example at board games, with their multifarious relationships. Now pass to card games; here you find many correspondences with the first group, but many common features drop out, and others appear. When we pass next to ball games, much that is common is retained, but much is lost.—Are they all "amusing"? Compare chess with noughts and crosses. Or is there always winning and losing, or competition between players? Think of patience. In ball games there is winning and losing; but when a child throws his ball at the wall and catches it again, this feature has disappeared. Look at the parts played by skill and luck; and at the difference between skill in chess and skill in tennis. Think now of games like ring-a-ring-a-roses; here is the element of amusement, but how many other characteristic features have disappeared! And we can go through the many, many other groups of games in the same way; can see how similarities crop up and disappear.

---

[1] Wittgenstein expressed the wish that his German text always be available to the reader of his work. His publisher, Basil Blackwell of Oxford, wishes me to note that the original German text, along with the English translation, is available in the standard edition of *Philosophical Investigations* (Editor.)

And the result of this examination is: we see a complicated network of similarities overlapping and criss-crossing: sometimes overall similarities, sometimes similarities of detail.

67. I can think of no better expression to characterize these similarities than "family resemblances"; for the various resemblances between members of a family: build, features, color of eyes, gait, temperament, etc. etc. overlap and criss-cross in the same way.—And I shall say: "games" form a family.

And for instance the kinds of number form a family in the same way. Why do we call something a "number"? Well, perhaps because it has a—direct—relationship with several things that have hitherto been called number; and this can be said to give it an indirect relationship to other things we call the same name. And we extend our concept of number as in spinning a thread we twist fibre on fibre. And the strength of the thread does not reside in the fact that some one fibre runs through its whole length, but in the overlapping of many fibres.

But if someone wished to say, "There is something common to all these constructions—namely the disjunction of all their common properties"—I should reply, Now you are only playing with words. One might as well say, "Something runs through the whole thread—namely the continuous overlapping of those fibres."

68. "All right: the concept of number is defined for you as the logical sum of these individual interrelated concepts: cardinal numbers, rational numbers, real numbers, etc.; and in the same way the concept of a game as the logical sum of a corresponding set of sub-concepts."—It need not be so. For I *can* give the concept "number" rigid limits in this way, that is, use the word "number" for a rigidly limited concept, but I can also use it so that the extension of the concept is *not* closed by a frontier. And this is how we do use the word "game." For how is the concept of a game bounded? What still counts as a game and what no longer does? Can you give the boundary? No. You can *draw* one; for none has so far been drawn. (But that never troubled you before when you used the word "game.")

"But then the use of the word is unregulated, the 'game' we play with it is unregulated."—It is not everywhere circumscribed by rules; but no more are there any rules for how high one throws the ball in tennis, or how hard; yet tennis is a game for all that and has rules too.

69. How should we explain to someone what a game is? I imagine that we should describe *games* to him, and we might add: "This *and similar things* are called 'games.' " And do we know any more about it ourselves? Is it only other people whom we cannot tell exactly what a game is?—But this is not ignorance. We do not know the boundaries because none have been drawn. To repeat, we can draw a boundary—for a special purpose. Does it take that to make the concept usable? Not at all! (Except for that special purpose.) No

more than it took the definition: 1 pace = 75 cm. to make the measure of length 'one pace' usable. And if you want to say "But still, before that it wasn't an exact measure," then I reply: very well, it was an inexact one.—Though you still owe me a definition of exactness.

70. "But if the concept 'game' is uncircumscribed like that, you don't really know what you mean by a 'game.' "—When I give the description: "The ground was quite covered with plants"—do you want to say I don't know what I am talking about until I can give a definition of a plant?

My meaning would be explained by, say, a drawing and the words "The ground looked roughly like this." Perhaps I even say "it looked *exactly* like this."—Then were just *this* grass and *these* leaves there, arranged just like this? No, that is not what it means. And I should not accept any picture as exact in *this* sense.

Someone says to me: "Show the children a game." I teach them gaming with dice, and the other says "I didn't mean that sort of game." Must the exclusion of the game with dice have come before his mind when he gave me the order? [2]

---

71. One might say that the concept 'game' is a concept with blurred edges. —"But is a blurred concept a concept at all?"—Is an indistinct photograph a picture of a person at all? Is it even always an advantage to replace an indistinct picture by a sharp one? Isn't the indistinct one often exactly what we need?

Frege compares a concept to an area and says that an area with vague boundaries cannot be called an area at all. This presumably means that we cannot do anything with it.—But is it senseless to say, "Stand roughly there?" Suppose that I were standing with someone in a city square and said that. As I say it I do not draw any kind of boundary, but perhaps point with my hand—as if I were indicating a particular *spot*. And this is just how one might explain to someone what a game is. One gives examples and intends them to be taken in a particular way.—I do not, however, mean by this that he is supposed to see in those examples that common thing which I—for some reason—was unable to express; but that he is now to *employ* those examples in a particular way. Here giving examples is not an *indirect* means of explaining—in default of a better. For any general definition can be misunderstood too. The point is that *this* is how we play the game. (I mean the language-game with the word "game.")

72. *Seeing what is common.* Suppose I show someone various multi-colored pictures, and say: "The color you see in all these is called 'yellow ochre.' "—This is a definition, and the other will get to understand it by looking for and seeing

---

[2] This paragraph—here set off by lines—was written on a slip and inserted by Wittgenstein without a definite indication of where it should come in. (Editor's note.)

what is common to the pictures. Then he can look *at,* can point *to,* the common thing.

Compare with this a case in which I show him figures of different shapes all painted the same color, and say: "What these have in common is called 'yellow ochre.'"

And compare this case: I show him samples of different shades of blue and say, "The color that is common to all these is what I call 'blue.'"

73. When someone defines the names of color for me by pointing to samples and saying "This color is called 'blue,' this 'green' . . ." this case can be compared in many respects to putting a table in my hands, with the words written under the color-samples.—Though this comparison may mislead in many ways.—One is now inclined to extend the comparison: to have understood the definition means to have in one's mind an idea of the thing defined, and that is a sample or picture. So if I am shown various different leaves and told "This is called a 'leaf,'" I get an idea of the shape of a leaf, a picture of it in my mind.—But what does the picture of a leaf look like when it does not show us any particular shape, but "what is common to all shapes of leaf?" Which shade is the "sample in my mind" of the color green—the sample of what is common to all shades of green?

"But might there not be such 'general' samples? Say a schematic leaf, or a sample of *pure* green?"—Certainly there might. But for such a schema to be understood as a *schema,* and not as the shape of a particular leaf, and for a slip of pure green to be understood as a sample of all that is greenish and not as a sample of pure green—this in turn resides in the way the samples are used.

Ask yourself what *shape* must the sample of the color green be? Should it be rectangular? Or would it then be the sample of a green rectangle?—So should it be "irregular" in shape? And what is to prevent us then from regarding it—that is, from using it—only as a sample of irregularity of shape?

74. Here also belongs the idea that if you see this leaf as a sample of "leaf shape in general" you *see* it differently from someone who regards it as, say, a sample of this particular shape. Now this might well be so—though it is not so —for it would only be to say that, as a matter of experience, if you *see* the leaf in a particular way, you use it in such-and-such a way or according to such-and-such rules. Of course, there is such a thing as seeing in *this* way or *that;* and there are also cases where whoever sees a sample like *this* will in general use it in *this* way, and whoever sees it otherwise in another way. For example, if you see the schematic drawing of a cube as a plane figure consisting of a square and two rhombi you will, perhaps, carry out the order "Bring me something like this" differently from someone who sees the picture three-dimensionally.

75. What does it mean to know what a game is? What does it mean, to know it and not be able to say it? Is this knowledge somehow equivalent to an unformulated definition? So that if it were formulated I should be able to recog-

nize it as the expression of my knowledge? Isn't my knowledge, my concept of a game, completely expressed in the explanations that I could give? That is, in my describing examples of various kinds of game; showing how all sorts of other games can be constructed on the analogy of these; saying that I should scarcely include this or this among games; and so on.

76. If someone were to draw a sharp boundary I could not acknowledge it as the one that I too always wanted to draw, or had drawn in my mind. For I did not want to draw one at all. His concept can then be said to be not the same as mine, but akin to it. The kinship is that of two pictures, one of which consists of color patches with vague contours, and the other of patches similarly shaped and distributed, but with clear contours. The kinship is just as undeniable as the difference.

77. And if we carry this comparison still further it is clear that the degree to which the sharp picture *can* resemble the blurred one depends on the latter's degree of vagueness. For imagine having to sketch a sharply defined picture "corresponding" to a blurred one. In the latter there is a blurred red rectangle: for it you put down a sharply defined one. Of course—several such sharply de fined rectangles can be drawn to correspond to the indefinite one.—But if the colors in the original merge without a hint of any outline won't it become a hopeless task to draw a sharp picture corresponding to the blurred one? Won't you then have to say, "Here I might just as well draw a circle or heart as a rectangle, for all the colors merge." Anything—and nothing—is right.—And this is the position you are in if you look for definitions corresponding to our concepts in esthetics or ethics.

In such a difficulty always ask yourself, How did we *learn* the meaning of this word ("good" for instance)? From what sort of examples? in what language-games? Then it will be easier for you to see that the word must have a family of meanings.

—*Philosophical Investigations* (1953)

MORRIS WEITZ

The Role of Theory in Esthetics

Theory has been central in esthetics and is still the preoccupation of the philosophy of art. Its main avowed concern remains the determination of the nature of art which can be formulated into a definition of it. It construes definition as the statement of the necessary and sufficient properties of what is being defined, where the statement purports to be a true or false claim about the essence of art, what characterizes and distinguishes it from everything else. Each of the great theories of art—Formalism, Voluntarism, Emotionalism, Intellectualism, Intuitionism, Organicism—converges on the attempt to state the defining properties of art. Each claims that it is the true theory because it has formulated correctly into a real definition the nature of art; and that the others are false because they have left out some necessary or sufficient property. Many theorists contend that their enterprise is no mere intellectual exercise but an absolute necessity for any understanding of art and our proper evaluation of it. Unless we know what art is, they say, what are its necessary and sufficient properties, we cannot begin to respond to it adequately or to say why one work is good or better than another. Esthetic theory, thus, is important not only in itself but for the foundations of both appreciation and criticism. Philosophers, critics, and even artists who have written on art, agree that what is primary in esthetics is a theory about the nature of art.

Is esthetics theory, in the sense of a true definition or set of necessary and sufficient properties of art, possible? If nothing else does, the history of esthetics itself should give one enormous pause here. For, in spite of the many theories, we seem no nearer our goal today than we were in Plato's time. Each age, each art-movement, each philosophy of art, tries over and over again to establish the stated ideal only to be succeeded by a new or revised theory, rooted, at least in part, in the repudiation of preceding ones. Even today, almost everyone interested in esthetic matters is still deeply wedded to the hope that the correct theory of art is forthcoming. We need only examine the numerous new books on art in which new definitions are proffered; or, in our own country especially, the basic textbooks and anthologies to recognize how strong the priority of a theory of art is.

In this essay I want to plead for the rejection of this problem. I want to show that theory—in the requisite classical sense—is *never* forthcoming in esthetics, and that we would do much better as philosophers to supplant the question, "What is the nature of art?," by other questions, the answers to which will provide us with all the understanding of the arts there can be. I want to show that the inadequacies of the theories are not primarily occasioned by any legitimate difficulty such as, for example, the vast complexity of art, which might be corrected by further probing and research. Their basic inadequacies reside instead in a fundamental misconception of art. Esthetic theory—all of it—is wrong in principle in thinking that a correct theory is possible because it radically misconstrues the logic of the concept of art. Its main contention that "art" is amenable to real or any kind of true definition is false. Its attempt to discover the necessary and sufficient properties of art is logically misbegotten for the very simple reason that such a set and, consequently, such a formula about it, is never forthcoming. Art, as the logic of the concept shows, has no set of necessary and sufficient properties, hence a theory of it is logically impossible and not merely factually difficult. Esthetic theory tries to define what cannot be defined in its requisite sense. But in recommending the repudiation of esthetic theory I shall not argue from this, as too many others have done, that its logical confusions render it meaningless or worthless. On the contrary, I wish to reassess its role and its contribution primarily in order to show that it is of the greatest importance to our understanding of the arts.

Let us now survey briefly some of the more famous extant esthetic theories in order to see if they do incorporate correct and adequate statements about the nature of art. In each of these there is the assumption that it is the true enumeration of the defining properties of art, with the implication that previous theories have stressed wrong definitions. Thus, to begin with, consider a famous version of Formalist theory, that propounded by Bell and Fry. It is true that they speak mostly of painting in their writings but both assert that what they find in that art can be generalized for what is "art" in the others as well. The essence of painting, they maintain, is the plastic elements in relation. Its defining property is significant form, that is, certain combinations of lines, colors, shapes, volumes —everything on the canvas except the representational elements—which evoke a unique response to such combinations. Painting is definable as plastic organization. The nature of art, what it *really* is, so their theory goes, is a unique combination of certain elements (the specifiable plastic ones) in their relations. Anything which is art is an instance of significant form; and anything which is not art has no such form.

To this the Emotionalist replies that the truly essential property of art has been left out. Tolstoy, Ducasse, or any of the advocates of this theory, find that the requisite defining property is not significant form but rather the expression of emotion in some sensuous public medium. Without projection of emotion into some piece of stone or words or sounds, etc., there can be no art. Art is really such embodiment. It is this that uniquely characterizes art, and any true, real definition of it, contained in some adequate theory of art, must so state it.

The Intuitionist disclaims both emotion and form as defining properties. In Croce's version, for example, art is identified not with some physical, public object but with a specific creative, cognitive, and spiritual act. Art is really a first stage of knowledge in which certain human beings (artists) bring their images and intuitions into lyrical clarification or expression. As such, it is an awareness, non-conceptual in character, of the unique individuality of things; and since it exists below the level of conceptualization or action, it is without scientific or moral content. Croce singles out as the defining essence of art this first stage of spiritual life and advances its identification with art as a philosophically true theory or definition.

The Organicist says to all of this that art is really a class of organic wholes consisting of distinguishable, albeit inseparable, elements in their causally efficacious relations which are presented in some sensuous medium. In A. C. Bradley, in piecemeal versions of it in literary criticism, or in my own generalized adaptation of it in my *Philosophy of the Arts,* what is claimed is that anything which is a work of art is in its nature a unique complex of interrelated parts—in painting, for example, lines, colors, volumes, subjects, etc., all interacting upon one another on a paint surface of some sort. Certainly, at one time at least it seemed to me that this organic theory constituted the one true and real definition of art.

My final example is the most interesting of all, logically speaking. This is the Voluntarist theory of Parker. In his writings on art, Parker persistently calls into question the traditional simpleminded definitions of esthetics. "The assumption underlying every philosophy of art is the existence of some common nature present in all the arts." [1] "All the so popular brief definitions of art— 'significant form,' 'expression,' 'intuition,' 'objectified pleasure'—are fallacious, either because, while true of art, they are also true of much that is not art, and hence fail to differentiate art from other things; or else because they neglect some essential aspect of art." [2] But instead of inveighing against the attempt at definition of art itself, Parker insists that what is needed is a complex definition rather than a simple one. "The definition of art must therefore be in terms of a complex of characteristics. Failure to recognize this has been the fault of all the well-known definitions." [3] His own version of Voluntarism is the theory that art is essentially three things: embodiment of wishes and desires imaginatively satisfied, language, which characterizes the public medium of art, and harmony, which unifies the language with the layers of imaginative projections. Thus, for Parker, it is a true definition to say of art that it is ". . . the provision of satisfaction through the imagination, social significance, and harmony. I am claiming that nothing except works of art possess all three of these marks." [4]

Now, all of these sample theories are inadequate in many different ways. Each purports to be a complete statement about the defining features of all works of art and yet each of them leaves out something which the others take to be central. Some are circular, for example, the Bell-Fry theory of art as significant form which is defined in part in terms of our response to significant form. Some of them, in their search for necessary and sufficient properties, emphasize too few properties, like (again) the Bell-Fry definition which leaves out subject-representation in painting, or the Croce theory which omits inclusion of the very important feature of the public, physical character, say, of architecture. Others are too general and cover objects that are not art as well as works of art. Organicism is surely such a view since it can be applied to *any* causal unity in

---

[1] DeWitt H. Parker, "The Nature of Art," reprinted in E. Vivas and M. Krieger, *The Problems of Aesthetics* (N. Y., 1953), p. 90.

[2] *Ibid.,* pp. 93-94.

[3] *Ibid.,* p. 94.

[4] *Ibid.,* p. 104.

the natural world as well as to art.[5] Still others rest on dubious principles, for example, Parker's claim that art embodies imaginative satisfactions, rather than real ones; or Croce's assertion that there is nonconceptual knowledge. Consequently, even if art has one set of necessary and sufficient properties, none of the theories we have noted or, for that matter, no esthetic theory yet proposed, has enumerated that set to the satisfaction of all concerned.

Then there is a different sort of difficulty. As real definitions, these theories are supposed to be factual reports on art. If they are, may we not ask, Are they empirical and open to verification or falsification? For example, what would confirm or disconfirm the theory that art is significant form or embodiment of emotion or creative synthesis of images? There does not even seem to be a hint of the kind of evidence which might be forthcoming to test these theories; and indeed one wonders if they are perhaps honorific definitions of "art," that is, proposed redefinitions in terms of some *chosen* conditions for applying the concept of art, and not true or false reports on the essential properties of art at all.

But all these criticisms of traditional esthetic theories—that they are circular, incomplete, untestable, pseudo-factual, disguised proposals to change the meaning of concepts—have been made before. My intention is to go beyond these to make a much more fundamental criticism, namely, that esthetic theory is a logically vain attempt to define what cannot be defined, to state the necessary and sufficient properties of that which has no necessary and sufficient properties, to conceive the concept of art as closed when its very use reveals and demands its openness.

The problem with which we must begin is not "What is art?," but "What sort of concept is 'art'?" Indeed, the root problem of philosophy itself is to explain the relation between the employment of certain kinds of concepts and the conditions under which they can be correctly applied. If I may paraphrase Wittgenstein, we must not ask, What is the nature of any philosophical x?, or even, according to the semanticist, What does "x" mean?, a transformation that leads to the disastrous interpretation of "art" as a name for some specifiable class of objects; but rather, What is the use or employment of "x"? What does "x" do in the language? This, I take it, is the initial question, the begin-all if not the end-all of any philosophical problem and solution. Thus, in esthetics, our first problem is the elucidation of the actual employment of the concept of art, to give a logical description of the actual functioning of the concept, including a description of the conditions under which we correctly use it or its correlates.

My model in this type of logical description or philosophy derives from Wittgenstein. It is also he who, in his refutation of philosophical theorizing in he sense of constructing definitions of philosophical entities, has furnished conmporary esthetics with a starting point for any future progress. In his new

[5] See M. Macdonald's review of my *Philosophy of the Arts* in *Mind*, Oct., 1951, pp. 561-564, for a brilliant discussion of this objection to the Organic theory.

work, *Philosophical Investigations,*[6] Wittgenstein raises as an illustrative question, What is a game? The traditional philosophical, theoretical answer would be in terms of some exhaustive set of properties common to all games. To this Wittgenstein says, let us consider what we call "games": "I mean board games, card games, ball games, Olympic games, and so on. What is common to them all?—Don't say: 'there *must* be something common, or they would not be called "games"' but *look and see* whether there is anything common to all.—For if you look at them you will not see something that is common to *all,* but similarities, relationships, and a whole series of them at that . . ."

Card games are like board games in some respects but not in others. Not all games are amusing, nor is there always winning or losing or competition. Some games resemble others in some respects—that is all. What we find are no necessary and sufficient properties, only "a complicated network of similarities overlapping and crisscrossing," such that we can say of games that they form a family with family resemblances and no common trait. If one asks what a game is, we pick out sample games, describe these, and add, "This and *similar things* are called 'games.'" This is all we need to say and indeed all any of us knows about games. Knowing what a game is is not knowing some real definition or theory but being able to recognize and explain games and to decide which among imaginary and new examples would or would not be called "games."

The problem of the nature of art is like that of the nature of games, at least in these respects: If we actually look and see what it is that we call "art," we will also find no common properties—only strands of similarities. Knowing what art is is not apprehending some manifest or latent essence but being able to recognize, describe, and explain those things we call "art" in virtue of these similarities.

But the basic resemblance between these concepts is their open texture. In elucidating them, certain (paradigm) cases can be given, about which there can be no question as to their being correctly described as "art" or "game," but no exhaustive set of cases can be given. I can list some cases and some conditions under which I can apply correctly the concept of art but I cannot list all of them, for the all-important reason that unforeseeable or novel conditions are always forthcoming or envisageable.

A concept is open if its conditions of application are emendable and corrigible; that is, if a situation or case can be imagined or secured which would call for some sort of *decision* on our part to extend the use of the concept to cover this, or to close the concept and invent a new one to deal with the new case and its new property. If necessary and sufficient conditions for the application of a concept can be stated, the concept is a closed one. But this can happen only in logic or mathematics where concepts are constructed and completely

[6] L. Wittgenstein, *Philosophical Investigations,* (Oxford, 1953), tr. by E. Anscombe. (All quotations appear in the preceding selection, pp. 195-199—Editor's note.)

defined. It cannot occur with empirically-descriptive and normative concepts unless we arbitrarily close them by stipulating the ranges of their uses.

I can illustrate this open character of "art" best by examples drawn from its sub-concepts. Consider questions like "Is Dos Passos' *U. S. A.* a novel?," "Is V. Woolf's *To the Lighthouse* a novel?," "Is Joyce's *Finnegan's Wake* a novel?" On the traditional view, these are construed as factual problems to be answered yes or no in accordance with the presence or absence of defining properties. But certainly this is not how any of these questions is answered. Once it arises, as it has many times in the development of the novel from Richardson to Joyce (for example, "Is Gide's *The School for Wives* a novel or a diary?"), what is at stake is no factual analysis concerning necessary and sufficient properties but a decision as to whether the work under examination is similar in certain respects to other works, already called "novels," and consequently warrants the extension of the concept to cover the new case. The new work is narrative, fictional, contains character delineation and dialogue but (say) it has no regular time-sequence in the plot or is interspersed with actual newspaper reports. It is like recognized novels, A, B, C . . . , in some respects but not like them in others. But then neither were B and C like A in some respects when it was decided to extend the concept applied to A to B and C. Because work N + 1 (the brand new work) is like A, B, C . . . N in certain respects—has strands of similarity to them—the concept is extended and a new phase of the novel engendered. "Is N + 1 a novel?," then, is no factual, but rather a decision problem, where the verdict turns on whether or not we enlarge our set of conditions for applying the concept.

What is true of the novel is, I think, true of every sub-concept of art: "tragedy," "comedy," "painting," "opera," etc., of "art" itself. No "Is X a novel, painting, opera, work of art, etc.?" question allows of a definitive answer in the sense of a factual yes or no report. "Is this *collage* a painting or not?" does not rest on any set of necessary and sufficient properties of painting but on whether we decide—as we did!—to extend "painting" to cover this case.

"Art," itself, is an open concept. New conditions (cases) have constantly arisen and will undoubtedly constantly arise; new art forms, new movements will emerge, which will demand decisions on the part of those interested, usually professional critics, as to whether the concept should be extended or not. Estheticians may lay down similarity conditions but never necessary and sufficient ones for the correct application of the concept. With "art" its conditions of application can never be exhaustively enumerated since new cases can always be envisaged or created by artists, or even nature, which would call for a decision on someone's part to extend or to close the old or to invent a new concept. (For example, "It's not a sculpture, it's a mobile.")

What I am arguing, then, is that the very expansive, adventurous character of art, its ever-present changes and novel creations, makes it logically impossible to ensure any set of defining properties. We can, of course, choose to close the concept. But to do this with "art" or "tragedy" or "portraiture," etc., is ludicrous since it forecloses on the very conditions of creativity in the arts.

Of course there are legitimate and serviceable closed concepts in art. But these are always those whose boundaries of conditions have been drawn for a *special* purpose. Consider the difference, for example, between "tragedy" and "(extant) Greek tragedy." The first is open and must remain so to allow for the possibility of new conditions, for example, a play in which the hero is not noble or fallen or in which there is no hero but other elements that are like those of plays we already call "tragedy." The second is closed. The plays it can be applied to, the conditions under which it can be correctly used are all in, once the boundary, "Greek," is drawn. Here the critic can work out a theory or real definition in which he lists the common properties at least of the extant Greek tragedies. Aristotle's definition, false as it is as a theory of all the plays of Aeschylus, Sophocles, and Euripides, since it does not cover some of them,[7] properly called "tragedies," can be interpreted as a real (albeit incorrect) definition of this closed concept; although it can also be, as it unfortunately has been, conceived as a purported real definition of "tragedy," in which case it suffers from the logical mistake of trying to define what cannot be defined—of trying to squeeze what is an open concept into an honorific formula for a closed concept.

What is supremely important, if the critic is not to become muddled, is to get absolutely clear about the way in which he conceives his concepts; otherwise he goes from the problem of trying to define "tragedy," etc., to an arbitrary closing of the concept in terms of certain preferred conditions or characteristics which he sums up in some linguistic recommendation that he mistakenly thinks is a real definition of the open concept. Thus, many critics and estheticians ask, "What is tragedy?," choose a class of samples for which they may give a true account of its common properties, and then go on to construe this account of the chosen closed class as a true definition or theory of the whole open class of tragedy. This, I think, is the logical mechanism of most of the so-called theories of the subconcepts of art: "tragedy," "comedy," "novel," etc. In effect, this whole procedure, subtly deceptive as it is, amounts to a transformation of correct criteria for *recognizing* members of certain legitimately closed classes of works of art into recommended criteria for *evaluating* any putative member of the class.

The primary task of esthetics is not to seek a theory but to elucidate the concept of art. Specifically, it is to describe the conditions under which we employ the concept correctly. Definition, reconstruction, patterns of analysis are out of place here since they distort and add nothing to our understanding of art. What, then, is the logic of "X is a work of art"?

As we actually use the concept, "Art" is both descriptive (like "chair")

[7] See H. D. F. Kitto, *Greek Tragedy*, (London, 1939), on this point.

and evaluative (like "good"); that is, we sometimes say, "This is a work of art," to describe something and we sometimes say it to evaluate something. Neither use surprises anyone. . . .

There is nothing wrong with the evaluative use; in fact, there is good reason for using "Art" to praise. But what cannot be maintained is that theories of the evaluative use of "Art" are true and real definitions of the necessary and sufficient properties of art. Instead they are honorific definitions, pure and simple, in which "Art" has been redefined in terms of chosen criteria.

But what makes them—these honorific definitions—so supremely valuable is not their disguised linguistic recommendations; rather it is the *debates* over the reasons for changing the criteria of the concept of art which are built into the definitions. In each of the great theories of art, whether correctly understood as honorific definitions or incorrectly accepted as real definitions, what is of the utmost importance are the reasons proffered in the argument for the respective theory, that is, the reasons given for the chosen or preferred criterion of excellence and evaluation. It is this perennial debate over these criteria of evaluation which makes the history of esthetic theory the important study it is. The value of each of the theories resides in its attempt to state and to justify certain criteria which are either neglected or distorted by previous theories. Look at the Bell-Fry theory again. Of course, "Art is significant form" cannot be accepted as a true, real definition of art; and most certainly it actually functions in their esthetics as a redefinition of art in terms of the chosen condition of significant form. But what gives it its esthetic importance is what lies behind the formula: In an age in which literary and representational elements have become paramount in painting, *return* to the plastic ones since these are indigenous to painting. Thus, the role of the theory is not to define anything but to use the definitional form, almost epigrammatically, to pin-point a crucial recommendation to turn our attention once again to the plastic elements in painting.

Once we, as philosophers, understand this distinction between the formula and what lies behind it, it behooves us to deal generously with the traditional theories of art; because incorporated in every one of them is a debate over and argument for emphasizing or centering upon some particular feature of art which has been neglected or perverted. If we take the esthetic theories literally, as we have seen, they all fail; but if we reconstrue them, in terms of their function and point, as serious and argued-for recommendations to concentrate on certain criteria of excellence in art, we shall see that esthetic theory is far from worthless. Indeed, it becomes as central as anything in esthetics, in our understanding of art, for it teaches us what to look for and how to look at it in art. What is central and must be articulated in all the theories are their debates over the reasons for excellence in art—debates over emotional depth, profound truths, natural beauty, exactitude, freshness of treatment, and so on, as criteria of evaluation—the whole of which converges on the perennial problem of what makes a work of art good.

To understand the role of esthetic theory is not to conceive it as definition, logically doomed to failure, but to read it as summaries of seriously made recommendations to attend in certain ways to certain features of art.

—*The Journal of Aesthetics and Art Criticism,* Volume XV (1956)

PART TWO

THE WORK OF ART

CHAPTER EIGHT

The "Body" of the Work

MARGARET MACDONALD
The Work of Art as Physical

BERNARD BOSANQUET
The Esthetic Attitude in Its Embodiments

DAVID WIGHT PRALL
Sensuous Elements and Esthetic Orders

Introductory Note

PART TWO IS DEVOTED TO THE WORK of art—its materials, expressiveness, form, and function. In this chapter we shall be concerned with its physical properties and sensuous materials.

According to the idealistic interpretation, the work of art is not physical but spiritual. For example, Croce maintains that the physical objects—the statue, the building, the printed poem, etc.—are not to be confused with art. They are simply "memoranda," physical stimulants for imaginative activity. The work of art, which is an apparition, lives in the imagination and there alone. Croce quite agrees with Walt Whitman:

All architecture is what you do to it when you look upon it.
(Did you think it was in the white or gray stone? or the lines of the
    arches and cornices?)

All music is what awakens from you when you are reminded by the
instruments,
It is not the violins and the cornets, it is not the oboe nor the beating
drums, nor the score of the baritone singing his sweet romanza,
nor that of the men's chorus, nor that of the women's chorus,
It is nearer and farther than they.

The physical object is esthetically important only because it stimulates imagination, and the object in nature is important for the same reason.

This point of view is implied by Croce in his identification of intuition and expression, and it has been explicitly developed by R. G. Collingwood in *The Principles of Art* and by Jean-Paul Sartre in *The Psychology of Imagination*. Likewise the selection from Samuel Alexander reproduced in our first chapter maintains that the work of art is a *phenomenal* object created by the co-working of imagination and physical stimuli.

Such insistence upon the imaginary character of the work of art may seem paradoxical. To say that a piece of sculpture is not a physical object is confusing to a person who goes to a museum to see it and perhaps lays his hand on the good hard stone. Recently a movement called "the philosophy of ordinary language," which derives in large measure from Wittgenstein, has insisted that meaning, as in this instance, is shown by the way in which people actually use words. Sharing this point of view, Margaret Macdonald (1903-1956), professor at New Bedford College and editor of the influential journal *Analysis,* discusses the variety of meanings which attach to "the work of art." When we apply the term to a novel or a piece of music we are using our words differently than when we apply the term to a painting which, together with cobwebs, hangs on a wall. The work of art may be quite tangible, and even a poem is, in a sense, real. Such considerations impel Miss Macdonald to criticize the ideas of Croce, Collingwood, and Sartre.

A somewhat similar criticism of Croce, although written from a very different philosophical standpoint, is advanced by Bernard Bosanquet (1848-1923), a distinguished British philosopher. Art, he maintains, evokes an integrated response of the whole "body-and-mind." He calls this response "feeling"; and the feeling, he says, is always embodied in an object. "It is a *relevant* feeling," he explains. "I mean it is attached, annexed, to the quality of some object—to all its detail . . . My feeling in its special quality is evoked by the special quality of which it is the feeling, and in fact is one with it." [1] Thus emphasizing the *embodiment* of feeling, he opposes the tendency of Benedetto Croce to minimize the esthetic importance of the sensuous medium and the physical objects of nature. Although Bosanquet is an idealist, he believes that Croce's is a "false

[1] Bernard Bosanquet, *Three Lectures on Aesthetic* (Macmillan, London, 1915), pp. 3, 5.

idealism," because it neglects the yearning of the creative imagination toward externalization and the influence of the external medium upon the imagination. As he says elsewhere, "To reject the function of the body—our own and nature's —is not to honor but to bereave the spirit." [2]

His emphasis upon the importance of the medium is no new principle: it is at least as old as Aristotle and received its classic expression in Lessing's *Laocoön*. But in a sense it has been rediscovered by modern artists and estheticians, and it has had an extraordinary cleansing and renovating effect upon the arts. For example, the work of an architect such as Frank Lloyd Wright, a designer such as Moholy-Nagy, a sculptor such as Henry Moore, or a painter such as Henri Matisse, has been profoundly influenced by this principle. "Respect your medium" has been a principal imperative of modern art.

Whereas the medium is the *particular* natural stuff out of which the work of art is made, the more abstract sensuous qualities, such as line, shape, and color in the visual arts, or pitch, timbre, and degree of loudness in the auditory arts, may be considered apart from the particular medium and form of art (color, for example, is common to many mediums and various arts).

These abstract sensuous elements have been perspicaciously discussed by David Wight Prall (1886-1940), Professor of Philosophy at the University of California and later at Harvard, in his important books *Aesthetic Analysis* and *Aesthetic Judgment*. He begins with an analysis of the sensuous materials, then describes the composition of these materials in orders or forms, and finally discusses the expressive features that result from reference to the surrounding world. Although he thus deals with referential expression, his books are characterized by their emphasis upon immediate sensuous surface and form. "It is characteristic of esthetic apprehension," he declares, "that the surface fully presented to sense is the total object of apprehension. . . . As we leave this surface in our attention, to go deeper into meanings or more broadly into connections and relations, we depart from the typically esthetic attitude." [3]

Although he thus tends to abstract from relations *external* to the work of art, he emphasizes relations that are internal and native to the materials. The pitch, timbre, and intensity (degree of loudness) of sound; the hue, saturation, and "brightness" (lightness or darkness) of color; the geometrical properties of lines, surfaces, and masses; and the spatial or temporal extension common to various arts, afford a natural basis for formal composition or order. The order, in each case, is intrinsic to the elements as such; and one reason that odors, tastes, and tactile qualities are artistically less important than tones and colors is that they lack any intrinsic principle of order, such as pitch or hue.

[2] "Croce's Aesthetic," *Proceedings of the British Academy*, Volume IX (1919-1920), p. 272.
[3] David Wight Prall, *Aesthetic Judgment* (Crowell, New York, 1929), p. 20.

MARGARET MACDONALD

The Work of Art as Physical

. . . The notion of Imagination enters differently into different esthetic (and critical) theories according to other notions with which it is contrasted. Moreover, some of these differences connect more directly than others with ordinary uses of the words "imagination," "imagine," and their cognates. I am not at present prepared to say that these differences themselves represent different uses of such words. But certainly some theories about art and imagination are more "metaphysical" than others. [Also], such theories may differ in width. At least, some of them may be more narrowly expounded and applied though it is not certain that nevertheless they do not have wider implications. For example, the most popular doctrines of the relation between art and imagination in English are confined to literature and particularly to poetry. I refer to the doctrines of Coleridge and other poets and critics of the romantic movement which have been continued by their modern followers.[1] Nevertheless, none of these writers explicitly denies that what is true of imagination in literature is true of it also in other arts. But if applied to those other arts, the doctrines would seem much less plausible without much modification. But even less explicit theorists make a similar restriction. For Shakespeare, for example, it is the *poet*, not the painter, sculptor or musician, who is, like the lunatic and the lover "of Imagination all compact." [2] This may be due to the fact that Englishmen are more interested in literature than any other art. When Bacon, for example, divided the human mind into the Faculties of Sensation, Reason, Memory, and Imagination, he allotted Philosophy to Reason, History to Memory (*whose* memory, one wonders?) and Poesy, not art in general, to Imagination.[3] He thus suggests either that poetry is the sole art or that other arts do not use imagination. But then it would be odd to describe music and painting as either philosophy or history, that is, as forms of analytic reasoning or remembering. Probably, if pressed, Bacon would have pushed these other arts into the pigeon-hole of Sensation. But they would not stay there quietly. For Sensation as the lowliest of the faculty hierarchy was invariably thought to provide by passive reception the "raw material" upon which the higher faculties worked. But painters and

---

[1] *Cf.* D. G. James, *Scepticism and Poetry* (1937) and R. L. Brett, *The Third Earl of Shaftesbury* (1951).

[2] *A Midsummer Night's Dream*, Act 5, Scene 1.

[3] *Advancement of Learning*, Bk. II.

composers do not passively see and hear what is "given" but actively produce what may be seen and heard by themselves and others. So their works cannot simply be allotted to Sensation as their origin. Indeed, the mythical matings of faculty psychology are totally inadequate to explain any of their alleged progeny, including the arts. It does not, of course, follow that artists are not sometimes correctly called "imaginative" and that this is not esthetically important. It is also much more natural to speak of an "imaginative writer" than of an "imaginative painter" or an "imaginative composer" and this may also be important.

Examples of the wider doctrine which does define all works of art as works of imagination are the theories of R. G. Collingwood,[4] Jean-Paul Sartre,[5] both influenced by Croce. According to them a work of art must be distinguished from all physical objects, even from such objects as the picture on the gallery wall, the sounds filling the concert hall, the printed volume from which the novel is being read. One reason given for this is that although a work of art cannot be communicated to others without a physical vehicle it can be imagined, and thus internally produced, by an artist who did not choose to manifest it externally. I think the relation is somewhat complex between works of art and physical objects, or, rather, between what is correctly said about works of art and the physical world.[6] But this is not elucidated by this metaphor popular with certain esthetic philosophers of a work of art as a mysterious message transmitted by an intrinsically worthless instrument, the physical medium. The very notion of a *medium* suggests the spiritualist séance rather than the study or studio. Nevertheless, it does make sense (though it may be false) to say that Shakespeare made up a play which he did not write down or get performed and that no one but he knew of this. So, it is argued, this situation may be generalized. Every work of art might similarly exist privately and remain uncommunicated. Physical labor is, therefore, not essential to a work of art which must be an imaginary object, a mental creation or private fantasy. But none of these consequences follow. There may, indeed, be good evidence to show that an artist had contemplated and even thought out a work which he never committed to word, paint, sound or other material. He may have described the work in a letter, diary or orally. But I doubt if an ordinary person would unhesitatingly assert that he had thereby *produced* the work. If the work were of one of the plastic arts I think this would certainly be denied. For it seems absurd to say of someone that he had painted a picture or carved a statue without the use of tools or materials. An imaginary picture or statue just isn't a picture or statue because these words stand for works which need hands as well as heads to bring

[4] *Principles of Art* (Oxford University Press, 1938).

[5] *The Psychology of Imagination*, trans. (Philosophical Library, N. Y., 1948), Conclusion, Sec. 2, "The Work of Art."

[6] Cf. *"Art and the 'Object of Art'"* by Paul Ziff, *Mind*, N.S., vol. LX, 1951, pp. 466-480, but I think Mr. Ziff simplifies the problem by confining his remarks to objects of the plastic arts.

them into existence. This may not be quite so clear for other works of art. I have said that Shakespeare might have made up a play which he did not write down or get performed. Similarly, Mozart might have composed a melody, say a setting for a song, which was never sung and for which he did not produce a score. Would one say that these works had existed and been lost to the world? Perhaps. Normally, a lost literary or musical work is one of which the text or score has disappeared or been forgotten, not one of which no text or score, written or oral, existed. But while no one would say that a picture which had not been painted however clearly a painter had imagined or even described it, had existed and been lost one might hesitate to deny that a poem or a song had existed because it was known only to its author and had never been spoken or sung aloud. For if this had been done, only once, and had been overheard there would be no good reason to deny the existence of the work though it were never heard again. This seems to attribute an exaggerated artistic importance to the mechanical processes of making visible and audible. An imaginary picture is not a picture and is of an entirely different logical type because the *work* of producing a picture cannot be done or, at least, completed without physical labor. But the task of making up a poem or story or composing a tune may sometimes be over before these are spoken, sung or written down. Moreover, there seems to be no substantial difference between what is imagined and what is uttered, heard, written, and read. I do not think these facts justify the conclusions of idealist esthetic philosophers but they may give some excuse for them and do also show discrepancies between the works of different arts which are important for esthetics. Yet although one may sometimes wonder whether an unrevealed poem or tune may properly be called a poem or tune, it does not follow that every literary and musical work still less every work of art is imaginary. For the circumstances I have described in which one might ask this question include the fact that it is asked of the work of an established artist. Of one who had never produced a public work it would be absurd to ask whether he might be a silent rival to all known artists. One who never exhibits his artistic skill is not a very "pure" artist but a fraud. Of a reputable author or composer, however, it might be sensible to ask whether all his works were known and there might be reason to believe they were not. I do not assert that we positively should add an imagined sonnet to the Shakespearean corpus but only that we might, rightly, hesitate and be inclined to do so as we should not hesitate to exclude an imagined statue from the works of Rodin. The hesitation would be due to a strong conflicting tendency to call works of art only certain public objects. This is, I am sure the primary use of the word for all and the sole use for some, works. Works of art are, primarily, public, perceptual objects made by someone using technical skill. There may be a distinction between artists and craftsmen, as Collingwood insisted,[7] but the borderland is wide and

[7] *Principles of Art*, Pt. I, Ch. 2, (Oxford University Press, 1938).

all artists, as makers, are also craftsmen. What they make and with what kind of skill, however, varies widely. In the plastic arts (painting and sculpture), the finished work is, normally, a physical object of the same sort as stones and stars. If asked to count the number of objects in a room one would include the Ming jar and the Turner as well as the rest. These works are enduring, particular objects each with its spatio-temporal position. They are, moreover, distinguished, as originals, from all replicas or copies.[8] They are made in the comparatively simple sense of being constructed from physical materials and only attention by a spectator is needed to perceive them as they were created.[9] In a fairly straight-forward sense one now "sees" the same picture or statue as the artist painted or modelled. The situation is less simple for literary and musical works of art. To revert to the room already mentioned. One would probably include in the collection of its objects the books in the bookcase and the scores on the music stand. It would not, however, be so clear that one had thereby included Shakespeare's plays or Verdi's operas. First, because no author or composer directly produces a printed volume. Secondly, though he might produce a pile of written or type-written manuscript and this might be referred to as the work, it would also, and perhaps more correctly, be called the text or score of the work. More correctly, because written or printed texts and scores are not necessary to the existence of literature and music. The primary form of such works is vocal and their survival formerly depended entirely upon memory and oral transmission. Spoken narratives, recitations, songs are not, however, physical objects. They are rather physical events which begin, continue, and then cease to exist. They are more like flashes of lightning and showers of rain than rocks and planets. But such events are public to all observers while they last. So are literary and musical performances. If, however, the corresponding work is identified with any one such performance it is obvious that compared with pictures and statues literary and musical works have a very brief existence. Well, it is possible that some have. A work might never be repeated after its first performance and be forgotten. Many thrilling camp fire stories and epic poems must have so perished. True, a picture or statue might be completed and immediately destroyed. The difference is that this need not happen whereas it is (I think, logically) impossible that the performance of a literary or musical work should continue for more than a very limited time. It would be absurd, for example, to suppose a play or symphony whose performance lasted a year. Yet there are many works of literature and music which have outlasted many works of the plastic arts.

[8] It has been pointed out to me that such works as etchings and woodcuts are exceptions to this. What the artist directly produces in these is an engraved plate or worked block. These, however, are not identified with or exhibited as the etching or woodcut but only prints taken from them of which they may be many, each an original. They would not be so called, however, unless taken from the object prepared by the artist.

[9] I ignore for this purpose such later operations as the cleaning of an old work, the emending of a text or score, etc.

"Not marble, nor the gilded monuments
Of princes, shall outlive this powerful rhyme." [10]

(An optimistic remark in view of the author's well-known habit of leaving his offspring for players and patrons to preserve.) How does this happen? The poem (or symphony) outlives its competitors if at some time or place there is, or could be, a physical presentation of it. Such occurrences are not copies, replicas or reproductions of an original. A performance of *Hamlet* now is not a reproduction of the first or any other production. Nor is it a copy of the text. To say that would be absurd. Nor are these performances many but related to a single source as the etching to its incised plate. Yet they are each and all manifestations of "the same work." Thus works of literature and music lack the definite spatio-temporal position of most works of the plastic arts. They exist wherever and whenever they are physically manifested. One cannot sensibly ask for the whereabouts of Shakespeare's plays and Beethoven's symphonies as one can for that of the Mona Lisa and St. Paul's Cathedral.

This distinction between the sense of "play" (and any comparable term) in which Shakespeare wrote only one play called *Hamlet* and that in which *Hamlet* has been played one hundred times this season has been likened to that between particular and universal and between type and token in the use of words. The first is wrong. The relation between a performance of *Hamlet* and the play may seem, superficially, to resemble that between the color of this paper and "whiteness." The paper with its color may be destroyed, but not whiteness; the performance ends but *Hamlet* remains. But differences make the comparison more misleading than helpful. It would be nonsense to talk of a performance of the play as an "instance" of *Hamlet* as the color of this paper is an instance of whiteness. Universals are qualities and relations. *Hamlet* does not characterize the performances of the play nor does it relate any objects. Finally, universals are timeless. It makes no sense to ask when whiteness and equality began to exist. Yet it is both sensible and true to say that Shakespeare's *Hamlet* came into existence about 1600, has continued to exist, in the manner already suggested, since that date and may cease to exist. [11] The comparison with the type-token distinction in the use of "word" is less misleading. Words in the type sense have a beginning, a history, and sometimes a decease—they become obsolete. Nor do they characterize or relate. For the sense of "the" in which there is only one word THE in the English language—the type word—does not characterize the token "the," which has just been printed, as does, for example, blackness. But the function of this, and every similar token, is to present the type-word. Tokens of the same type are related by similarity plus a convention which associates cer-

[10] W. Shakespeare, *Sonnet 55*.
[11] Cf. Warren and Wellek, *Theory of Literature* (London, 1949), p. 154.

tain noises with certain marks as being of the "same" word. So, too, the performances of *Hamlet* or the Ninth Symphony are of those works if they resemble
each other in certain fundamental respects. They will also differ, but if too eccentric they will be excluded from those which present these works. Perhaps
the chief difference between "work of art" in this sense and "word" is that individual presentations of a work of art may have their own independent artistic
value, while token-words do not fulfill independent grammatical and stylistic
functions. The performance of a great actor or violinist may be a work of art in
its own right, apart from being yet another version of *Hamlet* or the Brahms
Concerto, for acting and musical execution are also arts.

That a distinction must be made between some works of art and their manifestations may have led some esthetic philosophers, especially those chiefly interested in literature, into bad metaphysics. For this looks like a distinction between
two kinds of objects. Then it is tempting to construe a work of art as type as
something above or behind its perceptible token occurrences, for example, a
platonic Idea, a Norm,[12] a private mental state. Or, alternatively, with the phe-
nomenalists, to identify the work with the set of its occurrences. Neither
alternative will do. For by the ordinary use of the term "literature" or "music"
the ultimate test of whether works of these arts exist is sensory observation and
not introspection or super-sensuous intuition. But neither did Shakespeare and
Beethoven produce, nor do we see and hear, a *class* of occurrences when enjoying a play or symphony. The solution is to emphasize that because a word has
two uses it does not follow that it is used for two different objects. "Work of
art" is just used ambiguously in the manner described without implying any
expansion or contraction of the universe.

As for the process of making or creating a work of art. I have suggested,
somewhat crudely, that in some arts this is more physically laborious than in
others. I wanted to show that there might be an excuse for saying that some composition, for example, in literature and music, is internal. That it occurs "in the
mind" or "in imagination." I have said that this may sometimes happen. I also
think that whether it happens or not is an unimportant accident. What is done
"in the head" could have been done as well on paper, vocally or with a musical
instrument. There is, however, a more fundamental answer to idealist and sub-
jectivist conclusions drawn from the peculiarities of these arts. I have said that
one cannot separate the making of a work of the plastic arts from the skillful
handling of physical materials. There seem to be no comparable public materials
and exhibitions of skill in literature and music. One may always watch a person
painting, drawing, sculpting; one may not, even in his presence, be able to ob-

[12] Warren and Wellek, *loc. cit.*, p. 154.

serve that someone is composing a novel or symphony. Hence esthetic philosophers have supposed that musicians and authors, and, more particularly,
authors [13] use more refined methods and materials to produce their etherial
works. The fact of occasional unrecorded composition is used to support this
view. Authors are conceived to compose, like spiders, by each spinning his web
of private fancies from his Imagination. These may then, if their author so
chooses, be externalized, by an almost mechanical operation, in written or spoken
words, for public appraisal. But this is a totally misleading picture. There is one
physical element common to both literature and music, which is sound. Works
of both arts are manifested in audible performances. But the sounds in literature
are not mere physical noises but words of a particular language. The material
with which the literary artist creates is certainly not crude physical sound, comparable to stone, marble or paint, but neither is it private fancies or images.
What an English writer uses is the English language. I shall not discuss
whether this is part of the physical world, but it is certainly not a private invention by an individual. A writer inherits his native language as the independent,
public system of words and meanings of the society into which he is born. He
absorbs and accepts it perhaps even more completely than the plastic artist receives his materials from nature. It is in this system that he learns to prattle, discourse, and finally to create. If he is a good writer he may slightly modify the
system; he will do that with the material which has not been done before. If he
is a great writer, such as Shakespeare, appearing at the right historical moment,
he may effect a major transformation, leaving his successors an incomparably
more powerful and delicate instrument. Still, it will be the English language, not
the language of Shakespeare. Not even the greatest literary genius creates an entirely new language. The work of a literary artist is thus a construction of words,
the words of an established language most of which are in common use and all
of which may be understood by others and adopted into the language. His
labor is

> "the intolerable wrestle
> With words and meanings" [14]

which are public, not private, and where,

> "Words strain
> Crack and sometimes break, under the burden,
> Under the tension, slip, slide, perish,
> Decay with imprecision, will not stay in place,
> Will not stay still." [15]

---

[13] I have considered literature and music together as in many ways similar and
different from the plastic arts. But this is not general. Indeed, most esthetic philosophers
practically ignore music.

[14] T. S. Eliot, *The Four Quartets: East Coker*, Sec. 2.

[15] *Loc. cit., Burnt Norton*, Sec. 5.

I said that whether some literary composition was unrecorded was unimportant and did not support idealist conclusions. The reason should now be clear. If what is done, externally or internally, audibly or silently, is literary composition, it will be a construction from the words of an established language. For this is what we mean by the term "literary composition." But if all that happens is the passage of a series of private images, feelings, or symbols, this is not literary composition nor its result a work of art.

Much of this applies also to music. The material of the composer, too, is not mere physical sound or noise. Nor is it sounds used with the rules of significance which makes language a medium of communication about all topics. Musical sounds are notes of a scale and musical composition the arrangement of such notes according to further conventions of melody, harmony and the like which are common to a musical community.[16] These the composer finds and accepts as the writer accepts his native language. Like language, too, they change and develop and may even be revolutionized by great composers but are never entirely superseded. No more than literature is music a series of private feelings, sensations, images; it is a structure of sounds ordered by common conventions and addressed to a suitably trained audience. As with literature, composition, whether external or internal, must follow this pattern if it is to be correctly termed "musical composition" and its result a musical work.

I have tried to show that the esthetic theories of Croce, Collingwood, Sartre and other idealists who equate works of art with works of imagination and these with what is mental or physically unreal do not satisfactorily elucidate our use of the term "work of art." They confuse the indubitable fact that in composing a work of art an artist may imagine more than he now perceives or can remember, with the admission of imaginary objects and fictitious entities. *The Tempest* is a work of imagination, it shows great imaginative and creative power, but it is certainly not an imaginary or fictitious object. Shakespeare's play is as real as its author. True, it "contains" or is "about" imaginary objects, Prospero, Caliban, Ariel, a magic island. These require other treatment. I will say here only that their logical status differs from that of the work of art, for it is very obvious that we talk of them differently.

—"Art and Imagination," *Proceedings of the Aristotelian Society* (1953)

16 *Cf.* E. Hanslick, *The Beautiful in Music*, pp. 144-145.

BERNARD BOSANQUET

The Esthetic Attitude in Its Embodiments

Why are there different arts? The simple answer to this question takes us, I believe, to the precise root and source of the whole principle of esthetic expressiveness. . . .

We should begin, I am convinced, from the very simplest facts. Why do artists make different patterns, or treat the same pattern differently, in wood-carving, say, and clay-modeling, and wrought-iron work? If you can answer this question thoroughly, then, I am convinced, you have the secret of the classification of the arts and of the passage of feeling [1] into its esthetic embodiment; that is, in a word, the secret of beauty.

Why, then, in general does a worker in clay make different decorative patterns from a worker in wrought-iron? I wish I could go into this question with illustrations and details, but I will admit at once that I am not really competent to do so, though I have taken very great interest in the problem. But in general there can surely be no doubt of the answer. You cannot make the same things in clay as you can in wrought-iron, except by a *tour de force*. The feeling of the work is, I suppose, altogether different. The metal challenges you, coaxes you, as William Morris said of the molten glass, to do a particular kind of thing with it, where its tenacity and ductility make themselves felt. The clay, again, is delightful, I take it, to handle, to those who have a talent for it; but it is delightful of course in quite different manipulations from those of the wrought-iron. I suppose its facility of surface, how it lends itself to modeling or to throwing on the wheel, must be its great charm. Now the decorative patterns which are carried out in one way or the other may, of course, be suggested *ab extra* by a draughtsman, and have all sorts of properties and interests in themselves as mere lines

---

[1] What Bosanquet means by "feeling" and by "body-and-mind," terms which appear several times in the pages here reproduced, is made clear by the following quotation from the Preface to his book: "I must appear unfortunate in having laid so much stress on 'feeling,' just when high authorities are expressing a doubt whether the word has any meaning at all. . . . I can only say here that the first and main thing which the word suggests to me is the concernment of the whole 'body-and-mind,' as Plato puts it in building up his account of psychical unity on the single sentence, 'The man has a pain in his finger' [*Republic*, 462 D]. It is the whole man, the 'body-and-mind,' who has the pain, and in it is one, though it is referred to the finger and localized there. When a 'body-and-mind' is, as a whole, in any experience, that is the chief feature, I believe, of what we mean by feeling. Think of him as he sings, or loves, or fights. When he is one, I believe it is always through feeling, whatever distinctions may supervene upon it. That unity, at all events, is the main thing the word conveys to me."

on paper. But when you come to carry them out in the medium, then, if they are appropriate, or if you succeed in adapting them, they become each a special phase of the embodiment of your whole delight and interest of "body-and-mind" in handling the clay or metal or wood or molten glass. It is alive in your hands, and its life grows or rather magically springs into shapes which it, and you in it, seem to desire and feel inevitable. The feeling for the medium, the sense of what can rightly be done in it only or better than in anything else, and the charm and fascination of doing it so—these, I take it, are the real clue to the fundamental question of esthetics, which is "how feeling and its body are created adequate to one another." It is parallel to the question in general philosophy, "Why the soul has a body." It is the same sort of thing as the theory of the rising mountain,[2] but it is much less open to caprice, being absolute fact all through, and it explains not merely the interpretation of lines and shapes, but the whole range and working of the esthetic imagination in the province of fine art, which is its special province.

To this doctrine belongs the very fruitful modern topic of the relation of beautiful handicraft with the workman's life, as the outcome and expression of his body-and-mind, and amid all the disparagement which the most recent views of art are apt to throw upon Ruskin, we must remember that it was first and foremost to his inspired advocacy that this point of view owes its recognition today, and William Morris, for instance, recognized him, in this respect at least, as his master.

The differences of the great arts then are simply such differences as those between clay-modeling, wood-carving, and wrought-iron work, developed on an enormous scale, and with their inevitable consequences for whole provinces of esthetic imagination.

For this is a fact of the highest importance. Every craftsman, we saw, feels the peculiar delight and enjoys the peculiar capacity of his own medium. This delight and sense of capacity are of course not confined to the moments when he is actually manipulating his work. His fascinated imagination lives in the powers of his medium; he thinks and feels in terms of it; it is the peculiar body of which *his* esthetic imagination and no other is the peculiar soul.

Thus there grow up the distinct traditions, the whole distinctive worlds of imaginative thought and feeling, in which the great imaginative arts have their life and being. . . .

The ideal of every art must be revealed, I take it, in terms of the art itself; and it must be what underlies the whole series of efforts which the artist's imagination has made and is making, to create, in his own medium, an embodied feeling in which he can rest satisfied. It is the world as he has access to it through his art. It may seem to him more than any of his works; but it only has existence in them and in the effort which they imply when taken all together.

[2] See the account of Empathy, by Vernon Lee, reproduced in this volume. (Editor.)

The danger is to try and make a picture of this effort, apart from any of its achievements, which is really nothing. Then you get the enfeebled ideal, which means the omission of all character and individuality.

Now let us take a particular case. If our view of the distinction and connection of the arts is right, and it is simply a question of the medium adopted by each, and the capacities of that medium as proved by experience, what is to be said of the distinctive character of *poetry*? It seems in a sense to have almost no material element, to work directly with significant ideas in which the objects of the imagination are conveyed. Language is so transparent, that it disappears, so to speak, into its own meaning, and we are left with no characteristic medium at all.

I do not think there can be any doubt about the true attitude here. Poetry, like the other arts, has a physical or at least a sensuous medium, and this medium is sound. It is, however, significant sound, uniting inseparably in itself the factors of formal expression through an immediate pattern, and of representation through the meanings of language, exactly as sculpture and painting deal at once and in the same vision both with formal patterns and with significant shapes. That language is a physical fact with its own properties and qualities is easily seen by comparing different tongues, and noting the form which different patterns, such as sapphic or hexameter verse, necessarily receive in different languages, such as Greek and Latin. To make poetry in different languages, for example, in French and German, is as different a task as to make decorative work in clay and iron. The sound, meter, and meaning are the same inseparable product in a poem as much as the color, form, and embodied feeling in a picture. And it is only an illusion to suppose that because you have significant sentences in poetry, therefore you are dealing with meanings which remain the same outside the poem, any more than a tree or a person whom you think you recognize in a picture, is, as you know them at home so to speak, *the* tree or *the* person *of* the picture. Poetry no more keeps its meaning when turned into corresponding prose, than a picture or a sonata keeps its meaning in the little analyses they print in the catalogues or programs.

Shelley, according to Professor Bradley, had a feeling of the kind referred to. Poetry seemed to him to deal with a perfectly apt and transparent medium, with no qualities of its own, and therefore approaching to being no medium at all, but created out of nothing by the imagination for the use of the imagination. While the media employed by the other arts, being gross and physical and having independent qualities of their own, seemed to him rather obstacles in the way of expression than apt instruments of it. The answer to such a view is what we have just given.

It is the qualities of the media which give them the capacity to serve as embodiments of feeling; and sonorous language, the medium of poetry, has its peculiarities and definite capacities precisely like the others.

Here, I cannot but think, we are obliged to part company, with some regret, from Benedetto Croce. He is possessed, as so often is the case with him, by
a fundamental truth, so intensely that he seems incapable of apprehending
what more is absolutely necessary to its realization. Beauty, he sees, is for the
mind and in the mind. A physical thing, supposed unperceived and unfelt, cannot be said in the full sense to possess beauty. But he forgets throughout, I must
think, that though feeling is necessary to its embodiment, yet also the embodiment is necessary to feeling. To say that because beauty implies a mind,
therefore it is an internal state, and its physical embodiment is something
secondary and incidental, and merely brought into being for the sake of
permanence and communication—this seems to me a profound error of principle, a false idealism. It meets us, however, throughout Croce's system, according to which "intuition"—the inward vision of the artist—is the only true
expression. External media, he holds, are, strictly speaking, superfluous, so that
there is no meaning in distinguishing between one mode of expression and
another (as between paint and musical sound and language). Therefore there
can be no classification of the arts, and no fruitful discussion of what can better
be done by one art than by another. And esthetic—the philosophy of expression
—is set down as all one with linguistic—the philosophy of speech. For there is no
meaning in distinguishing between language in the sense of speech, and other
modes of expression. Of course, if he had said that speech is not the only form
of language, but that every art speaks to us in a language of its own, that would
have had much to be said for it. But I do not gather that that is his intention.

His notion is not a new one among theorists. It really is deeply rooted in
a philosophical blunder. No doubt it seems obvious, when once pointed out,
that things are not all there, not complete in all qualities, except when they are
appreciated in a mind. And then, having rightly observed that this is so, we are
apt to go on and say that you have them complete, and have all you want of
them, if you have them before your mind and have not the things in bodily presence at all. But the blunder is, to think that you can have them completely before your mind without having their bodily presence at all. And because of this
blunder, it seems fine and "ideal" to say that the artist operates in the bodiless
medium of pure thought or fancy, and that the things of the bodily world are
merely physical causes of sensation, which do not themselves enter into the
effects he uses. It is rather a natural thing to say about poetry, because we discount the physical side of language. We glance at its words and do not sound
them. And Shelley, as we saw, says something very like that.

But at the very beginning of all this notion, as we said, there is a blunder.
Things, it is true, are not complete without minds, but minds, again, are not
complete without things; not any more, we might say, than minds are complete
without bodies. Our resources in the way of sensation, and our experiences in
the way of satisfactory and unsatisfactory feeling, are all of them won out of our

intercourse with things, and are thought and imagined by us as qualities and properties of the things. Especially we see this in music. Here we have an art entirely made up of a material—musical tone—which one may say does not exist at all in the natural world, and is altogether originated by our inventive and imaginative manipulation of physical things, pressing on in the line of creative discovery which something very like accident must at first have opened up to us.[3] Apart from this imaginative operation upon physical things, our fancy in the realm of music could have done as good as nothing.

And in principle it is the same with all the arts. All the material and the physical process which the artist uses—take our English language as used in poetry for an example—has been elaborated and refined, and, so to speak, consecrated by ages of adaptation and application in which it has been fused and blended with feeling—and it carries the life-blood of all this endeavor in its veins; and that is how, as we have said over and over again, feelings get their embodiment, and embodiments get their feeling. If you try to cut the thought and fancy loose from the body of the stuff in which it molds its pictures and poetic ideas and musical constructions, you impoverish your fancy, and arrest its growth, and reduce it to a bloodless shade. When I pronounce even a phrase so commonplace in itself as "Rule, Britannia!" the actual vibrations of the sound, the bodily experience I am aware of in saying it, is alive with the history of England which passed into the words in the usage and formation of the language. Up to a certain point, language is poetry ready-made for us.

And I suppose that a great painter, in his actual handling of his brush, has present with him a sense of meaning and fitness which is one with the joy of execution, both of which the experience of a lifetime has engrained in the cooperation of his hand and eye. I take it, there is a pleasure in the brush stroke, which *is also* a sense of success in the use of the medium, and of meaning in hitting the exact effect which he wants to get. We common people have something analogous to all this, when we enjoy the too-rare sensation of having found the right word. In such "finding" there is a creative element. A word is, quite strictly speaking, not used twice in the same sense.

Croce says, indeed, that the artist has every stroke of the brush in his mind as complete before he executes it as after. The suggestion is that using the brush adds nothing to his inward or mental work of art. I think that this is false idealism. The bodily thing adds immensely to the mere idea and fancy, in wealth of qualities and connections. If we try to cut out the bodily side of our world, we shall find that we have reduced the mental side to a mere nothing.

And so, when we said that you can carry away the soul of a thing and leave its body behind, we always added that you must in doing so confer its soul upon

---

[3] This applies even to the development of song, so far as that involves a musical system.

a new and spiritualized body.[4] Your imagination must be an imagination of something, and if you refuse to give that something a definite structure, you pass from the esthetic semblance to the region of abstract thought. I have spoken of sound as physical; if this is a difficulty it is enough to call it sensuous, and sensuous in immediate connection with other physical properties and experiences. This applies both to music and to language.

All this later argument of ours, starting from the importance of medium and technique, has aimed at exhibiting in detail the double process of creation and contemplation which is implied in the esthetic attitude, and the impossibility of separating one factor of it from another. And it is the same question as that stated in other words, how a feeling can be got into an object. This is the central problem of the esthetic attitude; and, as we have seen, the best material for solving it for us who are not great artists comes from any minor experience we may have at command in which we have been aware of the outgoing of feeling into expression. We must think not merely of the picture in the gallery or the statue in the museum, but of the song and the dance, the dramatic reading, the entering into music, or the feel of the material in the minor arts, or simply, of the creative discovery of the right word.

The festal or social view of art will help us here. Suppose a tribe or a nation has won a great victory; "they are feeling big, and they want to make something big," as I have heard an expert say. That, I take it, is the rough account of the beginning of the esthetic attitude. And according to their capacity and their stage of culture, they may make a pile of their enemies' skulls, or they may build the Parthenon. The point of the esthetic attitude lies in the adequate fusion of body and soul, where the soul is a feeling, and the body its expression, without residue on either side.

—Three Lectures on Æsthetic (1915)

DAVID WIGHT PRALL

Sensuous Elements and Esthetic Orders

What is the language of esthetics? What are its nouns or terms? What are their adjectives or relations? If it is admitted that nature and the arts give us

[4] This sentence refers back to an idea developed in a preceding part of Bosanquet's lecture, namely, that "the real sting of even the crudest glorification of copying is this wonder that you can carry off with you a thing's soul, and leave its body behind."

concrete structural complexes, and that esthetic understanding is grasping the nature of these, as constituted of sensory elements in relation, then we must abstract such aspects of quality as are clearly relational, and survey the elements in the orders constituted by such relations. And since . . . these relations are peculiar to certain qualitative aspects of sensuous material, we shall not expect to find them limited to the spatial or the temporal merely. What is characteristic of color contrasts is not only that they are spatially exhibited, but that the colors as such really do contrast, really are far apart in some aspect of color as such. And since this is not so obviously the case with tastes and smells and other sorts of sensory content like the feeling of muscular strain or of rhythmic pulse, we shall turn our attention at first to sound and color to see what we can discover in them that will explain, namely, make intelligible, the structures of music and painting.

What we do find are non-numerical, non-spatial, non-temporal serial relations constituting serial orders. But the situation is complicated by the fact that these serial orders are not of the concrete sounds, not of hearable notes nor of concrete visible colors as such, but of aspects of these which are conveniently called dimensions on the analogy to spatial dimensions. As a geometrical structure may vary in length while it remains the same in breadth, so sound can vary in pitch while it remains the same in loudness, or *vice versa*. It is such independent variation that establishes the grouping of elements or terms in all analysis, and in our case a grouping in serial orders.

A relation constituting a serial order has certain properties. If it applies to a group of elements, then every one of these elements is related to every other by this same relation. This is called the connexity of the relation. A relation is said to have connexity when between any two elements of the field whatever this relation holds. Now all sounds have pitch, and every distinct pitch is either above or below any other pitch that we may choose. Thus all sounds are related in a single order, every sound to every other sound. We might simply say that sounds are pitch-related. But the point of a serial relation is that the sense of the relation, its direction, is part of what gives it its special character. Instead of being reversible or symmetrical, above-in-pitch is asymmetrical. A relation is called asymmetrical when, if it is the relation of, say, x to y, it cannot be the relation of y to x. Thus if it is the fact that x is taller than y, this involves the fact that y is not taller than x, but shorter. If B is higher in pitch than A, A cannot be higher in pitch than B. If this seems too obvious to notice, we need only call attention to such a series as that of selected points on the surface of the earth. Chicago is related to New York by the relation west-of. And it seems at first obvious that New York cannot be related to Chicago by this same relation, but only by its converse, east-of. But if we go east from New York to Southampton and Gibraltar and Singapore and San Francisco, and keep on going east through Omaha, we shall get to Chicago by a route on which New York is west and not east of

Chicago. The series of pitches is not like this. It runs out in both directions instead of coming back upon itself.

The relation higher-in-pitch-than has a further property, called transitiveness. If B is higher in pitch than A, and C is higher in pitch than B, then C is higher in pitch than A. It is clear then that every sound (and we distinguish sounds from noises by just this criterion that they have clearly perceptible pitch) lies in this single linear series of pitches, each at its own fixed point. The order is one-dimensional, to use a convenient term, and it is also not cyclical. And no sound can be removed from this given pitch order. Nor can anything enter this order except sounds. By virtue of being what we call a single sound, a note has to be at a particular pitch; and to be at a particular pitch is to be at a point fixed in the single series of all the pitches that there are.

The important fact for esthetics is not merely that a musical sound has its particular place in the single order of all pitches, but that we cannot help hearing it at this place, not too exactly always, but necessarily as relatively high or relatively low, and always as higher or lower than any other note whose pitch we can distinguish from its. The serial order is thus native to sound as such. It is intrinsic to sounds in the sense that every sound is in this serial order and that nothing that is not a sound can possibly be in this order. It is this orderliness, as we have seen, that makes concrete pitch patterns in successive notes a possibility. Sounds differing in pitch always lie near-in-pitch-to, and far-in-pitch-from, other sounds. In any given set of notes we can therefore speak of the pitch distance or interval between them, once we have established a measure for such distances. . . . We have here a basic structural possibility, the necessary condition of melody, for example, insofar as melody is pitch pattern made up of a succession of notes at distinguishable intervals from one another, and heard as at these intervals. And this quite regardless of any special set of intervals chosen, or of our having technical musical names for the intervals.

That this is more significant than the mere fact that sounds vary is plain, if we think of smells or tastes. Loudness and softness in sounds, the dimension called their intensity, may be said to be paralleled by intensity in smells or tastes; but only very roughly even for our perception. And our control over the production of smells, for example, for direct patterned presentation, is so far behind our control of sound intensities, as with our own voices or by means of instruments, as to be almost negligible. Of pitch, our control, far from being thus negligible, is both accurate and of the wide range defined by many instruments. And what in smell or taste corresponds to pitch in sound? That aspect of an odor or a taste, no doubt, that is specifically characteristic; what defines it as resinous or fragrant or putrid, or salty or sour. Even so we have rather a complex of dimensions than a relatively simple line of variation, a somewhat confusing or confused quality, more comparable to the complexity of timbre, perhaps, than to pitch. And what could be said to lie exactly, or even very roughly, as far from the odor of pine needles in one direction and some other given odor lies in another? The directions of variation here are not plain to ordinary perception. As our systematic knowledge of smells and tastes grows, we can discern order in them, and even without this they themselves furnish esthetic content as elements more or less alike, more or less contrasting. But just as there is no clear, complete order in them directly apprehended by us, which is intrinsic to their nature as pitch order is to the nature of sounds, so in composition with them we have no adequate control of structural forms or distinctly perceptible intelligible patterns.

It is plainly enough the felt pitch relations, depending upon the intrinsic order of sounds in pitch, that give to music the possibility of melody, so far, we must repeat, as melody depends on pitch for its heard character. That it does so depend characteristically will hardly be denied. A pattern of noises or of sounds of unvarying pitch, or of sounds not at recognizable intervals in pitch, we do not even call melody; and if we did, it must be granted that this would be a melody lacking the distinctive character that melodies in the more usual application of the word are defined by.

Sounds then do not merely vary; they vary systematically. They vary in the two directions of a serial order, along the line of a single dimension. . . . This allows us to select a limited number of points on the line at recognized intervals, those relations of pitch distance out of which all of our western musical compositions have been made.

But in this emphasis on pitch, we must not neglect the other dimensions of variation in sound. For these are equally conditions, though less strikingly characteristic conditions, of musical structure. The relation louder-than, with its converse, softer-than, is a relation establishing for all sounds—and for all noises, too, so that noise can enter strictly into structure—another one-dimensional serial order intrinsic to sounds and noises, found, that is, in nothing else and always present when sound or noise is present. It is the fact that noises, even with no distinguishable pitch, have their fixed places in this dimension of loudness-softness that makes them possible as integral elements in genuine musical composition. And here again there is not mere variation or mere contrast or similarity, but distinguishable degrees of similarity and contrast, distances in loudness-softness as measured along a single dimension, at one fixed point of which every noise and every sound lies by virtue of its degree of loudness, where also it is heard to lie, if we hear it at all.

For color variation the serially ordered aspects are not quite so easy to exhibit. But at least we have an adequate scheme of them, in which every aspect of variation appears to be systematically included. While the distances between variations differ according as we use one or another of the various color diagrams—the color cones of psychology or the color body of Ostwald's theoretically more regular and systematically more easily intelligible scheme—still the fact of serial orders or dimensions dictated by the intrinsic nature of color variation remains the same. There are the hues from yellow through orange and red, and on through purple and violet to blue and blue-green and green and green-yellow back to yellow. There are the lighter tints for each hue, running up into white in all of them, and the darker shades running down into black. And there are the variations for hues at all degrees of lightness and darkness from maximum saturation to the neutral grays. This gives us three convenient main dimensions of color variation, all compactly illustrated in the familiar diagram of a double cone. The neutral variations, white to black through the grays, are represented along the vertical axis from upper to lower apex; the saturated hues lie on the circumference of the double base; the pure light variations (which may be thought of as mixtures of pure saturated hues with white) run upward to white itself on the surface of the upper cone; and the pure dark variations (which may be thought of as saturated hues mixed with increasing amounts of black) correspondingly run downward on the outer lower surface to black. The points beneath the surface, inside the cone, would represent all the rest of the possibilities of color variation. In general, the downward direction is from light to dark, the direction inward to the axis is from saturation to neutral, and the variations along the circles with centers on the axis, in planes parallel to the base of the double cone, are variations in hue, at all the various intensities and various saturations. To fix convenient points on the circumference of the base of the cone, the complementaries red and green, and yellow and blue, may be placed at the extremities of diameters of this base circle, the two diameters lying at right angles to each other. Thus the circumference is quartered red to yellow, yellow to green, green to blue, and blue back to red.

The scheme fails to represent accurately some of the relative distances as measured in terms of felt degrees of similarity and contrast. Full saturated yellow is not for our vision so far from white as any of the other full hues; and the hues on the red-yellow sector are brighter and warmer than those on the blue-green sector. Moreover, it is obvious that any line through the cone at any angle will give a set of variations along a dimension that constitutes a series just as clearly as the sets of variations along the traditionally selected three lines. But these three are those that have been conventionally named, and they serve our purposes well enough. For all that we wish to establish is that every color variation is to be found somewhere in the scheme, and that therefore every color variation lies at a determinately felt distance from others along any single dimension chosen.

But it will be clear at once that the selection of scales of color variations is guided by relations peculiar to color and not strictly parallel to the relations that make up musical scales. For in color, although hue is perhaps fundamentally characteristic, variations in hue are no more significant for color composition, no more characteristic of color design, than variations of saturation or of brightness.

The order of the hues is cyclical, too, while the orders of the variations in saturation and brightness are not. In sound the two serial orders, that of pitch and
that of loudness, are like these latter in being non-cyclical. But while notes are
regularly named by their pitch—an indication of the greater significance of pitch
than of loudness to musical pattern—colors are named sometimes for their hue,
sometimes for their other aspects, or for at least two of their aspects in combination. A name like brown is nowhere applicable on the main lines of variation
that we have indicated. Nor is brown a "hue." Its "hue" is orange, and yet the
name orange does not fit it at all. In fact, of course, it is a name covering a range
in the sector about orange, which depends for its characteristic concrete quality
largely on being not a saturated color. The fact that we so often speak of browns
and grays together as contrasted with reds and greens and yellows and blues,
shows how the feeling of its lack of saturation has been taken as its distinguishing characteristic without reference explicitly to any scheme. But the ordinary
scheme definitely includes it, and its name, instead of removing it from the
scheme, fairly indicates its place there, provided we attend to its characteristic
meaning and not merely to the name itself, which might lead us to think of it
as one among the other hues.

But another point occurs at once. A pitch pattern is easily recognizable as an
aspect of melodic structure and hence of music. But pictures are not so regularly
or so readily apprehended as being color patterns. In fact, in much of what we
think of under the term painting, it is spatial design not color design that is the
characteristic distinction. The parallel with music is still clear, though obviously
not at all adequate. As colors are spread over surfaces, so notes are extended
through time, and rhythm may enter into melody as distinctly as pitch itself,
though a definite rhythmic beat may be entirely absent, as in plain song. At any
rate, it is perfectly clear that painting has not traditionally been sheer color design to any such degree as that in which musical composition has been pitch pattern; and although temporal spread is as necessary a condition of music as spatial
spread is of painting, it seems at least fair to say that the relative emphasis on the
intrinsic nature of sound in music as distinguished from its one-dimensional
extension in time, is greater than the relative emphasis on color as such as
distinguished from spatial design in painting.

In both cases, however, it is clear not only that the qualitative orders require
either spatial or temporal extension of their elements in order to be concretely
present to an organism, but also that the spatial and temporal aspects of the
concrete content are themselves structural.

Like pitch, time, whatever else it may be, is an order. That space is an
order we all realize from an elementary acquaintance with geometry. Two lines
on a surface cannot remain merely separate lines. They are necessarily related as
parallel to each other or at an angle, and at a determinate angle. And these intrinsic properties of all spatial elements lend themselves to structure, carry structure

in their very nature. But without visually perceptible, that is to say colored, area, no spatial pattern can be sensuously present. Even figures in geometry must be black against white or gray if they are to be seen. So that the qualitative elements of our intrinsic qualitative orders are as necessary to the sensuous presentation of spatial character as spatial character is to the presentation of elements of color, or duration and succession in a time order to the presentation of elements of sound.

Two different orders must combine, so to speak, if we are to have any concrete pattern at all. Philosophically this was recognized by Plato in the notion of the communication of the categories. Since every sound in order to be heard, and every color in order to be seen, must be more than pitch and loudness in the one case, more than hue and saturation and brightness in the other, spatial and temporal structure and the orders intrinsic to space and time are as essential to concrete esthetic surface as what we usually call sensuous content as *distinguished* from spatio-temporal structure. Since, however, we can conceive color and sound abstractly in qualitative orders neither spatial nor temporal, this distinction between so-called content and formal structure lies within concrete content. In fact the distinction of form from matter or of structure from content is entirely relative. We never have the one without the other in actuality. They are both abstractions. And just as this is nothing derogatory to them, since it is true of all the aspects of concretely experienced data, so it is fairly absurd to speak as if qualitative elements and orders were less fundamentally significant in composition than spatial and temporal elements and forms.

Our vastly greater systematization of what we have distinguished by abstraction of the features of the spatial and temporal aspects of our world in mathematics and science inclines us to neglect the significance, even for the arts, of the serial qualitative orders intrinsic to color and sound. We have used mathematical and geometrical abstractions so much that the elements among which these abstract relations subsist have literally vanished, as points have become by definition the vanishing points of lines, and lines the vanishing points or disappearing boundaries between intersecting planes. Space and time have become purely formal as we have realized their abstractness in systematic analysis. There are no real but only nominal elements of space and time. But it takes very little meditation on the nature of pitch and hue to see that once we abstract their formal nature in the same way from sound and color, these latter become purely formal too. It is the lack of full attention to what we mean by color contrast itself, as distinguished from the spatial presentation of such contrast, that makes us unwilling to admit that color as such has no extension, but is only an abstract formal scheme, just as pitch is a purely formal continuum, which is one of the analytical aspects of sound. And adequate analysis would resolve sound totally into such formal aspects, if we treated sound as we do space, and dropped out of our account of it its feeling in concrete presentation.

Thus our scheme of esthetic analysis may be accused indifferently of formalizing esthetics, or of reducing all the formal aspects of art and nature to sensuous content. The point is that any content concretely presented, anything experienced directly, is qualitative; that no concrete quality is absolutely simple, that all the surface of the experienced world as clearly apprehended consists, upon analysis, of elements intrinsically ordered and also ordered spatially and temporally. The temporal cannot be present except as it attaches itself to what is qualitatively and spatially extended any more than the qualitative can be altogether unenduring. What is extended in no way at all is nothing. Our purest spiritual longings are the longings of an organism, and they are inconceivable as concretely existent in separation from it. Only in abstraction are they clearly conceivable and at all intelligible, just as color contrast or pitch pattern is conceivable in abstraction from the concrete. Thinking about things in order to know them involves just such abstracting; and it appears to be our good fortune to live in a time when men have penetrated far enough into the nature of logic to allow analysis to be clearly discerned as constituted of the forms which such abstracting makes out. All science involves the discriminating of elements and relations necessary to generality and systematization. The established sciences are the fields where this process has developed sufficiently to give us confidence in the usefulness and validity of the method.

One further point seems required here if we are to be sure that we have not misplaced our emphasis on qualitative orders. We have spoken of these orders as intrinsic to sound and intrinsic to color. We have spoken of spatial and temporal orders as intrinsic to elements that are spatial and temporal. And we have noticed that for actual concretely apparent surfaces for ear and eye we require spatio-temporal structure as well as qualitative structure. A note must have duration just as truly as it must have pitch or timbre; and spatial and temporal structures can appear only as qualitied. We keep "quality" as a term for the very purpose of distinguishing such aspects of color and sound from extensional aspects whether spatial or temporal.

Why, then, are the qualitative orders any more intrinsic to sound and color than spatial or temporal order? And why, if we are to be rigorous, are temporal and spatial order any more intrinsic to spatial and temporal elements than the qualitative orders, since only as qualitied and hence as involving qualitative orders, can either spatial or temporal elements appear concretely? That the answer is in the end a matter of definition must be plain. But good definitions serve honest purposes, and we do not distinguish and define usefully where there is no significant difference. The difference in our case is, however, easy to indicate. Every sound has a pitch and lies in the pitch order, as every color has brightness and saturation and hue and lies in these orders. Also every sound has temporal duration and every color, spatial extension. But everything in the world has duration, while nothing but sound has pitch, as nothing in the world but sound has loudness in the specific use of the word as here applied. Vast numbers of things in the world have spatial extension, while nothing in the world but color has hue or what is meant by brightness or darkness as these terms apply to color. What we are doing is simply to limit the application of the terms that we use to abstract aspects of experience in a way that appears at once to be un-ambiguous and to serve the purposes of the sort of knowledge that we seek by indicating relevant distinctions for esthetics. . . .

Thus our analytical base is outlined. The elements in it are elements of sensuous content intrinsically ordered, elements that are found by means of discrimination in the concrete, but ordered and conceived in abstract series. The serial orders are of at least two sorts, qualitative and spatio-temporal, the former intrinsic to certain qualities, the latter to space-time configurations. And from their intrinsic orders elements cannot be removed. A note carries with it its position in the pitch series into any composition, and maintains its determinate distance in pitch from notes of other pitch placed near or far from it in any temporal succession of notes. In the same way any configuration in space or time simply exhibits selected parts out of the ordered manifolds that constitute the nature of space and time. And as qualities cannot appear concretely except within spatio-temporal structure, so spatial and temporal configurations require for concrete exhibition qualitative content. The qualitative orders and the spatio-temporal orders are equally abstract, but they are clearly distinct in nature, and while they are dependent reciprocally for concrete exhibition, they are independently variable.

The possibilities for structure are thus infinite; and the arts have selected out of these infinite possibilities a relatively limited number of determinate modes or fundamental patterns on the basis of which works of art have been constructed. Moreover, artists have had to consider many non-esthetic aspects of the physical media that are the bearers of esthetic form and quality. And esthetics is forced into considering such media, and various non-esthetic purposes, if for no other reason than to distinguish practical technique and practical knowledge of struc-tural materials from what is strictly esthetic knowledge of esthetic structures and their constituents as esthetic surface. The relatively simple analytical basis just outlined is no doubt fundamental and even necessary to esthetic comprehension. But we shall have to account on non-esthetic grounds for a great deal that would otherwise remain inexplicable. Our present need is to exhibit those natural conditions that have set up for us ordered and limited selections of elements and basic patterns for composition with these elements.

—*Aesthetic Analysis* (1936)

CHAPTER NINE

Expressiveness

CHARLES W. MORRIS
Science, Art, and Technology

SUSANNE K. LANGER
Expressiveness and Symbolism

RUDOLF ARNHEIM
Expression

I. A. RICHARDS
Science and Poetry

J. W. N. SULLIVAN
The Nature of Music

Introductory Note

IN THE PRECEDING CHAPTER we have been mainly concerned with the *matter* or "body" of the work of art. There are two other "dimensions" that are commonly recognized—*expressiveness* and *form*.

The expressiveness is largely a function of *representations*, which iconically denote actual things, such as trees, mountains, and human figures, and *connotations*, which merely suggest such recognizable things or qualities. Art not only "imitates" things by straightforward depiction—it hints at things by analogy, symbol, or association.

Form results from the ordering of parts or elements into significant relations, as in the thematic variation of a symphony or the unfolding plot of a tragedy. Since form is basic to art, we shall consider it at length in Chapters X and XI.

During the second and third decades of this century, estheticians were especially preoccupied with the problem of form. This was the period when such "formalists" as Clive Bell and Roger Fry exercised their greatest influence. They challenged the esthetic relevance of sentimental associations and directed attention to the great importance of plastic organization. It was a movement toward purification in esthetic theory that was paralleled by "abstract" or "non-objective" trends in the arts (for example, in the works of Kandinsky, Mondrian, and Brancusi). But, as the century wore on, the interest in meaning and symbolism became ever more pronounced. A brilliant generation of thinkers—Whitehead, Russell, Wittgenstein, Freud, Cassirer, Carnap, to name the more prominent—established the new "keynote" of philosophical thought. Esthetics has reflected this general trend. The writers represented in the present chapter are typical of the predominant interest in expressiveness that has characterized esthetics in the last two decades.

Writing in support of "the Unity of Science Movement," a research and publication project sponsored by a group of positivists and other empiricists, Charles William Morris (1901-   ), Professor of Philosophy at the University of Chicago, distinguishes between scientific, esthetic, and technological discourse. Scientific discourse is for the purpose of making accurate predictions; esthetic discourse is for the purpose of presenting values for direct appreciation; and technological discourse is for the purpose of controlling behavior. It follows that the content of a work of art, as distinguished from the content of a scientific or technological treatise, is essentially value-expressive.

There are two principal features of this theory of art. The work of art is said to be (1) *iconic* and (2) *valuational*. An iconic sign is similar in some respects to what it denotes (for example, Saint-Saëns' "The Swan" resembles serene and graceful motion; it also resembles an emotion that is similarly serene). The function of the esthetic icon is to express an appraisal or valuation. An example would be the artful way in which a little boy prances along behind an effeminate man, mimicking and thereby expressing his dislike of the man's mincing gait. Art is thus an appraisive picturing of things. A non-esthetic icon, such as a road-map, may be merely informative, but an esthetic icon "pictures" the values that it designates. In directly presenting value in a concrete image, art is quite different from abstract scientific or philosophical discourse *about* values.

With its emphasis upon iconicity, this theory is a kind of modern version of the ancient theory of imitation. But in his later work Morris modifies this position. He still maintains that iconic appraisive signs are of great importance in the arts, but he now thinks that esthetic signs, especially in literature, can be designative without being iconic. Thus "the arts are not limited in their valuative aim to the use of icons." [1]

Morris is primarily interested in the theory of signs ("semiotics"), and his interest in esthetics is rather incidental. On the other hand, Susanne Knauth Langer (1895-   ), a distinguished author and Professor of Philosophy at Connecticut College, has become mainly interested in the philosophy of art. She began her philosophical career by exploring logic and the whole field of signs, symbols, languages, and meanings, and in her most popular book, *Philosophy in a New Key* (1942), she has expounded the fundamental notion of symbolization as the connective link between fields as disparate as music, science, and religion (here following the lead of Ernst Cassirer in his monumental *Philosophy of Symbolic Forms*). Then in *Feeling and Form* (1953) she generalized the theory of music to cover all the arts, and in her *Problems of Art* (1957), she responded to critics by reformulating some of her basic ideas.

Her theory is based upon a distinction between two types of "symbolism," the *discursive,* which we find in pure science, and the *presentational,* which confronts us in art. Discursive symbolism is language in its literal use. It employs conventional meaningful units (the "dictionary" meanings) according to rules of grammar and syntax. Each word has a relatively fixed meaning, and the total meaning of the discourse is built up stepwise by using the words successively. The import can be paraphrased by using synonyms and logically equivalent sentences, and it refers to the neutral aspects of our world of observation and thought—the ideas and facts that are *least* tinged by subjective feeling. Presentational symbolism, in contrast, employs no fixed constituents to be combined according to rules; it therefore cannot be broken up into units with independent and conventional meanings; its meaning inheres in the total form, and cannot be paraphrased; it expresses, in its total range, the whole subjective side of existence that discourse is incapable of expressing—our moods, emotions, desires, the sense of movement, growth, felt tensions and resolutions, even sensations and thoughts in their characteristic passage. It does this not by a gushing forth of emotion but by an articulation of the "logical forms" of subjectivity.

This articulation is made possible by a congruence between the patterns of art and the patterns of sentience. At this point Professor Langer invokes a well-known theory of *Gestalt* psychology—that there may be a similarity of form between different fields of experience. It will be helpful to cite a concrete example: "In the space below are two meaningless forms. The reader will be able to decide without any trouble which of the meaningless sounds, *uloomu* and *takete,* applies to each form. The demonstration shows that impressions from different

---

[1] Charles W. Morris, *Signs, Language, and Behaviour* (Prentice-Hall, New York, 1946), p. 194.

 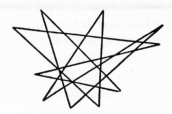

sense departments may be very similar with respect to form. Each of the sounds, *takete* and *uloomu*, fits perfectly one of the visual designs, but not the other. The impressions are different in content—one is visual and the other auditory— but similar in form." [2] Dr. Langer points out that such congruence of form holds not only between one sense department and another but between a pattern of sense and a pattern of feeling. "The tonal structures we call 'music,' " for example, "bear a close logical similarity to the forms of human feeling—forms of growth and of attenuation, flowing and stowing, conflict and resolution, speed, arrest, terrific excitement, calm, or subtle activation and dreamy lapses." [3] Thus subjective experience has a structure that can be abstracted and articulated by the congruent form of a work of art. But resemblance is not reference, and in the moment of esthetic vision, any sense of reference is superseded by the immediate reality of the esthetic apparition. Since the word "symbol" is almost always used to denote reference, the work of art is a "symbol" in a somewhat unusual meaning of the word. Symbols, in the ordinary sense, may occur within the work of art, but they function at a different level from the work that contains them.

Another esthetician who has been influenced by *Gestalt* theory is Rudolf Arnheim (1904-   ), Professor of Psychology at Sarah Lawrence College. In the Preface to his *Art and Visual Experience,* he states: "As long as I can remember I have concerned myself with art, studied its nature and history, tried my eyes and hands at it, and sought the company of artists, art theorists, art educators. This interest has been enhanced by my psychological studies." His initial studies occurred in Germany, the land of his birth, where he became familiar with the writings of Von Ehrenfels, Max Wertheimer, Wolfgang Köhler, Kurt Koffka, and other *Gestalt* theorists. The combination of this theoretical background with intensive experience of the arts has lent solidity and concreteness to Arnheim's esthetics.

In the selection included in this chapter he is taking issue with the traditional theory of the relation of sensory perception to expression. According to this theory, you perceive pure sense-data and then associate feelings and ideas with these original data. The expressiveness is due to this association. For exam-

[2] Carroll C. Pratt, *Music as the Language of Emotion* (Library of Congress, Washington, D. C., 1952), p. 18.
[3] Susanne K. Langer, *Feeling and Form* (Scribner's, New York, 1953), p. 27.

ple, what you perceive when you watch the flames in a fireplace would simply be bright reddish shapes in rapid movement. But you know from past experience "that fire hurts and destroys. It may remind you of violence. Perhaps you associate red with blood, which will reinforce the element of violence. The flames may seem to be moving like snakes. Also, your cultural environment has accustomed you to thinking of red as a color of passion. In consequence of all this, you not only see colors and shapes in motion, but are also struck by the expression of something frightening, violent, passionate." [4] In other words, you *perceive* only sensory data such as color, shape, sound; and expression is a superadded and secondary response due to the association of ideas. Arnheim opposes this theory of expression.

As he explains in the following selection, expression is original and primary. In the case of the fire, one sees "the graceful play of aggressive tongues, flexible striving, lively color." The expressiveness appears in the visible pattern itself and strikes our attention immediately. An expressive whole is not attained by adding up isolated parts, thus combining associated ideas and feelings with sensory data. The expressiveness is intrinsic to the integrated structure of the whole, and this is cognized *en bloc*. The important consequences of this *Gestalt* theory for art and esthetic education are discussed by Arnheim.

A more semantic and positivistic approach to expression is to be found in the very influential writings of Ivor Armstrong Richards (1893-   ), an English scholar and literary critic who has in recent years taught at Harvard. Maintaining that words and other symbols have many meanings that should be carefully distinguished, he and C. K. Ogden have discriminated sixteen principal meanings of the word "meaning," and have taken a whole book, *The Meaning of Meaning*, to explain these distinctions. Particularly important for esthetics is the difference between "emotive" and "descriptive" meaning. The distinction is between meaning used to *describe facts* and meaning used to *evoke emotions*. In science, descriptive meaning is requisite; in art, emotive meaning is essential.

The positivistic background of Richards' thinking is a skeptical, scientific view of nature. He can find no sufficient reason to suppose that the universe has the qualities of spirituality that religion and idealistic philosophy have imputed to it. The poets who write in this vein are entirely mistaken.

In *Science and Poetry*, Richards has characterized poetry as a satisfying, harmonious articulation of emotional-volitional attitudes rather than as a revelation of verifiable truth. His discussion of "the crisis in belief" caused by the progress of science, and the consequent need for a reinterpretation of the relation of poetry to belief, has provoked an immense amount of controversy. Perhaps too many of the writers who have engaged in this controversy have lost sight of the background of Richards' thought—especially the conviction, which he shares

---

[4] Arnheim, "The Priority of Expression," *Journal of Aesthetics*, Vol. VIII, December 1949, p. 106.

with Matthew Arnold, that art acts formatively in enlarging one's sensibilities, deepening one's sympathies, and inducing a more capacious and harmonious ability to experience life.

Richards now thinks that his views in *Science and Poetry* were stated somewhat too simply and interpreted too crudely. In a letter to the present editor he has declared, "I first revised and then discontinued *Science and Poetry* because I found that it was helping to spread oversimplified and sometimes crudely wrong views in a subject I cared much about: views as much as 180 degrees off mine! Philosophical discussion often seizes on a book as an excuse for a battle which its author might think silly from the start. Something of this sort seems to have happened here. But 'They know not well the subtle ways'; the Aeneas they fight over is not there." I have included in the present chapter a selection from Richards' *Practical Criticism,* which interprets the relation between poetry and doctrine in a more guarded way.

The discussion of the nature of music by John William Navin Sullivan (1886-1937), the son of a poor Irish sailor who became a gifted mathematician, can be interpreted as a reaction against the positivistic esthetics of Richards and the isolationist esthetics of Bell and Fry (or of Eduard Hanslick and Edmund Gurney in musical theory). Sullivan believes that the function of music as expressive as Beethoven's "is to communicate valuable spiritual states which testify to the depth of the artist's nature and to the quality of his experience of life." So lucid an argument needs no commentary, but its full force can be gauged only if one should read Sullivan's entire book, with its detailed analysis of Beethoven's spiritual development and the effects on his music. The implications go far beyond musical esthetics—they challenge the whole isolationist interpretation of art and the materialistic interpretation of science and reality.

CHARLES W. MORRIS

Science, Art, and Technology

§ 1

A consideration of science, art, and technology is inevitably a study of basic human activities and their interrelations. The theme is an old one, and many pages by many writers in many centuries supply variations and commentary. Yet the theme is a timely one for an America that stands before decades of high promise and peril, and for this *Review* which has recently opened its pages to a discussion of the place of the arts in the unity of science movement. There also exists today an instrument—the theory of signs—which may prove of great power in meeting the recurrent demands for insight into the essentials of human culture.[1]

§ 2

The utilization of the theory of signs for an approach to cultural activities is grounded in the enormous role which signs play in human behavior. The use of certain properties of things as clues to further properties, and the functioning in behavior of subsidiary spoken or written languages correlated both with human activities and the things upon which the activities are directed, are distinctive features of human activity. This fact makes it possible to view human culture as a web of sign-sustained and sign-sustaining activities, and to utilize the different modes of sign-functioning as clues to the character of the different accompanying modes of activity. It is common, for instance, to distinguish various forms of discourse (scientific, poetic, mathematical, religious, metaphysical, philosophical, etc.); French and German would be different languages, but each of them permits of all such forms of discourse. The project naturally suggests itself of approaching the nature and relations between the dominant forms of human activity through a study of the forms of discourse which are components and products of the activities in question. This approach has the merit of concreteness, since in comparing, for instance, art and science it directs attention to the work of art and the piece of scientific writing, searching in them for the reflection of the differences between art and science as human activities.

§ 3

A form of discourse is a specialization of language for the better accomplishment of some specific purpose. The everyday language of a people is an amazingly complex sign structure performing a multitude of individual and social functions. Its very protean character is its strength, for it provides the matrix in which and through which all human activities are interlocked in symbolic expression as they are interlocked in practice. This strength, however, involves a fundamental weakness: the very multiplicity of functions performed prevents the adequate performance of any one specialized function. So it is that men have gradually devised certain specializations of their common language for the more adequate performance of various specific tasks. Such specializations are here referred to as forms of discourse.

Forms of discourse can be analyzed in terms of the functions they have been elaborated to perform, and light can be thrown on the characteristic human ac-

[1] The reference is to pages 159-182 and 194-199 of the Spring 1939 number of *The Kenyon Review*, and *Foundations of the Theory of Signs (International Encyclopedia of Unified Science,* vol. I, no. 2), University of Chicago Press, 1938.

tivities and their interrelations by a study of the nature of the forms of discourse which are the products and the instruments of these activities. In practice each approach aids the other, and both will be used in the account which follows.

It seems unlikely that all the characteristic forms of discourse are equally basic. A distinction can be made—analogous to that in the theory of colors—between primary and secondary forms of discourse. Secondary forms of discourse are those built up out of other forms of discourse; primary forms of discourse are those which are not a function of other forms of discourse. The present position is that there are three primary forms of discourse (the scientific, the esthetic, and the technological), and that all other forms are secondary, that is, are a function of these primary forms.[2] A brief characterization of the three primary forms of discourse will provide an opportunity to show something of the interrelation of science, art, and technology, and to emphasize some of the cultural implications of these interrelations.

§ 4

The scientific form of discourse has received the most careful and elaborate analysis of any of the forms of discourse. Logicians have for the most part restricted their attention to the language of science; such a work as the *International Encyclopedia of Unified Science* is mainly devoted to such analysis. . . .

Scientific discourse is, in summary, statemental or predictive in character, and the statements are either confirmable (or disconfirmable) in terms of empirical evidence, or are statements used in obtaining confirmable statements upon the basis of other confirmable statements.[3] Scientific discourse provides man with a map such that he can determine his expectations with increasing accuracy on the basis of what he encounters in direct experience. Science as an institution involves all the procedures by which such discourse is obtained; science as a habit of mind involves a preference for the scientific form of discourse and the procedures utilized in the control of such discourse. Science as a whole ministers to man's need to be able to determine correctly his expectations, and hence his activity, in terms of the evidence which lies at hand. It is in the realization of this purpose that scientific discourse has been evolved and is being progressively controlled.

[2] The number of the primary forms of discourse corresponds to the three dimensions of sign functioning: scientific discourse brings into prominence the relation of signs to objects denoted (the semantical dimension), esthetic discourse accents in a distinctive way the sign structure itself (the syntactical dimension), technological discourse emphasizes the efficacy of the signs in the practice of the users (the pragmatical dimension). The theory of discourse is thus one development of the general theory of signs (technically called semiotic).

[3] For the detailed development of such a view of scientific discourse—without however the emphasis on the control of predictions—see the writings of R. Carnap, especially *Foundations of Logic and Mathematics*, in the *International Encyclopedia of Unified Science*, vol. I, no. 3 (University of Chicago Press, 1939).

§ 5

Men have, however, other needs than that of accurate prediction. As beings with needs, and so values, they are concerned with the vivid portrayal of what they value, and in devices by which their needs can be satisfied. Esthetic discourse ministers to the first interest; technological discourse to the second. By "esthetic discourse" is meant that specialized type of language which is the actual work of art (the poem, the painting, the music); the term does not refer to discourse about art, unless, indeed, this discourse is itself esthetic rather than scientific or technological.

That art is a language, that the work of art is in some sense a sign, is the basic doctrine of estheticians from Plato to Dewey. It is an intelligible interpretation of the doctrine of "imitation" to regard it as a theory of the sign-character of the work of art. For "imitation" was never originally limited to literal reproduction of existing objects (thus Aristotle speaks of the imitation of what is or what men think to be or what ought to be); to affirm that the work of art was an imitation was to affirm that it was a sign, and, indeed, a sign of a specific character: an image or icon "imitating" what is designated by embodying in itself the characters of any object the sign could be said to denote. From this point of view it is possible to regard Aristotle's *Poetics* as a treatise in esthetics written from the standpoint of the theory of signs. Thus the approach to art as a form of discourse is an ancient and common heritage in esthetics; the modern theory of signs, in proportion as it is more precise and elaborate, should be able to make clear the foundational material which was hardly more than implicit in ancient formulations, should be able to make more specific the nature of esthetic discourse, and should be able to free the sign theory of art from the Platonic metaphysics of universals which has enshrouded the doctrine from Plato to Schopenhauer and Santayana and which itself arose out of inadequacies in the existing theories of signs.[4]

If the work of art can be regarded as a sign, the central question is as to the nature of the designating sign and the nature of what is designated (in technical terms, the nature of the sign vehicle and the designatum). The view proposed is that the esthetic sign designates the value properties of actual or possible situations and that it is an iconic sign (an "image") in that it embodies these values in some medium where they may be directly inspected (in short, the esthetic sign is an iconic sign whose designatum is a value). To give content to this statement it would be necessary to analyze in detail the notion of value and the characteristics of iconic signs, but this is neither practical nor advisable in the present

---

[4] An article, "Aesthetics and the Theory of Signs," published in *The Journal of Unified Science* (formerly *Erkenntnis*), 1939, attempts to sketch an esthetics based on the general theory of signs. I shall not in the present remarks on art attempt to cover the same ground or make use of the more precise terminology there developed. This theory had in genesis no connection with the classical doctrine of imitation.

context. For whatever theory of value be maintained, it must be recognized that objects have value properties among their total set of properties (an object can be insipid, sublime, menacing, oppressive, or gay in some contexts just as it may have a certain mass or length or velocity in other contexts), and that esthetic media, since they themselves are objects, can embody certain value properties (a small piece of cork could hardly be sublime, but it could be insipid or even gay).

From this point of view the artist is one who molds some medium so that it takes on the value of some significant experience (an experience which may of course arise in the process of molding the medium and need not antedate this process). The work of art is a sign which designates the value or value structure in question, but has the peculiarity, as an iconic sign, that in spite of its generality of reference, the value it designates is embodied in the work itself, so that in perceiving a work of art one perceives directly a value structure and need not be concerned with other objects which the esthetic sign might denote (technically, other denotata than the sign vehicle itself).[5] In works of art men and women have embodied their experience of value, and these experiences are communicable to those who perceive the molded medium. Art is the language for the communication of values.

If such is the function of art, detailed examination should show that esthetic discourse is language specialized for the adequate accomplishment of this purpose. Since the work of art is an icon and not a statement, esthetic discourse is not restricted to signs whose truth is confirmable, and it needs no elaborate set of indexical signs for accuracy in space-time references. Since the aim is not prediction, the requirements of consistency or non-contradictoriness take on a special form: it is only necessary that the component signs in the total sign structure be such as to build up the total icon with the value in question, and such consistency in the presentation of a value may even involve sign combinations which the logician of scientific discourse would class as contradictory. Since the esthetic sign itself embodies the values it designates, in esthetic discourse the perceptual properties of the sign vehicles themselves become of great importance, and the artist constantly experiments with special syntactical combinations of these signs to obtain desired value effects. Since the work of art does designate, and in many cases denotes, the value properties of actual situations, esthetic discourse is by no means a mere "expression of the emotions": value properties are objectively relative properties of objects and in dealing with them esthetic discourse is concerned with the same world with which science and technology are concerned. It is for this reason that esthetic discourse can often be given a paraphrase in scientific discourse, as in the prose restatement of the content of a poem.

---

[5] "Abstract" art (perhaps automorphic or metamorphic art would be a more exact name) might seem an exception to a sign theory of art. That this is not so is argued in the previously mentioned article, "Aesthetics and the Theory of Signs."

Nevertheless, the type of concern is different, for the presentation of value is not to be confused with making statements about value: science itself may make statements about values as about anything else. Art does not, except incidentally, make statements about values, but presents values for direct experience; it is not a language about values, but the language of value.

§ 6

The third form of primary discourse may be called technological discourse. It is distinguished by such signs as "ought," "should," "do," "do not." A sentence in technological discourse has in function, if not in fact, the form of a command; its purpose is not to report a situation or present a value but to induce a mode of action. Such a sentence ("Paint of this kind ought to be applied in this way") implies an accepted value, whether stated or not (the permanency of the painting, etc.); it may suggest a scientific statement ("This mode of application best realizes the value in question"); it has an irreducible rhetorical or imperative component ("Apply the paint in the way described!"). Various subdivisions of technological discourse are defined in terms of the ends for which techniques are indicated—medical discourse, engineering discourse, agricultural discourse, and the like. Each profession has its own imperatives, its own *oughts,* relative to the values it seeks to control.

The question as to the relation of morality to technology may be put in terms of the relation of moral discourse to technological discourse. The simplest possibility would be to equate the two forms of discourse, so that any action is moral insofar as it aims to utilize techniques adequate to realize some value. While there is much to be said for such a position, it does not seem to correspond to general usage as well as a view which would make moral discourse a subspecies of technological discourse (and so morality a form of technology). The question then arises as to the basis of differentiation. The moral attitude may be held to arise when the endeavor is made to maximize the positive value of a situation in which values are in conflict. Morality would then become a technology of technologies, consisting of those techniques for the maximum integration and utilization of the various techniques which a community has available for the satisfaction of its interests. . . .

§ 7

The three primary forms of discourse are simply the development of three basic functions found in the everyday language, which permits making statements, presenting values, and controlling behavior. The primary forms of discourse are related as these three basic human concerns are related. The purposes to be realized are distinct and the corresponding forms of discourse are irreducible. Proficiency in the use of one form of discourse by no means involves proficiency in the use of the others; indeed, in the life of the individual the forms of discourse are often in competition, both because of the differences in human abilities and because of the shortness of human life. But while the individual may have to make a choice, society as a whole need not, for the adequate accomplishment of each of the three basic purposes requires the fulfillment of the others.

If interests are to be satisfied and values realized it is helpful to present vividly what has been attained and what is being sought, and esthetic discourse provides such presentation. It is also desirable to know the consequences of proposed courses of action under the conditions which have to be met, and scientific discourse favors such accuracy in prediction. Technological discourse gives the stimulation to act upon the techniques deemed effective in the realization of the values sought.

Scientific discourse does not entice by the presentation of value nor seduce to action by the advocacy of a technique; it represents the subordination of interest to the mapping of the structure of the existential. Yet it is clear that the direction of science is in a general sense determined by what values men at the time hold, and that science provides the basis for the control of all techniques, since the determination of whether a given procedure does or does not reach a certain goal is a scientific question. Further, the scientist may be helped in the scientific study of values by the vivid portrayal of the value whose conditions he endeavors to trace. He may obtain stimulation through the esthetic presentation of the value of scientific activity and results. And as a scientist aiming to realize the ends of science, he is a technologist since he must develop and control the techniques adequate to his purposes. If science provides the basis for the control of technological discourse, it is also true that the development of science is inseparable from the development of technology.

Esthetic discourse has as its field the presentation for direct inspection of the whole realm of values, negative as well as positive. Since men's values are a function of their interests and the world in which such interests arise and operate, the presentation of value will, by and large, require reference to persons and the world, so that esthetic discourse may incorporate within itself and for its own purpose the statemental character of scientific discourse. It may, further, concern itself with the value of scientific and technological activity and their results. Its presentation of negative value might seem to endanger the work of the moralist, and indeed it does endanger encrusted moral customs. But if morality means the active endeavor to maximize positive values, the moralist needs to have before him for consideration all that interests, so that in the larger sense the free development of art is a vital aid in the development of a vigorous and progressive morality. Finally, the artist is himself technologist in that he must work his will upon some material or other. As technologist he can utilize whatever scientific knowledge can be obtained about his media and about the adequacy of his techniques to attain their ends.

The technologist in turn can only be grateful for the vivid presentation of the values whose status in nature he attempts to control, and for what scientific material he can draw upon to control the efficacy of his techniques. The same is true of the moral technologist. A vital morality can only be helped by a vigorous art and a courageous science which stop before no value or fact. For a morality which is not alert to all that men need and find good or evil is blind and fossilized, while a morality whose injunctions are not constantly corrected by scientific knowledge of the situations with which the injunctions deal, and of the adequacy of the commanded techniques in such situations, is dogmatic and superstitious.

The activities of the scientist, the artist, and the technologist are mutually supporting activities, and their differences and interrelations may be discerned in the differences and interrelations of scientific, esthetic, and technological discourse. . . .

—*Kenyon Review,* Volume I (1939)

SUSANNE K. LANGER

Expressiveness and Symbolism

I. *Expressiveness*

When we talk about "Art" with a capital "A"—that is, about any or all of the arts: painting, sculpture, architecture, the potter's and goldsmith's and other designers' arts, music, dance, poetry, and prose fiction, drama and film—it is a constant temptation to say things about "Art" in this general sense that are true only in one special domain, or to assume that what holds for one art must hold for another. For instance, the fact that music is made for performance, for presentation to the ear, and is simply not the same thing when it is given only to the tonal imagination of a reader silently perusing the score, has made some estheticians pass straight to the conclusion that literature, too, must be physically heard to be fully experienced, because words are originally spoken, not written; an obvious parallel, but a careless and, I think, invalid one. It is dangerous to set up principles by analogy, and generalize from a single consideration.

But it is natural, and safe enough, to ask analogous questions: "What is the function of sound in music? What is the function of sound in poetry? What is the function of sound in prose composition? What is the function of sound in drama?" The answers may be quite heterogeneous; and that is itself an important fact, a guide to something more than a simple and sweeping theory. Such findings guide us to exact relations and abstract, variously exemplified basic principles.

At present, however, we are dealing with principles that have proven to be the same in all the arts, when each kind of art—plastic, musical, balletic, poetic, and each major mode, such as literary and dramatic writing, or painting, sculpturing, building plastic shapes—has been studied in its own terms. Such candid study is more rewarding than the usual passionate declaration that all the arts are alike, only their materials differ, their principles are all the same, their techniques all analogous, etc. That is not only unsafe, but untrue. It is in pursuing the differences among them that one arrives, finally, at a point where no more differences appear; then one has found, not postulated, their unity. At that deep level there is only one concept exemplified in all the different arts, and that is the concept of Art.

The principles that obtain wholly and fundamentally in every kind of art are few, but decisive; they determine what is art, and what is not. Expressiveness, in one definite and appropriate sense, is the same in all art works of any kind. What is created is not the same in any two distinct arts—this is, in fact, what makes them distinct—but the principle of creation is the same. And "living form" means the same in all of them.

A work of art is an expressive form created for our perception through sense or imagination, and what it expresses is human feeling. The word "feeling" must be taken here in its broadest sense, meaning *everything that can be felt,* from physical sensation, pain and comfort, excitement and repose, to the most complex emotions, intellectual tensions, or the steady feeling-tones of a conscious human life. In stating what a work of art is, I have just used the words "form," "expressive," and "created"; these are key words. One at a time, they will keep us engaged.

Let us consider first what is meant, in this context, by a *form.* The word has many meanings, all equally legitimate for various purposes; even in connection with art it has several. It may, for instance—and often does—denote the familiar, characteristic structures known as the sonnet form, the sestina, or the ballad form in poetry, the sonata form, the madrigal, or the symphony in music, the contredance or the classical ballet in choreography, and so on. This is not what I mean; or rather, it is only a very small part of what I mean. There is another sense in which artists speak of "form" when they say, for instance, "form follows function," or declare that the one quality shared by all good works of art is "significant form," or entitle a book *The Problem of Form in Painting and Sculpture,* or *The Life of Forms in Art,* or *Search for Form.* They are using "form" in a wider sense, which on the one hand is close to the commonest, popular meaning, namely just the *shape* of a thing, and on the other hand to the quite unpopular meaning it has in science and philosophy, where it designates something more abstract; "form" in its most abstract sense means structure, articulation, a whole resulting from the relation of mutually dependent factors, or more precisely, the way that whole is put together.

The abstract sense, which is sometimes called "logical form," is involved in the notion of expression, at least the kind of expression that characterizes art. That is why artists, when they speak of achieving "form," use the word with something of an abstract connotation, even when they are talking about a visible and tangible art object in which that form is embodied.

The more recondite concept of form is derived, of course, from the naive one, that is, material shape. Perhaps the easiest way to grasp the idea of "logical form" is to trace its derivation.

Let us consider the most obvious sort of form, the shape of an object, say a lampshade. In any department store you will find a wide choice of lampshades, mostly monstrosities, and what is monstrous is usually their shape. You select the least offensive one, maybe even a good one, but realize that the color, say violet, will not fit into your room; so you look about for another shade of the same shape but a different color, perhaps green. In recognizing this same shape in another object, possibly of another material as well as another color, you have quite naturally and easily abstracted the concept of this shape from your actual impression of the first lampshade. Presently it may occur to you that this shade is too big for your lamp; you ask whether they have *this same shade* (meaning another one of this shape) in a smaller size. The clerk understands you.

But what is *the same* in the big violet shade and the little green one? Nothing but the interrelations among their respective various dimensions. They are not "the same" even in their spatial properties, for none of their actual measures are alike; but their shapes are congruent. Their respective spatial factors are put together in the same way, so they exemplify the same form.

It is really astounding what complicated abstractions we make in our ordinary dealing with forms—that is to say, through what twists and transformations we recognize the same logical form. Consider the similarity of your two hands. Put one on the table, palm down, superimpose the other, palm down, as you may have superimposed cut-out geometric shapes in school—they are not alike at all. But their shapes are *exact opposites*. Their respective shapes fit the same description, provided that the description is modified by a principle of application whereby the measures are read one way for one hand and the other way for the other—like a timetable in which the list of stations is marked: "Eastbound, read down; Westbound, read up."

As the two hands exemplify the same form with a principle of reversal understood, so the list of stations describes two ways of moving, indicated by the advice to "read down" for one and "read up" for the other. We can all abstract the common element in these two respective trips, which is called the *route*. With a return ticket we may return only by the same route. The same principle relates a mold to the form of the thing that is cast in it, and establishes their formal correspondence, or common logical form.

So far we have considered only objects—lampshades, hands, or regions of the earth—as having forms. These have fixed shapes; their parts remain in fairly stable relations to each other. But there are also substances that have no definite shapes, such as gases, mists, and water, which take the shape of any bounded space that contains them. The interesting thing about such amorphous fluids is that when they are put into violent motion they do exhibit visible forms, not bounded by any container. Think of the momentary efflorescence of a bursting rocket, the mushroom cloud of an atomic bomb, the funnel of water or dust screwing upward in a whirlwind. The instant the motion stops, or even slows beyond a certain degree, those shapes collapse and the apparent "thing" disappears. They are not shapes of things at all, but forms of motions, or dynamic forms.

Some dynamic forms, however, have more permanent manifestations, because the stuff that moves and makes them visible is constantly replenished. A waterfall seems to hang from the cliff, waving streamers of foam. Actually, of course, nothing stays there in mid-air; the water is always passing; but there is more and more water taking the same paths, so we have a lasting shape made and maintained by its passage—a permanent dynamic form. A quiet river, too, has dynamic form; if it stopped flowing it would either go dry or become a lake. Some twenty-five hundred years ago, Heracleitos was struck by the fact that you cannot step twice into the same river at the same place—at least, if the river means the water, not its dynamic form, the flow.

When a river ceases to flow because the water is deflected or dried up, there remains the river bed, sometimes cut deeply in solid stone. That bed is shaped by the flow, and records as graven lines the currents that have ceased to exist. Its shape is static, but it *expresses* the dynamic form of the river. Again, we have two congruent forms, like a cast and its mold, but this time the congruence is more remarkable because it holds between a dynamic form and a static one. That relation is important; we shall be dealing with it again when we come to consider the meaning of "living form" in art.

The congruence of two given perceptible forms is not always evident upon simple inspection. The common *logical* form they both exhibit may become apparent only when you know the principle whereby to relate them, as you compare the shapes of your hands not by direct correspondence, but by correspondence of opposite parts. Where the two exemplifications of the single logical form are unlike in most other respects one needs a rule for matching up the relevant factors of one with the relevant factors of the other; that is to say, a *rule of translation,* whereby one instance of the logical form is shown to correspond formally to the other.

The logical form itself is not another thing, but an abstract concept, or better an *abstractable* concept. We usually don't abstract it deliberately, but only use it, as we use our vocal cords in speech without first learning all about their operation and then applying our knowledge. Most people perceive intuitively the similarity of their two hands without thinking of them as conversely related; they can guess at the shape of the hollow inside a wooden shoe from the shape of a human foot, without any abstract study of topology. But the first time they see a map in the Mercator projection—with parallel lines of longitude, not meeting at the poles—they find it hard to believe that this corresponds logically to the circular map they used in school, where the meridians bulged apart toward the equator and met at both poles. The visible shapes of the continents are different on the two maps, and it takes abstract thinking to match up the two representations of the same earth. If, however, they have grown up with both maps, they will probably see the geographical relationships either way with equal ease, because these relationships are not *copied* by either map, but *expressed,* and expressed equally well by both; for the two maps are different *projections* of the same logical form, which the spherical earth exhibits in still another—that is, a spherical—projection.

An expressive form is any perceptible or imaginable whole that exhibits relationships of parts, or points, or even qualities or aspects within the whole, so that it may be taken to represent some other whole whose elements have analogous relations. The reason for using such a form as a symbol is usually that the thing it represents is not perceivable or readily imaginable. We cannot see the earth as an object. We let a map or a little globe express the relationships of places on the earth, and think about the earth by means of it. The understanding of one thing through another seems to be a deeply intuitive process in the human brain; it is so natural that we often have difficulty in distinguishing the symbolic expressive form from what it conveys. The symbol seems to be the thing itself, or contain it, or be contained in it. A child interested in a globe will not say, "This means the earth," but "Look, this is the earth." A similar identification of symbol and meaning underlies the widespread conception of holy names, of the physical efficacy of rites, and many other primitive but culturally persistent phenomena. It has a bearing on our perception of artistic import; that is why I mention it here.

The most astounding and developed symbolic device humanity has evolved is language. By means of language we can conceive the intangible, incorporeal things we call our *ideas,* and the equally inostensible elements of our perceptual world that we call *facts.* It is by virtue of language that we can think, remember, imagine, and finally conceive a universe of facts. We can describe things and represent their relations, express rules of their interactions, speculate and predict and carry on a long symbolizing process known as reasoning. And above all, we can communicate, by producing a serried array of audible or visible words, in a pattern commonly known, and readily understood to reflect our multifarious concepts and percepts and their interconnections. This use of language is *discourse;* and the pattern of discourse is known as *discursive form.* It is a highly versatile, amazingly powerful pattern. It has impressed itself on our tacit thinking, so that we call all systematic reflection "discursive thought." It has made, far more than most people know, the very frame of our sensory experience—the frame of objective facts in which we carry on the practical business of life.

Yet even the discursive pattern has its limits of usefulness. An expressive form can express any complex of conceptions that, via some rule of projection, appears congruent with it, that is, appears to be of that form. Whatever there is in experience that will not take the impress—directly or indirectly—of discursive form, is not discursively communicable or, in the strictest sense, logically thinkable. It is unspeakable, ineffable; according to practically all serious philosophical theories today, it is unknowable.

Yet there is a great deal of experience that is knowable, not only as immediate, formless, meaningless impact, but as one aspect of the intricate web of life, yet defies discursive formulation, and therefore verbal expression: that is what we sometimes call the *subjective aspect* of experience, the direct feeling of it— what it is like to be waking and moving, to be drowsy, slowing down, or to be sociable, or to feel self-sufficient but alone; what it feels like to pursue an elusive thought or to have a big idea. All such directly felt experiences usually have no names—they are named, if at all, for the outward conditions that normally accompany their occurrence. Only the most striking ones have names like "anger," "hate," "love," "fear," and are collectively called "emotion." But we feel many things that never develop into any designable emotion. The ways we are moved are as various as the lights in a forest; and they may intersect, sometimes without cancelling each other, take shape and dissolve, conflict, explode into passion, or be transfigured. All these inseparable elements of subjective reality compose what we call the "inward life" of human beings. The usual factoring of that life-stream into mental, emotional, and sensory units is an arbitrary scheme of simplification that makes scientific treatment possible to a considerable extent; but we may already be close to the limit of its usefulness, that is, close to the point where its simplicity becomes an obstacle to further questioning and discovery instead of the revealing, ever-suitable logical projection it was expected to be.

Whatever resists projection into the discursive form of language is, indeed, hard to hold in conception, and perhaps impossible to communicate, in the proper and strict sense of the word "communicate." But fortunately our logical intuition, or form-perception, is really much more powerful than we commonly believe, and our knowledge—genuine knowledge, understanding—is considerably wider than our discourse. Even in the use of language, if we want to name something that is too new to have a name (for example, a newly invented gadget or a newly discovered creature), or want to express a relationship for which there is no verb or other connective word, we resort to metaphor; we mention it or describe it as something else, something analogous. The principle of metaphor is simply the principle of saying one thing and meaning another, and expecting to be understood to mean the other. A metaphor is not language, it is an idea expressed by language, an idea that in its turn functions as a symbol to express something. It is not discursive and therefore does not really make a statement of the idea it conveys; but it formulates a new conception for our direct imaginative grasp.

Sometimes our comprehension of a total experience is mediated by a metaphorical symbol because the experience is new, and language has words and phrases only for familiar notions. Then an extension of language will gradually follow the wordless insight, and discursive expression will supersede the non-discursive pristine symbol. This is, I think, the normal advance of human thought and language in that whole realm of knowledge where discourse is possible at all.

But the symbolic presentation of subjective reality for contemplation is not only tentatively beyond the reach of language—that is, not merely beyond the words we have; it is impossible in the essential frame of language. That is why those semanticists who recognize only discourse as a symbolic form must regard the whole life of feeling as formless, chaotic, capable only of symptomatic expression, typified in exclamations like "Ah!" "Ouch!" "My sainted aunt!" They usually do believe that art is an expression of feeling, but that "expression" in art is of this sort, indicating that the speaker has an emotion, a pain, or other personal experience, perhaps also giving us a clue to the general kind of experience it is—pleasant or unpleasant, violent or mild—but not setting that piece of inward life objectively before us so we may understand its intricacy, its rhythms and shifts of total appearance. The differences in feeling-tones or other elements of subjective experience are regarded as differences in quality, which must be felt to be appreciated. Furthermore, since we have no intellectual access to pure subjectivity, the only way to study it is to study the symptoms of the person who is having subjective experiences. This leads to physiological psychology—a very important and interesting field. But it tells us nothing about the phenomena of subjective life, and sometimes simplifies the problem by saying they don't exist.

Now, I believe the expression of feeling in a work of art—the function that makes the work an expressive form—is not symptomatic at all. An artist working on a tragedy need not be in personal despair or violent upheaval; nobody, indeed, could work in such a state of mind. His mind would be occupied with the causes of his emotional upset. Self-expression does not require composition and lucidity; a screaming baby gives his feeling far more release than any musician, but we don't go into a concert hall to hear a baby scream; in fact, if that baby is brought in we are likely to go out. We don't want self-expression.

A work of art presents feeling (in the broad sense I mentioned before, as everything that can be felt) for our contemplation, making it visible or audible or in some way perceivable through a symbol, not inferable from a symptom. Artistic form is congruent with the dynamic forms of our direct sensuous, mental, and emotional life; works of art are projections of "felt life," as Henry James called it, into spatial, temporal, and poetic structures. They are images of feeling, that formulate it for our cognition. What is artistically good is whatever articulates and presents feeling to our understanding.

Artistic forms are more complex than any other symbolic forms we know. They are, indeed, not abstractable from the works that exhibit them. We may abstract a shape from an object that has this shape, by disregarding color, weight and texture, even size; but to the total effect that is an artistic form, the color matters, the thickness of lines matters, and the appearance of texture and weight. A given triangle is the same in any position, but to an artistic form its location, balance, and surroundings are not indifferent. Form, in the sense in which we artists speak of "significant form" or "expressive form," is not an abstracted structure, but an apparition; and the vital processes of sense and emotion that a good work of art expresses seem to the beholder to be directly contained in it, not symbolized but really presented. The congruence is so striking that symbol and meaning appear as one reality. Actually, as one psychologist who is also a musician has written, "Music sounds as feelings feel." And likewise, in good painting, sculpture, or building, balanced shapes and colors, lines and masses look as emotions, vital tensions and their resolutions feel.

An artist, then, expresses feeling, but not in the way a politician blows off steam or a baby laughs and cries. He formulates that elusive aspect of reality that is commonly taken to be amorphous and chaotic; that is, he objectifies the subjective realm. What he expresses is, therefore, not his own actual feelings, but what he knows about human feeling. Once he is in possession of a rich symbolism, that knowledge may actually exceed his entire personal experience. A work of art expresses a conception of life, emotion, inward reality. But it is neither a confessional nor a frozen tantrum; it is a developed metaphor, a non-discursive symbol that articulates what is verbally ineffable—the logic of consciousness itself.

II. *The Art Symbol and the Symbol in Art*

... The work as a whole is the image of feeling, which may be called the Art Symbol. It is a single organic composition, which means that its elements are not independent constituents, expressive, in their own right, of various emotional ingredients, as words are constituents of discourse, and have meanings in their own right, which go to compose the total meaning of the discourse. Language is a *symbolism,* a system of symbols with definable though fairly elastic meanings, and rules of combination whereby larger units—phrases, sentences, whole speeches—may be compounded, expressing similarly built-up ideas. Art, contrariwise, is not a symbolism. The elements in a work are always newly created with the total image, and although it is possible to analyze what they contribute to the image, it is not possible to assign them any of its import apart from the whole. That is characteristic of organic form. The import of a work of art is its "life," which, like actual life, is an indivisible phenomenon. Who could say how much of a natural organism's life is in the lungs, how much in the legs, or how much more life would be added to us if we were given a lively tail to wave? The Art Symbol is a single symbol, and its import is not compounded of partial symbolic values. It is, I think, what Cecil Day Lewis means by "the poetic image," and what some painters, valiantly battling against popular misconceptions, call "the absolute image." It is the objective form of life-feeling in terms of space, or musical passage, or other fictive and plastic medium.

. . . If the Art Symbol is a single, indivisible symbol, and its import is never compounded of contributive cargoes of import, what shall we make of the fact that many artists incorporate symbols in their works? Is it a mistake to interpret certain elements in poems or pictures, novels or dances, as symbols? Are the symbolists, imagists, surrealists, and the countless religious painters and poets before them all mistaken—everybody out of step except Johnnie?

Symbols certainly do occur in art, and in many, if not most, cases contribute notably to the work that incorporates them. Some artists work with a veritable riot of symbols; from the familiar halo of sacrosanct personages to the terrible figures of the *Guernica,* from the obvious rose of womanhood or the lily of chastity to the personal symbols of T. S. Eliot, sometimes concentric as a nest of tables, painters and poets have used symbols. Iconography is a fertile field of research; and where no influence-hunting historian has found any symbols, the literary critics find Bloom as a symbol of Moses, and the more psychological critics find Moses a symbol of birth.

They may all be right. One age revels in the use of symbolism in pictures, drama, and dance, another all but dispenses with it; but the fact that symbols and even whole systems of symbols (like the gesture-symbolism in Hindu dances) may occur in works of art is certainly patent.

All such elements, however, are genuine symbols; they have meanings, and the meanings may be stated. Symbols in art connote holiness, or sin, or rebirth, womanhood, love, tyranny, and so forth. These meanings enter into the work of art as elements, creating and articulating its organic form, just as its subject-matter—fruit in a platter, horses on a beach, a slaughtered ox, or a weeping Magdalen—enter into its construction. Symbols used in art lie on a different semantic level from the work that contains them. Their meanings are not part of its import, but elements in the form that has import, the expressive form. The meanings of incorporated symbols may lend richness, intensity, repetition or reflection or a transcendent unrealism, perhaps an entirely new balance to the work itself. But they function in the normal manner of symbols: they mean something beyond what they present in themselves. It makes sense to ask what a Hound of Heaven or brown sea-girls or Yeat's Byzantium may stand for, though in a poem where symbols are perfectly used it is usually unnecessary. Whether the interpretation has to be carried out or is skipped in reception of the total poetic image depends largely on the reader. The important point for us is that there is a literal meaning (sometimes more than one) connoted by the symbol that occurs in art.

The use of symbols in art is, in fine, a principle of construction—a device, in the most general sense of that word, "device." But there is a difference, often missed by theorists, between principles of construction and principles of art. The principles of art are few: the creation of what might be termed "an apparition" (this term would bear much discussion, but we have no time for it, and I think any one conversant with the arts knows what I mean), the achievement of organic unity or "livingness," the articulation of feeling. These principles of art are wholly exemplified in every work that merits the name of "art" at all, even though it be not great or in the current sense "original" (the anonymous works of ancient potters, for instance, were rarely original designs). Principles of construction, on the other hand, are very many; the most important have furnished our basic devices, and given rise to the Great Traditions of art. Representation in painting, diatonic harmony in music, metrical versification in poetry are examples of such major devices of composition. They are exemplified in thousands of works; yet they are not indispensable. Painting can eschew representation, music can be atonal, poetry can be poetry without any metrical scaffold.

The excited recognition and exploitation of a new constructive device—usually in protest against the traditional devices that have been used to a point of exhaustion, or even the point of corruption—is an artistic revolution. Art in our own day is full of revolutionary principles. Symbols, crowding metaphorical images, indirect subject-matter, dream elements instead of sights or events of waking life, often the one presented through the other, have furnished us lately with a new treasure-trove of motifs that command their own treatments, and the result is a new dawning day in art. The whole old way of seeing and hearing and word-thinking is sloughed off as the possibilities inherent in the modern devices of creation and expression unfold. In that excitement it is natural for the young—the young spirits, I mean, who are not necessarily the people of military or marriageable age—to feel that they are the generation that has discovered, at last, the principles of art, and that heretofore art labored under an incubus, the false principles they repudiate, so there never really was a pure and perfectable art before. They are mistaken, of course; but what of it? So were their predeces-

sors—the Italian Camerata, the English Lake Poets, the early Renaissance painters—who discovered new principles of artistic organization and thought they had
discovered how to paint, or how to make real music, or genuine poetry, for the
first time. It is we, who philosophize about art and seek to understand its
mission, that must keep distinctions clear.

In summary, then, it may be said that the difference between the Art Symbol and the symbol used in art is a difference not only of function but of kind.
Symbols occurring in art are symbols in the usual sense, though of all degrees of
complexity, from simplest directness to extreme indirectness, from singleness to
deep interpenetration, from perfect lucidity to the densest over-determination.
They have meanings, in the full sense that any semanticist would accept. And
those meanings, as well as the images that convey them, enter into the work of
art as elements in its composition. They serve to create the work, the expressive
form.

The art symbol, on the other hand, *is* the expressive form. It is not a symbol
in the full familiar sense, for it does not convey something beyond itself. Therefore it cannot strictly be said to have a meaning; what it does have is import. It
is a symbol in a special and derivative sense, because it does not fulfill all the
functions of a true symbol: it formulates and objectifies experience for direct
intellectual perception, or intuition, but it does not abstract a concept for discursive thought. Its import is seen in it; not, like the meaning of a genuine symbol, by means of it but separable from the sign. The symbol in art is a metaphor,
an image with overt or covert literal signification; the art symbol is the absolute
image—the image of what otherwise would be irrational, as it is literally ineffable:
direct awareness, emotion, vitality, personal identity—life lived and felt,. the
matrix of mentality.

—Problems of Art (1957)

RUDOLF ARNHEIM

Expression

Every work of art must express something. This means, first of all, that the
content of the work must go beyond the presentation of the individual objects of
which it consists. But such a definition is too large for our purpose. It broadens
the notion of "expression" to include any kind of communication. True, we
commonly say, for example, that a man "expresses his opinion." Yet artistic

expression seems to be something more specific. It requires that the communication of the data produce an "experience," the active presence of the forces that make up the perceived pattern. How is such an experience achieved?

Inside Linked to Outside

In a limited sense of the term, expression refers to features of a person's external appearance and behavior that permit us to find out what the person is feeling, thinking, striving for. Such information may be gathered from a man's face and gestures, the way he talks, dresses, keeps his room, handles a pen or a brush, as well as from the opinions he holds, the interpretation he gives to events. This is less and also more than what I mean here by expression: less, because expression must be considered even when no reference is made to a mind manifesting itself in appearance; more, because much importance cannot be attributed to what is merely inferred intellectually and indirectly from external clues. Nevertheless this more familiar meaning of the term must be discussed briefly here.

We look at a friend's face, and two things may happen: we understand what his mind is up to; and we find in ourselves a duplicate of his experiences. The traditional explanation of this accomplishment may be gathered from a playful review of Lavater's *Physiognomic Fragments for the Advancement of the Knowledge and Love of Our Fellow Man* written by the poet Matthias Claudius around 1775. "Physiognomics is a science of faces. Faces are *concreta* for they are related *generaliter* to natural reality and *specialiter* are firmly attached to people. Therefore the question arises whether the famous trick of the 'abstractio' and the 'methodus analytica' should not be applied here, in the sense of watching out whether the letter *i*, whenever it appears, is furnished with a dot and whether the dot is never found on top of another letter; in which case we should be sure that the dot and the letter are twin brothers so that when we run into Castor we can expect Pollux not to be far away. For an example we posit that there be one hundred gentlemen, all of whom are very quick on their feet, and they had given sample and proof of this, and all of these hundred gentlemen had a wart on their noses. I am not saying that gentlemen with a wart on their noses are cowards but am merely assuming it for the sake of the example. . . . Now *ponamus* there comes to my house a fellow who calls me a wretched scribbler and spits me into the face. Suppose I am reluctant to get into a fist fight and also cannot tell what the outcome would be, and I am standing there and considering the issue. At that moment I discover a wart on his nose, and now I cannot refrain myself any longer, I go after him courageously and, without any doubt, get away unbeaten. This procedure would represent, as it were, the royal road in this field. The progress might be slow but just as safe as that on other royal roads."

In a more serious vein, the theory was stated early in the eighteenth century by the philosopher Berkeley. In his essay on vision he speaks about the way in which the observer sees shame or anger in the looks of a man. "Those passions are themselves invisible: they are nevertheless let in by the eye along with colors and alterations of countenance, which are the immediate object of vision, and which signify them for no other reason than barely because they have been observed to accompany them: without which experience, we should no more have taken blushing for a sign of shame than gladness." Charles Darwin, in his book on the expression of emotions, devoted a few pages to the same problem. He believed that external manifestations and their physical counterparts are connected by the observer either on the basis of an inborn instinct or of learning. "Moreover, when a child cries or laughs, he knows in a general manner what he is doing and what he feels; so that a very small exertion of reason would tell him what crying or laughing meant in others. But the question is, do our children acquire their knowledge of expression solely by experience through the power of association and reason? As most of the movements of expression must have been gradually acquired, afterwards becoming instinctive, there seems to be some degree of *a priori* probability that their recognition would likewise have become instinctive."

Recently a new version of the traditional theory has developed from a curious tendency on the part of many social scientists to assume that when people agree on some fact it is probably based on an unfounded convention. According to this view, judgments of expression rely on "stereotypes," which individuals adopt ready-made from their social group. For example, we have been told that aquiline noses indicate courage and that protruding lips betray sensuality. The promoters of the theory generally imply that such judgments are wrong, as though information not drawn from the individual's firsthand experience could never be trusted. The real danger does not lie in the social origin of the information, but rather in the fact that people have a tendency to acquire simply structured concepts on the basis of insufficient evidence, which may have been gathered firsthand or secondhand, and to preserve these concepts unchanged in the face of contrary experience. Whereas this may make for many one-sided or entirely wrong evaluations of individuals and groups of people, the existence of stereotypes does not explain the origin of physiognomic judgments. If these judgments stem from tradition, what is the tradition's source? Are they right or wrong? Even though often misapplied, traditional interpretations of physique and behavior may still be based on sound observation. In fact, perhaps they are so hardy because they are so true.

Within the framework of associationist thinking, a step forward was made by Lipps, who pointed out that the perception of expression involves the activity of forces. His theory of "empathy" was designed to explain why we find expression even in inanimate objects, such as the columns of a temple. The reasoning was as follows. When I look at the columns, I know from past experience the kind of mechanical pressure and counterpressure that occurs in them. Equally from past experience, I know how I should feel myself if I were in the place of the columns and if those physical forces acted upon and within my own body. I project my own kinesthetic feelings into the columns. Furthermore, the pressures and pulls called up from the stores of memory by the sight tend to provoke responses also in other areas of the mind. "When I project my strivings and forces into nature I do so also as to the way my strivings and forces make me feel, that is, I project my pride, my courage, my stubbornness, my lightness, my playful assuredness, my tranquil complacence. Only thus my empathy with regard to nature becomes truly esthetic empathy."

The characteristic feature of traditional theorizing in all its varieties is the belief that the expression of an object is not inherent in the visual pattern itself. What we see provides only clues for whatever knowledge and feelings we may mobilize from memory and project upon the object. The visual pattern has as little to do with the expression we confer upon it as words have to do with the content they transmit. The letters "pain" mean "suffering" in English and "bread" in French. Nothing in them suggests the one rather than the other meaning. They transmit a message only because of what we have learned about them.

Expression Embedded in Structure

William James was not so sure that body and mind have nothing intrinsically in common. "I cannot help remarking that the disparity between motions and feelings, on which these authors lay so much stress, is somewhat less absolute than at first sight it seems. Not only temporal succession, but such attributes as intensity, volume, simplicity or complication, smooth or impeded change, rest or agitation, are habitually predicated of both physical facts and mental facts." Evidently James reasoned that although body and mind are different media—the one being material, the other not—they might still resemble each other in certain structural properties.

This point was greatly stressed by *gestalt* psychologists. Particularly Wertheimer asserted that the perception of expression is much too immediate and compelling to be explainable merely as a product of learning. When we watch a dancer, the sadness or happiness of the mood seems to be directly inherent in the movements themselves. Wertheimer concluded that this was true because formal factors of the dance reproduced identical factors of the mood. The meaning of this theory may be illustrated by reference to an experiment by Binney in which members of a college dance group were asked individually to give improvisations of such subjects as sadness, strength, or night. The performances of the dancers showed much agreement. For example, in the representation of sadness the movement was slow and confined to a narrow range. It was mostly curved in shape and showed little tension. The direction was indefinite, changing, wavering, and the body seemed to yield passively to the force of gravitation rather than being propelled by its own initiative. It will be admitted that the physical mood of sadness has a similar pattern. In a depressed person the mental processes are slow and rarely go beyond matters closely related to immediate experiences and interests of the moment. In all his thinking and striving are softness and a lack of energy. There is little determination, and activity is often controlled by outside forces.

Naturally there is a traditional way of representing sadness in a dance, and the performances of the students may have been influenced by it. What counts, however, is that the movements, whether spontaneously invented or copied from other dancers, exhibited a formal structure so strikingly similar to that of the intended mood. And since such visual qualities as speed, shape, or direction are immediately accessible to the eye, it seems legitimate to assume that they are the carriers of an expression directly comprehensible to the eye.

If we examine the facts more closely, we find that expression is conveyed not so much by the "geometric-technical" properties of the percept as such, but by the forces they can be assumed to arouse in the nervous system of the observer. Regardless of whether the object moves (dancer, actor) or is immobile (painting, sculpture), it is the kind of directed tension or "movement"—its strength, place, and distribution—transmitted by the visible patterns that is perceived as expression. . . .

The Priority of Expression

The impact of the forces transmitted by a visual pattern is an intrinsic part of the percept, just as shape or color. In fact, expression can be described as the primary content of vision. We have been trained to think of perception as the recording of shapes, distances, hues, motions. The awareness of these measurable characteristics is really a fairly late accomplishment of the human mind. Even in the Western man of the twentieth century it presupposes special conditions. It is the attitude of the scientist and the engineer or of the salesman who estimates the size of a customer's waist, the shade of a lipstick, the weight of a suitcase. But if I sit in front of a fireplace and watch the flames, I do not normally register certain shades of red, various degrees of brightness, geometrically defined shapes moving at such and such a speed. I see the graceful play of aggressive tongues, flexible striving, lively color. The face of a person is more readily perceived and remembered as being alert, tense, concentrated rather than as being triangularly shaped, having slanted eyebrows, straight lips, and so on. This priority of expression, although somewhat modified in adults by a scientifically oriented education, is striking in children and primitives, as has been shown by Werner and Köhler. The profile of a mountain is soft or threateningly harsh; a blanket thrown over a chair is twisted, sad, tired.

The priority of physiognomic properties should not come as a surprise. Our senses are not self-contained recording devices operating for their own sake. They have been developed by the organism as an aid in properly reacting to the environment. The organism is primarily interested in the forces that are active around it—their place, strength, direction. Hostility and friendliness are attributes of forces. And the perceived impact of forces makes for what we call expression.

If expression is the primary content of vision in daily life, the same should be all the more true for the way the artist looks at the world. The expressive qualities are his means of communication. They capture his attention, through them he understands and interprets his experiences, and they determine the form patterns he creates. Therefore the training of art students should be expected to consist basically in sharpening their sense of these qualities and in teaching them to look to expression as the guiding criteria for every stroke of the pencil, brush, or chisel. In fact many good art teachers do precisely this. But there are also plenty of times when the spontaneous sensitivity of the student to expression not only is not developed further, but is even disturbed and suppressed. There is, for example, an old-fashioned but not extinct way of teaching students to draw from the model by asking them to establish the exact length and direction of contour lines, the relative position of points, the shape of masses. In other words, students are to concentrate on the geometric-technical qualities of what they see. In its modern version this method consists in urging the young artist to think of the model or of a freely invented design as a configuration of masses, planes, directions. Again interest is focussed on geometric-technical qualities.

This method of teaching follows the principles of scientific definition rather than those of spontaneous vision. There are, however, other teachers who will proceed differently. With a model sitting on the floor in a hunched-up position, they will not begin by making the students notice that the whole figure can be inscribed in a triangle. Instead they will ask about the expression of the figure; they may be told, for example, that the person on the floor looks tense, tied together, full of potential energy. They will suggest, then, that the student try to render this quality. In doing so the student will watch proportions and directions, but not as geometric properties in themselves. These formal properties will be perceived as being functionally dependent upon the primarily observed expression, and the correctness and incorrectness of each stroke will be judged on the basis of whether or not it captures the dynamic "mood" of the subject. Equally, in a lesson of design, it will be made clear that to the artist, just as to any unspoiled human being, a circle is not a line of constant curvature, whose points are all equally distant from a center, but first of all a compact, hard, restful thing Once the student has understood that roundness is not identical with circularity, he may try for a design whose structural logic will be controlled by the primary concept of something to be expressed. For whereas the artificial concentration on formal qualities will leave the student at a loss as to which pattern to select among innumerable and equally acceptable ones, an expressive theme will serve as a natural guide to forms that fit the purpose.

It will be evident that what is advocated here is not the so-called "self-expression." The method of self-expression plays down, or even annihilates, the function of the theme to be represented. It recommends a passive, "projective" pouring-out of what is felt inside. On the contrary, the method discussed here requires active, disciplined concentration of all organizing powers upon the expression that is localized in the object of representation.

It might be argued that an artist must practice the purely formal technique before he may hope to render expression successfully. But that is exactly the notion that reverses the natural order of the artistic process. In fact all good practicing is highly expressive. This first occurred to me many years ago when I watched the dancer Gret Palucca perform one of her most popular pieces, which she called "Technical Improvisations." This number was nothing but the systematic exercise that the dancer practiced every day in her studio in order to loosen up the joints of her body. She would start out by doing turns of her head, then move her neck, then shrug her shoulders, until she ended up wriggling her toes. This purely technical practice was a success with the audience because it was thoroughly expressive. Forcefully precise and rhythmical movements presented, quite naturally, the entire catalogue of human pantomime. They passed through all the moods from lazy happiness to impertinent satire.

In order to achieve technically precise movements, a capable dance teacher may not ask students to perform "geometrically" defined positions, but to strive for the muscular experience of uplift, or attack, or yielding, that will be created by correctly executed movements. (Comparable methods are nowadays applied therapeutically in physical rehabilitation work. For example, the patient is not asked to concentrate on the meaningless, purely formal exercise of flexing and stretching his arm, but on a game or piece of work that involves suitable motions of the limbs as a means to a sensible end.)

The Physiognomics of Nature

The perception of expression does not therefore necessarily—and not even primarily—serve to determine the state of mind of another person by way of externally observable manifestations. Köhler has pointed out that people normally deal with and react to expressive physical behavior in itself rather than being conscious of the psychical experiences reflected by such behavior. We perceive the slow, listless, "droopy" movements of one person as contrasted to the brisk, straight, vigorous movements of another, but do not necessarily go beyond the meaning of such appearance by thinking explicitly of the physical weariness or alertness behind it. Weariness and alertness are already contained in the physical behavior itself; they are not distinguished in any essential way from the weariness of slowly floating tar or the energetic ringing of the telephone bell. It is true, of course, that during a business conversation one person may be greatly concerned with trying to read the other's thoughts and feelings through what can be seen in his face and gestures. "What is he up to? How is he taking it?" But in such circumstances we clearly go beyond what is apparent in the perception of expression itself, and secondarily apply what we have seen to the mental processes that may be hidden "behind" the outer image.

Particularly the content of the work of art does not consist in states of mind that the dancer may pretend to be experiencing in himself or that our imagination may bestow on a painted Mary Magdalen or Sebastian. The substance of the work consists in what appears in the visible pattern itself. Evidently, then, expression is not limited to living organisms that we assume to possess consciousness. A steep rock, a willow tree, the colors of a sunset, the cracks in a wall, a tumbling leaf, a flowing fountain, and in fact a mere line or color or the dance of an abstract shape on the movie screen have as much expression as the human body, and serve the artist equally well. In some ways they serve him even better, for the human body is a particularly complex pattern, not easily reduced to the simplicity of shape and motion that transmits compelling expression. Also it is overloaded with nonvisual associations. The human figure is not the easiest, but the most difficult, vehicle of artistic expression.

The fact that nonhuman objects have genuine physiognomic properties has been concealed by the popular assumption that they are merely dressed up with human expression by an illusory "pathetic fallacy," by empathy, anthropomorphism, primitive animism. But if expression is an inherent characteristic of perceptual patterns, its manifestations in the human figure are but a special case of a more general phenomenon. The comparison of an object's expression with a human state of mind is a secondary process. A weeping willow does not look sad because it looks like a sad person. It is more adequate to say that since the shape, direction, and flexibility of willow branches convey the expression of passive hanging, a comparison with the structurally similar state of mind and body that we call sadness imposes itself secondarily. The columns of a temple do not strive upward and carry the weight of the roof so dramatically because we put ourselves in their place, but because their location, proportion, and shape are carefully chosen in such a way that their image contains the desired expression. Only because and when this is so, are we enabled to "sympathize" with the columns, if we so desire. An inappropriately designed temple resists all empathy.

To define visual expression as a reflection of human feelings would seem to be misleading on two counts: first, because it makes us ignore the fact that expression has its origin in the perceived pattern and in the reaction of the brain field of vision to this pattern; second, because such a description unduly limits the range of what is being expressed. We found as the basis of expression a configuration of forces. Such a configuration interests us because it is significant not only for the object in whose image it appears, but for the physical and mental world in general. Motifs like rising and falling, dominance and submission, weakness and strength, harmony and discord, struggle and conformance, underlie all existence. We find them within our own mind and in our relations to other people, in the human community and in the events of nature. Perception of expression fulfills its spiritual mission only if we experience in it more than the resonance of our own feelings. It permits us to realize that the forces stirring in ourselves are only individual examples of the same forces acting throughout the universe. We are thus enabled to sense our place in the whole and in the inner unity of that whole.

Some objects and events resemble each other with regard to the underlying patterns of forces; others do not. Therefore, on the basis of their expressive appearance, our eye spontaneously creates a kind of Linnean classification of all things existing. This perceptual classification cuts across the order suggested by other kinds of categories. Particularly in our modern Western civilization we are accustomed to distinguishing between animate and inanimate things, human and nonhuman creatures, the mental and the physical. But in terms of expressive qualities, the character of a given person may resemble that of a particular tree more closely than that of another person. The state of affairs in a human society may be similar to the tension in the skies just before the outbreak of a thunderstorm. Further, our kind of scientific and economic thinking makes us define things by measurements rather than by the dynamics of their appearance. Our criteria for what is useful or useless, friendly or hostile, have tended to sever the connections with outer expression, which they possess in the minds of children or primitives. If a house or a chair suits our practical purposes, we may not stop to find out whether its appearance expresses our style of living. In business relations we define a man by his census data, his income, age, position, nationality, or race—that is, by categories that ignore the inner nature of the man as it is manifest in his outer expression.

Primitive languages give us an idea of the kind of world that derives from a classification based on perception. Instead of restricting itself to the verb "to walk," which rather abstractly refers to locomotion, the language of the African Ewe takes care to specify in every kind of walking the particular expressive qualities of the movement. There are expressions for "the gait of a little man whose limbs shake very much, to walk with a dragging step like a feeble person, the gait of a long-legged man who throws his legs forward, of a corpulent man who walks heavily, to walk in a dazed fashion without looking ahead, an energetic and firm step," and many others. These distinctions are not made out of sheer esthetic sensitivity, but because the expressive properties of the gait are believed to reveal important practical information on what kind of man is walking and what is his intent at the moment.

Although primitive languages often surprise us by their wealth of sub-divisions for which we see no need, they also reveal generalizations that to us may seem unimportant or absurd. For example, the language of the Klamath Indians has prefixes for words referring to objects of similar shape or movement. Such a prefix may describe "the outside of a round or spheroidal, cylindrical, discoid or bulbed object, or a ring; also voluminous; or again, an act accomplished with an object which bears such a form; or a circular or semi-circular or waving movement of the body, arms, hands, or other parts. Therefore this prefix is to be found connected with clouds, celestial bodies, rounded slopes on the earth's surface, fruits rounded or bulbed in shape, stones and dwellings (these last being usually circular in form.) It is employed too, for a crowd of animals, for en-closures, social gatherings (since an assembly usually adopts the form of a circle), and so forth."

Such a classification groups things together that to our way of thinking belong in very different categories and have little or nothing in common. At the same time, these features of primitive language remind us that the poetical habit of uniting practically disparate objects by metaphor is not a sophisticated invention of artists, but derives from and relies on the universal and spontaneous way of approaching the world of experience.

George Braque advises the artist to seek the common in the dissimilar. "Thus the poet can say, The swallow knifes the sky, and thereby makes a knife out of a swallow." It is the function of the metaphor to make the reader penetrate the concrete shell of the world of things by combinations of objects that have little in common but the underlying pattern. Such a device, however, would not work unless the reader of poetry was still alive, in his own daily experience, to the symbolic or metaphoric connotation of all appearance and activity. For ex-ample, hitting or breaking things normally evokes, if ever so slightly, the over-tone of attack and destruction. There is a tinge of conquest and achievement to all rising—even the climbing of a staircase. If the shades are pulled in the morn-ing and the room is flooded with light, more is experienced than a simple change of illumination. One aspect of the wisdom that belongs to a genuine culture is the constant awareness of the symbolic meaning expressed in concrete happen-ing, the sensing of the universal in the particular. This gives significance and dignity to all daily pursuits, and prepares the ground on which the arts can grow. In its pathological extreme this spontaneous symbolism manifests itself in what is known to the psychiatrist as the "organ speech" of psychosomatic and other neurotic symptoms. There are people who cannot swallow because there is some-thing in their lives they "cannot swallow" or whom an unconscious sense of guilt compels to spend hours every day on washing and cleaning. . . .

All Art Is Symbolic

If art could do nothing better than reproduce the things of nature, either directly or by analogy, or to delight the senses, there would be little justification for the honorable place reserved to it in every known society. Art's reputation must be due to the fact that it helps man to understand the world and himself, and presents to his eyes what he has understood and believes to be true. Now everything in this world is a unique individual; no two things can be equal. But anything can be understood only because it is made up of ingredients not reserved to itself but common to many or all other things. In science, greatest knowledge is achieved when all existing phenomena are reduced to a common law. This is true for art also. The mature work of art succeeds in subjecting everything to a dominant law of structure. In doing so, it does not distort the variety of existing things into uniformity. On the contrary, it clarifies their differences by making them all comparable. Braque has said, "By putting a lemon next to an orange they cease to be a lemon and an orange and become fruit. The mathematicians follow this law. So do we." He fails to remember that the virtue of such correlation is two-fold. It shows the way in which things are similar and, by doing so, defines their individuality. By establishing a common "style" for all objects, the artist creates a whole, in which the place and function of every one of them are lucidly defined. Goethe said: "The beautiful is a manifestation of secret laws of nature, which would have remained hidden to us forever without its appearance."

Every element of a work of art is indispensable for the one purpose of pointing out the theme, which embodies the nature of existence for the artist. In this sense we find symbolism even in works that, at first sight, seem to be little more than arrangements of fairly neutral objects. We need only glance at the bare outlines of the two still lifes sketched in Figures *a* and *b* to experience two different conceptions of reality. Cézanne's picture (*a*) is dominated by the stable framework of verticals and horizontals in the background, the table, and the axes of bottles and glass. This skeleton is strong enough to give support even to the sweeping folds of the fabric. A simple order is conveyed by the upright symmetry of each bottle and that of the glass. There is abundance in the swelling volumes and emphasis on roundness and softness even in the inorganic matter. Compare this image of prosperous peace with the catastrophic turmoil in Picasso's work (*b*). Here we find little stability. The vertical and horizontal orientations are avoided. The room is slanted, the right angles of the table, which is turned over, are either hidden by oblique position or distorted. The four legs do not run parallel, the bottle topples, the desperately sprawling corpse of the bird is about to fall off the table. The contours tend to be hard, sharp, lifeless, even in the body of the animal.

Since the basic perceptual pattern carries the theme, we must not be sur-

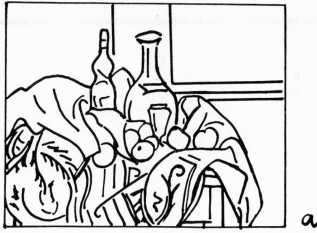

prised to find that art continues to fulfill its function even when it ceases to represent objects of nature. "Abstract" art does in its own way what art has always done. It is not better than representational art, which also does not hide but reveals the meaningful skeleton of forces. It is no less good, for it contains the essentials. It is not "pure form," because even the simplest line expresses visible meaning and is therefore symbolic. It does not offer intellectual abstractions, because there is nothing more concrete than color, shape, and motion. It does not limit itself to the inner life of man, or to the unconscious, because for art the distinctions between the outer and the inner world and the conscious and the unconscious mind are artificial. The human mind receives, shapes, and interprets its image of the outer world with all its conscious and unconscious powers, and the realm of the unconscious could never enter our experience without the reflection of perceivable things. There is no way of presenting the one without the other. But the nature of the outer and the inner world can be reduced to a play of forces, and this "musical" approach is attempted by the misnamed abstract artists.

We do not know what the art of the future will look like. But we know that "abstraction" is not art's final climax. No style will ever be that. It is one valid way of looking at the world, one view of the holy mountain, which offers a different image from every place but can be seen as the same everywhere.

—*Art and Visual Perception* (1954)

I. A. RICHARDS

Science and Poetry

The future of poetry is immense, because in poetry, where it is worthy of its high destinies, our race, as time goes on, will find an ever surer and surer stay. There is not a creed which is not shaken, not an accredited dogma which is not shown to be questionable, not a received tradition which does not threaten to dissolve. Our religion has materialized itself in the fact, in the supposed fact; it has attached its emotion to the fact, and now the fact is failing it. But for poetry the idea is everything.—MATTHEW ARNOLD.

I. *The Neutralization of Nature*

Poetry is failing us, or we it, if after our reading we do not find ourselves changed; not with a temporary change, such as luncheon or slumber will produce, from which we inevitably work back to the *status quo ante,* but with a permanent alteration of our possibilities as responsive individuals in good or bad adjustment to an all but overwhelming concourse of stimulations. How much contemporary poetry has the power to make such deep changes? Let us set aside youthful enthusiasms; there is a time in most lives when, rightly enough, Mr. Masefield, Mr. Kipling, Mr. Drinkwater, or even Mr. Noyes or Mr. Studdert Kennedy may profoundly affect the awakening mind; it is being introduced to poetry, or rather to the possibility [1] of emotional experience instigated, if not wholly controlled, through ordered words. Later on, looking back, we can see that any one of a hundred other poets would have served as well. Let us con-

---

[1] See the admirable and important *Note on the development of taste in poetry* at the end of Chapter I of Mr. Eliot's *The Use of Poetry.*

sider only the experienced reader, shaped by and responsive to a wide variety of the pressures from the contemporary situation, and familiar also with many different modes of the poetry of the past.

Contemporary poetry which will, accidents apart, modify the attitudes of this reader will be such as would not have been written in another age than our own. It will have sprung in part from the contemporary situation. It will be the outgrowth of needs, impulses, attitudes, which did not arise in the same form for poets in the past. And correspondingly—though this we are less willing to acknowledge—the poetry of the past will be read by such a reader in new ways. "The eye altering alters all." A poem no more than any other object is independent of the interests by which it is apprehended. Our attitudes to man, to nature, and to the universe which contains them both, change with every generation, and have changed more extensively and more deeply in recent years. We cannot leave these changes out of account in speculating about modern poetry, though, of course, arguments from them are no valid ground for appraisal. When attitudes are changing neither criticism nor poetry remain stationary. To those who realize what the poet is this will be obvious; all literary history bears it out.

It would be of little use to give a list of the chief recent intellectual revolutions and to attempt to deduce therefrom what must be happening to poetry. The effects upon our attitudes of changes of opinion are too complex to be calculated so. What we have to consider is not men's current opinions but their attitudes—how they feel about this or that as part of the world; what relative importance its different aspects have for them; what they are prepared to sacrifice for what; what they trust, what they are frightened by, what they desire. To discover these things we must go to the poets. Unless they are failing us, they will show us just these things.

They will *show* them, but, of course, they will not state them. Their poetry will not be *about* their attitudes in the sense in which a treatise on anatomy is about the structure of the body. It arises out of attitudes and will evoke them in an adequate reader, but, as a rule, it will not mention any. And when it does they may be entering dramatically only as means. We must, of course, expect occasional essays in verse upon psychological topics, but these should not mislead us. Most of the attitudes with which poetry is concerned are indescribable . . . and can only be named or spoken about indirectly through the situations (typically poems) which evoke them. The poem, the actual experience as it forms itself in the mind of the fit reader, controlling his responses to the world and ordering his impulses, does not ordinarily speak about its purposes. It has no need to while it can effect them. Poetry is thus our best evidence as to how other men feel about things; and as we read it, we discover not so much how life seems to another, as how it is for ourselves.

Although we cannot describe attitudes in terms which do not apply also to others which we are not considering, and although we cannot deduce a poet's attitudes from the general intellectual background, nonetheless, after reading his poetry, when his experience has induced our own, we can sometimes profitably look round us to see why these attitudes should be so very different, in some ways, from those we find in the poetry of one hundred or of one thousand years ago. In so doing we gain a means of indicating what these attitudes are, useful both for those who are constitutionally unable to read poetry (an increasing number), and for those victims of education who neglect modern poetry because they "don't know what to make of it."

What, then, has been happening to the intellectual background, to the world-picture, and in what ways may changes here have caused a reorganization of our attitudes?

The central dominant change may be described as the *Neutralization of Nature*,[2] the transference from the Magical View of the world to the scientific, a change so great that it is perhaps only paralleled historically by the change, from whatever adumbration of a world-picture preceded the Magical View, to the Magical View itself. By the Magical View I mean, roughly, the belief in a world of Spirits and Powers which control events, and which can be evoked and, to some extent, controlled themselves by human practices. The belief in Inspiration and the beliefs underlying Ritual are representative parts of this view. It has been decaying slowly for some three hundred years, but its definite overthrow has taken place only in the last seventy. Vestiges and survivals of it prompt and direct a great part of our daily affairs, but it is no longer the world-picture which an informed mind most easily accepts. There is some evidence that Poetry, together with the other Arts, arose with this Magical View. It is a possibility to be seriously considered that Poetry may pass away with it.

The reasons for the downfall of the Magical View are familiar. It seems to have arisen as a consequence of an increase in man's knowledge of and command over nature (the discovery of agriculture). It fell through the extension of that knowledge of and command over nature. Throughout its (10,000 years?) reign its stability has been due to its capacity for satisfying men's emotional needs through its adequacy as an object for their attitudes. We must remember that human attitudes have developed always *inside* the social group; they are what a man feels, the mainsprings of his behavior towards his fellowmen, and their application to the inhuman is an extension by metaphor. Thus the Magical View, being an interpretation of nature in terms of man's own most intimate and most important affairs, suits man's emotional make-up better than any other view possibly can. The attraction of the Magical View lay very little in the actual command over nature which it gave. That Galton was the first person to test the efficacy of prayer experimentally is an indication of this. What did give the Magical View its standing was the ease and adequacy with which the universe

2 See Appendix.

therein presented could be emotionally handled, the scope offered for man's love and hatred, for his terror as well as for his hope and despair. It gave life a shape, a sharpness, and a coherence that no other means could so easily secure.

In its place we have the universe of the mathematician, a field for the tracing out of ever wider and more general uniformities. A field in which intellectual certainty is available, on an unlimited scale. Also the despondencies, the emotional excitements accompanying research and discovery, again on an unprecedented scale. Thus a number of men who might in other times have been poets may today be in biochemical laboratories—a fact of which we might avail ourselves, did we feel the need, in defense of an alleged present poverty in poetry. But apart from these thrills, what has the world-picture of science to do with human emotions? A god voluntarily or involuntarily subject to the General Theory of Relativity does not make an emotional appeal. So this form of compromise fails. Various emergent deities have been suggested—by Mr. Wells, by Professors Alexander and Lloyd Morgan—but, alas! the reasons for suggesting them have become too clear and conscious. They are there to meet a demand, not to make one; they do not do the work for which they were invented.

The revolution brought about by science is, in short, too drastic to be met by any such half-measures. It touches the central principle by which the Mind has been deliberately organized in the past, and no alteration in beliefs,[3] however great, will restore equilibrium while that principle is retained. I come now to the main purport of these remarks.

Ever since man first grew self-conscious and reflective he has supposed that his feelings, his attitudes, and his conduct spring from his knowledge. That as far as he could it would be wise for him to organize himself in this way, with knowledge [4] as the foundation on which should rest feeling, attitude, and behavior. In point of fact, he never has been so organized, knowledge having been until recently too scarce; but he has constantly been persuaded that he was built on this plan, and has endeavored to carry the structure further on these lines. He has sought for knowledge, supposing that it would itself *directly* excite a right orientation to existence, supposing that, if he only knew what the world was like, this knowledge in itself would show him how to feel towards it, what attitudes to adopt, and with what aims to live. He has constantly called what he found in this quest, "knowledge," unaware that it was hardly ever pure, unaware that his feelings, attitudes, and behavior were *already* orientated by his physiological and social needs, and were themselves, for the most part, the sources of whatever it was that he supposed himself to be knowing.

Suddenly, not long ago, he began to get genuine knowledge on a large scale

[3] See Appendix.

[4] That is, thoughts which are both true and evidenced, in the narrower stricter senses. For a discussion of some relevant senses of 'truth' and 'knowledge' see *Principles of Literary Criticism,* Chapters XXXIII and XXXIV, and *Mencius on the Mind,* Chapter IV, also *The Meaning of Meaning,* Chapters VII and X.

—knowledge, that is to say, purified from the influences of his wishes or his fears
The process went faster and faster; it snowballed. Now he has to face the fact
that the edifices of supposed knowledge, with which he so long buttressed and
supported his attitudes, will no longer stand up, and, at the same time, he has to
recognize that pure knowledge is irrelevant to his aims, that it has no *direct*
bearing upon what he should feel, or what he should attempt to do.

For science, as our most elaborate way of *pointing* to things systematically,
tells us and can tell us nothing about the nature of things in any *ultimate* sense.
It can never answer any question of the form: *What* is so and so? it can only tell
us *how* such and such behave. And it does not attempt to do more than this.
Nor, indeed, can more than this be done. Those ancient, deeply troubling, formulations that begin with "What" and "Why"—as contrasted with "How"—prove,
when we examine them, to be not questions at all; but requests—for emotional
satisfaction. They indicate our desire not for knowledge, the indifferent and
emotionally neutral knowledge which is yielded by science, but for assurance,[5]
a point which appears clearly when we look into the "How" of questions and
requests, of knowledge and desire. Science can tell us about man's place in the
universe and his chances; that the place is precarious, and the chances prob-
lematical. It can enormously increase our chances if we can make wise use of it.
But it cannot tell us what we are or what this world is; not because these are in-
soluble questions, but because they are not scientific questions at all. Science
cannot answer these pseudo-questions; they do not belong to its province. Nor
can philosophy or religion "answer" them in the sense in which science has
taught us to expect answers to its questions. As the senses of "question" shift,
so do those of "answer," and those of "fact," "truth," "belief," and "knowledge"
with them. The new prestige and power of science which are due to its separation from confusion with other modes of inquiry are shifting these senses and
forcing a more general awareness of their differences upon us. And, with that,
all the varied "answers" which have for ages been regarded as the keys of wisdom are, for many minds, in danger of dissolving together.

The result is a biological crisis which is not likely to be decided without
trouble. It is one which we can, perhaps, decide for ourselves, partly by thinking,
partly by reorganizing our minds in other ways; otherwise it may be decided for
us, not in the way we should choose. While it lasts it puts a strain on each
individual and upon society, which is part of the explanation of many modern
difficulties, the difficulties of the poet in particular, to come back to our present
subject. I have not really been far away.

[5] On this point the study of the child's questions included in *The Language and
Thought of the Child* by J. Piaget (Kegan Paul, 1926), is illuminating.

II. *Poetry and Beliefs*

The business of the poet . . . is to give order and coherence, and so freedom, to a body of experience. To do so through words which act as its skeleton, as a structure by which the impulses which make up the experience are adjusted to one another and act together. The means by which words do this are many and varied. To work them out is a problem for linguistic psychology, that embarrassed young heir to philosophy. What little can be done shows already that most critical dogmas of the past are either false or nonsense. A little knowledge is not here a danger, but clears the air in a remarkable way.

Roughly and inadequately, even in the dim light of present knowledge, we can say that words work in the poem in two main fashions. As sensory stimuli and as (in the *widest* sense) symbols. We must refrain from considering the sensory side of the poem, remarking only that it is *not* in the least independent of the other side, and that it has for definite reasons prior importance in most poetry. We must confine ourselves to the other function of words in the poem, or rather, omitting much that is of secondary relevance, to one form of that function, let me call it *pseudo-statement*.

It will be admitted—by those who distinguish between scientific statement, where truth is ultimately a matter of verification as this is understood in the laboratory, and emotive utterance, where "truth" is primarily acceptability *by* some attitude, and more remotely is the acceptability *of* this attitude itself—that it is *not* the poet's business to make scientific statements. Yet poetry has constantly the air of making statements, and important ones; which is one reason why some mathematicians cannot read it. They find the alleged statements to be *false*. It will be agreed that their approach to poetry and their expectations from it are mistaken. But what exactly is the other, the right, the poetic, approach and how does it differ from the mathematical?

The poetic approach evidently limits the framework of possible consequences into which the pseudo-statement is taken. For the scientific approach this framework is unlimited. Any and every consequence is relevant. If any of the consequences of a statement conflicts with acknowledged fact then so much the worse for the statement. Not so with the pseudo-statement when poetically approached. The problem is—just how does the limitation work? One tempting account is in terms of a supposed universe of discourse, a world of make-believe, of imagination, of recognized fictions common to the poet and his readers. A pseudo-statement which fits into this system of assumptions would be regarded as "poetically true"; one which does not, as "poetically false." This attempt to treat "poetic truth" on the model of general "coherence theories" is very natural for certain schools of logicians but is inadequate, on the wrong lines from the outset. To mention two objections, out of many; there is no means of discovering what the "universe of discourse" is on any occasion, and the kind of coherence which must hold within it, supposing it to be discoverable, is not an affair of logical relations. Attempt to define the system of propositions into which

"O Rose, thou art sick!"

must fit, and the logical relations which must hold between them if it is to be "poetically true"; the absurdity of the theory becomes evident.

We must look further. In the poetic approach the relevant consequences are not logical or to be arrived at by a partial relaxation of logic. Except occasionally and by accident logic does not enter at all. They are the consequences which arise through our emotional organization. The acceptance which a pseudo-statement receives is entirely governed by its effects upon our feelings and attitudes. Logic only comes in, if at all, in subordination, as a servant to our emotional response. It is an unruly servant, however, as poets and readers are constantly discovering. A pseudo-statement is "true" if it suits and serves some attitude or links together attitudes which on other grounds are desirable. This kind of "truth" is so opposed to scientific "truth" that it is a pity to use so similar a word, but at present it is difficult to avoid the malpractice.[6]

This brief analysis may be sufficient to indicate the fundamental disparity and opposition between pseudo-statements as they occur in poetry and statements as they occur in science. A pseudo-statement is a form of words which is justified entirely by its effect in releasing or organizing our impulses and attitudes (due regard being had for the better or worse organizations of these *inter se*); a statement, on the other hand, is justified by its truth, that is, its correspondence, in a highly technical sense, with the fact to which it points.

Statements true and false alike do, of course, constantly touch off attitudes and action. Our daily practical existence is largely guided by them. On the whole true statements are of more service to us than false ones. None the less we do not and, at present, cannot order our emotions and attitudes by true statements alone. Nor is there any probability that we ever shall contrive to do so. This is one of the great new dangers to which civilization is exposed. Countless pseudo-statements—about God, about the universe, about human nature, the relations of mind to mind, about the soul, its rank and destiny—pseudo-statements which are pivotal points in the organization of the mind, vital to its well-being, have suddenly become, for sincere, honest and informed minds, impossible to believe as for centuries they have been believed.[7] The accustomed incidences of the modes

---

[6] A pseudo-statement, as I use the term, is not necessarily false in any sense. It is merely a form of words whose scientific truth or falsity is irrelevant to the purpose in hand.

"Logic" in this paragraph is, of course, being used in a limited and conventional, or popular, sense.

[7] See Appendix. For the mind I am considering here the question "Do I believe *x*?" is no longer the same. Not only the "What" that is to be believed but the "How" of the believing has changed—through the segregation of science and its clarification of the techniques of proof. This is the danger; and the remedy suggested is a further differ-

of believing are changed irrecoverably; and the knowledge which has displaced them is not of a kind upon which an equally fine organization of the mind can be based.

This is the contemporary situation. The remedy, since there is no prospect of our gaining adequate knowledge, and since indeed it is fairly clear that scientific knowledge cannot meet this need, is to cut our pseudo-statements free from that kind of belief which is appropriate to verified statements. So released they will be changed, of course, but they can still be the main instruments by which we order our attitudes to one another and to the world. This is not a desperate remedy, for, as poetry conclusively shows, even the most important among our attitudes can be aroused and maintained without any believing of a factual or verifiable order entering in at all. We need no such beliefs, and indeed we must have none, if we are to read *King Lear*. Pseudo-statements to which we attach no belief and statements proper, such as science provides, cannot conflict. It is only when we introduce inappropriate kinds of believing into poetry that danger arises. To do so is from this point of view a profanation of poetry.

Yet an important branch of criticism which has attracted the best talents from prehistoric times until today consists of the endeavor to persuade men that the functions of science and poetry are identical, or that the one is a "higher form" of the other, or that they conflict and we must choose between them.

The root of this persistent endeavor has still to be mentioned; it is the same as that from which the Magical View of the world arose. If we give to a pseudo-statement the kind of unqualified acceptance which belongs by right only to certified scientific statements—and those judgments of the routine of perception and action from which science derives—, if we can contrive to do this, the impulses and attitudes with which we respond to it gain a notable stability and vigor. Briefly, if we can contrive to believe poetry, then the world *seems*, while we do so, to be transfigured. It used to be comparatively easy to do this, and the habit has become well established. With the extension of science and the neutralization of nature it has become difficult as well as dangerous. Yet it is still alluring; it has many analogies with drug-taking. Hence the endeavors of the critics referred to. Various subterfuges have been devised along the lines of regarding Poetic Truth as figurative, symbolic; or as more immediate, as a truth of Intuition transcending common knowledge; or as a higher form of the same truth that science yields. Such attempts to use poetry as a denial or as a corrective of science are very common. One point can be made against them all: they are never worked out in detail. There is no equivalent of Mill's *Logic* ex-

entiation of the "Hows." To these differences correspond differences in the senses of "is so" and "being" where, as is commonly the case, "is so" and "being" assert believings. As we admit this, the world that "is" divides into worlds incommensurable in respect of so called "degrees of reality." Yet, and this is all-important, these worlds have an order, with regard to one another, which is the order of the mind; and interference between them imperils sanity.

pounding any of them. The language in which they are framed is usually a blend of obsolete psychology and emotive exclamations.

The long-established and much-encouraged habit of giving to emotive utterances—whether pseudo-statements simple, or looser and larger wholes taken as saying something figuratively—the kind of assent which we give to unescapable facts, has for most people debilitated a wide range of their responses. A few scientists, caught young and brought up in the laboratory, are free from it; but then, as a rule, they pay no *serious* attention to poetry. For most men the recognition of the neutrality of nature brings about—through this habit—a divorce from poetry. They are so used to having their responses propped up by beliefs, however vague, that when these shadowy supports are removed they are no longer able to respond. Their attitudes to so many things have been forced in the past, over-encouraged. And when the world-picture ceases to assist there is a collapse. Over whole tracts of natural emotional response we are today like a bed of dahlias whose sticks have been removed. And this effect of the neutralization of nature is perhaps only in its beginnings. However, human nature has a prodigious resilience. Love poetry seems able to out-play psychoanalysis.

A sense of desolation, of uncertainty, of futility, of the groundlessness of aspirations, of the vanity of endeavor, and a thirst for a life-giving water which seems suddenly to have failed, are the signs in consciousness of this necessary reorganization of our lives.[8] Our attitudes and impulses are being compelled to become self-supporting; they are being driven back upon their biological justification, made once again sufficient to themselves. And the only impulses which seem strong enough to continue unflagging are commonly so crude that, to more finely developed individuals, they hardly seem worth having. Such people cannot live by warmth, food, fighting, drink, and sex alone. Those who are least affected by the change are those who are emotionally least removed from the animals. As we shall see at the close of this essay, even a considerable poet may attempt to find relief by a reversion to primitive mentality.

It is important to diagnose the disease correctly and to put the blame in the

---

[8] My debt to *The Waste Land* here will be evident. The original footnote seems to have puzzled Mr. Eliot and some other readers. Well it might! In saying, though, that he "had effected a complete severance between his poetry and all beliefs" I was referring not to the poet's own history, but to the technical detachment of the poetry. And the way in which he then seemed to me to have "realized what might otherwise have remained a speculative possibility" was by finding a new order through the contemplation and exhibition of disorder.

"Yes! Very funny this terrible thing is. A man that is born falls into a dream like a man who falls into the sea. If he tries to climb out into the air as inexperienced people endeavor to do, he drowns—*nicht wahr?* . . . No! I tell you! The way is to the destructive element submit yourself, and with the exertions of your hands and feet in the water make the deep, deep sea keep you up. So if you ask me how to be? In the destructive element immerse . . . that was the way." *Lord Jim*, p. 216. Mr. Eliot's later verse has sometimes shown still less "dread of the unknown depths." That, at least, seems in part to explain to me why *Ash Wednesday* is better poetry than even the best sections of *The Waste Land.*

right quarter. Usually it is some alleged "materialism" of science which is denounced. This mistake is due partly to clumsy thinking, but chiefly to relics of the Magical View. For even if the Universe were "spiritual" all through (whatever that assertion might mean; all such assertions are probably nonsense), that would not make it any more accordant to human attitudes. It is not what the universe is made of but how it works, the law it follows, which makes verifiable knowledge of it incapable of spurring on our emotional responses, and further, the nature of knowledge itself makes it inadequate. The contact with things which we therein establish is too sketchy and indirect to help us. We are beginning to know too much about the bond which unites the mind to its object in knowledge [9] for that old dream of a perfect knowledge which would guarantee perfect life to retain its sanction. What was thought to be pure knowledge, we see now to have been shot through with hope and desire, with fear and wonder; and these intrusive elements indeed gave it all its power to support our lives. In knowledge, in the "How?" of events, we can find hints by which to take advantage of circumstances in our favor and avoid mischances. But we cannot get from it a *raison d'être* or a justification of more than a relatively lowly kind of life.

The justification, on the reverse, of any attitude lies, not in the object, but in itself, in its serviceableness to the whole personality. Upon its place in the whole system of attitudes, which is the personality, all its worth depends. This is as true for the subtle, finely compounded attitudes of the civilized individual as for the simpler attitudes of the child.

In brief, the imaginative life is its own justification; and this fact must be faced, although sometimes—by a lover, for example—it may be very difficult to accept. When it is faced, it is apparent that all the attitudes to other human beings and to the world in all its aspects, which have been serviceable to humanity, remain as they were, as valuable as ever. Hesitation felt in admitting this is a measure of the strength of the evil habit I have been describing. But many of these attitudes, valuable as ever, are, now that they are being set free, more difficult to maintain, because we still hunger after a basis in belief.

APPENDIX

Two chief words seem likely occasions of misunderstanding in the above; and they have in fact misled some readers. One is *Nature,* the other is *Belief.*

Nature is evidently as variable a word as can be used. Its senses range from the mere inclusive THAT, in which we live and of which we are a part, to whatever would correspond to the most detailed and interconnected account we could

---

[9] Verifiable scientific knowledge, of course. Shift the sense of "knowledge" to include hope and desire and fear as well as reference, and what I am saying would no longer be true. But then the relevant sense of "true" would have changed too. Its sanction would no longer be verifiability.

attain of this. Or we omit ourselves (and other minds) and make Nature *either* what influences us (in which case we should not forget our metabolism), *or* an object we apprehend (in which case there are as many Natures are there are types of apprehension we care to distinguish). And what is "natural" to one culture is strange and artificial to another. (See *Mencius on the Mind*, chap. III.) More deceptively, the view here being inseparable from the eye, and this being a matter of habitual speculation, we may talk, as we think, the same language and yet put very different things into Nature; and what we then find will not be unconnected with what we have put in. I have attempted some further discussion of these questions in Chapters VI and VII of *Coleridge on Imagination*.

Belief. Two "beliefs" may differ from one another: (1) In their objects (2) In their statements or expressions (3) In their modes (4) In their grounds (5) In their occasions (6) In their connections with other "beliefs" (7) In their links with possible action (8) And in other ways. Our chief evidence usually for the beliefs of other people (and often for our own) must be some statement or other expression. But very different beliefs may fittingly receive the same expression. Most words used in stating any speculative opinion are as ambiguous as "Belief"; and yet by such words belief-objects must be distinguished.

But in the case of "belief" there is an additional difficulty. Neither it nor its partial synonyms suggest the great variety of the attitudes (3) that are commonly covered (and confused) by the term. They are often treated as though they were mere variations in degree. Of what? Of belief, it would be said. But this is no better than the parallel trick of treating all varieties of love as a mere more or less only further differentiated by their objects. Such crude over-simplifications distort the structure of the mind and, although favorite suasive devices with some well-intentioned preachers, are disastrous.

There is an ample field here awaiting a type of dispassionate inquiry which it has seldom received. A world threatened with ever more and more leisure should not be too impatient of important and explorable subtleties.

Meanwhile, as with "Nature," misunderstanding should neither provoke nor surprise. I should not be much less at my reader's mercy if I were to add notes doubling the length of this little book. On so vast a matter, even the largest book could contain no more than a sketch of how things have seemed to be sometimes to the writer.

—Science and Poetry (revised edition, 1935)

III. *Doctrine in Poetry*

With most of our critical difficulties what we have had to explain is how mistakes come to be so frequent. But here we are in the opposite case, we have to explain how they come to be so rare. For it would seem evident that poetry which has been built upon firm and definite beliefs about the world, *The Divine*

Comedy or *Paradise Lost,* or Donne's *Divine Poems,* or Shelley's *Prometheus Unbound,* or Hardy's *The Dynasts,* must appear differently to readers who do and readers who do not hold similar beliefs. Yet in fact most readers, and nearly all good readers, are very little disturbed by even a direct opposition between their own beliefs and the beliefs of the poet. Lucretius and Virgil, Euripides and Aeschylus, we currently assume, are equally accessible, given the necessary scholarship, to a Roman Catholic, to a Buddhist and to a confirmed skeptic. Equally accessible in the sense that these different readers, after due study, may respond in the same way to the poetry and arrive at similar judgments about it. And when they differ, their divergencies will commonly not be a result of their different positions with regard to the doctrines [1] of the authors, but are more likely to derive from other causes—in their temperaments and personal experience.

I have instanced religious poetry because the beliefs there concerned have the widest implications, and are the most seriously entertained of any. But the same problem arises with nearly all poetry; with mythology very evidently; with such supernatural machinery as appears in *The Rime of the Ancient Mariner:*

> The horned Moon, with one bright star
> Within the nether tip,

with Blake's manifestoes; but equally, though less obtrusively, with every passage which seems to make a statement, or depend upon an assumption, that a reader may dissent from, without thereby giving proof of mental derangement.

It is essential to recognize that the problem [2] is the same whether the possible stumbling-block, the point of dissent, be trivial or important. When the point is trivial, we easily satisfy ourselves with an explanation in terms of "poetic fictions." When it is a matter of no consequence whether we assent or dissent, the theory that these disputable statements, so constantly presented to us in poetry, are merely *assumptions* introduced for poetic purposes, seems an adequate explanation. And when the statements, for example, Homer's account of "the monkey-shines of the Olympian troupe," are frankly incredible, if paraded solemnly before the bar of reasoned judgment, the same explanation applies. But as the assumptions grow more plausible, and as the consequences for our view of the world grow important, the matter seems less simple. Until, in the end, with Donne's Sonnet,[3] for example, it becomes very difficult not to think that

---

[1] I am not accusing these authors of doctrinal poetry in the narrow sense of verse whose sole object is to teach. But that a body of doctrine is presented by each of these poets, even by Virgil, can hardly escape any reader's notice.

[2] A supplementary and fuller discussion of this whole matter will be found in *Principles of Literary Criticism,* Ch. XXXII-XXXV, where difficulties, which here must be passed by, are treated in detail.

[3] Richards is referring to the following sonnet:
> At the round earth's imagined corners blow
> Your trumpets, angels, and arise, arise

actual belief in the doctrine that appears in the poem is required for its full and perfect imaginative realization. The mere assumption of Donne's theology, as a poetic fiction, may seem insufficient in view of the intensity of the feeling which is supported and conveyed to us by its means. It is at least certain . . . that many who try to read religious poetry find themselves strongly invited to the beliefs presented, and that doctrinal dissent is a very serious obstacle to their reading. Conversely, many successful but dissenting readers find themselves in a mental attitude towards the doctrine which, if it is not belief, closely resembles belief.

Yet if we suppose that, beyond this mere "poetic" assumption, a definite state of belief in this particular doctrine of the Resurrection of the Body is required for a full reading of Donne's poem, great difficulties at once arise. We shall have to suppose that readers who hold different beliefs incompatible with this particular doctrine must either not be able to read the poem, or must temporarily while reading it abandon their own beliefs and adopt Donne's. Both suppositions *seem* contrary to the facts, though these are matters upon which certainty is hazardous. We shall do better, however, to examine the "poetic fiction," or assumption, theory more closely and see whether when fully stated it is capable of meeting the complaint of inadequacy noticed above.

In the first place the very word "assumption" is unsuitable here. Ordinarily an assumption is a proposition, an object of thought, entertained intellectually in order to trace its logical consequences as a hypothesis. But here we are concerned very little with logical consequences and almost exclusively with emotional consequences. In the effect of the thought upon our feelings and attitudes, all its importance, for poetry, lies. But there are clearly two ways in which we may entertain an assumption: intellectually, that is in a context of other thoughts ready to support, contradict, or establish other logical relations with it; and emotionally, in a context of sentiments, feelings, desires, and attitudes ready to group themselves around it. Behind the intellectual assumption stands the desire for logical consistency and order in the receptive side of the mind. But behind the emotional assumptions stands the desire or need for order of the whole outgoing emotional side of the personality, the side that is turned towards action.

Corresponding to this distinction there are two forms of belief and similarly

---

From death, you numberless infinities
Of souls, and to your scattered bodies go;
All whom the flood did, and fire shall o'erthrow,
All whom war, dearth, age, agues, tyrannies,
Despair, law, chance hath slain, and you, whose eyes
Shall behold God, and never taste death's woe.
But let them sleep, Lord, and me mourn a space;
For, if above all these my sins abound,
'Tis late to ask abundance of Thy grace,
When we are there. Here on this lowly ground,
Teach me how to repent, for that's as good
As if Thou hadst seal'd my pardon with Thy blood.

two forms of disbelief. Intellectual belief more resembles a weighting of an idea than anything else, a loading [4] which makes other, less heavily weighted, ideas, adjust themselves to it rather than *vice versa*. The loading may be legitimate; the quantity of evidence, its immediacy, the extent and complexity of the supporting systems of ideas are obvious forms of legitimate loading: or it may be illegitimate; our liking for the idea, its brilliance, the trouble that changing it may involve, emotional satisfactions from it, are illegitimate—*from the standpoint of intellectual belief* be it understood. The whole use of intellectual belief is to bring *all* our ideas into as perfect an ordered system as possible. We disbelieve only because we believe something else that is incompatible, as Spinoza long ago pointed out. Similarly, we perhaps only believe because it is necessary to disbelieve whatever is logically contradictory to our belief. *Neither belief nor disbelief arises,* in this intellectual sense, *unless the logical context of our ideas is in question.* Apart from these logical connections the idea is neither believed nor disbelieved, nor doubted nor questioned; it is just present. Most of the ideas of the child, of primitive man, of the peasant, of the non-intellectual world and of most poetry are in this happy condition of real intellectual disconnection.

Emotional belief is a very different matter. In primitive man, as innumerable observers have remarked, any idea which opens a ready outlet to emotion or points to a line of action in conformity with custom is quickly believed. We remain much more primitive in this phase of our behavior than in intellectual matters. Given a need [5] (whether conscious *as a desire* or not), any idea which can be taken as a step on the way to its fulfillment is accepted, unless some other need equally active at the moment bars it out. This acceptance, this use of the idea—by our interests, desires, feelings, attitudes, tendencies to action and what not—is emotional belief. So far as the idea is useful to them it is believed, and the sense of attachment, of adhesion, of conviction, which we feel, and to which we give the name of belief, is the result of this implication of the idea in our activities.

Most beliefs, of course, that have any strength or persistence are mixtures of intellectual and emotional belief. A purely intellectual belief need have little strength, no quality of conviction about it, for unless the idea is very original and contrary to received ideas, it needs little loading to hold its own. When we find a modern physicist, for example, passionately attached to a particular theory, we may suspect illegitimate loading, his reputation is perhaps involved in its

---

[4] To introspection this loading seems like a feeling of trust—or trustworthiness. We "side" with the belief intellectually, and though traditionally belief has been discussed along with judgment it is, as William James pointed out, more allied to choice.

[5] I use "need" here to stand for an imbalance mental or physical, a tendency, given suitable conditions, for a movement towards an end-state of equilibrium. A swinging pendulum might thus be said to be actuated by a need to come to rest, and to constantly overdo its movements toward that end. We are much more like pendulums than we think, though, of course, our imbalances are infinitely more intricate.

acceptance. Conversely, a very strong emotional belief may have little persistence. Last night's revelation grows dim amid this morning's affairs, for the need which gave it such glamorous reality was only a need of the moment. Of this kind are most of the revelations received from poetry and music. But though the sense of revelation has faded, we should not suppose that the shaping influence of such experiences must be lost. The mind has found through them a pattern of response which may remain, and it is this pattern rather than the revelation which is important.

The great difference between these two kinds of belief, as I have defined them, appears most plainly if we consider what *justification* amounts to for each. Whether an intellectual belief is justified is entirely a matter of its logical place in the largest, most completely ordered, system of ideas we can attain to. Now the central, most stable, mass of our ideas has already an order and arrangement fixed for it by the facts of Nature. We must bring our ideas of these facts into correspondence with them or we promptly perish. And this order among the everyday facts of our surroundings determines the arrangement of yet another system of our ideas: namely, physical theory. These ideas are thereby weighted beyond the power of irreconcilable ideas to disturb them. Anyone who understands them cannot help believing in them, and disbelieving *intellectually* in irreconcilable ideas, provided that he brings them close enough together to perceive their irreconcilability. There are obviously countless ideas in poetry which, if put into this logical context, must be disbelieved at once.

But this intellectual disbelief does not imply that emotional belief in the same idea is either impossible or even difficult—much less that it is undesirable. For an emotional belief is not justified through any logical relations between its idea and other ideas. Its only justification is its success in meeting our needs—due regard being paid to the relative claims of our many needs one against another. It is a matter, to put it simply, of the *prudence* (in view of *all* the needs of our being) of the kind of emotional activities the belief subserves. The desirability or undesirability of an emotional belief has nothing to do with its intellectual status, provided it is kept from interfering with the intellectual system. And poetry is an extraordinarily successful device for preventing these interferences from arising.

Coleridge, when he remarked that "a willing suspension of disbelief" accompanied much poetry, was noting an important fact, but not quite in the happiest terms, for we are neither aware of a disbelief nor voluntarily suspending it in these cases. It is better to say that the question of belief or disbelief, in the intellectual sense, never arises when we are reading well. If unfortunately it does arise, either through the poet's fault or our own, we have for the moment ceased to be reading poetry and have become astronomers, or theologians, or moralists, persons engaged in quite a different type of activity.

But a possible misconception must be noted here. The intellectual exploration of the *internal* coherence of the poem, and the intellectual examination of the relations of its ideas to other ideas of ordinary experience which are *emotionally* relevant to it, are not only permissible but necessary in the reading of such poetry. . . . But this restricted intellectual inquiry is a different thing from the all-embracing attempt to systematize our ideas which alone brings up the problem of intellectual belief.

We can now turn back to [Donne's poem], to the point from which this long analysis started. There are many readers who feel a difficulty in giving to Donne's theology just that kind of acceptance, *and no more*, that they give to Coleridge's "star within the nether tip." They feel an invitation to accord to the poem that belief in its ideas which we can hardly help supposing to have been, in Donne's mind, a powerful influence over its shaping. These readers may, perhaps, be content if we insist that the fullest possible *emotional* belief is fitting and desirable. At the same time there are many who are unable to accord *intellectual* belief to these particular theological tenets. Such readers may feel that a threatened liberty is not thereby denied them. The fact that Donne probably gave both forms of belief to these ideas need not, I think, prevent a good reader from giving the fullest emotional belief while withholding intellectual belief, or rather while not allowing the question of intellectual belief to arise. The evidence is fragmentary upon the point, largely because it has been so strangely little discussed. But the very fact that the need to discuss it has not insistently arisen—seeing how many people from how many different intellectual positions have been able to agree about the value of such doctrinal poems—points strongly in this direction. The absence of intellectual belief need not cripple emotional belief, though evidently enough in some persons it may. But the habit of attaching emotional belief only to intellectually certified ideas is strong in some people; it is encouraged by some forms of education; it is perhaps becoming, through the increased prestige of science, more common.[6] For those whom it conquers it means "Good-bye to poetry."

—Practical Criticism (1929)

[6] I have discussed this danger at length in *Science and Poetry*. There is reason to think that poetry has often arisen through fusion (or confusion) between the two forms of belief, the boundary between what is intellectually certified and what is not being much less sharply defined in former centuries and *defined in another manner*. The standard of *verification* used in science today is comparatively a new thing. As the scientific view of the world (including our own nature) develops, we shall probably be forced into making a division between fact and fiction that, unless we can meet it with a twofold theory of belief on the lines suggested above, would be fatal not only to poetry but to all our finer, more spiritual, responses. That is the problem.

J. W. N. SULLIVAN

The Nature of Music

I. *Art and Reality*

§ 1

On May 28, 1810, Elizabeth Brentano, a young woman who is described as having been beautiful, highly cultured and fascinating, wrote a letter to Goethe describing her meeting with Beethoven. In the course of this letter she professes to report a conversation with Beethoven and attributes to him the following remarks:

> When I open my eyes I must sigh, for what I see is contrary to my religion, and I must despise the world which does not know that music is a higher revelation than all wisdom and philosophy, the wine which inspires one to new generative processes, and I am the Bacchus who presses out this glorious wine for mankind and makes them spiritually drunken. When they are again become sober they have drawn from the sea all that they brought with them, all that they can bring with them to dry land. I have not a single friend, I must live alone. But well I know that God is nearer to me than to other artists; I associate with Him without fear; I have always recognized and understood Him and have no fear for my music —it can meet no evil fate. Those who understand it must be freed by it from all the miseries which the others drag about with themselves.
>
> "Music, verily, is the mediator between intellectual and sensuous life.
>
> "Speak to Goethe about me. Tell him to hear my symphonies and he will say that I am right in saying that music is the one incorporeal entrance into the higher world of knowledge which comprehends mankind but which mankind cannot comprehend."

On the following day, when Elizabeth showed Beethoven what she had written he exclaimed, "Did I say that? Well, then I had a raptus!"

But the question is whether Beethoven said any of it at all. It is an unfortunate fact that the fascinating Elizabeth was not a perfectly truthful person. Even her champion, Thayer, admits that she was not above forging documents, or parts of documents. And the remarks attributed to Beethoven in this letter certainly differ in style from anything to be found in his writings. Schindler, the constant associate of Beethoven in his last years, stated that he had never heard "the master" talk like it. On the other hand, Beethoven was at this time only forty years of age; he had not yet entered into the silence of his last years.

And Elizabeth was indisputedly far more intelligent and responsive than Schind-ler. Moreover there are certain points about the report which, when examined, are seen to be characteristic and such as would be difficult to invent. The rea-sonable hypothesis is to suppose that Beethoven did make certain claims for his music and that Elizabeth, very romantic and somewhat unscrupulous, gave them what she thought was an effective presentation.

The point is important because in this report is almost the only evidence we have as to Beethoven's conception of the function of music. It is a conception which was not consonant with the intellectual outlook of his own time, and which is, indeed, incompatible with the general intellectual climate of the last three centuries. We may assume, as the irreducible minimum basis of Elizabeth's fantasies, that Beethoven regarded art as a way of communicating knowledge about reality. Beethoven was a firm believer in what Mr. I. A. Richards [1] calls the "revelation theory" of art. This is a theory which, if true, means that art has a significance very much more important than that usually attributed to it. Art must rank with science and philosophy as a way of communicating knowledge about reality. Other artists besides Beethoven have held this view, but there is no room for it in the great scientific world-outlook that was initiated in the seventeenth century and which is still the dominant outlook of our time. And a theory of esthetics which is serious and does not simply ignore the great revolution in thought produced by science, finds it difficult, if not impossible, to attach to art the significance Beethoven claimed for it. Nevertheless, the fact that Beet-hoven, who created the music, held these ideas about his music, is not unim-portant. It seems easy for some writers, men of quite average sensibility and intelligence, to dismiss the testimony of the greatest artists to the meaning of their own work when this testimony conflicts with the philosophy the critic has found adequate to accommodate his own experience. Such an attitude shows a pathetic confidence in the validity of "established truths." A certain humility in the pres-ence of utterances which presumably spring from a richer context of experience than we possess is surely to be excused. So that we may sympathize with Goethe when he replied to Elizabeth's report of Beethoven's conversation:

> The ordinary human mind might, perhaps, find contradictions in it; but before that which is uttered by one possessed of such a demon, an ordi-nary layman must stand in reverence, and it is immaterial whether he speaks from feeling or knowledge, for here the gods are at work strewing seeds for future discernment and we can only wish that they may proceed undisturbedly to development. But before they can become general, the clouds which veil the human mind must be dispersed. . . . To think of teaching him would be an insolence even in one with greater insight than mine, since he has the guiding light of his genius, which frequently il-lumines his mind like a stroke of lightning while we sit in darkness and scarcely suspect the direction from which daylight will break upon us.

[1] *Principles of Literary Criticism.*

The letter is a little constrained, but it is evident that Goethe feels that Beethoven must be treated with respect. It is impossible, Goethe feels, to be quite sure about the limitations of a genius of the Beethoven order. It would be advisable, then, before we dismiss Beethoven's ideas about the significance of music, to inquire into them more closely.

§ 2

By the end of the eighteenth century the mental climate characteristic of the modern world was well established in the general mind. We have borrowed [2] the term "mental climate" to indicate those fundamental assumptions which are current during any particular period and which are the common ground, as it were, of the different world outlooks which are constructed during that period. Such assumptions do not exist as explicit philosophies; they are, rather, the basis of the philosophies created in their time. Such an assumption, unquestioned during the last three centuries, is, for example, that there exists an order of nature. The mental climate characteristic of the modern world is most clearly manifested in modern science, for here the activity is conditioned by the assumptions in a perfectly direct manner. But the same assumptions, for the most part unconscious, can be found in much modern philosophy and esthetic criticism. For our present purpose the aspect of these assumptions that most interests us is that they make plausible the idea that art is an activity expressive wholly of peculiarities of the human constitution. It is not a revelation of reality; the values attributed by the artist to nature are not inherent in nature. The basis of this outlook is scientific materialism, which supposes that the reality of the world may be exhaustively described in terms of the abstractions found so successful in building up modern science—such abstractions as mass, force, location in space and time, and so on. In this universe the human mind, itself, in some way, the product of these abstractions, creates values expressive of its own constitution. These values are not part of reality; to suppose that they are is to adopt the "magical" view of the world. Our aspirations are expressive of nothing but our own needs—in the last resort, of our biological needs—and are, in that sense, purely accidental. They throw no light on the constitution of the universe; they point to no universal purpose in things. That the artist reveals to us the nature of reality, or anything but the peculiarities of his neural organization, is a notion incompatible with the scientific outlook on the world.

It follows from this that art is a somewhat trivial mystery. It is a mystery because the pleasure we indisputably get from a work of art cannot easily be related to our biological needs. Especially is this the case with music. It is difficult to understand why, in the struggle for existence, a peculiar sensibility to certain sequences of non-natural sounds should ever have been developed. And the mystery is trivial because nothing but an accidental and nonessential appetite

[2] A. N. Whitehead, *Science and the Modern World*.

appears to be involved. On the basis of this estimate of art the theory of "the esthetic emotion" has been proposed. This theory supposes that amongst the emotions proper to a human being is one particular emotion which is excited by works of art or, more generally, by all "manifestations of the beautiful," and which is excited by nothing else. The emotion appears to be capable of degrees, but also of a maximum. Some works of art are better than others, but it is also possible for a work of art to be "perfect." The perfect work of art excites the esthetic emotion to its maximum. The nearest analogy to this state would seem to be provided by the sexual orgasm. The classification of works of art proper on this theory, therefore, is the classification into perfect and imperfect, those that produce orgasm and those that do not. Amongst perfect works of art may be a symphony, a line of melody, an epic poem or a Serbian mat. The same value must naturally be attributed to all these works, since they are all completely successful in the function of a work of art, which is to excite the esthetic emotion to its maximum. The objection to this theory is that it entirely fails to take into account the most important of our reactions to a work of art. It is not true that works of art excite in us one specific emotion, and works of art are not adequately classified as perfect and imperfect. The difference in our responses to a late quartet by Beethoven and an early quartet by Haydn, for instance, is not described by saying that a specific emotion is more or less excited. The one is not a more perfect form of the other. It may be replied that both compositions possess the quality of *beauty*, and that our only relevant reaction, from the point of view of esthetic theory, is our reaction to this quality, a reaction which is susceptible of degrees, but which is always of the same kind. Such a reply derives all its plausibility merely from the poverty of language. Language, as an historical accident, is poor in names for subjective states, and consequently in names for the imputed properties of objects that produce those states. Even such words as love and hate, dealing with emotions to which mankind has always paid great attention, are merely portmanteau words. Within their meanings are not only differences of degree, but differences of kind. To conclude, because the word "beauty" exists almost in isolation, that it refers to some definite quality of objects, or that it is descriptive of some one subjective state, is to mistake a deficiency in language for a key to truth.

If we forgo the pleasing but puerile pastime of constructing a philosophy out of the accidents of grammar, and remain faithful to our actual experience, we shall find no reason to believe in a specific esthetic emotion, nor to believe in the existence of some unique quality of beauty inhabiting all works of art. Such beliefs are merely the first and easiest steps in man's efforts to frame a theory of art which shall be compatible with the materialistic universe of science, in which values do not form part of reality. But it is quite possible for a truer and more flexible theory to flourish, even in this mechanistic desert. We need postulate no mystical similarity amongst works of art, nor suppose that one unique and apparently useless appetite is satisfied by them. We may admit the correctness of our direct perceptions that works of art are great and small, and not merely perfect and imperfect. The feeling we indisputably have, from a great work of art, that a large area of experience has been illuminated and harmonized for us, need not be wholly dismissed. It is true that experience is susceptible of different degrees of organization, and the superior degree of organization of his experience that has been achieved by a great artist may be, at least temporarily, communicated to us. We may suppose that his nervous system is, in some ways, better constructed than our own. He has not discovered and revealed some mystic quality of beauty; he has bestowed upon our experience a higher degree of organization. For the time being we see through his eyes. But, in order to remain faithful to materialism, we must not suppose that the artist has communicated knowledge; he has not given us a revelation about the nature of reality. Reality is the material of science, and values do not enter into the scientific scheme. The harmony of experience, as the artist reveals it, is not an indication that "all's right with the world"; it is merely an indication that his nervous system is organized in a certain way. The advantage of this theory over the "esthetic emotion" theory is that it does not require us to do so much violence to the direct reactions we experience in the presence of a work of art. It is true that it does not allow us to take those reactions at their face value; we have, at least partially, to explain them away. But we are not required to reduce ourselves to the comparatively imbecile condition of the "pure esthete." We are not required to pretend that a fine song is as valuable as a fine symphony, that comprehensiveness and profundity are as nothing compared with "perfection." The richness of the artist's material, and the extent and depth of his organization of it, are admitted to be the factors that give his work its value.

This theory is probably the most adequate that can be devised on the basis of materialism. A work of art does not, as a scientific discovery does, exhibit new factors in reality; it merely presents a different and more desirable organization of experience from that we normally possess. This theory is, it must be admitted, a trifle obscure. If we think of the new ordering of known facts that a mathematical genius may give us we see that the distinction between organization of experience and the discovery of new factors in reality is not perfectly clear-cut. Probably a long and doubtful analysis would be required to make the point perfectly clear. This analysis, however, is not necessary, for there is reason to suppose that the materialistic doctrine on which the whole theory rests has no longer any compelling force.

§ 3

The materialistic doctrine that has most influenced esthetic theory is the doctrine that the artist's perceptions give us no knowledge of the nature of reality. This doctrine assumes that the whole of reality may be exhaustively described in terms of the fundamental scientific concepts elaborated in Europe during the seventeenth century. Stated thus nakedly the assumption seems an enormous one. The suspicion immediately arises that its ground is much more emotional than rational, but, in truth, the assumption did have a certain rational basis which has only recently been destroyed. That basis is found in the fact that the elements ignored by science never come in to disturb it. If other elements than those considered by science form an integral part of reality how is it that the scientific description seems to be complete? The fact that science forms a coherent and closed system is surely a presumption against the existence of what it ignores. By the end of the eighteenth century the convincing force of this argument was at its maximum. The triumphs achieved by the French mathematicians, on the basis of the concepts introduced by Galileo and made explicit by Newton, justified the belief that the key to the universe had now been discovered. Laplace's remark to Napoleon that in writing the *Mécanique Céleste,* he had found no need to assume the existence of God, expressed both the materialist position and the best available evidence for it. But this evidence was, after all, very slight. The fact that Laplace had not found God in the heavens was no proof that he would not find him on the earth. The phenomena of life and mind were so far from being included in the scientific scheme that it was only their almost total ignorance of these phenomena which enabled the eighteenth-century materialists to hope that they would be included. This objection can still be made to the materialist scheme; it has not yet shown itself competent to describe the whole of reality. But the objection has now acquired more force, for the great change that has come over the scientific outlook is due precisely to the fact that the materialist conceptions have been found to be inadequate in the very fields in which they achieved their greatest triumphs. And it is perfectly possible, in the resulting reorganization of scientific thought, that values will be regarded as inherent in reality. Even without this, however, recent analysis has resolved the paradox created by the fact that science forms a closed system. It has been shown that it does so in virtue of the fact that physics (the science on which the materialist outlook was based) deals with but one aspect of reality, namely, its structure, and remains perpetually within its own domain by the device of cyclic definition.

But for the purposes of a theory of art it is the fact that the materialist outlook has been abandoned rather than the reasons for its abandonment that is of importance. Our reactions to a work of art, or rather our interpretations of those reactions, have been largely conditioned by the mental climate brought about by scientific materialism. Nothing is more pervasive or more powerful than such a climate. It is indeed a climate in that it allows only certain growths to come to maturity, stunting and warping all others. The characteristic of this particular climate that interests us at present is that it has made difficult or impossible the correct evaluation of our esthetic experiences and for this reason has hindered us in understanding the significance of a great artist. It has distorted our esthetic perceptions by forcing us to accommodate them to a system of thought in which they really have no place, so that our reactions to a work of art are no longer accepted by us in their purity, but are immediately interpreted and sophisticated to serve our general outlook. For this reason most criticism is concerned with secondary issues, which are the only ones that can appear in the prevalent mental climate.

§ 4

For the purposes of esthetic criticism the most important fact that emerges from the present reorganization of scientific thought is that those elements of our experience that science ignores are not thereby shown to have no bearing upon the nature of reality. The fundamental concepts hitherto employed by science have been shown to be both unnecessary and insufficient. They are in process of being replaced by a different set, and it is perfectly possible that, when the replacement is complete, values will be established as inherent in reality. Even should science be able to progress without importing values into its scheme, that fact would afford no presumption against the existence of values. For one major result of recent physical speculation has been to show the precise nature of the limitations to scientific knowledge. Science gives us knowledge of structure, but not of substance. It may be assumed that this is the only kind of knowledge possible to us, but there seem to be no good reasons for such an assumption. Science, indeed, tells us a very great deal less about the universe than we have been accustomed to suppose, and there is no reason to believe that all we can ever know must be couched in terms of its thin and largely arbitrary abstractions.

With the disintegration of the three-centuries-old scientific outlook the way is clear for the construction of an adequate esthetic criticism. It is true, as Mr. Richards insists, that the artist gives us a superior organization of experience. But that experience includes perceptions which, although there is no place for them in the scientific scheme, need none the less be perceptions of factors in reality. Therefore a work of art may communicate knowledge. It may indeed be a "revelation." The "higher consciousness" of the great artist is evidenced not only by his capacity for ordering his experience, but also by having his experience. His world may differ from that of the ordinary man as the world of the ordinary man differs from that of a dog, in the extent of his contact with reality as well as in his superior organization of it. We may continue to maintain, then, the "revelation" theory of art. Indeed, our business as critics is to make it more explicit. The highest art has a transcendental function, as science has. In saying this, however, we must be careful to distinguish between these functions. We cannot say that art communicates knowledge, as science does, for we should be open to the objection made to the revelation theory of art that we cannot say what the revelation is of. But what art does do is to communicate to us an attitude, an attitude taken up by the artist consequent upon his perceptions, which perceptions may be perceptions of factors in reality. It is characteristic of the greatest art that the attitude it communicates to us is felt by us to be valid, to be the reaction to a more subtle and comprehensive contact with reality than we can normally make. We no longer need dismiss this feeling or attempt to explain it away. The colossal and mastered experience which seems to be reflected in the Heilgesang of the A minor quartet, for instance, is, we may be confident, indicative of more than the peculiarities of Beethoven's neural organization. The perceptions which made that experience possible were in no sense illusory; they were perceptions of the nature of reality, even though they have no place in the scientific scheme. Beethoven does not communicate to us his perceptions or his experiences. He communicates to us the attitude based on them. We may share with him that unearthly state where the struggle ends and pain dissolves away, although we know but little of this struggle and have not experienced his pain. He lived in a universe richer than ours, in some ways better than ours and in some ways more terrible. And yet we recognize his universe and find his attitudes towards it prophetic of our own. It is indeed our own universe, but as experienced by a consciousness which is aware of aspects of which we have but dim and transitory glimpses.

II. *Music As Expression*

We have seen that there is no reason to believe that uniqueness implies isolation.[3] Poetic experiences are quite as unique as musical experiences, but nobody imagines that they form a closed world of their own, that they are wholly dissociated from the rest of the poet's nature and from his experience of life. It is true that, for the appreciation of a work of art in any medium, special sensibilities are required, and such sensibilities can be pleasurably exercised in almost complete independence of any other interests. Thus much of Spenser's poetry may perhaps be regarded as existing in a moral and spiritual vacuum; it has, so to say, almost no discoverable context. Here the specific poetic sensibilities are being exercised "for their own sakes." Music, much more than poetry, affords

[3] In the preceding chapter, here omitted, Sullivan discusses the argument of Edmund Gurney, in *The Power of Sound*, that music is unique and therefore isolated. Sullivan admits the uniqueness of music but denies that this implies its isolation. He declares, "Musical phrases, like lines of poetry, are unique, but they are not thereby isolated. It is perfectly possible that there is a unique musical faculty, as unique as the sense of hearing itself, but it is not thereby an isolated faculty. . . . The strictly unique character of musical experiences is a rather trivial fact about them. But that they exist in isolation would be, if true, a very important characteristic. For it would follow that music exists to do nothing but employ, agreeably, a special faculty. The musician's experience of life and what he has made of it, the extent and depth of his inner life, could find, on this theory, no reflection in his music. . . . As this conclusion is quite incompatible with our judgments of the value of our musical experiences we must investigate their nature more closely."

specimens of works which lead this curiously independent existence, but it need be no more true of music than of poetry that it must be essentially meaningless. If, therefore, we find that some compositions irresistibly suggest to us some spiritual context we need not resist this impulse on theoretical grounds. We need not suppose that we are the victims of a literary culture and an imperfectly developed musical faculty. As a matter of fact, all the greatest music in the world, and some of the worst, does suggest a spiritual context. It does more than suggest; its whole being is conditioned by this context, and it lives to express it. This context is directly perceived even by those who, for theoretical reasons, do not explicitly admit its existence. The most ardent advocate of the isolation theory will, for example, describe one composition as more "profound" than another, will describe one melody as "noble" and another as "sentimental." Such judgments are incompatible with the isolation theory, for on that theory nothing could be said except that a piece of music afforded a greater or less degree of a unique and incommunicable pleasure. A composition could be no more profound or noble or sentimental than a wine. Yet such judgments, in the case of many compositions, are quite unavoidable.

If this be admitted we may, for our present purposes, divide musical compositions into three classes. We may admit that, so far as our present analysis penetrates, there are compositions which exist in isolation. Secondly, there are compositions which spring from a spiritual context and express spiritual experiences. And, thirdly, there is the class of music ordinarily called program music. Of these classes the second is the most important.

In our reactions to compositions belonging to the first group we find nothing is involved but our perceptions of musical quality and the delight those perceptions afford. An analysis of these perceptions could only be undertaken on the basis of a theory of musical esthetics, and no satisfactory theory exists. No theory that has yet been proposed, such as Darwin's theory that music is a highly developed form of the sexual calls of animals, or Spencer's theory that it is an elaboration of emotional speech, gives any explanation of why one musical phrase is pleasing and another not nor, more important still, why one sequence of phrases seems satisfactory, stimulating and "logical," while another sequence appears arbitrary and boring. It is possible that, in the remote future, the physiology of the nervous system will throw some light on the matter, but at present it is impossible to give any recipes for writing good melodies or for developing a musical theme in a satisfactory manner. The rules which have from time to time been propounded, based on the examination of large numbers of examples, are as faithfully obeyed by bad music as by good. What is quite certain is that musical phrases differ in quality and that successions of phrases differ in the degree of their musical fitness and coherence. Whether any music really exists which involves *only* these perceptions we are not here concerned to argue. We are prepared to admit that, so far as our analysis extends, there are compositions which appeal only to our musical perceptions of quality and coherence, variety, invention, and so on, leaving it to the science of the future to say what connection these musical perceptions may have with the rest of our perceptions.

Our response to music of the second kind involves more factors than does our response to music of the first kind. Music which impresses us as expressing spiritual experiences and as springing from a spiritual context is still music. It must satisfy the musical faculty; it must obey all the criteria that "pure" music obeys. But the musical experiences it communicates are less isolated than those of pure music; a greater extent, as it were, of the artist's nature has been concerned in their creation; more comprehensive and, probably, deeper needs are satisfied by them. Amongst musical phrases are some which do more than please our musical faculty. They stir other elements in us; they reverberate throughout a larger part of our being. Certain emotions and expectations are aroused besides those that accompany our reactions to pure music. And the sequences of such phrases, besides satisfying our musical faculty's criteria of coherence and fitness, also satisfy these other expectations, give a natural development to these other emotions, continue, by a process of organic growth, this wilder life that has been awakened in us. But the poverty of language in names for subjective states has tempted many writers to describe these experiences, communicated to us by music, by describing some situation or event which would, they think, arouse a similar response. And because such situations are very largely conditioned by the critic's sensibility and imagination the same composition may be given a great apparent variety of interpretations. But, in any case, the bare statement of a situation the composition is supposed to be about tells us nothing of any value. Even if the composer had a definite situation in mind, and one knew precisely what that situation was, a description of the situation tells us nothing of the quality of the response awakened by the music.

Beethoven's imaginative realization of the death of a hero, in the slow movement of the Eroica symphony, for instance, is utterly different in quality from Wagner's realization of the same situation in the Siegfried funeral march. What these compositions mean to us is precisely their communication, in each case, of the personal and individual conception of the situation. And it is this personal conception which reveals to us directly the depth and subtlety of the composer's feelings and perceptions. Such communications inform us directly of the spiritual context from which they spring, and they do this even if we are completely ignorant of any situation that may be involved. On the other hand, knowledge of the situation tells us nothing that we want to know. If we use the word "heroic" to describe the music of the Eroica symphony, that is not because the symphony is "about" Napoleon or Abercrombie, but because Heroism, as a state of being, was realized by Beethoven to the extent that he has expressed it, and it is the quality of his realization that is important. It is *his* conception of the heroic that matters to us, and which is a clue to the greatness of the soul which is expressing itself. The comparative tawdriness of Wagner's music is not due to any difference there might be in the imagined situation, but to the comparative poverty of his inner resources.

A knowledge of the situation that a musical composition is "about," therefore, can tell us little of value. And in practice we almost always know nothing of the situation, if any, that was in the mind of the composer. Nevertheless, a great deal of writing on music consists in presentations of imagined situations, and this is one reason why writing on music is properly classed as one of the dreariest branches of literature. It is possible that a great literary artist could so select and present a situation that experiences similar to those evoked by a given composition would be experienced by the reader. Beethoven, for instance, when asked for the "meaning" of the Appassionata sonata told his questioner to read Shakespeare's *Tempest*. No two compositions could be more unlike, and Beethoven was either joking or knew nothing of the play but its title. But he could, with more point, have referred a questioner to *Macbeth* as an illustration of the first movement of the C minor symphony. Even such vague correspondences are rare, however, and the usual "program" presented by the writer on music seems to have little more relation to the composition than would a newspaper report of a street accident. But just as the journalist may have had emotions justifying his use of the word "Tragedy," so these programs may represent something to their authors. These strange landscapes and violent variations in the weather conditions that so many compositions seem to suggest are, we may suppose, the symbols for experiences that are less trivial than they seem. They are merely unsuccessful devices of communication. We cannot know, for instance, what significance dancing elves, murmuring brooks and thunderstorms may have in the imagination of the descriptive writer. Such programs are merely unintelligible. A man thinks of what symbols he can, and the symbols he invents are conditioned not only by his sensibility and imagination, but by his experience. To this is due the great variety of interpretations of the same composition. It is possible that the different interpreters had similar spiritual experiences evoked by the composition, but it requires a great artist to express such experiences unambiguously. We may conclude then, that it is very doubtful whether any compositions of the kind we are discussing are "about" any of the programs that have been suggested for them. And as we have said, if we did know the program we should know nothing of importance about the composition. The "meaning" of these compositions is to be found in the spiritual experiences they evoke. The musical critic who wishes to describe these experiences is faced with precisely the same task as the literary critic who wishes to describe the significance of a poem and, like the literary critic, he is likely to achieve but a stammering success. But his task is no harder. Both critics should eschew "programs" as irrelevant, although as the situation is explicit in a poem it is much easier to regard it as vital. But it is really no more illuminating to be told that Wordsworth wrote a sonnet about the view of London from Westminster Bridge than it is to be told that Chopin wrote a waltz about a puppy chasing its tail. The difference is that the poet himself cannot express his reaction to the situation without mentioning the situation, whereas the musician can do so. Music, compared with the other arts, is a kind of disembodied ghost, and has all the advantages and disadvantages of that state.

The reluctance of many musicians to admit that music of the kind we are discussing (which includes almost the whole of Beethoven's music) is in any sense program music is due to their feeling that any proposed "situation" is not only inadequate but even irrelevant. In denying the adequacy of any proposed situation to the musical effect they have been led to the strained position that music has no extra-musical content whatever, that it witnesses to nothing in the composer except his possession of an isolated faculty called musical imagination. This view, as we have said, is not compatible with our direct reactions to music, and even the exponents of this view seem to find it almost impossible, as their writings prove, to hold it consistently. It is also in direct contradiction to the expressed views of some of the great composers themselves. Beethoven most certainly regarded his music as expressing states of consciousness which might conceivably have been expressed by some other art. Indeed, he seems to have regarded music not only as a medium for the presentation of "beauty," but as a language with which he was more familiar than any other. The evidence of his letters and reported remarks is quite clear on this point. Thus, in describing his method of composition to Louis Schlosser he refers to himself as "incited by moods, which are translated by the poet into words, by me into tones that sound, and roar and storm about me until I have set them down in notes." And in conversation with Neate he said, "I always have a picture in my mind when composing, and follow its lines." That we are not to take the word "picture" in this remark too literally is shown by his letter of July 15, 1817, to Wilhelm Gerhard where he says, "The description of a picture belongs to the field of painting; in this the poet can count himself more fortunate than my muse for his territory is not so restricted as mine in this respect, though mine, on the other hand, extends into other regions, and my dominion is not easily reached." And Schindler reports that Beethoven, in his later years, complained that people were less able to grasp the meaning of music than they were in his young days, and he even thought of giving poetic titles to his earlier works to supply this deficiency in his hearers' imaginations. It is certain, therefore, that Beethoven, at any rate, considered that his music had an extra-musical content, that is to say, a content that could conceivably be expressed in some other medium. But we may be quite certain that whatever poetic titles Beethoven or anybody else had given to his compositions would not have assisted his hearers in grasping this content. For the content, as we have said, is the composer's reaction to the situation, not the situation. And this reaction is conditioned by the spiritual nature of the man and is a revelation of it. In his capacity to express this content Beethoven reveals himself as a great musical genius, and the content itself reveals him as a great spirit.

Music, as an expressive art, evokes states of consciousness in the hearer which are analogous to states that may be produced by extra-musical means. It is usual to describe these states as "emotions" but this word, unless carefully used, is misleading. Psychologists have tabulated human emotions, that is, they have given a list of those emotions for which names exist. But it is difficult to find a musical composition whose effect is adequately described as evoking one or more of these emotions. No composition, for instance, can be adequately described as "melancholy" or "joyful." Such emotions, if they enter at all into the total effect, never enter as isolated elements. Gurney has proposed the term "fused emotion" to describe the musical experience, but the term is not very illuminating. We are again in presence of the mystery that attends our reaction to any work of art. There are as few melancholy or joyful poems as there are musical compositions. It may be that our reaction to a work of art is a synthesis of relatively simple emotions, but the analysis would probably teach us little. For the effect exists as a whole and not as an assemblage of its elements, just as a living creature is more than an assemblage of its constituent molecules. Such synthetic wholes are doubtless the highest experiences of which we are capable, but they are probably too rare and of too little practical importance to have received names. There is no harm in calling them emotions, provided it is realized that we are only rarely referring to named emotions. Some fairly complex emotions, such as "awe," have received names and have been more or less plausibly analyzed into a number of simpler constituent emotions. But our reactions to a work of art have hitherto resisted analysis into these simple terms, and for that reason many people have supposed that some unique "esthetic emotion" is involved. But we have already objected to that theory that it does not account for the differences in our reactions to different works of art.

The most valuable states or "emotions" that music arouses are those that spring from the richest and deepest spiritual context. We are immediately aware, with great compositions of this kind, that the state of consciousness expressed by the composer is the result of certain perceptions and experiences. So far as we can recognize the emotion communicated to us we can say something of the conditions it, as it were, presupposes. If there is nothing in our experience akin to that of the composer his composition can be for us nothing but an example of "pure music." But the experiences we attribute to the composer tell us nothing, of course, about the causes of those experiences. To suppose that they do is to fall into the error of the program writer. Thus when Marx describes the A minor quartet as inspired by Beethoven's progress from a sick bed to health we feel that the description is both inadequate and arbitrary. He has failed to do justice to the quality of the experience from which the work sprang, and he has quite arbitrarily invented a cause of the experience. But the critic who should deny any spiritual content whatever to the A minor quartet, who should fail to see that it could only germinate in the soil of some profound experience, would fail even more signally than Marx.

The function of the kind of music we have been discussing is to communicate valuable spiritual states, and these states testify to the depth of the artist's nature and to the quality of his experience of life. Such states cannot usually be correlated with definite situations, and for that reason no program for them can be given. They are the fruits of countless experiences as realized and coordinated by the artist, and they enter into the very texture of his spiritual being. But there are certain classes of experiences, not perhaps of the highest order, for which situations can be assigned. Music expressing such experiences, deliberately relating them to the situation, is the highest form of what is ordinarily called program music. We may take Beethoven's Pastoral symphony as being, on the whole, a composition of this class. It is concerned, for the most part, to depict its composer's reactions to various pastoral scenes. But, together with this, it contains a good deal of program music of a different order whose purpose it is to give a musical representation of certain physical perceptions. The notorious cuckoo notes, the effect of flowing water in the Beside the Brook movement, the storm, are specimens of music of this class. It would not be sufficient to say of such music that its purpose is to represent physical perceptions. The representation must be musical, and only as realistic as is compatible with that condition. This means that the representation can never be completely realistic except when the physical perceptions concerned are musical sounds. Thus a tolling bell can be represented very realistically by tolling a bell. But it is only the most stupid modern composers who give equally realistic representations of trains and motor-horns. In any case, the actual physical perceptions that can be communicated by music are very few, although there is evidence that music can, for some people, suggest other than auditory perceptions. Thus there can be no doubt that, for some minds, sounds and colors are associated. Many lists have been given of the color equivalents of the different orchestral instruments. The lists do not agree, but that does nothing to invalidate the existence of the correspondences. Even keys have their characteristic colors for some minds. It is possible, therefore, that by correct choice of key and instrumentation compositions could be designed which would powerfully suggest to such minds certain landscape effects. We also find that some music irresistibly reminds certain musical critics of food. Or it may arouse olfactory images. Writings on music abound in which colors, wines, peaches and perfumes are suggested to the authors by musical compositions. But such powers of evocation belong to the more freakish resources of music. No compositions worth talking about are designed to arouse such images, and probably those who experience them would regard them as amongst the least valuable of their reactions to the music. Such by-products of auditory stimuli do not help us to understand the peculiar character of program music. That character does not consist in any correspondences that may exist between auditory and other physical perceptions, but in the analogy between the musical emotions communicated and the emotions aroused by the external situation that forms the program of the composition. If it be said, for instance, that Debussy's L'Après-midi d'un Faune makes the impression of "a vegetable world alive in quivering hot sunshine . . . the life of trees, streams and lakes, the play of light upon water and on clouds, the murmur of plants drinking and feeding in the sunlight," it is not because musical sounds can evoke images of heat and light and vegetables, but because a man in such surroundings may typically experience emotions analogous to those communicated by the music. Program music, in the strict sense, may be defined as music that communicates musical experiences analogous to extra-musical experiences that may be associated with some definite external situation. It does not, any more than any other music, depict any part of the external world.

—*Beethoven: His Spiritual Development* (1927)

CHAPTER TEN

Form

ROGER FRY

Pure and Impure Art

A. C. BRADLEY

Poetry for Poetry's Sake

DEWITT H. PARKER

The Problem of Esthetic Form

D. W. GOTSHALK

Type Designs

MEYER SCHAPIRO

Style

Introductory Note

THE WORK OF ART, as we have said, is an organized complex of sensuous and expressive elements, and its organization is its form. Recent art and esthetics have tended to emphasize formal values, but estheticians have disagreed as to the meaning of form. A number of writers have interpreted form as sheer abstract design, to the exclusion of connotations and representations. This point of view was championed in musical esthetics by Hanslick and Gurney. A similar interpretation, with reference particularly to the visual arts, has been formulated by the famous English critic, Roger Fry (1886-1934).

The ideas of Fry were greatly influenced by "the Bloomsbury circle," a

group of intimate friends, including the philosopher G. E. Moore, the econ-
omist John Maynard Keynes, the novelist Virginia Woolf, and the art critic
Clive Bell. A close study will reveal the indebtedness of both Fry and Bell to
the ideas of Moore, especially to the remarks about esthetic emotion and formal
beauty in his *Principia Ethica* (1903) and the contention that a value, such as
goodness or beauty, is a unique and "non-natural" quality (*cf.* Moore's remarks
about the "naturalistic fallacy"). It is not surprising that Bell and Fry, thus
linked together, came to much the same conclusions.

Since Bell has had a great influence upon esthetics, I shall briefly summarize his ideas. He agrees with Véron and Tolstoy that art is emotional, but he
thinks that there is a peculiarly esthetic emotion, quite different from the emotions of ordinary life, that is directed to "significant form." By significant form he
means a unique quality resulting from certain combinations of lines, colors, and
spatial elements. The representation of space is necessary to achieve certain kinds
of visual form but any other kind of representation is esthetically irrelevant. Like
'anslick and Gurney, Bell insists upon the "isolated" character of esthetic
experience and works of art.

What, then, does he mean by the word "significant"? The significance in
question, it would appear, consists of the expression of the artist's emotion, but
the only emotion that Bell considers legitimate in art—the peculiarly "esthetic"
emotion—is aroused by the vision of significant form. He suggests, however, a
possible escape from the circularity of this definition. Art may be a revelation, he
says, of the universal "rhythm of reality." But since he insists that the significance
of art "is unrelated to the significance of life," this so-called "metaphysical hypothesis" remains extremely vague. Perhaps we may interpret it as meaning that
the artist emulates, without definitely imitating, the structural harmonies of his
natural environment, such as the pattern of a sea shell or the floret of a sun-
flower.

In essentials, Fry agrees with Bell. His emphasis is upon not only purity of
form but exclusiveness of appeal. "In proportion as art becomes purer," he writes,
"the number of people to whom it appeals gets less. It cuts out all the romantic
overtones of life which are the usual bait by which men are induced to accept
a work of art. It appeals only to the esthetic sensibility, and that in most men is
comparatively weak." [1] In the selection here reprinted, he undertakes to define
the nature of such "pure" art and to distinguish it from the impure varieties. He
shares with Bell the belief that there is an exclusively esthetic emotion which is
aroused by the "unexpected inevitabilities of formal relations," [2] and he tends,
like Bell, to find in the abstract character of music the ideal of pure art. In this
respect both writers are the heirs of Walter Pater, who believed that all the arts

[1] From the essay "Art and Life" in *Vision and Design* (Brentano's, New York, 1920).
[2] Roger Fry, *Vision and Design*, p. 181.

should aspire to the condition of music, in which matter is most completely absorbed into form.[3]

A less isolationist theory is expressed by Andrew Cecil Bradley (1851-1935), a distinguished critic and professor of poetry at Oxford University. Although he primarily discusses form and content in poetry, his conception of form can be extended to all the arts.

He agrees with Fry that works of art have their own *intrinsic* value and significance, and that art neither *is* life nor a copy of it. But unlike Fry, he does not discount the importance of subject matter. He admits that the subject as such, apart from artistic treatment, has no esthetic value, but he thinks that a great subject may be the focus which brings to the artist's imagination a great artistic vision. He also rejects the antithesis between form and content. In the well-composed poem or work of art, content and form are not two separate things, but one thing regarded from two different points of view. The content is the elements-in-relation; the form is the relations-among-the-elements; and the total work is the organic unity of relational elements. Content and form, *separately* conceived, are not in the poem. It follows that the content cannot be paraphrased —that a poem, for example, cannot *really* be translated. For we have in the poem a form-meaning or a meaning-in-form; and to separate the meaning from the form is to mutilate it.

Much has been written in recent years by the so-called "new critics"—such as Cleanth Brooks and John Crowe Ransom—about "the heresy of paraphrase," the inseparability of form and content, and the intrinsic and organic form of works of art; but it seems to me that all that is most valuable in their general theory, apart from their very acute criticism of particular works, has been stated by Bradley.

A substantially similar point of view is expressed by DeWitt Henry Parker (1885-1949), Professor of Philosophy at the University of Michigan, who contends that the all-embracing principle of form—its very essence and meaning—is organic unity. This consists of completeness without redundancy, harmony without the sacrifice of richness, achieved in an experience isolated and self-sufficient. All the other principles of form—theme, thematic variation, balance, rhythm, hierarchy, and evolution—serve this one master principle. Form thus conceived is not limited to mere design or pattern, such as the abstract relation of colors or sounds apart from their suggestiveness or dramatic import. On the contrary, it is the organization of all the elements—pure sensuous materials, representations, and connotations—into a single and inclusive experience. Thus form is no independent thing, imposed as from the outside upon an independent subject matter, but is the perfectly natural and inevitable development of expression.

In addition to the principles of form discussed by Parker we can distinguish

[3] See Pater's essay "The School of Giorgione" in *The Renaissance,* and compare the concluding paragraph in Fry's essay "The Art of Florence" in *Vision and Design.*

certain "type designs," such as the sonnet, the waltz, the sonata, and the fugue—or certain traditional styles, such as the Romanesque or the Baroque. Also individual artists develop characteristic modes of expression which serve to typify their work. In his excellent book, *Art and the Social Order,* Dilman Walter Gotshalk (1901-   ), Professor of Philosophy at the University of Illinois, points out that such type patterns may be either rigid constricting molds or plastic receptacles which the artist and the imaginative beholder can fill with rich new content.

The concept of style receives a much fuller elucidation in the essay by Meyer Schapiro (1904-   ), Professor of Fine Arts and Archeology at Columbia University and author of such important works as *Van Gogh* (1950) and *Cézanne* (1952). Style, as a persistent form and manner of expression, may be exhibited by an individual, group, civilization, or historical period. Although such an inclusive term suffers from vagueness, Schapiro's discussion is admirably clear and precise. I have reproduced less than half of his essay: the remainder is devoted to an erudite interpretation of the causes and morphology of styles, reviewing the theories of Wölfflin, Riegl, and others. I know of no better introduction to the subject.

ROGER FRY

Pure and Impure Art

There is such a thing as impure or useful science, and, if you were to analyze that activity, you would find all sorts of biological motives at work, although the fundamental truth-seeking passion of pure science is distinguished precisely by its independence of, and its indifference to, biological necessity.

Similarly there is an impure and, perhaps, useful art (though the use of impure art is not so easily demonstrated as that of impure science); here too, analysis would reveal a number of elements which really form no part of the essential esthetic activity, and you will make a serious mistake if, after such an analysis, you declare these to be constituent parts of that phenomenon.

If you have a substance which you know to be chemically pure it is clear that you have a right to say that every element which you discover in that substance by analysis is a constituent part of it, but, if you have any reason to suspect an impure mixture, you know that any particular element which the analysis reveals may be due to the impurity and form no part of the substance which you are investigating.

Now that the esthetic activity does mix in various degrees with a number of other activities is surely evident. Take for instance advertisements: many of these show no esthetic effort and do not even try to afford esthetic pleasure; they merely convey more or less inaccurate information about a particular object. You can think of advertisements where not only are the merits of the objects enumerated but the object, let us say a bottle of Somebody's Beer, is depicted. Every detail of the bottle and its label is given so that we may recognize it when we see it in the bar, but there is no sign that in the manner of representation any thought has been expended for our esthetic pleasure. On the other hand I take certain advertisements in American journals, where advertisements are taken seriously and romantically, and I find a very genuine effort, in the proportion and spacing of the letters, in the harmonious consistence of the forms, and in the exact presentation of the object, towards esthetic pleasure. None the less this esthetic appeal is mixed with all sorts of appeals to other feelings than the love of beauty—appeals to our sense of social prestige, to our avarice, to our desire for personal display, and so forth.

Or take again the case of dress—here no doubt there is often a considerable care for pure beauty of line and harmony of color, but such considerations have continually to give place to far more pressing concerns connected with social rivalry, in fact to all the complicated mass of instincts which go to make up what we call snobbishness.

These, then, are cases of obvious mixtures, in which the esthetic impulse has a part—but you will say these belong to applied art; if we take pictures which subserve no ultimate use we shall surely be safe. But alas the vast majority of pictures are not really works of art at all. No doubt in most a careful analysis would reveal some trace of esthetic preoccupations, but for the most part the appeal they make is to quite other feelings.

For the moment I must be dogmatic and declare that the esthetic emotion is an emotion about form. In certain people, purely formal relations of certain kinds arouse peculiarly profound emotions, or rather I ought to say the recognition by them of particular kinds of formal relations arouse these emotions. Now these emotions about forms may be accompanied by other emotions which have to do more or less with what I call the instinctive life.

The simplest examples of this can be taken from music. If, as frequently happens, an unmusical child strikes six notes in succession on the piano, the chances are that no one would be able to perceive any necessary relation between these notes—they have been struck by accident, as we say. But if I strike the first six notes of "God Save the King," every one who is not quite music-deaf recognizes that they have, as one would say, a meaning, a purpose. They occur in such a sequence that after each note has been struck we feel that only certain notes can follow and, as the notes follow one another, they more or less adequately fulfill our expectation, that is, from the beginning the idea of a formal design or scheme is impressed on our minds, and anything which departed violently from that would be not merely meaningless, but an outrage to our sense of order and proportion. We have then an immediate recognition of formal design, of a trend in every part towards a single unity or complete thing which we call the tune.

Now let us suppose that you hear "God Save the King" for the first time; it is possible that you would get an emotion from the mere recognition of that formal system. I do not say it would be a very profound or important emotion, but it might be an emotion, and it would probably stir up no image whatever in your mind, would be associated with no particular person or thing or idea. But those particular notes have become associated with many other things in our minds, so that when they are played we no longer can fix our minds on the form, we are instantly invaded by the associated feelings of loyalty, devotion to country, boredom from the memory of tiresome functions, or relief that we can now at last leave the theater. We shall say that that particular formal design of notes has become symbolical of numerous other things with which it has become associated.

Now this simple case presents in easy form some of the problems which confront us in works of art of all kinds. The form of a work of art has a meaning of its own and the contemplation of the form in and for itself gives rise in some people to a special emotion which does not depend upon the association of the form with anything else whatever. But that form may by various means either by casual opposition or by some resemblance to things or people or ideas in the outside world, become intimately associated in our minds with those other things, and if these things are objects of emotional feeling, we shall get from the contemplation of the form the echo of all the feelings belonging to the associated objects.

Now since very few people are so constituted by nature or training as to have developed the special feeling about formal design, and since every one has in the course of his life accumulated a vast mass of feeling about all sorts of objects, persons, and ideas, for the greater part of mankind the associated emotions of a work of art are far stronger than the purely esthetic ones.

So far does this go that they hardly notice the form, but pass at once into the world of associated emotions which that form calls up in them. Thus, to go back to our example, the vast majority of people have no notion whether the form of "God Save the King" is finely constructed and capable of arousing esthetic emotion or not. They have never, properly speaking, heard the form because they have always passed at once into that richly varied world of racial and social emotion which has gathered round it.

And what is true of certain pieces of music is even more true of the graphic arts. Here we have forms which quite visibly resemble certain objects in nature, and not unfrequently these objects, such for instance as a beautiful woman, are charged for us with a great deal of emotion. When to this we add that people are far less sensitive to the meaning of visible formal design than they are to audible design, we need not be surprised that pictures are almost always estimated for qualities which have nothing, or almost nothing, to do with their formal design or their esthetic quality in the strict sense.

To satisfy this emotional pleasure in the associated ideas of images which the mass of mankind feel so strongly there has arisen a vast production of pictures, writings, music, etc., in which formal design is entirely subordinated to the excitation of the emotions associated with objects. And this is what we may call popular, commercial, or impure art, and to this category belongs nowadays the vast majority of so-called artistic productions. On the other hand in each generation there are likely to be a certain number of people who have a sensitiveness to purely formal relations. To such people these relations have meaning and arouse keen emotions of pleasure. And these people create such systems of formal relations and do not sacrifice willingly or consciously anything of those formal relations to the arousing of emotions connected with objects in the outside world. Their whole attention is directed towards establishing the completest relationship of all parts within the system of the work of art.

It so happens that these systems of formal relations the meaning of which is apprehended by a comparatively few people in each generation, have a curious vitality and longevity, whereas those works in which appeal is made chiefly to the associated ideas of images rarely survive the generation for whose pleasure they were made. This may be because the emotions about objects change more rapidly than the emotions about form. But whatever the reason, the result is that the accumulated and inherited artistic treasure of mankind is made up almost entirely of those works in which formal design is the predominant consideration.

This contrast between the nature of inherited art and the mass of contemporary art has become so marked that the word "classic" is often used (loosely and incorrectly, no doubt) to denote work which has this peculiar character. People speak of classical music, for instance, when they mean the works of any of the great composers. It is significant of the rarity of comprehension of such formal design that to many people classical music is almost synonymous with "dull" music. . . .

Since most people are unable to perceive the meaning of purely formal relations, are unable to derive from them the profound satisfaction that the creator and those that understand him feel, they always look for some meaning that can be attached to the values of actual life, they always hope to translate a work of art into terms of *ideas* with which they are familiar. . . .

Now I venture to say that no one who has a real understanding of the art of painting attaches any importance to what we call the subject of a picture—

what is represented. To one who feels the language of pictorial form all depends on *how* it is presented, *nothing* on what. Rembrandt expressed his profoundest feelings just as well when he painted a carcass hanging up in a butcher's shop as when he painted the Crucifixion or his mistress. Cézanne whom most of us believe to be the greatest artist of modern times expressed some of his grandest conceptions in pictures of fruit and crockery on a common kitchen table.

I remember when this fact became clear to me, and the instance may help to show what I mean. In a loan exhibition I came upon a picture of Chardin. It was a signboard painted to hang outside a druggist's shop. It represented a number of glass retorts, a still, and various glass bottles, the furniture of a chemist's laboratory of that time. You will admit that there was not much material for wish-fulfillment (unless the still suggested remote possibilities of alcohol). Well, it gave me a very intense and vivid sensation. Just the shapes of those bottles and their mutual relations gave me the feeling of something immensely grand and impressive and the phrase that came into my mind was, "This is just how I felt when I first saw Michelangelo's frescoes in the Sistine Chapel." Those represented the whole history of creation with the tremendous images of Sybils and Prophets, but esthetically it meant something very similar to Chardin's glass bottles.

And here let me allude to a curious phenomenon which I have frequently noticed, namely, that even though at the first shock of a great political design the subject appears to have a great deal to do with one's emotional reaction, that part of one's feeling evaporates very quickly; one soon exhausts the feelings connected by associated ideas with the figures, and what remains, what never grows less nor evaporates, are the feelings dependent on the purely formal relations. This indeed may be the explanation of that curious fact that I alluded to, the persistence throughout the ages of works in which formal perfection is attained, and the rapid disappearance and neglect which is the fate of works that make their chief appeal through the associated ideas of the images. . . .

. . . The question occurs, "What is the source of the affective quality of certain systems of formal design for those who are sensitive to pure form? Why are we moved deeply by certain sequences of notes which arouse no suggestion of any experience in actual life? Why are we moved deeply by certain dispositions of space in architecture which refer so far as we can tell to no other experience?"

One thing I think we may clearly say, namely, that there is a pleasure in the recognition of order, of inevitability in relations, and that the more complex the relations of which we are able to recognize the inevitable interdependence and correspondence, the greater is the pleasure; this of course will come very near to the pleasure derived from the contemplation of intellectual constructions united by logical inevitability. What the source of that satisfaction is would clearly be a problem for psychology.

But in art there is, I think, an affective quality which lies outside that. It is not a mere recognition of order and interrelation; every part, as well as the whole, become suffused with an emotional tone. Now, from our definition of this pure beauty, the emotional tone is not due to any recognizable reminiscence or suggestion of the emotional experiences of life; but I sometimes wonder if it nevertheless does not get its force from arousing some very deep, very vague, and immensely generalized reminiscences. It looks as though art had got access to the substratum of all the emotional colors of life, to something which underlies all the particular and specialized emotions of actual life. It seems to derive an emotional energy from the very conditions of our existence by its relation of an emotional significance in time and space. Or it may be that art really calls up, as it were, the residual traces left on the spirit by the different emotions of life, without however recalling the actual experiences, so that we get an echo of the emotion without the limitation and particular direction which it had in experience.

—"The Artist and Psychoanalysis" from *The Hogarth Essays* (1924)

ANDREW CECIL BRADLEY
Poetry for Poetry's Sake

The words "Poetry for poetry's sake" recall the famous phrase "Art for Art." It is far from my purpose to examine the possible meanings of that phrase, or all the questions it involves. I propose to state briefly what I understand by "Poetry for poetry's sake," and then, after guarding against one or two misapprehensions of the formula, to consider more fully a single problem connected with it. And I must premise, without attempting to justify them, certain explanations. We are to consider poetry in its essence, and apart from the flaws which in most poems accompany their poetry. We are to include in the idea of poetry the metrical form, and not to regard this as a mere accident or a mere vehicle. And, finally, poetry being poems, we are to think of a poem as it actually exists; and, without aiming here at accuracy, we may say that an actual poem is the succession of experiences—sounds, images, thoughts, emotions—through which we pass when we are reading as poetically as we can. Of course this imaginative experience—if I may use the phrase for brevity—differs with every reader and every time of reading: a poem exists in innumerable degrees. But that insurmountable fact lies in the nature of things and does not concern us now.

What then does the formula "Poetry for poetry's sake" tell us about this experience? It says, as I understand it, these things. First, this experience is an end in itself, is worth having on its own account, has an intrinsic value. Next, its *poetic* value is this intrinsic worth alone. Poetry may have also an ulterior value as a means to culture or religion; because it conveys instructions, or softens the passions, or furthers a good cause; because it brings the poet fame or money or a quiet conscience. So much the better: let it be valued for these reasons too. But its ulterior worth neither is nor can directly determine its poetic worth as a satisfying imaginative experience; and this is to be judged entirely from within. And to these two positions the formula would add, though not of necessity, a third. The consideration of ulterior ends, whether by the poet in the act of composing or by the reader in the act of experiencing, tends to lower poetic value. It does so because it tends to change the nature of poetry by taking it out of its own atmosphere. For its nature is to be not a part, nor yet a copy, of the real world (as we commonly understand that phrase), but to be a world by itself, independent, complete, autonomous; and to possess it fully you must enter the world, conform to its laws, and ignore for the time the beliefs, aims, and particular conditions which belong to you in the other world of reality.

Of the more serious misapprehensions to which these statements may give rise I will glance only at one or two. The offensive consequences often drawn from the formula "Art for Art" will be found to attach not to the doctrine that Art is an end in itself, but to the doctrine that Art is the whole or supreme end of human life. And as this latter doctrine, which seems to me absurd, is in any case quite different from the former, its consequences fall outside my subject. The formula "Poetry is an end in itself" has nothing to say on the various questions of moral judgment which arise from the fact that poetry has its place in a many-sided life. For anything it says, the intrinsic value of poetry might be so small, and its ulterior effects so mischievous, that it had better not exist. The formula only tells us that we must not place in antithesis poetry and human good, for poetry is one kind of human good; and that we must not determine the intrinsic value of this kind of good by direct reference to another. If we do, we shall find ourselves maintaining what we did not expect. If poetic value lies in the stimulation of religious feelings, *Lead, Kindly Light*[1] is no better a poem than many a tasteless version of a Psalm: if in the excitement of patriotism, why is *Scots, Wha Hae*[2] superior to *We Don't Want to Fight?* if in the mitigation of the passions, the Odes of Sappho will win but little praise: if in instruction, Armstrong's *Art of Preserving Health* should win much.

Again, our formula may be accused of cutting poetry away from its connection with life. And this accusation raises so huge a problem that I must ask leave to be dogmatic as well as brief. There is plenty of connection between life and poetry, but it is, so to say, a connection underground. The two may be called

[1] Newman.
[2] Burns.

different forms of the same thing: one of them having (in the usual sense) reality, but seldom fully satisfying imagination; while the other offers something which satisfies imagination but has not full "reality." They are parallel developments which nowhere meet, or, if I may use loosely a word which will be serviceable later, they are analogous. Hence we understand one by help of the other, and even, in a sense, care for one because of the other; but hence also, poetry neither is life, nor, strictly speaking, a copy of it. They differ not only because one has more mass and the other a more perfect shape, but because they have different *kinds* of existence. The one touches us as beings occupying a given position in space and time, and having feelings, desires, and purposes due to that position: it appeals to imagination, but appeals to much besides. What meets us in poetry has not a position in the same series of time and space, or, if it has or had such a position, it is taken apart from much that belonged to it there; and therefore it makes no direct appeal to those feelings, desires, and purposes, but speaks only to contemplative imagination—imagination the reverse of empty or emotionless, imagination saturated with the results of "real" experience, but still contemplative. Thus, no doubt, one main reason why poetry has poetic value for us is that it presents to us in its own way something which we meet in another form in nature or life; and yet the test of its poetic value for us lies simply in the question whether it satisfies our imagination; the rest of us, our knowledge or conscience, for example, judging it only so far as they appear transmuted in our imagination. So also Shakespeare's knowledge or his moral insight, Milton's greatness of soul, Shelley's "hate of hate" and "love of love," and that desire to help men or make them happier which may have influenced a poet in hours of meditation—all these have, as such, no poetical worth: they have that worth only when, passing through the unity of the poet's being, they reappear as qualities of imagination, and then are indeed mighty powers in the world of poetry.

I come to a third misapprehension, and so to my main subject. This formula, it is said, empties poetry of its meaning: it is really a doctrine of form for form's sake. "It is of no consequence what a poet says, so long as he says the thing well. The *what* is poetically indifferent: it is the *how* that counts. Matter, subject, content, substance, determines nothing; there is no subject with which poetry may not deal: the form, the treatment, is everything. Nay, more: not only is the matter indifferent, but it is the secret of Art to 'eradicate the matter by means of the form,'"—phrases and statements like these meet us everywhere in current criticism of literature and the other arts. They are the stock-in-trade of writers who understand of them little more than the fact that somehow or other they are not "bourgeois." But we find them also seriously used by writers whom we must respect, whether they are anonymous or not; something like one or another of them might be quoted, for example, from Professor Saintsbury, the late R. A. M. Stevenson, Schiller, Goethe himself; and they are the watchwords of a school in the one country where esthetics has flourished. They come, as a rule, from men who either practice one of the arts, or, from study of it, are interested in its methods. The general reader—a being so general that I may say what I will of him—is outraged by them. He feels that he is being robbed of almost all that he cares for in a work of art. "You are asking me," he says, "to look at the Dresden Madonna as if it were a Persian rug. You are telling me that the poetic value of *Hamlet* lies solely in its style and versification, and that my interest in the man and his fate is only an intellectual or moral interest. You allege that, if I want to enjoy the poetry of *Crossing the Bar,* I must not mind what Tennyson says there, but must consider solely his way of saying it. But in that case I can care no more for a poem than I do for a set of nonsense verses; and I do not believe that the authors of *Hamlet* and *Crossing the Bar* regarded their poems thus."

These antitheses of subject, matter, substance on the one side, form, treatment, handling on the other, are the field through which I especially want, in this lecture, to indicate a way. It is a field of battle; and the battle is waged for no trivial cause; but the cries of the combatants are terribly ambiguous. Those phrases of the so-called formalist may each mean five or six different things. Taken in one sense they seem to me chiefly true; taken as the general reader not unnaturally takes them, they seem to me false and mischievous. It would be absurd to pretend that I can end in a few minutes a controversy which concerns the ultimate nature of Art, and leads perhaps to problems not yet soluble; but we can at least draw some plain distinctions which, in this controversy, are too often confused.

In the first place, then, let us take "subject" in one particular sense; let us understand by it that which we have in view when, looking at the title of an unread poem, we say that the poet has chosen this or that for his subject. The subject, in this sense, so far as I can discover, is generally something, real or imaginary, as it exists in the minds of fairly cultivated people. The subject of *Paradise Lost* would be the story of the Fall as that story exists in the general imagination of a Bible-reading people. The subject of Shelley's stanzas *To a Skylark* would be the ideas which arise in the mind of an educated person when, without knowing the poem, he hears the word "skylark." If the title of a poem conveys little or nothing to us, the "subject" appears to be either what we should gather by investigating the title in a dictionary or other book of the kind, or else such a brief suggestion as might be offered by a person who had read the poem, and who said, for example, that the subject of *The Ancient Mariner* was a sailor who killed an albatross and suffered for his deed.

Now the subject, in this sense (and I intend to use the word in no other), is not, as such, inside the poem, but outside it. The contents of the stanzas *To a Skylark* are not the ideas suggested by the word "skylark" to the average man; they belong to Shelley just as much as the language does. The subject, therefore, is not the matter *of* the poem at all; and its opposite is not the *form* of the poem, but the whole poem. The subject is one thing; the poem, matter and form alike, another thing. This being so, it is surely obvious that the poetic value cannot lie in the subject, but lies entirely in its opposite, the poem. How can the subject determine the value when on one and the same subject poems may be written of all degrees of merit and demerit; or when a perfect poem may be composed on a subject so slight as a pet sparrow,[3] and, if Macaulay [4] may be trusted, a nearly worthless poem on a subject so stupendous as the omnipresence of the Deity? The "formalist" is here perfectly right. Nor is he insisting on something unimportant. He is fighting against our tendency to take the work of art as a mere copy or reminder of something already in our heads, or at the best as a suggestion of some idea as little removed as possible from the familiar. The sightseer who promenades a picture-gallery, remarking that this portrait is so like his cousin, or that landscape the very image of his birthplace, or who, after satisfying himself that one picture is about Elijah, passes on rejoicing to discover the subject, and nothing but the subject, of the next—what is he but an extreme example of this tendency? Well, but the very same tendency vitiates much of our criticism, much criticism of Shakespeare, for example, which, with all its cleverness and partial truth, still shows that the critic never passed from his own mind into Shakespeare's; and it may be traced even in so fine a critic as Coleridge, as when he dwarfs the sublime struggle of Hamlet into the image of his own unhappy weakness. Hazlitt by no means escaped its influence. Only the third of that great trio, Lamb, appears almost always to have rendered the conception of the composer.

Again, it is surely true that we cannot determine beforehand what subjects are fit for Art, or name any subject on which a good poem might not possibly be written. To divide subjects into two groups, the beautiful or elevating, and the ugly or vicious, and to judge poems according as their subjects belong to one of these groups or the other, is to fall into the same pit, to confuse with our preconceptions the meaning of the poet. What the thing is in the poem he is to be judged by, not by the thing as it was before he touched it; and how can we venture to say beforehand that he cannot make a true poem out of something which to us was merely alluring or dull or revolting? The question whether, having done so, he ought to publish his poem; whether the thing in the poet's work will not be still confused by the incompetent Puritan or the incompetent sensualist with the thing in *his* mind, does not touch this point; it is a further question, one of ethics, not of art. No doubt the upholders of "Art for Art's sake" will generally be in favor of the courageous course, of refusing to sacrifice the better or stronger part of the public to the weaker or worse; but their maxim in no way binds them to this view. Rossetti suppressed one of the best of his sonnets, a sonnet chosen for admiration by Tennyson, himself extremely sensitive about the moral effect of poetry; suppressed it, I believe, because it was called

---

[3] Catullus.
[4] *Robert Montgomery.*

fleshly. One may regret Rossetti's judgment and at the same time respect his scrupulousness; but in any case he judged in his capacity of citizen, not in his capacity of artist.

So far then the "formalist" appears to be right. But he goes too far, I think, if he maintains that the subject is indifferent and that all subjects are the same to poetry. And he does not prove his point by observing that a good poem might be written on a pin's head, and a bad one on the Fall of Man. That truth shows that the subject *settles* nothing, but not that it counts for nothing. The Fall of Man is really a more favorable subject than a pin's head. The Fall of Man, that is to say, offers opportunities of poetic effects wider in range and more penetrating in appeal. And the fact is that such a subject, as it exists in the general imagination, has some esthetic value before the poet touches it. It is, as you may choose to call it, an inchoate poem or the debris of a poem. It is not an abstract idea or a bare isolated fact, but an assemblage of figures, scenes, actions, and events, which already appeal to emotional imagination; and it is already in some degree organized and formed. In spite of this a bad poet would make a bad poem on it; but then we should say he was unworthy of the subject. And we should not say this if he wrote a bad poem on a pin's head. Conversely, a good poem on a pin's head would almost certainly transform its subject far more than a good poem on the Fall of Man. It might revolutionize its subject so completely that we should say, "The subject may be a pin's head, but the substance of the poem has very little to do with it."

This brings us to another and a different antithesis. Those figures, scenes, events, that form part of the subject called the Fall of Man, are not the substance of *Paradise Lost;* but in *Paradise Lost* there are figures, scenes, and events resembling them in some degree. These, with much more of the same kind, may be described as its substance, and may then be contrasted with the measured language of the poem, which will be called its form. Subject is the opposite not of form but of the whole poem. Substance is within the poem, and its opposite, form, is also within the poem. I am not criticizing this antithesis at present, but evidently it is quite different from the other. It is practically the distinction used in the old-fashioned criticism of epic and drama, and it flows down, not unsullied, from Aristotle. Addison,[5] for example, in examining *Paradise Lost* considers in order the fable, the characters, and the sentiments; these will be the substance: then he considers the language, that is, the style and numbers; this will be the form. In like manner, the substance or meaning of a lyric may be distinguished from the form.

Now I believe it will be found that a large part of the controversy we are dealing with arises from a confusion between these two distinctions of substance and form, and of subject and poem. The extreme formalist lays his whole weight on the form because he thinks its opposite is the mere subject. The general

[5] *Spectator,* 267, &c.

reader is angry, but makes the same mistake, and gives to the subject praises that rightly belong to the substance.[6] I will give an example of what I mean. I can only explain the following words of a good critic [7] by supposing that for the moment he has fallen into this confusion: "The mere matter of all poetry—to wit, the appearances of nature and the thoughts and feelings of men—being unalterable, it follows that the difference between poet and poet will depend upon the manner of each in applying language, meter, rhyme, cadence, and what not, to this invariable material." What has become here of the substance of *Paradise Lost*—the story, scenery, characters, sentiments as they are in the poem? They have vanished clean away. Nothing is left but the form on one side, and on the other not even the subject, but a supposed invariable material, the appearances of nature and the thoughts and feelings of men. Is it surprising that the whole value should then be found in the form?

So far we have assumed that this antithesis of substance and form is valid, and that it always has one meaning. In reality it has several, but we will leave it in its present shape, and pass to the question of its validity. And this question we are compelled to raise, because we have to deal with the two contentions that the poetic value lies wholly or mainly in the substance, and that it lies wholly or mainly in the form. Now these contentions, whether false or true, may seem at least to be clear; but we shall find, I think, that they are both of them false, or both of them nonsense: false if they concern anything outside the poem, nonsense if they apply to something in it. For what do they evidently imply? They imply that there are in a poem two parts, factors, or components, a substance and a form; and that you can conceive them distinctly and separately, so that when you are speaking of the one you are not speaking of the other. Otherwise how can you ask the question, In which of them does the value lie? But really in a poem, apart from defects, there are no such factors or components; and therefore it is strictly nonsense to ask in which of them the value lies. And on the other hand, if the substance and the form referred to are not in the poem, then both the contentions are false, for its poetic value lies in itself.

What I mean is neither new nor mysterious; and it will be clear, I believe, to any one who reads poetry poetically and who closely examines his experience. When you are reading a poem, I would ask—not analyzing it, and much less criticizing it, but allowing it, as it proceeds, to make its full impression on you through the exertion of your re-creating imagination—do you then apprehend and enjoy as one thing a certain meaning or substance, and as another thing certain articulate sounds, and do you somehow compound these two? Surely

---

[6] What is here called "substance" is what people generally mean when they use the word "subject" and insist on the value of the subject. I am not arguing against this usage, or in favor of the usage which I have adopted for the sake of clearness. It does not matter which we employ, so long as we and others know what we mean. (I use "substance" and "content" indifferently.)

[7] George Saintsbury.

you do not, any more than you apprehend apart, when you see someone smile, those lines in the face which express a feeling, and the feeling that the lines express. Just as there the lines and their meaning are to you one thing, not two, so in poetry the meaning and the sounds are one: there is, if I may put it so, a resonant meaning, or a meaning resonance. If you read the line, "The sun is warm, the sky is clear," [8] you do not experience separately the image of a warm sun and clear sky, on the one side, and certain unintelligible rhythmical sounds on the other; nor yet do you experience them together, side by side; but you experience the one *in* the other. And in like manner when you are really reading *Hamlet*, the action and the characters are not something which you conceive apart from the words; you apprehend them from point to point *in* the words, and the words as expressions of them. Afterwards, no doubt, when you are out of the poetic experience but remember it, you may by analysis decompose this unity, and attend to a substance more or less isolated, and a form more or less isolated. But these are things in your analytic head, not in the poem, which is *poetic* experience. And if you want to have the poem again, you cannot find it by adding together these two products of decomposition; you can only find it by passing back into poetic experience. And then what you recover is no aggregate of factors, it is a unity in which you can no more separate a substance and a form than you can separate living blood and the life in the blood. This unity has, if you like, various "aspects" or "sides," but they are not factors or parts; if you try to examine one, you find it is also the other. Call them substance and form if you please, but these are not the reciprocally exclusive substance and form to which the two contentions *must* refer. They do not "agree," for they are not apart: they are one thing from different points of view, and in that sense identical. And this identity of content and form, you will say, is no accident; it is of the essence of poetry insofar as it is poetry, and of all art insofar as it is art. Just as there is in music not sound on one side and a meaning on the other, but expressive sound, and if you ask what is the meaning you can only answer by pointing to the sounds; just as in painting there is not a meaning *plus* paint, but a meaning *in* paint, or significant paint, and no man can really express the meaning in any other way than in paint and in *this* paint; so in a poem the true content and the true form neither exist nor can be imagined apart. When then you are asked whether the value of a poem lies in a substance got by decomposing the poem, and present, as such, only in reflective analysis, or whether the value lies in a form arrived at and existing in the same way, you will answer, "It lies neither in one, nor in the other, nor in any addition of them, but in the poem, where they are not."

We have then, first, an antithesis of subject and poem. This is clear and valid; and the question in which of them does the value lie is intelligible; and its answer is, *In the poem.* We have next a distinction of substance and form.

[8] Shelley, "Lines Written in Dejection Near the Bay of Naples."

If the substance means ideas, images, and the like taken alone, and the form means the measured language taken by itself, this is a possible distinction, but it is a distinction of things not in the poem, and the value lies *in neither of them.* If substance and form mean anything *in* the poem, then each is involved in the other, and the question in which of them the value lies has no sense. No doubt you may say, speaking loosely, that in this poet or poem the aspect of substance is the more noticeable, and in that the aspect of form; and you may pursue interesting discussions on this basis, though no principle or ultimate question of value is touched by them. And apart from that question, of course, I am not denying the usefulness and necessity of the distinction. We cannot dispense with it. To consider separately the action or the characters of a play, and separately its style or versification, is both legitimate and valuable, so long as we remember what we are doing. But the true critic in speaking of these apart does not really think of them apart; the whole, the poetic experience, of which they are but aspects, is always in his mind; and he is always aiming at a richer, truer, more intense repetition of that experience. On the other hand, when the question of principle, of poetic value, is raised, these aspects *must* fall apart into components, separately inconceivable; and then there arise two heresies, equally false, that the value lies in one of two things, both of which are outside the poem, and therefore where its value cannot lie.

On the heresy of the separable substance a few additional words will suffice. This heresy is seldom formulated, but perhaps some unconscious holder of it may object: "Surely the action and the characters of *Hamlet* are in the play; and surely I can retain these, though I have forgotten all the words. I admit that I do not possess the whole poem, but I possess a part, and the most important part." And I would answer: "If we are not concerned with any question of principle, I accept all that you say except the last words, which do raise such a question. Speaking loosely, I agree that the action and characters, as you perhaps conceive them, together with a great deal more, are in the poem. Even then, however, you must not claim to possess all of this kind that is in the poem; for in forgetting the words you must have lost innumerable details of the action and the characters. And, when the question of value is raised, I must insist that the action and characters, as you conceive them, are not in *Hamlet* at all. If they are, point them out. You cannot do it. What you find at any moment of that succession of experiences called *Hamlet* is words. In these words, to speak loosely again, the action and characters (more of them than you can conceive apart) are focused; but your experience is not a combination of them, as ideas, on the one side, with certain sounds on the other; it is an experience of something in which the two are indissolubly fused. If you deny this, to be sure I can make no answer, or can only answer that I have reason to believe that you cannot read poetically, or else are misinterpreting your experience. But if you do not deny this, then you will admit that the action and characters of the poem, as you separately imagine them, are no part of it, but a product of it in your reflective imagination, a faint analogue of one aspect of it taken in detachment from the whole. Well, I do not dispute, I would even insist, that, in the case of so long a poem as *Hamlet*, it may be necessary from time to time to interrupt the poetic experience, in order to enrich it by forming such a product and dwelling on it. Nor, in a wide sense of 'poetic,' do I question the poetic value of this product, as you think of it apart from the poem. It resembles our recollections of the heroes of history or legend, who move about in our imaginations, 'forms more real than living man,' and are worth much to us though we do not remember anything they said. Our ideas and images of the 'substance' of a poem have this poetic value, and more, if they are at all adequate. But they cannot determine the poetic value of the poem, for (not to speak of the competing claims of the 'form') nothing that is outside the poem can do that, and they, as such, are outside it." [9]

Let us turn to the so-called form—style and versification. There is no such thing as mere form in poetry. All form is expression. Style may have indeed a certain esthetic worth in partial abstraction from the particular matter it conveys, as in a well-built sentence you may take pleasure in the build almost apart from the meaning. Even so, style is expressive—presents to sense, for example, the order, ease, and rapidity with which ideas move in the writer's mind—but it is not expressive of the meaning of that particular sentence. And it is possible, interrupting poetic experience, to decompose it and abstract for comparatively separate consideration this nearly formal element of style. But the esthetic value of style so taken is not considerable; [10] you could not read with pleasure for an hour a composition which had no other merit. And in poetic experience you never apprehend this value by itself; the style is here expressive also of a particular meaning, or rather is one aspect of that unity whose other aspect is meaning. So that what you apprehend may be called indifferently an expressed meaning or a significant form. Perhaps on this point I may in Oxford appeal to authority, that of Matthew Arnold and Walter Pater, the latter at any rate an authority whom the formalist will not despise. What is the gist of Pater's teaching about style, if it is not that in the end the one virtue of style is truth or adequacy; that the word, phrase, sentence, should express perfectly the writer's perception, feeling, image, or thought; so that, as we read a descriptive phrase of Keats's, we exclaim, "That is the thing itself"; so that, to quote Arnold, the words are "symbols equivalent with the thing symbolized," or, in our technical language, a form identical with its content? Hence in true poetry it is, in strictness, impossible to express the meaning in any but its own words, or to change the words without changing the meaning. A translation of such poetry is not really the old meaning in a fresh dress; it is a new

9 These remarks will hold good, *mutatis mutandis,* if by "substance" is understood the "moral" or the "idea" of a poem, although perhaps in one instance out of five thousand this may be found in so many words in the poem.

10 On the other hand, the absence, or worse than absence, of style, in this sense, is a serious matter.

product, something like the poem, though, if one chooses to say so, more like it in the aspect of meaning than in the aspect of form.

No one who understands poetry, it seems to me, would dispute this, were it not that, falling away from his experience, or misled by theory, he takes the word "meaning" in a sense almost ludicrously inapplicable to poetry. People say, for instance, "steed" and "horse" have the same meaning; and in bad poetry they have, but not in poetry that *is* poetry.

> "Bring forth the horse!" The horse was brought:
> In truth he was a noble steed!

says Byron in *Mazeppa*. If the two words mean the same here, transpose them:

> "Bring forth the steed!" The steed was brought:
> In truth he was a noble horse!

and ask again if they mean the same. Or let me take a line certainly very free from "poetic diction":

> To be or not to be, that is the question.

You may say that this means the same as "What is just now occupying my attention is the comparative disadvantages of continuing to live or putting an end to myself." And for practical purposes—the purpose, for example, of a coroner—it does. But as the second version altogether misrepresents the speaker at that moment of his existence, while the first does represent him, how can they for any but a practical or logical purpose be said to have the same sense? Hamlet was well able to "unpack his heart with words," but he will not unpack it with our paraphrases.

These considerations apply equally to versification. If I take the famous line which describes how the souls of the dead stood waiting by the river, imploring a passage from Charon:

> *Tendebantque manus ripae ulterioris amore,*[11]

and if I translate it, "and were stretching forth their hands in longing for the further bank," the charm of the original has fled. Why has it fled? Partly (but we have dealt with that) because I have substituted for five words, and those the words of Virgil, twelve words, and those my own. In some measure because I have turned into rhythmless prose a line of verse which, as mere sound, has unusual beauty. But much more because in doing so I have also changed the *meaning* of Virgil's line. What that meaning is *I* cannot say: Virgil has said it. But I can see this much, that the translation conveys a far less vivid picture of the outstretched hands and of their remaining outstretched, and a far less poignant sense of the distance of the shore and the longing of the souls. And it does

[11] *Aeneid*, VI, 314.

so partly because this picture and this sense are conveyed not only by the obvious meaning of the words, but through the long-drawn sound of "tendebantque," through the time occupied by the five syllables and therefore by the idea of "ulterioris," and through the identity of the long sound "or" in the penultimate syllables of "ulterioris amore"—all this, and much more, apprehended not in this analytical fashion, nor as *added* to the beauty of mere sound and to the obvious meaning, but in unity with them and so as expressive of the poetic meaning of the whole.

It is always so in fine poetry. The value of versification, when it is indissolubly fused with meaning, can hardly be exaggerated. The gift for feeling it, even more perhaps than the gift for feeling the value of style, is the *specific* gift for poetry, as distinguished from other arts. But versification, taken, as far as possible, all by itself, has a very different worth. Some esthetic worth it has; how much, you may experience by reading poetry in a language of which you do not understand a syllable. The pleasure is quite appreciable, but it is not great; nor in actual poetic experience do you meet with it, as such, at all. For, I repeat, it is not *added* to the pleasure of the meaning when you read poetry that you do understand: by some mystery the music is then the music *of* the meaning, and the two are one. However fond of versification you might be, you would tire very soon of reading verses in Chinese; and before long of reading Virgil and Dante if you were ignorant of their languages. But take the music as it is *in* the poem, and there is a marvelous change. Now

> It gives a very echo to the seat
> Where Love is throned,[12]

or "carries far into your heart," almost like music itself, the sound

> Of old, unhappy, far-off things
> And battles long ago.[13]

What then is to be said of the following sentence of the critic quoted before: [14] "But when anyone who knows what poetry is reads—

> Our noisy years seem moments in the being
> Of the eternal silence,[15]

he sees that, quite independently of the meaning, . . . there is one note added to the articulate music of the world—a note that never will leave off resounding till the eternal silence itself gulfs it"? I must think that the writer is deceiving himself. For I could quite understand his enthusiasm, if it were an enthusiasm for the music of the meaning; but as for the music, "quite independently of the

---

[12] *Twelfth Night,* II. iv.
[13] Wordsworth, "The Solitary Reaper."
[14] Saintsbury, *History of English Prosody,* iii. pp. 74-71.
[15] Wordsworth, "Ode on the Intimations of Immortality."

meaning," so far as I can hear it thus (and I doubt if any one who knows English can quite do so), I find it gives some pleasure, but only a trifling pleasure. And indeed I venture to doubt whether, considered as mere sound, the words are at all exceptionally beautiful, as Virgil's line certainly is. . . .

Pure poetry is not the decoration of a preconceived and clearly defined matter: it springs from the creative impulse of a vague imaginative mass pressing for development and definition. If the poet already knew exactly what he meant to say, why should he write the poem? The poem would in fact already be written. For only its completion can reveal, even to him, exactly what he wanted. When he began and while he was at work, he did not possess his meaning; it possessed him. It was not a fully formed soul asking for a body: it was an inchoate soul in the inchoate body of perhaps two or three vague ideas and a few scattered phrases. The growing of this body into its full stature and perfect shape was the same thing as the gradual self-definition of the meaning. And this is the reason why such poems strike us as creations, not manufactures, and have the magical effect which mere decoration cannot produce. This is also the reason why, if we insist on asking for the meaning of such a poem, we can only be answered, "It means itself."

And so at last I may explain why I have troubled myself and you with what may seem an arid controversy about mere words. It is not so. These heresies which would make poetry a compound of two factors—a matter common to it with the merest prose, *plus* a poetic form, as the one heresy says: a poetical substance *plus* a negligible form, as the other says—are not only untrue, they are injurious to the dignity of poetry. In an age already inclined to shrink from those higher realms where poetry touches religion and philosophy, the formalist heresy encourages men to taste poetry as they would a fine wine, which has indeed an esthetic value, but a small one. And then the natural man, finding an empty form, hurls into it the matter of cheap pathos, rancid sentiment, vulgar humor, bare lust, ravenous vanity—everything which, in Schiller's phrase,[16] the form should extirpate, but which no mere form can extirpate. And the other heresy—which is indeed rather a practice than a creed—encourages us in the habit so dear to us of putting our own thoughts or fancies into the place of the poet's creation. What he meant by *Hamlet,* or the *Ode to a Nightingale,* or *Abt Vogler,* we say, is this or that which we knew already; and so we lose what he had to tell us. But he meant what he said, and said what he meant.

Poetry in this matter is not, as good critics of painting and music often affirm, different from the other arts; in all of them the content is one thing with the form. What Beethoven meant by his symphony, or Turner by his picture, was not something which you can name, but the picture and the symphony. Meaning they have, but *what* meaning can be said in no language but their own: and we know this, though some strange delusion makes us think the meaning has

[16] Not that to Schiller "form" meant mere style and versification.

less worth because we cannot put it into words. Well, it is just the same with poetry. But because poetry is words, we vainly fancy that some other words than its own will express its meaning. And they will do so no more—or, if you like to speak loosely, only a little more—than words will express the meaning of the Dresden Madonna. Something a little like it they may indeed express. And we may find analogues of the meaning of poetry outside it, which may help us to appropriate it. The other arts, the best ideas of philosophy or religion, much that nature and life offer us or force upon us, are akin to it. But they are only akin. Nor is it the expression of them. Poetry does not present to imagination our highest knowledge or belief, and much less our dreams and opinions; but it, content and form in unity, embodies in its own irreplaceable way something which embodies itself also in other irreplaceable ways, such as philosophy or religion. And just as each of these gives a satisfaction which the other cannot possibly give, so we find in poetry, which cannot satisfy the needs they meet, that which by their natures they cannot afford us. But we shall not find it fully if we look for something else.

And now, when all is said, the question will still recur, though now in quite another sense, What does poetry mean? This unique expression, which cannot be replaced by any other, still seems to be trying to express something beyond itself. And this, we feel, is also what the other arts, and religion, and philosophy are trying to express: and that is what impels us to seek in vain to translate the one into the other. About the best poetry, and not only the best, there floats an atmosphere of infinite suggestion. The poet speaks to us of one thing, but in this one thing there seems to lurk the secret of all. He said what he meant, but his meaning seems to beckon away beyond itself, or rather to expand into something boundless which is only focused in it; something also which, we feel, would satisfy not only the imagination, but the whole of us; that something within us, and without, which everywhere

> makes us seem
> To patch up fragments of a dream,
> Part of which comes true, and part
> Beats and trembles in the heart.[17]

Those who are susceptible to this effect of poetry find it not only, perhaps not most, in the ideals which she has sometimes described, but in a child's song by Christina Rossetti about a mere crown of wind-flowers, and in tragedies like *Lear,* where the sun seems to have set forever. They hear this spirit murmuring its undertone through the *Aeneid,* and catch its voice in the song of Keats's nightingale, and its light upon the figures on the Urn, and it pierces them no less in Shelley's hopeless lament, *O world, O life, O time,* than in the rapturous ecstasy of his *Life of Life.* This all-embracing perfection cannot be expressed in poetic

---

[17] Shelley, "Is it that in some brighter sphere?"

words or words of any kind, nor yet in music or in color, but the suggestion of it
is in much poetry, if not all, and poetry has in this suggestion, this "meaning," a
great part of its value. We do it wrong, and we defeat our own purposes when
we try to bend it to them:

> We do it wrong, being so majestical,
> To offer it the show of violence;
> For it is as the air invulnerable,
> And our vain blows malicious mockery.[18]

It is a spirit. It comes we know not whence. It will not speak at our bidding, nor
answer in our language. It is not our servant; it is our master.

—*Oxford Lectures on Poetry* (1909)

DeWITT H. PARKER

The Problem of Esthetic Form

I shall try to reduce the general characteristics of esthetic form to their simplest principles, hoping to provide the elements of what might be called a logic of
esthetic form. These principles are, I think, very few; as few, indeed, as six: the
principle of organic unity, or unity in variety, as it has been called; the principle
of the theme; the principle of thematic variation; balance; the principle of hierarchy; and evolution. I do not assert that there are no more principles, but I at
least have been unable to find any of equal generality. Others that have been
suggested can be shown either to be identical with the six mentioned or to be
special cases of them. I shall consider each at some length.

First, the long-established principle of organic unity. By this is meant the
fact that each element in a work of art is necessary to its value, that it contains
no elements that are not thus necessary, and that all that are needful are there.
The beautiful object is organized all through, "baked all through like a cake."
Since everything that is necessary is there, we are not led to go beyond it to seek
something to complete it; and since there are no unnecessary elements, there is
nothing present to disturb its value. Moreover, the value of the work as a whole
depends upon the reciprocal relations of its elements: each needs, responds to,
demands, every other element. For example, in the Young Woman with a Water
Jug (by Johannes Vermeer: Metropolitan Museum), the cool green needs the

---

[18] *Hamlet*, 1. 1.

warm yellow and both need the red; the casement demands the table, the map requires the dark shadow under the casement, to balance it. In a melody, each tone requires its successor to continue the trend that is being established. In short, the meaning of the whole is not something additional to the elements of the work of art, but their cooperative deed.

This principle cannot, however, be described in so external a fashion. For the unity of a work of art is the counterpart of a unity within the experience of the beholder. Since the work of art becomes an embodiment not only of the imagination of the artist, but of the imagination of the spectator as well, his own experience is, for the moment, concentrated there. He is potentially as completely absorbed in it as he is in a dream; it is for the moment, in fact, his dream. And he can and does remain in the dream because the artist has so fashioned his work that everything there tends to continue and deepen it, and nothing to disturb and interrupt it. Art is the expression of the whole man, because it momentarily makes of man a whole. The "isolation" of the esthetic experience of Hugo Münsterberg [1] and the "repose in the object" of Ethel Puffer [2] are descriptions of the fact to which I am calling attention. This does not mean, of course, that the work of art is not related to other things or that it is actually isolated; but only that its relations are irrelevant to its value, and that it cuts itself off from the rest of the world during appreciation; and this it does, first, because it embodies my dream and, second, because it is so constructed as to make me dream on. The marble of which the statue is made comes from a certain quarry and has an interesting geological history there; it stands in a certain part of space, and hence is related to other parts of space; but all such facts are of no account to its beauty. By placing the statue on a pedestal, we indicate its isolation from the space of the room, as by putting a frame around a picture we isolate it, too, from everything else in the world. It is true that, in order to understand a work of art in its historical relations, I must connect it with the artist's personality, with other works of his, with the "moral temperature" of the age, with the development of artistic styles, and the full appreciation of its beauty depends upon acquaintance with its spiritual background. Who, for example, can appreciate the whole meaning of Signorelli's Pan without some knowledge of classical antiquity and the Italian renaissance? Yet at the moment of appreciation, all such knowledge becomes focused in the work of art, gathered and contained there like rays in a prism, and does not divert us from it.

The ancient law of organic unity is the master principle of esthetic form; all the other principles serve it. First among them is what I would call the principle of the theme. This corresponds to the "dominant character" or *idee mère* of Taine.[3] In every complex work of art there is some one (or there may be sev-

---

[1] *The Eternal Values*, chap. IX.
[2] *The Psychology of Beauty*, chap. III.
[3] *Philosophie de l'art*, part I, p. 5.

eral) pre-eminent shape, color, line, melodic pattern or meaning, in which is concentrated the characteristic value of the whole. It contains the work of art in little; represents it; provides the key to our appreciation and understanding of it. Thus every good pattern is built up of one or more shapes, the disposition of which constitutes the design. When there is color as well as shape, there is some dominant color that appears again and again or in related degrees of saturation, or else there is a color chord that is similarly repeated or is analyzed. In architecture, each style has its characteristic shape, line, or volume, as the pointed arch of the Gothic, the round arch of the Roman, the ellipse of the baroque. In music, there are the one or more themes that express the essential significance of each composition. Likewise, every sculptor, every draughtsman, has his unique and inimitable line. In every poem, there is a peculiar inflection and a regnant idea which constitute the basis of the design. In the drama or the novel, there is someone, or there may be several persons, whose character and fate create the plot.

The third principle is thematic variation. It is not sufficient to state the theme of a work of art; it must be elaborated and embroidered. One of the prominent ways of doing this is to make it echo and re-echo in our minds. Usually, if the theme can be repeated once only we are better pleased than with a single appearance. Yet to find the same thing barely repeated is monotonous; hence what we want is the same, to be sure, but the same with a difference: thematic variation. The simplest type of thematic variation is recurrence of the theme, as in any pattern built upon a repeat. Here is the maximum of sameness with the minimum of difference: mere difference of spatial or temporal position. A slight acquaintance with primitive art is sufficient to convince one of the overwhelming importance of recurrence there. Yet it is needless to say that recurrence is not confined to primitive art. We find it in all civilized art: the recurrence of the same shape and proportions in architecture and sculpture; the recurrence of the theme in music; the recurrence of the same type of foot in meter; repetition of the same color in painting; recurrence of lines and directions of lines (parallelism) in painting and sculpture and architecture; the refrain in poetry; the reappearance of the hero in different scenes in the drama and novel. However, because of the monotony of mere repetition, recurrence gives place to what may be called, in a generalized sense, transposition of theme, as when a melody is transposed to another key or tempo; or when in a design the same shape appears in a different color, or a color appears in different degrees of saturation or brightness; or in architecture, where a shape occurs in different sizes or members—in doors, windows, gables, choir-stalls, and the like. Still another kind of thematic variation is alternation, which requires, of course, more than one theme, or at least two different transpositions of the same theme. Of this, again, the illustrations are legion. Finally, there is inversion of theme, as when melody is inverted or, in painting or sculpture, a curve is reversed. These are not all the possible types of thematic variation, but they are, I think, the most important and usual.

Another principle of esthetic form is balance. Balance is equality of opposing or contrasting elements. Balance is one kind of esthetic unity, for despite the opposition of the elements in balance, each needs the other and together they create a whole. Thus the blue demands the gold and the gold the blue, and together they make a new whole, gold-and-blue. Opposition or contrast is never absent from balance, for even in symmetry, where the balancing elements are alike, the directions of these elements are opposed, right and left. But contrast is never by itself esthetically satisfactory, for the contrasting elements must offset each other, they must balance. In color, the warm offsets the cold; in a picture, the small object, properly placed, offsets the large one. Hence, just as only equal weights will balance in a scale pan, so only elements that are somehow equal in value, despite their opposition, will balance esthetically. Not every tint of blue will balance every shade of yellow; that depth of blue must reappear in a corresponding depth of yellow; a light, superficial blue would never balance a deep yellow. But the identity of the opposites is even greater than this. For, as has been remarked, the elements of a balanced unity demand each other; the blue demands the yellow; the line which falls in one direction demands the line that falls in the opposite direction. Now the demand which the color or line makes for its opposite is itself a foreshadowing of the latter; in its demand it already contains the prophecy of its opposite. And even when, as may occur in painting, there is balance between elements of unlike quality—balance, say, of brightness of color against distance or size—the attention value of each must be the same, though opposed in direction. The essential thing about balance is equality of opposed values, however unlike be the things that embody or carry the values.

The pervasiveness of the principle of balance is too generally recognized to need much illustration or argument. In painting we expect, with a reservation that I shall consider in a moment, a threefold balance: horizontal, perpendicular, and radial or diagonal—between the right and left sides, the upper and lower portions, and between what may roughly be called the corners. This last has not received the attention which it deserves; but in many pictures, as for example, Tintoretto's "Mercury" and the "Three Graces," the diagonal axis is the main axis; and in all cases of circular composition, radial balance is fundamental. In architecture, we find balance between right and left, and often between upper and lower parts. In music, there is not seldom a balance between earlier and later parts of a composition, or between opposing themes. In sculpture, there is the balance characteristic of the human body made more perfect by the artist.

Pervasive as balance is, its universality has not stood unquestioned. Nevertheless, many apparent exceptions can be explained away, as is well known, as cases of disguised or subtle balance. The older interpretation of balance after the analogy of symmetry—the balance of like parts—is only a special kind of balance.

and has to be supplemented by the wider conception of balance of unlike parts.[4] With this richer conception in mind, we can understand the balance—as in Bruegel's "Harvesters"—between prominent objects in the right-hand part and little except a vista on the left. Similarly, there is a balance—as in the same picture—between the upper and lower halves of a painting, even when the horizon line is high, and the upper part seems therefore to be relatively empty of masses; for the distance values in the sky balance the heavier lower part. No more difficult of explanation are some cases where asymmetry appears to be definitely sought, as when a girl will put a patch on one cheek but not on another, or will tie the lock of hair on the right with a ribbon, but not the lock on the left. For the piquancy of this procedure comes from the fact that there is a background of decisive symmetry, against which the asymmetrical element stands out. This is quite different from absolute lack of balance. One finds similar eccentric elements in all complex patterns; but always with a background of emphatic balance. And if it is true that such elements disturb symmetry, it is equally true that they serve to emphasize it. The triangle of passion is another illustration; for there also a balanced relationship is the background against which the unbalanced derives its interest.

There are, however, more difficult cases to consider. Many works of art, of the temporal arts in particular, are superficially considered rhythmical rather than balanced, and rhythm may seem to be opposed to balance. Yet an analysis of rhythm shows it to be built upon the two fundamental esthetic forms, thematic repetition and balance. For what are the typical characteristics of rhythm? Every rhythm is a motion of waves, all of a relatively constant or lawfully varying shape and temporal and spatial span, with balancing crests and troughs. The crest may be an accent or the swing up of a line; the trough may be one or more unaccented syllables, a pause, or the swing back of a line in the opposite direction. The rhythm may begin with the trough, as in iambic meter. The swing up and the swing back may both be very complex, as in free verse, yet the fundamental pattern, as it has just been described, is maintained: in every case there is the recurrence of a certain type of wave form, and the opposition—and balance—between the rising and falling swings. The simplest repeat, if you take its elements in succession, is a rhythm. In the diaper pattern, for example, there is the recurrence of the rising and falling lines, and their opposition and balance, two by two. Or a colonnade, as you apprehend the columns in succession, is a rhythm of identical and balancing filled and empty spaces, the columns corresponding to the arsis, and the spatial interval to the thesis.

Hence when balance seems to be replaced by rhythm, balance is still present, only it is not the simple type of balance so easily recognized, but balance as an element in the complex structure we call rhythm. This more subtle type of

[4] Compare Ethel Puffer, "Studies in Symmetry," *Harvard Psychological Studies*, vol. I, 1902.

balance exists oftentimes in pictorial composition—in "open" as opposed to "closed" forms—where the ordinary mode of balance is rejected. I remember one of Monet's "Lily Ponds," in which I searched vainly for the usual type of balance with reference to some axis, only to find that the elements of the picture were arranged in a clear-cut rhythm. Rhythm often replaces right-and-left balance in wall paintings, as in those of Puvis de Chavannes. In the Metropolitan Museum he has two paintings, both decorative sketches, which illustrate this: "Inter Artes et Naturam" and "The River." In the former, notice how we do not view the picture from a vertical central axis, but rather from left or right, taking each group of figures in turn as an element in a rhythmically disposed sequence of filled and empty spaces. In "The River," the rhythmical arrangement is in deep space.

Another and last type of unity I call evolution. By this I mean the unity of a process when the earlier parts determine the later, and all together create a total meaning. For illustrations, one naturally turns first to the temporal arts. The course of a well-fashioned story is a good example, for each incident determines its follower and all the incidents determine the destiny of the characters involved. The drama offers similar illustrations: the form is the same, only transposed to theatrical presentation. In the older, orthodox story or play there were three stages in the development, an initial one of introduction of characters, a second stage of complication, ending in the climax, and then the unraveling. But these stages may be compressed. The story may begin with the complication already there; the play may begin with the climax and proceed to the unraveling, and go back, as in Ibsen, to the preparation. But in every case, there is a necessary relation between means and consequences, causes and effects, and a total resulting meaning. Illustrations of this type of unity abound also in the static arts. Any line which we appreciate as having a beginning, middle, and end, and any composition of figures where we are led on from one figure or group of figures to another, is an illustration; for there, too, although the figures be physically static, our appreciation of them is a process in time, and through the process the meaning of the whole is evolved. Of all painters, I think El Greco offers the best illustrations of evolution, as in the "Crucifixion" (Prado museum), where we follow an intensely dramatic movement from the lower to the upper part of the picture.

Is evolution a genuinely distinct type of esthetic unity? Can it be reduced to one or more of the preceding forms? The most closely allied form is rhythm; yet that evolution is distinct from rhythm can easily be seen. For in rhythm, unless combined with evolution, there is no obvious development, no tendency toward a goal. Rhythm is recurrence and balance of systole and diastole, with no growth from one phase to another. It is true that we sometimes speak of any movement of growth as a rhythm, as when we talk of the rhythm of life, but in such cases rhythm exists in combination with evolution. For there is, of course, a rhythm in all life—birth and death, sleep and waking, activity and repose. And if life be taken generically or historically, there are other equally well-known rhythms, as in the history of art, with the alternation of the opposed directions from realism to romanticism. In melody also, except in the most eccentric types of music, harmonic evolution is joined with an accentual or time rhythm. More-over, even in the most mechanical types of rhythm, like the simple repeat, pro-vided they be esthetic, there is some felt growth of value through the recurrence and balance of parts, and some, however slight, looking forward to the end term as a goal. Only in purely natural rhythms, as of the tides, is there no growth at all, but these, unless they enter into the mind and emotion of man, are not es-thetic in character. Nevertheless, although there is always some evolution in every esthetic rhythm, evolution is not itself necessarily rhythmical. In literature, the rhythm of prose and poetry overlies a development of meanings which does not itself have a quasi-mechanical character of rhythm; the rhythm of time and accent is united with the melodic development of the musical theme, but does not constitute it. The essential character of evolution is, as Bergson has shown, growth or accumulation of meaning, which need not be rhythmical.

Two different types of evolutionary unity must be discriminated, the dra-matic and the non-dramatic. In the dramatic type there is an element of over-shadowing importance, the climax or goal; in the other type, this element is lacking. To be sure, every process must have an end, and the end has a distinctive importance as such, but it is not always true that the end has a greater importance than some other element or elements. The consummation of the meaning may occur through the agency of all parts evenly, rather than through a particular one. Many stories are of this character; there is an unfolding, a working out of something, with no obvious high points. Here and there the meaning rises, but there is no place where it becomes so central that we feel that the whole story depends upon it. And, if I mistake not, there is much music of this character; there is a definite drift or unfolding, but no climax or finale.

Closeness of connection, yet ultimate difference, marks the relation between evolution and the other types of esthetic unity, balance and thematic variation. The static character of balance is opposed to the dynamic character of evolution; indeed, all movement depends upon the upsetting of an established equilibrium. Yet seldom, even in the static arts, is balance found without movement; for there exists a tendency to proceed from one to another of the balanced elements. In a simple color contrast, for example, there is ever so slight a movement from the cold to the warm color. And, on the other hand, there is often a balance within evolution, between the complication and the unraveling of the plot, or the earlier and later parts of a musical theme. But the union of evolution and balance does not militate against the uniqueness of either. There remains for comparison, thematic variation. This form, too, might seem at first sight to be opposed to evolution, yet not so, for there is probably no case of variation in which the evolutionary element is not present. For the series of variations is not fruitless; each contributes something to a meaning which accumulates and is complete when the variations are over. So many, and no more, exist as are necessary to this end. Insofar as, in this way, a meaning is worked out, evolution and thematic variation approach and meet. Yet a difference remains. For the mode of the creation of the meaning is different. In the one case, it occurs through the recurrence of the central meaning in new shapes; in the other, through the realization of some single dominant idea, which extends over the entire work and is expressed once and once only. In the one case, we start with an idea already given, and work it out by repetition; in the other, we have no definite, but only a very vague idea to start with, and construct it step by step. The one method may be called analytic, the other synthetic. For example, we do not know what a musical theme is like until we have heard it entire; building it up is one thing; then, having got it, it is another thing to modulate, invert, and vary it. The same is true of a line.

Nevertheless, in the construction of a theme, both thematic variation and balance may be employed. For example, in building a melody, we may proceed from tone to tone consonant with a given tone, thus repeating the fundamental psychophysical rhythm of the two tones which is the basis of their harmony; or we may proceed through opposition by introducing dissonances. Again, in construcing a linear theme, it is possible to proceed either by repeating or continuing the curve with which we start, or else by introducing opposing and balancing lines. Or for the elucidation of a story it may be expedient to place the persons in various situations, in order that they may manifest their characters—the method of thematic variation—or to balance them against unlike characters. Yet by themselves neither mere variation of theme nor balance of opposites will create evolution. Thematic variation, balance, and evolution remain, therefore, the fundamental and irreducible types of esthetic unity. I personally have been unable to find other types. Types which seem to be different, like rhythm or circular composition, can easily be shown to be species of one or another of these pre-eminent forms. The reduction of rhythm has already been effected. As for circular composition, it is evidently a case of evolution; for there is always a beginning and an end; but evolution is combined with repetition, for the beginning and the end are the same. A melody that begins and ends on the tonic is a simple illustration. I have shown that all three forms are intermingled; and most works of art contain all three; yet they remain, nevertheless, distinct.[5]

The principle of hierarchy is not so much a mode of organic unity, like thematic variation, balance, and evolution, as rather a species of organization of elements in each of these modes. Sometimes, although not always, there is some one element, or there may be more, of a complex work of art which occupies a position of commanding importance there. These elements always embody the

[5] I am reminded by my friend, Miss Shio Sakanishi, that in many forms of Japanese art symmetry and repetition are carefully avoided, yet balance is scrupulously observed.

theme in an emphatic way, and have a significance far greater than any of the other elements. Thus, in a portrait, the figure is more important than the background, and the face is more significant than anything else. In a novel or drama there may be a scene of unusual significance for the development of the plot, or in a musical composition a single passage, like the Liebestod in Tristan, which overshadows the remainder of the composition or is the climax of its movement. Every dramatic species of evolution illustrates this, as we have seen. In balance also, as again we have already observed, one or the other of the elements may dominate, though slightly. However, dominance is a relative matter, and an element, not itself of unusual importance in the whole, may nevertheless overshadow another element, relatively. Thus, in the "Young Woman with a Water Jug" of Vermeer, the pitcher is more prominent than the box. Any quality whatever—large size, unusual brightness, richness of elaboration, central position, fullness of meaning—that attracts the attention to itself more strongly than the attention is attracted to other elements, creates relative dominance. However, there may be no elements of outstanding importance in the whole, as is the case in many a landscape painting and in the non-dramatic types of evolution, but only varying degrees of importance among all the elements.

—*The Analysis of Art* (1924)

D. W. GOTSHALK

Type Designs

Every over-all design, simple or complex, is as individual and unique as the work of art possessing it. To reproduce the design of a picture by Tintoretto, one would have to copy the shapes and lines and colors in the various patterns given them by the painter and the personages represented in their dramatic relationships, since these also enter into the total structure put there by the artist. Change a shape, substitute in Tintoretto's "Miracle of the Slave" or "Miracle of St. Mark" (Academy, Venice) a tiny rigid body for the great St. Mark, and the pattern of the shapes is perceptibly altered. Change a personage, substitute Christ for the executioner, and the structure of the drama is perceptibly altered. To reproduce the over-all design of a work with absolute completeness, one must reproduce the work itself with absolute completeness. To alter any feature is immediately to alter the presentational or representational relations radiating from that feature and so to alter the precise over-all design that the artist has given to his work.

Nevertheless, designs can be considered at a certain level of abstraction as mere schemata, or, more exactly, patterns within designs can be so regarded. In this sense the "same" design may occur again and again in the works of an artist. The swirl pattern in the "Miracle of St. Mark" recurs in one form or another in innumerable Tintoretto compositions. Artists generally tend to reuse similar patterns. As an artist matures, he develops a characteristic manner of organizing the aspects of his materials. "Each artist creates his own type of coordination, it is special to himself, it is his own personal language." [1] The artist uses this personal method of coordination again and again, usually suitably varied, in diverse works. The terse, monumentally simple linear patterns of Giotto; the vertically elongated shape patterns of El Greco; the dense, weighty, color rhythms of the later Titian, are repeated by these artists in different pictures with endless modifications. Similar type patterns are used by creators in the other arts. A person may recognize an excerpt from a poem as a quotation from Whitman or Dante by the rhythm of the language or by other formal features of the verse. A person may equally recognize a piece of music as by Bach or Beethoven or Wagner by its rhythmic, melodic, or harmonic structure. The characteristic form traits that artists impart to their diverse individual designs, it is true, often change considerably over time. Historians speak of the early, middle, and late manner of a Titian, a Beethoven, or a Wagner. An artist's manner of construction, like any habit, may be discarded for a new one or for a very different one. Still it is usually possible to abstract a set of recurrent formal traits from some group of any great artist's individual designs. Manners may change, but a manner is a manner and results in a type of form.[2]

Type patterns, however, include much more than type forms peculiar to individual artists. Indeed, the most familiar of all type patterns are traditional forms, often obscure in origin, that are employed equally in the work of numerous artists. Illustrations are the sonnet and ballad, the minuet and mazurka, the sonata and fugue and *passacaglia* and rondo, the orders of Greek architecture, the canons of Greek sculpture, the formal conventions of Byzantine or Japanese painting.

Type designs, individual and traditional, are important to all concerned with the arts. To the ordinary perceptive person they can be the starting-point of an apprehension of the total individual design of a creation. The swirl of a Tin-

---

[1] Vernon Blake, *The Art and Craft of Drawing* (London: Oxford University Press, 1927), p. 65.

[2] Ernest Newman, *The Unconscious Beethoven* (New York: Alfred A. Knopf, 1927), is a good example of an interesting detailed study of a creative artist's peculiar habits and unconscious traits of construction.

toretto, the *terza rima* of a Dante, the sonata form of the first movement of a Haydn symphony, can be tools for entering more fully into the over-all design and apprehending it in great detail. They supply a spacious frame which can be clothed in the flesh and blood of the individual form. To be sure, type patterns can be used by percipients as mere tags of identification and can become the dead ends of devitalized perception instead of tools to implement detailed appreciation. Often they are no more than this in so-called "appreciation courses" in colleges. But, if type patterns are used as instrumentalities instead of as finalities and as methods for starting on the quest of an over-all design, they can open up the general outlay of an individual structure and become the dim beginnings of esthetic wisdom regarding form.

The critic and the historian of art can also make good use of type designs. Not only can these designs serve as starting-points for that full appreciation of form which should precede the distinctive critical and historical tasks, they can also be used in the critical and historical tasks themselves.

The critic, for example, can use type patterns as a basis for judging the originality of an artist. Has this artist merely borrowed a stencil from tradition and filled it with timely commonplaces or inconsequential novelties? Has he given new and glowing life to a traditional form that seemed played out and dead before he revived it? Has he invented a powerful type form peculiarly his own? Often the difference between a genius and a hack is revealed more clearly in the difference of the handling of a traditional type pattern or in the difference of strength of their individual type patterns than in any other formal difference or in any differences in the material, expressive, or functional features of their works.

As to the historian of art, he can use type patterns as tools of clarification and correlation of individual designs. A type pattern, such as a sonata or an epic, is a schema of recurrent formal traits. In his analysis of form, the main business of the historian, I believe, is the analysis of concrete forms, not of schemata. But type patterns, as schemata of recurrent formal traits, can highlight generic formal features of concrete forms and formal similarities between different concrete forms. The general pattern of the sonata can help to point up certain general properties of a Beethoven or a Mozart sonata and supply a language in terms of which to compare the individual design of this Beethoven sonata with that, or this Mozart sonata with this Beethoven sonata. Thus, while the analysis of type patterns is not the main concern of the historian, these patterns can supply bases for the clarification and correlation of individual designs, which is his main business, and so make a substantial contribution to his analysis of form.

Type patterns, finally, can be of considerable service to the creative artist. To the apprentice in an art, traditional type patterns can provide good discipline. They can require him to hew to a line while allowing him a certain freedom of invention of details. They can teach him general conceptions of artistic ordering and can help to inculcate precision and a certain amount of elementary technical facility. To the alert apprentice they can even be means to the discovery of new forms by stirring his imagination to conceive alternatives and variants of traditional forms.

To the mature artist, traditional type patterns can equally be an asset. Such types as the ode and ballad and prose epic in literature or the sonata and theme and variations and fugue in music can serve as fruitful bases of original productions. A certain superior richness of inventive imagination and a certain temperament are probably required to create works in such traditional forms that are outstanding and permanently valuable. But when artists with these qualities do take over these forms, they can usually make something very fine out of them. In literature there have been myriad examples of artists of this sort from the Greek poets to Fielding and Coleridge and Keats. In music, Bach is an obvious example. "Bach was one of the most conventional composers who ever existed. He accepted forms and formulas ready-made from his predecessors, chiefly German and Italian, but French and English also, and he was none the worse for it, because he succeeded, in spite of these self-imposed blinkers to his fancy, in making something greater out of precedent than it had ever been before." [3] An artist less virile than Bach, or a slavish copyist who took traditional type patterns as rigid schemata and traditional examples as absolute models, would be unlikely to turn traditional forms to very significant account. But an artist who extracted their principles, adapted them to his own needs, and filled them with rich new matter from his own abundant fancy would be perennially able to find them profitable.

Besides traditional forms, individual type patterns or the characteristic formal twists that artists employ in designing their works have an obvious creative usefulness. Ordinarily, these patterns are developed as a consequence of the artist's personality maturing and gaining stability. Their usefulness to the artist is similar to the usefulness of a habit in everyday life. Our habits of walking and running facilitate our everyday responses to stimuli. The individual type patterns of artists, at least as technical "manners" or traits, can facilitate artistic responses to stimuli. They can constitute mechanisms of action ready to cope with creative impulses, and they can enable the artist to ride the crest of his inspiration by supplying devices adequate to his personality that automatically shape the energy going into his work.

It should certainly be added that type patterns, traditional and individual, can be a disadvantage and even a danger to the creative artist. An ambitious apprentice may be handcuffed and ill at ease writing drama in neoclassic patterns or music in seventeenth-century forms and may produce only undistinguished

---

[3] Eric Blom, *The Limitations of Music* (New York: Macmillan Co., 1928), p. 114.

work in these molds. A change to designs of his own invention, adapted to some compelling contemporary purpose, may release unsuspected creative powers, and the young artist may eventually become the founder of a new type of drama or musical form. In the work of a mature artist who lacks fertility of invention, the use of traditional type patterns may not curb his creativity, but it may underlie his mediocrity. His Greek-temple banks and memorials, his statues of grand antique design, his facile heroic couplets, or his carefully classical sonatas and fugues may have the slickness of high-grade studio pieces. Flavored by a cool or dulcet personality, they may even have a mild gracious charm. But in the end they will bespeak a feebleness of imagination, and their charm will be clouded by recognition of the hackneyed, derivative, out-of-date, otiose, and irrelevant.

One of the most frequent uses of traditional type forms is as easy short cuts. A veneer of novelty spread upon a tried and true artistic pattern usually produces a very salable product. The monetarily successful hackworks of the great often follow this formula. So do many of the popular songs of the commercial theater, which sell immensely, then vanish immediately. Motion pictures frequently use for plots stereotyped dramatic forms which have been spruced up by novelties of setting and dialogue, by popular actors, and the like. Such works are entertaining when their additions are lively or clever, but they usually do not stand up under close or repeated scrutiny. To the gifted professional artist, traditional type patterns can be a means to quick commercial success but also to quick artistic death or to low-grade creative performance.

Nor are individual type patterns free of disadvantages and perils for the creative artist. A painter such as Corot may hit upon a type of composition warmly approved by the public and, deserting his earlier and more solid work, spend his days repeating his new formula. For any number of reasons the manner of any artist may degenerate into a conscious mannerism or, remaining unconscious, be used too profusely or mechanically. People there are who would gladly do without some of the more synthetic of Haydn's compositions or some of the more pretentious of Liszt's forms. Others would gladly forego some of the patterns of sweet *bambini* of the Della Robbias or some of the clouds of corpulent nudes garnishing the more lush works of Rubens or pupils of Rubens. Every artist—a Bach as well as a Haydn or a Liszt, a Michelangelo as well as a Rubens or a Della Robbia—has a limited set of gestures manifesting his personality and modifying his forms; and no artist has a personality so profoundly complex that these gestures are without danger, upon occasion, of protruding too insistently and, by so doing, marring the esthetic effectiveness of his forms. . . .

Type patterns are partial forms, abstractions from concrete forms. In the public object, it is the concrete form, the total individual system of relations pervading the materials of the work of art, that is artistic form in the fullest sense.

—*Art and the Social Order* (1947)

MEYER SCHAPIRO

Style

I

By style is meant the constant form—and sometimes the constant elements, qualities, and expression—in the art of an individual or a group. The term is also applied to the whole activity of an individual or society, as in speaking of a "life-style" or the "style of a civilization."

For the archeologist, style is exemplified in a motive or pattern, or in some directly grasped quality of the work of art, which helps him to localize and date the work and to establish connections between groups of works or between cultures. Style here is a symptomatic trait, like the nonesthetic features of an artifact. It is studied more often as a diagnostic means than for its own sake as an important constituent of culture. For dealing with style, the archeologist has relatively few esthetic and physiognomic terms.

To the historian of art, style is an essential object of investigation. He studies its inner correspondences, its life-history, and the problems of its formation and change. He, too, uses style as a criterion of the date and place of origin of works, and as a means of tracing relationships between schools of art. But the style is, above all, a system of forms with a quality and a meaningful expression through which the personality of the artist and the broad outlook of a group are visible. It is also a vehicle of expression within the group, communicating and fixing certain values of religious, social, and moral life through the emotional suggestiveness of forms. It is, besides, a common ground against which innovations and the individuality of particular works may be measured. By considering the succession of works in time and space and by matching the variations of style with historical events and with the varying features of other fields of culture, the historian of art attempts, with the help of common-sense psychology and social theory, to account for the changes of style or specific traits. The historical study of individual and group styles also discloses typical stages and processes in the development of forms.

For the synthesizing historian of culture or the philosopher of history, the style is a manifestation of the culture as a whole, the visible sign of its unity. The style reflects or projects the "inner form" of collective thinking and feeling. What is important here is not the style of an individual or of a single art, but forms and qualities shared by all the arts of a culture during a significant span of time.

In this sense one speaks of Classical or Medieval or Renaissance Man with respect to common traits discovered in the art styles of these epochs and documented also in religious and philosophical writings.

The critic, like the artist, tends to conceive of style as a value term; style as such is a quality and the critic can say of a painter that he has "style" or of a writer that he is a "stylist." Although "style" in this normative sense, which is applied mainly to individual artists, seems to be outside the scope of historical and ethnological studies of art, it often occurs here, too, and should be considered seriously. It is a measure of accomplishment and therefore is relevant to understanding of both art and culture as a whole. Even a period style, which for most historians is a collective taste evident in both good and poor works, may be regarded by critics as a great positive achievement. So the Greek classic style was, for Winckelmann and Goethe, not simply a convention of form but a culminating conception with valued qualities not possible in other styles and apparent even in Roman copies of lost Greek originals. Some period styles impress us by their deeply pervasive, complete character, their special adequacy to their content; the collective creation of such a style, like the conscious shaping of a norm of language, is a true achievement. Correspondingly, the presence of the same style in a wide range of arts is often considered a sign of the integration of a culture and the intensity of a high creative moment. Arts that lack a particular distinction or nobility of style are often said to be styleless, and the culture is judged to be weak or decadent. A similar view is held by philosophers of culture and history and by some historians of art.

Common to all these approaches are the assumptions that every style is peculiar to a period of a culture and that, in a given culture or epoch of culture, there is only one style or a limited range of styles. Works in the style of one time could not have been produced in another. These postulates are supported by the fact that the connection between a style and a period, inferred from a few examples, is confirmed by objects discovered later. Whenever it is possible to locate a work through nonstylistic evidence, this evidence points to the same time and place as do the formal traits, or to a culturally associated region. The unexpected appearance of the style in another region is explained by migration or trade. The style is therefore used with confidence as an independent clue to the time and place of origin of a work of art. Building upon these assumptions, scholars have constructed a systematic, although not complete, picture of the temporal and spatial distribution of styles throughout large regions of the globe. If works of art are grouped in an order corresponding to their original positions in time and space, their styles will show significant relationships which can be coordinated with the relationships of the works of art to still other features of the cultural points in time and space.

II

Styles are not usually defined in a strictly logical way. As with languages, the definition indicates the time and place of a style or its author, or the historical relation to other styles, rather than its peculiar features. The characteristics of styles vary continuously and resist a systematic classification into perfectly distinct groups. It is meaningless to ask exactly when ancient art ends and medieval begins. There are, of course, abrupt breaks and reactions in art, but study shows that here, too, there is often anticipation, blending, and continuity. Precise limits are sometimes fixed by convention for simplicity in dealing with historical problems or in isolating a type. In a stream of development the artificial divisions may even be designated by numbers— Styles I, II, III. But the single name given to the style of a period rarely corresponds to a clear and universally accepted characterization of a type. Yet direct acquaintance with an unanalyzed work of art will often permit us to recognize another object of the same origin, just as we recognize a face to be native or foreign. This fact points to a degree of constancy in art that is the basis of all investigation of style. Through careful description and comparison and through formation of a richer, more refined typology adapted to the continuities in development, it has been possible to reduce the areas of vagueness and to advance our knowledge of styles.

Although there is no established system of analysis and writers will stress one or another aspect according to their viewpoint or problem, in general the description of a style refers to three aspects of art: form elements or motives, form relationships, and qualities (including an all-over quality which we may call the "expression").

This conception of style is not arbitrary but has arisen from the experience of investigation. In correlating works of art with an individual or culture, these three aspects provide the broadest, most stable, and therefore most reliable criteria. They are also the most pertinent to modern theory of art, although not in the same degree for all viewpoints. Technique, subject matter, and material may be characteristic of certain groups of works and will sometimes be included in definitions; but more often these features are not so peculiar to the art of a period as the formal and qualitative ones. It is easy to imagine a decided change in material, technique, or subject matter accompanied by little change in the basic form. Or, where these are constant, we often observe that they are less responsive to new artistic aims. A method of stone-cutting will change less rapidly than the sculptor's or architect's forms. Where a technique does coincide with the extension of a style, it is the formal traces of the technique rather than the operations as such that are important for description of the style. The materials are significant mainly for the textural quality and color, although they may affect the conception of the forms. For the subject matter, we observe that quite different themes—portraits, still lifes, and landscapes—will appear in the same style.

It must be said, too, that form elements or motives, although very striking and essential for the expression, are not sufficient for characterizing a style. The pointed arch is common to Gothic and Islamic architecture, and the round arch to Roman, Byzantine, Romanesque, and Renaissance buildings. In order to distinguish these styles, one must also look for features of another order and, above all, for different ways of combining the elements.

Although some writers conceive of style as a kind of syntax or compositional pattern, which can be analyzed mathematically, in practice one has been unable to do without the vague language of qualities in describing styles. Certain features of light and color in painting are most conveniently specified in qualitative terms and even as tertiary (intersensory) or physiognomic qualities, like cool and warm, gay and sad. The habitual span of light and dark, the intervals between colors in a particular palette—very important for the structure of a work—are distinct relationships between elements, yet are not comprised in a compositional schema of the whole. The complexity of a work of art is such that the description of forms is often incomplete on essential points, limiting itself to a rough account of a few relationships. It is still simpler, as well as more relevant to esthetic experience, to distinguish lines as hard and soft than to give measurements of their substance. For precision in characterizing a style, these qualities are graded with respect to intensity by comparing different examples directly or by reference to a standard work. Where quantitative measurements have been made, they tend to confirm the conclusions reached through direct qualitative description. Nevertheless, we have no doubt that, in dealing with qualities, much greater precision can be reached.

Analysis applies esthetic concepts current in the teaching, practice, and criticism of contemporary art; the development of new viewpoints and problems in the latter directs the attention of students to unnoticed features of older styles. But the study of works of other times also influences modern concepts through discovery of esthetic variants unknown in our own art. As in criticism, so in historical research, the problem of distinguishing or relating two styles discloses unsuspected, subtle characteristics and suggests new concepts of form. The postulate of continuity in culture—a kind of inertia in the physical sense—leads to a search for common features in successive styles that are ordinarily contrasted as opposite poles of form; the resemblances will sometimes be found not so much in obvious aspects as in fairly hidden ones—the line patterns of Renaissance compositions recall features of the older Gothic style, and in contemporary abstract art one observes form relationships like those of Impressionist painting.

The refinement of style analysis has come about in part through problems in which small differences had to be disengaged and described precisely. Examples are the regional variations within the same culture; the process of historical development from year to year; the growth of individual artists and the discrimination of the works of master and pupil, originals and copies. In these studies the criteria for dating and attribution are often physical or external—matters of small symptomatic detail—but here, too, the general trend of research has been to look for features that can be formulated in both structural and expressive-physiognomic terms. It is assumed by many students that the expression terms are all translatable into form and quality terms, since the expression depends on particular shapes and colors and will be modified by a small change in the latter. The forms are correspondingly regarded as vehicles of a particular effect (apart from the subject matter). But the relationship here is not altogether clear. In general, the study of style tends toward an ever stronger correlation of form and expression. Some descriptions are purely morphological, as of natural objects—indeed, ornament has been characterized, like crystals, in the mathematical language of group theory. But terms like "stylized," "archaistic," "naturalistic," "mannerist," "baroque," are specifically human, referring to artistic processes, and imply some expressive effect. It is only by analogy that mathematical figures have been characterized as "classic" and "romantic."

III

The analysis and characterization of the styles of primitive and early historical cultures have been strongly influenced by the standards of recent Western art. Nevertheless, it may be said that the values of modern art have led to a more sympathetic and objective approach to exotic arts than was possible fifty or a hundred years ago.

In the past, a great deal of primitive work, especially representation, was regarded as artless even by sensitive people; what was valued were mainly the ornamentation and the skills of primitive industry. It was believed that primitive arts were childlike attempts to represent nature—attempts distorted by ignorance and by an irrational content of the monstrous and grotesque. True art was admitted only in the high cultures, where knowledge of natural forms was combined with a rational ideal which brought beauty and decorum to the image of man. Greek art and the art of the Italian High Renaissance were the norms for judging all art, although in time the classic phase of Gothic art was accepted. Ruskin, who admired Byzantine works, could write that in Christian Europe alone "pure and precious ancient art exists, for there is none in America, none in Asia, none in Africa." From such a viewpoint careful discrimination of primitive styles or a penetrating study of their structure and expression was hardly possible.

With the change in Western art during the last seventy years, naturalistic representation has lost its superior status. Basic for contemporary practice and for knowledge of past art is the theoretical view that what counts in all art are the elementary esthetic components, the qualities and relationships of the fabricated lines, spots, colors, and surfaces. These have two characteristics: they are intrinsically expressive, and they tend to constitute a coherent whole. The same tendencies to coherent and expressive structure are found in the arts of all cultures. There is no privileged content or mode of representation (although the greatest works may, for reasons obscure to us, occur only in certain styles). Perfect art is possible in any subject matter or style. A style is like a language, with an internal order and expressiveness, admitting a varied intensity or delicacy of statement. This approach is a relativism that does not exclude absolute judgments of value; it makes these judgments possible within every framework by abandoning a fixed norm of style. Such ideas are accepted by most students of art today, although not applied with uniform conviction.

As a result of this new approach, all the arts of the world, even the drawings of children and psychotics, have become accessible on a common plane of expressive and form-creating activity. Art is now one of the strongest evidences of the basic unity of mankind.

This radical change in attitude depends partly on the development of modern styles, in which the raw material and distinctive units of operation—the plane of the canvas, the trunk of wood, tool marks, brush strokes, connecting forms, schemas, particles and areas of pure color—are as pronounced as the elements of representation. Even before nonrepresentative styles were created, artists had become more deeply conscious of the esthetic-constructive components of the work apart from denoted meanings.

Much in the new styles recalls primitive art. Modern artists were, in fact, among the first to appreciate the works of natives as true art. The development of Cubism and Abstraction made the form problem exciting and helped to refine the perception of the creative in primitive work. Expressionism, with its high pathos, disposed our eyes to the simpler, more intense modes of expression, and together with Surrealism, which valued, above all, the irrational and instinctive in the imagination, gave a fresh interest to the products of primitive fantasy. But, with all the obvious resemblances, modern paintings and sculptures differ from the primitive in structure and content. What in primitive art belongs to an established world of collective beliefs and symbols arises in modern art as an individual expression, bearing the marks of a free, experimental attitude to forms. Modern artists feel, nevertheless, a spiritual kinship with the primitive, who is now closer to them than in the past because of their ideal of frankness and intensity of expression and their desire for a simpler life, with more effective participation of the artist in collective occasions than modern society allows.

One result of the modern development has been a tendency to slight the content of past art; the most realistic representations are contemplated as pure constructions of lines and colors. The observer is often indifferent to the original meanings of works, although he may enjoy through them a vague sentiment of the poetic and religious. The form and expressiveness of older works are regarded, then, in isolation, and the history of an art is written as an immanent development of forms. Parallel to this trend, other scholars have carried on fruitful research into the meanings, symbols, and iconographic types of Western art, relying on the literature of mythology and religion; through these studies the knowledge of the content of art has been considerably deepened, and analogies to the character of the styles have been discovered in the content. This has strengthened the view that the development of forms is not autonomous but is connected with changing attitudes and interests that appear more or less clearly in the subject matter of the art.

IV

Students observed early that the traits which make up a style have a quality in common. They all seem to be marked by the expression of the whole, or there is a dominant feature to which the elements have been adapted. The parts of a Greek temple have the air of a family of forms. In Baroque art, a taste for movement determines the loosening of boundaries, the instability of masses, and the multiplication of large contrasts. For many writers a style, whether of an individual or a group, is a pervasive, rigorous unity. Investigation of style is often a search for hidden correspondences explained by an organizing principle which determines both the character of the parts and the patterning of the whole.

This approach is supported by the experience of the student in identifying a style from a small random fragment. A bit of carved stone, the profile of a molding, a few drawn lines, or a single letter from a piece of writing often possesses for the observer the quality of the complete work and can be dated precisely; before these fragments, we have the conviction of insight into the original whole. In a similar way, we recognize by its intrusiveness an added or repaired detail in an old work. The feel of the whole is found in the small parts.

I do not know how far experiments in matching parts from works in different styles would confirm this view. We may be dealing, in some of these observations, with a microstructural level in which similarity of parts only points to the homogeneity of a style or a technique, rather than to a complex unity in the esthetic sense. Although personal, the painter's touch, described by constants of pressure, rhythm, and size of strokes, may have no obvious relation to other unique characteristics of the larger forms. There are styles in which large parts of a work are conceived and executed differently, without destroying the harmony of the whole. In African sculpture an exceedingly naturalistic, smoothly carved head rises from a rough, almost shapeless body. A normative esthetic might regard this as imperfect work, but it would be hard to justify this view. In Western paintings of the fifteenth century, realistic figures and landscapes are set against a gold background, which in the Middle Ages had a spiritualistic sense. In Islamic art, as in certain African and Oceanic styles, forms of great clarity and simplicity in three dimensions—metal vessels and animals or the domes of buildings—have surfaces spun with rich mazy patterns; in Gothic and Baroque art, on the contrary, a complex surface treatment is associated with a correspondingly complicated silhouette of the whole. In Romanesque art the proportions of figures are not submitted to a single canon, as in Greek art, but two or three distinct systems of proportioning exist even within the same sculpture, varying with the size of the figure.

Such variation within a style is also known in literature, sometimes in great works, like Shakespeare's plays, where verse and prose of different texture occur together. French readers of Shakespeare, with the model of their own classical drama before them, were disturbed by the elements of comedy in Shakespeare's tragedies. We understand this contrast as a necessity of the content and the poet's conception of man—the different modes of expression pertain to contrasted types of humanity—but a purist classical taste condemned this as inartistic. In modern literature both kinds of style, the rigorous and the free, coexist and express different viewpoints. It is possible to see the opposed parts as contributing elements in a whole that owes its character to the interplay and balance of contrasted qualities. But the notion of style has lost in that case the crystalline uniformity and simple correspondence of part to whole with which we began. The integration may be of a looser, more complex kind, operating with unlike parts.

Another interesting exception to the homogeneous in style is the difference between the marginal and the dominant fields in certain arts. In early Byzantine works, rulers are represented in statuesque, rigid forms, while the smaller accompanying figures, by the same artist, retain the liveliness of an older episodic, naturalistic style. In Romanesque art this difference can be so marked that scholars have mistakenly supposed that certain Spanish works were done partly by a Christian and partly by a Moslem artist. In some instances the forms in the margin or in the background are more advanced in style than the central parts, anticipating a later stage of the art. In medieval work the unframed figures on the borders of illuminated manuscripts or on cornices, capitals, and pedestals are often freer and more naturalistic than the main figures. This is surprising, since we would expect to find the most advanced forms in the dominant content. But in medieval art the sculptor or painter is often bolder where he is less bound to an external requirement; he even seeks out and appropriates the regions of freedom. In a similar way an artist's drawings or sketches are more advanced than the finished paintings and suggest another side of his personality. The execution of the landscape backgrounds behind the religious figures in paintings of the fifteenth century is sometimes amazingly modern and in great contrast to the precise forms of the large figures. Such observations teach us the importance of considering in the description and explanation of a style the unhomogeneous, unstable aspect, the obscure tendencies toward new forms.

If in all periods artists strive to create unified works, the strict ideal of consistency is essentially modern. We often observe in civilized as well as primitive art the combination of works of different style into a single whole. Classical gems were frequently incorporated into medieval reliquaries. Few great medieval buildings are homogeneous, since they are the work of many generations of artists. This is widely recognized by historians, although theoreticians of culture have innocently pointed to the conglomerate cathedral of Chartres as a model of stylistic unity, in contrast to the heterogeneous character of stylelessness of the arts of modern society. In the past it was not felt necessary to restore a damaged work or to complete an unfinished one in the style of the original. Hence the strange juxtapositions of styles within some medieval objects. It should be said, however, that some styles, by virtue of their open, irregular forms, can tolerate the unfinished and heterogeneous better than others.

Just as the single work may possess parts that we would judge to belong to different styles, if we found them in separate contexts, so an individual may produce during the same short period works in what are regarded as two styles. An obvious example is the writing of bilingual authors or the work of the same man in different arts or even in different genres of the same art—monumental and easel painting, dramatic and lyric poetry. A large work by an artist who works mainly in the small, or a small work by a master of large forms, can deceive an expert in styles. Not only will the touch change, but also the expression and method of grouping. An artist is not present in the same degree in everything he does, although some traits may be constant. In the twentieth century, some artists have changed their styles so radically during a few years that it would be difficult, if not impossible, to identify these as works of the same hand, should their authorship be forgotten. In the case of Picasso, two styles—Cubism and a kind of classicizing naturalism—were practiced at the same time. One might discover common characters in small features of the two styles—in qualities of the brushstroke, the span of intensity, or in subtle constancies of the spacing and tones—but these are not the elements through which either style would ordinarily be characterized. Even then, as in a statistical account small and large samples of a population give different results, so in works of different scale of parts by one artist the scale may influence the frequency of the tiniest elements or the form of the small units. The modern experience of stylistic variability and of the unhomogeneous within an art style will perhaps lead to a more refined conception of style. It is evident, at any rate, that the conception of style as a visibly unified constant rests upon a particular norm of stability of style and shifts from the large to the small forms, as the whole becomes more complex.

What has been said here of the limits of uniformity of structure in the single work and in the works of an individual also applies to the style of a group. The group style, like a language, often contains elements that belong to different historical strata. While research looks for criteria permitting one to distinguish accurately the works of different groups and to correlate a style with other characteristics of a group, there are cultures with two or more collective styles of art at the same moment. This phenomenon is often associated with arts of different function or with different classes of artists. The arts practiced by women are of another style than those of the men; religious art differs from profane, and civic from domestic; and in higher cultures the stratification of social classes often entails a variety of styles, not only with respect to the rural and urban, but within the same urban community. This diversity is clear enough today in the coexistence of an official-academic, a mass-commercial, and a freer avant-garde art. But more striking still is the enormous range of styles within the latter—although a common denominator will undoubtedly be found by future historians.

While some critics judge this heterogeneity to be a sign of an unstable, unintegrated culture, it may be regarded as a necessary and valuable consequence of the individual's freedom of choice and of the world scope of modern culture, which permits a greater interaction of styles than was ever possible before. The present diversity continues and intensifies a diversity already noticed in the preceding stages of our culture, including the Middle Ages and the Renaissance, which are held up as models of close integration. The unity of style that is contrasted with the present diversity is one type of style formation, appropriate to particular aims and conditions; to achieve it today would be impossible without destroying the most cherished values of our culture.

If we pass to the relation of group styles of different visual arts in the same period, we observe that, while the Baroque is remarkably similar in architecture, sculpture, and painting, in other periods, for example, the Carolingian, the early Romanesque, and the modern, these arts differ in essential respects. In England, the drawing and painting of the tenth and eleventh centuries—a time of great accomplishment, when England was a leader in European art—are characterized by an enthusiastic linear style of energetic, ecstatic movement, while the architecture of the same period is inert, massive, and closed and is organized on other principles. Such variety has been explained as a sign of immaturity; but one can point to similar contrasts between two arts in later times, for example, in Holland in the seventeenth century where Rembrandt and his school were contemporary with classicistic Renaissance buildings.

When we compare the styles of arts of the same period in different media—literature, music, painting—the differences are no less striking. But there are epochs with a far-reaching unity, and these have engaged the attention of students more than the examples of diversity. The concept of the Baroque has been applied to architecture, sculpture, painting, music, poetry, drama, gardening, script, and even philosophy and science. The Baroque style has given its name to the entire culture of the seventeenth century, although it does not exclude contrary tendencies within the same country, as well as a great individuality of national arts. Such styles are the most fascinating to historians and philosophers, who admire in this great spectacle of unity the power of a guiding idea or attitude to impose a common form upon the most varied contexts. The dominant style giving force is identified by some historians with a world outlook common to the whole society; by others with a particular institution, like the church or the absolute monarchy, which under certain conditions becomes the source of a universal viewpoint and the organizer of all cultural life. This unity is not necessarily organic; it may be likened also, perhaps, to that of a machine with limited freedom of motion; in a complex organism the parts are unlike and the integration is more a matter of functional interdependence than of the repetition of the same pattern in all the organs.

Although so vast a unity of style is an impressive accomplishment and seems to point to a special consciousness of style—the forms of art being felt as a necessary universal language—there are moments of great achievement in a single art with characteristics more or less isolated from those of the other arts. We look in vain in England for a style of painting that corresponds to Elizabethan poetry and drama; just as in Russia in the nineteenth century there was no true parallel in painting to the great movement of literature. In these instances we recognize that the various arts have different roles in the culture and social life of a time and express in their content as well as style different interests and values. The dominant outlook of a time—if it can be isolated—does not affect all the arts in the same degree, nor are all the arts equally capable of expressing the same outlook. Special conditions within an art are often strong enough to determine a deviant expression.

—Anthropology Today, edited by A. L. Kroeber (1953)

CHAPTER ELEVEN

Form and Function

Introductory Note

IN ARCHITECTURE AND THE INDUSTRIAL ARTS, the beauty of form is primarily an expression of function. This principle is no recent discovery: it was enunciated by Vitruvius in ancient Rome and it was practiced by primitive man long before any esthetic theory was formulated. But it has often been violated or forgotten; and it has been, in a sense, rediscovered by such modern architects and designers as Le Corbusier and Moholy-Nagy.

The great prophet in this revival of functionalism has been Horatio Greenough (1805-1852)—a worthy contemporary of Emerson and Thoreau. Leaving the United States before he received his Harvard diploma, he set up a studio in Florence and practiced the art of sculpture for the next twenty-two years. Then he returned and surprised the people of Boston by praising the clipper-ship as a work of art. "*There* is something," he exclaimed, "I should not be ashamed to show Phidias!" In ship-building the form is determined by the function: the adaptation to wind and wave results in harmony and grace. So should it be in architecture. The rule must be "to plant a building firmly on the ground," that is, to adapt its design to the site; then "instead of forcing the functions of every sort of building into one general form, without reference to the inner distribution, let us begin from the heart as a nucleus, and *work outward*," achieving "the *external expression* of the *inward functions* of the building." All meaningless, inorganic decoration should be stripped away: there must be "the entire and immediate banishment of all makeshift and make-believe."

To his countrymen Greenough, a lover of Greek architecture, gives this advice: "The fundamental laws of building found at the basis of every style of architecture must be the basis of ours. The adaptation of the forms and magnitude of structures to the climate they are exposed to, and the offices for which they are intended, teaches us to study our own varied wants in these respects. The harmony of their ornaments with the nature that they embellished, and the institutions from which they sprang, calls on us to do the like justice to our country, our government, and our faith. . . . So the American builder by a truly philosophic investigation of ancient art will learn of the Greeks to be American. . . . I contend for Greek principles, not Greek things. . . . The men who have reduced locomotion to its simplest elements, in the trotting wagon and the yacht *America,* are nearer to Athens at this moment than they who would bend the Greek temple to every use." We should respect the eternal laws of building but plagiarize nothing from the past.

Greenough breaks down any sharp distinction between the applied and the fine arts, and insists that a machine should be a thing of beauty. "If we compare the form of a newly invented machine with the perfected type of the same instrument, we observe, as we trace it through the phases of improvement, how weight is shaken off where strength is less needed, how functions are made to approach without impeding each other, how straight becomes curved, and the curve is straightened, till the straggling and cumbersome machine becomes the compact, effective, and beautiful engine." This passage could be taken as a summary of much of the argument of Lewis Mumford (1895-   ), the distinguished American critic and social philosopher. He similarly traces the emergence of sound canons of machine-design—a stripping down to essentials and an adaptation of form to function.

Like Ruskin and William Morris, he has been greatly disturbed by the tendency for mechanized production to displace creative art, but he has prophesied a higher union of art and machine technology. In his *Technics and Civilization,* he divides "the development of the machine and the machine civilization into three successive but overlapping and interpenetrating phases: eotechnic, paleotechnic, neotechnic. . . . Speaking in terms of power and characteristic materials, the eotechnic phase is a water-and-wood complex; the paleotechnic phase is a coal-and-iron complex; and the neotechnic phase is an electric-and-alloy complex." Each phase has the most profound social ramifications, involving art, religion, and all humane pursuits. Beginning with the eotechnic phase, whose goal was at first a greater intensification of life, the rift between mechanization and humanization has gradually widened, until it has reached its climax in the "smoke-pall, air-sewage, and disorder" of some of our modern industrial cities. But new cleanliness and beauty is made possible by electricity and modern materials (for example, "the steel frame construction in architecture, which permits the fullest use of glass and the most complete utilization of sunlight").

When these new resources are finally controlled by humane social planning, and the biological and social sciences come to maturity, a new phase will begin—the "biotechnic": "Life, which has always paid the fiddler, now begins to call the tune." But before we can enter into this higher stage, art must be enriched by the machine, and the machine in turn humanized by art. The political and economic order necessary to effect this profound transformation Mumford calls "basic communism," but his ideal is that of a free society very different from the Soviet system.

HORATIO GREENOUGH

Structure and Organization

The developments of structure in the animal kingdom are worthy of all our attention if we would arrive at sound principles in building. The most striking feature in the higher animal organizations is the adherence to one abstract type. The forms of the fish and the lizard, the shape of the horse, and the lion, and the camelopard, are so nearly framed after one type that the adherence thereto seems carried to the verge of risk. The next most striking feature is the modification of the parts, which, if contemplated independently of the exposure and functions whose demands are thus met, seems carried to the verge of caprice. I believe few persons not conversant with natural history ever looked through a collection of birds, or fish, or insects, without feeling that they were the result of Omnipotence at play for mere variety's sake.

If there be any principle of structure more plainly inculcated in the works of the Creator than all others, it is the principle of unflinching adaptation of forms to functions. I believe that colors also, so far as we have discovered their chemical causes and affinities, are not less organic in relation to the forms they invest than are those forms themselves.

If I find the length of the vertebrae of the neck in grazing quadrupeds increased, so as to bring the incisors to the grass; if I find the vertebrae shortened in beasts of prey, in order to enable the brute to bear away his victims; if I find the wading birds on stilts, the strictly aquatic birds with paddles; if, in pushing still further the investigation, I find color arrayed either for disguise or aggression, I feel justified in taking the ground that organization is the primal law of structure, and I suppose it, even where my imperfect light cannot trace it, unless embellishment can be demonstrated. Since the tints as well as the forms of plants and flowers are shown to have an organic significance and value, I take it for granted that tints have a like character in the mysteriously clouded and pearly shell, where they mock my ken. I cannot believe that the myriads are furnished, at the depths of the ocean, with the complicated glands and absorbents to nourish those dyes, in order that the hundreds may charm my idle eye as they are tossed in disorganized ruin upon the beach.

Let us dwell for a moment upon the forms of several of the higher types of animal structure. Behold the eagle as he sits on the lonely cliff, towering high in the air; carry in your mind the proportions and lines of the dove and mark how the finger of God has, by the mere variation of diameters, converted the type of meekness into the most expressive symbol of majesty. His eye, instead of rushing as it were out of his head, to see the danger behind him, looks steadfastly forward from its deep cavern, knowing no danger but that which it pilots. The structure of his brow allows him to fly upward with his eyes in shade. In his beak and his talons we see at once the belligerent, in the vast expanse of his sailing pinions the patent of his prerogative. *Dei Gratia Raptor!* Whence the beauty and majesty of the bird? It is the oneness of his function that gives him his grandeur, it is transcendental mechanism alone that begets his beauty. Observe the lion as he stands! Mark the ponderous predominance of his anterior extremities, his lithe loins, the lever of his hock, the awful breadth of his jaws, and the depth of his chest. His mane is a curiass, and when the thunder of his voice is added to the glitter of his snarling jaws, man alone with all his means of defense stands self-possessed before him. In this structure again are beheld, as in that of the eagle, the most terrible expression of power and dominion, and we find that it is here also the result of transcendental mechanism. The form of the hare might well be the type of swiftness for him who never saw the greyhound. The greyhound overtakes him, and it is not possible in organization that this result should obtain, without the promise and announcement of it, in the lengths and diameters of this breed of dogs.

Let us now turn to the human frame, the most beautiful organization of earth, the exponent and minister of the highest being we immediately know. This stupendous form, towering as a lighthouse, commanding by its posture a wide horizon, standing in relation to the brutes where the spire stands in relation to the lowly colonnades of Greece and Egypt, touching earth with only one-half the soles of its feet—it tells of majesty and dominion by that upreared spine, of duty by those unencumbered hands. Where is the ornament of this frame? It is all beauty, its motion is grace, no combination of harmony ever equaled, for expression and variety, its poised and stately gait; its voice is music, no cunning mixture of wood and metal ever did more than feebly imitate its tone of command or its warble of love. The savage who envies or admires the special attributes of beasts maims unconsciously his own perfection to assume their tints, their feathers, or their claws; we turn from him with horror, and gaze with joy on the naked Apollo.

I have dwelt a moment on these examples of expression and of beauty that I may draw from them a principle in art, a principle which, if it has been often illustrated by brilliant results, we constantly see neglected, overlooked, forgotten —a principle which I hope the examples I have given have prepared you to accept at once and unhesitatingly. It is this: in art, as in nature, the soul, the purpose of a work will never fail to be proclaimed in that work in proportion to the subordination of the parts to the whole, of the whole to the function. If you will trace the ship through its various stages of improvement, from the dugout canoe and the old galley to the latest type of the sloop-of-war, you will remark that every advance in performance has been an advance in expression, in grace, in beauty, or grandeur, according to the functions of the craft. This artistic gain, effected by pure science in some respects, in others by mere empirical watching of functions where the elements of the structure were put to severe tests, calls loudly upon the artist to keenly watch traditional dogmas and to see how far analogous rules may guide his own operations. You will remark, also, that after mechanical power had triumphed over the earlier obstacles, embellishment began to encumber and hamper ships, and that their actual approximation to beauty has been effected, first, by strict adaptation of forms to functions, second, by the gradual elimination of all that is irrelevant and impertinent. The old chairs were formidable by their weight, puzzled you by their carving, and often contained too much else to contain convenience and comfort. The most beautiful chairs invite you by a promise of ease, and they keep that promise; they bear neither flowers nor dragons, nor idle displays of the turner's caprice. By keeping within their province they are able to fill it well. Organization has a language of its own, and so expressive is that language that a makeshift or make-believe can scarce fail of detection. The swan, the goose, the duck, when they walk toward the water are awkward, when they hasten toward it are ludicrous. Their feet are paddles, and their legs are organized mainly to move those paddles in the water; they, therefore, paddle on land, or as we say, waddle. It is only when their breasts are launched into the pond that their necks assume the expression of ease and grace. A serpent upon a smooth hard road has a similar awkward expression of impotence; the grass, or pebbles, or water, as he meets either, afford him his *sine quâ non*, and he is instantly confident, alert, effective.

If I err not, we should learn from these and the like examples, which will meet us wherever we look for them, that God's world has a distinct formula for every function, and that we shall seek in vain to borrow shapes; we must make the shapes, and can only effect this by mastering the principles.

It is a confirmation of the doctrine of strict adaptation that I find in the purer Doric temple. The sculptures which adorned certain spaces in those temples had an organic relation to the functions of the edifice; they took possession of the worshiper as he approached, lifted him out of everyday life, and prepared him for the presence of the divinity within. The world has never seen plastic art developed so highly as by the men who translated into marble, in the tympanum and the metope, the theogony and the exploits of the heroes. Why, then, those columns uncarved? Why, then, those lines of cornice unbroken by foliages, unadorned by flowers? Why that matchless symmetry of every member, that music of gradation, without the tracery of the Gothic detail, without the endless caprices of arabesque? Because those sculptures *spake,* and speech asks a groundwork of silence and not of babble, though it were of green fields.

I am not about to deny the special beauties and value of any of the great types of building. Each has its meaning and expression. I am desirous now of analyzing that majestic and eloquent simplicity of the Greek temple, because, though I truly believe that it is hopeless to transplant its forms with any other result than an expression of impotent dilettantism, still I believe that its principles will be found to be those of all structures of the highest order.

When I gaze upon the stately and beautiful Parthenon, I do not wonder at the greediness of the moderns to appropriate it. I do wonder at the obtuseness which allowed them to persevere in trying to make it work in the towns. It seems like the enthusiasm of him who should squander much money to transfer an Arabian stallion from his desert home, that, as a blindfolded gelding, he might turn his mill. The lines in which Byron paints the fate of the butterfly that has fallen into the clutches of its childish admirer [1] would apply not inaptly to the Greek temple at the mercy of a sensible building committee, wisely determined to have their money's worth.

When high art declined, carving and embellishment invaded the simple organization. As the South Sea Islanders have added a variety to the human form by tattooing, so the cunning artisans of Greece undertook to go beyond perfection. Many rhetoricians and skilled grammarians refined upon the elements of the language of structure. They all spake: and demigods, and heroes, and the gods themselves, went away and were silent.

If we compare the simpler form of the Greek temple with the ornate and carved specimens which followed it, we shall be convinced, whatever the subtlety, however exquisite the taste that long presided over those refinements, that they were the beginning of the end, and that the turning-point was the first introduction of a fanciful, not demonstrable, embellishment, and for this simple

---

[1] In *The Giaour*, the passage (lines 388-421) including:
"For every touch that wooed its stay
    Hath brushed its brightest hues away."

reason, that, embellishment being arbitrary, there is no check upon it; you begin with acanthus leaves, but the appetite for sauces, or rather the need of them, increases as the palate gets jaded. You want jasper, and porphyry, and serpentine, and giallo antico, at last. Nay, you are tired of Aristides the Just, and of straight columns; they must be spiral, and by degrees you find yourself in the midst of a barbaric pomp whose means must be slavery—nothing less will supply its waste, —whose enjoyment is satiety, whose result is corruption.

It was a day of danger for the development of taste in this land, the day when Englishmen perceived that France was laying them under contribution by her artistic skill in manufacture. They organized reprisals upon ourselves, and, in lieu of truly artistic combinations, they have overwhelmed us with embellishment, arbitrary, capricious, setting at defiance all principle, meretricious dyes and tints, catchpenny novelties of form, steam-woven fineries and plastic ornaments, struck with the die or pressed into molds. In even an ordinary house we look around in vain for a quiet and sober resting-place for the eye; we see naught but flowers, flourishes—the renaissance of Louis Quatorze gingerbread embellishment. We seek in vain for aught else. Our own manufacturers have caught the furor, and our foundries pour forth a mass of ill-digested and crowded embellishment which one would suppose addressed to the sympathies of savages or of the colored population, if the utter absence of all else in the market were not too striking to allow such a conclusion.

I do not suppose it is possible to check such a tide as that which sets all this corruption toward our shores. I am aware of the economical sagacity of the English, and how fully they understand the market; but I hope that we are not so thoroughly asphyxiated by the atmosphere they have created as to follow their lead in our own creation of a higher order. I remark with joy that almost all the more important efforts of this land tend, with an instinct and a vigor born of the institutions, toward simple and effective organization; and they never fail whenever they toss overboard the English dictum and work from their own inspirations to surpass the British, and there, too, where the world thought them safe from competition.

I would fain beg any architect who allows fashions to invade the domain of principles to compare the American vehicles and ships with those of England, and he will see that the mechanics of the United States have already outstripped the artists, and have, by the results of their bold and unflinching adaptation, entered the true track, and hold up the light for all who operate for American wants, be they what they will.

In the American trotting wagon I see the old-fashioned and pompous coach dealt with as the old-fashioned palatial display must yet be dealt with in this land. In vain shall we endeavor to hug the associations connected with the old form. The redundant must be pared down, the superfluous dropped, the necessary itself reduced to its simplest expression, and then we shall find, whatever the organization may be, that beauty was waiting for us, though perhaps veiled, until our task was fully accomplished.

—Memorial of Horatio Greenough (1853)

LEWIS MUMFORD

The Esthetic Assimilation of the Machine

. . . In the arts, it is plain that the machine is an instrument with manifold and conflicting possibilities. It may be used to counterfeit older forms of art; it may also be used, in its own right, to concentrate and intensify and express new forms of experience. As substitutes for primary experience, the machine is worthless: indeed it is actually debilitating. Just as the microscope is useless unless the eye itself is keen, so all our mechanical apparatus in the arts depends for its success upon the due cultivation of the organic, physiological, and spiritual aptitudes that lie behind its use. The machine cannot be used as a shortcut to escape the necessity for organic experience. Mr. Waldo Frank has put the matter well: "Art," he says, "cannot become a language, hence an experience, unless it is practiced. To the man who plays, a mechanical reproduction of music may mean much, since he already has the experience to assimilate. But where reproduction becomes the norm, the few music makers will grow more isolate and sterile, and the ability to experience music will disappear. The same is true with the cinema, dance, and even sport."

Whereas in industry the machine may properly replace the human being when he has been reduced to an automaton, in the arts the machine can only extend and deepen man's original functions and intuitions. Insofar as the phonograph and the radio do away with the impulse to sing, insofar as the camera does away with the impulse to see, insofar as the automobile does away with the impulse to walk, the machine leads to a lapse of function which is but one step away from paralysis. But in the application of mechanical instruments to the arts it is not the machine itself that we must fear. The chief danger lies in the failure to integrate the arts themselves with the totality of our life-experience: the perverse triumph of the machine follows automatically from the abdication of the spirit. Consciously to assimilate the machine is one means of reducing its omnipotence. We cannot, as Karl Buecher wisely said, "give up the hope that it will be possible to unite technics and art in a higher rhythmical unity, which will restore to the spirit the fortunate serenity and to the body the harmonious cultivation that manifest themselves at their best among primitive peoples." The machine has not destroyed that promise. On the contrary, through the more conscious cultivation of the machine arts and through greater selectivity in their use, one sees the pledge of its wider fulfillment throughout civilization. For at the bottom of that cultivation there must be the direct and immediate experience of living itself: we must directly see, feel, touch, manipulate, sing, dance, communicate before we can extract from the machine any further sustenance for life. If we are empty to begin with, the machine will only leave us emptier; if we are passive and powerless to begin with, the machine will only leave us more feeble.

But modern technics, even apart from the special arts that it fostered, had a cultural contribution to make in its own right. Just as science underlined the respect for fact, so technics emphasized the importance of function: in this domain, as Emerson pointed out, the beautiful rests on the foundations of the necessary. The nature of this contribution can best be shown, perhaps, by describing the way in which the problem of machine design was first faced, then evaded, and finally solved.

One of the first products of the machine was the machine itself. As in the organization of the first factories the narrowly practical considerations were uppermost, and all the other needs of the personality were firmly shoved to one side. The machine was a direct expression of its own functions: the first cannon, the first crossbows, the first steam engines were all nakedly built for action. But once the primary problems of organization and operation had been solved, the human factor, which had been left out of the picture, needed somehow to be reincorporated. The only precedent for this fuller integration of form came naturally from handicraft: hence over the incomplete, only partly realized forms of the early cannon, the early bridges, the early machines, a meretricious touch of decoration was added: a mere relic of the happy, semi-magical fantasies that painting and carving had once added to every handicraft object. Because perhaps the energies of the eotechnic period [1] were so completely engrossed in the technical problems, it was, from the standpoint of design, amazingly clean and direct: ornament flourished in the utilities of life, flourished often perversely and extravagantly, but one looks for it in vain among the machines pictured by Agricola or Besson or the Italian engineers: [2] they are as direct and factual as was architecture from the tenth to the thirteenth century.

The worst sinners—that is, the most obvious sentimentalists—were the en-

[1] For an explanation of the terms eotechnic, paleotechnic, neotechnic, and biotechnic, employed by Mumford, see the editor's introductory note to this chapter.

[2] Georgius Agricola is the author of *De Re Mettalica* (1546), which describes the advanced technology of the early sixteenth century. Jacques Besson wrote *Theatre des Instruments Mathématiques et Méchaniques,* an account of sixteenth-century technics. Among the Italian engineers here referred to the most famous is Leonardo da Vinci. (Editor's note.)

gineers of the paleotechnic period. In the act of recklessly deflowering the environment at large, they sought to expiate their failures by adding a few sprigs or posies to the new engines they were creating: they embellished their steam engines with Doric columns or partly concealed them behind Gothic tracery: they decorated the frames of their presses and their automatic machines with cast-iron arabesque, they punched ornamental holes in the iron framework of their new structures, from the trusses of the old wing of the Metropolitan Museum to the base of the Eiffel tower in Paris. Everywhere similar habits prevailed: the homage of hypocrisy to art. One notes identical efforts on the original steam radiators, in the floral decorations that once graced typewriters, in the nondescript ornament that still lingers quaintly on shotguns and sewing machines, even if it has at length disappeared from cash registers and Pullman cars—as long before, in the first uncertainties of the new technics, the same division had appeared in armor and in crossbows.

The second stage in machine design was a compromise. The object was divided into two parts. One of them was to be precisely designed for mechanical efficiency. The other was to be designed for looks. While the utilitarian claimed the working parts of the structure the esthete was, so to speak, permitted slightly to modify the surfaces with his unimportant patterns, his plutonic flowers, his aimless filigree, provided he did not seriously weaken the structure or condemn the function to inefficiency. Mechanically utilizing the machine, this type of design shamefully attempted to conceal the origins that were still felt as low and mean. The engineer had the uneasiness of a parvenu, and the same impulse to imitate the most archaic patterns of his betters.

Naturally the next stage was soon reached: the utilitarian and the esthete withdrew again to their respective fields. The esthete, insisting with justice that the structure was integral with the decoration and that art was something more fundamental than the icing the pastrycook put on the cake, sought to make the old decoration real by altering the nature of the structure. Taking his place as workman, he began to revive the purely handicraft methods of the weaver, the cabinet maker, the printer, arts that had survived for the most part only in the more backward parts of the world, untouched by the tourist and the commercial traveler. The old workshops and ateliers were languishing and dying out in the nineteenth century, especially in progressive England and in America, when new ones, like those devoted to glass under William de Morgan in England, and John La Farge in America, and Lalique in France, or to a miscellany of handicrafts, such as that of William Morris in England, sprang into existence, to prove by their example that the arts of the past could survive. The industrial manufacturer, isolated from this movement yet affected by it, contemptuous but half-convinced, made an effort to retrieve his position by attempting to copy mechanically the dead forms of art he found in the museum. So far from gaining from the handicrafts movement by this procedure he lost what little virtue his untutored designs possessed, issuing as they sometimes did out of an intimate knowledge of the processes and the materials.

The weakness of the original handicrafts movement was that it assumed that the only important change in industry had been the intrusion of the soulless machine. Whereas the fact was that everything had changed, and all the shapes and patterns employed by technics were therefore bound to change, too. The world men carried in their heads, their idolum, was entirely different from that which set the medieval mason to carving the history of creation or the lives of the saints above the portals of the cathedral, or a jolly image of some sort above his own doorway. An art based like handicraft upon a certain stratification of the classes and the social differentiation of the arts could not survive in a world where men had seen the French Revolution and had been promised some rough share of equality. Modern handicraft, which sought to rescue the worker from the slavery of shoddy machine production, merely enabled the well-to-do to enjoy new objects that were as completely divorced from the dominant social milieu as the palaces and monasteries that the antiquarian art dealer and collector had begun to loot. The *educational aim* of the arts and crafts movement was admirable; and, insofar as it gave courage and understanding to the amateur, it was a success. If this movement did not add a sufficient amount of good handicraft it at least took away a great deal of false art. William Morris's dictum, that one should not possess anything one did not believe to be beautiful or know to be useful was, in the shallow showy bourgeois world he addressed, a revolutionary dictum.

But the social outcome of the arts and crafts movement was not commensurate with the need of the new situation; as Mr. Frank Lloyd Wright pointed out in his memorable speech at Hull House in 1901, the machine itself was as much an instrument of art, in the hands of an artist, as were the simple tools and utensils. To erect a social barrier between machines and tools was really to accept the false notion of the new industrialist who, bent on exploiting the machine, which they owned, and jealous of the tool, which might still be owned by the independent worker, bestowed on the machine an exclusive sanctity and grace it did not merit. Lacking the courage to use the machine as an instrument of creative purpose, and being unable to attune themselves to new objectives and new standards, the esthetes were logically compelled to restore a medieval ideology in order to provide a social backing for their anti-machine bias. In a word, the arts and crafts movement did not grasp the fact that the new technics, by expanding the role of the machine, had altered the entire relation of handwork to production, and that the exact processes of the machine were not necessarily hostile to handicraft and fine workmanship. In its modern form handicraft could no longer serve as in the past when it had worked under the form of an intensive caste-specialization. To survive, handicraft would have to adapt itself to the amateur, and it was bound to call into existence, even in pure handwork, those forms of economy and simplicity which the machine was claiming for its own, and to which it was adapting mind and hand and eye. In this process of re-integration certain "eternal" forms would be recovered: there are handicraft forms dating back to a distant past which so completely fulfill their functions that no amount of further calculation or experiment will alter them for the better. These type-forms appear and reappear from civilization to civilization; and if they had not been discovered by handicraft, the machine would have had to invent them.

The new handicraft was in fact to receive presently a powerful lesson from the machine. For the forms created by the machine, when they no longer sought to imitate old superficial patterns of handwork, were closer to those that could be produced by the amateur than were, for example, the intricacies of special joints, fine inlays, matched woods, beads and carvings, complicated forms of metallic ornament, the boast of handicraft in the past. While in the factory the machine was often reduced to producing fake handicraft, in the workshop of the amateur the reverse process could take place with a real gain: he was liberated by the very simplicities of good machine forms. Machine technique as a means to achieving a simplified and purified form relieved the amateur from the need of respecting and imitating the perversely complicated patterns of the past—patterns whose complications were partly the result of conspicuous waste, partly the outcome of technical virtuosity, and partly the result of a different state of feelings. But before handicraft could thus be restored as an admirable form of play and an efficacious relief from a physically untutored life, it was necessary to dispose of the machine itself as a social and esthetic instrument. So the major contribution to art was made, after all, by the industrialist who remained on the job and saw it through.

With the third stage in machine design an alteration takes place. The imagination is not applied to the mechanical object after the practical design has been completed: it is infused into it at every stage in development. The mind works through the medium of the machine directly, respects the conditions imposed upon it, and—not content with a crude quantitative approximation—seeks out a more positive esthetic fulfillment. This must not be confused with the dogma, so often current, that any mechanical contraption that works necessarily is esthetically interesting. The source of this fallacy is plain. In many cases, indeed, our eyes have been trained to recognize beauty in nature, and with certain kinds of animals and birds we have an especial sympathy. When an airplane becomes like a gull it has the advantage of this long association and we properly couple the beauty with the mechanical adequacy, since the poise and swoop of a gull's flight casts in addition a reflective beauty on its animal structure. Having no such association with a milkweed seed, we do not feel the same beauty in the autogyro, which is kept aloft by a similar principle. While genuine beauty in a thing of use must always be joined to mechanical adequacy and therefore involves a certain amount of intellectual recognition and appraisal, the relation is not a simple one: it points to a common source rather than an identity.

In the conception of a machine or of a product of the machine there is a point where one may leave off for parsimonious reasons without having reached esthetic perfection: at this point perhaps every mechanical factor is accounted for, and the sense of incompleteness is due to the failure to recognize the claims of the human agent. Esthetics carries with it the implication of alternatives between a number of mechanical solutions of equal validity: and unless this awareness is present at every stage of the process, in smaller matters of finish, fineness, trimness, it is not likely to come out with any success in the final stage of design. Form follows function, underlining it, crystallizing it, clarifying it, making it real to the eye. Makeshifts and approximations express themselves in incomplete forms: forms like the absurdly cumbrous and ill-adjusted telephone apparatus of the past, like the old-fashioned airplane, full of struts, wires, extra supports, all testifying to an anxiety to cover innumerable unknown or uncertain factors; forms like the old automobile in which part after part had been added to the effective mechanism without having been absorbed into the body of the design as a whole; forms like our oversized steel-work which were due to our carelessness in using cheap materials and our desire to avoid the extra expense of calculating them finely and expending the necessary labor to work them up. The impulse that creates a complete mechanical object is akin to that which creates an esthetically finished object; and the fusion of the two at every stage in the process will necessarily be effected by the environment at large: who can gauge how much the slatternliness and disorder of the paleotechnic environment undermined good design, or how much the order and beauty of our neotechnic plants—like that of the Van Nelle factory in Rotterdam—will eventually aid it? Esthetic interests cannot suddenly be introduced from without: they must be constantly operative, constantly visible.

Expression through the machine implies the recognition of relatively new esthetic terms: precision, calculation, flawlessness, simplicity, economy. Feeling attaches itself in these new forms to different qualities than those that made handicraft so entertaining. Success here consists in the elimination of the non-essential, rather than, as in handicraft decoration, in the willing production of superfluity, contributed by the worker out of his own delight in the work. The elegance of a mathematical equation, the inevitability of a series of physical inter-relations, the naked quality of the material itself, the tight logic of the whole—these are the ingredients that go into the design of machines: and they go equally into products that have been properly designed for machine production. In handicraft it is the worker who is represented: in machine design it is the work. In handicraft, the personal touch is emphasized, and the imprint of the worker and his tool are both inevitable: in machine work the impersonal prevails, and if the worker leaves any tell-tale evidence of his part in the operation, it is a defect or a flaw. Hence the burden of machine design is in the making of the original pattern: it is here that trials are made, that errors are discovered and buried, that the creative process as a whole is concentrated. Once the master-pattern is set, the rest is routine: beyond the designing room and the laboratory there is—for goods produced on a serial basis for a mass market—no opportunity for choice and personal achievement. Hence apart from those commodities that can be produced automatically, the effort of sound industrial production must be to increase the province of the designing room and the laboratory, reducing the scale of the production, and making possible an easier passage back and forth between the designing and the operative sections of the plant.

Who discovered these new canons of machine design? Many an engineer and many a machine worker must have mutely sensed them and reached toward them: indeed, one sees the beginning of them in very early mechanical instruments. But only after centuries of more or less blind and unformulated effort were these canons finally demonstrated with a certain degree of completeness in the work of the great engineers toward the end of the nineteenth century—particularly the Roeblings in America and Eiffel in France—and formulated after that by theoreticians like Reidler and Meyer in Germany. The popularization of the new esthetic awaited . . . the post-impressionist painters. They contributed by breaking away from the values of purely associative art and by abolishing an undue concern for natural objects as the basis of the painter's interest: if on one side this led to completer subjectivism, on the other it tended toward a recognition of the machine as both form and symbolic.[3] In the same direction Marcel Duchamp, for example, who was one of the leaders of this movement, made a collection of cheap, ready-made articles, produced by the machine, and called attention to their esthetic soundness and sufficiency. In many cases, the finest designs had been achieved before any conscious recognition of the esthetic had

[3] In a preceding section of his book, Mumford writes as follows: "The Cubists were perhaps the first school to overcome [the] association of the ugly and the mechanical: they not merely held that beauty could be produced through the machine: they even pointed to the fact that it had been produced. The first expression of Cubism indeed dates back to the seventeenth century: Jean Baptiste Bracelle, in 1624, did a series of Bizarreries which depicted mechanical men, thoroughly cubist in conception. This anticipated in art, as Glanvill did in science, our later interests and inventions. What did the modern Cubists do? They extracted from the organic environment just those elements that could be stated in abstract geometrical symbols: they transposed and readjusted the contents of vision as freely as the inventor readjusted organic functions: they even created on canvas or in metal mechanical equivalents of organic objects: Léger painted human figures that looked as if they had been turned in a lathe, and Duchamp-Villon modeled a horse as if it were a machine. This whole process of rational experiment in abstract mechanical forms was pushed further by the constructivists. Artists like Grabo and Moholy-Nagy put together pieces of abstract sculpture, composed of glass, metal plates, spiral springs, wood, which were the nonutilitarian equivalents of the apparatus that the physical scientist was using in his laboratory. They created in forms the semblance of the mathematical equations and physical formulæ that had produced our new environment, seeking in this new sculpture to observe the physical laws of equipose or to evolve dynamic equivalents for the solid sculpture of the past by rotating a part of the object through space."

taken place. With the coming of the commercialized designer, seeking to add "art" to a product which *was* art, the design has more often than not been trifled with and spoiled. The studious botching of the kodak, the bathroom fixture, and the steam radiator under such stylicizing is a current commonplace.

The key to this fresh appreciation of the machine as a source of new esthetic forms has come through a formulation of its chief esthetic principle: the principle of economy. This principle is of course not unknown in other phases of art: but the point is that in mechanical forms it is at all times a controlling one, and it has for its aid the more exact calculations and measurements that are now possible. The aim of sound design is to remove from the object, be it an automobile or a set of china or a room, every detail, every molding, every variation of the surface, every extra part except that which conduces to its effective functioning. Toward the working out of this principle, our mechanical habits and our unconscious impulses have been tending steadily. In departments where esthetic choices are not consciously uppermost our taste has often been excellent and sure. Le Corbusier has been very ingenious in picking out manifold objects, buried from observation by their very ubiquity, in which this mechanical excellence of form has manifested itself without pretense or fumbling. Take the smoking pipe: it is no longer carved to look like a human head or does it bear, except among college students, any heraldic emblems: it has become exquisitely anonymous, being nothing more than an apparatus for supplying drafts of smoke to the human mouth from a slow-burning mass of vegetation. Take the ordinary drinking glass in a cheap restaurant: it is no longer cut or cast or engraved with special designs: at most it may have a slight bulge near the top to keep one glass from sticking to another in stacking: it is as clean, as functional, as a high tension insulator. Or take the present watch and its case and compare it with the forms that handicraft ingenuity and taste and association created in the sixteenth or seventeenth centuries. In all the commoner objects of our environment the machine canons are instinctively accepted: even the most sentimental manufacturer of motor cars has not been tempted to paint his coach work to resemble a sedan chair in the style of Watteau, although he may live in a house in which the furniture and decoration are treated in that perverse fashion.

This stripping down to essentials has gone on in every department of machine work and has touched every aspect of life. It is a first step toward that completer integration of the machine with human needs and desires which is the mark of the neotechnic phase, and will be even more the mark of the biotechnic period, already visible over the edge of the horizon. As in the social transition from the paleotechnic to the neotechnic order, the chief obstacle to the fuller development of the machine lies in the association of taste and fashion with waste and commercial profiteering. For the rational development of genuine technical standards, based on function and performance, can come about only by a wholesale devaluation of the scheme of bourgeois civilization upon which our present system of production is based.

Capitalism, which along with war played such a stimulating part in the development of technics, now remains with war the chief obstacle toward its further improvement. The reason should be plain. The machine devaluates rarity: instead of producing a single unique object, it is capable of producing a million others just as good as the master model from which the rest are made. The machine devaluates age: for age is another token of rarity, and the machine, by placing its emphasis upon fitness and adaptation, prides itself on the brand-new rather than on the antique: instead of feeling comfortably authentic in the midst of rust, dust, cobwebs, shaky parts, it prides itself on the opposite qualities —slickness, smoothness, gloss, cleanness. The machine devaluates archaic taste: for taste in the bourgeois sense is merely another name for pecuniary reputability, and against that standard the machine sets up the standards of function and fitness. The newest, the cheapest, the commonest objects may, from the standpoint of pure esthetics, be immensely superior to the rarest, the most expensive, and the most antique. To say all this is merely to emphasize that the modern technics, by its own essential nature, imposes a greater purification of esthetics: that is, it strips off from the object all the barnacles of association, all the sentimental and pecuniary values which have nothing whatever to do with esthetic form, and it focuses attention upon the object itself.

The social devaluation of caste, enforced by the proper use and appreciation of the machine, is as important as the stripping down of essential forms in the process itself. One of the happiest signs of this during the last decade was the use of cheap and common materials in jewelry, first introduced, I believe, by Lalique: for this implied a recognition of the fact that an esthetically appropriate form, even in the adornment of the body, has nothing to do with rarity or expense, but is a matter of color, shape, line, texture, fitness, symbol. The use of cheap cottons in dress by Chanel and her imitators, which was another postwar phenomenon, was an equally happy recognition of the essential values in our new economy: it at last put our civilization, if only momentarily, on the level of those primitive cultures which gladly bartered their furs and ivory for the white man's colored glass beads, by the adroit use of which the savage artist often proved to any disinterested observer that they—contrary to the white man's fatuous conceit—had gotten the better of the bargain. Because of the fact that woman's dress has a peculiarly compensatory role to play in our megalopolitan society, so that it more readily indicates what is absent than calls attention to what is present in it, the victory for genuine esthetics could only be a temporary one. But these forms of dress and jewelry pointed to the goal of machine production: the goal at which each object would be valued in terms of its direct mechanical and vital and social function, apart from its pecuniary status, the snobberies of caste, or the dead sentiments of historical emulation.

This warfare between a sound machine esthetic and what Veblen has called the "requirements of pecuniary reputability" has still another side. Our modern technology has, in its inner organization, produced a collective economy and its typical products are collective products. Whatever the politics of a country may be, the machine is a communist: hence the deep contradictions and conflicts that have kept on developing in machine industry since the end of the eighteenth century. At every stage in technics, the work represents a collaboration of innumerable workers, themselves utilizing a large and ramifying technological heritage: the most ingenious inventor, the most brilliant individual scientist, the most skilled designer contributes but a moiety to the final result. And the product itself necessarily bears the same impersonal imprint: it either functions or it does not function on quite impersonal lines. There can be no qualitative difference between a poor man's electric bulb of a given candlepower and a rich man's, to indicate their differing pecuniary status in society, although there was an enormous difference between the rush or stinking tallow of the peasant and the wax candles or sperm oil used by the upper classes before the coming of gas and electricity.

Insofar as pecuniary differences are permitted to count in the machine economy, they can alter only the scale of things—not, in terms of present production, the kind. What applies to electric light bulbs applies to automobiles: what applies there applies equally to every manner of apparatus or utility. The frantic attempts that have been made in America by advertising agencies and "designers" to stylicize machine-made objects have been, for the most part, attempts to pervert the machine process in the interests of caste and pecuniary distinction. In money-ridden societies, where men play with poker chips instead of with economic and esthetic realities, every attempt is made to disguise the fact that the machine has achieved potentially a new collective economy, in which the possession of goods is a meaningless distinction, since the machine can produce all our essential goods in unparalleled quantities, falling on the just and the unjust, the foolish and the wise, like the rain itself.

The conclusion is obvious: we cannot intelligently accept the practical benefits of the machine without accepting its moral imperatives and its esthetic forms insofar as they, too, fulfill human purposes. Otherwise both ourselves and our society will be the victims of a shattering disunity, and one set of purposes, that which created the order of the machine, will be constantly at war with trivial and inferior personal impulses bent on working out in covert ways our psychological weaknesses. Lacking on the whole this rational acceptance, we have lost a good part of the practical benefits of the machine and have achieved esthetic expression only in a spotty, indecisive way. The real social distinction of modern technics, however, is that it tends to eliminate social distinctions. Its immediate goal is effective work. Its means are standardization: the emphasis of the generic and the typical: in short, conspicuous economy. Its ultimate aim is leisure—that is, the release of other organic capacities.

The powerful esthetic side of this social process has been obscured by speciously pragmatic and pecuniary interests that have inserted themselves into our technology and have imposed themselves upon its legitimate aims. But in spite of this deflection of effort, we have at last begun to realize these new values, these new forms, these new modes of expression. Here is a new environment—man's extension of nature in terms discovered by the close observation and analysis and abstraction of nature. The elements of this environment are hard and crisp and clear: the steel bridge, the concrete road, the turbine and the alternator, the glass wall. Behind the façade are rows and rows of machines, weaving cotton, transporting coal, assembling food, printing books, machines with steel fingers and lean muscular arms, with perfect reflexes, sometimes even with electric eyes. Alongside them are the new utilities—the coke oven, the transformer, the dye vats—chemically cooperating with these mechanical processes, assembling new qualities in chemical compounds and materials. Every effective part in this whole environment represents an effort of the collective mind to widen the province of order and control and provision. And here, finally, the perfected forms begin to hold human interest even apart from their practical performances: they tend to produce that inner composure and equilibrium, that sense of balance between the inner impulse and the outer environment, which is one of the marks of a work of art. The machines, even when they are not works of art, underlie our art—that is, our organized perceptions and feelings—in the way that Nature underlies them, extending the basis upon which we operate and confirming our own impulse to order. The economic: the objective: the collective: and finally the integration of these principles in a new conception of the organic—these are the marks, already discernible, of our assimilation of the machine not merely as an instrument of practical action but as a valuable mode of life.

—Technics and Civilization (1934)

PART THREE

APPRECIATION AND CRITICISM

CHAPTER TWELVE

Empathy and Abstraction

VERNON LEE
Empathy

THEODOR LIPPS
Empathy, Inner Imitation, and Sense-Feelings

WILHELM WORRINGER
Abstraction and Empathy

Introductory Note

MOST OF THE THEORIES PRESENTED in earlier chapters have thrown light on the nature of esthetic appreciation. The characterization of esthetic experience by Lange, Santayana, Hirn, Croce, Dewey, Morris, and Richards—to mention only a few names—illuminates not only the creative activity of the artist but the contemplative activity of the beholder. Although no sharp line can be drawn between the contemplative and the creative phases of art, the selections to which we shall now turn focus upon the esthetic attitude. They also shed further light on the nature of the work of art.

An interesting interpretation of form, the subject of Chapters X and XI, has been advanced by the proponents of "empathy." (The term "empathy" was coined by the psychologist Edward Titchener, in his *Experimental Psychology of the Thought Processes,* as an English rendering of *"einfühlung,"* which means literally "feeling into.") According to this interpretation, the formal elements acquire meaning for the imagination only because we project our activities and feelings into them. Thus form as an esthetic value is not an objective fact. It is a free creation of the imagination, and belongs to the realm of appearances. It is inseparable from expression, since all its spiritual content is derived from the mind.

The most original proponent of empathy writing in English has been Violet Paget, whose pen-name is Vernon Lee (1856-1935). Lipps' *Raumaesthetik,* which contained the first detailed exposition of the theory of empathy, was published in 1893-7, but did not become known to Lee until 1899. Her own account, published two years before she discovered Lipps, appears in an article "Beauty and Ugliness" in the *Contemporary Review.*

She believes that many aims operate to create art (for example, the making of useful objects, the transmission of knowledge, the expression of emotions), but that there is always a regulative principle, an "esthetic imperative," namely, the attainment of beauty and the avoidance of ugliness. Objects found to be beautiful are essentially formal; they are *configurations* of sounds, colors, lines, words, etc. The main question of esthetics becomes, then, what makes certain forms beautiful and other forms ugly. Her answer is: Forms are beautiful when we project into them our own activities, and when this projection arouses pleasure by facilitating our sense of vitality. In the case of ugliness, we feel an opposite sense of obstruction and displeasure.

The main feature of her theory in its earlier formulations was the great stress upon the importance of organic sensations and bodily postures. "We cannot satisfactorily focus a stooping figure like the Medicean Venus," she pointed out, "if we stand before it bolt upright and with tense muscles, nor a very erect and braced figure like the Apoxyomenos if we stand before it humped up and with slackened muscles. In such cases the statue seems to evade our eye, and it is impossible to realize its form thoroughly; whereas, when we adjust our muscles in imitation of the tenseness or slackness of the statue's attitude, the statue immediately becomes a reality to us." [1] But under the influence of Lipps she later modified her position, being convinced that she had laid too much stress upon kinesthetic sensations and muscular adjustments. What we project into the object, she realized, are mainly the emotions and ideas of which the organic mimicry and bodily accommodations are the symptoms.

In the account here reprinted, she differs from Lipps in one important respect. She objects to the conception of empathy "as a metaphysical and quasi-mythological *projection of the ego* into the object or shape under consideration." This is in opposition to the tendency of Lipps to speak of the ego as at one with the object. Empathy, according to his view, is based partly upon a feeling of "self-value"; the unity and worth of personality are projected into the object of appreciation.

---

[1] Vernon Lee and C. Anstruther-Thomson, *Beauty and Ugliness and other Studies in Psychological Aesthetics* (John Lane, London, 1912), p. 218.

In the pages of Theodor Lipps (1851-1941), the theory of empathy becomes explicit and profound, but the germ of his doctrine is to be found in various German predecessors. Thus in Herder we find the arresting sentence, "the beauty of a line is movement, and the beauty of movement expression," which suggests that outward forms must be given a dynamic content derived from the activity of the mind. A more explicit statement is to be found in a little book by Robert Vischer, *Über das optische Formgefühl* (1873). Later contributors include the philosopher Hermann Lotze, who gives a brief but luminous account of how the mind projects itself into nature.

Since Lipps' exposition is not easy to follow, I shall summarize it in some detail. He begins the present article by defining the nature of the "esthetic object." It consists of the "sensuous appearance," not the bare physical object, but the image as remodeled by imagination and charged with vital meaning. It is the beautiful thing contemplated, and is therefore to be distinguished from the act of contemplation. Attention is not aware of itself; it is directed outward to the object and absorbed therein. Nevertheless, what gives esthetic import to the object, and what constitutes the *ground* of its enjoyment, is this very act of contemplation. The mind unconsciously enlivens the outward form by fusing into it the modes of its own activity—its striving and willing, its sense of freedom and power, etc. The moods thus transported into the object do not spring from the real or practical ego, but only from the ego so far as contemplative.

We are now prepared to define more precisely the nature of the esthetic object. It may be analyzed into two factors: first, there is the inner activity, the emotion of pride, the feeling of vigor or freedom, etc.; second, there is the external sensuous content as bare physical stimulus. The *esthetic* object springs into existence as a result of the fusion of these two factors. The ego unconsciously supposes itself at one with the object, and there is no longer any duality. Empathy simply means the disappearance of the twofold consciousness of self and object, and the enrichment of experience that results from this interpenetration. So completely is the self transported into the object that the contemplator of a statue, for example, may unconsciously imitate its posture and implied movement by definite muscular adjustments.

Although Lipps recognizes the existence of such spontaneous mimicry, he insists that empathy does not consist in the bodily feelings thus aroused. In fact, we forget all about our bodies and attend simply to the object. Our bodily behavior is a symptom of what we are feeling rather than the object of our awareness. We do not, in fact, attribute kinesthetic feelings even to the object, but attribute to it only the total emotional state that is appropriate to the representation at hand.

Wilhelm Worringer (1881-   ), a famous German art historian, takes as his point of departure the theory of Lipps. His essay draws an interesting contrast between empathy and "abstraction." Whereas in empathy the mind lends to the object its own spirit and feels itself at one with it, in abstraction the mind feels the inviolable and separate integrity of the object. Empathy involves a transference of vital feelings from the subject *into* the object; abstraction involves the withdrawal of subjective feelings *from* the object. When engaged in such abstraction, the mind creates or contemplates abstract geometrical forms—stiff lines, flat surfaces, cubical shapes, etc.—which, appearing durable and permanent, afford a refuge from the flux and impermanence of sensuous phenomena.

Empathy is the result of a happy sympathetic relation between man and the outside world, whereas abstraction occurs mainly among peoples who feel no such delight in nature and life. "It expresses no joyful affirmation of sensuous vitality," declares Worringer, "but belongs rather to the other domain, which through all the transitoriness and chances of life strives for a higher world, freed from all illusions of the senses, from all false impressions, a domain in which inevitableness and permanency reign." [2] On the whole, abstraction is characteristic of Primitive, Egyptian, Byzantine, Gothic, and Oriental art, and also the "dehumanized" contemporary art discussed by Ortega y Gasset. On the other hand, empathy is more characteristic of late Greco-Roman, Renaissance, and "naturalistic" Western art.

Despite the antithesis between empathy and abstraction, Worringer finds the two esthetic processes alike in being modes of "self-privation"—escapes from the limitations of man's ordinary circumscribed being. In empathy, man "loses himself" in the object; in abstraction, he imaginatively transcends his "human, all too-human" nature through the contemplation of "eternal" forms.

VERNON LEE

Empathy

The mountain rises. What do we mean when we employ this form of words? Some mountains, we are told, have originated in an *upheaval.* But even if this particular mountain did, we never saw it and geologists are still disputing about HOW and WHETHER. So the *rising* we are talking about is evidently not that probable or improbable *upheaval.* On the other hand all geologists tell us that every mountain is undergoing a steady *lowering* through its particles being weathered away and washed down; and our knowledge of landslips and avalanches shows us that the mountain, so far from rising, is *descending.* Of course

<hr/>

[2] Wilhelm Worringer, *Form in Gothic* (G. P. Putnam's Sons, London, 1927), p. 37.

we all know that, objects the Reader, and of course nobody imagines that the rock and the earth of the mountain is rising, or that the mountain is getting up or growing taller! All we mean is that the mountain *looks* as if it were rising.

The mountain *looks!* Surely here is a case of putting the cart before the horse. No; we cannot explain the mountain *rising* by the mountain *looking,* for the only *looking* in the business is *our* looking *at* the mountain. And if the Reader objects again that these are all *figures of speech,* I shall answer that *Empathy* is what explains why we employ figures of speech at all, and occasionally employ them, as in the case of this rising mountain, when we know perfectly well that the figure we have chosen expresses the exact reverse of the objective truth. Very well; then, (says the Reader) we will avoid all figures of speech and say merely: when we look at the mountain *we somehow or other think of the action of rising.* Is that sufficiently literal and indisputable?

So literal and indisputable a statement of the case, I answer, that it explains, when we come to examine it, why we should have a thought of rising when we look at the mountain, since we cannot look at the mountain, nor at a tree, a tower or anything of which we similarly say that it *rises,* without lifting our glance, raising our eye and probably raising our head and neck, all of which raising and lifting unites into a general awareness of something *rising.* The rising of which we are aware is going on in us. But, as the Reader will remember also, when we are engrossed by something outside ourselves, as we are engrossed in looking at the shape (for we can *look* at only the shape, not the *substance*) of that mountain we cease thinking about ourselves, and cease thinking about ourselves exactly in proportion as we are thinking of the mountain's shape. What becomes therefore of our awareness of raising or lifting or *rising?* What can become of it (so long as it continues to be there!) except that it coalesces with the shape we are looking at; in short that the *rising* continuing to be thought, but no longer to be thought of with reference to ourselves (since we aren't thinking of ourselves), is thought of in reference to what we *are* thinking about, namely, the mountain, or rather the mountain's shape, which is, so to speak, responsible for any thought of rising, since it obliges us to lift, raise or rise ourselves in order to take stock of it. It is a case exactly analogous to our transferring the measuring done by our eye to the line of which we say that it *extends* from A to B, when in reality the only *extending* has been the extending of our glance. It is a case of what I have called the tendency to merge the *activities* of the perceiving subject with the qualities of the perceived object. Indeed if I insisted so much upon this tendency of our mind, I did so largely because of its being at the bottom of the phenomenon of *Empathy,* as we have just seen it exemplified in the *mountain which rises.*

If this is Empathy, says the Reader (relieved and reassured), am I to understand that Empathy is nothing beyond *attributing what goes on in us when we look at a shape to the shape itself?*

I am sorry that the matter is by no means so simple! If what we attributed to each single shape was only the precise action which we happen to be accomplishing in the process of looking at it, Empathy would indeed be a simple business, but it would also be a comparatively poor one. No. The *rising* of the mountain is an idea started by the awareness of our own lifting or raising of our eyes, head or neck, and it is an idea containing the awareness of that lifting or raising. But it is far more than the idea merely of that lifting or raising which we are doing at this particular present moment and in connection with this particular mountain. That present and particular raising and lifting is merely the nucleus to which gravitates our remembrance of all similar acts of raising, or *rising* which we have ever accomplished or seen accomplished, *raising* or *rising* not only of our eyes and head, but of every other part of our body, and of every part of every other body which we ever perceived to be rising. And not merely the thought of past *rising* but the thought also of future rising. All these risings, done by ourselves or watched in others, actually experienced or merely imagined, have long since united together in our mind, constituting a sort of composite photograph whence all differences are eliminated and wherein all similarities are fused and intensified: the general idea of *rising*, not "I rise, rose, will rise, it rises, has risen or will rise" but merely *rising* as such, *rising* as it is expressed not in any particular tense or person of the verb *to rise*, but in that verb's infinitive. It is this universally applicable notion of rising, which is started in our mind by the awareness of the particular present acts of raising or rising involved in our looking at that mountain, and it is this general idea of rising, that is, of *upward movement,* which gets transferred to the mountain along with our own particular present activity of raising some part of us, and which thickens and enriches and marks that poor little thought of a definite raising with the interest, the emotional fullness gathered and stored up in its long manifold existence. In other words: what we are transferring (owing to that tendency to merge the activities of the perceiving subject with the qualities of the perceived object) from ourselves to the looked at shape of the mountain, is not merely the thought of the rising which is really being done by us at that moment, but the thought and emotion, the *idea of rising as such* which had been accumulating in our mind long before we ever came into the presence of that particular mountain. And it is this complex mental process, by which we (all unsuspectingly) invest that inert mountain, that bodiless shape, with the stored up and averaged and essential modes of our activity—it is this process whereby we make the mountain *raise itself,* which constitutes what, accepting Professor Titchener's translation of the German word *Einfühlung,* I have called Empathy.

The German word *Einfühlung,* "feeling into"—derived from a *verb to feel oneself into something* ("sich in Etwas einfühlen") was in current use even before Lotze and Vischer applied it to esthetics, and some years before Lipps (1897) and Wundt (1903) adopted it into psychological terminology; and as it is now consecrated, and no better occurs to me, I have had to adopt it, although the literal connotations of the German word have surrounded its central meaning (as I have just defined it) with several mischievous misinterpretations. Against two of these I think it worth while to warn the Reader, especially as, while so doing, I can, in showing what it is not, make it even clearer what Empathy really is. The first of these two main misinterpretations is based upon the reflexive form of the German verb *"sich einfühlen"* (to feel *oneself* into) and it defines, or rather does not define, Empathy as a metaphysical and quasi-mythological *projection of the ego* into the object or shape under observation; a notion incompatible with the fact that Empathy, being only another of those various mergings of the activities of the perceiving subject with the qualities of the perceived object wherewith we have already dealt, depends upon a comparative or momentary abeyance of all thought of an ego; if we became aware that it is *we* who are thinking the rising, we who are *feeling* the rising, we should not think or feel that the mountain did the rising. The other (and as we shall later see) more justifiable misinterpretation of the word Empathy is based on its analogy with *sympathy,* and turns it into a kind of sympathetic, or as it has been called, *inner,* that is, merely *felt, mimicry* of, for instance, the mountain's *rising.* Such mimicry, not only *inner* and *felt,* but outwardly manifold, does undoubtedly often result from very lively *empathic* imagination. But as it is the mimicking, inner or outer, of movements and actions which, like the *rising* of the mountain, take place only in our imagination, it presupposes such previous animation of the inanimate, and cannot therefore be taken either as constituting or explaining Empathy itself.

Such as I have defined and exemplified it in our Rising Mountain, Empathy is, together with mere Sensation, probably the chief factor of preference, that is of an alternative of satisfaction and dissatisfaction, in esthetic contemplation, the muscular adjustments and the measuring, comparing and coordinating activities by which Empathy is started, being indeed occasionally difficult and distressing, but giving in themselves little more than a negative satisfaction, at the most that of difficulty overcome and suspense relieved. But although nowhere so fostered as in the contemplation of shapes, Empathy exists or tends to exist throughout our mental life. It is, indeed, one of our simpler, though far from absolutely elementary, psychological processes, entering into what is called imagination, sympathy, and also into that inference from our own inner experience which has shaped all our conceptions of an outer world, and given to the intermittent and heterogeneous sensations received from without the framework of our constant and highly unified inner experience, that is to say, of our own activities and aims. Empathy can be traced in all modes of speech and thought, particularly in the universal attribution of *doing* and *having* and *tending* where all we can really assert is successive and varied *being.* Science has indeed explained away the anthropomorphic implications of *Force* and *Energy, Attraction* and *Re-*

pulsion; and philosophy had reduced *Cause* and *Effect* from implying intention and effort to meaning mere constant succession. But Empathy still helps us to many valuable analogies; and it is possible that without its constantly checked but constantly renewed action, human thought would be without logical cogency, as it certainly would be without poetical charm. Indeed if Empathy is so recent a discovery, this may be due to its being part and parcel of our thinking; so that we are surprised to learn its existence, as Molière's good man was to hear that he talked prose.

—*The Beautiful* (1913)

THEODOR LIPPS

Empathy, Inner Imitation, and Sense-Feelings [1]

I direct my attention in the following to empathy in general. What I shall say applies to empathic projection into definite sorts of objects, especially into the movements, postures, and positions of man, whether real or represented as in sculpture; also into the forms of architecture.

Esthetic enjoyment is a feeling of pleasure or joy in each individual case colored in some specific way and ever different in each new esthetic object— a pleasure caused by viewing the object. In this experience the esthetic object is always sensuous, that is, sensuously perceived or imagined, and it is only this. I have a feeling of joy before a beautiful object: this means that I have this feeling in viewing the sensuous perception or image, in which form the beautiful object immediately presents itself to me. I have it while I view this object, that is, bring it into clear attention, apperceive it. But only the sensuous appearance of the esthetic object, for example, of the work of art, is attended to in esthetic contemplation. It alone is the "object" of the esthetic enjoyment; it is the only thing that stands "opposite" me as something distinct from myself and with which I, and my feeling of pleasure, enter into some "relationship." It is through this relationship that I am joyous or pleased, in short, enjoying myself.

The question of the "object" of esthetic enjoyment is one thing, the question of the *ground* of it is quite another. The sensuous appearance of the beautiful thing is certainly the *object* of esthetic enjoyment, but just as certainly it is

---

[1] *Einfühlung, innere Nachahmung, und Organempfindungen.* "*Organempfindungen,*" here translated as "sense-feelings," refers to the feelings localized in the body, to kinesthetic sensations, motor disturbances, physical cravings such as hunger, and so forth.

not the *ground* of it. Rather, the cause of esthetic enjoyment is myself, or the ego; exactly the same ego that feels joyous or pleased "in view" of the object or "opposite" it.

This means first of all that I may not only feel joyful or pleased, but may feel otherwise stimulated. There is no doubt that I feel myself, among other things, striving or willing, exerting or bestirring myself. In such endeavor or exertion I feel myself resisting or overcoming obstacles perhaps also yielding to them; I have a sense of reaching a goal, of satisfying my striving and my will, I feel my efforts succeeding. In short, I feel a multifarious "inner activity." And in all this I feel vigorous, free, certain, resilient, perhaps proud and the like. This sort of feeling is always the ground of esthetic enjoyment.

One can see that this ground occupies a middle position between the object of the esthetic enjoyment and the enjoyment itself. Let us stress this first: The above mentioned feelings have not, like the enjoyment, the beautiful thing for an object. I feel in the esthetic contemplation of the beautiful object in some way vigorously active, or free, or proud. And then, I do not feel vigorously active and so forth, *in view* of the object or *opposite* it, but I feel thus *in* it.

Likewise, this feeling of activity is not *the object of enjoyment*, that is, of my pleasure in the beautiful object. As certainly as I feel joy in view of the *sensuous* object, which I call beautiful, just as certainly I do not feel pleasure in response *to* the experienced activity, the power, etc., or *in view* of this activity, of the power, etc. This activity is not objective. It is not anything that stands opposite me. Just as I do not feel active over against the object, but *in* the object, so I do not experience joy over against my activity, but in it. I feel happy or blessed *in* it.

To be sure, my own activity may become objective to me, namely, when it is no longer my present activity but when I contemplate it in retrospect. But then it is no longer immediately experienced, but only remembered in imagination. And thus is it objective. This imagined activity, or more generally this imagined self, can then also be the object of my joy. But this we are not discussing. We are now only concerned with the immediately experienced activity, the success, the power, freedom, and so forth.

The term "object" of joy is taken here in an entirely restricted sense. It may be possible to take it less strictly; then the "object" of joy might be that *from* which I derive joy, and this means that to which the joy is related and which at the same time is the reason for the joy.

In this sense the question about the object of esthetic enjoyment may be answered in a twofold manner. On the one hand it can be said: Esthetic pleasure has no object at all. The esthetic enjoyment is not enjoyment of an object, but enjoyment of a self. It is an immediate feeling of a value that is lodged in oneself. But this is not a feeling that is related to an object. Rather, its characteristic consists in this—that there is no separation in it between my pleased ego and that with which I am pleased; in it both are one and the same self, the immediately experienced ego.

On the other hand it may be pointed out that after all, in esthetic enjoyment, this sense of value is objectified. In contemplating the strong, proud, free human form standing before me I do not feel strong, proud and free as such, or in my own place, or in my own body, but I feel myself thus in the contemplated form and only in it.

And accordingly, may I not say also this: The esthetic enjoyment has an object that is at the same time its ground. I can even give to this object a two-fold characterization. First, the object in question is the strong, proud, free ego; not the ego as such, however, but just so far as it objectifies itself, that is, so far as it is bound up with the sensuously perceived figure. Secondly, the object of esthetic enjoyment is this sensously perceived, this observed figure; not the figure as such, however, but the figure so far as I feel and experience it in myself, this strong, proud, free ego.

The specific characteristic of esthetic pleasure has now been defined. It consists in this: that it is the enjoyment of an object, which however, so far as it is the object of *enjoyment,* is not an object, but myself. Or, it is the enjoyment of the ego, which however, so far as it is esthetically enjoyed, is not myself but objective.

Now, all this is included in the concept empathy. It constitutes the very meaning of this concept. Empathy is the fact here established, that the object is myself and by the very same token this self of mine is the object. Empathy is the fact that the antithesis between myself and the object disappears, or rather does not yet exist.

How is empathy possible? An answer to this question presupposes complete clearness about the sharp distinction between the content or object of feeling (*Empfindungsinhalt*), on the one hand, and the immediately intuited attitudes or feelings of the subject (*Ichqualitäten oder Gefühlen*), on the other hand. But only one side of this antithesis shall be here considered.

I have the sensation of a color. This color belongs to a sensuously perceived object. Or, I feel hunger and thirst. These feelings, these contents of my sensation belong to my body. They are felt as determinations of this sensuously perceived thing, as a modification of the physical organism.

Different is the doing or the activity, the endeavor, the striving, the succeeding, that I feel. These belong to the ego; more than that, they are the ego or constitute it: I feel *myself* active. They absolutely do not belong to a sensuously perceived object or to one remembered in imagination, in short to no object that stands apart from me.

For this very reason these subjective qualities may belong to any material object. They belong, and with them the self, or the self belongs, and with it

THEODOR LIPPS · 377

these qualities, to that object with which I feel myself and my subjective states inextricably bound, whenever I stop to contemplate the object. But we shall determine more definitely these circumstances and with them the meaning of empathy.

I stretch out my arm or I hold my arm extended. Doing this I feel active, that is, I feel myself striving, endeavoring, and feel my striving succeed or gratify itself.

Here I can say I feel myself active, striving, endeavoring, attaining the end—in my arm. But this activity does not, in the full sense, take place in the arm, that is, it is not tied up with the contemplation of the arm or the contemplated arm. Rather, it is connected with my mood if I extend my arm from caprice, or with some purpose in mind if I extend my arm for a certain purpose. And the caprice or the purposefulness is something different from my contemplation of the arm or from myself who is contemplating. . . . It belongs to my personality as distinct from the contemplating self, or to my personality as object (*meiner "realen" Persönlichkeit*). This also implies that in this case my activity does not in the full sense "belong" to the extended arm. It is in a certain way, but not esthetically, empathized [2] in it.

Now we change the situation. My arm is freely extended for a time. Then I feel a desire, an impulse, a "compulsion" to drop it. This desire originates in the arm. I feel it coming from it or from its extended position. Therefore it lies in it or has its ground in it. In this case, too, the striving is my striving. But just this striving of mine I feel in my arm. For this reason I can also say the arm strives downward. And when the arm sinks, then this striving of the arm is realized. The sinking is therefore *its* activity.

Let us complicate the conditions. Upon the extended hand lies a stone. I now feel this striving, which in this case, too, remains "my" striving, to be the result of the pressure of the stone or of the stone which exerts this pressure. Accordingly I now say: The stone strives. And when it falls, the falling is an activity of the stone itself. It falls of its own power.

Now, with these two cases we have come nearer to the esthetic empathy. But we have not yet reached it. Let us dwell in particular upon the first case. Here, too, my striving is not altogether a matter of the arm. I cannot say: While I contemplate the arm and its extended position, and only as a result of my contemplation, does the striving spring into my consciousness. It springs also from something entirely different, namely, from the manner in which the continued extension of the arm affects me, from my feeling of discomfort. And this again is a factor entirely different from the contemplated self. The striving, so far as it comes from the arm, does not have its basis in the arm; rather, it is

---

[2] *Eingefühlt*; that is, the feeling of my activity in the extended arm is empathy, but not esthetic empathy; because the activity is felt as motivated by the self, which is distinguished from the arm. The antithesis between self and object remains. (Editor's note.)

motivated within me. It is not my striving in the arm, but my striving in view of the arm, or my striving directed upon the arm from without. Analogous is the downward pull of the stone.[3]

Now I substitute someone else's arm for my own. I *see* another person's arm extended. Let the manner of extension be perceptibly free, easy, sure, proud. Or more generally, I see a person perform some kind of vigorous, nimble, free, or bold movements. Let these be the object of my concentrated attention.

Now I again feel a striving. Possibly I realize this striving. I imitate the movements. In doing so I feel active. I feel the effort, the resistance to obstacles, the act of overcoming, the joy of succeeding. I feel all this actually. I do not merely imagine things of this sort.

Here again two possibilities present themselves. The imitation may be voluntary, that is, I, too, should like to have the feeling of freedom, assurance, and pride, which the other person has.

In this case I have again gotten far away from esthetic empathy. The immediate ground of my striving and doing is in this case not the observed movement, but this wish. And this wish is again something different from the observed arm and the merely contemplative self.

Now, at last, let us assume that the imitation is involuntary. The more I am absorbed in the contemplation of the seen movement the more involuntary will be the imitation. Conversely, the more involuntary the action is, the more is the observer *wholly* in the seen movement. But now, when I am completely engrossed by the contemplation of the movement, I am completely carried away from that which I am doing, namely, from the movement which I actually execute, from all that is going on in my body; I am no longer conscious of my outward imitation.

Nevertheless, in this state, the sense of striving and effort persists in my consciousness; there remains the feeling of activity, of effort, of inner accomplishment, of success. There remains the consciousness of "inner imitation."

Now this inner imitation takes place, for my consciousness, solely in the observed object. The feeling of striving, of effort, of success is no longer bound up with my movement, but merely with the objective bodily movement observed by me.

But this does not suffice. My inner activity in this imitation is exclusively bound up in a twofold sense with the observed object. First—the activity which I feel, I experience as derived entirely from the contemplation of the perceived movement. It is immediately and necessarily connected with it; and it is solely connected with it.

Secondly—the *object* of my activity is not my own activity, which is different

---

[3] In other words, the discomfort involved in these two cases makes me aware of how I am being affected, and of the subjective motivation of my activities. I become conscious of myself as separate from the object. (Editor's note.)

from the observed one, but only this activity which I behold. I feel active in the movement or in the moving figure, and through projecting myself into it I feel myself striving and performing this same movement. There is no other way; because under the assumed conditions there cannot be any other movement but the observed one as the object of my consciousness.

In a word, I am now with my feeling of activity entirely and wholly in the moving figure. Even spatially, if we can speak of the spatial extent of the ego, I am in its place. I am transported into it. I am, so far as my consciousness is concerned, entirely and wholly identical with it. Thus feeling myself active in the observed human figure, I feel also in it free, facile, proud. This is esthetic imitation and this imitation is at the same time esthetic empathy.

Here the whole emphasis must be laid on the "identity" which exists for my consciousness. This must be taken in the strictest sense.

In voluntary imitation I see the movement and have knowledge of the way the performer feels. I have a mental image (*Vorstellung*) of the activity which the other experiences, of his freedom and pride. On the other hand I also experience my own movement and feel my activity, my freedom and my pride, etc.

Contrariwise, in esthetic imitation this opposition is absolutely done away with. The two are simply one. The mere mental image no longer exists; my actual feeling has taken its place. And it is just because of this that I feel myself performing this movement in the other's movement.

In this "esthetic imitation" the facts seem to be analogous to what occurs in an unimitative movement of my own. The only difference seems to be that I now am conscious of experiencing and performing a movement which in fact, and for subsequent reflection, is the movement of another.

But in this comparison the most essential difference is overlooked. It is true that in both cases my inner activity—my striving and success, or in other words, the experienced satisfaction of my striving—is my own activity. But in the two cases it is not the same self that acts. In the unimitative movement my "real" self acts, my total personality as it is actually disposed at the time, with all its feelings, fancies, thoughts, and especially the motive or inner occasion from which the movement springs. In the esthetic imitation, quite differently, the self is an ideal one. This term is not clear. This "ideal" self, too, is real. But it is not the real "practical" self. It is the contemplative self, lingering and merged in the contemplation of the object. . . .

So far we have thought of esthetic imitation not only as an inward but also as an outward activity, in the sense that I overtly imitate the observed activity. But this outward consummation of the movements may not take place.

For this there are several reasons; for example, regard for good manners. But the chief hindrance is the practical absurdity and uselessness, or the actual impracticability of the movements.

For instance, from my seat in the theater I observe a dance which is performed upon the stage. In this case it is impossible for me to take part in the dance. Nor do I have the desire to dance; I am not in the mood for it. Both my situation and attitude prevent any bodily movements. But this does not eliminate my inner activity, the striving and satisfaction I feel as I contemplate the movements enacted before me.

To be sure, every striving is by its nature a striving after the realization of its end. But this realization is not lacking here. I experience the actual movement. I see it before me; not as my own, of course. But in this lies the peculiarity of esthetic imitation, that the alien activity takes the place of one's own.

At this point one may remark: The realization of a striving directed towards a bodily movement certainly does not consist in having a visual image of the movement, but consists in the experiencing of kinesthetic sensations, such as the sensations of muscle tension, friction of joints and so forth, as they occur in movements.

I shall reply to this remark by more precisely defining what has been said before. . . .

It lies in the nature of esthetic imitation that it aims chiefly at arousing the activity of the self. In the instinctive urge for self-activity lies its ultimate basis. But also it lies in the nature of the impulse to such imitation, that the desire for self-activity can be satisfied in the contemplation of the very movement that releases the desire for imitation.

So this desire needs no further satisfaction, and in particular not the satisfaction afforded by the kinesthetic events occurring in one's own body. The contemplation of the observed movement awakens the tendency to a corresponding self-activity; and by corresponding we mean that which would be connected with the execution of such a movement in my own person. And this tendency is at the same time realized in the act of contemplation. This takes place the more certainly, the more I am absorbed in the contemplation. The "absorption" liberates the above-mentioned tendency or removes in me the obstacles to its realization. Now, every tendency is realized when the obstacles to its realization are removed, or, speaking in positive terms, when the tendency is free, that is left to itself. For this is the meaning of tendency. . . .

In the perception of the other person's movement, I say, the tendency of the "corresponding" self-activity is awakened and satisfied. And this is why the satisfaction through the kinesthetic experiences is no longer needed. . . .

In esthetic imitation I become progressively less aware of muscular tensions or of sense-feelings in general the more I surrender in contemplation to the esthetic object. All such preoccupations disappear entirely from my consciousness. I am completely and wholly carried away from this sphere of my experience.

And it is not only so, it must be so. Sense-feelings are objective experiences and these of necessity compete with other objective experiences. And this means, for example, that the feelings of my bodily states must disappear from consciousness to the degree in which I am engrossed in the contemplation of the esthetic object—to which the states of my body simply cannot belong.

But this turning of consciousness away from the states of my body excludes certain possibilities: that the feeling of my bodily condition is identical with the feeling of activity which I obtain in esthetic contemplation; that the joy which I feel in view of the esthetic object is in truth, wholly or partially, joy in these bodily states; and lastly that my joy in the esthetic object *consists* wholly or in part in the feeling of these states. . . .

The beauty of an object is every time the beauty of this object and never the charm of anything that is not this beautiful object, or part of it. This means in particular that pleasure in the states of my body—a thing so different from the contemplated object and perhaps spatially far removed from it—cannot be felt by me as pleasure in this *object*. Pleasure from physical states is pleasure which I feel while I am paying attention to these states. To say that something is pleasurable means simply that I have a feeling of pleasure by being inwardly orientated towards it. But the pleasure which I feel while I am paying attention to my physical states or the processes in my physical organs cannot be identical, either wholly or in part, with the joy which I feel when I do not pay attention to the processes in my physical organs, but devote my whole attention to the esthetic object. In short, A cannot equal non-A.

Empathy means, not a sensation in one's body, but feeling something, namely, oneself, into the esthetic object.

Hitherto I have assumed that the object of the esthetic contemplation is a human movement, posture, or mien. But empathy is of the same nature in other cases, for example, in the contemplation of architectural forms. In viewing a large hall I feel an inner "expansion," my heart "expands"; I have this peculiar sense of what is happening within me. Connected with it are muscle-tensions, perhaps those involved in the expansion of the chest. To be sure, they do not exist for my consciousness, so long as my attention is directed to the spacious hall. But it is possible that this fact may not prevent an esthetician from confusing the feeling of inner expansion with this sensation of the body expanding with its muscle tensions. For in this case, as also when we refer to the thirst for water and the thirst for revenge and in very many other instances, common usage —and for good reasons—employs the same terms.

But all this means simply confusion of meanings. As a matter of truth, so far as I am concerned the sensations of my own bodily state are entirely absent in esthetic contemplation.

But perchance the sense-feelings which I impute to the *object* of contemplation, have some significance for esthetic enjoyment. This I must deny no less emphatically. When I see the sculptured image of a man in the act of rising, the sense-feelings which a real man would have who thus arises, do not exist for my esthetic contemplation, any more than my own sense-feelings so exist. What I immediately intuit in the plastic form is its willing, the power, the pride. Only this lies for my contemplation immediately in the contemplated object. And to the esthetic object belongs absolutely nothing but what lies immediately in the object of contemplation. The thought that also the sense-feelings would unquestionably appear in such a man if he were a real man, is an ingredient added by my reflection.

For the rest, such sense-feelings are simply uninteresting . . . unless they happen to be tormenting. And in the latter case it may also happen that I am conscious of them. Only this means the end of pure esthetic enjoyment.

If, for instance, I see a dancer dancing on tiptoe, my impression of the disagreeable feeling which she must have does intrude. Consequently I am hurled out of the state of esthetic contemplation. Not because of the unpleasantness of the feeling, but because of the feeling. Sorrow is also disagreeable, but the sorrow that I see in a figure does not arrest the esthetic contemplation. This sorrow is empathized.

A representation of a hungry man is not a representation of hunger; simply the manner in which he feels is represented. In esthetic contemplation I participate only in this emotional phase. But that the physical disturbance of hunger is ordinarily the cause of such a state of mind is an interpretation dictated by reason.

In short, sense-feelings, of whatever kind they may be, do not in any way enter into esthetic contemplation and into esthetic enjoyment. It absolutely belongs to the nature of esthetic contemplation to eliminate them.

And it is the duty of scientific esthetics and necessary for its sound development, that it gradually recover from this disease of preoccupation with sense-feelings.

—Archiv für die gesamte Psychologie, Vol. I (1903)

WILHELM WORRINGER

Abstraction and Empathy

The aim of the following discussion is to disprove the assumption that [the] process of empathy has been at all times and places the basis of artistic creation. With the theory of empathy in mind, we stand helpless in face of the artistic creations of many ages and nations. For the understanding of that vast complex of works of art which were produced outside the narrow limits of Greco-Roman and modern occidental art, it offers us no clue. Here we are forced to discern a quite different psychological process, which explains the peculiar quality of that style which is only negatively appreciated by us. Before we seek to characterize this process we must devote a few words to certain basic ideas of esthetics, because it is only by an agreement on these basic ideas that an understanding of what follows is possible.

Since the flowering-time of art history fell in the nineteenth century, the theories of the origin of the work of art were obviously based on a materialistic outlook. It need not be mentioned how healthy and rational was the effect of this attempt to penetrate into the essential nature of art, as a reaction against the speculative esthetics and esthetic beautiful-soulism of the eighteenth century. In this way an extremely valuable foundation was assured for the young science. A work like Semper's *Stil* remains an achievement of art history which, like every structure of thought built on a grand scale and fully elaborated, stands beyond the historical valuations of "true" and "false." [1]

Nevertheless this book with its materialistic theory of the origin of the work of art, which made its way into all circles and for decades until our own time was taken as the tacit presupposition of most researches in art history, is for us today an obstacle to progress and thought. All deeper penetration into the innermost nature of the work of art is obstructed by the excessive estimation of subordinate elements. And besides, not everyone who appeals to Semper has Semper's genius.

Everywhere there is a reaction against this flat and easy artistic materialism. The greatest breach in this system indeed was made by the Vienna scholar who died young, Alois Riegl, whose profound and masterly work on the late Roman art-industry—partly because of the difficulty of access to the publication—unfortunately did not gain the attention which, with its epoch-making importance, it deserved. [2]

Riegl for the first time introduced into the method of art-historical research the concept of the "artistic purpose." By the "absolute purpose of art" must be understood that latent inner demand which, totally independent of the object and the mode of creation, exists for itself and acts as the will to form. It is the primary element of all artistic creation and every work of art is in its innermost

[1] Gottfried Semper (1803-1879) is often referred to as a leading exponent of "esthetic materialism," but this term is a misnomer when applied to his doctrine as a whole. His principal work, *Der Stil in den technischen und tektonischen Künsten, oder Praktische Aesthetik,* 2 Vols., 1860-1863, is remarkable for its scope and profundity (Editor's note).

[2] My work at many points is based on the view of Riegl, as laid down in *Stilfragen* (1893) and in *Spätrömischen Kunstindustrie* (1901). An acquaintance with these works is very desirable, even if not absolutely necessary, for understanding my work. Even though the present writer does not agree with Riegl in all points, he stands on the same ground so far as the method of investigation is concerned, and owes to him the greatest stimulation.

essence but an objectification of this absolute art-purpose present *a priori*. The materialistic method of art, which, as must be expressly emphasized, is not to be simply identified with Gottfried Semper, but is based partly on a pedantic mis-interpretation of his work, saw in the primitive work of art a product of three factors: utilitarian purpose, raw material, and technique. The history of art was for it in the last resort a history of skill. The new view on the other hand regards the history of art as a history of artistic purpose, starting from the psychological presupposition that skill is only a phenomenon secondary to purpose. The peculiarities of style of past epochs are thus not to be traced to a deficiency of skill, but to a differently directed purpose. Thus what is decisive is what Riegl calls "the absolute purpose of art," which is only modified by those three factors, utilitarian purpose, raw material, and technique. "These three factors no longer have that positive creative role which the materialistic theory has attributed to them, but a hindering, negative role: they form, as it were, the coefficient of friction within the total product." (*Spätrömischen Kunstindustrie.*) [3]

In general we shall not understand why the concept of artistic purpose is given such an exclusive importance so long as we start with the naïve deep-rooted presupposition that the artistic purpose—that is, the impulse from which the work of art springs—has been the same at all times, subject only to certain variations which we call stylistic peculiarities, and that, so far as the plastic arts are concerned, the impulse has always been to approximate the natural proto-type. . . .

Every mode of regarding the history of art which consistently breaks with this one-sidedness is decried as artificial, as an affront to the "healthy human understanding." But what is this healthy human understanding if not the lazi-ness of our minds, which will hardly go beyond the small and limited range of our ideas and recognize the possibilities of other presuppositions. . . .

Before we go farther, let us clarify the relation of the imitation of nature to esthetics. It is necessary to agree on this, that the instinct of imitation, this ele-mentary need of man, stands outside of esthetics in the proper sense and that its satisfaction has in principle nothing to do with art.

But at this point it is well to distinguish between the instinct of imitation and naturalism as a type of art. . . . They are by no means identical and must be sharply distinguished, however difficult this may seem. Every confusion of ideas is in this regard of the most crucial importance. . . .

[3] *Cf.* Heinrich Wölfflin: "To deny a technical origin of particular forms, is naturally very far from my intention. The nature of the material, the mode of its working, the con-struction are never without influence. But what I should maintain—particularly as against several recent tendencies—is this, that technique never creates a style, but where we speak of art a definite feeling of form is always the primary element. The technically produced forms must not contradict this feeling of form; they can continue to exist only where they accommodate themselves to the form-taste which is already present." (*Renaissance und Barock,* 2nd ed., p. 57.)

The primitive instinct of imitation has prevailed in all ages and its history is a history of manual skill without esthetic significance. In the very earliest ages this instinct was quite separate from the artistic impulse in the true sense; it satisfied itself especially in miniature art, as in those small idols and symbolic trifles which we know from all early art-epochs, and which often enough stand in direct contrast to the creations in which the purely artistic impulse of the peoples in question manifested itself. We remember how for example in Egypt the imitative instinct and the artistic impulse developed side by side, simultaneously but separately. While the so-called folk-art with startling realism created such well-known statues as the "Scribe" or the "Country Judge," the true art, falsely called "court art," showed a strict style which departed from all realism. That here there can be no question either of crudity or of stiffness, and that a certain psychological instinct demanded satisfaction, will be maintained in the further course of our discussions. True art has at all times satisfied a deep psychological need, but not the pure instinct of imitation, the petty pleasure of copying the natural prototype. The glory which crowns the concept of art, all the admiring devotion which it has enjoyed in all ages, can be psychologically explained only as we think of an art which, arising from psychological needs, satisfies psychological needs. . . .

The worth of an art-work, which we call its beauty, lies generally speaking in its values as a means to happiness. These values stand naturally in a causal relation to the psychological needs which they satisfy. The "absolute purpose of art" is thus the index to the quality of those psychological needs.

A psychology of the need of art—that is to say, from our modern standpoint, the need of style—has not yet been written. It would be a history of world-feeling (Weltgefühl) and as such would have an equal rank by the side of the history of religion. By world-feeling I understand the psychological state with which humanity confronts the cosmos, the phenomena of the external world. This state betrays itself in the quality of psychological needs, that is, in the nature of the absolute purpose of art and finds its external precipitate in the work of art, namely, in the style itself, whose peculiarity is just the peculiarity of the psychological need. Thus in the evolution of artistic style the various gradations of the so-called world-feeling may be read off just as in the theogony of peoples.

Every style represents for mankind, who created it out of its psychological needs, the highest happiness. This must become the prime article of belief for all objective consideration of the history of art. What from our standpoint appears as the grossest distortion must have been for its producer the highest beauty and the fulfillment of his artistic purpose. Thus from our standpoint, that of our modern esthetics, which gives its judgments exclusively in the sense of Greco-Roman antiquity or of the Renaissance, all valuations from a higher standpoint are inanities and platitudes.

After this necessary digression we return to the starting-point, namely, to the thesis of the limited applicability of the theory of empathy.

The need of empathy may be regarded as the presupposition of the artistic purpose only where this purpose inclines to the truth of organic life, that is, to naturalism in the higher sense. The feeling of happiness, which is revived in us by the expression of organic vitality, what modern man calls beauty, is a satisfaction of that inner need of self-exercise, in which Lipps sees the presupposition of the process of empathy. We enjoy ourselves in the forms of a work of art. Esthetic enjoyment is objectified self-enjoyment. The value of a line, of a form, consists for us in the value of the life which it contains for us. It keeps its beauty only through our vital feeling, which we obscurely project into it.

The recollection of the inorganic form of a pyramid, or of the suppression of life exemplified in Byzantine mosaics, tells us at once that the need of empathy, which for obvious reasons always inclines to the organic, cannot possibly have determined the artistic purpose. Indeed we are compelled to think that here there is an impulse which is directly opposed to the impulse of empathy and which seeks to suppress just that in which the need of empathy finds its satisfaction.[4]

The tendency to abstraction appears to us as the polar opposite of the need of empathy. To analyze it and to establish the significance which it assumes in the development of art, is the primary task of the present work. . . .

We find that the artistic purpose of uncivilized peoples, so far as they have such a thing at all, the artistic purpose of all primitive art-epochs, and finally the artistic purpose of certain peoples of Oriental culture, exhibits this abstract tendency. The tendency to abstraction is thus dominant in the initial stage of all art, and remains so with certain peoples at higher levels of culture, while, for example, among the Greeks and other Occidentals it gradually expires to make way for the tendency to empathy.

Now what are the psychological presuppositions of the tendency to abstraction? We have to seek them in the world-feeling of those peoples, in their psychological relation to the cosmos. While the tendency of empathy has as its condition a happy pantheistic relation of confidence between man and the phenomena of the external world, the tendency to abstraction is the result of a great inner conflict between man and his surroundings, and corresponds in religion to a strongly transcendental coloring of all ideas. This state we might call a prodigious mental fear of space. Tibullus says: "First in the world God made fear"; this same feeling of anxiety can be considered the root of artistic creation.

A comparison with that physical dread of open spaces, which as a disease

---

[4] That we today can empathize ourselves even into the form of a pyramid is not to be denied, and in general the possibility of an empathy into abstract forms, of which much will be said later, should not be denied. But everything contradicts the supposition that this impulse of empathy was effective in the creators of the pyramidal form. . . .

afflicts certain persons, will perhaps explain more fully what we understand by the psychological fear of space. This physical dread may be popularly regarded as a vestige of a normal stage of human evolution, in which man, trying to become accustomed to surrounding space, could not rely on visual impressions alone, but still needed to be reassured by his sense of touch. As soon as he became a biped and thus for the first time appeared in human form, a slight feeling of insecurity must have remained. But in his further evolution he freed himself, by habit and intellectual reflection, from this primitive anxiety toward immense space.[5]

With the psychological fear of space before the vast, incoherent, bewildering world of phenomena, the case is similar. The rationalistic development of mankind repressed that instinctive anxiety which results from the lost state of man within the world-whole. Only the civilized Oriental peoples, whose deeper world-instinct opposed such a rationalistic development, and who always saw in the phenomenal world only the glistening veil of Maya, remained conscious of the inextricable confusion of all the phenomena of life, and thus were not under the illusion of any intellectual external domination over the cosmos. . . .

Vexed by the confused connection and interplay of external phenomena, such peoples were dominated by a great need of rest. The possibility of happiness, which they sought in art, did not consist in immersing themselves in the things of the external world, to enjoy themselves in them, but in freeing the particular thing in the outer world from its arbitrariness and apparent contingency, immortalizing it by approximation to abstract forms, and in this way finding a resting-place in the flight of phenomena. Their strongest impulse was, as it were, to tear the external object out of the context of nature, out of the endless interplay of existence, to purify it of all dependence on life, all arbitrariness, to make it necessary and stable, to make it approximate to its absolute value. Where they attained this, they felt that happiness and satisfaction which the beauty of the form full of organic vitality imparts to us; indeed they knew only one kind of beauty and thus we must call it their beauty.

Riegl says in his *Stilfragen:* "The geometrical style, strictly constructed according to the primary laws of symmetry and rhythm, is from the standpoint of regularity the most perfect. But in our estimation it stands the lowest, and even the historical development of the arts teaches us that this style has mostly been peculiar to peoples at a time when they remained at a relatively lower state of civilization."

If we consider this proposition, which indeed minimizes the role which

---

[5] In this connection we may recollect that the fear of space manifests itself clearly in Egyptian architecture. By countless columns, which have no constructive function, it was sought to destroy the impression of free space and to steady man's helpless gaze. *Cf.* Riegl, *Spätrömische Kunstindustrie,* Chap. I.

geometric style has played with peoples of advanced culture, we are faced with this fact: the style which is most perfect in its regularity, the style of the highest abstraction, the strictest exclusion of life, is peculiar to peoples at their most primitive stage of culture. Thus there must be a causal connection between primitive culture and the highest, most purely regular form of art. And we may further set up the principle that the less the human race, by virtue of its spiritual perception, is on friendly and trustful terms with the external object, the more powerful is the dynamic force from which that highest abstract beauty springs.

Not that primitive man sought more strenuously for regularity in nature or felt regularity more strongly in it, quite the contrary: because he stands so lost and spiritually helpless among the things of the external world, because he feels only mystery and arbitrariness in the connection and interplay of external phenomena, the impulse is so strong in him to release the things of the external world from their arbitrariness and obscurity, to give them the value of necessity and the value of regularity. To make use of a bold comparison: in primitive man, as it were, the instinct for the "thing in itself" is most powerful. The increasing spiritual domination over the external world and the force of habit signify a deadening, a dulling of this instinct. Only after the human spirit, in an evolution of thousands of years, has traversed the whole path of rationalistic understanding, there awakens anew in man, as he gives up the attempt at ultimate knowledge, the feeling for the "thing in itself." What was previously instinct is now the final product of understanding. Cast down from the pride of knowledge, man now stands again quite as lost and helpless in face of the cosmos as primitive man, after he has recognized "that this visible world in which we find ourselves is the work of Maya, a spell, an appearance without consistency and in itself without substance, to be compared to an optical illusion or a dream, a veil which surrounds the human consciousness, a something of which it is as false and as true to say 'that it is, as that it is not.'" (Schopenhauer, *Kritik der Kantischen Philosophie.*)

But this perception was artistically unfruitful, since man had already become an individual and had released himself from the mass. Only the dynamic force which resides in an undifferentiated mass held together by a common instinct could have created those forms of the highest abstract beauty. The individual standing alone was too weak for such abstraction.

We would misinterpret the psychological conditions of the origin of this abstract art-form if we were to say that the yearning for regularity made men consciously grasp at geometrical regularity, for this would presuppose an intellectual preoccupation with geometrical form, would make it appear a product of deliberation and calculation. We are much more justified in assuming that here we have a purely instinctive creation, that the tendency to abstraction has created this form with elementary necessity without the intervention of the intellect. Just because the intellect had not yet disturbed the instinct, the innate disposition toward regularity could find abstract expression. . . .

These abstract regular forms are thus the only and the highest forms in which man can rest in face of the immense confusion of the cosmos. . . . The plain and simple line and its elaboration with purely geometrical regularity must have offered the greatest possibility of happiness for men disturbed by the obscurity and confusion of phenomena. For here the last vestige of connection with and dependence upon life is wiped out; here the highest absolute form, the purest abstraction is attained; here there is law, there is necessity, where otherwise the arbitrariness of the organic prevails. But such abstraction does not now serve as the prototype of any natural object. "From the natural object the geometrical line is distinguished just by this, that it does not stand in the context of nature. What constitutes its essence belongs indeed to nature; the mechanical forces are forces of nature. But in the geometrical line and geometrical forms they are taken altogether out of the context of nature and the endless interplay of natural forces and accentuated for themselves." (Lipps, *Aesthetik*, p. 249.)

This pure abstraction could naturally never be attained when an actual natural prototype was the model. Therefore the question arises: How does the impulse to abstraction stand in relation to external objects? We have already emphasized that it was not the imitative instinct—the history of the imitative instinct is something else than the history of art—that required the artistic rendering of a natural prototype. Instead we see in this abstract art the effort to release the individual external object, so far as it arouses a special interest, from its connection with and dependence on other things, to snatch it from the stream of transiency, to make it absolute. . . .

A decisive consequence of such an artistic purpose was on the one hand the approximation to flat representation, and on the other hand strict suppression of the representation of space and exclusive rendering of the individual form.

Men were impelled toward flat representation because three-dimensionality is the greatest obstacle to a grasp of the object in its self-enclosed material individuality. Its perception as three-dimensional requires a sequence of connected moments of perception in which the separate individuality of the object dissolves. Then too, on the other hand, the dimensions of depth betray themselves only by foreshortenings and shadows; hence their comprehension requires a strong cooperation of understanding and habit. Thus in both respects the independence of outer things is disturbed by a subjective interpretation whose avoidance was as far as possible the task of the peoples of ancient culture.

The suppression of space-representation was for this reason a dictate of the tendency to abstraction; because it is space itself which connects things with one another, which gives them their relativity in the cosmos, and because space does not permit itself to be individualized. Thus so far as a sensible object is still dependent on space, it cannot appear to us in its isolated material individuality. All effort was thus directed to the individual form redeemed from space.

Now if we repeat the formula which we found as the basis of empathic experience: "Esthetic enjoyment is objectified self-enjoyment," we are at once aware of the polar opposition between these two forms of esthetic enjoyment [that is, abstraction and empathy]. On the one hand, the I as a disturbing force, an obstacle to the happiness that might be found in the work of art; on the other hand, the inmost connection between the I and the work of art, which takes all its life from the I alone.

This dualism of esthetic experience . . . is not final. These two poles are only different expressions of one common need, which reveals itself to us as the deepest and ultimate essence of all esthetic experience: that is the need of self-privation.

In the tendency to abstraction, the intensity of the impulse of self-privation is much greater and more consistent. Here it is characterized, not as in the case of the need for empathy as a tendency to part with one's separate individuality, but as a tendency, in the contemplation of something necessary and immutable, to escape from the accidental in human existence in general, from the apparent arbitrariness of organic existence. Life as such is felt as the disturber of esthetic enjoyment.

That even the need for empathy, as the starting-point of esthetic experience, represents at bottom an impulse to self-privation, will be all the more incomprehensible to us at first glance since we still have ringing in our ears that formula: "Esthetic enjoyment is objectified self-enjoyment." For these words assert that the process of empathy represents a self-affirmation, an affirmation of the universal will to activity which is in us. "We have always a need for self-exercise. This is indeed the fundamental need of our nature." But while we empathically project our will to activity into another object, we are *in* that other object. We are released from our individual existence so long as we with our inner impulse to experience are absorbed in an external object, in an external form. We feel as if our individuality were flowing within fixed limits as against the limitless differentiation of the individual consciousness. In this self-objectification lies self-privation. This affirmation of our individual need of activity represents at the same time a restriction of its illimitable possibilities, a denial of its boundless differentiations. We rest with our inner impulse to activity within the limits of this objectification. "Thus in empathy I am not the real I, but am inwardly released from this ego; that is, I am released from all that I am apart from the contemplation of form. I am only this ideal I, this contemplating I." (Lipps, *Aesthetik*, p. 247.) Common parlance speaks pertinently of a losing of the self in the contemplation of a work of art.

Thus in this sense it cannot be too strongly emphasized that all esthetic enjoyment, as perhaps even all human feeling of happiness in general, is to be traced back to the impulse of self-privation as its deepest and ultimate essence. . . .[6]

—Abstraktion und Einfühlung (1908: twelfth edition, 1921)

[6] Schopenhauer's esthetics offers an analogy to such a conception. For Schopenhauer the happiness of esthetic contemplation consists in just this, that in it man is released from his individuality, from his will, and remains only as a pure subject, as a clear mirror of the object. "And just thereby is the one engaged in such contemplation no longer an individual, for this individual has in just such contemplation lost himself: but he is the pure, will-less, painless, timeless subject of perception." (*Cf.* the third book of *The World as Will and Idea.*)

CHAPTER THIRTEEN

Distance and Dehumanization

EDWARD BULLOUGH
"Psychical Distance" as a Factor in Art
and an Esthetic Principle

JOSÉ ORTEGA Y GASSET
The Dehumanization of Art

KENNETH CLARK
The Naked and the Nude

Introductory Note

SINCE THE PUBLICATION OF Kant's *Critique of Judgment, disinterestedness* (which of course is not *un*interestedness) has been commonly recognized as characteristic of the esthetic attitude. The object of an *"entirely disinterested . . . satisfaction,"* declared Kant, "is called beautiful." [1] Such detachment from practical interests is emphasized by Edward Bullough (1880-1934), a distinguished British psychologist, in his concept of "psychical distance." Esthetic distance, he explains, has two aspects: First, there is a negative, inhibitory side— which consists of "a putting of the object out of gear with our practical needs

[1] Kant, *Critique of Judgment* (translated by J. H. Bernard) (Macmillan, London, 1931), p. 55.

and ends." Second, there is a positive side—"the elaboration of the experience on the new basis created by the inhibitory action of distance." This positive aspect consists in the objectification of one's mental states. The contemplator's feelings are interpreted not as modes of his being but as characteristics of the object.

Distance, being a matter of degree, varies according to two different sets of conditions: the characteristics of the object, and the attitudes of the subject. As the object becomes more stylized, unrealistic, and isolated, the distance correspondingly increases. As the contemplator independently adopts a more impersonal attitude, the distance again increases proportionately. The right mean consists of "the utmost decrease of distance without its disappearance," that is, the maximum personal appeal compatible with distance—a rule which Bullough calls the "antinomy of distance."

A somewhat different theory of esthetic distance is formulated by the famous Spanish philosopher, José Ortega y Gasset (1883-   ). Far from accepting Bullough's "antinomy of distance," he defends the extreme increase of detachment in recent art. The tendency of modern artists, he thinks, is to return to the "royal road of art," which is "the Will to Style"; and stylistic art is highly distanced art. Whereas Bullough believes that art of great distance characterizes periods of a low level of general culture, Ortega believes that the choice of such art is a mark of intellectual aristocracy. He welcomes the new art as a harbinger of the coming time when, as he believes, "society in politics, as well as in art, will manage to organize itself, as it should be, in two orders or ranks, that of the superior and that of the ordinary men." His aristocratic point of view stands in interesting contrast to the democratic ideals expressed by Tolstoy, Whitehead, and Mumford elsewhere in this volume.

The result of high distancing, declares Ortega, is a rejection of the "human" in art. The idea of "dehumanization," which is obviously akin to Worringer's concept of "abstraction," has been vigorously challenged by Sir Kenneth Clark (1903-   ), formerly Professor of Fine Arts at Oxford and eminent art historian. In his remarkable study of the nude as an art-form (originally presented as the A. W. Mellon Lectures at the National Art Gallery in Washington, D. C.), Clark maintains that the idea of the inhumanity of the work of art is false and enervating. No man can divest himself of his essential humanity, and he should not try. If he should attempt to cut himself off from his body, or divorce himself from his deepest instincts, he will only divide his own nature and destroy the vitality of his art. But the esthetic impulse is no mere attempt to grasp things as they are. "We do not wish to imitate, we wish to perfect." The *ideal* of the oneness of the spirit and body stimulated the Greeks to their highest artistic achievements. The esthetic attitude, so interpreted, is neither an intense participation nor an absolute detachment—it is neither low nor high distance—it is a balance between the two, a synthesis of contraries.

EDWARD BULLOUGH

"Psychical Distance" and a Factor in Art and an Esthetic Principle

I. 1. Meaning of the term "Distance."
   2. Distance as a factor in Art.
   3. Distance as an esthetic principle.
II. 1. Distance describes a personal relation.
   2. The antinomy of Distance.
   3. The variability of Distance.
   4. Distance as the psychological formulation of the antirealism of Art: naturalistic and idealistic Art.
   5. Distance as applied to the antithesis "sensual" and "spiritual."
   6. Distance as applied to the antithesis "individualistic" and "typical."

I

1. The conception of "Distance" suggests, in connection with Art, certain trains of thought by no means devoid of interest or of speculative importance. Perhaps the most obvious suggestion is that of *actual spatial* distance, that is, the distance of a work of Art from the spectator, or that of *represented spatial* distance, that is, the distance represented within the work. Less obvious, more metaphorical, is the meaning of *temporal* distance. The first was noticed already by Aristotle in his *Poetics;* the second has played a great part in the history of painting in the form of perspective; the distinction between these two kinds of distance assumes special importance theoretically in the differentiation between sculpture in the round, and relief-sculpture. Temporal distance, remoteness from us in point of time, though often a cause of misconceptions, has been declared to be a factor of considerable weight in our appreciation.

It is not, however, in any of these meanings that "Distance" is put forward here, though it will be clear in the course of this essay that the above mentioned kinds of distance are rather special forms of the conception of Distance as advocated here, and derive whatever *esthetic* qualities they may possess from Distance in its general connotation. This general connotation is "Psychical Distance."

A short illustration will explain what is meant by "Psychical Distance." Imagine a fog at sea: for most people it is an experience of acute unpleasantness. Apart from the physical annoyance and remoter forms of discomfort such as delays, it is apt to produce feelings of peculiar anxiety, fears of invisible dangers, strains of watching and listening for distance and unlocalized signals. The listless movements of the ship and her warning calls soon tell upon the nerves of the passengers; and that special, expectant, tacit anxiety and nervousness, always associated with this experience, make a fog the dreaded terror of the sea (all the more terrifying because of its very silence and gentleness) for the expert sea-farer no less than for the ignorant landsman.

Nevertheless, a fog at sea can be a source of intense relish and enjoyment. Abstract from the experience of the sea fog, for the moment, its danger and practical unpleasantness, just as every one in the enjoyment of a mountain-climb disregards its physical labor and its danger (though, it is not denied, that these may incidentally enter into the enjoyment and enhance it); direct the at-tention to the features "objectively" constituting the phenomenon—the veil surrounding you with an opaqueness as of transparent milk, blurring the outline of things and distorting their shapes into weird grotesqueness; observe the car-rying-power of the air, producing the impression as if you could touch some far-off siren by merely putting out your hand and letting it lose itself behind that white wall; note the curious creamy smoothness of the water, hypocritically denying as it were any suggestion of danger; and, above all, the strange solitude and remoteness from the world, as it can be found only on the highest moun-tain tops; and the experience may acquire, in its uncanny mingling of repose and terror, a flavor of such concentrated poignancy and delight as to contrast sharply with the blind and distempered anxiety of its other aspects. This con-trast, often emerging with startling suddenness, is like a momentary switching on of some new current, or the passing ray of a brighter light, illuminating the outlook upon perhaps the most ordinary and familiar objects—an impression which we experience sometimes in instants of direst extremity, when our prac-tical interest snaps like a wire from sheer over-tension, and we watch the con-summation of some impending catastrophe with the marveling unconcern of a mere spectator.

It is a difference of outlook, due—if such a metaphor is permissible—to the insertion of Distance. This Distance appears to lie between our own self and its affections, using the latter term in its broadest sense as anything which affects our being, bodily or spiritually, for example, as sensation, perception, emotional state or idea. Usually, though not always, it amounts to the same thing to say that the Distance lies between our own self and such objects as are the sources or vehicles of such affections.

Thus, in the fog, the transformation by Distance is produced in the first instance by putting the phenomenon, so to speak, out of gear with our practical, actual self; by allowing it to stand outside the context of our personal needs and ends—in short, by looking at it "objectively," as it has often been called, by permitting only such reactions on our part as emphasize the "objective" features

396 · DISTANCE AND DEHUMANIZATION

of the experience, and by interpreting even our "subjective" affections not as modes of *our* being but rather as characteristics of the phenomenon.

The working of Distance is, accordingly, not simple, but highly complex. It has a *negative,* inhibitory aspect—the cutting-out of the practical sides of things and of our practical attitude to them—and a *positive* side—the elaboration of the experience on the new basis created by the inhibitory action of Distance.

2. Consequently, this distanced view of things is not, and cannot be, our normal outlook. As a rule, experiences constantly turn the same side towards us, namely, that which has the strongest practical force of appeal. We are not ordinarily aware of those aspects of things which do not touch us immediately and practically, nor are we generally conscious of impressions apart from our own self which is impressed. The sudden view of things from their reverse, usually unnoticed, side, comes upon us as a revelation, and such revelations are precisely those of Art. In this most general sense, Distance is a factor in all Art.

3. It is, for this very reason, also an esthetic principle. The esthetic contemplation and the esthetic outlook have often been described as "objective." We speak of "objective" artists as Shakespeare or Velasquez, of "objective" works or art forms as Homer's *Iliad* or the drama. It is a term constantly occurring in discussions and criticisms, though its sense, if pressed at all, becomes very questionable. For certain forms of Art, such as lyrical poetry, are said to be "subjective"; Shelley, for example, would usually be considered a "subjective" writer. On the other hand, no work of Art can be genuinely "objective" in the sense in which this term might be applied to a work on history or to a scientific treatise; nor can it be "subjective" in the ordinary acceptance of that term, as a personal feeling, a direct statement of a wish or belief, or a cry of passion is subjective. "Objectivity" and "subjectivity" are a pair of opposites which in their mutual exclusiveness when applied to Art soon lead to confusion.

Nor are they the only pair of opposites. Art has with equal vigor been declared alternately "idealistic" and "realistic," "sensual" and "spiritual," "individualistic" and "typical." Between the defense of either terms of such antitheses most esthetic theories have vacillated. It is one of the contentions of this essay that such opposites find their synthesis in the more fundamental conception of Distance.

Distance further provides the much needed criterion of the beautiful as distinct from the merely agreeable.

Again, it marks one of the most important steps in the process of artistic creation and serves as a distinguishing feature of what is commonly so loosely described as the "artistic temperament."

Finally, it may claim to be considered as one of the essential characteristics of the "esthetic consciousness"—if I may describe by this term that special mental attitude towards, and outlook upon, experience, which finds its most pregnant expression in the various forms of Art.

II

Distance, as I said before, is obtained by separating the object and its appeal from one's own self, by putting it out of gear with practical needs and ends. Thereby the "contemplation" of the object becomes alone possible. But it does not mean that the relation between the self and the object is broken to the extent of becoming "impersonal." Of the alternatives "personal" and "impersonal" the latter surely comes nearer to the truth; but here, as elsewhere, we meet the difficulty of having to express certain facts in terms coined for entirely different uses. To do so usually results in paradoxes, which are nowhere more inevitable than in discussions upon Art. "Personal" and "impersonal," "subjective" and "objective" are such terms, devised for purposes other than esthetic speculation; and becoming loose and ambiguous as soon as applied outside the sphere of their special meanings. In giving preference therefore to the term "impersonal" to describe the relation between the spectator and a work of Art, it is to be noticed that it is not impersonal in the sense in which we speak of the "impersonal" character of Science, for instance. In order to obtain "objectively valid" results, the scientist excludes the "personal factor," that is, his personal wishes as to the validity of his results, his predilection for any particular system to be proved or disproved by his research. It goes without saying that all experiments and investigations are undertaken out of a personal interest in the science, for the ultimate support of a definite assumption, and involve personal hopes of success; but this does not affect the "dispassionate" attitude of the investigator, under pain of being accused of "manufacturing his evidence."

1. Distance does not imply an impersonal, purely intellectually interested relation of such a kind. On the contrary, it describes a *personal* relation, often highly emotionally colored, but of a *peculiar character*. Its peculiarity lies in that the personal character of the relation has been, so to speak, filtered. It has been cleared of the practical, concrete nature of its appeal, without, however, thereby losing its original constitution. One of the best-known examples is to be found in our attitude towards the events and characters of the drama: they appeal to us like persons and incidents of normal experience, except that that side of their appeal, which would usually affect us in a directly personal manner, is held in abeyance. This difference, so well known as to be almost trivial, is generally explained by reference to the knowledge that the characters and situations are "unreal," imaginary. . . . But, as a matter of fact, the "assumption" upon which the imaginative emotional reaction is based is not necessarily the condition, but often the consequence, of Distance; that is to say, the converse of the reason usually stated would then be true: namely, that Distance, by changing our relation to the characters, renders them seemingly fictitious, not that the fictitousness of the characters alters our feelings toward them. It is, of course, to be granted that the actual and admitted unreality of the dramatic action reinforces

the effect of Distance. But surely the proverbial unsophisticated yokel whose chivalrous interference in the play on behalf of the hapless heroine can only be prevented by impressing upon him that "they are only pretending," is not the ideal type of theatrical audience. The proof of the seeming paradox that it is Distance which primarily gives to dramatic action the appearance of unreality and not *vice versa,* is the observation that the same filtration of our sentiments and the same seeming "unreality" of *actual* men and things occur, when at times, by a sudden change of inward perspective, we are overcome by the feeling that "all the world's a stage."

2. This personal but "distanced" relation (as I will venture to call this nameless character of our view) directs attention to a strange fact which appears to be one of the fundamental paradoxes of Art: it is what I propose to call "the antinomy of Distance."

It will be readily admitted that a work of Art has the more chance of appealing to us the better it finds us prepared for its particular kind of appeal. Indeed, without some degree of predisposition on our part, it must necessarily remain incomprehensible, and to that extent unappreciated. The success and intensity of its appeal would seem, therefore, to stand in direct proportion to the completeness with which it corresponds with our intellectual and emotional peculiarities and the idiosyncrasies of our experience. The absence of such a concordance between the characters of a work and of the spectator is, of course, the most general explanation for differences of "tastes."

At the same time, such a principle of concordance requires a qualification, which leads at once to the antinomy of Distance.

Suppose a man who believes that he has cause to be jealous about his wife, witnesses a performance of *Othello.* He will the more perfectly appreciate the situation, conduct and character of Othello, the more exactly the feelings and experiences of Othello coincide with his own—at least he *ought* to on the above principle of concordance. In point of fact, he will probably do anything but appreciate the play. In reality, the concordance will merely render him acutely conscious of his own jealousy; by a sudden reversal of perspective he will no longer see Othello apparently betrayed by Desdemona, but himself in an analogous situation with his own wife. This reversal of perspective is the consequence of the loss of Distance.

If this be taken as a typical case, it follows that the qualification required is that the coincidence should be as complete as is compatible with maintaining Distance. The jealous spectator of *Othello* will indeed appreciate and enter into the play the more keenly, the greater the resemblance with his own experience— *provided* that he succeeds in keeping the Distance between the action of the play and his personal feelings: a very difficult performance in the circumstances. It is on account of the same difficulty that the expert and the professional critic make a bad audience, since their expertness and critical professionalism are

practical activities, involving their concrete personality and constantly endanger-
ing their Distance. (It is, by the way, one of the reasons why Criticism is an art,
for it requires the constant interchange from the practical to the distanced attitude
and *vice versa,* which is characteristic of artists.)

The same qualification applies to the artist. He will prove artistically most
effective in the formulation of an intensely *personal* experience, but he can
formulate it artistically only on condition of a detachment from the experience
qua personal. Hence the statement of so many artists that artistic formulation was
to them a kind of catharsis, a means of ridding themselves of feelings and ideas
the acuteness of which they felt almost as a kind of obsession. Hence, on the
other hand, the failure of the average man to convey to others at all adequately
the impression of an overwhelming joy or sorrow. His personal implication in the
event renders it impossible for him to formulate and present it in such a way as to
make others, like himself, feel all the meaning and fullness which it possesses for
him.

What is therefore, both in appreciation and production, most desirable is
the *utmost decrease of Distance without its disappearance.*

3. Closely related, in fact a presupposition to the "antinomy," is the *variability of Distance.* Herein especially lies the advantage of Distance compared
with such terms as "objectivity" and "detachment." Neither of them implies a
personal relation—indeed both actually preclude it; and the mere inflexibility and
exclusiveness of their opposites render their application generally meaningless.

Distance, on the contrary, admits naturally of degrees, and differs not only
according to the nature of the *object,* which may impose a greater or smaller
degree of Distance, but varies also according to the *individual's capacity* for maintaining a greater or lesser degree. And here one may remark that not only do
persons differ from each other in their habitual measure of Distance, but that
the *same individual differs* in his ability to maintain it in the face of different
objects and of different arts.

There exist, therefore, two different sets of conditions affecting the degree
of Distance in any given case: those offered by the object and those realized by
the subject. In their interplay they afford one of the most extensive explanations
for varieties of esthetic experience, since loss of Distance, whether due to the one
or the other, means loss of esthetic appreciation.

In short, Distance may be said to be *variable both according to the distanc-
ing-power of the individual, and according to the character of the object.*

There are two ways of losing Distance: either to "under-distance" or to
"over-distance." "Under-distancing" is the commonest failing of the *subject,* an
excess of Distance is a frequent failing of Art, especially in the past. Historically
it looks almost as if Art had attempted to meet the deficiency of Distance on the
part of the subject and had overshot the mark in this endeavor. It will be seen
later that this is actually true, for it appears that over-distanced Art is specially

designed for a class of appreciation which has difficulty to rise spontaneously to any degree of Distance. The consequence of a loss of Distance through one or other cause is familiar: the verdict in the case of under-distancing is that the work is "crudely naturalistic," "harrowing," "repulsive in its realism." An excess of Distance produces the impression of improbability, artificiality, emptiness or absurdity.

The individual tends, as I just stated, to under-distance rather than to lose Distance by over-distancing. *Theoretically* there is no limit to the decrease of Distance. In theory, therefore, not only the usual subjects of Art, but even the most personal affections, whether ideas, percepts, or emotions, can be sufficiently distanced to be esthetically appreciable. Especially artists are gifted in this direction to a remarkable extent. The average individual, on the contrary, very rapidly reaches his limit of decreasing Distance, his "Distance-limit," that is, that point at which Distance is lost and appreciation either disappears or changes its character.

In the *practice*, therefore, of the average person, a limit does exist which marks the minimum at which his appreciation can maintain itself in the esthetic field, and this average minimum lies considerably higher than the Distance-limit of the artist. It is practically impossible to fix this average limit, in the absence of data, and on account of the wide fluctuations from person to person to which this limit is subject. But it is safe to infer that, in art practice, explicit references to organic affections, to the material existence of the body, especially to sexual matters, lies normally below the Distance-limit, and can be touched upon by Art only with special precautions. Allusions to social institutions of any degree of personal importance—in particular, allusions implying any doubt as to their validity—the questioning of some generally recognized ethical sanctions, references to topical subjects occupying public attention at the moment, and such like, are all dangerously near the average limit and may at any time fall below it, arousing, instead of esthetic appreciation, concrete hostility or mere amusement.

This difference in the Distance-limit between artists and the public has been the source of much misunderstanding and injustice. Many an artist has seen his work condemned, and himself ostracized for the sake of so-called "immoralities" which to him were *bona fide* esthetic objects. His power of distancing, nay, the necessity of distancing feelings, sensations, situations which for the average person are too intimately bound up with his concrete existence to be regarded in that light, have often quite unjustly earned for him accusations of cynicism, sensualism, morbidness, or frivolity. The same misconception has arisen over many "problem plays" and "problem novels" in which the public have persisted in seeing nothing but a supposed "problem" of the moment, whereas the author may have been—and often has demonstrably been—able to distance the subject matter sufficiently to rise above its practical problematic import and to regard it simply as a dramatically and humanly interesting situation.

The variability of Distance in respect to Art, disregarding for the moment the subjective complication, appears both as a general feature in Art, and in the differences between the special arts.

It has been an old problem why the "arts of the eye and of the ear" should have reached the practically exclusive predominance over arts of other senses. Attempts to raise "culinary art" to the level of a Fine Art have failed in spite of all propaganda, as completely as the creation of scent or liquor "symphonies." There is little doubt that, apart from other excellent reasons of a partly psycho-physical, partly technical nature, the actual, *spatial distance* separating objects of sight and hearing from the subject has contributed strongly to the development of this monopoly. In a similar manner *temporal remoteness* produces Distance, and objects removed from us in point of time are *ipso facto* distanced to an extent which was impossible for their contemporaries. Many pictures, plays, and poems had, as a matter of fact, rather an expository or illustrative significance— as for instance much ecclesiastical Art—or the force of a direct practical appeal —as the invectives of many satires or comedies—which seem to us nowadays irreconcilable with their esthetic claims. Such works have consequently profited greatly by lapse of time and have reached the level of Art only with the help of temporal distance, while others, on the contrary, often for the same reason have suffered a loss of Distance, through *over*-distancing.

Special mention must be made of a group of artistic conceptions which present excessive Distance in their form of appeal rather than in their actual presentation—a point illustrating the necessity of distinguishing between distancing an object and distancing the appeal of which it is the source. I mean here what is often rather loosely termed "idealistic Art," that is, Art springing from abstract conceptions, expressing allegorical meanings, or illustrating general truths. Generalizations and abstractions suffer under this disadvantage that they have too much general applicability to invite a personal interest in them, and too little individual concreteness to prevent them applying to us in all their force. They appeal to everybody and therefore to none. An axiom of Euclid belongs to nobody, just because it compels every one's assent; general conceptions like Patriotism, Friendship, Love, Hope, Life, Death, concern as much Dick, Tom and Harry as myself, and I, therefore, either feel unable to get into any kind of personal relation to them, or, if I do so, they become at once, emphatically and concretely, *my* Patriotism, *my* Friendship, *my* Love, *my* Hope, *my* Life and Death. By mere force of generalization, a general truth or a universal ideal is so far distanced from myself that I fail to realize it concretely at all, or, when I do so, I can realize it only as part of my *practical actual being*, that is, it falls below the Distance-limit altogether. "Idealistic Art" suffers consequently under the peculiar difficulty that its excess of Distance turns generally into an *under*-distanced appeal—all the more easily, as it is the usual failing of the subject to *under*- rather than to *over*-distance.

The different special arts show at the present time very marked variations in the degree of Distance which they usually impose or require for their appreciation. Unfortunately here again the absence of data makes itself felt and indicates the necessity of conducting observations, possibly experiments, so as to place these suggestions upon a securer basis. In one single art, namely, the *theater*, a small amount of information is available, from an unexpected source, namely the proceedings of the censorship committee,[1] which on closer examination might be made to yield evidence of interest to the psychologist. In fact, the whole censorship problem, as far as it does not turn upon purely economic questions, may be said to hinge upon Distance; if every member of the public could be trusted to keep it, there would be no sense whatever in the existence of a censor of plays. There is, of course, no doubt that, speaking generally, theatrical performances *eo ipso* run a special risk of a loss of Distance owing to the material presentment [2] of its subject-matter. The physical presence of living human beings as vehicles of dramatic art is a difficulty which no art has to face in the same way. A similar, in many ways even greater, risk confronts *dancing*: though attracting perhaps a less widely spread human interest, its animal spirits are frequently quite unrelieved by any glimmer of spirituality and consequently form a proportionately stronger lure to under-distancing. In the higher forms of dancing technical execution of the most wearing kind makes up a great deal for its intrinsic tendency towards a loss of Distance, and as a popular performance, at least in southern Europe, it has retained much of its ancient artistic glamour, producing a peculiarly subtle balancing of Distance between the pure delight of bodily movement and high technical accomplishment. In passing, it is interesting to observe (as bearing upon the development of Distance), that this art, once as much a fine art as music and considered by the Greeks as a particularly valuable educational exercise, should—except in sporadic cases—have fallen so low from the pedestal it once occupied. Next to the theater and dancing stands *sculpture*. Though not using a *living* bodily medium, yet the human form in its full spatial materiality constitutes a similar threat to Distance. Our northern habits of dress and ignorance of the human body have enormously increased the difficulty of distancing Sculpture, in part through the gross misconceptions to which it is exposed, in part owing to a complete lack of standards of bodily perfection, and an inability to realize the distinction between sculptural form and bodily shape, which is the only but fundamental point distinguishing a statue from a cast taken from life. In *painting* it is apparently the form of its presentment and the usual reduction in scale which would explain why this art can venture to approach more closely than sculpture to the normal Distance-

1 Report from the Joint Select Committee of the House of Lords and the House of Commons on the Stage Plays (Censorship), 1909.
2 I shall use the term "presentment" to denote the manner of presenting, in distinction to "presentation" as that which is presented.

limit. As this matter will be discussed later in a special connection this simple reference may suffice here. *Music* and *architecture* have a curious position. These two most abstract of all arts show a remarkable fluctuation in their Distances. Certain kinds of music, especially "pure" music, or "classical" or "heavy" music, appear for many people over-distanced; light, "catchy" tunes, on the contrary, easily reach that degree of decreasing Distance below which they cease to be Art and become a pure amusement. In spite of its strange abstractness which to many philosophers has made it comparable to architecture and mathematics, music possesses a sensuous, frequently sensual character: the undoubted physiological and muscular stimulus of its melodies and harmonies, no less than its rhythmic aspects, would seem to account for the occasional disappearance of Distance. To this might be added its strong tendency, especially in unmusical people, to stimulate trains of thought quite disconnected with itself, following channels of subjective inclinations—daydreams of a more or less directly personal character. *Architecture* requires almost uniformly a very great Distance; that is to say, the majority of persons derive no esthetic appreciation from architecture as such, apart from the incidental impression of its decorative features and its associations. The causes are numerous, but prominent among them are the confusion of building with architecture and the predominance of utilitarian purposes, which overshadow the architectural claims upon the attention.

4. That all art requires a Distance-limit beyond which, and a Distance within which only, esthetic appreciation becomes possible, is the *psychological formulation of a general characteristic of Art*, namely, its *anti-realistic nature*. Though seemingly paradoxical, this applies as much to "naturalistic" as to "idealistic" Art. The difference commonly expressed by these epithets is at bottom merely the difference in the degree of Distance; and this produces, so far as "naturalism" and "idealism" in Art are not meaningless labels, the usual result that what appears obnoxiously "naturalistic" to one person, may be "idealistic" to another. To say that Art is anti-realistic simply insists upon the fact that Art is not nature, never pretends to be nature and strongly resists any confusion with nature. It emphasizes the *art*-character of Art: "artistic" is synonymous with "anti-realistic"; it explains even sometimes a very marked degree of artificiality.

"Art is an imitation of nature," was the current art-conception in the eighteenth century. It is the fundamental axiom of the standard-work of that time upon esthetic theory by the Abbé Du Bos, *Réflexions critiques sur la poésie et la peinture*, 1719; the idea received strong support from the literal acceptance of Aristotle's theory of μίμησις [imitation] and produced echoes everywhere, in Lessing's *Laocoön* no less than in Burke's famous statement that "all Art is great as it deceives." Though it may be assumed that since the time of Kant and of the Romanticists this notion has died out, it still lives in unsophisticated minds. Even when formally denied, it persists, for instance, in the belief that "Art idealizes nature," which means after all only that Art copies nature with certain improvements and revisions. Artists themselves are unfortunately often responsible for the spreading of this conception. Whistler indeed said that to produce Art by imitating nature would be like trying to produce music by sitting upon the piano, but the selective, idealizing imitation of nature finds merely another support in such a saying. Naturalism, pleinairism, impressionism—even the guileless enthusiasm of the artist for the works of nature, her wealth of suggestion, her delicacy of workmanship, for the steadfastness of her guidance, only produce upon the public the impression that Art is, after all, an imitation of nature. Then how can it be anti-realistic? The antithesis, Art *versus* nature, seems to break down. Yet if it does, what is the sense of Art?

Here the conception of Distance comes to the rescue. The solution of the dilemma lies in the "antinomy of Distance" with its demand: utmost decrease of Distance without its disappearance. The simple observation that Art is the more effective, the more it falls into line with our predispositions which are inevitably molded on general experience and nature, has always been the original motive for "naturalism." "Naturalism," "impressionism" is no new thing; it is only a new name for an innate leaning of Art, from the time of the Chaldeans and Egyptians down to the present day. Even the Apollo of Tenea apparently struck his contemporaries as so startlingly "naturalistic" that the subsequent legend attributed a superhuman genius to his creator. A constantly closer approach to nature, a perpetual refining of the limit of Distance, yet without overstepping the dividing line of art and nature, has always been the inborn bent of art. To deny this dividing line has occasionally been the failing of naturalism. But no theory of naturalism is complete which does not at the same time allow for the intrinsic idealism of Art: for both are merely degrees in that wide range lying beyond the Distance-limit. To imitate nature so as to trick the spectator into the deception that it is nature which he beholds, is to forsake Art, its anti-realism, its distanced spirituality, and to fall below the limit into sham, sensationalism, or platitude.

But what, in the theory of antinomy of Distance requires explanation is the existence of an *idealistic, highly distanced* Art. There are numerous reasons to account for it; indeed in so complex a phenomenon as Art, single causes can be pronounced almost *a priori* to be false. Foremost among such causes which have contributed to the formation of an idealistic Art appears to stand the subordination of Art to some extraneous purpose of an impressive, exceptional character. Such a subordination has consisted—at various epochs of Art history —in the use to which Art was put to subserve commemorative, hieratic, generally religious, royal or patriotic functions. The object to be commemorated had to stand out from among other still existing objects or persons; the thing or the being to be worshiped had to be distinguished as markedly as possible from profaner objects of reverence and had to be invested with an air of sanctity by a removal from its ordinary context of occurrence. Nothing could have assisted more powerfully the introduction of a high Distance than this attempt to differentiate objects of common experience in order to fit them for their exalted position. Curious, unusual things of nature met this tendency half-way and easily assumed divine rank; but others had to be distanced by an exaggeration of their size, by extraordinary attributes, by strange combinations of human and animal forms, by special insistence upon particular characteristics, or by the careful removal of all noticeably individualistic and concrete features. Nothing could be more striking than the contrast, for example, in Egyptian Art between the monumental, stereotyped effigies of the Pharaohs, and the startlingly realistic rendering of domestic scenes and of ordinary mortals, such as "the Scribe" or "the Village Sheik." Equally noteworthy is the exceeding artificiality of Russian ikon-painting with its prescribed attributes, expressions and gestures. Even Greek dramatic practice appears to have aimed, for similar purposes and in marked contrast to our stage-habits, at an increase rather than at a decrease of Distance. Otherwise Greek Art, even of a religious type, is remarkable for its *low* Distance value; and it speaks highly for the esthetic capacities of the Greeks that the degree of realism which they ventured to impart to the representations of their gods, while humanizing them, did not, at least at first,[3] impair the reverence of their feelings towards them. But apart from such special causes, idealistic Art of great Distance has appeared at intervals, for apparently no other reason than that the great Distance was felt to be essential to its *art*-character. What is noteworthy and runs counter to many accepted ideas is that such periods were usually epochs of a low level of general culture. These were times, which, like childhood, required the marvelous, the extraordinary, to satisfy their artistic longings, and neither realized nor cared for the poetic or artistic qualities of ordinary things. They were frequently times in which the mass of the people were plunged in ignorance and buried under a load of misery, and in which even the small educated class sought rather amusement or a pastime in Art; or they were epochs of a strong practical common sense too much concerned with the rough-and-tumble of life to have any sense of its esthetic charms. Art was to them what melodrama is to a section of the public at the present time, and its wide Distance was the safeguard of its artistic character. The flowering periods of Art have, on the contrary, always borne the evidence of a narrow Distance. Greek Art, as just mentioned, was realistic to an extent which we, spoilt as we are by modern developments, can grasp with difficulty, but which the contrast with its oriental contemporaries sufficiently proves. During the Augustan period—which Art historians at last are coming to regard no longer as merely "degenerated" Greek Art —Roman Art achieved its greatest triumphs in an almost naturalistic portrait-sculpture. In the Renaissance we need only think of the realism of portraiture, sometimes amounting almost to cynicism, of the *désinvolture* with which the mis-

[3] That this practice did, in course of time, undermine their religious faith, is clear from the plays of Euripides and from Plato's condemnation of Homer's mythology.

tresses of popes and dukes were posed as madonnas, saints and goddesses apparently without any detriment to the esthetic appeal of the works, and of the remarkable interpenetration of Art with the most ordinary routine of life, in order to realize the scarcely perceptible dividing line between the sphere of Art and the realm of practical existence. In a sense, the assertion that idealistic Art marks periods of a generally low and narrowly restricted culture is the converse to the oft-repeated statement that the flowering periods of Art coincide with epochs of decadence: for this so-called decadence represents indeed in certain respects a process of disintegration, politically, racially, often nationally, but a disruption necessary to the formation of larger social units and to the breakdown of outgrown national restrictions. For this very reason it has usually also been the sign of the growth of personal independence and of an expansion of individual culture.

To proceed to some more special points illustrating the distanced and therefore anti-realistic character of art—both in subject matter and in the form of presentation Art has always safeguarded its distanced view. Fanciful, even phantastic, subjects have from time immemorial been the accredited material of Art. No doubt things, as well as our view of them, have changed in the course of time: *Polyphemus* and the *Lotus-Eaters* for the Greeks, the *Venusberg* or the *Magnetic Mountain* for the Middle Ages were less incredible, more realistic than to us. But *Peter Pan* or *L'Oiseau Bleu* still appeal at the present day in spite of the prevailing note of realism of our time. "Probability" and "improbability" in Art are not to be measured by their correspondence (or lack of it) with actual experience. To do so had involved the theories of the fifteenth to the eighteenth centuries in endless contradictions. It is rather a matter of *consistency* of Distance. The note of realism, set by a work as a whole, determines *intrinsically* the greater or smaller degree of fancy which it permits; and consequently we feel the loss of Peter Pan's shadow to be infinitely more probable than some trifling improbability which shocks our sense of proportion in a naturalistic work. No doubt also, fairy tales, fairy plays, stories of strange adventures were primarily invented to satisfy the craving of curiosity, the desire for the marvelous, the shudder of the unwonted and the longing for imaginary experiences. But by their mere eccentricity in regard to the normal facts of experience they cannot have failed to arouse a strong feeling of Distance.

Again, certain conventional subjects taken from mythical and legendary traditions, at first closely connected with the concrete, practical life of a devout public, have gradually, by the mere force of convention as much as by their inherent anti-realism, acquired Distance for us today. Our view of Greek mythological sculpture, of early Christian saints and martyrs must be considerably distanced, compared with that of the Greek and medieval worshiper. It is in part the result of lapse of time, but in part also a real change of attitude. Already the outlook of the Imperial Roman had altered, and Pausanias shows a curious dualism of standpoint, declaring the Athene Lemnia to be the supreme achievement of Phidias's genius, and gazing awe-struck upon the roughly hewn tree trunk representing some primitive Apollo. Our understanding of Greek tragedy suffers admittedly under our inability to revert to the point of view for which it was originally written. Even the tragedies of Racine demand an imaginative effort to put ourselves back into the courtly atmosphere of red-heeled, powdered ceremony. Provided the Distance is not too wide, the result of its intervention has everywhere been to enhance the *art*-character of such works and to lower their original ethical and social force of appeal. Thus in the central dome of the Church (Sta Maria dei Miracoli) at Saronno are depicted the heavenly hosts in ascending tiers, crowned by the benevolent figure of the Divine Father, bending from the window of heaven to bestow His blessing upon the assembled community. The mere realism of foreshortening and of the boldest vertical perspective may well have made the naïve Christian of the sixteenth century conscious of the Divine Presence—but for us it has become a work of Art.

The unusual, exceptional, has found its especial home in tragedy. It has always—except in highly distanced tragedy—been a popular objection to it that "there is enough sadness in life without going to the theater for it." Already Aristotle appears to have met with this view among his contemporaries clamoring for "happy endings." Yet tragedy is not sad; if it were, there would indeed be little sense in its existence. For the tragic is just in so far different from the merely sad, as it is distanced; and it is largely the exceptional which produces the Distance of tragedy: exceptional situations, exceptional characters, exceptional destinies and conduct. Not of course, characters merely cranky, eccentric, pathological. The exceptional element in tragic figures—that which makes them so utterly different from characters we meet with in ordinary experience—is a consistency of direction, a fervor of ideality, a persistence and driving-force which is far above the capacities of average men. The tragic of tragedy would, transposed into ordinary life, in nine cases out of ten, end in drama, in comedy, even in farce, for lack of steadfastness, for fear of conventions, for the dread of "scenes," for a hundred-and-one petty faithlessnesses toward a belief or an ideal: even if for none of these, it would end in a compromise simply because man forgets and time heals.[4] Again, the sympathy which aches with the sadness of tragedy is another such confusion, the under-distancing of tragedy's appeal. Tragedy trembles always on the knife-edge of a *personal* reaction, and sympathy which finds relief in tears tends almost always towards a loss of Distance. Such

[4] The famous "unity of time," so senseless as a "canon," is all the same often an indispensable condition of tragedy. For in many a tragedy the catastrophe would be even intrinsically impossible, if fatality did not overtake the hero with that rush which gives no time to forget and none to heal. It is in cases such as these that criticism has often blamed the work for "improbability"—the old confusion between Art and nature—forgetting that the death of the hero is the convention of the art-form, as much as grouping in a picture is such a convention and that probability is not the correspondence with average experience, but consistency of Distance.

a loss naturally renders tragedy unpleasant to a degree: it becomes sad, dismal, harrowing, depressing. But real tragedy (melodrama has a very strong tendency to speculate upon sympathy), truly appreciated, is not sad. "The pity of it—oh, the pity of it," that essence of all genuine tragedy is not the pity of mild, regretful sympathy. It is a chaos of tearless, bitter bewilderment, of upsurging revolt and rapturous awe before the ruthless and inscrutable fate; it is the homage to the great and exceptional in the man who in a last effort of spiritual tension can rise to confront blind, crowning Necessity even in his crushing defeat.

As I explained earlier, the form of presentation sometimes endangers the maintenance of Distance, but it more frequently acts as a considerable support. Thus the bodily vehicle of *drama* is the chief factor of risk to Distance. But, as if to counterbalance a confusion with nature, other features of stage-presentation exercise an opposite influence. Such are the general theatrical *milieu,* the shape and arrangement of the stage, the artificial lighting, the costumes, *mise-en-scène* and make-up, even the language, especially verse. Modern reforms of staging, aiming primarily at the removal of artistic incongruities between excessive decoration and the living figures of the actors and at the production of a more homogeneous stage-picture, inevitably work also towards a greater emphasis and homogeneity of Distance. The history of staging and dramaturgy is closely bound up with the evolution of Distance, and its fluctuations lie at the bottom not only of the greater part of all the talk and writing about "dramatic probability" and the Aristotelian "unities," but also of "theatrical illusion." In *sculpture,* one distancing factor of presentment is its lack of color. The esthetic, or rather inesthetic effect of realistic coloring, is in no way touched by the controversial question of its use historically; its attempted resuscitation, such as by Klinger, seems only to confirm its disadvantages. The distancing use even of pedestals, although originally no doubt serving other purposes, is evident to anyone who has experienced the oppressively crowded sensation of moving in a room among life-size statues placed directly upon the floor. The circumstance that the space of statuary is the same space as ours (in distinction to relief sculpture or painting, for instance) renders a distancing by pedestals, that is, a removal from our spatial context, imperative.[5] Probably the framing of *pictures* might be shown to serve a similar purpose—though paintings have intrinsically a much greater Distance—because neither their space (perspective and imaginary space) nor their lighting coincides with our (actual) space or light, and the usual reduction in scale of the represented objects prevents a feeling of undue proximity. Besides, painting always retains to some extent a *two*-dimensional character, and this character supplies *eo ipso* a Distance. Nevertheless, life-size pictures, especially if they possess

[5] An instance which might be adduced to disprove this point only shows its correctness on closer inspection: for it was on purpose and with the intention of removing Distance, that Rodin originally intended his *Citoyens de Calais* to be placed, without pedestals, upon the marketplace of that town.

strong relief, and their light happens to coincide with the actual lighting, can occasionally produce the impression of actual presence which is a far from pleasant, though fortunately only a passing, illusion. For decorative purposes, in pictorial renderings of vistas, garden-perspectives and architectural extensions, the removal of Distance has often been consciously striven after, whether with esthetically satisfactory results is much disputed.

A general help towards Distance (and therewith an anti-realistic feature) is to be found in the "unification of presentment" [6] of all art-objects. By unification of presentment are meant such qualities as symmetry, opposition, proportion, balance, rhythmical distribution of parts, light-arrangements, in fact all so-called "formal" features, "composition" in the widest sense. Unquestionably, Distance is not the only, nor even the principal function of composition; it serves to render our grasp of the presentation easier and to increase its intelligibility. It may even in itself constitute the principal esthetic feature of the object, as in linear complexes or patterns, partly also in architectural designs. Yet, its distancing effect can hardly be underrated. For, every kind of visibly intentional arrangement or unification must, by the mere fact of its presence, enforce Distance, by distinguishing the object from the confused, disjointed, and scattered forms of actual experience. This function can be gauged in a typical form in cases where composition produces an exceptionally marked impression of artificiality (not in the bad sense of that term, but in the sense in which all art is artificial); and it is a natural corollary to the differences of Distance in different arts and of different subjects, that the arts and subjects vary in the degree of artificiality which they can bear. It is this sense of artificial finish which is the source of so much of that elaborate charm of Byzantine work, of Mohammedan decoration, of the hieratic stiffness of so many primitive madonnas and saints. In general the emphasis of composition and technical finish increases with the Distance of the subject matter: heroic conceptions lend themselves better to verse than to prose; monumental statues require a more general treatment, more elaboration of setting and artificiality of pose than impressionistic statuettes like those of Troubetzkoi; an ecclesiastic subject is painted with a degree of symmetrical arrangement which would be ridiculous in a Dutch interior, and a naturalistic drama carefully avoids the tableau impression characteristic of a mystery play. In a similar manner the variations of Distance in the arts go hand in hand with a visibly greater predominance of composition and "formal" elements, reaching a climax in architecture and music. It is again a matter of "consistency of Distance." At the same time, while from the point of view of the artist this is undoubtedly the case, from the point of view of the public the emphasis of composition and technical finish appears frequently to relieve the impression of highly distanced subjects by *diminishing the Distance of the whole.* The spectator has a tendency to see in composition and finish merely evidence of the artist's "cleverness," of his mastery

[6] See note 2, *ante.*

over his material. Manual dexterity is an enviable thing to possess in every one's experience, and naturally appeals to the public *practically,* thereby putting it into a directly personal relation to things which intrinsically have very little personal appeal for it. It is true that this function of composition is hardly an esthetic one: for the admiration of mere technical cleverness is not an artistic enjoyment, but by a fortunate chance it has saved from oblivion and entire loss, among much rubbish, also much genuine Art, which otherwise would have completely lost contact with our life.

5. This discussion, necessarily sketchy and incomplete, may have helped to illustrate the sense in which, I suggested, Distance appears as a fundamental principle to which such antitheses as idealism and realism are reducible. The difference between "idealistic" and "realistic" Art is not a clear-cut dividing-line between the art-practices described by these terms, but is a difference of degree in the Distance-limit which they presuppose on the part both of the artist and of the public. A similar reconciliation seems to me possible between the opposites "sensual" and "spiritual," "individual" and "typical." That the appeal of Art is sensuous, even sensual, must be taken as an indisputable fact. Puritanism will never be persuaded, and rightly so, that this is not the case. The sensuousness of Art is a natural implication of the "antinomy of Distance," and will appear again in another connection. The point of importance here is that the whole sensual side of Art is purified, spiritualized, "filtered" as I expressed it earlier, by Distance. The most sensual appeal becomes the translucent veil of an underlying spirituality, once the grossly personal and practical elements have been removed from it. And—a matter of special emphasis here—*this spiritual aspect of the appeal is the more penetrating, the more personal and direct its sensual appeal would have been* BUT FOR THE PRESENCE OF DISTANCE. For the artist, to trust in this delicate transmutation is a natural act of faith which the Puritan hesitates to venture upon: which of the two, one asks, is the greater idealist?

6. The same argument applies to the contradictory epithets "individual" and "typical." A discussion in support of the fundamental individualism of Art lies outside the scope of this essay. Every artist has taken it for granted. Besides it is rather in the sense of "concrete" or "individualized," that it is usually opposed to "typical." On the other hand, "typical," in the sense of "abstract," is as dia metrically opposed to the whole nature of Art, as individualism is characteristic of it. It is in the sense of "generalized" as a "general human element" that it is claimed as a necessary ingredient in Art. This antithesis is again one which naturally and without mutual sacrifice finds room within the conception of Distance. Historically the "typical" has had the effect of counteracting *under*-distancing as much as the "individual" has opposed *over*-distancing. Naturally the two ingredients have constantly varied in the history of Art; they represent, in fact, two sets of conditions to which Art has invariably been subject: the personal and the social factors. It is Distance which on one side prevents the emptying of

Art of its concreteness and the development of the typical into abstractness; which, on the other, suppresses the directly personal element of its individualism; thus reducing the antitheses to the peaceful interplay of these two factors. It is just this interplay which constitutes the "antinomy of Distance."

—*British Journal of Psychology*, Volume V (1913)

JOSÉ ORTEGA Y GASSET

The Dehumanization of Art

Artistic Art

What do the majority of people call esthetic pleasure? What happens when they like a work of art, for instance, a theatrical production? The answer is beyond doubt; the people like a drama when they have succeeded in becoming interested in the human destinies which are proposed to them. The loves, hatreds, sorrows, and joys of the characters move their hearts. They become at one with what they see, as if the characters were real human beings. And they say that the work is "good" when it succeeds in producing the quantity of illusion necessary for the fictitious characters to be worth as much as living persons. In lyric poetry they will look for the loves and sorrows of the man who throbs under the poet. In painting they will be attracted by pictures of men and women with whom they think in some sense it would be interesting to live. A picture of a landscape will appear "pretty" to them when the real landscape portrayed in it deserves, because of its loveliness or sentimental appeal, to be visited on some excursion.

This means that for the majority of people esthetic pleasure is not a spiritual attitude different in essence from that which is usually adopted in the remainder of their lives. It is only distinguished from the latter in non-essential qualities: it is perhaps less utilitarian, more intense, and without painful consequences. But in the last analysis the objects with which art occupies itself are the same objects that appear in daily existence: human figures and passions. And they will call art the ensemble of means through which they are put into contact with interesting human things. Thus they will tolerate artistic forms properly so called, irrealities, fantasies, so long as these do not interfere with their perception of human forms and situations. As soon as the purely esthetic elements predominate, and the people cannot grasp the history of John and Mary, they are be wildered; they do not know what to do in the presence of the stage settings, the book, or the painting. This reaction is natural; for they know of no other attitude than the practical towards external realities, that attitude which makes us become impassioned and compels us to intervene sentimentally. A work of art which does not invite them to such an intervention leaves them with no role to perform.

Now in this respect we should come to a perfect and clear understanding. To enjoy and to suffer with human destinies, which perhaps the work of art is presenting to us, is something very different from true artistic enjoyment. Furthermore these sympathies toward the human element in the work of art are in principle incompatible with strict esthetic delight.

This is a matter of optics which is very simple. In order to see an object we have appropriately to readjust our organs of vision. If our visual readjustment is inadequate we cannot see the object or else we do not see it well. Let the reader imagine that we are now looking at a garden through a windowpane. Our eyes will be readjusted in such a way that the ray of vision goes right through the glass to be fixed upon the flowers and the foliage. Since the goal of vision is the garden, whereupon the visual ray is cast, our glance will penetrate through the glass without stopping to perceive it. The clearer the glass is, the less we will see. But then making an effort we may withdraw attention from the garden; and by retracting the ocular ray, we may fixate it upon the glass. Then the garden will disappear in our eyes and we will see instead only some confused masses of color which seem to stick to the glass. Consequently to see the garden and to see the glass in the windowpane are two incompatible operations: one excludes the other and each requires a different ocular readjustment.

Likewise he who in the work of art aims to be moved by the fate of John and Mary, or of Tristan and Iseult, and readjusts to them his spiritual perception will not be able to see the work of art. The misfortunes of Tristan are only such, and consequently they will be able to move us in so far as they may be taken for reality. But the artistic object is artistic only in so far as it is not real. In order to enjoy the equestrian portrait of Charles V by Titian it is an unavoidable condition that we should not see there Charles V in person, authentic and living, but that we should see instead a portrait, a known real image, a fiction. The man portrayed and his portrait are two objects completely different: either we get interested in one or the other. If, in the former, "we live with" Charles V; if in the latter, "we contemplate" an artistic object as such.

Now the majority of people are unable to adjust their attention to the glass and the transparency which is the work of art; instead they penetrate through it to wallow passionately in the human reality to which the work of art refers. If they are invited to let loose their prey and fix their attention upon the work of art itself, they will say that they see nothing in it, because, indeed, they see no human realities there, but only artistic transparencies, pure essences.

During the nineteenth century artistic processes have been too impure. Artists reduced to a minimum the strict artistic elements and made their works consist almost entirely of the fiction of human realities. In this sense we must say that in one way or another all the normal art of the last century was realistic. Beethoven and Wagner were realists. So were Chateaubriand and Zola. Seen from the heights of today romanticism and realism approach each other and reveal their common realistic roots.

Products of this nature are only partially works of art, or artistic objects. To enjoy them it is not necessary to have any power to adjust one's self to the essential and transparent qualities which constitute esthetic sensibility. It is enough to possess human sensibility and to allow the anxieties and joys of others to echo within one's self. One can understand then why the art of the nineteenth century has been so popular: it was made for the undifferentiated masses in proportion to the fact that it is not art, but an extract from life itself. It should be remembered that in the case of all epochs which have had two different types of art, one for the minority and one for the majority, the latter was always realistic. For example during the Middle Ages, corresponding to the binary structure of society which was divided into castes, the nobles and the plebeians, there were two types of art, a noble art which was "conventional," "idealistic," that is to say artistic, and a popular art which was realistic and satirical.

We are not going to discuss now whether a pure art is possible. Perhaps it is not, but the reasons which may lead us to such a negation are long and difficult. Perhaps it is better then to leave the theme intact. Moreover, it really does not matter for the subject we are now talking about. Even if pure art is impossible there is no doubt room for a tendency to purify art. This tendency will lead towards a progressive elimination of the human, all too human elements, which dominate romantic and naturalistic production. In this process the point will be reached when the human element of the work of art will be so scanty that it will be hardly visible. Then we shall have an object which will be perceived only by the individual who possesses the peculiar gift of artistic sensibility. It will be an art for artists and not for the masses of the people. It will be an art of caste and not a democratic art. This is why the new art divides people into two classes of individuals: those who understand it and those who do not; that is, the artists and those who are not. New art is artistic art. . . .

Some Scraps of Phenomenology

An illustrious man is dying. His wife is by his bedside. A doctor counts the pulsations of the dying man. In the background of the room there are two people, a newspaper reporter, who attends the obituary scene, by reason of his business, and a painter whom chance has brought there. The wife, the doctor, the newspaper reporter, and the painter are witnessing the very same fact.

Nevertheless, this one fact, the agony of the man, offers itself to each one of them in a different aspect. So different are these aspects that they scarcely have a common nucleus. The difference between what the fact is for the woman, pierced by sorrow, and for the painter who contemplatively gazes at the scene, is so great that perhaps it would be more exact to say the wife and the painter witness two facts entirely different.

It happens then that the same reality breaks into many diverging realities when it is seen from different points of view. And here we may ask which of these multiple realities is the true one, the authentic one. Our decision will be arbitrary, no matter what it may be. Our preference for one or the other can only be based upon caprice. All of these realities are equivalent. Each one is the authentic one for its corresponding point of view. The only thing we can do is to classify these points of view and to select among them the one that may appear to us as more normal, or more spontaneous. Thus we may reach a notion not at all absolute, but at least practical and normative of reality.

The clearest way to differentiate the points of view of the four persons who attend the death scene consists of measuring their dimensions: the spiritual distance at which each one is from the common fact—that of the agony. To the wife of the dying man this distance is at a minimum, so much so that it is almost nonexistent. The lamentable event so tortures her heart and occupies such a large portion of her soul that it fuses with her own person; or, said in an inverse manner, the woman intervenes in the scene, she is a part of it. For us to see anything so that a given fact may be contemplated, we must set it at some remove from ourselves, so that it ceases to form a living part of our own being. Thus the woman does not attend the scene, but is within it. She does not contemplate it, but rather she lives it.

The doctor is a little more distant. This is a professional case for him. He does not intervene in the situation with the impassioned and blind anxiety which floods the soul of the poor woman, and yet his profession compels him to be seriously interested in what is happening. He feels towards it a certain responsibility, and perhaps his prestige is at stake. Consequently, even if he participates less intimately than the wife, he also takes part in the event. The scene overtakes him and drags him into its dramatic core, grasping him not by his heart, but by a professional fragment of his personality. He also lives in the sad happening, although with emotions which do not spring forth from his cordial self, but from the professional periphery of his being.

If we now place ourselves in the point of view of the newspaper reporter we will notice that we have moved away greatly from that painful reality. We have moved away so far that we have lost all sentimental contacts with the fact in question. The newspaper reporter is there like the doctor, compelled by his profession, not by any spontaneous and human impulse, but while the profession of the doctor compels him to intervene in the event, that of the newspaper reporter compels him precisely not to intervene: he must limit himself only to see. For him the fact, properly speaking, is a mere scene, a mere spectacle which he may describe later on in the columns of his newspaper. He does not share sentimentally in what is happening there; spiritually he is out and free from the event; he does not live it, but he contemplates it. And yet he contemplates it with the preoccupation of a person who has to tell it later on to his readers. He would like to interest them, to move them, and if possible, to make them shed tears as if they were transitory relatives of the deceased. At school he had read Horace's prescription: *Si vis me flere, dolendum est primum ipsi tibi.*[1] Docile to Horace the newspaper man tries to feign an emotion in order to try later on to adapt it to his journalism. And thus it happens although he does not live the scene "he feigns" to live it.

Lastly the painter, indifferent, merely glances sidewise at the human reality. What happens there does not worry him; he is, as they say, miles away from the event. His attitude is purely contemplative and one might even say that he does not contemplate the event in its integrity; the painful internal sense of it is left outside the field of his perception. He pays attention only to externals, to lights and shadows, to chromatic values. With the painter we have reached a point of maximum distance and of minimum sentimental intervention.

The unavoidable heaviness of this analysis would be compensated if it should enable us to speak clearly about a scale of spiritual distances between reality and ourselves. In this scale the degrees of proximity are equivalent to the degrees of sentimental participation in the event: the degrees of distance, on the contrary, signify the degrees of liberation through which we objectify the real event, thus converting it into a pure theme for contemplation. Situated at one of these extremes, we face a certain aspect of the world—persons, things, situations, that is to say, reality as being "lived": from the other extreme, on the other hand, we see everything in its aspects "as contemplated reality."

Upon arriving at this point, we must introduce a consideration which is essential to esthetics, without which it is not easy to penetrate into the physiology of art, whether it be old or new. Among those diverse aspects of reality which correspond to the various points of view, there is one from which are derived all the others and which is the base of them all. That is the "lived" reality. If there were no one to live in pure surrender and frenzy the agony of a man, the doctor would not be interested in it, the readers would not understand the pathetic gestures of the newspaper reporter who writes up the event, and the picture in which the painter represents a man in his bed, surrounded by doleful figures, would be unintelligible to us. The same we could say of any other object, whether it be a person or thing. The original form of an apple is that

[1] "If you wish me to weep, it is first necessary for you to grieve." (Editor's note.)

which the apple possesses when we are ready to eat it. In all the other possible forms which an apple may have, as for instance, the form given to it by an artist of the year 1600 in which he has combined it with a baroque ornament, the form that it represents in a still-life picture by Cézanne, or in that elemental metaphor which compares it to the cheek of a girl, the apple preserves more or less its original aspect. A picture or a poem where no "lived" forms were remaining would be unintelligible, that is to say, would not be anything, as a speech would be nothing if all of its words had been stripped of their habitual meanings.

This means that in the scale of realities there corresponds to the "lived" reality a primacy which compels us to consider it the reality *par excellence*. Instead of "lived" reality we might call it human reality. The painter who witnesses contemplatively the scene of the agony seems to be "inhuman." Let us say, then, that the human point of view is that in which we "live" the situations, persons, or things. And *vice versa*, all realities—woman, landscape, event—are human when they offer us the aspect which is usually "lived" by us. . . .

The Dehumanization of Art

With tremendous speed young art has diversified itself in a great number of directions and divergent attempts. There is nothing quite so easy as to emphasize the differences between some productions and others. But this emphasis on what is different and specific will become empty, if we fail to determine beforehand the common background which affirms itself in all these works, in such various ways, indeed, that at times they are even at cross purposes. Already it was taught by our good old Aristotle that different things are differentiated by that which makes them similar, that is by a certain common character in them. Because all bodies have color, we notice that some have a different color than others. Species are precisely specifications of the genus and we understand them only when we see, revealed in their diverse forms, their common patrimony.

The particular directions of young art are of little interest to me and with very few exceptions particular works of art possess even less interest. But in turn, my valuation of the new artistic products should not be of interest to anyone. Writers who reduce their inspiration to express their esteem or lack of esteem for works of art should not write. They really are not worthy of this difficult task. It is just as the Spanish critic "Clarín" (Leopold Alas) used to say about certain clumsy playwrights, that it would be better for them to devote their efforts to other tasks, as for instance to establishing a family. And if they already have one? Well, then, let them establish another.

What matters now is the indubitable presence in the world of a new esthetic sensibility. This new sensibility is found not only among the creators of art, but also among people for whom art is created. As distinguished from the plurality of special directions and individual works, this sensibility represents what is generic, and productive of the divergent tendencies. This is what seems to be of interest to define.

And searching for the generic and characteristic note of all new productions, I find that it is the tendency to dehumanize art. The preceding paragraphs give to this formula a certain precision.

Let us compare a picture in the new manner with one in the manner of 1860. We will begin, in a simple way, by comparing the objects represented in both of them, perhaps a man, a house, a mountain. Soon we notice that the artist of 1860 has tried first of all to give the objects in his picture the same air and aspect that they have outside of it when they form a part of the "lived" or human reality. . . . The man, the house, and the mountain are immediately recognized as such. They are old, habitual friends. In the recent picture, on the contrary, it is hard for us to recognize them. The spectator perhaps thinks that the painter has failed to achieve the likeness. But it may be also that the picture of 1860 was "badly painted"—that is to say, between the objects in the picture and the corresponding ones outside of it, there may be a great distance, an important divergence. And yet, whatever be the distance, the mistakes of the traditional artist point toward the "human object." They are failures on the road towards it. . . . In the new picture the contrary happens: it is not that the painter errs, nor that his deviations from the "natural" (natural = human) fail to reach it. The fact is that they point to a road leading away from the "human" object in the opposite direction.

The painter, far from trying, more or less clumsily, to move toward reality, seems to have evaded it. He seems to have tried gallantly to deform it, to break its human aspect, to dehumanize it. With the things represented in the traditional picture, we might live in the imagination. Many Englishmen have fallen in love with Mona Lisa. With things represented in the new pictures, it is impossible to live: on stripping them of their aspects as "lived" realities, the painter has broken the bridges and burned the ships which might transport us to our habitual world. He leaves us locked up in an abstruse universe, he forces us to associate with objects with which there is no possible human association. Thus we have to improvise a new form of association completely different from the usual one which allows us to live with things: we have to create and to invent original acts that are adequate to those unusual figures. This new life, a life invented after the annulment of spontaneous life, is precisely what we may call artistic understanding and pleasure. This life does not lack in sentiment and passion but evidently these passions and sentiments belong to a psychic flora very different from that which covers the landscapes of our primary and human life. They are secondary emotions which those ultra-objects provoke in the artist that is within us. They are sentiments specifically esthetic.

One may say that such a result could be more simply obtained by putting aside totally those human forms—man, house, mountain—and building figures completely original. But this is in the first place impractical. Perhaps in the most abstract ornamental line there vibrates as in disguise a tenacious reminiscence of certain "natural" forms. In the second place—and this is most important —the art of which we are talking is not only inhuman because it does not contain human things but it actively consists of the dehumanizing operation. In its flight away from the human it does not pay so much attention to the term "ad quem," the strange fauna to which it arrives, as it does to the term "a quo," the human aspect which it destroys. The thing is not to paint something completely different from a man, a house, or a mountain, but to paint a man with the least possible semblance of a man, a house which preserves of its nature only what is strictly necessary for us to witness its metamorphosis, a cone which miraculously springs forth from what was previously a mountain, as the snake sheds its skin. Esthetic pleasure for the new artist emanates from that victory over the "human": for that reason it is necessary in each case to make concrete such victory and to show the strangled victim.

Ordinary people think that it is very easy to flee away from reality when indeed it is the most difficult thing in the world. It is easy to say or to paint a thing which lacks sense completely, that is unintelligible: for this it will be enough to put alongside each other, as the Dadaists have done, words without connection, or to draw lines casually. But to be able to construct something that is not a copy of the "natural" and which nevertheless possesses some substance implies the most sublime gift.

"Reality" constantly waylays the artist to prevent his evasion. What a great cunningness the flight of genius presupposes. It must be like an inverted Ulysses who escapes from his daily Penelope and sails among reefs towards the bewitching realm of Circe. When he succeeds in escaping for a moment the perpetual waylaying of reality let us not blame the artist for his gesture of pride —that brief gesture that makes him look like St. George with the dragon conquered at his feet.

An Invitation to Understand

In the works of art preferred during the last century there is always a nucleus of "lived" reality which is like the substance of the esthetic body. Upon it art operates, and its operation is reduced to polishing that human nucleus, to giving it a coat of varnish, a certain brilliance, composure, and reverberation. To the great majority of people such structure in the work of art is the most natural, is the only possible one. To them art is the mirror of life, it is nature seen through a temperament, it is the representation of the human, etc. But with no less deep conviction, the young support a contrary theory. Why should the old be right against the young if the future will always make the young right against the old? Above all, it is good not to become indignant or shout. . . .

Our most deeply rooted and indubitable convictions are always the most suspicious. They constitute our limitations, our boundaries, our prisons. Life is of no consequence if a formidable eagerness to widen its frontiers does not stamp within its confines. A person lives in proportion to his longing for more life. All obstinacy in staying within the familiar horizon signifies weakness, the decadence of vital energy. The horizon is a biological line, a living organ of our very being; as long as we enjoy plenitude, the horizon migrates, it becomes widened, it undulates elastically almost to the rhythm of our respiration. On the other hand, when the horizon becomes fixed as in a shell it is because we come into the fold of senility.

It is not so evident as the academicians suppose that the work of art should perforce consist of a human nucleus whose hair the muses can comb and polish. This is, to begin with, to make art consist of the use of cosmetics. I have already said that the perception of the "lived" reality, and the perception of the artistic form, are in principle incompatible because each requires a different adjustment of our organs of perception. An art which would give us the opportunity to take that double glance would be a cross-eyed art. The art of the nineteenth century has often been such; that is why its artistic products, far from representing a normal type of art, are perhaps the greatest anomaly in the history of taste. All the great epochs of art have avoided the "human" as the center of gravity in their creations. And the imperative of exclusive realism which has ruled over the sensibility of the past century signifies precisely a monstrosity without equal in esthetic evolution. From which it results that the new inspiration, so extravagant in appearance, comes back at least in one point to the royal road of art. Because this road is called "The Will to Style." Well now: to stylize is to deform the real, to derealize. Stylization implies dehumanization. And *vice versa* there is no other way to dehumanize than to stylize. Realism, on the other hand, inviting the artist to follow submissively the form of things, invites him not to have style. That is why the Zurbarán enthusiast, not knowing what to say, says that his pictures have "character," just as Lucas or Sorolla, Dickens or Galdos have character but not style. On the other hand the eighteenth century, which possesses so little character, possesses style to the point of saturation.

—*La Deshumanización del Arte* (1925)

KENNETH CLARK

The Naked and the Nude

The English language, with its elaborate generosity, distinguishes between the naked and the nude. To be naked is to be deprived of our clothes, and the word implies some of the embarrassment most of us feel in that condition. The word "nude," on the other hand, carries, in educated usage, no uncomfortable overtone. The vague image it projects into the mind is not of a huddled and defenseless body, but of a balanced, prosperous, and confident body: the body re-formed. In fact, the word was forced into our vocabulary by critics of the early eighteenth century to persuade the artless islanders that, in countries where painting and sculpture were practiced and valued as they should be, the naked human body was the central subject of art.

For this belief there is a quantity of evidence. In the greatest age of painting, the nude inspired the greatest works; and even when it ceased to be a compulsive subject it held its position as an academic exercise and a demonstration of mastery. Velásquez, living in the prudish and corseted court of Philip IV and admirably incapable of idealization, yet felt bound to paint the *Rokeby Venus*. Sir Joshua Reynolds, wholly without the gift of formal draftsmanship, set great store by his *Cymon and Iphigenia*. And in our own century, when we have shaken off one by one those inheritances of Greece which were revived at the Renaissance, discarded the antique armor, forgotten the subjects of mythology, and disputed the doctrine of imitation, the nude alone has survived. It may have suffered some curious transformations, but it remains our chief link with the classic disciplines. When we wish to prove to the Philistine that our great revolutionaries are really respectable artists in the tradition of European painting, we point to their drawings of the nude. Picasso has often exempted it from that savage metamorphosis which he has inflicted on the visible world and has produced a series of nudes that might have walked unaltered off the back of a Greek mirror; and Henry Moore, searching in stone for the ancient laws of its material and seeming to find there some of those elementary creatures of whose fossilized bones it is composed, yet gives to his constructions the same fundamental character that was invented by the sculptors of the Parthenon in the fifth century before Christ.

These comparisons suggest a short answer to the question, "What is the nude?" It is an art form invented by the Greeks in the fifth century, just as opera is an art form invented in seventeenth-century Italy. The conclusion is certainly too abrupt, but it has the merit of emphasizing that the nude is not the subject of art, but a form of art.

It is widely supposed that the naked human body is in itself an object upon which the eye dwells with pleasure and which we are glad to see depicted. But anyone who has frequented art schools and seen the shapeless, pitiful model that the students are industriously drawing will know this is an illusion. The body is not one of those subjects which can be made into art by direct transcription—like a tiger or a snowy landscape. Often in looking at the natural and animal world we joyfully identify ourselves with what we see and from this happy union create a work of art. This is the process students of esthetics call empathy, and it is at the opposite pole of creative activity to the state of mind that has produced the nude. A mass of naked figures does not move us to empathy, but to disillusion and dismay. We do not wish to imitate; we wish to perfect. We become, in the physical sphere, like Diogenes with his lantern looking for an honest man; and, like him, we may never be rewarded. Photographers of the nude are presumably engaged in this search, with every advantage; and having found a model who pleases them, they are free to pose and light her in conformity with their notions of beauty; finally, they can tone down and accentuate by retouching. But in spite of all their taste and skill, the result is hardly ever satisfactory to those whose eyes have grown accustomed to the harmonious simplifications of antiquity. We are immediately disturbed by wrinkles, pouches, and other small imperfections, which, in the classical scheme, are eliminated. By long habit we do not judge it as a living organism, but as a design; and we discover that the transitions are inconclusive, the outline is faltering. We are bothered because the various parts of the body cannot be perceived as simple units and have no clear relationship to one another. In almost every detail the body is not the shape that art had led us to believe it should be. Yet we can look with pleasure at photographs of trees and animals, where the canon of perfection is less strict. Consciously or unconsciously, photographers have usually recognized that in a photograph of the nude their real object is not to reproduce the naked body, but to imitate some artist's view of what the naked body should be. Rejlander was the most Philistine of the early photographers, but, perhaps without knowing it, he was a contemporary of Courbet, and with this splendid archetype somewhere in the background he produced one of the finest (as well as one of the first) photographs of the nude. He succeeded partly because his unconscious archetype was a realist. The more nearly ideal the model, the more unfortunate the photographs that try to imitate it—as those in the style of Ingres or Whistler prove.

So that although the naked body is no more than the point of departure for a work of art, it is a pretext of great importance. In the history of art, the subjects that men have chosen as nuclei, so to say, of their sense of order have often been in themselves unimportant. For hundreds of years, and over an area stretching from Ireland to China, the most vital expression of order was an imaginary animal biting its own tail. In the Middle Ages drapery took on a life of its own, the same life that had inhabited the twisting animal, and became the vital pattern of Romanesque art. In neither case had the subject any independent existence. But the human body, as a nucleus, is rich in associations, and when it is turned into art these associations are not entirely lost. For this reason it seldom achieves the concentrated esthetic shock of animal ornament, but it can be made expressive of a far wider and more civilizing experience. It is ourselves and arouses memories of all the things we wish to do with ourselves; and first of all we wish to perpetuate ourselves.

This is an aspect of the subject so obvious that I need hardly dwell on it; and yet some wise men have tried to close their eyes to it. "If the nude," says Professor Alexander, "is so treated that it raises in the spectator ideas or desires appropriate to the material subject, it is false art, and bad morals." This high-minded theory is contrary to experience. In the mixture of memories and sensations aroused by Rubens' *Andromeda* or Renoir's *Bather* are many that are "appropriate to the material subject." And since these words of a famous philosopher are often quoted, it is necessary to labor the obvious and say that no nude, however abstract, should fail to arouse in the spectator some vestige of erotic feeling, even though it be only the faintest shadow—and if it does not do so, it is bad art and false morals. The desire to grasp and be united with another human body is so fundamental a part of our nature that our judgment of what is known as "pure form" is inevitably influenced by it; and one of the difficulties of the nude as a subject for art is that these instincts cannot lie hidden, as they do, for example, in our enjoyment of a piece of pottery, thereby gaining the force of sublimation, but are dragged into the foreground, where they risk upsetting the unity of responses from which a work of art derives its independent life. Even so, the amount of erotic content a work of art can hold in solution is very high. The temple sculptures of tenth-century India are an undisguised exaltation of physical desire; yet they are great works of art because their eroticism is part of their whole philosophy.

Apart from biological needs, there are other branches of human experiences of which the naked body provides a vivid reminder—harmony, energy, ecstasy, humility, pathos; and when we see the beautiful results of such embodiments, it must seem as if the nude as a means of expression is of universal and eternal value. But this we know historically to be untrue. It has been limited both in place and in time. There are naked figures in the paintings of the Far East; but only by an extension of the term can they be called nudes. In Japanese prints they are part of *ukioye,* the passing show of life, which includes, without comment, certain intimate scenes usually allowed to pass unrecorded. The idea of offering the body for its own sake, as a serious subject of contemplation, simply did not occur to the Chinese or Japanese mind, and to this day raises a slight barrier of misunderstanding. In the Gothic North the position was fundamentally very similar. It is true that German painters in the Renaissance, finding that the naked body was a respected subject in Italy, adapted it to their needs, and evolved a remarkable convention of their own. But Dürer's struggles show how artificial this creation was. His instinctive responses were curiosity and horror, and he had to draw a great many circles and other diagrams before he could brace himself to turn the unfortunate body into the nude.

Only in countries touching on the Mediterranean has the nude been at home; and even there its meaning was often forgotten. The Etruscans, owing three quarters of their art to Greece, never abandoned a type of tomb figure in which the defunct man displays his stomach with a complacency that would have shocked a Greek profoundly. Hellenistic and Roman art produced statues and mosaics of professional athletes who seem satisfied with their monstrous proportions. More remarkable still, of course, is the way in which the nude, even in Italy and Greece, is limited by time. It is the fashion to speak of Byzantine art as if it were a continuation of Greek; the nude reminds us that this is one of the refined excesses of specialization. Between the Nereids of late Roman silver and the golden doors of Ghiberti the nudes in Mediterranean art are few and insignificant—a piece of modest craftsmanship like the Ravenna ivory *Apollo and Daphne,* a few *objets de luxe,* like the Veroli Casket, with its cartoon-strip Olympus, and a number of Adams and Eves whose nakedness seldom shows any memory of antique form. Yet, during a great part of that millennium, the masterpieces of Greek art had not yet been destroyed, and men were surrounded by representations of the nude more numerous and, alas, infinitely more splendid than any that have come down to us. As late as the tenth century the *Knidian Aphrodite* of Praxiteles, which had been carried to Constantinople, it is said, by Theodosius, was praised by the Emperor Constantine Porphyrogenitus; and a famous bronze copy of it is mentioned by Robert de Clari in his account of the taking of Constantinople by the Crusaders. Moreover, the body itself did not cease to be an object of interest in Byzantium: this we may deduce from the continuation of the race. Athletes performed in the circus; workmen, stripped to the waist, toiled at the building of St. Sophia. There was no want of opportunity for artists. That their patrons did not demand representations of the nude during this period may be explained by a number of reasonable-looking causes—fear of idolatry, the fashion for asceticism, or the influence of Eastern art. But in fact such answers are incomplete. The nude had ceased to be the subject of art almost a century before the official establishment of Christianity. And during the Middle Ages there would have been ample opportunity to introduce it both into profane decoration and into such sacred subjects as show the beginning and the end of our existence.

Why, then, does it never appear? An illuminating answer is to be found in the notebook of the thirteenth-century architect, Villard de Honnecourt. This contains many beautiful drawings of draped figures, some of them showing a high degree of skill. But when Villard draws two nude figures in what he believes to be the antique style the result is painfully ugly. It was impossible for him to adapt the stylistic conventions of Gothic art to a subject that depended on an entirely different system of forms. There can be few more hopeless misunderstandings in art than his attempt to render that refined abstraction, the antique torso, in terms of Gothic loops and pothooks. Moreover, Villard has constructed his figures according to the pointed geometrical scheme of which he himself gives us the key on another page. He evidently felt that the divine element in the human body must be expressed through geometry. Cennino Cennini, the last chronicler of medieval practice, says, "I will not tell you about irrational animals, because I have never learned any of their measurements. Draw them from nature, and in this respect you will achieve a good style." The Gothic artists could draw animals because this involved no intervening abstraction. But they could not draw the nude because it was an idea: an idea that their philosophy of form could not assimilate.

As I have said, in our Diogenes search for physical beauty our instinctive desire is not to imitate but to perfect. This is part of our Greek inheritance, and it was formulated by Aristotle with his usual deceptive simplicity. "Art," he says, "completes what nature cannot bring to a finish. The artist gives us knowledge of nature's unrealized ends." A great many assumptions underlie this statement, the chief of which is that everything has an ideal form of which the phenomena of experience are more or less corrupted replicas. This beautiful fancy has teased the minds of philosophers and writers on esthetics for over two thousand years, and although we need not plunge into a sea of speculation, we cannot discuss the nude without considering its practical application, because every time we criticize a figure, saying that a neck is too long, hips are too wide or breasts too small, we are admitting, in quite concrete terms, the existence of ideal beauty. Critical opinion has varied between two interpretations of the ideal, one unsatisfactory because it is too prosaic, the other because it is too mystical. The former begins with the belief that although no individual body is satisfactory as a whole, the artist can choose the perfect parts from a number of figures and then combine them into a perfect whole. Such, we are told by Pliny, was the procedure of Zeuxis when he constructed his *Aphrodite* out of the five beautiful maidens of Kroton, and the advice reappears in the earliest treatise on painting of the post-antique world, Alberti's *Della Pittura*. Dürer went so far as to say that he had "searched through two or three hundred." The argument is repeated again and again for four centuries, never more charmingly than by the French seventeenth-century theorist, Du Fresnoy, whom I shall quote in Mason's translation:

> For tho' our casual glance may sometimes meet
> With charms that strike the soul and seem complete,

Yet if those charms too closely we define,
Content to copy nature line for line,
Our end is lost. Not such the master's care,
Curious he culls the perfect from the fair;
Judge of his art, thro' beauty's realm he flies,
Selects, combines, improves, diversifies;
With nimble step pursues the fleeting throng,
And clasps each Venus as she glides along.

Naturally, the theory was a popular one with artists: but it satisfies neither logic nor experience. Logically, it simply transfers the problem from the whole to the parts, and we are left asking by what ideal pattern Zeuxis accepted or rejected the arms, necks, bosoms, and so forth of his five maidens. And even admitting that we do find certain individual limbs or features that, for some mysterious reason, seem to us perfectly beautiful, experience shows us that we cannot often recombine them. They are right in their setting, organically, and to abstract them is to deprive them of that rhythmic vitality on which their beauty depends.

To meet this difficulty the classic theorists of art invented what they called "the middle form." They based this notion on Aristotle's definition of nature, and in the stately language of Sir Joshua Reynolds' *Discourses* it seems to carry some conviction. But what does it amount to, translated into plain speech? Simply that the ideal is composed of the average and the habitual. It is an uninspiring proposition, and we are not surprised that Blake was provoked into replying, "All Forms are Perfect in the Poet's Mind but these are not Abstracted or compounded from Nature, but are from the Imagination." Of course he is right. Beauty is precious and rare, and if it were like a mechanical toy, made up of parts of average size that could be put together at will, we should not value it as we do. But we must admit that Blake's interjection is more a believer's cry of triumph than an argument, and we must ask what meaning can be attached to it. Perhaps the question is best answered in Crocean terms. The ideal is like a myth, in which the finished form can be understood only as the end of a long process of accretion. In the beginning, no doubt, there is the coincidence of widely diffused desires and the personal tastes of a few individuals endowed with the gift of simplifying their visual experiences into easily comprehensible shapes. Once this fusion has taken place, the resulting image, while still in a plastic state, may be enriched or refined upon by succeeding generations. Or, to change the metaphor, it is like a receptacle into which more and more experience can be poured. Then, at a certain point, it is full. It sets. And, partly because it seems to be completely satisfying, partly because the mythopoeic faculty has declined, it is accepted as true. What both Reynolds and Blake meant by ideal beauty was really the diffused memory of that peculiar physical type developed in Greece between the years 480 and 440 B.C.. which in varying degrees of intensity and consciousness furnished the mind of Western man with a pattern of perfection from the Renaissance until the present century.

Once more we have returned to Greece, and it is now time to consider some peculiarities of the Greek mind that may have contributed to the formation of this indestructible image.

The most distinctive is the Greek passion for mathematics. In every branch of Hellenic thought we encounter a belief in measurable proportion that, in the last analysis, amounts to a mystical religion; and as early as Pythagoras it had been given the visible form of geometry. All art is founded on faith, and inevitably the Greek faith in harmonious numbers found expression in their painting and sculpture; but precisely how we do not know. The so-called canon of Polykleitos is not recorded, and the rules of proportion that have come down to us through Pliny and other ancient writers are of the most elementary kind. Probably the Greek sculptors were familiar with a system as subtle and elaborate as that of their architects, but we have scarcely any indication as to what it was. There is, however, one short and obscure statement in Vitruvius that, whatever it meant in antiquity, had a decisive influence on the Renaissance. At the beginning of the third book, in which he sets out to give the rules for sacred edifices, he suddenly announces that these buildings should have the proportions of a man. He gives some indication of correct human proportions and then throws in a statement that man's body is a model of proportion because with arms or legs extended it fits into those "perfect" geometrical forms, the square and the circle. It is impossible to exaggerate what this simple-looking proposition meant to the men of the Renaissance. To them it was far more than a convenient rule: it was the foundation of a whole philosophy. Taken together with the musical scale of Pythagoras, it seemed to offer exactly that link between sensation and order, between an organic and a geometric basis of beauty, which was (and perhaps remains) the philosopher's stone of esthetics. Hence the many diagrams of figures standing in squares or circles that illustrate the treatises on architecture or esthetics from the fifteenth to the seventeenth century.

Vitruvian man, as this figure has come to be called, appears earlier than Leonardo da Vinci, but it is in Leonardo's famous drawing in Venice that he receives his most masterly exposition; also, on the whole the most correct, for Leonardo makes only two slight deviations from Vitruvius, whereas most of the other illustrations follow him very sketchily. This is not one of Leonardo's most attractive drawings, and it must be admitted that the Vitruvian formula does not provide any guarantee of a pleasant-looking body. The most carefully worked-out illustration of all, in the Como Vitruvius of 1521, shows an ungraceful figure with head too small and legs and feet too big. Especially troublesome was the question of how the square and the circle, which were to establish the perfect form, should be related to one another. Leonardo, on no authority that I can discover, said that in order to fit into a circle the figure should stretch apart his legs so that he was a fourteenth shorter than if they were together. But this arbitrary solution did not please Cesariano, the editor of the Como Vitruvius, who inscribed the square in the circle, with unfortunate results. We see that from the point of view of strict geometry a gorilla might prove to be more satisfactory than a man.

How little systematic proportion alone can be relied on to produce physical beauty is shown by Dürer's engraving known as the *Nemesis* or *Large Fortune*. It was executed in 1501, and we know that in the preceding year Dürer had been reading Vitruvius. In this figure he has applied Vitruvian principles of measurement down to the last detail: according to Professor Panofsky, even the big toe is operative. He has also taken his subject from a work by Poliziano, the same humanist poet who inspired Botticelli's *Birth of Venus* and Raphael's *Galatea*. But in spite of these precautions he has not achieved the classical ideal. That he did so later was owing to the practice of relating his system to antique figures. It was not his squares and circles that enabled him to master classical proportions, but the fact that he applied them to memories of the *Apollo Belvedere* and the *Medici Venus*—forms "perfected in the poet's mind." And it was from these, in the end, that he derived the beautiful nude figure of Adam in his famous engraving of the *Fall*.

Francis Bacon, as we all know, said, "There is no excellent beauty that hath not some strangeness in the proportion. A man cannot tell whether Apelles or Albert Dürer were the more trifler; where of the one would make a personage by geometrical proportions: the other by taking the best part out of divers faces to make one excellent." This very intelligent observation is unfair to Dürer, and suggests that Bacon, like the rest of us, had not read his book on human proportions, only looked at the plates. For, after 1507, Dürer abandoned the idea of imposing a geometrical scheme on the body, and set about deducing ideal measurements from nature, with a result, as may be imagined, somewhat different from his analyses of the antique; and in his introduction he forcefully denies the claim that he is providing a standard of absolute perfection. "There lives no man upon earth," he says, "who can give a final judgment upon what the most beautiful shape of a man may be; God only knows that. . . . 'Good' and 'better' in respect of beauty are not easy to discern, for it would be quite possible to make two different figures, neither conforming with the other, one stouter, the other thinner, and yet we might scarce be able to judge which of the two excelled in beauty."

So the most indefatigable and masterly constructor of ideal proportions abandoned them halfway through his career, and his work, from the *Nemesis* onward, is a proof that the idea of the nude does not depend on analyzable proportions alone. And yet when we look at the splendidly schematized bodies of Greek sculpture, we cannot resist the conviction that some system did exist. Almost every artist or writer on art who has thought seriously about the nude has concluded that it must have some basis of construction that can be stated in terms of measurement; and I myself, when trying to explain why a photograph did not satisfy me, said that I missed the sense of simple units clearly related to one another. Although the artist cannot construct a beautiful nude by mathematical rules, any more than the musician can compose a beautiful fugue, he cannot ignore them. They must be lodged somewhere at the back of his mind or in the movements of his fingers. Ultimately he is as dependent on them as an architect.

Dipendenza [dependency]: that is the word used by Michelangelo, supreme as a draftsman of the nude and as an architect, to express his sense of the relationship between these two forms of order. And in the pages that follow I often make use of architectural analogies. Like a building, the nude represents a balance between an ideal scheme and functional necessities. The figure artist cannot forget the components of the human body, any more than the architect can fail to support his roof or forget his doors and windows. But the variations of shape and disposition are surprisingly wide. The most striking instance is, of course, the change in proportion between the Greek and the Gothic idea of the female body. One of the few classical canons of proportion of which we can be certain is that which, in a female nude, took the same unit of measurement for the distance between the breasts, the distance from the lower breast to the navel, and again from the navel to the division of the legs. This scheme we shall find carefully maintained in all figures of the classical epoch and in most of those which imitated them down to the first century. Contrast a typical Gothic nude of the fifteenth century, the *Eve* in the Vienna gallery attributed to Memlinc. The components are—naturally—the same. The basic pattern of the female body is still an oval, surmounted by two spheres; but the oval has grown incredibly long, the spheres have grown distressingly small. If we apply our unit of measurement, the distance between the breasts, we find that the navel is exactly twice as far down the body as it is in the classic scheme. This increased length of body is made more noticeable because it is unbroken by any suggestion of ribs or muscles. The forms are not conceived as individual blocks, but seem to have been drawn out of one another as if they were made of some viscous material. It is usual to speak of this kind of Gothic nude as "naturalistic," but is Memlinc's *Eve* really closer to the average (for this is what the word means) than the antique nude? Such, at all events, was certainly not the painter's intention. He aimed at producing a figure that would conform to the ideals of his time, that would be the kind of shape men liked to see; and by some strange interaction of flesh and spirit this long curve of the stomach has become the means by which the body has achieved the ogival rhythm of late Gothic architecture.

A rather less obvious example is provided by Sansovino's *Apollo* on the Loggetta in Venice. It is inspired by the *Apollo Belvedere*, but although Sansovino, like all his contemporaries, thought that the antique figure was of unsurpassable beauty, he has allowed himself a fundamental difference in his construction of the body. We may describe this by saying that the antique male nude is like a Greek temple, the flat frame of the chest being carried on the columns of the legs; whereas the Renaissance nude is related to the architectural system that produced the central-domed church; so that instead of the sculptural interest depending on a simple, frontal plane, a number of axes radiate from one center. Not only the elevations but, so to say, the ground plans of these figures would have an obvious relationship to their respective architectures. What we may call the multiple-axis nude continued until the classicistic revival of the eighteenth century. Then, when architects were reviving the Greek-temple form, sculptors once more gave to the male body the flatness and frontality of a frame building. Ultimately the *dipendenza* of architecture and the nude expresses the relationship we all so earnestly desire between that which is perfected by the mind and that which we love. Poussin, writing to his friend Chantelou in 1642, said, "The beautiful girls whom you will have seen in Nîmes will not, I am sure, have delighted your spirit any less than the beautiful columns of Maison Carrée; for the one is no more than an old copy of the other." And the hero of Claudel's *Partage de midi,* when at last he puts his arms round his beloved, utters, as the first pure expression of his bliss, the words "O Colonne!"

So our surmise that the discovery of the nude as a form of art is connected with idealism and faith in measurable proportions seems to be true, but it is only half the truth. What other peculiarities of the Greek mind are involved? One obvious answer is their belief that the body was something to be proud of, and should be kept in perfect trim.

We need not suppose that many Greeks looked like the *Hermes* of Praxiteles, but we can be sure that in fifth-century Attica a majority of the young men had the nimble, well-balanced bodies depicted on the early red-figure vases. On a vase in the British Museum is a scene that will arouse sympathy in most of us, but to the Athenians was ridiculous and shameful—a fat youth in the gymnasium embarrassed by his ungraceful figure, and apparently protesting to a thin one, while two young men of more fortunate development throw the javelin and the discus. Greek literature from Homer and Pindar downward contains many expressions of this physical pride, some of which strike unpleasantly on the Anglo-Saxon ear and trouble the minds of schoolmasters when they are recommending the Greek ideal of fitness. "What do I care for any man?" says the young man Kritobalos in the *Symposium* of Xenophon: "I am beautiful." And no doubt this arrogance was increased by the tradition that in the gymnasium and the sportsground such young men displayed themselves totally naked.

The Greeks attached great importance to their nakedness. Thucydides, in recording the stages by which they distinguished themselves from the barbarians, gives prominence to the date at which it became the rule in the Olympic games, and we know from vase paintings that the competitors at the Panathenaic festival had been naked ever since the early sixth century. Although the presence or absence of a loincloth does not greatly affect questions of form, and in this study I shall include figures that are lightly draped, psychologically the Greek cult of absolute nakedness is of great importance. It implies the conquest of an inhibition that oppresses all but the most backward people; it is like a denial of original sin. This is not, as is sometimes supposed, simply a part of paganism: for the Romans were shocked by the nakedness of Greek athletes, and Ennius attacked it as a sign of decadence. Needless to say, he was wide of the mark, for the most determined nudists of all were the Spartans, who scandalized even the Athenians by allowing women to compete, lightly clad, in their games. He and subsequent moralists considered the matter in purely physical terms; but, in fact, Greek confidence in the body can be understood only in relation to their philosophy. It expresses above all their sense of human wholeness. Nothing that related to the whole man could be isolated or evaded; and this serious awareness of how much was implied in physical beauty saved them from the two evils of sensuality and estheticism.

At the same party where Kritobalos brags about his beauty Xenophon describes the youth Autolykos, victor of the Pankration, in whose honor the feast was being given. "Noting the scene," he says, "the first idea to strike the mind is that beauty has about it something regal; and the more so if it chance to be combined (as now in the person of Autolykos) with modesty and self-respect. Even as when a splendid object blazes forth at night, the eyes of men are riveted, so now the beauty of Autolykos drew on him the gaze of all; nor was there one of those onlookers but was stirred to his soul's depth by him who sat there. Some fell into unwonted silence, while the gestures of the rest were equally significant."

This feeling, that the spirit and body are one, which is the most familiar of all Greek characteristics, manifests itself in their gift of giving to abstract ideas a sensuous, tangible, and, for the most part, human form. Their logic is conducted in the form of dialogues between real men. Their gods take visible shape, and on their appearance are usually mistaken for half-familiar human beings—a maidservant, a shepherd, or a distant cousin. Woods, rivers, even echoes are shown in painting as bodily presences, solid as the living protagonists, and often more prominent. Here we reach what I take to be the central point of our subject: "Greek statues," said Blake, in his *Descriptive Catalogue*, "are all of them representations of spiritual existences, of gods immortal, to the mortal, perishing organ of sight; and yet they are embodied and organized in solid marble." The bodies were there, the belief in the gods was there, the love of rational proportion was there. It was the unifying grasp of the Greek imagination that brought them together. And the nude gains its enduring value from the fact that it reconciles several contrary states. It takes the most sensual and immediately interesting object, the human body, and puts it out of reach of time and desire; it takes the most purely rational concept of which mankind is capable, mathematical order, and makes it a delight to the senses; and it takes the vague fears of the unknown and sweetens them by showing that the gods are like men and may be worshiped for their life-giving beauty rather than their death-dealing powers.

To recognize how completely the value of these spiritual existences depends on their nudity, we have only to think of them as they appear, fully clothed, in the Middle Ages or early Renaissance. They have lost all their meaning. When the Graces are represented by three nervous ladies hiding behind a blanket, they no longer convey to us the civilizing influence of beauty. When Herakles is a lumbering *Landsknecht* weighed down by fashionable armor, he cannot increase our sense of well-being by his own superabundant strength. Conversely, when nude figures, which had been evolved to express an idea, ceased to do so, and were represented for their physical perfection alone, they soon lost their value. This was the fatal legacy of neoclassicism, and Coleridge, who lived through the period, summed up the situation in some lines he added to the translation of Schiller's *Piccolomini:*

> *The intelligible powers of ancient poets,*
> *The fair humanities of old religion,*
> *The Power, the Beauty and the Majesty,*
> *That had their haunts in dale or piney mountain,*
> *. . . all these have vanished.*
> *They live no longer in the faith of reason.*

The academic nudes of the nineteenth century are lifeless because they no longer embodied real human needs and experiences. They were among the hundreds of devalued symbols that encumbered the art and architecture of the utilitarian century.

The nude had flourished most exuberantly during the first hundred years of the classical Renaissance, when the new appetite for antique imagery overlapped the medieval habits of symbolism and personification. It seemed then that there was no concept, however sublime, that could not be expressed by the naked body, and no object of use, however trivial, that would not be better for having been given human shape. At one end of the scale was Michelangelo's *Last Judgment;* at the other the door knockers, candelabra, or even handles of knives and forks. To the first it might be objected—and frequently was—that nakedness was unbecoming in a representation of Christ and His saints. This was the point put forward by Paolo Veronese when he was tried by the Inquisition for including drunkards and Germans in his picture of the marriage of Cana: to which the chief inquisitor gave his immortal reply, "Do you not know that in these figures by Michelangelo there is nothing that is not spiritual—*non vi è cosa se non de spirito?*" And to the second it might be objected—and frequently is—that the similitude of the naked Venus is not what we need in our hand when we are cutting up our food or knocking at a door, to which Benvenuto

Cellini would have replied that since the human body is the most perfect of all forms we cannot see it too often. In between these two extremes was that forest of nude figures, painted or carved, in stucco, bronze, or stone, which filled every vacant space in the architecture of the sixteenth century.

Such an insatiable appetite for the nude is unlikely to recur. It arose from a fusion of beliefs, traditions, and impulses very remote from our age of essence and specialization. Yet even in the new self-governing kingdom of the esthetic sensation the nude is enthroned. The intensive application of great artists has made it into a sort of pattern for all formal constructions, and it is still a means of affirming the belief in ultimate perfection. "For soule is forme, and doth the bodie make," wrote Spenser in his *Hymne in Honour of Beautie,* echoing the words of the Florentine Neoplatonists, and although in life the evidence for the doctrine is inconclusive, it is perfectly applicable to art. The nude remains the most complete example of the transmutation of matter into form.

Nor are we likely once more to cut ourselves off from the body, as in the ascetic experiment of medieval Christianity. We may no longer worship it, but we have come to terms with it. We are reconciled to the fact that it is our lifelong companion, and since art is concerned with sensory images the scale and rhythm of the body is not easily ignored. Our continuous effort, made in defiance of the pull of gravity, to keep ourselves balanced upright on our legs affects every judgment on design, even our conception of which angle shall be called "right." The rhythm of our breathing and the beat of our hearts are part of the experience by which we measure a work of art. The relation of head to body determines the standard by which we assess all other proportions in nature. The disposition of areas in the torso is related to our most vivid experiences, so that, abstract shapes, the square and the circle, seem to us male and female; and the old endeavor of magical mathematics to square the circle is like the symbol of physical union. The starfish diagrams of Renaissance theorists may be ridiculous, but the Vitruvian principle rules our spirits, and it is no accident that the formalized body of the "perfect man" became the supreme symbol of European belief. Before the *Crucifixion* of Michelangelo we remember that the nude is, after all, the most serious of all subjects in art; and that it was not an advocate of paganism who wrote, "The Word was made flesh, and dwelt among us . . . full of grace and truth."

—The Nude (1956)

CHAPTER FOURTEEN

Isolation and Synaesthesis

HUGO MÜNSTERBERG
Connection in Science and Isolation in Art

C. K. OGDEN, I. A. RICHARDS, and JAMES WOOD
Synaesthesis

Introductory Note

As a DISTINGUISHED MEMBER OF the Philosophy Department at Harvard, Hugo Münsterberg (1863-1916) has developed a theory somewhat like that of Bullough and Ortega y Gasset. He similarly recognizes the detachment of the esthetic attitude from practical considerations, but his main emphasis is upon the contrast between esthetic appreciation and scientific knowledge. "We find knowledge," he declares, "in transforming the object so that it can be linked with all others, but . . . we find beauty in transforming the object so that it stands for itself alone, gives us its own reality, separated from the rest of the world." The contemplator is not intent upon asking *why* or *whence* or *whither;* he does not as in science peer behind the object into its causes, or gaze beyond at its possible destiny. He is intent simply upon discovering the *what*—upon intuiting the immediate object, with all its concrete values, as abstracted from its connections with things that lie beyond the "frame" of the experience. Kant and Schopenhauer described the nature of this intense focusing upon the object, but Münsterberg has greatly enriched and extended this earlier account.

In a brief but pithy statement, three English writers, Charles Kay Ogden

433

(1889-   ), Ivor Armstrong Richards (1893-   ), and James Wood (1899-
), agree with Münsterberg that esthetic experience is, in a sense, isolated
and self-sufficient. This state of repose, they believe, is achieved not by the
simplification and exclusion of impulses but by their balance and harmonization.
The essence of esthetic enjoyment is "synaesthesis"—a condition of psychological
equilibrium in which the whole self is brought into vigorous and harmonious
activity. Experience of this type is disinterested and impersonal (although in a
sense the contemplator becomes more fully himself in becoming more fully
alive). There is no impulse to act, only the alert and poised awareness of the
completely coordinated personality.

In his various critical writings, Richards has used "synaesthesis" as the test
of esthetic value. A work of art, he has maintained, is to be judged excellent if
it arouses this sort of rich and harmonious experience.

HUGO MUNSTERBERG

Connection in Science and Isolation in Art

It is claimed that physics and chemistry and biology and psychology and
history give us an account of all the physical and psychical things which surround us and of ourselves; that there is nothing in the universe which cannot be
included in such a scientific report. The scientist, whether he deals with stones
or stars, with plants or men, with individuals or nations, claims to show us what
they really are: he assumes to give us the truth about them, and, as we cannot
prove that his so-called truth is wrong, it seems that all things in heaven and on
earth cannot be anything else than that which the scholar with his textbooks has
proved them to be. There cannot be an account of reality which is of equal
value with the "true" one.

We all know how the scientist reaches his important results on which it is
claimed our whole modern civilized life is built up, and which have made our
technique possible and have given us an understanding of the past. He analyzes
most carefully the objects which he observes, the material and the mental ones,
and thus finds their elements; the physical world dissolves itself into biological
cells and chemical elements and physical molecules and all, ultimately, into mechanical atoms, while the psychical world shows itself to be made up of elements which the psychologist calls sensations. The whole universe, and man's
life in it, becomes a gigantic combination of atoms and sensations. But the de-

scription of the elements is not the only task of the scientist. His second great aim is, as everybody knows, explanation, that is, the understanding of all processes as effects of foregoing causes and, correspondingly, as causes of subsequent effects. Description and explanation are thus assumed to cover the whole ground of physical and psychological researches, and if all is described in its elements and explained by its causes, we then know the real world and every other possible account must remain an arbitrary fancy below the level of truth.

But are description and explanation after all really two different processes? As soon as we look a little deeper into the mechanism of scientific thinking we discover that it is not so. The describer says, This object has these elements, this ocean yonder contains salt and its water contains hydrogen and oxygen and each drop contains trillions of atoms. What does he mean by that? If we ask him, he will say, I mean by that an account of reality, and that the account is true, I can prove. How does he prove it? Well, he takes a pailful of that sea water and evaporates it and shows us the salt as a result; he brings a galvanic current through the water and shows us the division of the water into hydrogen and oxygen; and if we ask him finally to prove that each drop of water is made from atoms, he begins to show the changes through which the water passes under strong pressure, with high temperature and low temperature, and so on, to give us mathematical proofs that these changes cannot be understood without the theory of atomism. Such proof he thinks must convince us: we can taste the crystallized salt, we can see how the balloons get filled by the gases, how the steam is formed. But does such proof really give us what we asked for? When the salt is crystallized, when the hydrogen is in the balloon, when the steam is evaporated, we do not have any longer the sea water about whose elements we inquired; the water has been transformed into something else, and, while the scientist was expected to show us what the water *is,* he has practically shown us by his proofs only into what the water can be transformed. When he says the water "contains" the salt and the gases, he means that certain processes, for instance evaporation, have the effect of transforming the given substance into such salt and such gases, while nobody could get salt out of a solution of sugar. The scientific descriptive account of the elements of an object thus does not give any knowledge of the object itself at all, but it tells us what changes can be produced through an analysis of that object, what effects we must expect from it, what new objects can be got from it. The description of the elements brings us thus not nearer to the thing itself, it takes us away from the thing and it teaches us with what effects the thing is connected; in other words: the "elements" are merely expressions of justified expectations as to the behavior of the thing. No proof and no demonstration can go behind that or beyond that; we may tear in pieces or crush the thing, we may pulverize or boil it to show what it contains, but we are always producing a new object in the place of the old one: the powder is *not* the stone—we have shown only that the stone can be transformed into powder; that is, we have proved that we can bring about a certain change and effect with the stone.

As soon as we have grasped the deeper meaning of all "analysis" we see that it is inseparable from the study of causes and effects. Description and explanation are not two separate logical tasks, but merely one—description works toward explanation, and there cannot be any descriptive analysis which does not find its real meaning in the reference to that which will happen with the thing—that is, to the effects which it causes. Every progress in the description of the world has meant a step forward towards the understanding of causal relations and nothing else; and every new insight into causal laws has brought new modes of description. The day when mechanics is able to describe every atom and every action in the world no causal problem will remain unsolved; the ideal description, at the same time, will be the ideal explanation. All that science can teach us about the object O is thus merely how it was caused by L and M and N and how it will bring about the effect P and Q and R; and those characteristic expectations as to P and Q and R and those references to L and M and N we express and condense in the account of the *elements* of O; but O itself remains always O: we cannot creep into it, we cannot get more of it than to know that it is O, and if we break it in pieces to show its parts, then it is a group of P's and R's but no longer the O. There is no escape: science does not care at all for O itself; even when science enumerates O's so-called elements, it speaks in reality not of O but of its causal and logical relations to L, M, N, P, Q, R, and the whole alphabet of things. Science makes us believe that it speaks of the thing, and yet informs us merely of the thing's relations to other things in the universe. Whenever we want to grasp one piece of the world, science takes it out of our hand, shows us instead of itself a thousand other things to which it is related, pushes us ever forward to discover new causes and effects, and hides the situation by calling this search for the future connections an "analysis" and those features which determine those connections the "elements." It may be said the only meaning of all knowledge, description and explanation, is the search for the connection of things—when the world has become to the human intellect a connected whole, the goal is reached.

Such insight into connections is, of course, of fundamental importance, because all our practical actions must be regulated by it. If I want to act, the things in the world are my means and tools—I do not care what they "are," I then care only for what they can produce, how far they can serve my ends. And if I deal with men, I do not ask what they really "are" but how I can influence them, what I can expect from them, how I can connect them with my hopes and fears. If I want to understand a product of civilization, an institution, a law, a religion, a government, again I must needs establish their connections with the human efforts of the past, their causes and effects, their relations to all the institutions; and, if I want to grasp a thought, I must understand its relations to the other thoughts which are involved and connected with it. All that the philologist, the historian, the psychologist, the naturalist are offering is indeed invaluable at every step in the walk of life, and from the primitive knowledge that guides the child's behavior in the nursery and the savage's life in the forests up to the most complex knowledge which directs the actions of the modern engineer or physician, every new understanding of connection has been an assistance in the world of men and things, of nature and civilization in which we live.

There is thus no reproach to the scientist in our insisting that he gives us knowledge not only of the thing itself, but also of its connections; but the fact remains that his truth—his description and explanation—does not bring us nearer to the reality of the thing itself—in fact, it leads us away from the object we are interested in, leads us away to other objects with which it may be connected.

How vain sounds now the claim that the truth of science is the only possible truth and that every presentation of objects which is not based on scientific knowledge carries us away from the objective facts. No, it is science which veils the real thing which we want to know, and turns our attention to that which the thing is not. Is it not possible to come nearer to the object itself, to grasp its true reality, to feel its life, to sink into it, to penetrate into its fullness? Instead of crumbling it into pieces—for its scattered fragments are no longer the thing—is it not possible to give the whole of our mind to the presentation of the one thing alone, with all that it gives us, with all that it shows and suggests, while the world about it and the world around us are forgotten? The highest truth about the thing must be the knowledge of the thing itself, not of its causes and its effects; the thing itself with all its richness and all its meanings to the human mind, and not the substitution which the scientist proposes for the explanation of future events. The thing itself is not its past or its future, it wants to be understood just as it offers itself to our mind in the present experience, and there cannot be any rest for us until we accept what it offers this moment instead of looking with the eyes of science to what it promises for the future. The highest truth thus lies not in the inference to future transformations, but in the appreciation of present offerings; not in the study of the elements, but in the acceptance of the whole in its human relations. Thus, if you really want the thing itself, there is only one way to get it: you must separate it from everything else, you must disconnect it from causes and effects, you must bring it before the mind so that nothing else but this one presentation fills the mind, so that there remains no room for anything besides it. If that ever can be reached, the result must be clear: for the object it means complete isolation; for the subject, it means complete repose in the object, and that is complete satisfaction with the object; and that is, finally, merely another name for the enjoyment of beauty. To isolate the object for the mind, means to make it beautiful, for it fills the mind without an idea of anything else: we are interested in the impression as it is in itself, without any reference to anything outside of it in space and time; and this complete repose, where the objective impression becomes for us an ultimate end in itself, is the only possible content of the true experience of beauty.

Yes, connection is science, but the work of art is isolation; more than that, isolation is beauty whether nature or the imagination of the artist offers it. We have here reached the highest point of a philosophical discussion, the point from which we can overlook the two worlds together, the world of knowledge and the world of beauty. Neither the scientist nor the artist gives us the world of immediate experience, as in our real life we experience neither a system of connected things nor a series of isolated objects. To produce a connected system or to have an object isolated, and thus cut loose and separated from everything else in the world, is to demand an artificial transformation of reality to serve the purpose of our will. As every descriptive and explanatory knowledge, yes, every analysis, serves indeed the purpose of connection, every esthetic rendering of the world really serves this other end, to isolate the factors of experience, to make them independent of every possible connection, and thus to present them to our mind just as they really are in themselves. Wherever nature gives us such an experience which is closed in itself and does not point to anything else, and brings to silence every practical desire and makes us forget all things besides the one which offers itself to our mind, there nature herself is the artist. But more often, the genius of men must transform chance experience, must paint the landscape, must form in marble the figure, must express in songs the emotional affection, must render in dramas the actions of men.

That ocean yonder was my experience which I wanted to know in all its truth and reality. The scientist came and showed me the salt which was crystallized out of it, and the gases into which the galvanic current dissolved it, and the mathematical curves in which the drops were moving—most useful knowledge, indeed, for all my practical purposes—but in every one of his statements, that ocean itself with its waves and its surf and its radiant blueness had disappeared. But let us not ask what can be done with the water, how it can be used, what is its economic value, how it will carry my boat, what has caused its movements; but let us ask only once, what is it really that I see; the water itself must give us the answer. Let it express itself, give to it, too, a chance to communicate to us all that it can bring to our mind, to show us to its best advantage every one of its features, to tell us its own story, to bring to the highest expression every hidden meaning of reality; let us only once give our whole attention to that one courageous, breezy wave, which thunders there against the rock; let us forget what there was and what there will be; let us live through one pulse-beat of experience in listening merely to that wave alone, seeing its foam alone, tasting its breeze alone—and in that one thrill we have grasped the thing itself as it really is in its fullest truth. The painter alone can succeed in holding that wave in its wonderful swing on his canvas, and his golden frame can separate that painted wave forever from the rest of the universe. He has created, then, a thing of beauty, because it satisfies us as it is; and what his brush tells us is not less true than the formula of the mathematician who calculated the movement of the wave, and the formula of the chemist who separated the elements. But, of course, the painter must really succeed, the frame alone cannot isolate that bit of experience. If his painting is nothing but a colored photograph which makes us ask, what the name of that shore is, whether there is good bathing and fishing there, and where the way from that rock leads, then, of course, we are in the midst of connections, the thing of beauty has again become a thing of information; we may have a good advertisement of a seashore place, but a poor painting; the real work of art on the other hand holds our mind to the object itself, its way leads nowhere and its frame ends its world. And so we may say: to isolate an object for our mind; to show the object as it really is; to give us repose in the object; to make the object beautiful—are only four different expressions of the same fact.

One aspect more ought to be emphasized at once. Science is connection, but not every connection is science; art is isolation, but not every isolation is art. In fancy, or in superstition, we might mentally connect any objects whatever in the world, but that would not be knowledge; and, on the other hand, we might, in a sensual enjoyment, give over our whole mind to anything which captured our senses, and yet that alone would not constitute the basis for a declaration of beauty. Both science and art, knowledge and beauty, are independent of individual, personal desires and instincts and fancies. Both make a general claim; they are not meant as individual decisions, they demand an over-individual value; that which is knowledge for one is taken to be knowledge for all; that which is declared beautiful by one is assumed to appear beautiful to all. Knowledge and beauty are thus postulates: you ought to connect the things of the world in this way if you want knowledge, and you ought to isolate the things of the world in that way if you want beauty. It is exactly as with the prescriptions of morality; any one may construct individual rules, but he can demand only that the others fulfill his prescriptions if they want to escape his punishment, there is no moral obligation in such an individual, arbitrary rule. Morality, on the other hand, is over-individual, and claims you ought to follow it even to your personal disadvantage. This "ought" which morality attaches to human actions, logic attaches to the scientific connections of things, and esthetics attaches to the artistic isolation of things. If we give our whole mind to an object which we isolate with the understanding that we do not claim that it ought to absorb the mind of others, that object may be agreeable but cannot be beautiful, just as the individual rule which the master gives to his servants may be useful and practical, but cannot as such be of moral value. That which we eat and drink, though delicious, can as such never be beautiful, because we destroy it while we are enjoying it, and in our pleasure we thus exclude the demand that others ought to enjoy it with us; the more lasting the object, the larger the circle of those individuals which can take part in it with us, the greater are its esthetic possibilities. The statue of snow stands on a lower plane than that of marble.[1]

And one more consequence ought to be considered from the beginning—if science means over-individual connection and art over-individual isolation, one most important difference of scientific and of artistic work must follow at once. The scientist seeks a connection whose ideal is thus the complete system which comprises the whole universe, and which leaves, therefore, no room for anything outside of the one system; there can be, therefore, only one science and all scholars of the world are cooperating in working out that one system of knowledge; every progress made is for all time and for everybody. For the world of art, exactly the opposite must be true; if beauty means isolation, the perfect rendering of one object has in itself no relation to the rendering of other objects and every one can try the process of isolating again. While a scientific problem once solved is solved for all time, an esthetic subject can be taken up with ever-new freshness. The Pythagorean theorem cannot be created a second time after Pythagoras, but Madonnas can be painted; and will be painted, without end after Raphael, and again and again Spring and Love will be sung in lyrical poems. Science, therefore, moves forward in a straight direction, every generation knows more than the foregoing did, but art does not know such continuity. The continuity in the history of art is formed by the influence which the works of art have on the imagination of the artists of a later generation; a cumulative influence thus certainly exists and every artist stands today under the influence of the esthetic productions of two thousand years: but the artist of today does not continue the work of the artist of yesterday; every work is closed in itself and has no objective reference to any other work of art.

But we must return to our central proposition. We said that science connects but art isolates; that we find knowledge in transforming the object so that it can be linked with all others, but that we find beauty in transforming the object so that it stands for itself alone, gives us its own reality, separated from the rest of the world. We can characterize the difference also by saying the scientist analyzes where the artist interprets, the scientist seeks elements where the artist aims at the meaning, the scientist works towards laws where the artist seeks values, the scientist explains where the artist appreciates; but both, that must be clear, aim to give us an understanding of the objective world, both give us truths. Both are, on the other hand, more than mere passive mirrors of the world; both come with subjective energies towards the world, as the

---

[1] This paragraph is largely a restatement of Kant's doctrine of the claim of the esthetic judgment to universal validity. (Editor's note.)

scientific account with its aiming at connection involves just as many subjective activities as the artistic rendering with its aim towards isolation of the special thing.

Whether the one truth is more valuable than the other depends upon our purpose. The purpose for which we looked out in scientific knowledge was practical mastery of the world for the outer achievements; we had to know what causes were connected with what effects. No other kind of truth can help us for this end; what can be the use of sinking with our mind into an isolated object, which by its isolation is separated from its causes and effects if we want to manage the affairs of practical life? But is that really the only end in our existence; is the world really for us merely a material to be used and never a material to be enjoyed; is the object merely a cause to produce certain effects, never an end in itself; can our life be complete in itself if everything comes in question for us merely as a means to something else and never as valuable in its own offering; does not our mind in all the striving and rushing of daily life long for the rest of satisfaction? Certainly our life would not be worth living if the transitory stages of using the world were not alternating with periods through which our mind rests in the world. Religion and philosophy seek this rest of the mind, this repose of our existence in the contemplation of the eternal totality. The lover of beauty seeks it in the contemplation of the single object; he isolates it from the world and by that act of isolation it does not come in question any more as means to an effect, as tool for an end, as product of a cause, as a steppingstone to something else, but merely in its own existence, and, therefore, because it does not suggest anything outside of itself, it brings a final rest to the mind of the subject. Now the tree is not lumber, the animal is not food, the waterfall is not machine power, but in their beauty alone are they appreciated.

Exactly as the power of knowledge must be developed through training and education for the purposes of later practical life, so the power of esthetic appreciation must be developed in early youth for this not less important and not less valuable other aim of human life—to seek rest in the things of our world. Nowhere, perhaps, is this need greater than among our American youth. Not only the impressions of the life of adults, not only the rush and push of the public life which they see, suggest a one-sided aspect, an unbalanced over-estimation of the practical, of the looking on things as means of practical ends; but even their play and their childish enjoyment is but imitation, fully shaped by this same one-sided idea. The European children are accustomed to devices of play which stimulate the imagination first of all; the American child grows up with movement plays which train the skill and the practical initiative, but are useless for the development of imaginative power. A youth who does not learn early to appreciate the objects in their own meaning, but sees them as causes for effects, cannot be expected to have in later life other than practical interests and must lack that repose which gives the only complete satisfaction, that repose which a mere restless striving for practical ends ever promises but can never give. The most systematic effort must be made to train the young man from the first for the true aspect of the world which takes the things as they really are in their highest import and not as they appear in the system of causes and effects.

To be trained to the understanding of this highest truth it is not necessary to learn anything by heart or to make experiments; and yet serious and severe training is required. We have said that to understand anything as it is in itself, we must be able to abstract it from all its connections; the one power of the mind which we ought to train is thus the power of abstraction, of isolation, the power which suppresses the thought of everything which lies outside of the object and inhibits every desire which is not satisfied by the object in its immediate presentation. From this point of view, it is immaterial whether the beauty appears in nature and life or in the rendering of the artist and poet. The landscape which the painter gives us on the canvas is separated from the world by its frame, the roads in that landscape do not lead anywhere outside of the frame and there are no people behind those hills; if we begin to connect it with anything outside of itself, it becomes merely a geographical illustration, and thus a part of science. But the beautiful sunset there over the ocean in real nature is not less separated from the world, and, if we connect it with that which was before and with that which will follow, it becomes astronomical knowledge and the restful absorption of our mind is gone. This suppression of the thought of where the road is leading needs more careful preparation and more insistent training than the stimulation of such inquiries, which must be brought into the service of knowledge. To see the marble statue but not to ask for the color of the living being, to see the bust and not to ask for the arms and legs, to hear the poem and not to ask to whom the poet addresses it, to read the drama and not to inquire what will happen after the last act, is possible only if the scientific attitude with its desire for connection is suppressed and the attitude of satisfaction in the isolated object is developed. Art instruction in the school is the great social scheme which the community has at its disposal to train this power; that is, to open the mind for that truth which is more complete in itself than the truth of scientific knowledge, for that truth which understands the immediate reality of the objects. . . .

Philosophy, to condense all into one phrase, has shown that all scientific knowledge leads us away from the real object, giving us merely its connections; that if we want the real object, we must separate it from all its connections, must grasp it in its complete isolation; and that it is the function of art to bring about this isolation and to show us the object in its immediate truth.

—The Principles of Art Education (1905)

C. K. OGDEN, I. A. RICHARDS, AND JAMES WOOD

Synaesthesis

My master the celebrated Chang says: "Having no leanings is called Chung, admitting of no change is called Yung. By Chung is denoted Equilibrium; Yung is the fixed principle regulating everything under heaven."

What heaven has ordained is man's Nature; an accordance with this is the Path; the regulation of it is Instruction.

There is nothing more visible than what is secret—nothing more manifest than what is minute. The superior man is careful: he is but one.

When anger, sorrow, joy, pleasure are in being but are not manifested, the mind may be said to be in a state of Equilibrium; when the feelings are stirred and cooperate in due degree the mind may be said to be in a state of Harmony. Equilibrium is the great principle.

If both Equilibrium and Harmony exist everything will occupy its proper place and all things will be nourished and flourish.

—From the *Chung Yung*
The Doctrine of Equilibrium and Harmony

It remains only to formulate a doctrine which seems essentially that to be attributed to Confucius in the quotations from the *Chung Yung* at the head of this article. . . . It is expected that the experience now about to be described will be recognized by those who look for it; it has, indeed, been noticed by many poets and critics. It marks off a field which cannot otherwise be defined and also explains why the objects therein contained can reasonably be regarded as of great importance. The limits of this field do not correspond with those set by a naïve use of the term Beauty, but it will be found that the actual usage of careful and sensitive persons not affected by special theories corresponds as closely with this definition as with any other which can be given.

> "And when there came a pause
> Of silence such as baffled his best skill:
> Then sometimes, in that silence, while he hung
> Listening, a gentle shock of mild surprise
> Has carried far into his heart the voice
> Of mountain torrents; or the visible scene
> Would enter unawares into his mind
> With all its solemn imagery, its rocks,

Its woods, and that uncertain heaven received
Into the bosom of the steady lake." [1]

The experience though fugitive and evanescent in the extreme may yet be analyzed by a consideration of the occasions on which we became aware of it in a more gradual manner. Limiting ourselves for the moment to the visual field we are aware of certain shapes and colors. These when more closely studied usually reveal themselves as in three dimensions, or as artists say, in forms. These forms must in some cases, but in others may not, be identified as this or that physical object. Throughout this process impulses are aroused and sustained, which gradually increase in variety and degree of systematization. To these systems in their early stages will correspond the emotions such as joy, horror, melancholy, anger, and mirth; or attitudes, such as love, veneration, sentimentality. . . .

What [the artist] puts into his work is a selection made from an indefinitely large number of possible elements, and their specific arrangement is also only one of many possible. This selection and arrangement is due to the direction and accentuation of his interest—in other words to the play of impulses which controls his activity at the moment; and it is often such that the same group of impulses are aroused in the spectator. We do not make the artist's selection because that is done for us. This seems to be the only way, unless by telepathy, of coming into contact with other minds than our own. Some rest content with this contact, which is plainly a matter of degree.

So far, however, we need not have experienced Beauty, but it is here that our emotion assumes a more general character, and we find that correspondingly our attitude has become impersonal. The explanation of this change is of the greatest importance. The various impulses before alluded to have become further systematized and intensified. Not all impulses, it is plain, as usually excited, are naturally harmonious, for conflict is possible and common. A complete systematization must take the form of such an adjustment as will preserve free play to every impulse, with entire avoidance of frustration. In any equilibrium of this kind, however momentary, we are experiencing beauty.

The state of equilibrium is not one of passivity, inertia, over-stimulation or conflict, and most people would be rightly dissatisfied with such terms as Nirvana, Ecstasy, Sublimation or At-oneness with Nature, which might at first sight be thought appropriate. As descriptive of an esthetic state in which impulses are experienced *together,* the word *Synaesthesis,* however, conveniently covers both equilibrium and harmony. . . .

In equilibrium, there is no tendency to action, and any concert-goer must have realized the impropriety of the view that action is the proper outcome of esthetic appreciation. When impulses are "harmonized" on the other hand they

[1] Wordsworth, "There Was a Boy." (Editor.)

work together, and such disciplined coordination in action is much to be desired in other places. When works of art produce such action, or conditions which lead to action, they have either not completely fulfilled their function or would in the view of equilibrium here being considered be called not "beautiful" but "stimulative." [2]

As we realize beauty we become more fully ourselves the more our impulses are engaged. If, as is sometimes alleged, we are the whole complex of our impulses, this fact would explain itself. Our interest is not canalized in one direction rather than another. It becomes ready instead to take any direction we choose. This is the explanation of that detachment so often mentioned in artistic experience. We become impersonal or disinterested.

> "Yet once more, O ye Laurels, and once more
> Ye Myrtles brown, with Ivy never-sear,
>
> I come to pluck your Berries harsh and crude,
> And with forc'd fingers rude,
> Shatter your leaves before the mellowing year." [3]

Simultaneously, as another aspect of the same adjustment, our individuality becomes differentiated or isolated from the individualities of things around us. We become less "mixed into" other things. As we become more ourselves they become more themselves, because we are less dependent upon the particular impulses which they each arouse in us.

[2] Although the experience here described is readily recognizable, this account is admittedly speculative. The argumentative will need no prompting to the remark that the distinction between a balance and a deadlock is difficult to explain. Two particular cases which may produce misapprehension are worth noting.

The first is the case of irresolution. It may be supposed that here we have a balance of impulses by which we seem to be impelled first one way and then another with too rapid an alternation or too weak a thrust for either impulse to take effect. This condition must be marked off as totally distinct from that which we describe as equilibrium. The difference between them is theoretically as follows. In an equilibrium the impulses active, however they are specifically related, do yet sustain one state of mind. They combine to produce one phase of consciousness. In irresolution the sets of impulses sustain severally their independent phases. In some cases, what is essentially an oscillation may become a balance. The difference may be found in the cross connections between the subsidiary impulses contained in these oscillating systems. Two perfectly simple impulses, we may suppose, must either oscillate or lock. A more complex initial conflict may on the other hand discharge itself through its branch connections. We might describe balance as a conflict of impulses solving itself in the arousal of the other impulses of the personality. Balance as we have said above tends to bring the whole of the personality into play.

The other confusing case is that in which no conflict arises because only one self-sufficing set of impulses is in action. The state of mind which then arises seems in many ways to resemble balance. In intense anger or joy for instance, we have a certain lucidity, self-possession and freedom which might be mistaken for some of the conditions which arise in balance. But the resemblances are illusory as time shows. Balance refreshes and never exhausts.

[3] The first lines of Milton's *Lycidas*. (Editor.)

As a corollary of this individualization, particular sets of impulses are felt in relation to other sets, which, unless both were already active in the equilibrium, would not occur. . . .

In conclusion, the reason why equilibrium is a justification for the preference of one experience before another, is the fact that it brings into play all our faculties. In virtue of what we have called the synaesthetic character of the experience, we are enabled, as we have seen, to appreciate relationships in a way which would not be possible under normal circumstances. Through no other experience can the full richness and complexity of our environment be realized. The ultimate value of equilibrium is that it is better to be fully than partially alive.

—*The Foundations of Æsthetics* (1922)

CHAPTER FIFTEEN

Criticism

DAVID HUME
Of the Standard of Taste

THEODORE MEYER GREENE
The Nature and Criteria of Criticism

STEPHEN C. PEPPER
Organistic Criticism

LOUIS ARNAUD REID
Greatness

Introductory Note

THE ESTHETIC ATTITUDE (which we have been studying in Chapters XII-XIV) is appreciative; the critical attitude is not merely appreciative but judgmental. In appreciation, we *enjoy* a work of art; in criticism, we *appraise* it.

The question whether there can be any objective standard of judgment is discussed by David Hume (1711-1776). Although we may be stretching a word when we term Hume "modern" and when we include his essay in *A Modern Book of Esthetics,* there can be no doubt about his relevance to contemporary thought. Perhaps no other thinker is more often mentioned by the most up-to-date philosophers.

Hume seeks to mediate between the extremes of relativism and absolutism. As against the absolutists, he maintains that emotion, the most variable side of our nature, accounts for our tastes. Although the basis of taste lies in the mind, certain qualities in objects are fitted to produce the requisite sentiment. The awareness of these qualities and the assistance of our intellectual faculties are necessary to pave the way for the right emotional reaction. Hence the good critic must have delicate sensibility, freedom from prejudice, practice and familiarity with the arts, and good sense. Even so, a certain relativity in taste remains, but it is as innocent as it is unavoidable.

The nature and standards of criticism are discussed in *The Arts and the Art of Criticism,* by Theodore Meyer Greene (1897-   ), formerly Professor of Philosophy at Princeton and now Master of Sillman College at Yale. With broad insight, he has distinguished between historical, re-creative, and judicial criticism, and has discussed artistic style, formal excellence, truth, and greatness. In admitting truth as a criterion, he differs from Croce and Richards, who deny the esthetic relevance of beliefs, and in admitting both truth and greatness, he differs from Fry and Ortega y Gasset, who minimize "life-values" and referential meanings. In upholding the objectivity of critical standards, he also differs from the more relativisitic strain in Hume. The reader can very profitably consult Greene's book for a full exposition and defense of the distinctions that he here briefly summarizes.

Stephen Coburn Pepper (1891-   ), Professor of Philosophy at the University of California, recognizes diverse standards of critical judgment, but believes that each standard may be applied with a fair degree of objectivity. A significant standard does not reflect mere personal taste, but springs from a comprehensive orientation toward reality, a philosophical *Weltanschauung* or world hypothesis. He distinguishes four relatively adequate world hypotheses, which he calls mechanism, contextualism, organicism, and formism. Mechanism also goes by the name of "naturalism" or "materialism"; contextualism is usually called "pragmatism" or "instrumentalism"; organicism is most fully expressed in "absolute idealism"; formism, with its emphasis upon universals or similarities, is often called "realism" or "Platonic idealism." In his discussion of esthetic criticism, Pepper cites Santayana as an example of a mechanist, Dewey as a contextualist, Bosanquet as an organicist, and Aristotle as a formist. The mechanist asks of the work that it give pleasure; the contextualist, that it exhibit vividness of quality; the organicist, that it be a rich and well-integrated unity; the formist, that it typify the normal or universal. In his *Principles of Art Appreciation,* Pepper has employed the "mechanist" criterion of pleasure; in his *Aesthetic Quality,* he has skillfully elaborated the contextualist standard; and in the following selection from *The Basis of Criticism in the Arts,* he expounds the standard of organicism.

The criterion of organic unity which Pepper thus attributes to organicism is one of the prime standards insisted upon by Aristotle and by innumerable critics since his time. Its use is by no means confined to absolute idealists, although idealistic writers such as Hegel and Coleridge have emphasized it most strongly. Perhaps no other standard has exercised a greater sway in the history of criticism, but another very influential standard is "greatness," as enunciated by Longinus and interpreted in this chapter by Louis Arnaud Reid (1895-   ), Professor of Philosophy in London University. His discussion is so clear that no comment is necessary.

DAVID HUME

Of the Standard of Taste

The great variety of Taste, as well as of opinion, which prevails in the world, is too obvious not to have fallen under everyone's observation. Men of the most confined knowledge are able to remark a difference of taste in the narrow circle of their acquaintance, even where the persons have been educated under the same government, and have early imbibed the same prejudices. But those, who can enlarge their view to contemplate distant nations and remote ages, are still more surprised at the great inconsistence and contrariety. We are apt to call *barbarous* whatever departs widely from our own taste and apprehension; but soon find the epithet of reproach retorted on us. And the highest arrogance and self-conceit is at last startled, on observing an equal assurance on all sides, and scruples, amidst such a contest of sentiment, to pronounce positively in its own favor.

As this variety of taste is obvious to the most careless inquirer; so will it be found, on examination, to be still greater in reality than in appearance. The sentiments of men often differ with regard to beauty and deformity of all kinds, even while their general discourse is the same. There are certain terms in every language, which import blame, and others praise; and all men, who use the same tongue, must agree in their application of them. Every voice is united in applauding elegance, propriety, simplicity, spirit in writing; and in blaming fustian, affectation, coldness, and a false brilliancy: But when critics come to particulars, this seeming unanimity vanishes; and it is found, that they had affixed a very different meaning to their expressions. In all matters of opinion and science, the case is opposite: The difference among men is there oftener found to lie in generals than in particulars; and to be less in reality than in appearance. An explanation of the terms commonly ends the controversy; and the disputants are surprised to find, that they have been quarrelling, while at bottom they agreed in their judgment. . . .

It is natural for us to seek a *Standard of Taste*; a rule, by which the various sentiments of men may be reconciled; at least, a decision afforded, confirming one sentiment, and condemning another.

There is a species of philosophy, which cuts off all hopes of success in such an attempt, and represents the impossibility of ever attaining any standard of taste. The difference, it is said, is very wide between judgment and sentiment. All sentiment is right; because sentiment has a reference to nothing beyond itself, and is always real, wherever a man is conscious of it. But all determinations of the understanding are not right; because they have a reference to something beyond themselves, to wit, real matter of fact; and are not always conformable to that standard. Among a thousand different opinions which different men may entertain of the same subject, there is one, and but one, that is just and true; and the only difficulty is to fix and ascertain it. On the contrary, a thousand different sentiments, excited by the same object, are all right: Because no sentiment represents what is really in the object. It only marks a certain conformity or relation between the object and the organs or faculties of the mind; and if that conformity did not really exist, the sentiment could never possibly have being. Beauty is no quality in things themselves: It exists merely in the mind which contemplates them; and each mind perceives a different beauty. One person may even perceive deformity, where another is sensible of beauty; and every individual ought to acquiesce in his own sentiment, without pretending to regulate those of others. To seek the real beauty, or real deformity, is as fruitless an inquiry as to pretend to ascertain the real sweet or real bitter. According to the disposition of the organs, the same object may be both sweet and bitter: and the proverb has justly determined it to be fruitless to dispute concerning tastes. It is very natural, and even quite necessary, to extend this axiom to mental, as well as bodily taste; and thus common sense, which is so often at variance with philosophy, especially with the skeptical kind, is found, in one instance at least, to agree in pronouncing the same decision.

But though this axiom, by passing into a proverb, seems to have attained the sanction of common sense; there is certainly a species of common sense, which opposes it, at least serves to modify and restrain it. Whoever would assert an equality of genius and elegance between Ogilby and Milton, or Bunyan and Addison, would be thought to defend no less an extravagance, than if he had maintained a mole-hill to be as high as Teneriffe, or a pond as extensive as the ocean. Though there may be found persons, who give the preference to the former authors; no one pays attention to such a taste; and we pronounce, without scruple, the sentiment of these pretended critics to be absurd and ridiculous. The principle of the natural equality of tastes is then totally forgot, and while we admit it on some occasions, where the objects seem near an equality, it appears an extravagant paradox, or rather a palpable absurdity, where objects so disproportioned are compared together.

It is evident that none of the rules of composition are fixed by reasonings *a priori*, or can be esteemed abstract conclusions of the understanding, from comparing those habitudes and relations of ideas, which are eternal and immutable. Their foundation is the same with that of all the practical sciences, experience; nor are there anything but general observations, concerning what has been universally found to please in all countries and in all ages. Many of the beauties of poetry, and even of eloquence, are founded on falsehood and fiction, on hyperboles, metaphors, and an abuse or perversion of terms from their natural meaning. To check the sallies of the imagination, and to reduce every expression to geometrical truth and exactness, would be the most contrary to the laws of criticism; because it would produce a work, which, by universal experience, has been found the most insipid and disagreeable. But though poetry can never submit to exact truth, it must be confined by rules of art, discovered to the author either by genius or observation. If some negligent or irregular writers have pleased, they have not pleased by their transgressions of rule or order, but in spite of these transgressions: They have possessed other beauties, which were conformable to just criticism; and the force of these beauties has been able to overpower censure, and give the mind a satisfaction superior to the disgust arising from the blemishes. Ariosto pleases; but not by his monstrous and improbable fictions, by his bizarre mixture of the serious and comic styles, by the want of coherence in his stories, or by the continual interruptions of his narration. He charms by the force and clearness of his expression, by the readiness and variety of his inventions, and by his natural pictures of the passions, especially those of the gay and amorous kind: And however his faults may diminish our satisfaction, they are not able entirely to destroy it. Did our pleasure really arise from those parts of his poem, which we denominate faults, this would be no objection to criticism in general: It would only be an objection to those particular rules of criticism, which would establish such circumstances to be faults, and would represent them as universally blameable. If they are found to please, they cannot be faults; let the pleasure, which they produce, be ever so unexpected and unaccountable.

But though all the general rules of art are founded only on experience, and on the observation of the common sentiments of human nature, we must not imagine, that, on every occasion, the feelings of men will be conformable to these rules. Those finer emotions of the mind are of a very tender and delicate nature, and require the concurrence of many favorable circumstances to make them play with facility and exactness, according to their general and established principles. The least exterior hindrance to such small springs, or the least internal disorder, disturbs their motion, and confounds the operation of the whole machine. When we would make an experiment of this nature, and would try the force of any beauty or deformity, we must choose with care a proper time and place, and bring the fancy to a suitable situation and disposition. A perfect serenity of mind, a recollection of thought, a due attention to the object; if any of these circumstances be wanting, our experiment will be fallacious, and we shall be unable to judge of the catholic and universal beauty. The relation, which nature has placed between the form and the sentiment, will at least be more obscure; and it will require greater accuracy to trace and discern it. We shall be able to ascertain its influence, not so much from the operation of each particular beauty, as from the durable admiration, which attends those works, that have survived all the caprices of mode and fashion, all the mistakes of ignorance and envy.

The same Homer, who pleased at Athens and Rome two thousand years ago, is still admired at Paris and at London. All the changes of climate, government, religion, and language, have not been able to obscure his glory. Authority or prejudice may give a temporary vogue to a bad poet or orator; but his reputation will never be durable or general. When his compositions are examined by posterity or by foreigners, the enchantment is dissipated, and his faults appear in their true colors. On the contrary, a real genius, the longer his works endure, and the more wide they are spread, the more sincere is the admiration which he meets with. Envy and jealousy have too much place in a narrow circle; and even familiar acquaintance with his person may diminish the applause due to his performances: But when these obstructions are removed, the beauties, which are naturally fitted to excite agreeable sentiments, immediately display their energy; while the world endures, they maintain their authority over the minds of men.

It appears then, that, amidst all the variety and caprice of taste, there are certain general principles of approbation or blame, whose influence a careful eye may trace in all operations of the mind. Some particular forms or qualities, from the original structure of the internal fabric, are calculated to please, and others to displease; and if they fail of their effect in any particular instance, it is from some apparent defect or imperfection in the organ. A man in a fever would not insist on his palate as able to decide concerning flavors; nor would one, affected with the jaundice, pretend to give a verdict with regard to colors. In each creature, there is a sound and a defective state; and the former alone can be supposed to afford us a true standard of taste and sentiment. If, in the sound state of the organ, there be an entire or a considerable uniformity of sentiment among men, we may thence derive an idea of the perfect beauty; in like manner as the appearance of objects in daylight, to the eye of a man in health, is denominated their true and real color, even while color is allowed to be merely a phantasm of the senses.

Many and frequent are the defects in the internal organs, which prevent or weaken the influence of those general principles, on which depends our sentiment of beauty or deformity. Though some objects, by the structure of the mind, be naturally calculated to give pleasure, it is not to be expected, that in every individual the pleasure will be equally felt. Particular incidents and situations occur, which either throw a false light on the objects, or hinder the true from conveying to the imagination the proper sentiment and perception.

One obvious cause, why many feel not the proper sentiment of beauty, is the want of that *delicacy* of imagination, which is requisite to convey a sensibility of those finer emotions. This delicacy everyone pretends to: Everyone talks of it; and would reduce every kind of taste or sentiment to its standard. But as our intention in this essay is to mingle some light of the understanding with the feelings of sentiment, it will be proper to give a more accurate definition of delicacy than has hitherto been attempted. And not to draw our philosophy from too profound a source, we shall have recourse to a noted story in Don Quixote.

It is with good reason, says Sancho to the squire with the great nose, that I pretend to have a judgment in wine: This is a quality hereditary in our family. Two of my kinsmen were once called to give their opinion of a hogshead, which was supposed to be excellent, being old and of a good vintage. One of them tastes it; considers it; and, after mature reflection, pronounces the wine to be good, were it not for a small taste of leather, which he perceived in it. The other, after using the same precautions, gives also his verdict in favor of the wine; but with the reserve of a taste of iron, which he could easily distinguish. You cannot imagine how much they were both ridiculed for their judgment. But who laughed in the end? On emptying the hogshead, there was found at the bottom an old key with a leathern thong tied to it.

The great resemblance between mental and bodily taste will easily teach us to apply this story. Though it be certain, that beauty and deformity, more than sweet and bitter, are not qualities in objects, but belong entirely to the sentiment, internal or external; it must be allowed, that there are certain qualities in objects, which are fitted by nature to produce those particular feelings. Now as these qualities may be found in a small degree, or may be mixed and confounded with each other, it often happens that the taste is not affected with such minute qualities, or is not able to distinguish all the particular flavors, amidst the disorder in which they are presented. Where the organs are so fine, as to allow nothing to escape them; and at the same time so exact, as to perceive every ingredient in the composition: This we call delicacy of taste, whether we employ these terms in the literal or metaphorical sense. Here then the general rules of beauty are of use, being drawn from established models, and from the observation of what pleases or displeases, when presented singly and in a high degree: And if the same qualities, in a continued composition, and in a smaller degree, affect not the organs with a sensible delight or uneasiness, we exclude the person from all pretensions to this delicacy. To produce these general rules or avowed patterns of composition, is like finding the key with the leathern thong; which justified the verdict of Sancho's kinsmen, and confounded those pretended judges who had condemned them. Though the hogshead had never been emptied, the taste of the one was still equally delicate, and that of the other equally dull and languid: But it would have been more difficult to have proved the superiority of the former, to the conviction of every bystander. In like manner, though the beauties of writing had never been methodized, or reduced to general principles; though no excellent models had ever been acknowledged; the different degrees of taste would still have subsisted, and the judgment of one man been preferable to that of another; but it would not have been so easy to silence the bad critic, who might always insist upon his particular sentiment, and refuse to submit to his antagonist. But when we show him an avowed principle of art; when we illustrate this principle by examples, whose operation, from his own particular taste, he acknowledges to be conformable to the principle; when we prove that the same principle may be applied to the present case, where he did not perceive or feel its influence: He must conclude, upon the whole, that the fault lies in himself, and that he wants the delicacy, which is requisite to make him sensible of every beauty and every blemish, in any composition or discourse.

It is acknowledged to be the perfection of every sense or faculty, to perceive with exactness its most minute objects, and allow nothing to escape its notice and observation. The smaller the objects are, which become sensible to the eye, the finer is that organ, and the more elaborate its make and composition. A good palate is not tried by strong flavors, but by a mixture of small ingredients, where we are still sensible of each part, notwithstanding its minuteness and its confusion with the rest. In like manner, a quick and acute perception of beauty and deformity must be the perfection of our mental taste; nor can a man be satisfied with himself while he suspects that any excellence or blemish in a discourse has passed him unobserved. In this case, the perfection of the man, and the perfection of the sense or feeling, are found to be united. A very delicate palate, on many occasions, may be a great inconvenience both to a man himself and to his friends: But a delicate taste of wit or beauty must always be a desirable quality, because it is the source of all the finest and most innocent enjoyments of which human nature is susceptible. In this decision the sentiments of all mankind are agreed. Wherever you can ascertain a delicacy of taste, it is sure to meet with approbation; and the best way of ascertaining it is to appeal to those models and principles which have been established by the uniform consent and experience of nations and ages.

But though there be naturally a wide difference in point of delicacy between one person and another, nothing tends further to increase and improve this talent, than *practice* in a particular art, and the frequent survey or contemplation of a particular species of beauty. When objects of any kind are first presented to the eye or imagination, the sentiment which attends them is obscure and confused; and the mind is, in a great measure, incapable of pronouncing concerning their merits or defects. The taste cannot perceive the several excellencies of the performance, much less distinguish the particular character of each excellency, and ascertain its quality and degree. If it pronounce the whole in general to be beautiful or deformed, it is the utmost that can be expected; and even this judgment, a person so unpracticed will be apt to deliver with great hesitation and reserve. But allow him to acquire experience in those objects, his feeling becomes more exact and nice: He not only perceives the beauties and defects of each part, but marks the distinguishing species of each quality, and assigns it suitable praise or blame. A clear and distinct sentiment attends him through the whole survey of the objects; and he discerns that very degree and kind of approbation or displeasure which each part is naturally fitted to produce. The mist dissipates which seemed formerly to hang over the object: The organ acquires greater perfection in its operations; and can pronounce, without danger or mistake, concerning the merits of every performance. In a word, the same address and dexterity, which practice gives to the execution of any work, is also acquired by the same means, in the judging of it.

So advantageous is practice to the discernment of beauty, that, before we can give judgment on any work of importance, it will even be requisite that that very individual performance be more than once perused by us, and be surveyed in different lights with attention and deliberation. There is a flutter or hurry of thought which attends the first perusal of any piece, and which confounds the genuine sentiment of beauty. The relation of the parts is not discerned: The true characters of style are little distinguished. The several perfections and defects seem wrapped up in a species of confusion, and present themselves indistinctly to the imagination. Not to mention, that there is a species of beauty, which, as it is florid and superficial, pleases at first; but being found incompatible with a just expression either of reason or passion, soon palls upon the taste, and is then rejected with disdain, at least rated at a much lower value.

It is impossible to continue in the practice of contemplating any order of beauty, without being frequently obliged to form *comparisons* between the several species and degrees of excellence, and estimating their proportion to each other. A man, who had had no opportunity of comparing the different kinds of beauty, is indeed totally unqualified to pronounce an opinion with regard to any object presented to him. By comparison alone we fix the epithets of praise or blame, and learn how to assign the due degree of each. The coarsest daubing contains a certain lustre of colors and exactness of imitation, which are so far beauties, and would affect the mind of a peasant or Indian with the highest admiration. The most vulgar ballads are not entirely destitute of harmony or nature; and none but a person familiarized to superior beauties would pronounce their numbers harsh, or narration uninteresting. A great inferiority of beauty gives pain to a person conversant in the highest excellence of the kind, and is for that reason pronounced a deformity: As the most finished object with which we are acquainted is naturally supposed to have reached the pinnacle of perfection, and to be entitled to the highest applause. One accustomed to see, and examine, and weigh the several performances, admired in different ages and nations, can alone rate the merits of a work exhibited to his view, and assign its proper rank among the productions of genius.

But to enable a critic the more fully to execute this undertaking, he must preserve his mind free from all *prejudice,* and allow nothing to enter into his consideration but the very object which is submitted to his examination. We may observe, that every work of art, in order to produce its due effect on the mind, must be surveyed in a certain point of view, and cannot be fully relished by persons, whose situation, real or imaginary, is not conformable to that which is required by the performance. An orator addresses himself to a particular audience, and must have a regard to their particular genius, interests, opinions, passions, and prejudices; otherwise he hopes in vain to govern their resolutions, and inflame their affections. Should they even have entertained some prepossessions against him, however unreasonable, he must not overlook this disadvantage; but, before he enters upon the subject, must endeavour to conciliate their affection, and acquire their good graces. A critic of a different age or nation, who should peruse this discourse, must have all these circumstances in his eye, and must place himself in the same situation as the audience, in order to form a true judgment of the oration. In like manner, when any work is addressed to the public, though I should have a friendship or enmity with the author, I must depart from this situation; and considering myself as a man in general, forget, if possible, my individual being, and my peculiar circumstances. A person influenced by prejudice, complies not with this condition, but obstinately maintains his natural position, without placing himself in that point of view which the performance supposes. If the work be addressed to persons of a different age or nation, he makes no allowance for their peculiar views and prejudices; but, full of the manners of his own age and country, rashly condemns what seemed admirable in the eyes of those for whom alone the discourse was calculated. If the work be executed for the public, he never sufficiently enlarges his comprehension, or forgets his interest as a friend or enemy, as a rival or commentator. By this means, his sentiments are perverted; nor have the same beauties and blemishes the same influence upon him, as if he had imposed a proper violence on his imagination, and had forgotten himself for a moment. So far his taste evidently departs from the true standard, and of consequence loses all credit and authority.

It is well known, that in all questions submitted to the understanding, prejudice is destructive of sound judgment, and perverts all operations of the intellectual faculties: It is no less contrary to good taste; nor has it less influence to corrupt our sentiment of beauty. It belongs to *good sense* to check its influence in both cases; and in this respect, as well as in many others, reason, if not an essential part of taste, is at least requisite to the operations of this latter faculty. In all the nobler productions of genius, there is a mutual relation and correspondence of parts; nor can either the beauties or blemishes be perceived by him, whose thought is not capacious enough to comprehend all those parts, and compare them with each other, in order to perceive the consistence and uniformity of the whole. Every work of art has also a certain end or purpose for which it is calculated; and is to be deemed more or less perfect, as it is more or less fitted to attain this end. The object of eloquence is to persuade, of history to instruct, of poetry to please, by means of the passions and the imagination. These ends we must carry constantly in our view when we peruse any performance; and we must be able to judge how far the means employed are adapted to their respective purposes. Besides, every kind of composition, even the most poetical, is nothing but a chain of propositions and reasonings; not always indeed, the justest and most exact, but still plausible and specious, however disguised by the coloring of the imagination. The persons introduced in tragedy and epic poetry, must be represented as reasoning, and thinking, and concluding, and acting, suitably to their character and circumstances; and without judgment, as well as taste and invention, a poet can never hope to succeed in so delicate an undertaking. Not to mention, that the same excellence of faculties which contributes to the improvement of reason, the same clearness of conception, the same exactness of distinction, the same vivacity of apprehension, are essential to the operations of true taste, and are its infallible concomitants. It seldom or never happens, that a man of sense, who has experience in any art, cannot judge of its beauty; and it is no less rare to meet with a man who has a just taste without a sound understanding.

Thus, though the principles of taste be universal, and nearly, if not entirely, the same in all men; yet few are qualified to give judgment on any work of art, or establish their own sentiment as the standard of beauty. The organs of internal sensation are seldom so perfect as to allow the general principles their full play, and produce a feeling correspondent to those principles. They either labor under some defect, or are vitiated by some disorder; and by that means, excite a sentiment, which may be pronounced erroneous. When the critic has no delicacy, he judges without any distinction, and is only affected by the grosser and more palpable qualities of the object: The finer touches pass unnoticed and disregarded. Where he is not aided by practice, his verdict is attended with confusion and hesitation. Where no comparison has been employed, the most frivolous beauties, such as rather merit the name of defects, are the object of his admiration. Where he lies under the influence of prejudice, all his natural sentiments are perverted. Where good sense is wanting, he is not qualified to discern the beauties of design and reasoning, which are the highest and most excellent. Under some or other of these imperfections, the generality of men labor; and hence a true judge in the finer arts is observed, even during the most polished ages, to be so rare a character: Strong sense, united to delicate sentiment, improved by practice, perfected by comparison, and cleared of all prejudice, can alone entitle critics to this valuable character; and the joint verdict of such, wherever they are to be found, is the true standard of taste and beauty.

But where are such critics to be found? By what remarks are they to be known? How distinguish them from pretenders? These questions are embarrassing; and seem to throw us back into the same uncertainty, from which, during the course of this essay, we have endeavored to extricate ourselves.

But if we consider the matter aright, these are questions of fact, not of sentiment. Whether any particular person be endowed with good sense and a delicate imagination, free from prejudice, may often be the subject of dispute, and be liable to great discussion and inquiry: But that such a character is valuable and estimable, will be agreed in by all mankind. Where these doubts occur, men can do no more than in other disputable questions which are submitted to the understanding: They must produce the best arguments that their invention suggests to them; they must acknowledge a true and decisive standard to exist somewhere, to wit, real existence and matter of fact; and they must have indulgence to such as differ from them in their appeals to this standard. It is sufficient for our present purpose, if we have proved that the taste of all individuals is not upon an equal footing, and that some men in general, however difficult to be particularly pitched upon, will be acknowledged by universal sentiment to have a preference above others. . . .

Though men of delicate taste be rare, they are easily to be distinguished in society by the soundness of their understanding, and the superiority of their faculties above the rest of mankind. The ascendant, which they acquire, gives a prevalence to that lively approbation with which they receive any productions of genius, and renders it generally predominant. Many men, when left to themselves, have but a faint and dubious perception of beauty, who yet are capable of relishing any fine stroke which is pointed out to them. Every convert to the admiration of the real poet or orator is the cause of some new conversion. And though prejudices may prevail for a time, they never unite in celebrating any rival to the true genius, but yield at last to the force of nature and just sentiment. Thus, though a civilized nation may easily be mistaken in the choice of their admired philosopher, they never have been found long to err, in their affection for a favorite epic or tragic author.

But notwithstanding all our endeavors to fix a standard of taste, and reconcile the discordant apprehensions of men, there still remain two sources of variation which are not sufficient indeed to confound all the boundaries of beauty and deformity, but will often serve to produce a difference in the degrees of our approbation or blame. The one is the different humors of particular men; the other, the particular manners and opinions of our age and country. The general principles of taste are uniform in human nature: Where men vary in their judgments, some defect or perversion in the faculties may commonly be remarked; proceeding either from prejudice, from want of practice, or want of delicacy: and there is just reason for approving one taste, and condemning another. But where there is such a diversity in the internal frame or external situation as is entirely blameless on both sides, and leaves no room to give one the preference above the other; in that case a certain degree of diversity in judgment is unavoidable, and we seek in vain for a standard by which we can reconcile the contrary sentiments.

A young man whose passions are warm will be more sensibly touched with amorous and tender images than a man more advanced in years who takes pleasure in wise, philosophical reflections, concerning the conduct of life and moderation of the passions. At twenty, Ovid may be the favorite author; Horace at forty; and perhaps Tacitus at fifty. Vainly would we, in such cases, endeavor to enter into the sentiments of others, and divest ourselves of those propensities which are natural to us. We choose our favorite author as we do our friend, from a conformity of humor and disposition. Mirth or passion, sentiment or reflection; which ever of these most predominates in our temper, it gives us a peculiar sympathy with the writer who resembles us.

One person is more pleased with the sublime; another with the tender; a third with raillery. One has a strong sensibility to blemishes, and is extremely studious of correctness: Another has a more lively feeling of beauties, and pardons twenty absurdities and defects for one elevated or pathetic stroke. The ear of this man is entirely turned towards conciseness and energy; that man is delighted with a copious, rich, and harmonious expression. Simplicity is affected by one; ornament by another. Comedy, tragedy, satire, odes, have each its partisans, who prefer that particular species of writing to all others. It is plainly an error in a critic, to confine his approbation to one species or style of writing, and condemn all the rest. But it is almost impossible not to feel a predilection for that which suits our particular turn and disposition. Such preferences are innocent and unavoidable, and can never reasonably be the object of dispute, because there is no standard by which they can be decided. . . .

—*Essays* (1757)

THEODORE MEYER GREENE

The Nature and Criteria of Criticism

I. *The Three Aspects of Criticism* [1]

A work of art is a unique, individual whole—a self-contained artistic "organism" with a "life" and reality of its own. But it is also an historical phenomenon—the product of a specific artist in a specific school, period, and culture, and an exemplification of stylistic characteristics which it shares with other works by the same artist and of the same school, period, and culture. Finally, works of art vary in artistic excellence, truth, and significance: every work of art possesses its own degree of perfection and its own measure of truth or falsity, triviality or greatness.

The competent critic takes all three aspects of the work of art into account, and so, though with less systematic and historical rigor, does the artistically sensitive layman.[2] He apprehends the individual work of art in all its self-contained uniqueness through sensitive artistic re-creation. But to re-create it adequately he must understand the artist's "language," and this implies familiarity with the generic style of the composition and its cultural setting. Historically oriented re-creation, in turn, does not exhaust critical response, for such response also implies appraisal of the work of art with respect both to its artistic quality and to its truth and spiritual significance. Criticism has therefore three aspects, the historical, the re-creative, and the judicial. Each aspect relates itself to a corresponding aspect of the work of art itself—historical criticism, to the work's historical character and orientation; re-creative criticism, to its unique artistic individuality; and judicial criticism, to its artistic value. These aspects of criticism are mutually conditioning factors of a single organic process: their relation to one another is strictly analogous to the interrelation of style, individuality, and value in the work of art itself.

---

[1] I am especially indebted to Professor A. E. Hinds for the following analysis of artistic and literary criticism. Professor Hinds is at present engaged in writing a book on literary criticism in which these distinctions wll be examined both systematically and historically.

[2] The difference between lay and critical response to art is one of degree rather than of kind. Ideally, at least, the critic differs from the layman merely in possessing greater artistic sensitivity, a more accurate and a richer historical orientation, and a capacity for more objective judicial appraisal. That some laymen surpass some professional critics in one or other of these respects is irrelevant to my argument. My only concern is to formulate the basic principles of artistic response as these are exemplified in artistic and literary criticism at its best.

The special task of historical criticism is that of determining the nature and expressive intent of works of art in their historical context. It involves, on the one hand, the authentication of texts and monuments, and, on the other, their interpretation in the light of available biographical, social, cultural, and other types of evidence. It is only thus that we can hope to understand what it was that the authors or makers of works of art intended to express, and to interpret this intention in the light of *their* interests and cultural background.

The special task of re-creative criticism is that of apprehending imaginatively, through sensitive artistic response, what the artist has actually succeeded in expressing in a specific work of art. The re-creative critic will inevitably, and quite properly, *also* relate what he thus apprehends to his own interests and needs. But this act is not in itself integral to re-creative criticism, save insofar as it contributes positively to the critic's understanding of the work of art itself and *its* expressed content. The prefix "re," in the term "re-creation," is of crucial importance.

The special task of judicial criticism is that of estimating the value of a work of art in relation to other works of art and to other human values. This determination of value involves, as we shall see, an appeal to at least three distinguishable normative criteria—a strictly esthetic criterion of formal artistic excellence, an epistemic criterion of truth, and a normative criterion of larger significance, greatness, or profundity.

It must be emphasized that these three aspects of criticism are in reality three complementary approaches to the work of art, and that each approach can be explored effectively only in conjunction with the other two. Historical inquiry divorced from sensitive re-creation and judicial appraisal can merely produce an uninspired chronicle of "objective" historical "facts" which, by themselves, must fail to determine the artistic nature and value of the works of art under consideration. The effort to re-create a work of art without any understanding of its historical context must fail to be truly *re*-creative and must remain a purely subjective reaction. And man's esthetic response to art must lack all artistic significance if it is not accompanied by an appraisal of it in terms of appropriate artistic standards. But this evaluation of a work of art must remain purely academic, scientific, or moralistic, if it is undertaken without historical perspective and without artistic sensitivity.

Thus, re-creative apprehension and judicial appraisal are both conditioned by historical orientation. Really to *re*-create a work of art is to apprehend the content which its author actually expressed in it, that is, to interpret it correctly as a vehicle of communication. Such apprehension implies not only a general understanding of the medium employed but a familiarity with the artist's language and idiom, and these, in turn, are determined by his school, period, and culture as well as by his own personality. It also implies a knowledge of the artist's times and of his intellectual and spiritual environment. Without such historical orientation no critic, however artistically sensitive, can escape critical "sentimentality," that is, an illegitimate intrusion into the work of art of what does not exist in it and a failure to apprehend certain of its essential ingredients. Judicial appraisal, in turn, must be arbitrary and unfair unless it is based upon an historically objective understanding of what is appraised. The question, What is it worth? presupposes the question, What is it? and this question can be answered only within an historical frame of reference.

Similarly, the re-creation of a work of art in all its individuality is essential to both historical and judicial criticism. It conditions the work of the historian of art and literature because the subject matter of such historical study can be determined only in terms of immediate artistic response. Only man's artistic sensitivity can reveal what is and what is not a "work of art," and so, what does and what does not constitute the appropriate subject matter of artistic and literary history. On the other hand, only that can be subjected to valid artistic appraisal [3] which has been faithfully re-created. Appraisal cannot be based on rules or principles permitting of a purely mechanical application. We must "feel" what we would judge; our appraisal must be based upon an immediate artistic experience in the presence of the work of art itself.

Finally, though judicial appraisal is in a sense the culmination of criticism, it actually pervades the entire critical enterprise. Try as we may to postpone appraisal until the historical and re-creative tasks have been completed, we shall discover that we have been appraising the objects of artistic contemplation from the very outset. We are inescapably normative in all our thought and conduct. No sooner are we confronted with what purports to be a work of art than we evaluate it, however incipient may be this evaluation and however often this preliminary judgment may be revised in the light of new historical evidence and fresh re-creative discovery. This normative compulsion is not only inescapable; it is essential to profitable historical inquiry and to fruitful artistic re-creation. For historical investigations which are not guided throughout by a sense of values and standards, both artistic and non-artistic, that is, which lack normative perspective, tend to be trivial and inconsequential.[4] Significant historical research, in art as in other fields, must be guided by normative principles if it is to produce significant results. Artistic re-creation, in turn, can be no more than idle, self-indulgent play if the artistic quality and the truth and significance of art are ignored. Even the esthete, who deprecates the categories of artistic

---

[3] That is, appraisal which purports to be an objectively valid estimate of the work of art itself. Without such re-creation, appraisal is irrelevant to the work of art in question and records either a merely subjective preference or a merely mechanical application of academic rules.

[4] When the minute researches of a factually-minded scholar unearth facts which more synoptic minds can use and interpret profitably, these discoveries must be regarded as happy accidents. It is clear that the best historical research is not conducted in this way.

truth and greatness, is, at his best, aware of "pure" artistic quality and prides himself on the refinement of his esthetic taste.

The ideally all-round critic, then, is equally proficient in orienting himself historically to the work of art, in re-creating it, and in appraising it; and no critic can afford to be entirely deficient in any one of these three respects. But critics tend, as the result of temperament and training, to be predominantly historical, re-creative, or judicial in their basic approach to works of art in the several media. This predominant critical aptitude and interest, in turn, tends to identify them more or less closely with one or other of the great critical movements of a given culture. These movements, distinguished from one another by a major emphasis upon some aspect of the critical enterprise, may persist for centuries, but they acquire special importance during certain periods in history. Thus, in our modern European culture, "neo-classic" criticism, which was preponderantly judicial and which was distinguished for its allegiance to Aristotelian principles derived from the *Poetics,* flourished in the seventeenth and eighteenth centuries. "Romantic" criticism, which was preponderantly re-creative and which was distinguished for its interest in original genius, its emphasis upon the conceptually unanalyzable character of artistic quality, and its belief in the intuitive character of artistic apprehension, was the dominant critical movement of the first half of the nineteenth century. Finally, modern historical scholarship in literature and the fine arts achieved increasing importance during the second half of the nineteenth century and is still the dominant critical approach to art. These movements, I must repeat, differ from one another only in major emphasis, and the greatest figures in each movement owe their distinction to their unusual aptitude for all three types of criticism. But even the greatest critics tend to reflect the intellectual climate of their period and culture and to exhibit an affinity with one or other of the great critical movements.

If the ultimate interdependence of these three aspects of criticism is steadfastly borne in mind, it is profitable to note that their logical order of priority differs from their psychological order of priority. Historical inquiry logically precedes artistic re-creation as its necessary (though insufficient) condition, because a work of art, especially when it belongs to another age or culture, simply cannot be understood without the requisite historical orientation. Re-creation, in turn, is the necessary (though insufficient) condition of judicial appraisal, since only that can be significantly appraised whose nature has been re-creatively apprehended. Psychological interest tends to reverse this order. We normally take pains to re-create what, at first glance, arouses our artistic interest (that is, elicits a preliminary, more or less favorable, judicial estimate), and historical research in the realm of art is usually motivated by the desire to understand more adequately what we have already partially re-created and enjoyed.[5]

[5] It might perhaps be argued that the professional critic's special prerogative is to offer and defend judicial estimates, and that the layman's chief interest in art is properly

II. *Artistic Style, Perfection, Truth, and Greatness*

. . . The style of a work of art is a function of the composition as a whole, regarded as an historical phenomenon. Every artist has his own individual style (or styles), and so has every school, nation, period, and culture. Style is thus essentially a generic manifestation of the individual temper and outlook of the artist and of his social and cultural milieu. The works of any given artist manifest stylistic similarities and differ stylistically from the works of other artists; the style of one school differs from that of another; and when the art of one nation, period, or culture is compared with that of another, distinctive stylistic similarities and differences become apparent. Of course, these several stylistic characteristics overlap, for a work of art simultaneously manifests the style of the artist, of the school to which he belongs, and of his nation, culture, and period. Thus a painting by Rubens illustrates his individual style as well as the Flemish variant of the seventeenth century Baroque. Hence, when we say that a work of art is "in" this or that style, the term "style" signifies a complex, historically determinant, generic character which must be interpreted in both a narrower and a wider frame of reference.

When, on the other hand, we say that a work of art "has" style, we declare it to be more or less *successfully* expressive in the manner of art. Style in this sense is synonymous with artistic quality or expressiveness. The artistic quality or perfection of a work of art is definable as pure artistic merit, that is, as proportional to the success with which an artist has succeeded in expressing, *via* artistic form in an artistic medium, what he wished to express, irrespective of the truth and the significance of the expressed artistic content. The work of an artist who has nothing to express must, by definition, be wholly inexpressive and therefore wholly lacking in artistic quality or merit. It will therefore "have" no style whatever because it is not a work of art at all. As a result, it will not be "in" any historical style in any really significant sense; it can be no more than a "manneristic" imitation of certain superficial generic characteristics of genuine works of art by other artists.

Style as an *historical* phenomenon and artistic quality as artistic *merit* are thus intimately related. The former not only presupposes the latter; it *is* the latter regarded from the historical point of view. When we consider a work of art stylistically we ask: To what extent does it express the individual outlook of its author and thus resemble his other creative compositions? In what ways does

---

confined to artistic re-creation and enjoyment. But such a distinction between the layman and the critic would, if pressed, radically distort the unitary nature of man's response to art. In actuality, the layman is continually appraising what he apprehends and enjoys, and most professional critics have chosen to be critics, partly at least, because of their unusual capacity for artistic re-creation and enjoyment. The more we consider the matter, the more inescapable is the conclusion that everyone who approaches art seriously, that is, both re-creatively and judicially, is really a "critic," even though his critical equipment be more or less deficient.

it manifest the generic traits and express the pervasive attitudes of his school, nation, period, and culture? On the other hand, when we consider its artistic merit, we concentrate our attention upon the composition as an artistic achievement, and ask: How successfully, according to artistic criteria, has its author expressed in this composition what he set out to express, that is, how appropriate is the work's specific form to the artist's expressive intent? These two questions, though clearly different in focus and objective, both relate to the work's distinctive mode of expression. The former is designed to establish generic similarities and differences between the work in question and other compositions, and these similarities and differences are viewed in historical perspective. The latter is designed to determine the degree of the composition's individual artistic excellence without *specific* reference to its larger historical orientation or to the artist's larger productivity. But the second question cannot be answered adequately save within a wider stylistic framework, since re-creation and evaluation are, as we have seen, dependent upon historical orientation; and, conversely, the generic style of a work of art cannot be determined without both artistic re-creation and judicial appraisal of the composition itself and of other compositions with which it is compared.

The truth and the greatness of a work of art, in turn, depend upon, yet transcend, both its stylistic character and its strictly artistic quality. Two compositions can be in the same style and yet vary greatly in truth and significance, and one may express a profound insight into human experience, the other, a distorted or superficial interpretation of human life. Thus the painting of Watteau and Boucher, though both artists were Frenchmen living in the eighteenth century and though both painted in the Rococo style, differ greatly in expressed significance. Again, two compositions may be similar in artistic quality or degree of perfection, expressing with equal competence the content which each artist wished to express, but the content of the one may be slight, that of the other, rich in human import. A Callot line drawing . . . is as perfect of its kind as one of Rembrandt's etched crucifixions . . . but the expressed content of the latter is certainly richer in human significance than that of the former. The truth and significance of a work of art are thus primarily functions of the work's expressed content; its artistic quality or perfection is primarily a function of its specific expressive form; its style is primarily a function of its historical and generic character.

Style, perfection, truth, and greatness are thus distinct but complementary concepts. Style is *primarily* an historical concept, while artistic perfection, truth, and greatness are *primarily* normative concepts. The standard of artistic perfection is *primarily* esthetic or infra-philosophic, while the standards of truth and greatness are *primarily* supra-esthetic or philosophic in character. All four concepts are applicable, positively or negatively, to all art. They are explicitly invoked by most critics, and implicitly invoked even by the layman in his response to art. The fact that they are seldom defined with precision or distinguished clearly in concrete application imposes upon the philosopher of art a peculiar obligation to clarify their meaning and determine as precisely as possible how they are related.

None of the critical concepts can be understood adequately save in its relation to the other three. But the general relation in which they stand to one another suggests the order in which they can most profitably be investigated. Style conditions but does not guarantee artistic merit; a work can be artistically expressive without being truthful in the manner of art; and the artist's expressed insight can be truthful without being profound. That is, artistic greatness presupposes artistic truth, artistic truth presupposes artistic quality, and artistic quality is necessarily a function of generic style. . . .

—The Arts and the Art of Criticism (1940)

STEPHEN C. PEPPER

Organistic Criticism

Organicism, traditionally known as objective idealism, is the world hypothesis that stresses the internal relatedness or coherence of things. It is impressed with the manner in which observations at first apparently unconnected turn out to be closely related, and with the fact that as knowledge progresses it becomes more systematized. It conceives the value of our knowledge as proportional to the degree of integration it has attained, and comes to identify value with integration in all spheres. Value in the sphere of knowledge is integration of judgments; in the sphere of ethics, it is integration of acts; in the sphere of art, it is integration of feelings. Finally, it conceives all of these as contained in a total integration of existence or reality.

Like contextualism, it is not impressed with the apparent boundaries of men's bodies. It deals with situations, but regards a contextualistic situation as merely a way station to a larger integration. It speaks of anything short of total integration as a fragment—meaning literally a fragment of the whole to which it ultimately and really belongs. By "really belongs," it means that when we have come to understand or achieve the whole of which the fragment was a part, we will recognize that the fragment was all along an integral part of that whole and that the apparent separateness of the part was merely due to our failure to perceive it in its relations to the other parts in the whole. It was due, as the organicist is fond of saying, to "the weakness of the spectator."

Now, we need not concern ourselves with the question of the final adequacy of this view of things. It is clear even from the few references I have made that it receives a great deal of corroboration. In the field of esthetic appreciation and criticism it has proved to be possibly the most fruitful of all views. Schelling was the first to bring out the full extent of its implications, but Coleridge with the sensitiveness of a poet should probably be credited with the discovery of its powers as an instrument of criticism. Hegel rolled it ponderously over the whole field of cultural history in art, and is perhaps largely responsible for the intense modern interest in that subject. But most of his followers in esthetic theory seem to me to have been more absorbed in developing the permutations of its concepts than in following its guidance among esthetic facts, until finally Bosanquet gathered together the scattered results of a century of organistic thought and in his brief *Three Lectures on Aesthetic* [1] brought out one of the masterpieces in the literature of esthetics. In its honesty, and modesty, and simple-minded consistency, and earnestness in keeping the reader in constant touch with the facts, it is not likely to be surpassed by any future exponent of the view. It is the more remarkable in that Bosanquet obviously lacks esthetic sensitivity of the sort which emanates from every sentence that Coleridge writes. But he has the thing which Coleridge lacks, the perseverance to carry an idea through. If Bosanquet and Coleridge could be combined, the one for his intuitive grasp of the theory in its concrete workings and the other for his theoretical insight into its esthetic meanings, we should have the perfect writer of organistic esthetics and criticism.

I should like to introduce you to the view through Bosanquet's *Three Lectures*. Soon after the opening he gives a succinct statement of the fundamental principle of organicism. "I only know in philosophy," he says, "one method; and that is to expand *all* relevant facts, taken together, into ideas which approve themselves to thought as exhaustive and self-consistent." [2] I cannot stop to comment on this condensed statement which is the mature fruit of a century of thought on the method of this world hypothesis. But I would have you note, for this point often escapes critics of organicism, that the self-consistency of which he speaks is not the mathematical self-consistency of abstract symbols. It is the self-consistency of *"all* the relevant facts." It is the coherence, the integrated connectedness, of *facts*. Bosanquet is enunciating a material principle. The kind of self-consistency he is pointing out is one that can be found only by following the guidance and the compulsion of the facts.

He proceeds to apply this principle to the esthetic field. He first says something that sounds a good deal like unqualified hedonism. "The simplest esthetic

[1] Bernard Bosanquet, *Three Lectures on Aesthetic* (Macmillan, London, 1931).
[2] Page 3.

experience," he writes, "is a pleasant feeling, or a feeling of something pleasant—when we attend to it, it begins to be the latter." The stress, however, is on the "*something* pleasant." He goes on, "It is a *relevant* feeling—I mean it is attached, annexed, to the quality of some subject—to all its detail." Stopping now, we might think this was Santayana's objectified pleasure. But next, "My feeling in its special quality is evoked by the special quality of the something of which it is the feeling, and in fact is one with it." [3] Now the feeling begins to take on a contextualistic tone, the "quality" of the experience, "in all its detail," is what comes out. Moreover, the feeling quality presently passes out of the individual into the situation in which many individuals share. "The esthetic attitude," he presently writes, "is that in which we have a feeling which is so embodied in the object that it will stand still to be looked at, and, in principle, to be looked at by everybody." [4] But one senses as he proceeds that the emphasis in his treatment of the esthetic situation is being shifted off the quality stressed in the contextualistic treatment to something else. Finally, Bosanquet comes to the definitive point.

> Feeling becomes "organized," "plastic," or "incarnate" [he writes]. This character of Esthetic feeling is all-important. For feeling which has found its incarnation or taken plastic shape cannot remain the passing reaction of a single "body-and-mind." . . . Say you are glad or sorry at something. In common life your sorrow is a more or less dull pain, and its object—what it is about—remains a thought associated with it. There is too apt to be no gain, no advance, no new depth of experience promoted by the connection. But if you have the power to draw out or give imaginative shape to the object and material of your sorrowful experience, then it *must* undergo a transformation. *The feeling is submitted to the laws of an object.* It must take on permanence, order, harmony, meaning, in short value. [5]

Do you see that now we have passed quite beyond pleasure? We are talking about an embodiment of sorrow. And do you see also that it is not the quality of the experience that Bosanquet stresses but its organization or embodiment? To reach the organistic idea, one is not far off if he starts with the vivid situation of the contextualist and instead of stressing the quality and defining the unity of the situation by the quality, stresses the organization and defines the unity of the situation in terms of its organization. Though it is not entirely satisfactory because of the ambiguity of the word "feeling," we probably cannot do better than accept the usual expression of the organistic definition of esthetic value as the *integration of feeling*.

By "feeling" must be carefully understood the qualitative side of experience in contrast with the practical and the logical; something more than the pleasant

[3] Pages 3 to 5.
[4] Page 6.
[5] Pages 7, 8.

and painful. The organicist is not much concerned about defining feeling precisely, because in the higher integrations it merges with the ethical and logical connections anyway, and in the simpler pleasant or painful experiences it is obviously distinct from practical activity or logical judgment. Incidentally, painful experiences are intrinsically disintegrative, so that pains get absorbed or sifted out inevitably in the progress of integration. The esthetic field is really defined by its origins among pleasures and the kind of connections indigenous to these origins rather than by any special sort of subject matter.

If you ask an organicist what these feeling connections are, he will ask you in effect if you have not felt the demand of pleasant things for other pleasant things to complete them or fill them out. Have you never been a bit of a creative artist in planting a garden, arranging flowers, putting a room in order, hanging up tools in the basement, making a speech, or even just carrying on a conversation? Do not gaps appear that ask to be filled in certain ways—ways that practically or logically are not called for, but that just make you feel better when they are followed out? There is no practical reason why you should put magazines in two piles on either side of the lamp on the parlor table, and as the logicians have been telling everybody there is certainly no logical reason for it since any arrangement is an order. But the magazines feel better that way. We say the two piles balance each other, and the lamp in the middle seems to ask for them too. Well, that is a feeling connection.

If you are walking alone down the front path, ten to one you walk down the middle of it. That is a series of feeling connections. When you selected your tie this morning did not you think a bit about the color of your suit and shirt and possibly also whether later in the day you were going to a reunion of old pals or to a tea party on Garden Street? That was a whole texture of feeling connections. If these connections are felt out with care, they will be found different for every situation. It takes imagination, we say, to feel them out. And here we come upon the organicist's special use of the term "imagination." It was, I believe, Coleridge who first called this activity the "creative imagination." It is the process of following out and building up feeling connections. With this in mind, another definition of esthetic value for an organicist could be "imaginative integration."

There are two quantitative dimensions that yield organistic standards of beauty—the degree of integration and the amount of material integrated. By degree of integration is meant the thoroughness with which feeling connections are carried out in an esthetic object. The maximum of integration is a condition where every detail of the object calls for every other and no feeling demands are unfulfilled. Or negatively, it is a condition where no detail can be removed or altered without marring or even destroying the value of the whole. Such a whole is called an organic unity, whence the name organicism. The degree of organicity is the intensive dimension of value in this theory.

The amount of material taken up into the organic whole is the extensive criterion. This standard may be a little deceptive, for the size or length of a work may not be indicative. A woven Indian basket may have more esthetic material taken up in it than the Eiffel Tower. Esthetic material is not just what the eye and ear respond to but also the images and meanings and emotions below the sensory surface. Anything that begets a feeling connection is esthetic material. And ultimately there is probably nothing that may not be drawn into an esthetic integration. Politics and business, medicine, factory labor, collecting tickets, working on the railroad, and obviously war and religion have often been esthetically embodied. A work of art that embodies a massive reference to these things is a large work though it be only fourteen lines long.

> Late and soon,
> Getting and spending we lay waste our powers,

and the rest of this sonnet is a big work. A view of our civilization and an ethical judgment is esthetically embodied here.

Just how much bigger one esthetic object is than another cannot be measured with scales and a ruler. Since there is no urgent practical reason why we should ever want to know to a unit and decimals the relative esthetic sizes of two objects, I doubt if we shall seriously try to improve on an experienced man's judgment in such matters. There is, after all, no more difficulty in judging that *Macbeth* is much bigger than *Anthony Adverse* just in the amount of esthetic material incorporated than in seeing with the eye that a full grown oak is bigger than a birch sapling. Nevertheless, though physical size is not an indication of esthetic bigness, it does take a good deal of physical size to incorporate a very large amount of esthetic material. Most of the works we think of as the greatest are also physically pretty big. The greatest fiction is among novels rather than short stories; the greatest poetry is among epics and dramas rather than sonnets; the greatest pictures are among oils, temperas, and frescoes rather than miniatures; the greatest architecture among tombs, temples, and cathedrals rather than domestic houses. Bigness is esthetically important and to obtain esthetic bigness a certain amount of physical bigness is likely to be necessary.

As between a highly integrated jewel box, however, and a poorly integrated cathedral with a lot of scattered charm, which is the better? When degree of organicity and amount of esthetic material vary inversely, how does one adjudicate between the standards? I think the organicist would not try to adjudicate. You already have the esthetic judgment when you have seen that the one object has esthetically utilized its small amount of esthetic material to the greatest advantage, and the other has failed to make the most of the large amount of positive esthetic values that it has. Why ask for anything more?

I think you must by now have got something of the spirit of the organistic theory of beauty. Let me next draw some of its esthetic consequences. I shall select three—its conception of the objectivity of esthetic judgment, its theory of esthetic criticism, and its interpretation of ugliness.

Organicism proposes a justification for a final objective judgment for a highly integrated work of art. Notice the limitation of objectivity to the integrated work. The point is that, in consistency with the general organistic concept of objectivity as identical with organicity, it would follow that objectivity of judgment can only arise in the apprehension of a high degree of organicity of fact. The organistic critic is, therefore, very secure in his positive judgments of the beauty of a highly organized work of art, but his negative judgments regarding the degree of failure of a rather unintegrated work would, he admits, be erratic and subjective, since he has very little to get a purchase on.

All of us must have had the experience of being asked to give a judgment of an immature or mediocre work. The difficulty is likely to be in finding anything specific to say. It is just generally not very good. There are no clues as to any particular way of pulling the thing together. Nothing calls particularly for anything else. Or, saying the same thing the other way around, there are so many ways in which some one little group of materials in the work might have developed in the hands of a man who felt their potentialities, that to explain to the maker of the object what he might have done with these materials would be virtually constructing a whole new work of art for him. For nothing else in the work confirms these particular potentialities. Moreover, you could just as well have taken another little group of materials from another part of the work and done the same thing with them, virtually constructing a totally different organization for him. The potentialities of the materials have nowhere been carried through and there are a bewildering number of conflicting potentialities of different materials. After looking over the work a while, you probably resort to asking him what he was trying to do.

Now, there is a rather widespread conception that this is the question one should always ask an artist before beginning to criticize his work. In fairness to the artist, it is said, you should not criticize him for not doing something he was not trying to do. So, you want to know first what he was trying to do, and then you will judge if he did it. This is good advice to inexperienced persons or to critics who are caught in a rut and need some assistance to get out. It calls attention to the possible weakness of the spectator. But if the spectator is not weak, there is no reason why the work of art should not explain itself. It can only obtain objectivity of judgment if it does, and, if it is thoroughly integrated, it both explains itself and has an objectivity of value.

So, if you are a man experienced in the potentialities of the materials of an art, and ask the artist what he was trying to do, it amounts to saying that whatever it was he was trying to do he did not succeed in doing it. What you are hoping is that he may have had an idea but lacked the ability to develop it, for then you can give him some assistance perhaps as to what materials to follow through and as to where he failed to answer demands of his materials and the like. When it is necessary to ask an artist what he was trying to do, either the spectator or the artist is weak. It is a question that an honest critic should never be afraid to ask, and that a critic secure in experience would be sure to ask when puzzled, for the most experienced critic has always something to learn about the potentialities of his art. But the question is intrinsically entirely irrelevant to the judgment of the esthetic worth of an object. The esthetic value of a work of art as an integration of feeling is as independent of any artist's subjective idea of what he wanted to do when he was making it, as the cognitive value of a scientific description of fact is independent of a scientist's idea of what he wanted to find when he started observing.

In the hands of a competent artist a work of art makes itself, so to speak, and the further it gets along the more nearly it does so literally. There are many anecdotes of novelists who found their characters taking the development of the story over into their own hands. The constant testimony of the force of inspiration points to the same thing. The esthetic materials seek their own satisfying structure and equilibrium through the artist, who does not dictate but follows their guidance.

The organicist's view of artistic creation is thus part of his conception of the objectivity of the esthetic work of art and of the judgment of it. Artistic creation is the creative imagination at work, and this consists in following through faithfully the demands of feeling in esthetic materials, bringing into the work materials called for by other materials till a complete organic unity is established. Then the work stops of itself, is self-explanatory, and objective.

At the earlier stages of artistic creation a fragment of material has many alternative completions and is indeterminate. "Shaft" by itself is indecisive. It might be part of a carriage. It might be hundreds of metaphorical things. Any decision about its meaning would be arbitrary and subjective. But "sunny shaft" converts it suddenly into a thing. Now it is part of a definite whole and is controlled by "sunny" so as not to become part of a wagon, and "sunny" in turn is controlled by "shaft" so as not to become a male part of a family.

But "sunny shaft" has its own range of indeterminacy and might enter many wholes. If we follow the feeling tensions of it, not the logical, to reach an imaginative whole in which it would find companionship, "sweet bird, enchanted" feels immensely right. And now "sunny shaft . . . sweet bird enchanted" leads to "poised therein" and "I behold" and then inevitably "from sky to earth it slanted." There has been a mood all through this construction gaining in precision. It may have vaguely preceded the whole thing, and gathered up "sunny shaft," "bird," and "enchanted" by affinity. But now partially embodied in these images it acquires shape itself and naturally begins to dance to itself,

Ta-túm-ta-tá-ta-túm-ti-tó-ta-túm-ti-tú-ti-tá-ta. The words and images already in the mood enter into the dance, and distribute themselves in time, and, through the vowel sounds and consonants of the words, modify and specify the indeterminate little rhythm, and presently all these fragments come out together in the integrated stanza:

> A sunny shaft did I behold
>   From sky to earth it slanted
> And poised therein a bird so bold—
>   Sweet bird, thou wert enchanted!

Looking back, we shall see a lot of other feeling connections, altogether too many to catalogue. We see, for instance, how right "behold" was in relation to the embodied mood—to "enchanted," for instance. "I beheld" is not as magical and romantic as "I did behold." So, the "did" was functional and not a syllable to fill a beat in the verse. Moreover, the long ō of "behold" is a tone the whole stanza longs for. It almost justifies "so bold" merely for its sound. In fact, it does. "A bird so bold" which in a juvenile rhymster would make you wince at the inversion for the sake of a rhyme not yielded by "so bold a bird," here gets a justification because that tone is needed in that place prominently, and the inversion landing the tone on the rhyme gives it a prominence that more than doubles its value. It is further weighted by the assonance of "so" just before it and the alliteration of the "b" in "bird," which binds the "bold" significantly back to the "bird." And there is a premonition of all this in the word "poised" at the beginning of the line, for "p" is allied to "b" and "oi" to "ō." The inversion, moreover, is slightly archaic and goes with "enchanted" and "did." What would *as a rule* be a defect becomes functional in the integrated embodiment of this feeling. Nor have we yet finished with the word, for it stands out in a way like a question, and the answer is in the rest of the poem beyond the first stanza. It might be called the very theme of the poem, or, to use a Victorian term, its moral. For doesn't the poem say subtly, "It's spring, be bold"?

Now think of the stanza again. Would not you know it was a fragment even if I had not told you, or you had not known there were other stanzas? When quoted [above], did it not feel incomplete in spite of the complete clarity of the image? Now, here is the rest of the poem. The same kind of imaginative construction we have done for the first stanza, following out the feeling connections of the materials, can be carried right on, and when the poem is finished, I ask you if there is not a rounded completeness about it, and if the first lines and the last and all the lines between do not cooperate with one another to make that completeness, and I ask further if there is a phrase or even a word taken in its context that could be changed without loss to the whole?

GLYCINE'S SONG

A sunny shaft did I behold,
　　From sky to earth it slanted:
And poised therein a bird so bold—
　　Sweet bird, thou wert enchanted!

He sank, he rose, he twinkled, he troll'd
　　Within that shaft of sunny mist;
His eyes of fire, his beak of gold,
　　All else of amethyst!

And thus he sang: "Adieu! adieu!
Love's dreams prove seldom true.
The blossoms, they make no delay:
The sparkling dew-drops will not stay.
　　Sweet month of May,
　　　We must away;
　　　Far, far away!
　　　To-day! to-day!"

This I offer as a rough illustration of the way of the creative imagination. I do not say that this is how Coleridge came into the construction of his poem. One of the characteristics of an organic whole is that, however you come into it, you will reach the same result in the end because every detail is organically related to every other. Had he started from the second stanza or the last, he would have come out the same. Ask yourself what could in emotional congruence have sung the song of the last stanza except a bird so bold, or a fairy, and, of course, the bird was a fairy and in the mood of the song is not the fairy better in the form of the bird?

Now I am not sure that all of you will agree with all of the comments I have made on this poem. But if you follow the way of the creative imagination in a highly integrated poem like this, I am assured that you and I could come to a large amount of agreement about it, and I would be as likely to change my attitude in the light of your comments as perhaps you in the light of mine. For the point is that the materials of this poem are highly controlled in their inter-relations, so that there is a constant test of relevancy within the work itself. It can be profitably discussed and constructed or reconstructed. This internal control is what is meant, according to the insight of the organicist, by the objectivity of a work of art. And now I think it must be clear why only highly integrated embodiments of feeling have this objectivity.[6]

[6] We have in this process of the creative imagination the explanation of that paradox in the esthetic experience noted by Kant in one of the antinomies of the *Critique of Judgment*—the sense of purposiveness without a purpose. Lately Bertram Morris in his

This objectivity of a work of art and accordingly of the esthetic judgment of it was, you recall, the first of three consequences we were going to trace resulting from the organistic definition and standards of esthetic value. We now come to the organistic theory of criticism. This follows immediately from the organistic conception of esthetic objectivity, and is, to my mind, one of the most fruitful contributions of any philosophy to esthetic theory.

The idea is that the critic re-creates in the process of judgment what the artist creates. In fact, I should expand the range of application of this re-creative process, for it is not only the critic but any appreciative spectator who is expected to do this. There is no essential difference between criticism on this view and the process of attaining a full appreciation of esthetic values on the part of any spectator. An understanding spectator is a critic, and a critic is simply an understanding spectator who is perhaps a little more articulate in communicating the experiences he has in a work of work. Everyone is expected to be active in his relations with a work of art. For how else can one sense the tensions, and connections, demands, fulfillments, satisfactions, and consummation in an organic integration of the esthetic materials, unless one actively enters into them and feels with them as the artist did?

Even the difference between artist and spectator is partially broken down on this view. Both actively enter into the feeling tensions of the materials, both imaginatively work these up toward an organic structure for the satisfaction of all elements in a total mutual fulfillment. The only difference is that the artist had to bring the materials together and construct a whole that did not actually exist before, while a spectator may follow the guidance of the artist. The artist creates, the spectator re-creates.

Now the way criticism comes in is like this: As the spectator imaginatively

---

Aesthetic Process (Evanston: Northwestern University, 1943) has made this the central theme of his analysis. He makes a reference to Kant (footnote, p. 77) which is a happy one and rather forgotten by most writers in this connection, and then summarizes his thesis in these sentences: "We have distinguished between art as the unfolding esthetic process, and beauty as the completed experience. The two tend to coalesce . . . between fulfilling and fulfilment. . . . Purpose is [here] nothing more or less than purposiveness realized; but we must not confuse the esthetic purpose with a set purpose which is intellectually anticipated in advance of, and apart from, the sensuous material. . . . [Esthetic] purpose is not cold, meticulous intellect at work, but is that which completes experience and satisfies the imagination. The relations within this complex have no loose ends, which would thwart perception. Purpose may not be abstracted as something separate from the art-process; it is precisely the end of the process as cumulative resolution" (p. 78). This is not a bad way of describing the process, for it lies midway between practical conation and that sort of passive or receptive sensuousness characteristic of the hedonistic esthetic and not entirely escaped in the intuited quality of the contextualistic esthetic. A hostile writer is likely to pose the dilemma: either explicit practical purpose with a definite conceptual goal aimed at and attained, or passive receptivity of enjoyment without a goal. The Kantian antinomy and Morris's paradox of an esthetic purpose that is not a set purpose, break the dilemma open and strikingly exhibit this third sort of mental being which is neither conation nor sensation but a specific esthetic activity. Morris's name for it is "the satisfied imagination," which is a good phrase if "satisfaction" does not connote *hedonic* satisfaction too strongly.

follows the feeling demands of the materials, sensing their potentialities, acknowledging and delighting in their fulfillments here, here, and here, becoming more and more excited as the organic structure begins to close in and the consummation comes in sight, he is perhaps suddenly blocked in one of his expectations. Here at this point the artist went one way where the spectator would have gone another.

Such a blockage is an automatic negative judgment on the part of the spectator. And notice how specific it is. An organistic critic makes no vague sweeping disapprovals. He is able to say precisely what is wrong for him and why. In his imaginative reconstruction he is frustrated at this point in expectations aroused by such and such and such materials in the work. He himself would have done so and so. That does not mean that he himself could do it, for he probably lacks the technical skill and training. But he can tell just where he is dissatisfied and why.

Incidentally, this sort of specific judgment also lays the critic himself wide open to criticism. He as well as the artist has shown how he imaginatively handles esthetic materials. And he may be wrong himself. This mode of criticism accordingly makes the critic very responsible. Actually the critic has to know just as much as the artist about the potentialities of materials, or more. Artist, critic, and spectator all come intimately together in this mode of appreciation and criticism, for they all have the common enterprise of finding the maximum integration and satisfaction for the materials before them.

When a spectator is dissatisfied, then the point of dissatisfaction is open to discussion. In regard to highly integrated works of art nothing is further from the truth than the *de gustibus non est disputandum* adage. When the spectator is dissatisfied, then the question is whether the spectator or the artist was wrong in his imaginative construction. The spectator who follows this method will undoubtedly begin spontaneously to check up his own imaginative reconstruction of the work. He will look for confirmations of his feeling expectations in other parts of his work, or for other expectations which other parts of his work may set up for the detail in question. If he finds the detail integrates with other parts of the work, he will then work back over his own original imaginative construction. Perhaps he slipped somewhere along the way. And then possibly he just does not know some of the potentialities of the materials and insofar is a weak spectator. If that is possible, he will wish to discuss the matter with other spectators so as to benefit from their sources of satisfaction which he is missing.

Now, of course, it was just such a criticism I was carrying on for a certain distance a few minutes ago in connection with Coleridge's lyric. And from the time I spent on the word "bold" you must suspect that something jarred my expectations about it. Something did. And, if you recall what followed, you will see it amounted to tracing out a large number of references from and to that word, and finding that they all confirmed it in its unusual position, and set it in its place in the total structure of the poem. From that vantage point my initial doubt and criticism was dispelled.[7] Coleridge was right and I was wrong. But if the confirmation had failed, the criticism would have stood. Even if I had not been satisfied with my own judgment and had sought the confirmation of other readers, the process would have been the same. And in the end the confirmation of other readers is always sought, for any reader may have inhibitions upon certain sorts of references in a work of art which other readers must fill in.

This re-creative conception of criticism has had many exponents since Coleridge first discovered it. Henry James, who besides being one of our best novelists is also one of our best critics, habitually employs it. Percy Lubbock inherited the method from James and explained it in its application to the novel in a little book, *The Craft of Fiction,* that deserves to be even better known than it is. I would like you to hear how Lubbock describes the method:

> The reader of a novel—by which I mean the critical reader—[he writes], is himself a novelist; he is the maker of a book which may or may not please his taste when it is finished, but of a book for which he must take his own share of the responsibility. The author does his part, but he cannot transfer his book like a bubble into the brain of the critic; he cannot make sure that the critic will possess his work. The reader must therefore become, for his part, a novelist, never permitting himself to suppose that the creation of the book is solely the affair of the author. . . . From point to point we follow the writer, always looking back to the subject itself in order to understand the logic of the course he pursues. We find that we are creating a design, large or small, simple or intricate, as the chapter finished is fitted into its place; or again there is a flaw and a break in the development, the author takes a turn that appears to contradict or to disregard the subject, and the critical question, strictly so called, begins. Is this proceeding of the author the right one, the best for the subject? Is it possible to conceive and to name a better? The hours of the author's labor are lived again by the reader, the pleasure of creation is renewed.[8]

Before leaving this topic a warning apparently needs to be given to some who enter upon this mode of criticism. It is strange that there should be any need of it, for the method is intrinsically self-regulative. But many excellent re-creative

---

[7] Strangely enough, such confirmed unexpectances are the food of vitality in art. This should be no surprise to us after our transit through contextualistic esthetics, though the organicist is always a little startled and mystified at them. They are, of course, genuine conflicts of expectation which turn out to be just right in the consummatory achievement. In a surpassingly good lyric like this one there is not a pivotal word that is not a little surprising, and somewhat the more so for turning out to be just right in its relations to all the other words.

[8] Percy Lubbock, *The Craft of Fiction* (Jonathan Cape and Harrison Smith, New York), pp. 17, 23-24.

critics have somehow got to setting arbitrary limits to the range of re-creation they allow. Roger Fry is an example. He seems to me one of the keenest and most rewarding critics yet to appear in the visual arts. But somehow he got the notion that the materials of a visual work of art must be limited to those that stimulate the eye—to colors, lines, planes, and volumes and, in general, the plastic values. The representative, dramatic, and symbolic values he dubbed "literary" and by arbitrary definitional fiat excluded them from the esthetic field of the visual arts. A generation of lesser critics has followed him, and those who have stood out against him have generally done so on unconvincing grounds and have not known how to answer him in his own terms.

The answer, of course, in the light of our present analysis, is simple. If the "literary" values integrate in their feeling references with the plastic values, or *vice versa*, they are intrinsic materials of the work of art. Moreover, an integration of both the representations (let us drop the question-begging "literary") and the plastic values is potentially a larger and richer integration than one that restricts itself to either the one or the other. And lastly, a critic who judges a work of art which in fact is an integration of both types of values, by following out the references of one type only, is bound to be frustrated whenever one of these types leads into the other for its organic fulfillment.

There is a tendency for organic critics to become formalistic like Roger Fry. One feels it a little even in Percy Lubbock. It comes out also in many musical critics, who write sometimes as if they were ashamed of any emotions in music. Of course, this is all absolutely contrary to the spirit of organistic criticism which sets no limits whatever upon the materials integrated so long as they are integrated in the mode of feeling.

Now a few words on the third and last consequence of the organistic criterion of beauty that I earlier alluded to—the interpretation of ugliness. Bosanquet spends his whole last lecture, a third of his exposition, on this question. There is, to be sure, an issue involving the basic categories of organicism in regard to negative values that is troubling Bosanquet. This we need not go into. But out of his struggles with the issue comes a conception of invincible ugliness that will stir up a sympathetic vibration somewhere in the heart of every true artist. Invincible ugliness is esthetic dishonesty.

First, objects which are not integrations of feeling are, of course, not ugly. They are not negative esthetic values. They are not esthetic values at all, since they fall outside the esthetic field. Secondly, experiences of objects which fail to realize the integrations of feeling potentially contained in them do not impute negative esthetic values to these objects. Let me refer you back to our analysis of the esthetic work of art in the previous lecture, and the contrast between the ideal consummatory perception and the partial perceptions on the way to it. So far as one of these partial perceptions is felt as a frustrated integration, it is a negative esthetic value and ugly to the spectator. But, as Bosanquet says, this only bespeaks a weakness of the spectator. The spectator has not mastered the intricacy of the design, or he cannot yet take the tension of the emotion, or he has not enough width of experience to understand the allusions.

> Intricacy, tension, and width [writes Bosanquet], account for a very large proportion of so-called ugliness, that is to say, of what shocks most people, or else seems to them repellantly uninteresting, or overstrained, or fantastic. All this part of ugliness then seems due to the weakness of the spectator, whether his object is nature or art.[9]

The esthetic work of art in these instances is not ugly though a spectator's experience of it may be. The beauty of the work of art is a "difficult beauty." And the ugliness of the spectator's response can be overcome by a fuller realization of the work.

Thirdly, what if the esthetic work of art itself is lacking in complete integration? Bosanquet, like most organicists (and I would guess all the most recent, and include many contextualists along with them), confuses this situation with the preceding. The confusion comes from a failure to make a complete analysis of the esthetic work of art such as we gave [above]. If the artist has not himself succeeded in fully integrating his esthetic materials and communicating their interrelations through a physical work of art, then the esthetic work itself is lacking in beauty. The work itself falls short of the total integration of which its materials were capable, and as such it must be regarded as ugly. But still it is not what Bosanquet calls an instance of invincible ugliness. It is an instance of what he might have called a weakness of the artist. Some other artist with these same materials might carry them forward to the consummation of which they were capable.

But, fourthly, we reach invincible ugliness when an artist assembles his materials so as to lead us to expect an imaginative integration and then by some positive action of his own directs us to another end. The end is likely to be something like popular applause, or propaganda, or a chance to make a little more money, or submissiveness to authority, or rebellion and pure cussedness, or even "that last infirmity," fame. For these the artist sacrifices the integrity of his work. So, writes Bosanquet, "the principal region in which to look for insuperable ugliness is . . . the region of insincere and affected art. Here you necessarily have the very root of ugliness." [10] The work itself contains ingredients positively frustrating to beauty. The artist himself probably had the capacity to bring his

[9] *Three Lectures on Aesthetic,* p. 95.
[10] *Ibid.,* p. 106.

materials to esthetic consummation. But he turned aside for an easier reward. The motive can be detected by anyone who can imaginatively follow the materials, and the negative judgment on the work of art is sharpened by a judgment on the character of the artist, the keener in that every artist is open to these temptations, and envies while he repudiates the superficial successes of the artist without integrity.

So out of organicism an esthetic conscience takes form, and we can speak of the dictates of taste. But these are really just the natural movement of the esthetic imagination undiverted in its aim to achieve an organic integration of feeling—an integration, that is, of the ways in which sensations, images, thoughts, and emotions seek to come together of their own accord about a perceptive center such as a physical work of art.

By way of summary, then, an object of great esthetic value, on this view, is one that achieves or closely approaches such an integration. Criticism is a following of the path of such achievement and a marking of questionable junctures along the way where frustrations or gaps occur in the experience of the critic. And appreciation is the same thing in the satisfactions of the partial achievements along the way and the triumph of final consummation in the total organic structure. In this imaginative activity artist and critic and spectator are nearly as one. They are a group of travelers all actively following the same trails with one of them, the artist, as their guide. Ugliness, or negative esthetic value, appears in the accidents or blocks along the way which may be due to the awkwardness of one of the group in not watching the guide, or to a failure of the guide to clear the trail properly, but invincible ugliness occurs when the guide betrays his followers and deliberately leads them astray for some reason of his own.

Whatever may happen to organicism in the future, I think this process of the creative imagination will never be forgotten. It joins artist, critic, and spectator, or all who seek esthetic values, into a community united in the creation of objects of the highest esthetic worth.

—*The Basis of Criticism in the Arts* (1946)

LOUIS ARNAUD REID

Greatness

What do we mean by greatness? Greatness is difficult to define, though as to what it is in actuality, there is a certain body of agreement. We all recognize to some degree the distinction between the great and the trifling, in art. We recognize that the passage where Samson cries,

"O dark, dark, dark, amid the blaze of noon,"

is "greater" than the last lyric of Comus, that Beethoven's *Hammerklavier* Sonata is "greater" than his first, that the reclining *Theseus* of Pheidias on the Parthenon is "greater" than the Hermes of Praxiteles, that Shakespeare's *Macbeth* is "greater" than his *A Midsummer Night's Dream,* or any lyric in it.

But can we say what we mean by the comparative "greater"? In the first place, we seem to mean *at least* expressiveness of the "great" values of life. As the question of greatness is easier to discuss in the case of an art like poetry, where ideas are more readily discernible, I shall select my examples mainly from poetry. This does not mean that, if true, our answers should not apply to arts like music and architecture. Certainly they ought. But for general reasons already made clear, the elements of greatness are always far harder to analyze in these cases.

It is very difficult, as has been said, and dangerous, to try to define greatness, to say exactly *why* what we call the "great" values of life are called "great," and what precisely constitutes their greatness. We do naturally assume that some values are "greater" than others. They are, I suppose, generally speaking, those values which, positively regarded, are the fulfillments of tendencies which are not only marked and strong, but profound and lofty and broad and far-reaching in the complexity of their implications. Great values are, probably, the fulfillments of those tendencies which are most important on the highest emergent plane with which we are acquainted,[1] the intricate life of man. Animal passions are strong, and strength is one character of greatness. But more than strength is needed. Greatness cannot be conceived without also thinking of the wide system

---

[1] It does not follow that there may not exist in the universe values higher and greater than these, or that the values cognized for example in great tragedy or through religion are not superhuman values. We are concerned with "greater" and not with "greatest."

of implications, seen or hidden, of the fine organization of a questing spirit, which reveals the universality of man's nature, which marks him off from the local animal, which reveals "the piece of work" that he is when he is most man. It must be, approximately, for these reasons that the spectacles of human love, hate, mortality, courage, romance, religious experience, or of the strife of man with himself, or his fellows, or nature, are spectacles which, as we say, penetrate to "the roots of our being."

That greatness in art consists at least in expression of the great values of life, is seen in the odd examples we mentioned; it is seen in extracts from larger works, as well as in whole and complete works. This quality of greatness may even be realized in the very simplest cases: we may realize something of it in viewing the massive pylons, crude and yet imposing, of an ancient Egyptian temple. We may get it even in the contemplation of some simple sense datum, such as a patch of color. It may be that a patch of gray-white may express death to me, carrying with it the flavor of all mortality. Or a patch of blue may express the infinite distances of blue skies, of cosmic sublimity. It may be that even in the apprehension of such extremely simple objects as these there is satisfied in some measure that longing for greatness of which Longinus speaks. "Nature . . . from the first implanted in our souls an invincible yearning for all that is great, all that is diviner than ourselves. . . . And that is why nature prompts us to admire, not the clearness and usefulness of a little stream, but the Nile, the Danube, the Rhine, and, far beyond all, the Ocean." Our minds yearn for these "Ocean"-experiences, and we are glad when we get them.

But though greatness, in the sense of expression of what we call the great values of life, can certainly be found in extremely simple esthetic objects, and although such expression technically satisfies the conditions of esthetic expressiveness, this is certainly not all, or even most, of what we mean when we speak of artistic "greatness." For one thing, as we know, the expressiveness of such simple data is relatively "subjective" and private, and lacking in community. Again, an *extract* from a work of art may exhibit greatness of quality, but to say, "This extract has 'greatness' *in* it" is very different from saying, "This is a great work of art." Mr. Lascelles Abercrombie has this in mind when he distinguishes between great "moments" of poetry, or "great poetry"; and a "great poem." [2] In *moments* of poetic experience we get "the accent or tone of greatness: it is matter so concentrated and organized as to effect an unusual richness and intensity of impression." In the great poem, on the other hand, there is more than this. "When we have some notable range and variety of richly compacted experience brought wholly into the final harmony of complex impression given us by a completed poem, with its perfect system of significances uniting into one significance, then we may expect to feel ourselves in the presence of great poetry; and the greater the range, the richer the harmony of its total significance, and the more evident

[2] *The Idea of Great Poetry*, p. 60.

our sense of its greatness. A similar effect may be given by a *series* of poems, when some connection of theme, in idea or mood, some relatedness in the kind of harmony effected over things, enables our minds to fuse the several impressions into one inclusive impression; but the effect can hardly be so decisive as when our minds are, without interruption, dominated by the single form of *one* poem." [3]

In the extract from the poem or in the simple sense datum which appears to express something great, or profound, or mysterious, or momentous, there is, as has been said, complexity of implication. Nevertheless, in such cases, their complexity and the depth of their penetration are rather implicit than explicit. It is not explicit in the body nor is it worked out in any detail. No one would dream of calling "great" a simple patch of color—to take an extreme example which verges on absurdity—even though it appeared genuinely expressive to him of great value. And the extract contains suggestions and possibilities, rather than anything else. But we want more than this in art; we want more than a flavor; we want a greatness made explicit, expressed, embodied in a body, and worked out in some detail.

A considerable complexity of embodiment is, then, required in works of art which are to be called "great." The great works of the great poets, Sophocles, Dante, Milton, Shakespeare, are organized embodiments of a large variety of human experience. And, being organizations of considerable complexity of human experience, they require for their development a certain space of "canvas," a certain length. Perhaps I may be allowed once more to quote a short passage from Mr. Abercrombie, for he puts the matter, as usual, with charming concreteness.

"Length," he says,[4] "in itself is nothing; but the plain fact is that a long poem, if it really is a poem (as for example *The Iliad* or *The Divine Comedy, Paradise Lost,* or *Hamlet,* are poems), enables a remarkable range, not merely of experiences, but of *kinds* of experience, to be collected into a single finality of harmonious impression: a vast plenty of things has been accepted as a single version of the ideal world, as a unity of significance. As far as unity is concerned, no less than as far as splendor of imagination is concerned, a sonnet by Wordsworth may be just as unmistakably an aspect of the ideal world; and it is a marvel, the range of matter in, for example, the sonnet to Toussaint l'Ouverture. But as for greatness, think for an instant of *The Iliad* as a whole, or *The Divine Comedy.* The thing simply is, that Homer and Dante can achieve an inclusive moment of final unity out of a whole series of moments as remarkable as that single one of Wordsworth's: obviously, then, irrespective of poetic quality as such, that final intricate harmony of theirs will be far richer, and so greater, than his—

[3] *Ibid.,* p. 72.
[4] *Ibid.,* pp. 72-74.

though by means of a unity far less direct than his, and a form less immediately impressive and therefore, no doubt, less lovely."

The character of complexity, of width and comprehensiveness, is a character of greatness which is of course not confined to the arts. In the realm of thought, we call him great who has the grasp of a wide and complex field of knowledge, and who has so organized his knowledge that any particular proposition readily falls into place in the system of the whole. Of the man of affairs who, in his realm, is also called great, the same is true: he too has capacity for comprehension of the complex, and he too has insight into the bearing of the whole upon this or that problem of practice. All real greatness seems to imply this grasp of the complex, with a sense of proportion and relevance.

The difference between thought and practice, on the one hand, and art on the other, is the difference between thought-and-practice-ends, and art-ends. The special situation upon which the complex system of knowledge must converge is a *knowledge*-situation, a problem, say, to be solved and understood. So knowledge of the system of practice converges upon some problem of *practice*. The situation upon which the systematized esthetic complex must converge, on the other hand, is an embodied *value*-situation. It is an embodied value to be savored and enjoyed.

And further, in "great" art, the embodied value to be savored is what we have called a "great" value, or group of great values. The thinker, or the man of affairs, must in one sense possess "a sense of values," for he has, as we have said, a sense of proportion; and what is that but a sense of values? But it is a sense of values relevant to facts to be *understood,* or *acted* upon, whereas in the case of the work of art the complexity apprehended is relevant to enjoyment or *appreciation* of value. In great art it is relevant to enjoyment or appreciation of great value or values. So that, whilst greatness of intellect, or of practicality, implies only great power of grasping the complex, with a sense of proportion and relevance, and has in itself nothing to do with capacity to discern and to savor and enjoy and appreciate what we have called the "great" values as such, the greatness of the great artist does involve possession of *both* these powers. What, for example, has a great physicist or a great mathematician or a great strategist to do with the appreciation of mortality or love or mystic rapture? (The physicist, or mathematician, or strategist, *qua* these things, I mean, not *qua* human beings or as possible artists.) The answer is, He has nothing to do with them. But appreciation of these values is just the artist's very province, so far as they are embodied. The function of art is expression of content in a body. The content, we have seen, is a content of values, and the content of great art, of great values. We may conclude then, that when great value or values are embodied in and through the complex whole of a work of art, then the work is great. And the greater the values, and the more of great values we have, provided they are united into one coherent meaning, the greater is the work.

This account, if at all true, ought to hold good of all art. It is far more difficult, as has been said, to work out and to illustrate in such cases as music and architecture; and to prove that it really works in these cases we should require to refer to a long series of experiments which have not, as far as I know, been made. We have therefore to fall back on a certain dogmatism, on a certain body of educated opinion, which says that in art these things are so. In some of Bach's Chorales and in some of his great Passion music, as well as in some of Beethoven's later work (to cite but two names), our intuition tells us that there is embodied this range and comprehensiveness of experience convergent upon, and making vivid and real, some of the profoundest values of human life. We cannot prove it; we can only say that our intuitions, our deepest feelings, our whole *being* of body-and-mind, tell us that it is so. If anyone says us nay, we have no very clear answer to give in reply. But lack of science need not unduly depress us here. Our present impotence at least does not *prove* us wrong. And we have on our side the prestige of the greatest and most distinguished minds.

—*A Study in Aesthetics* (1931)

Aristotle

From THE POETICS
(Translated by S. H. Butcher)

I *["Imitation" the common principle of the arts of poetry, music, dancing, painting, and sculpture. These arts distinguished according to the medium or material vehicle, the objects, and the manner of imitation. The medium of imitation is rhythm, language, and "harmony" (or melody), taken singly or combined.]*

I propose to treat of Poetry in itself and of its various kinds, noting the essential quality of each; to inquire into the structure of the plot as requisite to a good poem; into the number and nature of the parts of which a poem is composed; and similarly into whatever else falls within the same inquiry. Following, then, the order of nature, let us begin with the principles which come first.

Epic poetry and Tragedy, Comedy also and Dithyrambic poetry, and the music of the flute and of the lyre in most of their forms, are all in their general conception modes of imitation. They differ, however, from one another in three respects—the medium, the objects, the manner or mode of imitation, being in each case distinct.

For as there are persons who, by conscious art or mere habit, imitate and represent various objects through the medium of color and form, or again by the voice; so in the arts above mentioned, taken as a whole, the imitation is produced by rhythm, language, or "harmony," either singly or combined.

Thus in the music of the flute and of the lyre, "harmony" and rhythm alone are employed; also in other arts, such as that of the shepherd's pipe, which are essentially similar to these. In dancing, rhythm alone is used without "harmony"; for even dancing imitates character, emotion, and action, by rhythmical movement.

There is another art which imitates by means of language alone, and that either in prose or verse—which verse, again, may either combine different meters or consist of but one kind—but this has hitherto been without a name. For there is no common term we could apply to the mimes of Sophron and Xenarchus and the Socratic dialogues on the one hand; and, on the other, to poetic imitations in iambic, elegiac, or any similar meter. People do, indeed, add the word "maker" or "poet" to the name of the meter, and speak of elegiac poets, or epic (that is, hexameter) poets, as if it were not the imitation that makes the poet, but the verse that entitles them all indiscriminately to the name. Even when a treatise on medicine or natural science is brought out in verse, the name of the poet is by custom given to the author; and yet Homer and Empedocles have nothing in common but the meter, so that it would be right to call the one poet, the other physicist rather than poet. On the same principle, even if a writer in his poetic imitation were to combine all meters, as Chaeremon did in his *Centaur,* which is a medley composed of meters of all kinds, we should bring him too under the general term poet. So much then for these distinctions.

There are, again, some arts which employ all the means above mentioned, —namely, rhythm, tune, and meter. Such are Dithyrambic and Nomic poetry, and also Tragedy and Comedy; but between them the difference is, that in the first two cases these means are all employed in combination, in the latter, now one means is employed, now another.

Such, then, are the differences of the arts with respect to the medium of imitation.

II *[The objects of imitation. Higher or lower types are represented in all the imitative arts. In poetry this is the basis of the distinction between tragedy and comedy.]*

Since the objects of imitation are men in action, and these men must be either of a higher or a lower type (for moral character mainly answers to these divisions, goodness and badness being the distinguishing marks of moral differences), it follows that we must represent men either as better than in real life, or as worse, or as they are. It is the same in painting. Polygnotus depicted men as nobler than they are, Pauson as less noble, Dionysius drew them true to life.

Now it is evident that each of the modes of imitation above mentioned will exhibit these differences, and become a distinct kind in imitating objects that are thus distinct. Such diversities may be found even in dancing, flute-playing, and lyre-playing. So again in language, whether prose or verse unaccompanied by music. Homer, for example, makes men better than they are; Cleophon as they are; Hegemon the Thasian, the inventor of parodies, and Nicochares, the author of the Deiliad, worse than they are. The same thing holds good of Dithyrambs and Nomes; here too one may portray different types, as Timotheus and Philoxenus differed in representing their Cyclopes. The same distinction marks off Tragedy from Comedy; for Comedy aims at representing men as worse, Tragedy as better than in actual life.

III [*The manner of imitation. Poetry may be in form either dramatic narrative, pure narrative (including lyric poetry), or pure drama.*]

There is still a third difference—the manner in which each of these objects may be imitated. For the medium being the same, and the objects the same, the poet may imitate by narration—in which case he can either take another personality as Homer does, or speak in his own person, unchanged—or he may present all his characters as living and moving before us.

These, then, as we said at the beginning, are the three differences which distinguish artistic imitation,—the medium, the objects, and the manner. So that from one point of view, Sophocles is an imitator of the same kind as Homer —for both imitate higher types of character; from another point of view, of the same kind as Aristophanes—for both imitate persons acting and doing. . . .

This may suffice as to the number and nature of the various modes of imitation.

IV [*The origin and development of poetry. Psychologically, poetry may be traced to two causes, the instinct of imitation, and the instinct of "harmony" and rhythm. Historically viewed, poetry diverged early in two directions. Tragedy and comedy exhibit the distinction in a developed form.*]

Poetry in general seems to have sprung from two causes, each of them lying deep in our nature. First, the instinct of imitation is implanted in man from childhood, one difference between him and other animals being that he is the most imitative of living creatures, and through imitation learns his earliest lessons; and no less universal is the pleasure felt in things imitated. We have evidence of this in the facts of experience. Objects which in themselves we view with pain, we delight to contemplate when reproduced with minute fidelity: such as the forms of the most ignoble animals and of dead bodies. The cause of this again is, that to learn gives the liveliest pleasure, not only to philosophers but to men in general; whose capacity, however, of learning is more limited. Thus the reason why men enjoy seeing a likeness is, that in contemplating it they find themselves learning or inferring, and saying perhaps, "Ah, that is he." For if you happen not to have seen the original, the pleasure will be due not to the imitation as such, but to the execution, the coloring, or some such other cause.

Imitation, then, is one instinct of our nature. Next, there is the instinct for "harmony" and rhythm, meters being manifestly sections of rhythm. Persons, therefore, starting with this natural gift developed by degrees their special aptitudes, till their rude improvisations gave birth to Poetry.

Poetry now diverged in two directions, according to the individual character of the writers. The graver spirits imitated noble actions, and the actions of good men. The more trivial sort imitated the actions of meaner persons, at first composing satires, as the former did hymns to the gods and the praises of famous men. . . .

But when Tragedy and Comedy came to light, the two classes of poets still followed their natural bent: the lampooners became writers of Comedy, and the Epic poets were succeeded by Tragedians, since the drama was a larger and higher form of art.

Whether Tragedy has as yet perfected its proper types or not; and whether it is to be judged in itself, or in relation also to the audience—this raises another question. Be that as it may, Tragedy—as also Comedy—was at first mere improvisation. The one originated with the authors of the Dithyramb, the other with those of the phallic songs, which are still in use in many of our cities. Tragedy advanced by slow degrees; each new element that showed itself was in turn developed. Having passed through many changes, it found its natural form, and there it stopped. . . .

V [Definition of the ludicrous. Points of comparison between epic poetry and tragedy.]

Comedy is, as we have said, an imitation of characters of a lower type,— not, however, in the full sense of the word bad, the Ludicrous being merely a subdivision of the ugly. It consists in some defect or ugliness which is not painful or destructive. To take an obvious example, the comic mask is ugly and distorted, but does not imply pain. . . .

Epic poetry agrees with Tragedy insofar as it is an imitation in verse of characters of a higher type. They differ, in that Epic poetry admits but one kind of meter, and is narrative in form. They differ, again, in their length: for Tragedy endeavors, as far as possible, to confine itself to a single revolution of the sun, or but slightly to exceed this limit; whereas the Epic action has no limits of time. This, then, is a second point of difference; though at first the same freedom was admitted in Tragedy as in Epic poetry.

Of their constituent parts some are common to both, some peculiar to Tragedy: whoever, therefore, knows what is good or bad Tragedy, knows also about Epic poetry. All the elements of an Epic poem are found in Tragedy, but the elements of a Tragedy are not all found in the Epic poem. . . .

VI [Definition of tragedy. Six elements in tragedy. Plot, or the representation of the action, is of primary importance; character and thought come next in order.]

Tragedy, then, is an imitation of an action that is serious, complete, and of a certain magnitude; in language embellished with each kind of artistic ornament, the several kinds being found in separate parts of the play; in the form of action, not of narrative; through pity and fear effecting the proper purgation of these emotions. By "language embellished," I mean language into which rhythm, "harmony," and song enter. By "the several kinds in separate parts," I mean, that some parts are rendered through the medium of verse alone, others again with the aid of song.

Now as tragic imitation implies persons acting, it necessarily follows, in the first place, that Spectacular equipment will be a part of Tragedy. Next, Song and Diction, for these are the medium of imitation. By "Diction" I mean the mere metrical arrangement of the words: as for "Song," it is a term whose sense everyone understands.

Again, Tragedy is the imitation of an action; and an action implies personal agents, who necessarily possess certain distinctive qualities both of character and thought; for it is by these that we qualify actions themselves, and these —thought and character—are the two natural causes from which actions spring, and on actions again all success or failure depends. Hence, the Plot is the imitation of the action:—for by plot I here mean the arrangement of the incidents. By Character I mean that in virtue of which we ascribe certain qualities to the agents. Thought is required wherever a statement is proved, or, it may be, a general truth enunciated. Every Tragedy, therefore, must have six parts, which parts determine its quality—namely, Plot, Character, Diction, Thought, Spectacle, Song. Two of the parts constitute the medium of imitation, one the manner, and three the objects of imitation. And these complete the list. These elements have been employed, we may say, by the poets to a man; in fact, every play contains Spectacular elements as well as Character, Plot, Diction, Song, and Thought.

But most important of all is the structure of the incidents. For Tragedy is an imitation, not of men, but of an action and of life, and life consists in action, and its end is a mode of action, not a quality. Now character determines men's qualities, but it is by their actions that they are happy or the reverse. Dramatic action, therefore, is not with a view to the representation of character: character comes in as subsidiary to the actions. Hence the incidents and the plot are the end of a tragedy; and the end is the chief thing of all. Again, without action there cannot be a tragedy; there may be without character. The tragedies of most of our modern poets fail in the rendering of character; and of poets in general this is often true. It is the same in painting; and here lies the difference between Zeuxis and Polygnotus. Polygnotus delineates character well: the style of Zeuxis is devoid of ethical quality. Again, if you string together a set of speeches expressive of character, and well finished in point of diction and thought, you will not produce the essential tragic effect nearly so well as with a play which, however deficient in these respects, yet has a plot and artistically constructed incidents. Besides which, the most powerful elements of emotional interest in Tragedy— Peripeteia or Reversal of the Situation, and Recognition scenes—are parts of the plot. A further proof is, that novices in the art attain to finish of diction and precision of portraiture before they can construct the plot. It is the same with almost all the early poets.

The Plot, then, is the first principle, and, as it were, the soul of a tragedy: Character holds the second place. A similar fact is seen in painting. The most beautiful colors, laid on confusedly, will not give as much pleasure as the chalk outline of a portrait. Thus Tragedy is the imitation of an action, and of the agents mainly with a view to the action.

Third in order is Thought,—that is, the faculty of saying what is possible and pertinent in given circumstances. In the case of oratory, this is the function of the political art and of the art of rhetoric: and so indeed the older poets make their characters speak the language of civic life; the poets of our time, the language of the rhetoricians. Character is that which reveals moral purpose, showing what kind of things a man chooses or avoids. Speeches, therefore, which do not make this manifest, or in which the speaker does not choose or avoid anything whatever, are not expressive of character. Thought, on the other hand, is found where something is proved to be or not to be, or a general maxim is enunciated.

Fourth among the elements enumerated comes Diction; by which I mean, as has been already said, the expression of the meaning in words; and its essence is the same both in verse and prose.

Of the remaining elements Song holds the chief place among the embellishments.

The Spectacle has, indeed, an emotional attraction of its own, but, of all the parts, it is the least artistic, and connected least with the art of poetry. For the power of Tragedy, we may be sure, is felt even apart from representation and actors. Besides, the production of spectacular effects depends more on the art of the stage machinist than on that of the poet.

VII *[The plot must be a whole, complete in itself, and of adequate magnitude.]*

These principles being established, let us now discuss the proper structure of the Plot, since this is the first and most important thing in Tragedy.

Now, according to our definition, Tragedy is an imitation of an action that is complete, and whole, and of a certain magnitude; for there may be a whole that is wanting in magnitude. A whole is that which has a beginning, a middle, and an end. A beginning is that which does not itself follow anything by causal necessity, but after which something naturally is or comes to be. An end, on the contrary, is that which itself naturally follows some other thing, either by necessity, or as a rule, but has nothing following it. A middle is that which follows something as some other thing follows it. A well-constructed plot, therefore, must neither begin nor end at haphazard, but conform to these principles.

Again, a beautiful object, whether it be a living organism or any whole composed of parts, must not only have an orderly arrangement of parts, but must also be of a certain magnitude; for beauty depends on magnitude and order. Hence a very small animal organism cannot be beautiful; for the view of it is confused, the object being seen in an almost imperceptible moment of time. Nor, again, can one of vast size be beautiful; for as the eye cannot take it all in at once, the unity and sense of the whole is lost for the spectator; as for instance if there were one a thousand miles long. As, therefore, in the case of animate bodies and organisms a certain magnitude is necessary, and a magnitude which may be easily embraced in one view; so in the plot, a certain length is necessary, and a length which can be easily embraced by the memory. The limit of length in relation to dramatic competition and sensuous presentment, is no part of artistic theory. For had it been the rule for a hundred tragedies to compete together, the performance would have been regulated by the water-clock,—as indeed we are told was formerly done. But the limit as fixed by the nature of the drama itself is this:—the greater the length, the more beautiful will the piece be by reason of its size, provided that the whole be perspicuous. And to define the matter roughly, we may say that the proper magnitude is comprised within such limits, that the sequence of events, according to the law of probability or necessity, will admit of a change from bad fortune to good, or from good fortune to bad.

VIII *[The plot must be a unity. Unity of plot consists not in unity of hero, but in unity of action. The parts must be organically connected.]*

Unity of plot does not, as some persons think, consist in the unity of the hero. For infinitely various are the incidents in one man's life which cannot be reduced to unity; and so, too, there are many actions of one man out of which we cannot make one action. Hence the error, as it appears, of all poets who have composed a Heracleid, a Theseid, or other poems of the kind. They imagine that as Heracles was one man, the story of Heracles must also be a unity. But Homer, as in all else he is of surpassing merit, here too—whether from art or natural genius—seems to have happily discerned the truth. In composing the Odyssey he did not include all the adventures of Odysseus—such as his wound on Parnassus, or his feigned madness at the mustering of the host—incidents between which there was no necessary or probable connection: but he made the Odyssey, and likewise the Iliad, to center round an action that in our sense of the word is one. As therefore, in the other imitative arts, the imitation is one when the object imitated is one, so the plot, being an imitation of an action, must imitate one action and that a whole, the structural union of the parts being such that, if any one of them is displaced or removed, the whole will be disjointed and disturbed. For a thing whose presence or absence makes no visible difference, is not an organic part of the whole.

IX *[(Plot continued.) Dramatic unity can be attained only by the observance of poetic as distinct from historic truth; for poetry is an expression of the universal; history of the particular. The rule of probable or necessary sequence as applied to the incidents. The best tragic effect depends on the combination of the inevitable and the unexpected.]*

It is, moreover, evident from what has been said, that it is not the function of the poet to relate what has happened, but what may happen—what is possible according to the law of probability or necessity. The poet and the historian differ not by writing in verse or in prose. The work of Herodotus might be put into verse, and it would still be a species of history, with meter no less than without it. The true difference is that one relates what has happened, the other what may happen. Poetry, therefore, is a more philosophical and a higher thing than history: for poetry tends to express the universal, history the particular. By the universal I mean how a person of a certain type will on occasion speak or act, according to the law of probability or necessity; and it is this universality at which

poetry aims in the names she attaches to the personages. The particular is—for example—what Alcibiades did or suffered. In Comedy this is already apparent: for
here the poet first constructs the plot on the lines of probability, and then inserts
characteristic names—unlike the lampooners who write about particular individuals. But tragedians still keep to real names, the reason being that what is possible is credible: what has not happened we do not at once feel sure to be
possible: but what has happened is manifestly possible: otherwise it would not
have happened. Still there are even some tragedies in which there are only one or
two well-known names, the rest being fictitious. In others, none are well known—
as in Agathon's Antheus, where incidents and names alike are fictitious, and yet
they give none the less pleasure. We must not, therefore, at all costs keep to the
received legends, which are the usual subjects of Tragedy. Indeed, it would be
absurd to attempt it; for even subjects that are known are known only to a few,
and yet give pleasure to all. It clearly follows that the poet or "maker" should be
the maker of plots rather than of verses; since he is a poet because he imitates, and
what he imitates are actions. And even if he chances to take an historical subject, he is none the less a poet; for there is no reason why some events that have
actually happened should not conform to the law of the probable and possible,
and in virtue of that quality in them he is their poet or maker.

Of all plots and actions the episodic are the worst. I call a plot "episodic"
in which the episodes or acts succeed one another without probable or necessary
sequence. Bad poets compose such pieces by their own fault, good poets, to
please the players; for, as they write show pieces for competition, they stretch
the plot beyond its capacity, and are often forced to break the natural continuity.

But again, Tragedy is an imitation not only of a complete action, but of
events inspiring fear or pity. Such an effect is best produced when the events
come on us by surprise; and the effect is heightened when, at the same time, they
follow as cause and effect. The tragic wonder will then be greater than if they
happened of themselves or by accident; for even coincidences are most striking
when they have an air of design. We may instance the statue of Mitys at Argos,
which fell upon his murderer while he was a spectator at a festival, and killed
him. Such events seem not to be due to mere chance. Plots, therefore, constructed
on these principles are necessarily the best.

X [(Plot continued.) Definitions of simple and complex plots.]

Plots are either Simple or Complex, for the actions in real life, of which
the plots are an imitation, obviously show a similar distinction. An action which
is one and continuous in the sense above defined, I call Simple, when the

change of fortune takes place without Reversal of the Situation and without Recognition.

A Complex action is one in which the change is accompanied by such Reversal, or by Recognition, or by both. These last should arise from the internal structure of the plot, so that what follows should be the necessary or probable result of the preceding action. It makes all the difference whether any given event is a case of *propter hoc* or *post hoc*.

XI [(Plot continued.) Reversal of the situation, recognition, and tragic or disastrous incident explained.]

Reversal of the Situation is a change by which the action veers round to its opposite, subject always to our rule of probability or necessity. Thus in the Oedipus, the messenger comes to cheer Oedipus and free him from his alarms about his mother, but by revealing who he is, he produces the opposite effect. . . .

Recognition, as the name indicates, is a change from ignorance to knowledge, producing love or hate between the persons destined by the poet for good or bad fortune. The best form of recognition is coincident with a Reversal of the Situation, as in the Oedipus. There are indeed other forms. Even inanimate things of the most trivial kind may in a sense be objects of recognition. Again, we may recognize or discover whether a person has done a thing or not. But the recognition which is most intimately connected with the plot and action is, as we have said, the recognition of persons. This recognition, combined with Reversal, will produce either pity or fear; and actions producing these effects are those which, by our definition, Tragedy represents. Moreover, it is upon such situations that the issues of good or bad fortune will depend. Recognition, then, being between persons, it may happen that one person only is recognized by the other—when the latter is already known—or it may be necessary that the recognition should be on both sides. Thus Iphigenia is revealed to Orestes by the sending of the letter; but another act of recognition is required to make Orestes known to Iphigenia.

Two parts, then, of the Plot—Reversal of the Situation and Recognition—turn upon surprises. A third part is the Scene of Suffering. The Scene of Suffering is a destructive or painful action, such as death on the stage, bodily agony, wounds and the like. . . .

XIII *[(Plot continued.) What constitutes tragic action. The change of fortune and the character of the hero as requisite to an ideal tragedy. The unhappy ending more truly tragic than the "poetic justice" which is in favor with a popular audience, and belongs rather to comedy.]*

A perfect tragedy should, as we have seen, be arranged not on the simple but on the complex plan. It should, moreover, imitate actions which excite pity and fear, this being the distinctive mark of tragic imitation. It follows plainly, in the first place, that the change of fortune presented must not be the spectacle of a virtuous man brought from prosperity to adversity: for this moves neither pity nor fear; it merely shocks us. Nor, again, that of a bad man passing from adversity to prosperity: for nothing can be more alien to the spirit of Tragedy; it possesses no single tragic quality; it neither satisfies the moral sense nor calls forth pity or fear. Nor, again, should the downfall of the utter villain be exhibited. A plot of this kind would, doubtless, satisfy the moral sense, but it would inspire neither pity nor fear; for pity is aroused by unmerited misfortune, fear by the misfortune of a man like ourselves. Such an event, therefore, will be neither pitiful nor terrible. There remains, then, the character between these two extremes—that of a man who is not eminently good and just, yet whose misfortune is brought about not by vice or depravity, but by some error or frailty. He must be one who is highly renowned and prosperous—a personage like Oedipus, Thyestes, or other illustrious men of such families.

A well-constructed plot should, therefore, be single in its issue, rather than double as some maintain. The change of fortune should be not from bad to good, but, reversely, from good to bad. It should come about as the result not of vice, but of some great error or frailty, in a character either such as we have described, or better rather than worse. . . .

In the second rank comes the kind of tragedy which some place first. Like the Odyssey, it has a double thread of plot, and also an opposite catastrophe for the good and for the bad. It is accounted the best because of the weakness of the spectators; for the poet is guided in what he writes by the wishes of his audience. The pleasure, however, thence derived is not the true tragic pleasure. It is proper rather to Comedy, where those who, in the piece, are the deadliest enemies—like Orestes and Aegisthus—quit the stage as friends at the close, and no one slays or is slain.

XIV [(Plot continued.) The tragic emotions of pity and fear should spring out of the plot itself. To produce them by scenery or spectacular effect is entirely against the spirit of tragedy.]

Fear and pity may be aroused by spectacular means; but they may also result from the inner structure of the piece, which is the better way, and indicates a superior poet. For the plot ought to be so constructed that, even without the aid of the eye, he who hears the tale told will thrill with horror and melt to pity at what takes place. This is the impression we should receive from hearing the story of the Oedipus. But to produce this effect by the mere spectacle is a less artistic method, and dependent on extraneous aids. Those who employ spectacular means to create a sense not of the terrible but only of the monstrous, are strangers to the purpose of Tragedy; for we must not demand of Tragedy any and every kind of pleasure, but only that which is proper to it. And since the pleasure which the poet should afford is that which comes from pity and fear through imitation, it is evident that this quality must be impressed upon the incidents. . . .

XV [The element of character in tragedy. The rule of necessity or probability applicable to character as to plot. The "deus ex machina." How character is idealized.]

In respect of Character there are four things to be aimed at. First, and most important, it must be good. Now any speech or action that manifests moral purpose of any kind will be expressive of character: the character will be good if the purpose is good. This rule is relative to each class. Even a woman may be good, and also a slave; though the woman may be said to be an inferior being, and the slave quite worthless. The second thing to aim at is propriety. There is a type of manly valor; but valor in a woman, or unscrupulous cleverness, is inappropriate. Thirdly, character must be true to life: for this is a distinct thing from goodness and propriety, as here described. The fourth point is consistency: for though the subject of the imitation, who suggested the type, be inconsistent, still he must be consistently inconsistent. As an example of motiveless degradation of character, we have Menelaus in the Orestes: of character indecorous and inappropriate, the lament of Odysseus in the Scylla, and the speech of Melanippe: of inconsistency, the Iphigenia at Aulis—for Iphigenia the suppliant in no way resembles her later self.

As in the structure of the plot, so too in the portraiture of character, the poet should always aim either at the necessary or the probable. Thus a person of a given character should speak or act in a given way, by the rule either of necessity or of probability; just as this event should follow that by necessary or probable sequence. It is therefore evident that the unravelling of the plot, no less than the complication, must arise out of the plot itself, it must not be brought about by the *Deus ex Machina*—as in the Medea, or in the Return of the Greeks in the Iliad. The *Deus ex Machina* should be employed only for events external to the drama—for antecedent or subsequent events, which lie beyond the range of human knowledge, and which require to be reported or foretold; for to the gods we ascribe the power of seeing all things. Within the action there must be nothing irrational. If the irrational cannot be excluded, it should be outside the scope of the tragedy. Such is the irrational element in the Oedipus of Sophocles.

Again, since Tragedy is an imitation of persons who are above the common level, the example of good portrait-painters should be followed. They, while reproducing the distinctive form of the original, make a likeness which is true to life and yet more beautiful. So too the poet, in representing men who are irascible or indolent, or have other defects of character, should preserve the type and yet ennoble it. In this way Achilles is portrayed by Agathon and Homer. . . .

XVI [(Plot continued.) Recognition: its various kinds, with examples.]

What Recognition is has been already explained. We will now enumerate its kinds.

First, the least artistic form, which, from poverty of wit, is most commonly employed—recognition by signs. Of these some are congenital—such as "the spear which the earth-born race bear on their bodies," or the stars introduced by Carcinus in his Thyestes. Others are acquired after birth; and of these some are bodily marks, as scars; some external tokens, as necklaces, or the little ark in the Tyro by which the discovery is effected. Even these admit of more or less skillful treatment. Thus in the recognition of Odysseus by his scar, the discovery is made in one way by the nurse, in another by the swineherds. The use of tokens for the express purpose of proof—and, indeed, any formal proof with or without tokens—is a less artistic mode of recognition. A better kind is that which comes about by a turn of incident, as in the Bath Scene in the Odyssey.

Next come the recognitions invented at will by the poet, and on that account wanting in art. For example, Orestes in the Iphigenia reveals the fact that he is Orestes. She, indeed, makes herself known by the letter; but he, by speaking himself, and saying what the poet, not what the plot requires. This, therefore, is nearly allied to the fault above mentioned: for Orestes might as well have brought tokens with him. Another similar instance is the "voice of the shuttle" in the Tereus of Sophocles.

The third kind depends on memory when the sight of some object awakens a feeling: as in the Cyprians of Dicaeogenes, where the hero breaks into tears on seeing the picture; or again in the "Lay of Alcinous," where Odysseus, hearing the minstrel play the lyre, recalls the past and weeps; and hence the recognition.

The fourth kind is by process of reasoning. Thus in the Choëphori: "Some one resembling me has come: no one resembles me but Orestes: therefore Orestes has come." . . .

But, of all recognitions, the best is that which arises from the incidents themselves, where the startling discovery is made by natural means. Such is that in the Oedipus of Sophocles, and in the Iphigenia; for it was natural that Iphigenia should wish to dispatch a letter. These recognitions alone dispense with the artificial aid of tokens or amulets. Next come the recognitions by process of reasoning. . . .

XIX, XXII [Thought and diction in tragedy.]

It remains to speak of Diction and Thought, the other parts of Tragedy having been already discussed. Concerning Thought, we may assume what is said in the Rhetoric, to which inquiry the subject more strictly belongs. Under Thought is included every effect which has to be produced by speech, the subdivisions being—proof and refutation; the excitation of the feelings, such as pity, fear, anger, and the like; the suggestion of importance or its opposite. Now, it is evident that the dramatic incidents must be treated from the same points of view as the dramatic speeches, when the object is to evoke the sense of pity, fear, importance, or probability. The only difference is, that the incidents should speak for themselves without verbal exposition; while the effects aimed at in speech should be produced by the speaker, and as a result of the speech. For what were the business of a speaker, if the Thought were revealed quite apart from what he says?

Next, as regards Diction. One branch of the inquiry treats of the Modes of Utterance. But this province of knowledge belongs to the art of Delivery and to the masters of that science. . . . We may, therefore, pass this over as an inquiry that belongs to another art, not to poetry.

The perfection of style is to be clear without being mean. . . . But the greatest thing by far is to have a command of metaphor. This alone cannot be imparted by another; it is the mark of genius, for to make good metaphors implies an eye for resemblances. . . .

XXIII [Epic poetry. It agrees with tragedy in unity of action: herein contrasted with history.]

As to that poetic imitation which is narrative in form and employs a single meter, the plot manifestly ought, as in a tragedy, to be constructed on dramatic principles. It should have for its subject a single action, whole and complete, with a beginning, a middle, and an end. It will thus resemble a living organism in all its unity, and produce the pleasure proper to it. It will differ in structure from historical compositions, which of necessity present not a single action, but a single period, and all that happened within that period to one person or to many, little connected together as the events may be. For as the sea-fight at Salamis and the battle with the Carthaginians in Sicily took place at the same time, but did not tend to any one result, so in the sequence of events, one thing sometimes follows another, and yet no single result is thereby produced. Such is the practice, we may say, of most poets. Here again, then, as has been already observed, the transcendent excellence of Homer is manifest. He never attempts to make the whole war of Troy the subject of his poem, though that war had a beginning and an end. It would have been too vast a theme, and not easily embraced in a single view. If, again, he had kept it within moderate limits, it must have been over-complicated by the variety of the incidents. As it is, he detaches a single portion, and admits as episodes many events from the general story of the war—such as the Catalogue of the ships and others—thus diversifying the poem. All other poets take a single hero, a single period, or an action single indeed, but with a multiplicity of parts. . . .

XXIV [(Epic poetry continued.) Further points of agreement with tragedy. The points of difference are enumerated and illustrated.]

Again, Epic poetry must have as many kinds as Tragedy: it must be simple, or complex, or "ethical," or "pathetic." The parts also, with the exception of song and spectacle, are the same; for it requires Reversals of the Situation, Recognitions, and Scenes of Suffering. Moreover, the thoughts and the diction must be artistic. In all these respects Homer is our earliest and sufficient model. Indeed each of his poems has a twofold character. The Iliad is at once simple and "pathetic," and the Odyssey complex (for Recognition scenes run through it), and at the same time "ethical." Moreover, in diction and thought they are supreme.

Epic poetry differs from Tragedy in the scale on which it is constructed, and in its meter. As regards scale or length, we have already laid down an adequate limit: the beginning and the end must be capable of being brought within a single view. This condition will be satisfied by poems on a smaller scale than the old epics, and answering in length to the group of tragedies presented at a single sitting.

Epic poetry has, however, a great—a special—capacity for enlarging its dimensions, and we can see the reason. In Tragedy we cannot imitate several lines of actions carried on at one and the same time; we must confine ourselves to the action on the stage and the part taken by the players. But in Epic poetry, owing to the narrative form, many events simultaneously transacted can be presented; and these, if relevant to the subject, add mass and dignity to the poem. The Epic has here an advantage, and one that conduces to grandeur of effect, to diverting the mind of the hearer, and relieving the story with varying episodes. For sameness of incident soon produces satiety, and makes tragedies fail on the stage.

As for the meter, the heroic measure has proved its fitness by the test of experience. If a narrative poem in any other meter or in many meters were now composed, it would be found incongruous. . . .

The element of the wonderful is required in Tragedy. The irrational, on which the wonderful depends for its chief effects, has wider scope in Epic poetry, because there the person acting is not seen. Thus, the pursuit of Hector would be ludicrous if placed upon the stage—the Greeks standing still and not joining in the pursuit, and Achilles waving them back. But in the Epic poem the absurdity passes unnoticed. Now the wonderful is pleasing: as may be inferred from the fact that every one tells a story with some addition of his own, knowing that his hearers like it. It is Homer who has chiefly taught other poets the art of telling lies skillfully. The secret of it lies in a fallacy. For, assuming that if one thing is or becomes, a second is or becomes, men imagine that, if the second is, the first likewise is or becomes. But this is a false inference. Hence, where the first thing is untrue, it is quite unnecessary, provided the second be true, to add that the first is or has become. For the mind, knowing the second to be true, falsely infers the truth of the first. There is an example of this in the Bath Scene of the Odyssey.

Accordingly, the poet should prefer probable impossibilities to improbable possibilities. The tragic plot must not be composed of irrational parts. Everything irrational should, if possible, be excluded; or, at all events, it should lie outside the action of the play (as, in the Oedipus, the hero's ignorance as to the manner of Laius' death); not within the drama—as in the Electra, the messenger's account of the Pythian games; or, as in the Mysians, the man who has come from Tegea to Mysia and is still speechless. The plea that otherwise the plot would have been ruined, is ridiculous; such a plot should not in the first instance be constructed. But once the irrational has been introduced and an air of likelihood imparted to it, we must accept it in spite of the absurdity. Take even the irrational incidents in the Odyssey, where Odysseus is left upon the shore of Ithaca. How intolerable even these might have been would be apparent if an inferior poet were to treat the subject. As it is, the absurdity is veiled by the poetic charm with which the poet invests it.

The diction should be elaborated in the pauses of the action, where there is no expression of character or thought. For, conversely, character and thought are merely obscured by a diction that is over brilliant.

XXV [Critical objections brought against poetry, and the principles on which they are to be answered. In particular, an elucidation of the meaning of poetic truth, and its difference from common reality.]

With respect to critical difficulties and their solutions, the number and nature of the sources from which they may be drawn may be thus exhibited.

The poet being an imitator, like a painter or any other artist, must of necessity imitate one of three objects—things as they were or are, things as they are said or thought to be, or things as they ought to be. The vehicle of expression is language—either current terms or, it may be, rare words or metaphors. There are also many modifications of language, which we concede to the poets. Add to this, that the standard of correctness is not the same in poetry and politics, any more than in poetry and any other art. Within the art of poetry itself there are two kinds of faults—those which touch its essence, and those which are accidental. If a poet has chosen to imitate something, <but has imitated it incorrectly> through want of capacity, the error is inherent in the poetry. But if the failure is due to a wrong choice—if he has represented a horse as throwing out both his off legs at once, or introduced technical inaccuracies in medicine, for example, or in any other art—the error is not essential to the poetry. These are the points of view from which we should consider and answer the objections raised by the critics.

First as to matters which concern the poet's own art. If he describes the impossible, he is guilty of an error; but the error may be justified, if the end of the art be thereby attained (the end being that already mentioned)—if, that is, the effect of this or any other part of the poem is thus rendered more striking. A case in point is the pursuit of Hector. If, however, the end might have been as well, or better, attained without violating the special rules of the poetic art, the error is not justified: for every kind of error should, if possible, be avoided.

Again, does the error touch the essentials of the poetic art, or some accident of it? For example, not to know that a hind has no horns is a less serious matter than to paint it inartistically.

Further, if it be objected that the description is not true to fact, the poet may perhaps reply, "But the objects are as they ought to be": just as Sophocles said that he drew men as they ought to be; Euripides, as they are. In this way the objection may be met. If, however, the representation be of neither kind, the poet may answer, "This is how men say the thing is." This applies to tales about the gods. It may well be that these stories are not higher than fact nor yet true to fact: they are, very possibly, what Xenophanes says of them. But anyhow, "this is what is said." Again, a description may be no better than the fact: still, it was the fact; as in the passage about the arms: "Upright upon their butt-ends stood the spears." This was the custom then, as it now is among the Illyrians.

Again, in examining whether what has been said or done by some one is poetically right or not, we must not look merely to the particular act or saying, and ask whether it is poetically good or bad. We must also consider by whom it is said or done, to whom, when, by what means, or for what end; whether, for instance, it be to secure a greater good, or avert a greater evil. . . .

In general, the impossible must be justified by reference to artistic requirements, or to the higher reality, or to received opinion. With respect to the requirements of art, a probable impossibility is to be preferred to a thing improbable and yet possible. Again, it may be impossible that there should be men such as Zeuxis painted. "Yes," we say, "but the impossible is the higher thing; for the ideal type must surpass the reality." To justify the irrational, we appeal to what is commonly said to be. In addition to which, we urge that the irrational sometimes does not violate reason; just as "it is probable that a thing may happen contrary to probability."

Things that sound contradictory should be examined by the same rules as in dialectical refutation—whether the same thing is meant, in the same relation, and in the same sense. We should therefore solve the question by reference to what the poet says himself, or to what is tacitly assumed by a person of intelligence.

The element of the irrational, and, similarly, depravity of character, are justly censured when there is no inner necessity for introducing them. Such is the irrational element in the introduction of Aegeus by Euripides and the badness of Menelaus in the Orestes.

XXVI [A general estimate of the comparative worth of epic poetry and tragedy. The alleged defects of tragedy are not essential to it. Its positive merits entitle it to the higher rank of the two.]

The question may be raised whether the Epic or Tragic mode of imitation is the higher. If the more refined art is the higher, and the more refined in every case is that which appeals to the better sort of audience, the art which imitates anything and everything is manifestly most unrefined. The audience is supposed to be too dull to comprehend unless something of their own is thrown in by the performers, who therefore indulge in restless movements. . . . So we are told that Epic poetry is addressed to a cultivated audience, who do not need gesture; Tragedy, to an inferior public. Being then unrefined, it is evidently the lower of the two.

Now, in the first place, this censure attaches not to the poetic but to the histrionic art; for gesticulation may be equally overdone in epic recitation, as by Sosistratus, or in lyrical competition, as by Mnasitheus the Opuntian. Next, all action is not to be condemned—any more than all dancing—but only that of bad performers. Such was the fault found in Callippides, as also in others of our own day, who are censured for representing degraded women. Again, Tragedy like Epic poetry produces its effect even without action; it reveals its power by mere reading. If, then, in all other respects it is superior, this fault, we say, is not inherent in it.

And superior it is, because it has all the epic elements—it may even use the epic meter—with the music and spectacular effects as important accessories; and these produce the most vivid of pleasures. Further, it has vividness of impression in reading as well as in representation. Moreover, the art attains its end within narrower limits; for the concentrated effect is more pleasurable than one which is spread over a long time and so diluted. What, for example, would be the effect of the Oedipus of Sophocles, if it were cast into a form as long as the Iliad? Once more, the Epic imitation has less unity; as is shown by this, that any Epic poem will furnish subjects for several tragedies. Thus if the story adopted by the poet has a strict unity, it must either be concisely told and appear truncated; or, if it conform to the Epic canon of length, it must seem weak and watery. <Such length implies some loss of unity,> if, I mean, the poem is constructed out of several actions, like the Iliad and the Odyssey, which have many such parts, each with a certain magnitude of its own. Yet these poems are as perfect as possible in structure; each is, in the highest degree attainable, an imitation of a single action.

If, then, Tragedy is superior to Epic poetry in all these respects, and, moreover, fulfils its specific function better as an art—for each art ought to produce, not any chance pleasure, but the pleasure proper to it, as already stated—it plainly follows that Tragedy is the higher art, as attaining its end more perfectly.

Thus much may suffice concerning Tragic and Epic poetry in general; their several kinds and parts, with the number of each and their differences; the causes that make a poem good or bad; the objections of the critics and the answers to these objections.

Bibliography

The Historical Development of Esthetics

THE FOLLOWING BIBLIOGRAPHICAL SUGGESTIONS are intended as a brief guide to
the history of esthetic ideas and of the classical texts. I have not included works
from the Orient.

Plato's ideas about beauty, rhetoric, and art are scattered through the *Hippias Major, Republic* (see especially Book X), *Gorgias, Ion, Symposium, Phaedrus, Philebus,* and *Laws.* Lane Cooper, in his *Plato* (New York, 1938), has
edited and translated most of this material. R. G. Collingwood, "Plato's Philosphy
of Art," *Mind,* Volume 34, 1925, and Herbert Read, *Education for Peace,*
Chapter 6, are interesting comments on Plato's ideas of art and esthetic education. Aristotle's *Poetics* is probably the most influential treatise on esthetics ever
written. Perhaps the best single commentary is in S. H. Butcher, *Aristotle's
Theory of Poetry and Fine Art.* There is a discussion of esthetic education and
the concept of purgation in the final book of the *Politics,* and of the relation of
art to nature in the *Physics,* Book II, Chapter 1 and the *Metaphysics,* Book VII,
Chapters 7-9. The neo-Platonic conception of art and beauty finds eloquent expression in the *Enneads* of Plotinus as translated by Stephen MacKenna (sections on "Beauty" and "The Intellectual Beauty"). The best known Roman
works are Horace, *Art of Poetry,* and Longinus, *On the Sublime,* but the reader
may wish to know something of Plutarch's treatise on music, Pliny's remarks on
the fine arts, Vitruvius' treatise on architecture, and Cicero's and Quintilianus'
works on rhetoric. For commentary, especially on Horace and Longinus, see
J. W. H. Atkins, *Literary Criticism in Antiquity.*

The cursory remarks of Augustine and St. Thomas Aquinas about beauty
and art are scattered through various works. The main texts are quoted by
Jacques Maritain in *Art and Scholasticism* and by Etienne Gilson in *Painting
and Reality.* Another good source is C. S. Baldwin, *Medieval Rhetoric and
Poetic.*

The spirit of Renaissance esthetics can be gleaned from Leonardo da Vinci,

A Treatise on Painting and *Notebooks;* Cennino Cennini, *The Book of Art;* and Giorgio Vasari, *The Lives of the Painters* (see especially his short biographies of Giotto, Ucello, Alberti, Piero della Francesca, Leonardo, Michelangelo, and Raphael). For English thought, one can read Sir Philip Sidney, *Defence of Poetry;* Francis Bacon, "Of Beauty" in *Essays;* and Ben Jonson, *Timber,* or *Discoveries.* The neoclassic theory of literature is set forth in Pierre Corneille, *Discourse on the Three Unities,* and Nicolas Boileau, *Art of Poetry.* The later English neoclassic view is best expounded by John Dryden, *An Essay of Dramatic Poesy.*

The eighteenth century, sometimes called "the age of criticism," produced many works devoted to esthetics or literary criticism. Among the notable English works are David Hume, "Of Tragedy" and "Of the Standard of Taste" in *Essays;* Joseph Addison, *The Pleasures of the Imagination;* Edmund Burke, *A Philosophical Enquiry into the Origin of Our Ideas of the Sublime and Beautiful;* Lord Kames, *Elements of Criticism;* Sir Joshua Reynolds, *Discourses* (excellent on painting); and Thomas Reid, *Essays on the Intellectual Powers* (Essay VIII). On the continent there were such important works as G. E. Lessing, *Laocoön;* Denis Diderot, "The Paradox of the Actor" in *Rameau's Nephew and Other Works;* and Giambattista Vico, *The New Science* (a forerunner of Croce). Most important of all was Immanuel Kant, *The Critique of Judgment* (First Part), a difficult book that repays very careful study. Strongly influenced by Kant but important in its own right was Friedrich Schiller, *Letters on the Aesthetic Education of Man.* The final chapter of Ernest Cassirer, *The Philosophy of the Enlightenment,* is an illuminating discussion of the esthetics of the eighteenth century.

As we move into the nineteenth century the literature becomes more profuse. William Wordsworth in his "Preface" to *Lyrical Ballads* and "Essay Supplementary to the Preface," and Samuel Taylor Coleridge in *Biographia Literaria,* discuss the nature of imagination and the esthetics of poetry. Coleridge's more general theory is set forth in "On Poesy or Art" and *On the Principles of Genial Criticism Concerning the Fine Arts.* Faith in poetic imagination is very eloquently expressed in Shelley, "A Defence of Poetry." The letters of John Keats are full of insights into the creative process. Among the romantic essayists, William Hazlitt has much to say about art, imagination, and esthetic emotion (there is a good selection from his essays in W. J. Bate, *Criticism: the Major Texts*).

In Germany, the romantic movement intensified the interest in imagination and the arts. The serious student of German romanticism will study the ideas of Schelling, the two Schlegels, Jean Paul, Novalis, and Schleiermacher. Not to be overlooked by any student of esthetics is the profound discussion of the arts and esthetic experience in Arthur Schopenhauer, *The World as Will and Idea,* and the comprehensive discussion of esthetics in G. W. F. Hegel, *The Philos-*

ophy of Fine Art. A. C. Bradley's essay, "Hegel's Theory of Tragedy," in *Oxford Lectures on Poetry,* is an excellent discussion of one important phase of Hegelian esthetics; and Israel Knox, *The Aesthetic Theories of Kant, Hegel, and Schopenhauer,* is a useful brief survey.

The romantic movement had its repercussions in America and helped to produce New England transcendentalism. Emerson's essay "The Poet" is one of the best expressions of this movement. More "modern" in spirit is Walt Whitman's "Preface" to *Leaves of Grass* and his great plea for a high popular culture in *Democratic Vistas.* There is no better statement of the ideal of functional art than in the writings of Horatio Greenough. The ideas represented by the transcendentalists are very well reviewed in F. O. Matthieson, *American Renaissance.* A different area and phase of American life are represented by Edgar Allan Poe's essays on poetry (see especially "The Poetic Principle").

In the latter half of the nineteenth century, France became a great center of artistic activity, and there was much speculation about the arts. The student should find the ideas of Baudelaire, Gautier, Sainte-Beuve, Taine, and Mallarme good texts to study. The revolt of the French *avant-garde* against Philistinism was paralleled in England by such works as Oscar Wilde's *Intentions,* James McNeill Whistler's *Ten O'Clock Lectures,* and the critical essays of Walter Pater. In Germany, a similar interest in estheticism and pure form is reflected in the musical esthetics of Edmund Gurney and Eduard Hanslick, and the theory of painting of Konrad Fiedler.

Concern for the unity of art and life is to be found in the critical essays of Matthew Arnold. Another Victorian, George Meredith, pointed out the moral value of the comic spirit in *An Essay on Comedy.* But the moral and cultural interpretation of the arts found its most impassioned expression in the works of John Ruskin, such as *Lectures on Art, Stones of Venice,* and *Modern Painters.* A socialistic interpretation appeared in the lectures of William Morris—for example, in his *Hopes and Fears for Art.* The revolt against esthetic purism was also marked in various non-English books, such as Friedrich Nietzsche's *The Birth of Tragedy,* Sören Kierkegaard's *Stages of Life's Way,* and George Plekhanov's *Art and Society*—to group together three works which in most respects are quite diverse.

Commentary on these various books can be found in Bernard Bosanquet, *History of Aesthetics,* Katherine E. Gilbert and Helmut Kuhn, *History of Aesthetics,* George Saintsbury, *History of Criticism,* W. K. Wimsatt Jr. and Cleanth Brooks, *Literary Criticism: A Short History,* and Lionello Venturi, *History of Art Criticism.*

Bibliographies

Albert, Ethel M. and Kluckhohn, Clyde, *A Selected Bibliography on Values, Ethics, and Esthetics in the Behavioral Sciences and Philosophy, 1935-1958*, Chicago and Glencoe, Ill., 1959.

Beardsley, Monroe C., *Aesthetics*, New York, 1958 (contains detailed bibliographical notes at the end of each chapter).

Chandler, Albert R., *A Bibliography of Experimental Aesthetics, 1865-1932*, Columbus, 1933.

Gayley, Charles M. and Scott, Fred N., *A Guide to the Literature of Aesthetics*, Berkeley, 1890.

Hammond, William, *A Bibliography of Aesthetics and of the Philosophy of the Fine Arts from 1900 to 1932*, New York, 1933.

Hungerland, Helmut, *Selective Current Bibliography for Aesthetics and Related Fields* (published annually in the *Journal of Aesthetics*).

Robb, David M. and Garrison, J. J., *Art in the Western World*, New York, 1942 (contains excellent bibliography on the historical development of the arts).

For further bibliographies consult Baldwin's *Dictionary of Philosophy*, Vol. III; *Bibliographic Index*; *Journal of Philosophy*, annual bibliography 1934-1937; *Psychological Abstracts*; *International Index of Periodicals*; *Reader's Guide*; *Cumulative Book Index*; *Essay and General Literature Index*; *Art Index*; and *Bibliographie de la Philosophie* (annual).

General

Aiken, Henry, "Criteria for an Adequate Aesthetics" (comments by G. Boas, C. J. Ducasse, K. Gilbert, and S. C. Pepper), *Journal of Aesthetics*, Vol. 7 (1948), pp. 141-58.

Beardsley, Monroe C., *Aesthetics*, New York, 1958.

Bosanquet, Bernard, *History of Aesthetics*, London, 1904.

Carritt, E. F., *An Introduction to Aesthetics*, London, 1949.

——— *Philosophies of Beauty from Socrates to Robert Bridges*, New York, 1931 (an anthology).

——— *The Theory of Beauty*, Third Edition, London, 1928 (historical and critical).

Chandler, Albert R., *Beauty and Human Nature: Elements of Psychological Aesthetics*, New York, 1934 (summarizes the work in experimental esthetics).

Ducasse, Curt John, *The Philosophy of Art*, New York, 1929 (a critical account of leading theories of esthetics, with an elaboration of the emotionalist theory).

Gilbert, Katherine E., and Kuhn, Helmut, *A History of Esthetics*, Second Edition, Bloomington, Ind., 1953.

Jarrett, James L., *The Quest for Beauty,* New York, 1957 (general text).

Langer, Susanne K. (editor), *Reflections on Art,* Baltimore, 1958 (anthology).

Listowel, Earl of, *A Critical History of Modern Aesthetics,* London, 1933.

McMahon, Philip, *The Meaning of Art,* New York, 1930 (critical discussion of the hedonistic theory, imitation, illusion, the medium and technique, empathy, etc.).

—— *Preface to an American Philosophy of Art,* Chicago, 1945.

Munro, Thomas, *The Arts and Their Interrelations,* New York, 1949 (a broad survey).

—— *Toward Science in Aesthetics,* New York, 1956.

Ogden, C. K., Richards, I. A., and Wood, James, *The Foundations of Aesthetics,* New York, 1922 (short critical summaries of the leading theories of beauty).

Parker, DeWitt H., *The Principles of Aesthetics,* New York, 1946 (general text).

Torossian, Aram, *A Guide to Aesthetics,* Stanford University, 1937 (general text).

Vivas, Eliseo and Krieger, Murray, *The Problems of Aesthetics,* New York, 1953 (anthology).

Weitz, Morris, *Problems in Aesthetics,* New York, 1959 (anthology).

Chapter One

ART AS SEMBLANCE

Play and Art

Ducasse, C. J., *The Philosophy of Art,* New York, 1929, Ch. 7.

Groos, Karl, *The Play of Animals,* New York, 1898.

—— *The Play of Man,* New York, 1901.

Huizinga, J., *Homo Ludens: A Study of the Play Element in Culture,* London, 1949.

Lange, Konrad, *Das Wesen der Kunst,* Berlin, 1901.

Lowenfeld, Margaret, *Play in Childhood,* London, 1935.

Nahm, Milton C., *Aesthetic Experience and Its Presuppositions,* New York, 1946, Ch. 7.

Parker, DeWitt H., *Human Values,* New York, 1931, Chs. 14-15.

Piaget, Jean, *Play, Dreams, and Imagination in Childhood,* New York, 1951.

Rau, Catherine, "Psychological Notes on the Theory of Art as Play," *Journal of Aesthetics,* Vol. 8 (1950), pp. 229-38.

Richards, I. A., *Principles of Literary Criticism,* New York, 1926, Ch. 31.

Schiller, J. C. F. von, *On the Aesthetic Education of Man,* translated by Reginald Snell, New Haven, 1954 (best translation).

Spencer, Herbert, *Principles of Psychology,* Vol. 2, London, 1955, Ch. 9.

Viola, Wilhelm, *Child Art,* London, 1942.

Illusion, Imagination, and Creativity

Alexander, Samuel, *Beauty and Other Forms of Value,* London, 1933, Ch. 4.

Anderson, Harold H., *Creativity and Its Cultivation,* New York, 1959.

Bartlett, F. C., "Types of Imagination," *Journal of Philosophical Studies,* Vol. 3 (1928), pp. 78-85.

Blanshard, Brand, *The Nature of Thought,* New York, 1940, II, Chs. 23-24.

Carpenter, Rhys, and others, *The Bases of Artistic Creation,* New Brunswick, 1942.

Centeno, Augusto (editor), *The Intent of the Artist,* Princeton, 1941.

Chandler, Albert R., *Beauty and Human Nature,* New York, 1934, pp. 301-40.

Coleridge, Samuel Taylor, *Aesthetical Essays* (edited by J. Shawcross), Oxford, 1907.

Collingwood, R. G., *The Principles of Art,* Oxford, 1938, pp. 125-51, 195-280.

Dessoir, Max, *Aesthetik und allgemeine Kunstwissenschaft,* Stuttgart, 1923.

Downey, June, *Creative Imagination,* London, 1929.

Fry, Roger, *Last Lectures,* Cambridge, 1939.

——— *Transformations,* London, 1926.

———*Vision and Design,* London, 1920.

Gerard, R. W., "The Biological Basis of Imagination," *Scientific Monthly,* Vol. 62 (1946), pp. 477-99.

Gotshalk, D. W., *Art and the Social Order,* Chicago, 1947, Ch. 3.

Guggenheimer, Richard, *Creative Vision in Artist and Audience,* New York, 1950.

Hargreaves, H. L., "The 'Faculty' of Imagination," *British Journal of Psychology,* Monograph Supplement, III, 1927.

Jenkins, Iredell, *Art and the Human Enterprise,* Cambridge, Mass., 1958, Chs. 4-5.

Koffka, Kurt, "Problems in the Psychology of Art," *Art: A Symposium,* Bryn Mawr, 1940.

Kretschmer, E., *The Psychology of Men of Genius,* New York, 1931.

Langer, Susanne K., *Feeling and Form,* New York, 1953, especially Ch. 4 (on illusion).

——— *Problems of Art,* New York, 1957, Ch. 4.

Lee, Harry B., "The Creative Imagination," *Psychoanalytic Quarterly,* Vol. 18 (1949), pp. 351-60.

Lowenfeld, V., *The Nature of Creative Activity,* Third Edition, New York, 1957.

Lowes, John Livingston, *The Road to Xanadu,* Boston, 1927.

MacIver, R. M. (editor), *New Horizons in Creative Thinking,* New York, 1954.

Mauron, Charles, *Aesthetics and Psychology,* London, 1935.

Morgan, Charles, "The Nature of Dramatic Illusion," *Reflections on Art* (edited by Susanne K. Langer), Baltimore, 1958.

Morgan, Douglas, "Creativity Today," *Journal of Aesthetics,* Vol. 12 (1953), pp. 1-24.

Morris, Bertram, *The Aesthetic Process,* Evanston, 1943.

Portnoy, Julius, *A Psychology of Art Creation,* Philadelphia, 1942.

Read, Herbert, *Education Through Art,* London, 1943.

Rees, H. E., *A Psychology of Artistic Creation,* New York, 1942.

Ribot, R., *The Creative Imagination,* Paris, 1900.

Richards, I. A., *Coleridge on Imagination,* New York, 1935.

——— *Principles of Literary Criticism,* New York, 1924, Ch. 32.

Robertson, J. G., *Studies in the Genesis of Romantic Theory,* 1923

Schoen, Max, *Art and Beauty,* New York, 1932, Ch. 4.

―――― *Human Nature,* New York, 1930, Ch. 11.

Shahn, Ben, *The Shape of Content,* Cambridge, Mass., 1957.

Smith, Paul (editor), *Creativity,* New York, 1959.

Sparshott, Francis, "Mr. Ziff and the 'Artistic Illusion,'" *Mind,* Vol. 61 (1952), pp. 376-80.

Spearman, Charles E., *Creative Mind,* New York, 1931.

Tomas, Vincent, "Creativity in Art," *Philosophical Review,* Vol. 67 (1958), pp. 1-15.

Woolf, Virginia, *Mr. Bennett and Mrs. Brown,* London, 1924.

Chapter Two

ART AS BEAUTY

The Aristotelian and Scholastic Theory— Imitation and Reason

Adler, Mortimer J., *Art and Prudence,* New York, 1937, Ch. 2.

Auerbach, Erich, *Mimesis,* Princeton, 1953.

Baldwin, C. S., *Medieval Rhetoric and Poetic,* New York, 1924.

Bloosfeldt, Karl, *Art Forms in Nature,* London, 1936.

Brightfield, M. F., *The Issue in Literary Criticism,* Berkeley, 1932 (apropos of Aristotle's *Poetics*).

Butcher, S. H., *Aristotle's Theory of Poetry and Fine Art,* New York, 1923.

Bywater, Ingram, *Aristotle on the Art of Poetry,* Oxford, 1909.

Callahan, J. L., *A Theory of Esthetic According to the Principles of St. Thomas Aquinas,* Washington, 1927.

Chapman, Emmanuel, *St. Augustine's Philosophy of Beauty,* London, 1939.

Collingwood, R. G., *The Principles of Art,* Oxford, 1938, Ch. 3.

Coomaraswamy, Ananda, *The Transformation of Nature in Art,* Cambridge, Mass., 1934.

Cooper, Lane, *The Poetics of Aristotle, Its Meaning and Influence,* New York, 1923.

Evans, V. Burdwood, "A Scholastic Theory of Art," *Philosophy,* Vol. 8 (1933), pp. 397-411.

Fernandez, Ramon, *Messages,* New York, 1927.

Gilbert, Katherine E., "Aesthetic Imitation and Imitators in Aristotle," *Philosophical Review,* Vol. 45 (1936), pp. 558-73.

―――― "Recent Catholic Views on Art and Poetry," *Aesthetic Studies,* Durham, 1952.

Gilson, Etienne, *Painting and Reality,* New York, 1958.

Jenkins, Iredell, "Art and Ontology," *Review of Metaphysics,* Vol. 9 (1956), pp. 623-37.

Langer, Susanne K., *Problems of Art,* New York, 1927, Ch. 5.

Loewenberg, J., *Dialogues from Delphi,* Berkeley, 1949.

Loran, Erle, *Cézanne's Composition,* Berkeley, 1943.

Maritain, Jacques, *Art and Scholasticism,* New York, 1930.

―――― *Creative Intuition in Art and Poetry,* New York, 1953.

Marshall, John S., "Art and Aesthetic in Aristotle," *Journal of Aesthetics,* Vol. 12 (1953), pp. 228-31.

McKeon, Richard P., "Literary Criticism and the Concept of Imitation in Antiquity," *Modern Philology,* Vol. 34 (1936), pp. 1-35.

—— "Philosophic Bases of Art and Criticism," *Modern Philology*, Vol. 41 (1943), pp. 65-87.

—— "Rhetoric in the Middle Ages," *Speculum*, Vol 17 (1942), pp. 1-32.

Morris, Bertram, "Beauty and Nature," *Journal of Philosophy*, Vol. 34 (1937), pp. 653-60.

—— "Metaphysics of Beauty," *Journal of Philosophy*, Vol. 32 (1935), pp. 596-604.

Nahm, Milton C., *Aesthetic Experience and Its Presuppositions*, New York, 1946, Part I.

Noon, William T., *Joyce and Aquinas*, New Haven, 1957.

Read, Herbert, *Education Through Art*, New York, 1943, Ch. 1.

Stace, W. T., *The Meaning of Beauty*, London, 1929 (emphasizes the conceptual element).

Pleasure and Beauty—Santayana's Esthetics

Allen, Grant, *Physiological Aesthetics*, New York, 1877.

Arnett, Willard E., *Santayana and the Sense of Beauty*, Bloomington, Ind., 1955.

Farness, Lewis Richard, *Hedonism and Art*, London, 1928.

Gilbert, Katherine E., "Santayana's Doctrine of Aesthetic Expression," *Studies in Recent Aesthetic*, Chapel Hill, 1927.

Katkov, G., "The Pleasant and the Beautiful," *Proceedings of the Aristotelian Society*, Vol. 40 (1940), pp. 177-206.

Laird, John, *The Idea of Value*, Cambridge, 1929, pp. 134-72.

Lee, Harold Newton, *Perception and Aesthetic Value*, New York, 1938.

Marshall, Henry Rutgers, *Aesthetic Principles*, New York, 1895.

—— *The Beautiful*, New York, 1924.

—— *Pain, Pleasure, and Aesthetics*, London, 1894.

Osborne, Harold, *Theory of Beauty*, London, 1952.

Pepper, Stephen C., *The Basis of Criticism in the Arts*, Cambridge, Mass., 1946, Ch. 2.

—— *Principles of Art Appreciation*, New York, 1949, Chs. 1-2, 6.

Santayana, George, *Interpretations of Poetry and Religion*, New York, 1900.

—— "The Mutability of Aesthetic Categories," *Philosophical Review*, Vol. 34 (1925), pp. 281-91.

—— *Obiter Scripta*, New York, 1936.

—— *Reason in Art*, New York, 1922.

—— *The Sense of Beauty*, New York, 1896.

—— *Three Philosophical Poets*, Cambridge, Mass., 1910.

Schilpp, Paul Arthur (editor), *The Philosophy of George Santayana*, Evanston, 1940.

Singer, Irving, *Santayana's Aesthetics*, Cambridge, Mass., 1957.

Chapter Three

ART AS EMOTIONAL EXPRESSION

Emotion in Art—Must Art Create Beauty?

Aldrich, Virgil C., "Beauty as Feeling," *Kenyon Review*, Vol. 1 (1939), pp. 300-07.

Baensch, Otto, "Art and Feeling," *Reflections on Art* (edited by Susanne K. Langer), Baltimore, 1958.

Ducasse, C. J., *Art, the Critics, and You*, New York, 1944.

——— *The Philosophy of Art*, New York, 1929.

——— "Some Questions in Aesthetics," *Monist*, Vol. 42 (1932), pp. 42-59.

——— "What Has Beauty to Do with Art?" *Journal of Philosophy*, Vol. 25 (1928), pp. 181-85.

Garrod, H. W., *Tolstoi's Theory of Art*, Oxford, 1935.

Gordon, Kate, *Esthetics*, New York, 1909.

Gotshalk, D. W., "Art and Beauty," *Monist*, Vol. 41 (1931), pp. 624-32.

Hirn, Yrjö, *The Origins of Art*, London, 1900.

Knox, Israel, "Tolstoi's Esthetic Definition of Art," *Journal of Philosophy*, Vol. 27 (1930), pp. 65-70.

Montague, W. P., "Beauty Is Not All: A Plea for Esthetic Pluralism," *The Ways of Things*, New York, 1940.

Murry, John Middleton, "The Romantic Fallacy," *Criterion*, Vol. 4 (1926), pp. 521-37.

Nahm, Milton C., *Aesthetic Experience and Its Presuppositions*, New York, 1946, Part III.

Pepper, Stephen C., *Principles of Art Appreciation*, New York, 1949, Ch. 6.

Tolstoy, Leo, *What is Art? and Essays on Art*, London, 1925.

Ushenko, A., "Beauty in Art," *Monist*, Vol. 42 (1932), pp. 627-29.

Véron, Eugene, *Aesthetics*, London, 1879.

Wimsatt, W. K., and Beardsley, Monroe C., "The Affective Fallacy," *Sewanee Review*, Vol. 57 (1949), pp. 458-88.

Chapter Four

ART AS INTUITION

Abercrombie, Lascelles, "Communication versus Expression in Art," *British Journal of Psychology*, Vol. 14 (1923), pp. 68-78 (agrees with Tolstoy rather than Croce that communication is essential to art).

Bergson, Henri, *The Creative Mind*, New York, 1946.

——— *Introduction to Metaphysics*, New York, 1912.

——— *Laughter: An Essay on the Meaning of the Comic*, New York, 1911.

——— *The Two Sources of Morality and Religion*, New York, 1935.

——— *The World of Dreams*, New York, 1958.

Bosanquet, Bernard, "Croce's Aesthetic," *Mind*, Vol. 29 (1920), pp. 212-15.

——— "Croce's Aesthetic," *Proceedings of the British Academy*, Vol. 9 (1919-1920), pp. 261-88.

Carr, Herbert Wildon, "Mr. Bosanquet on Croce's Aesthetic," *Mind*, Vol. 29 (1920), pp. 207-11.

——— *The Philosophy of Benedetto Croce: The Problem of Art and History*, London, 1917.

Carritt, E. F., "Croce and His Aesthetic," *Mind*, Vol. 62 (1953), pp. 452-65.

——— *An Introduction to Aesthetics*, London, 1949.

——— *The Theory of Beauty*, London, 1928, Ch. 8.

——— *What is Beauty*, Oxford, 1932, Ch. 6.

Cary, Joyce, *Art and Reality*, New York, 1958.

Cock, Albert A., "The Aesthetic of Benedetto Croce," *Proceedings of the Aristotelian Society*, Vol. 15 (1914-1915), pp. 164-98.

Collingwood, R. G., "Art," *Speculum Mentis*, Oxford, 1924.

——— *Outline of a Philosophy of Art* London, 1925.

—— The Principles of Art, Oxford, 1938.

Croce, Benedetto, Aesthetic as Science of Expression and General Linguistic, Second Edition, London, 1922.

—— "Aesthetics" in the Fourteenth Edition of the Encyclopaedia Brittanica.

—— Ariosto, Shakespeare and Corneille, New York, 1920.

—— Autobiography, Oxford, 1927.

—— The Breviary of Aesthetic, Rice Institute Pamphlets, Houston, 1915.

—— The Defense of Poetry: Variations on the Theme of Shelley, Oxford, 1933.

—— The Essence of Aesthetics, London, 1921.

—— History: Its Theory and Practice, New York, 1921 (discusses relation of art and history).

—— The Philosophy of Giambattista Vico, New York, 1913.

—— "Poetry" (selection from La Poesia, 1937) in Guy Wilson Allen and Harry Hayden Clark, Literary Criticism, New York, 1941.

—— The Poetry of Dante, New York, 1922.

Dodson, George Rowland, Bergson and the Modern Spirit, London, 1914.

Ducasse, C. J., The Philosophy of Art, New York, 1929, Ch. 3.

Fiedler, Conrad, On Judging Works of Visual Art, Berkeley, 1949.

Gilbert, Katherine E., "The One and the Many in Croce's Aesthetic" and "Bergson's Penal Theory of Comedy," Studies in Recent Aesthetic, Chapel Hill, 1927.

Hope, Richard, "Laughter and the Comic: A Critique of Bergson's Theory of the Comic," Psyche, January 1927, pp. 72-85.

Hospers, John, "The Croce-Collingwood Theory of Art," Philosophy, Vol. 31 (1956), pp. 291-308.

Hulme, T. E., "Bergson's Theory of Art" and "The Philosophy of Intensive Manifolds," Speculations, New York, 1924.

Marcel, Gabriel, "Bergsonism and Music," Reflections on Art (edited by Susanne K. Langer), Baltimore, 1958.

Mathewson, Louise, Bergson's Theory of the Comic in the Light of English Comedy, University of Nebraska, 1920.

Mayo, Bernard, "Art, Language, and Philosophy in Croce," Philosophical Quarterly, Vol. 5 (1955), pp. 245-60.

Nahm, Milton C., "The Philosophy of Aesthetic Expression: The Crocean Hypothesis," Journal of Aesthetics, Vol. 13 (1955), pp. 458-68.

Orsini, G. N. G., "Theory and Practice in Croce's Aesthetics," Journal of Aesthetics, Vol. 13 (1955), pp. 300-13.

Santayana, George, "Croce's Aesthetics," The Idler and His Works, New York, 1957.

Seerveld, Calvin G., Benedetto Croce's Earlier Aesthetic Theories and Literary Criticism, Kampen, Holland, 1958.

Smith, J. A., "Croce" in the Fourteenth Edition of Encyclopaedia Brittanica.

—— The Nature of Art, Oxford, 1924.

Spingarn, J. E., Creative Criticism, New York, 1917.

Szathmary, Arthur, The Aesthetic Theory of Bergson, Cambridge, Mass., 1937.

Wimsatt, William K., and Brooks, Cleanth, Literary Criticism: A Short History, New York, 1957, Ch. 23 (on Croce).

Chapter Five

ART AS WISH-FULFILLMENT

On Nietzsche

Flaccus, Louis William, *Artists and Thinkers*, New York, 1916.

Kaufmann, Walter A., *Nietzsche*, Princeton, 1950, especially Ch. 4.

Knight, A. H. J., *Some Aspects of the Life and Works of Nietzsche*, Cambridge, Mass., 1933.

Lea, Frank Alfred, *The Tragic Philosopher*, London, 1957.

Ludovici, Anthony M., *Nietzsche and Art*, London, 1912.

Morgan, George Allen, *What Nietzsche Means*, Cambridge, Mass., 1941, Ch. 8.

Nietzsche, Friedrich, *The Birth of Tragedy* (translated by Francis Gollfing), New York, 1956. (There are also translations by Clifton P. Fadiman, New York, 1927, and W. A. Haussman, New York, 1925.)

——— *The Will to Power*, Vol. II, Books III and IV (translated by Anthony M. Ludovici), New York, 1910.

Vaihinger, Hans, *The Philosophy of "As If,"* New York, 1935, pp. 341-62.

On Freud and Related Theory

Adler, Alfred, *The Practice and Theory of Individual Psychology*, New York, 1924, Ch. 23.

Auden, W. H., "Psychology and Art Today," *The Arts Today*, London, 1935.

Baudouin, Charles, *Psycho-Analysis and Aesthetics*, London, 1924.

Bergler, Edmund, *The Writer and Psychoanalysis*, New York, 1950.

Bodkin, A. M., "The Relevance of Psycho-Analysis to Art Criticism," *British Journal of Psychology*, Vol. 25 (1924-1925), pp. 174-83.

Bruner, Jerome S., "Freud and the Image of Man," *Partisan Review*, Vol. 23 (1956), pp. 340-47.

Burke, Kenneth, "Freud and the Analysis of Poetry," *Philosophy of Literary Form*, Baton Rouge, 1941.

——— *A Grammar of Motives*, New York, 1945.

Caudwell, Christopher, *Further Studies in a Dying Culture*, London, 1949.

——— *Illusion and Reality*, New York, 1948.

Dalbiez, Roland, *Psychoanalytical Method and the Doctrine of Freud*, 2 vols., New York, 1951.

Ducasse, C. J., *The Philosophy of Art*, New York, 1929, Ch. 4.

Fraiberg, Louis, "Freud's Writings on Art," *International Journal of Psycho-Analysis*, Vol. 37 (1956), pp. 82-96.

Freud, Sigmund, *Civilization and Its Discontents*, London, 1930. (Some of these works by Freud do not deal with art but are valuable as a background.)

——— *The Basic Writings* (Modern Library), New York, 1938.

——— *Collected Papers*, 2 vols., London, 1925.

——— *Delusion and Dream*, New York, 1917.

——— "Dostoevsky and Parricide," in William Phillips (editor), *Art and Psychoanalysis*, New York, 1957.

——— *The Interpretation of Dreams*, New York, 1923.

——— *Introductory Lectures on Psycho-Analysis*, London, 1922.

——— *Leonardo da Vinci*, New York, 1916.

—— New Introductory Lectures on Psycho-Analysis, New York, 1933.

—— On Creativity and the Unconscious: Papers on the Psychology of Art, Literature, Love, Religion, New York, 1958.

—— Psychoanalytische Studien der Dichtung und Kunst, Leipzig, 1924.

—— Wit and Its Relation to the Unconscious, New York, 1916.

—— and D. E. Oppenheim, Dreams in Folklore, New York, 1958.

Fry, Roger, The Artist and Psycho-Analysis, London, 1924.

Gourmont, Remy de, "Subconscious Creation," Decadence, New York, 1921.

Graves, Robert, The Meaning of Dreams, London, 1924.

—— Poetic Unreason, London, 1925.

Hauser, Arnold, The Philosophy of Art History, New York, 1959, Ch. 3.

Hill, J. C., "Poetry and the Unconscious," British Journal of Medical Psychology, Vol. 4 (1924), pp. 125-33.

Hoffman, Frederick J., Freudianism and the Literary Mind, Baton Rouge, 1945.

Hyman, Stanley, "Freud and the Climate of Tragedy," Partisan Review, Vol. 23 (1956), pp. 198-214.

Jones, Ernest, Hamlet and Oedipus, New York, 1940.

—— The Life and Work of Sigmund Freud, 3 vols., New York, 1953-1957.

Kazin, A., "Psychoanalysis and Literary Culture Today," Partisan Review, Vol. 26 (1959), pp. 46-55.

Kris, Ernst, "Approaches to Art," Psychoanalysis Today, New York, 1944.

—— "Art and Regression," Transactions of the New York Academy of Sciences, Vol. 6 (1944), pp. 236-50.

—— Psychoanalytic Explorations in Art, New York, 1958.

Kubie, Lawrence S., Neurotic Distortion of the Creative Process, University of Kansas, 1958.

Lawrence, D. H., Psychoanalysis and the Unconscious, New York, 1921.

Lee, Harry B., "The Creative Imagina-

tion," Psychoanalytic Quarterly, Vol. 18 (1949), pp. 351-60.

Mann, Thomas, Freud, Goethe, Wagner, New York, 1937.

Marcuse, Ludwig, "Freud's Aesthetics," Journal of Aesthetics, Vol. 17 (1958), pp. 1-21.

Neumann, Erich, Art and the Creative Unconscious, New York, 1959.

Parker, DeWitt H., The Analysis of Art, New Haven, 1924.

—— Human Values, New York, 1931, Chs. 3, 14, 15.

—— "The Nature of Art," Revue Internationale de Philosophie, Vol. 1 (1939), pp. 684-702.

—— "Wish-Fulfillment and Intuition in Art," Proceedings of the Sixth International Congress of Philosophy, New York, 1931.

Phillips, William (editor), Art and Psychoanalysis, New York, 1957 (excellent essays by various writers).

Prescott, Frederick Clarke, The Poetic Mind, New York, 1922.

Rank, Otto, Art and Artist, New York, 1932.

—— The Myth of the Birth of the Hero, New York, 1952.

Read, Herbert, Art and Society, London, 1937, Ch. 5.

—— Art Now, New York, 1933.

—— (editor), Surrealism, London, 1936.

Ricklin, Franz, Wish-Fulfillment and Symbolism in Fairy Tales. Nervous and Mental Disease Monographs, No. 21, New York, 1915.

Sachs, Hans, The Creative Unconscious, Cambridge, Mass., 1942.

Schneider, Daniel E., Psychoanalysis and the Artist, New York, 1950.

Stekel, Wilhelm, "Poetry and Neurosis," Psychoanalytic Review, Vol. 10 (1923), pp. 73-96, 190-208, 316-28, 457-66.

Sterba, Richard, "The Problem of Art in Freud's Writings," Psychoanalytic Quarterly, Vol. 9 (April 1940), pp. 256-68.

Stokes, Adrian, "Form in Art: A Psychoanalytic Interpretation," *Journal of Aesthetics*, Vol. 18 (1959), pp. 193-203 (an introduction to an author who has written much on psychoanalysis and art).

Thorburn, John M., *Art and the Unconscious*, London, 1925.

—— Hannay, A. H., and Leon, P., "Artistic Form and the Unconscious,"

Modern Tendencies in Philosophy (Aristotelian Society Supplementary Volume 13), London, 1934.

Trilling, Lionel, "Art and Neurosis," *The Liberal Imagination*, New York, 1945.

—— "The Legacy of Freud: Literary and Aesthetic," *Kenyon Review*, Vol. 2 (1940), pp. 152-73.

Jung and the Concept of Archetypes

Abell, Walter, *The Collective Dream in Art*, Cambridge, Mass., 1957.

Bodkin, Maud, *Archetypal Patterns in Poetry*, Oxford, 1934.

—— *Studies of Type-Images in Poetry, Religion, and Philosophy*, London, 1951.

Campbell, Joseph, *The Hero with a Thousand Faces*, New York, 1956.

Frye, Northrop, "The Archetypes of Literature," *Kenyon Review*, Vol. 13 (1951), pp. 92-110.

Hyman, Stanley E., "Maud Bodkin and Psychological Criticism," *The Armed Vision*, New York, 1948.

Jacobi, Jolan, *Complex, Archetype, Symbol in the Psychology of C. G. Jung*, New York, 1959.

—— (editor), *Psychological Reflections: An Anthology of the Writings of C. G. Jung*, New York, 1953.

Jung, Carl Gustav, *The Archetypes and the Collective Unconscious* (Volume 9 of *Collected Works*), New York, 1959.

—— *The Integration of Personality*, New York, 1939, Ch. 3.

—— "On the Relation of Analytical Psychology to Poetic Art," *Contributions to Analytical Psychology*, London, 1928.

—— "Psychology and Literature," *Modern Man in Search of a Soul*, New York, 1934.

Lewis, C. Day, *The Poetic Image*, New York, 1947, Ch. 6.

Press, John, *The Fire and the Fountain*, New York, 1955, Ch. 6.

Read, Herbert, *Icon and Idea*, Cambridge, Mass., 1955.

Chapter Six

ART AS VIVID EXPERIENCE

Aiken, Henry, "The Concept of Relevance in Aesthetics," *Journal of Aesthetics*, Vol. 6 (1947), pp. 152-61.

Allen, A. H. B., "Art and Life," *Hibbert Journal*, Vol. 56 (1957), pp. 61-68.

Ames, Van Meter, *Introduction to Beauty*, New York, 1931.

Brown, Harold Chapman, "Act, Action, and Affective States," *Essays in Honor of John Dewey*, New York, 1929.

Brownell, Baker, *Art is Action*, New York, 1939.

—— *The Human Community*, New York, 1950, Part X.

Buermeyer, Laurence, *The Aesthetic Experience*, Merion, Pa., 1929.

Croce, Benedetto, "On the Aesthetics of Dewey," *Journal of Aesthetics,* Vol. 6, 1948, pp. 203-07; and Dewey, John, "A Comment on the Foregoing Criticisms," *Ibid.,* pp. 207-09.

Dewey, John, *Art as Experience,* New York, 1934.

――― *Experience and Nature,* Chicago, 1925.

――― and others, *Art and Education,* Merion, Pa., 1934.

Ducasse, C. J., *The Philosophy of Art,* New York, 1929, Ch. 6.

Eastman, Max, *Art and the Life of Action,* New York, 1934.

Edman, Irwin, *Arts and the Man,* New York, 1939.

Ellis, Havelock, *The Dance of Life,* Boston, 1923.

Gordon, Kate, "Pragmatism in Aesthetics," *Essays Philosophical and Psychological: In Honor of William James,* New York, 1908.

Kallen, Horace M., *Art and Freedom,* New York, 1942.

――― "Beauty and Use," *Philosophical Review,* Vol. 48 (1939), pp. 316-22.

――― *Indecency and the Seven Arts and Other Adventures of a Pragmatist in Aesthetics,* New York, 1930.

Krutch, Joseph Wood, *Experience and Art,* New York, 1932.

Mead, George H., "The Nature of Aesthetic Experience," *International Journal of Ethics,* Vol. 36 (1925-1926), pp. 382-93.

Montague, W. P., "The True, the Good,

and the Beautiful from a Pragmatic Standpoint," *The Ways of Things,* New York, 1940.

Pepper, Stephen C., *Aesthetic Quality,* New York, 1938.

――― "Art and Experience," *Review of Metaphysics,* Vol. 12 (1958), pp. 294-99.

――― "Art and Utility," *Journal of Philosophy,* Vol. 20 (1920), pp. 372-78.

――― *The Basis of Criticism in the Arts,* Cambridge, Mass., 1945, Ch. 3.

――― "The Concept of Fusion in Dewey's Aesthetic Theory," *The Work of Art,* Bloomington, 1955.

Prall, D. W., *Aesthetic Judgment,* New York, 1929, Ch. 15.

Rader, Melvin, "The Artist as Outsider," *Journal of Aesthetics,* Vol. 16 (1958), pp. 306-18.

――― "Isolationist and Contextualist Esthetics: Conflict and Resolution," *Journal of Philosophy,* Vol. 44 (1947), pp. 393-407.

Schilpp, Paul Arthur (editor), *The Philosophy of Alfred North Whitehead,* New York, 1951.

――― *The Philosophy of John Dewey,* Evanston, 1939.

Shearer, E. A., "Dewey's Esthetic Theory," *Journal of Philosophy,* Vol. 32 (1935), pp. 617-27, 650-64.

Whitehead, Alfred North, *Adventures of Ideas,* New York, 1933, Chs. 17, 18.

――― *Science and the Modern World,* New York, 1925, Chs. 5, 13.

Chapter Seven

CAN "ART" BE DEFINED?

Aschenbrenner, Karl, "Aesthetic Theory—Conflict and Conciliation," *Journal of Aesthetics,* Vol. 18 (1959), pp. 90-108.

D'Azevedo, W. L., "Structural Approach to Aesthetics: Toward a Definition of

Art in Anthropology," *American Anthropologist,* Vol. 60 (1958), pp. 702-14.

Elton, William (editor), *Aesthetics and Language,* New York, 1954.

Kahler, Erich, "What is Art?" in Morris

Weitz (editor), *Problems in Aesthetics*, New York, 1959 (an answer to Weitz).

Kennick, William E., "Does Traditional Aesthetics Rest on a Mistake?" *Mind*, Vol. 67 (1958), pp. 317-34.

Margolis, Joseph, "Mr. Weitz and the Definition of Art," *Philosophical Studies*, Vol. 9 (1958), pp. 88-94.

Ryle, Gilbert, "The Theory of Meaning," in C. A. Mace (editor), *British Philosophy in the Mid-Century*, London, 1957.

Weitz, Morris, "The Role of Theory in Aesthetics," *Journal of Aesthetics*, Vol. 15 (1956), pp. 27-35 (largely reprinted in the present volume).

Wittgenstein, Ludwig, *Philosophical Investigations*, Oxford, 1953.

Zerby, Lewis K., "A Reconsideration of the Role of Theory in Aesthetics—A Reply to Morris Weitz," *Journal of Aesthetics*, Vol. 16 (1957), pp. 253-55.

Ziff, Paul, "The Task of Defining a Work of Art," *Philosophical Review*, Vol. 62 (1953), pp. 58-78.

Chapter Eight

THE "BODY" OF THE WORK

What Is a "Work of Art"?

Beardsley, Monroe C., *Aesthetics*, New York, 1958, Ch. 1.

Bilsky, Manuel, "The Significance of Locating the Art Object," *Philosophy and Phenomenological Research*, Vol. 13 (1953), pp. 531-41.

Collingwood, R. G., *The Principles of Art*, Oxford, 1938, Ch. 7.

Duncker, Karl, "The Influence of Past Experience upon Perceptual Properties," *American Journal of Psychology*, Vol. 52 (1939), pp. 255-65.

Gallie, W. B., "The Function of Philosophical Aesthetics," *Mind*, Vol. 57 (1948), pp. 302-21.

Henze, Donald F., "Is the Work of Art a Construct?" *Journal of Philosophy*, Vol. 52 (1955), pp. 433-39.

——— "The Work of Art," *Journal of Philosophy*, Vol. 54 (1957), pp. 429-42.

Jenkins, Iredell, "The Aesthetic Object," *Review of Metaphysics*, Vol. 11 (1957), pp. 3-11.

Lewis, C. I., *Analysis of Knowledge and Valuation*, La Salle, Ill., 1947, Ch. 15, sections 5-7.

Margolis, Joseph, "Mode of Existence of a Work of Art," *Review of Metaphysics*, Vol. 12 (1958), pp. 26-34.

——— "The Identity of a Work of Art," *Mind*, Vol. 67 (1959), pp. 34-50.

Pepper, Stephen C., "Further Considerations on the Aesthetic Work of Art," *Journal of Philosophy*, Vol. 49 (1952), pp. 274-79.

——— *The Principles of Art Appreciation*, New York, 1949, pp. 8-12.

——— "Supplementary Essay," *The Basis of Criticism in the Arts*, Cambridge, Mass., 1949.

——— *The Work of Art*, Bloomington, 1955.

Rudner, Richard, "The Ontological Status of the Aesthetic Object," *Philosophy and Phenomenological Research*, Vol. 10 (1950), pp. 380-88.

Sartre, Jean-Paul, "Conclusion," *The Psychology of Imagination*, New York, 1948.

Stevenson, Charles S., "On 'What is a Poem?'," *Philosophical Review*, Vol. 66 (1957), Ch. 1.

Ushenko, Andrew P., *Dynamics of Art,* Bloomington, 1953, pp. 18-25, 42-51.

Vivas, Eliseo, "What is a Poem?" *Sewanee Review,* Vol. 62 (1954), pp. 578-97.

Wellek, Rene, and Warren, Austin, *The Theory of Literature,* New York, 1942, Ch. 12.

Ziff, Paul, "Art and the 'Object of Art'" in William Elton (editor), *Aesthetics and Language,* New York, 1954.

——— "The Task of Defining a Work of Art," *Philosophical Review,* Vol. 62 (1953), pp. 58-78.

The Medium

Alexander, Samuel, *Art and the Material,* Manchester, 1925.

Arnheim, Rudolf, *Film as Art,* Berkeley, 1958.

Babbitt, Irving, *The New Laokoön,* Boston, 1910.

Bosanquet, Bernard, *Three Lectures on Aesthetic,* London, 1915, Ch. 2 (the selection from Bosanquet in the present volume is taken from this chapter).

Bullough, Edward, "Mind and Medium in Art," *British Journal of Psychology,* Vol. 11 (1920-1921), pp. 26-46. Reprinted in *Aesthetics,* London, 1957.

Church, Ralph W., *An Essay on Critical Appreciation,* Ithaca, 1938, Ch. 3.

Doerner, Max, *The Materials of the Artist,* New York, 1934.

Ducasse, Curt John, *Art, the Critics, and You,* New York, 1944, Ch. 2.

Faure, Elie, *The Spirit of the Forms,* New York, 1930, Ch. 6.

Gilbert, Katherine E., "Bosanquet on the Artist's Medium," *Studies in Recent Aesthetic,* Chapel Hill, 1927.

Greene, Theodore M., *The Arts and the Art of Criticism,* Princeton, 1940, Part I.

Hitchcock, H. R., Jr., *In the Nature of Materials,* New York, 1942.

Le Corbusier (Jeanneret-Gris, C. E.), *Towards a New Architecture,* New York, 1927.

Lessing, G. E., *Laocoön,* Boston, 1894.

Marriott, Charles, and others, Symposium on "Mind and Medium in Art," *British Journal of Psychology,* Vol. 11 (1920-1921), pp. 1-54.

McMahon, A. Philip, *The Meaning of Art,* New York, 1930, Ch. 7.

Moore, Henry, *Sculpture and Drawings,* New York, 1944.

Munro, Thomas, "'The Afternoon of a Faun' and the Interrelation of the Arts," *Journal of Aesthetics,* Vol. 10 (1951), pp. 95-111.

——— *The Arts and Their Interrelations,* New York, 1949, Ch. 7.

Panofsky, Erwin, "Style and Medium in the Motion Pictures," *Critique* (January-February 1947).

Reid, Louis Arnaud, *A Study in Aesthetics,* New York, 1931, pp. 164-75.

Seiberling, Frank, *Looking into Art,* New York, 1959, Part Two.

Stallknecht, Newton P., "Art and the Four Causes," *Journal of Philosophy,* Vol. 31 (1934), pp. 710-17.

Symonds, J. A., "The Provinces of the Seven Arts" (Vol. 1), and "Is Music the Type and Measure of All Art" (Vol. 2), *Essays, Speculative and Suggestive,* London, 1890.

Weitz, Morris, *Philosophy of the Arts,* Cambridge, Mass., 1950, Ch. 7.

Esthetic Surface and Sensuous Materials

Aiken, Henry, "Art as Expression and Surface," *Journal of Aesthetics,* Vol. 4 (1945), pp. 87-95.

Berenson, Bernard, *Central Italian Painters of the Renaissance,* New York, 1909 (emphasis on tactile values).

Chandler, Albert R., *Beauty and Human Nature,* New York, 1934.

Clement, W. C., "Quality Orders," *Mind,* Vol. 65 (1956), pp. 185-99.

Dewey, John, *Art as Experience,* New York, 1934, Chs. 9-10.

Geldard, Frank A., *The Human Senses,* New York, 1953.

Goodman, Nelson, *The Structure of Appearance,* Cambridge, Mass., 1951, Part III.

Gotshalk, D. W., *Art and the Social Order,* Chicago, 1947, Ch. 4.

Greene, Theodore M., *The Arts and the Art of Criticism,* Princeton, 1940, Parts I and III.

Hartshorne, Charles, *The Philosophy and Psychology of Sensation,* Chicago, 1934.

Herring, Frances, "Touch—The Neglected Sense," *Journal of Aesthetics,* Vol. 7 (1949), pp. 199-215.

Jordan, Elijah, *The Aesthetic Object,* Bloomington, Ind., 1937.

Katz, David, *The World of Colour,* London, 1935.

Moore, Jared S., "The Work of Art and Its Material," *Journal of Aesthetics,* Vol. 6 (1948), pp. 331-38.

Ogden, C. K., and Wood, James, *Colour Harmony,* New York, 1926.

Ogden, R. M., *The Psychology of Art,* New York, 1938, especially Chs. 3, 7, 8.

Parkhurst, Helen H., *Beauty,* New York, 1930, Chs. 3 and 4.

Pepper, Stephen C., *Principles of Art Appreciation,* New York, 1949, Part III.

Prall, D. W., *Aesthetic Analysis,* New York, 1936.

——— *Aesthetic Judgment,* New York, 1929.

Santayana, George, *The Sense of Beauty,* New York, 1896, Part II.

Ushenko, Andrew P., "Dynamics in Art," *Power and Events,* Princeton, 1946.

——— *Dynamics of Art,* Bloomington, 1953, especially pp. 120-28, 212-21.

——— "Esthetic Immediacy," *Journal of Philosophy,* Vol. 38 (1941), pp. 68-72.

Chapter Nine

EXPRESSIVENESS

Meaning and Expressiveness

Abercrombie, Lascelles, *The Theory of Poetry,* London, 1924.

Abrams, Meyer H., *The Mirror and the Lamp,* New York, 1953.

Aldrich, Virgil, "Pictorial Meaning and Picture Thinking," *Kenyon Review,* Vol. 5 (1943), pp. 403-12. Reprinted in *Readings in Philosophical Analysis* (edited by H. Feigl and W. Sellars), New York, 1949.

——— "Pictorial Meaning, Picture-Thinking, and Wittgenstein's Theory of Aspects," *Mind,* Vol. 67 (1958), pp. 70-91.

Amyx, Clifford, "The Iconic Sign in Aesthetics," *Journal of Philosophy,* Vol. 6 (1947), pp. 54-60.

Arnheim, Rudolf, *Art and Visual Perception,* Berkeley, 1954.

—— "Gestalt and Art," *Journal of Aesthetics*, Vol. 2 (1943), pp. 70-75.

—— "The Gestalt Theory of Expression," *Psychological Review*, Vol. 56 (1949), pp. 156-71.

—— "The Priority of Expression," *Journal of Aesthetics*, Vol. 8 (1949), pp. 106-09.

—— "The Robin and the Saint: On the Twofold Nature of the Artistic Image," *Journal of Aesthetics*, Vol. 18 (1959), pp. 68-79.

Ayer, A. J., *Language, Truth, and Logic*, New York, 1936 (on the distinction between descriptive and emotive language).

Barfield, Owen, *Poetic Diction: A Study in Meaning*, London, 1928.

Beardsley, Monroe C., *Aesthetics*, New York, 1958, Chs. 3, 5-9.

Boas, George, "The Problem of Meaning in the Arts," *University of California Publications in Philosophy*, Vol. 25 (1950), pp. 301-25.

Bouwsma, O. K., "The Expression Theory of Art," *Philosophical Analysis* (edited by Max Black), Ithaca, 1950.

Brooks, Cleanth, "What Does Poetry Communicate?" *The Well Wrought Urn*, New York, 1949.

Burke, Kenneth, *A Grammar of Motives*, New York, 1945.

—— *A Rhetoric of Motives*, New York, 1950.

—— "Semantic and Poetic Meaning," *Southern Review*, Vol. 4 (1939), pp. 501-23.

Carver, G. A., *Aesthetics and the Problem of Meaning*, New Haven, 1952.

Cassirer, *An Essay on Man*, New Haven, 1944, Ch. 9.

—— *Language and Myth*, New York, 1946.

Daiches, David, *The Place of Meaning in Poetry*, London, 1935.

Empson, William, *Seven Types of Ambiguity*, London, 1930.

—— *The Structure of Complex Words*, Norfolk, Conn., 1951.

Gotshalk, D. W., *Art and the Social Order*, Chicago, 1947, Ch. 6.

—— "Aesthetic Expression," *Journal of Aesthetics*, Vol. 13 (1954), pp. 80-85.

Greene, Theodore M., *The Arts and the Art of Criticism*, Princeton, 1940, Parts III and IV.

Henle, Paul (editor), *Language, Thought, and Culture*, Ann Arbor, 1958.

Hospers, John, "The Concept of Artistic Expression," *Proceedings of the Aristotelian Society*, Vol. 55 (1954-1955), pp. 313-44. Reprinted in Morris Weitz (editor), *Problems in Aesthetics*, New York, 1959.

—— *Meaning and Truth in the Arts*, Chapel Hill, 1946.

Hungerland, Isabel Creed, "Iconic Signs and Expressiveness," *Journal of Aesthetics*, Vol. 3 (1944), pp. 15-21.

—— *Poetic Discourse*, Berkeley, 1958.

Isenberg, Arnold, "The Esthetic Function of Language," *Journal of Philosophy*, Vol. 46 (1949), pp. 5-19.

—— "Perception, Meaning, and the Subject Matter of Art," *Journal of Philosophy*, Vol. 41 (1944), pp. 561-75.

James, D. G., *Science and Poetry*, London, 1937.

Jessup, Bertram, "Meaning Range in the Work of Art," *Journal of Aesthetics*, Vol. 12 (1954), pp. 378-85.

Johnson, Martin, *Art and Scientific Thought*, London, 1944.

Kaplan, Abraham, "Referential Meaning in the Arts," *Journal of Aesthetics*, Vol. 12 (1954), pp. 457-74.

Kepes, Gyorgy, *The Language of Vision*, Chicago, 1944.

—— *The New Landscape in Art and Science*, Chicago, 1956.

Langer, Susanne K., *Feeling and Form*, New York, 1953.

—— *Philosophy in a New Key*, Cambridge, Mass., 1942.

—— *Problems of Art*, New York, 1957.

Lewis, C. Day, *The Poetic Image*, New York, 1947.

—— *The Poet's Way of Knowledge*, Cambridge, Eng., 1957.

Mayo, Bertram, "Poetry, Language, and Communication," *Philosophy*, Vol. 29 (1954), pp. 131-45.

Morris, Charles, "Esthetics and the Theory of Signs," *Journal of Unified Science (Erkenntnis)*, Vol. 8 (1939), pp. 131-50.

—— "Science, Art and Technology," *Kenyon Review*, Vol. 1 (1939), pp. 409-423 (largely reproduced in the present volume).

—— *Signs, Language, and Behavior*, New York, 1946.

Nahm, Milton C., *Aesthetic Experience and Its Presuppositions*, New York, 1946, Part III.

Ogden, C. K., and Richards, I. A., *The Meaning of Meaning*, New York, 1923.

Osborne, Harold, *Aesthetics and Criticism*, New York, 1955, Ch. 7.

Panofsky, Erwin, *Meaning in the Visual Arts*, Garden City, 1955.

—— *Studies in Iconology*, New York, 1939.

Pollock, T. C., "A Critique of I. A. Richards' Theory of Language and Literature," *A Theory of Meaning Analyzed*, General Semantics Monographs, Chicago: Institute of General Semantics, 1942.

Prall, D. W., *Aesthetic Judgment*, New York, 1929, Ch. 11.

Price, Kingsley B., "Is There Artistic Truth?" *Journal of Philosophy*, Vol. 46 (1949), pp. 285-91.

Rawlins, Ian, *Aesthetics and the Gestalt*, Edinburgh, 1953.

Reid, Louis Arnaud, "Aesthetic Meaning," *Proceedings of the Aristotelian Society*, Vol. 55 (1954-1955), pp. 219-50.

Richards, I. A., *How to Read a Page*, New York, 1942.

—— *Mencius on the Mind*, London, 1932.

—— *The Philosophy of Rhetoric*, London, 1936.

—— *Principles of Literary Criticism*, New York, 1926.

—— *Science and Poetry*, New York, 1926; Revised Edition, London, 1935.

—— *Speculative Instruments*, London, 1955.

Rieser, Max, "The Semantic Theory of Art in America," *Journal of Aesthetics*, Vol. 15 (1956), pp. 12-26.

Rudner, Richard, "On Semiotic Aesthetics," *Journal of Aesthetics*, Vol. 10 (1951), pp. 67-77.

Santayana, George, *The Sense of Beauty*, New York, 1896, Part IV.

Seiberling, Frank, *Looking into Art*, New York, 1959, Part One and Ch. 15.

Stern, Gustav, *Meaning and Change of Meaning*, Goteborg, 1931.

Stevenson, Charles L., *Ethics and Language*, New Haven, 1944 (on emotive meaning).

—— "Meaning: Descriptive and Emotive," *Philosophical Review*, Vol. 57 (1948), pp. 127-44.

Urban, Wilbur Marshall, *Language and Reality*, New York, 1939.

Ushenko, Andrew P., "Images in Art," *Philosophy*, Vol. 14 (1939), pp. 59-67.

—— "Metaphor," *Thought*, Vol. 30 (1955), pp. 421-39.

Vivas, Eliseo, "Aesthetics and Theory of Signs," *Creation and Discovery*, New York, 1955.

—— "Four Notes on I. A. Richards' Aesthetic Theory," *Philosophical Review*, Vol. 44 (1935), pp. 354-67.

Wallach, Michael A., "Art, Science, and Representation," *Journal of Aesthetics*, Vol. 18 (1959), pp. 159-73.

Walsh, Dorothy, "The Cognitive Content of Art," *Philosophical Review*, Vol. 52 (1943), pp. 433-51.

—— "The Poetic Use of Language," *Journal of Philosophy*, Vol. 35 (1938), pp. 73-81.

Wheelwright, Philip, "On the Semantics of Poetry," *Kenyon Review*, Vol. 2 (1940), pp. 263-83.

Wimsatt, W. K., *The Verbal Icon*, Lexington, Ky., 1954.
—— and Brooks, Cleanth, *Literary Criticism: A Short History*, New York, 1957, Chs. 27-28 (on Richards).

Symbolism

Ballard, E. G., "In Defense of Symbolic Aesthetics," *Journal of Aesthetics*, Vol. 12 (1953), pp. 38-43.

Berndtson, Arthur, "Semblance, Symbol, and Expression in the Aesthetics of Susanne Langer," *Journal of Aesthetics*, Vol. 14 (1956), pp. 489-502.

Bernheimer, Richard, "Concerning Symbols," *Art: A Symposium*, Bryn Mawr, 1940.

Cassirer, Ernst, *The Philosophy of Symbolic Forms*, 3 vols., New Haven, 1953-1957.

Garvin, Lucius, "Emotivism, Expression, and Symbolic Meaning," *Journal of Philosophy*, Vol. 55 (1958), pp. 111-18.

Morgan, Douglas N., "Icon, Index and Symbol in the Visual Arts," *Philosophical Studies*, Vol. 6 (1955), pp. 49-54.

Nagel, Ernst, Review of Langer, *Philosophy in a New Key*, in *Journal of Philosophy*, Vol. 40 (1943), pp. 323-29.

Naumburg, Margaret, "Art as Symbolic Speech," *Journal of Aesthetics*, Vol. 13 (1955), pp. 433-50.

Weitz, Morris, "Symbolism and Art," *Review of Metaphysics*, Vol. 7 (1954), pp. 466-81.

Welsh, Paul, "Discursive and Presentational Symbols," *Mind*, Vol. 64 (1955), pp. 181-99.

Wheelwright, Philip, *The Burning Fountain: A Study in the Language of Symbolism*, Bloomington, Ind., 1954.

Whitehead, Alfred North, *Symbolism: Its Meaning and Effect*, New York, 1927.

Wimsatt, W. K., and Brooks, Cleanth, *Literary Criticism: A Short History*, New York, 1957, Ch. 26.

Truth and Belief

Aiken, Henry, "The Aesthetic Relevance of Belief," *Journal of Aesthetics*, Vol. 9 (1951), pp. 301-15.

—— "Some Notes Concerning the Aesthetic and the Cognitive," *Journal of Aesthetics*, Vol. 13 (1955), pp. 378-94.

Beardsley, Monroe C., *Aesthetics*, New York, 1958, Chs. 8-9 (with bibliographical notes).

Bilsky, Manuel, "I. A. Richards on Belief," *Philosophy and Phenomenological Research*, Vol. 12 (1951), pp. 105-15.

Bostetter, Edward E., "The Eagle and the Truth: Keats and the Problem of Belief," *Journal of Aesthetics*, Vol. 16 (1958), pp. 362-72.

Gilbert, Katherine E., "The Intent and Tone of Mr. I. A. Richards," *Journal of Aesthetics*, Vol. 3 (1944), pp. 29-48.

Greene, Theodore M., "Beauty and the Cognitive Significance of Art," *Journal of Philosophy*, Vol. 37 (1940), pp. 365-81.

Heyl, B. C., "Artistic Truth Reconsidered," *Journal of Aesthetics*, Vol. 8 (1950), pp. 251-58.

Isenberg, Arnold, "The Problem of Belief," *Journal of Aesthetics*, Vol. 13 (1955), pp. 395-407.

Joost, N., "Poetry and Belief," *Dublin Review*, Vol. 226 (1952), pp. 35-53.

Jordan, R., "Poetry and Philosophy: Two Modes of Revelation," *Sewanee Review*, Vol. 67 (1959), pp. 1-27.

Phillips, William, "Artistic Truth and the Warped Vision," *Partisan Review*, Vol. 24 (1957), pp. 173-84.

Pursur, J. W. R., *Art and Truth*, Glasgow, 1957.

Rudolph, G. A., "The Aesthetic Field of I. A. Richards," *Journal of Aesthetics*, Vol. 14 (1956), pp. 348-58.

Ushenko, A. P., *Dynamics of Art*, Bloomington, Ind., 1953, Ch. 4.

Wimsatt, W. K., and Brooks, Cleanth, *Literary Criticism: A Short History*, New York, 1957, Chs. 27-28 (on Richards).

Musical Expressiveness

Beardsley, Monroe C., *Aesthetics*, New York, 1958, Ch. 7 (with bibliographical notes).

Buck, Perry C., *The Scope of Music*, London, 1927.

Goddard, Joseph, *The Deeper Sources of the Beauty and Expression of Music*, London, 1905.

Gurney, Edmund, *The Power of Sound*, London, 1880.

Hanslick, Eduard, *The Beautiful in Music*, London, 1891; reprint, New York, 1957.

Haydon, Glenn, *On the Meaning of Music*, Washington: Library of Congress, 1948.

Hospers, John, *Meaning and Truth in the Arts*, Chapel Hill, 1946, Part IV, section 1 (discusses Sullivan versus Hanslick and Gurney).

Howes, F., *Music and Its Meanings*, London, 1958.

Langer, Susanne K., *Feeling and Form*, New York, 1953, Chs. 7-8.

——— (editor), *Reflections on Art*, Baltimore, 1958 (contains excellent essays on music).

Meyer, Leonard, *Emotion and Meaning in Music*, Chicago, 1956.

Portnoy, Julius, *The Philosopher and Music*, New York, 1954.

Pratt, Carroll C., *Meaning in Music*, New York, 1931.

——— *Music as the Language of Emotion*, Washington: Library of Congress, 1952.

Santayana, George, *Reason in Art*, New York, 1905, Ch. 4.

Schneider, Marius, "Origin of the Symbol in the Spirit of Music," *Diogenes*, Fall, 1959.

Schweitzer, Albert, *Johann Sebastian Bach*, New York, 1911.

Sessions, Roger, "The Composer and His Message," *The Intent of the Artist* (edited by Augusto Centeno), Princeton, 1941.

——— *The Musical Experience*, Princeton, 1950.

Sullivan, J. W. N., *Beethoven: His Spiritual Development*, New York, 1927.

Tovey, Donald F., *Essays in Musical Analysis*, 6 vols., New York, 1935-1939.

——— *The Main Stream of Music*, New York, 1949.

Zuckerkandl, Victor, *Sound and Symbol*, New York, 1956.

Chapter Ten

FORM

Form in General

Abell, Walter, *Representation and Form,* New York, 1936 (reply to Fry and Bell).

Barnes, Albert C., "Plastic Form," *The Art in Painting,* New York, 1928.

Beardsley, Monroe C., *Aesthetics,* New York, 1958, Chs. 4-6.

Bell, Clive, *Art,* New York, 1914.

—— "The 'Difference' of Literature," *New Republic,* Vol. 33 (1922), pp. 18-19.

—— *Since Cézanne,* London, 1922.

Birkhoff, Charles D., *Aesthetic Measure,* Cambridge, Mass., 1933.

Blanshard, Frances, *Retreat from Likeness in the Theory of Painting,* New York, 1949.

Bradley, A. C., "Poetry for Poetry's Sake," *Oxford Lectures on Poetry,* London, 1909.

Brion, Marcel, "Abstract Art," *Diogenes,* No. 24 (1958), pp. 42-46.

Brooks, Cleanth, *The Well Wrought Urn,* New York, 1947.

Buermeyer, Laurence, "Pattern and Plastic Form" and "The Aesthetics of Roger Fry," *Art and Education,* Merion, Pa., 1929.

Burke, Kenneth, *Counter-Statement,* New York, 1931.

—— *The Philosophy of Literary Form,* Baton Rouge, 1941.

Carpenter, Rhys, *The Esthetic Basis of Greek Art of the 5th and 4th Centuries B.C.,* Bryn Mawr, 1921 (reply to Fry's viewpoint).

Carritt, E. F., "Art Without Form?" *Philosophy,* Vol. 16 (1941), pp. 19-26.

Dalcroze, Emile Jacques, *Rhythm, Music, and Education,* London, 1921.

Dewey, John, *Art as Experience,* New York, 1934, Chs. 6-8.

Ducasse, C. J., *The Philosophy of Art,* New York, 1929, Ch. 13 and Appendix.

Eliot, T. S., "The Music of Poetry," *On Poetry and Poets,* New York, 1957.

Fry, Roger, *Last Lectures,* Cambridge, Eng., 1939.

—— *Transformations,* London, 1926.

—— *Vision and Design,* London, 1920.

Gotshalk, D. W., *Art and the Social Order,* Chicago, 1947, Ch. 5.

Greene, Theodore M., *The Arts and the Art of Criticism,* Princeton, 1940, Part II.

Hadow, W. H., *Studies in Modern Music,* Second Series, London, 1907, pp. 32-56.

Hambidge, Jay, *Dynamic Symmetry,* New York, 1926.

Hiler, Hilaire, *Why Abstract?* New York, 1945.

Jessup, Bertram E., "Aesthetic Size," *Journal of Aesthetics,* Vol. 9 (1950), pp. 31-38.

Langer, Susanne K., *Feeling and Form,* New York, 1953.

—— *Problems of Art,* New York, 1957, Ch. 4.

—— *Reflections on Art,* Baltimore, 1958 (contains a number of essays on form).

Lubbock, Percy, *The Craft of Fiction,* New York, 1931.

Mauron, Charles, *The Nature of Beauty in Art and Literature,* London, 1927.

Moholy-Nagy, Lazlo, *The New Vision: Fundamentals of Design,* Fourth Revised Edition, New York, 1947.

Muir, Edwin, *The Structure of the Novel,* New York, 1929.

Munro, Thomas, "Form and Value in the Arts," *Journal of Aesthetics,* Vol. 13 (1955), pp. 316-41.

—— "Form in the Arts," *Journal of Aesthetics,* Vol. 2 (1943), pp. 5-26.

—— *The Interrelations of the Arts,* New York, 1949, Ch. 9.

—— *Scientific Method in Aesthetics,* New York, 1928, Ch. 2.

Nobbs, Percy, *Design,* London, 1937.

Parker, DeWitt H., *The Analysis of Art,* New Haven, 1926, Chs. 2-3.

Pepper, Stephen C., *Aesthetic Quality,* New York, 1938, Chs. 5-8.

—— *Principles of Art Appreciation,* New York, 1949, Chs. 3-5.

Ritchie, Benbow, "The Formal Structure of the Aesthetic Object," *Journal of Aesthetics,* Vol. 3 (1944), pp. 5-14.

Santayana, George, *The Sense of Beauty,* New York, 1896, Part III.

Shahn, Ben, *The Shape of Content,* Cambridge, Mass., 1957 (title essay).

Stechow, Wolfgang, "Problems of Structure in Some Relations Between the Visual Arts and Music," *Journal of Aesthetics,* Vol. 11 (1953), pp. 324-33.

Thompson, D'Arcy Wentworth, *On Growth and Form,* Cambridge, Eng., 1942.

Tovey, Donald F., *The Forms of Music,* New York, 1956.

Ushenko, A. P., *Dynamics of Art,* Bloomington, Ind., 1953, Ch. 2.

Weitz, Morris, *Philosophy of the Arts,* Cambridge, Mass., 1950, Chs. 1-3.

Weyl, Hermann, *Symmetry,* Princeton, 1952.

Williams, Donald C., "Form and Matter," *Philosophical Review,* Vol. 67 (1958), pp. 291-312, 499-521.

Woolf, Virginia, *Roger Fry: A Biography,* New York, 1940.

Style

Berenson, Bernard, *Aesthetics and History,* New York, 1948.

Boas, Franz, *Primitive Art,* Cambridge, Mass., 1927.

Boas, George, "Historical Periods," *Journal of Aesthetics,* Vol. 11 (1953), pp. 248-54.

Cooper, Lane (editor), *Theories of Style,* New York, 1907.

Frank, Paul L., "Historical or Stylistic Periods?" *Journal of Aesthetics,* Vol. 13 (1955), pp. 451-57.

Friedrich, Carl J., "Style as the Principle of Historical Interpretation," *Journal of Aesthetics,* Vol. 14 (1955), pp. 143-51.

Hauser, Arnold, *The Philosophy of Art History,* New York, 1959, especially Ch. 4.

Malraux, André, *The Psychology of Art,* 3 vols., New York, 1949-1950.

—— *Voices of Silence,* New York, 1953.

Murry, J. Middleton, *The Problem of Style,* New York, 1922.

Panofsky, Erwin, *Studies in Iconology,* New York, 1939.

Sachs, Curt, *The Commonwealth of Art: Style in the Fine Arts, Music, and the Dance,* New York, 1946.

Wolfflin, H., *Classic Art,* New York, 1959.

—— *Principles of Art History,* New York, 1954.

—— *The Sense of Form in Art,* New York, 1958.

Zucker, Paul, *Styles in Painting,* New York, 1950, especially Ch. 1.

Chapter Eleven

FORM AND FUNCTION

Barton, J. E., *Purpose and Admiration,* New York, 1933.

Brown, Theodore M., "Greenough, Paine, Emerson, and the Organic Aesthetic," *Journal of Aesthetics,* Vol. 14 (1956), pp. 304-17.

Cheney, Sheldon, *Art of the Machine,* New York, 1937.

DeZurko, Edward, *Origins of Functionalist Theory,* New York, 1957.

Geddes, Patrick, *Cities in Evolution,* London, 1915 (a source of Mumford's theory of technological phases).

Giedion, Siegfried, *Architecture, You and Me,* Cambridge, Mass., 1958.

—— *Mechanization Takes Command,* New York, 1948.

—— *Space, Time, and Architecture,* Cambridge, Mass., 1941.

Gill, Eric, *Beauty Looks After Herself,* New York, 1933.

Goodman, Percival, and Paul, *Communitas,* Chicago, 1947.

Greenough, Horatio, *Form and Function,* reprint: Berkeley, 1957.

—— *Memorial of Horatio Greenough,* New York, 1853.

—— *The Travels, Observations, and Experience of a Yankee Stonecutter,* New York, 1852.

Holme, Geoffrey, *Industrial Design and the Future,* London, 1934.

Le Corbusier (C. E. Jeanneret-Gris), *Towards a New Architecture,* New York, 1927.

Metzger, Charles R., *Emerson and Greenough,* Berkeley, 1954.

Moholy-Nagy, Lazlo, *The New Vision,* New York, 1947.

—— *Vision in Motion,* Chicago, 1947.

Moholy-Nagy, Sibyl, *Moholy-Nagy: Experiment in Totality,* New York, 1950.

Mumford, Lewis, *Art and Technics,* New York, 1952.

—— *City Development,* New York, 1945.

—— *The Culture of Cities,* New York, 1938.

—— *From the Ground Up,* New York, 1956.

—— "Human Prospect and Architecture," *Architectural Record,* Vol. 125 (1959), pp. 175-77.

—— *Roots of Contemporary American Architecture* (anthology), New York, 1952.

—— *Sticks and Stones,* New York, 1924.

—— *Technics and Civilization,* New York, 1934.

Neutra, Richard, *Survival Through Design,* New York, 1954.

Parker, DeWitt H., *The Analysis of Art,* New Haven, 1926, Ch. 5.

Pevsner, Nikolaus, *Pioneers of the Modern Movement: From William Morris to Walter Gropius,* London, 1936.

Read, Herbert, *Art and Industry,* New York, 1954.

Scott. Geoffrey, *The Architecture of Humanism,* London, 1924.

Sullivan, Louis H., *The Autobiography of an Idea,* New York, 1924.

—— *Kindergarten Chats,* Washington, 1934.

Teague, Walter D., *Design This Day,* New York, 1940.

Torroja, Eduardo, *Philosophy of Structures,* Berkeley, 1958.

Veblen, Thornstein, *The Instinct of Workmanship and the State of the Industrial Arts,* New York, 1914.

Wright, Frank Lloyd, *The Disappearing City,* New York, 1932.

—— *Modern Architecture,* Princeton, 1931.

—— *An Organic Architecture,* London, 1939.

—— *A Testament,* New York, 1957.

—— *When Democracy Builds*, Chicago, 1945.

—— and Brownell, Baker, *Architecture and Modern Life*, New York, 1932.

Chapter Twelve

EMPATHY AND ABSTRACTION

Ames, V. M., "On Empathy," *Psychological Review*, Vol. 52 (1943), pp. 490-94.

Anonymous, "Beauty and Expression," *Edinburgh Review*, Vol. 208 (1908), pp. 458-86.

Anstruther-Thompson, C., *Art and Man*, New York, 1924.

Basch, Victor, *Essai Critique sur l'Esthétique de Kant*, Paris, 1927.

Carritt, E. F., *The Theory of Beauty*, London, 1928, Ch. 11.

Ducasse, C. J., *The Philosophy of Art*, New York, 1929, Ch. 10.

Hulme, T. E., "Modern Art and Its Philosophy," *Speculations*, New York, 1924 (similar to Worringer).

Langfeld, Herbert, *The Aesthetic Attitude*, New York, 1920.

Lee, Vernon, *The Beautiful*, Cambridge, Eng., 1913.

—— *Music and Its Lovers*, New York, 1932.

—— and Anstruther-Thompson, C., *Beauty and Ugliness*, London, 1912.

Lipps, Theodor, *Aesthetik*, Hamburg and Leipzig, 1903.

Listowel, Earl of, *A Critical History of Modern Esthetics*, London, 1933, Chs. 7, 15.

Nahm, Milton C., *Aesthetic Experience and Its Presuppositions*, New York, 1946, Ch. 16.

Rader, Melvin, "The Root Values of Art," *Journal of Philosophy*, Vol. 38 (1941), pp. 324-32.

Worringer, Wilhelm, *Abstraktion und Einfühlung*, Munich, 1921. Translated as *Abstraction and Empathy*, New York, 1953.

—— *Form in Gothic*, New York, 1927.

Chapter Thirteen

DISTANCE AND DEHUMANIZATION

Buber, Martin, "Distance and Relation," *Hibbert Journal*, Vol. 49 (1951), pp. 105-13.

—— "Existence and Relation," *Psychiatry*, Vol. 20 (1957), pp. 97-104.

—— *I and Thou*, New York, 1937.

Bullough, Edward, *Aesthetics*, Palo Alto, 1957.

—— "Psychical Distance as a Factor in Art and an Aesthetic Principle," *British Journal of Psychology*, Vol. 5 (1912-1913), pp. 87-118 (selection reprinted in present volume omits last eleven pages of this article).

Chaudbury, P. J., "Psychical Distance in Indian Aesthetics," *Journal of Aesthetics*, Vol. 7 (1948), pp. 138-40.

Clark, Kenneth, *The Nude: A Study in Ideal Form*, New York, 1936; reprinted in Anchor paperback edition, New York, 1959.

Fry, Roger, "Some Questions in Esthetics," *Transformations*, London, 1926.

Knox, Israel, *The Aesthetic Theories of Kant, Hegel, and Schopenhauer*, New York, 1936, pp. 19-53.

Langfeld, Sydney, *The Aesthetic Attitude*, New York, 1920 (includes a criticism of Bullough).

Lipman, Matthew, "The Aesthetic Presence of the Body," *Journal of Aesthetics*, Vol. 15 (1957), pp. 425-34 (compare with Kenneth Clark).

Longman, Lester D., "The Concept of Psychical Distance," *Journal of Aesthetics*, Vol. 6 (1947), pp. 31-36.

Mauron, Charles, *Aesthetics and Psychology*, London, 1935, Chs. 3-6.

Mehlis, Georg, "The Aesthetic Problem of Distance," *Reflections on Art* (edited by Susanne K. Langer), Baltimore, 1958.

Michelis, P. A., "Aesthetic Distance and the Charm of Contemporary Art," *Journal of Aesthetics*, Vol. 18 (1959), pp. 1-45.

Ortega y Gasset, José, *The Dehumanization of Art*, Princeton, 1948.

Weitz, Morris, *Philosophy of the Arts*, Cambridge, Mass., 1950, Ch. 9.

Chapter Fourteen

ISOLATION AND SYNAESTHESIS

On Isolation and Synaesthesis

Bawden, H. Heath, "The Nature of Aesthetic Value," *Psychological Review*, Vol. 15 (1908), pp. 265-96.

Hamann, Richard, *Aesthetic*, Leipzig, 1911 (emphasizes isolation).

Knight, E. H., "Some Aesthetic Theories of Mr. Richards," *Mind*, Vol. 36 (1927), pp. 69-76.

Langfeld, Sydney, *The Aesthetic Attitude*, New York, 1920, pp. 48-57 (includes criticism of Münsterberg and Puffer).

Münsterberg, Hugo, *The Eternal Values*, Boston, 1909, Part III.

——— *The Principles of Art Education*, New York, 1905.

Ogden, C. K., Richards, I. A., and Wood, James, *The Foundations of Aesthetics*, New York, 1922.

Parkhurst, Helen Huss, *Beauty*, New York, 1930, pp. 25-31 (similar to Ogden, Richards, and Wood).

Puffer, Ethel, *The Psychology of Beauty*, Boston, 1905 (similar to Ogden, Richards, and Wood).

Richards, I. A., *Coleridge on Imagination*, New York, 1935.

——— *Principles of Literary Criticism*, New York, 1926, Chs. 2, 10-15, 18, 27.

——— *Science and Poetry*, New York, 1926, Ch. 2.

Urban, Wilbur, *Valuation: Its Nature and Laws*, New York, 1909, pp. 216-31 (similar to Ogden, Richards, and Wood).

Wimsatt, William K., and Brooks, Cleanth, *Literary Criticism: A Short History*, New York, 1957, pp. 616-25.

Other Interpretations of the Esthetic Attitude

Bartlett, Ethel M., *Types of Aesthetic Judgment*, London, 1937.

Beck, M., "Cognitive Character of Aesthetic Enjoyment," *Journal of Aesthetics*, Vol. 3 (1945), pp. 55-61.

Bosanquet, Bernard, *Three Lectures on Aesthetic*, London, 1915, Lecture 3.

Buermeyer, Laurence, *The Aesthetic Experience*, Merion, Pa., 1924.

Ducasse, C. J., *The Philosophy of Art*, New York, 1949, Chs. 9-12.

Guggenheimer, Richard, *Creative Vision in Artist and Audience*, New York, 1950.

—— *Sight and Insight*, New York, 1945.

Hahn, Lewis E., *A Contextualistic Theory of Perception*, Berkeley, 1942.

Hevner, K., "Aesthetic Experience: A Psychological Description," *Psychological Review*, Vol. 44 (1937), pp. 245-63.

Jenkins, Iredell, *Art and the Human Enterprise*, Cambridge, Mass., 1958, Ch. 8.

Koffka, Kurt, "Problems in the Psychology of Art," *Art: A Symposium*, Bryn Mawr, 1940.

Lee, Harry B., "On the Esthetic States of Mind," *Psychiatry*, Vol. 10 (1947), pp. 281-306.

Lundholm, Helge, *The Aesthetic Sentiment*, Cambridge, Mass., 1941.

Nahm, Milton C., *Aesthetic Experience and Its Presuppositions*, New York, 1946.

Neuhaus, Eugen, *The Appreciation of Art*, New York, 1924.

Parker, DeWitt H., *The Principles of Aesthetics*, New York, 1946, Chs. 4-5.

Pepper, Stephen C., *Principles of Art Appreciation*, New York, 1949, Part I.

Schoen, Max, "Aesthetic Experience in the Light of Current Psychology," *Journal of Aesthetics*, Vol. 1 (1941), pp. 24-33.

—— *The Understanding of Music*, New York, 1945.

Souriau, Etienne, "A General Methodology for the Scientific Study of Aesthetic Appreciation," *Journal of Aesthetics*, Vol. 14 (1955), pp. 1-18.

Stein, Leon, *Appreciation*, New York, 1947.

Stringham, E. J., *Listening to Music Creatively*, New York, 1959.

Tomas, Vincent, "Aesthetic Vision," *Philosophical Review*, Vol. 68 (1959), pp. 52-67.

Vivas, Eliseo, "A Definition of the Esthetic Experience," *Journal of Philosophy*, Vol. 34 (1937), pp. 628-34.

—— "A Natural History of the Aesthetic Transaction," *Naturalism and the Human Spirit* (edited by Yerwant H. Krikorian), New York, 1944.

Chapter Fifteen

CRITICISM

Abercrombie, Lascelles, *The Principles of Literary Criticism*, London, 1932.

—— *The Theory of Poetry*, London, 1924.

Aiken, Henry, "A Pluralistic Analysis of Aesthetic Value," *Philosophical Review*, Vol. 59 (1950), pp. 493-513.

—— "The Aesthetic Relevance of Artists' Intentions," *Journal of Philosophy*, Vol. 52 (1955), pp. 742-53.

Alexander, Samuel, "Beauty and Greatness in Art," *Proceedings of the Aristotelian Society*, Vol. 30 (1929-1930), pp. 205-28.

Balfour, A. J., *Criticism and Beauty*, Oxford, 1910.

Bartlett, Ethel M., *Types of Aesthetic Judgment*, London, 1937.

Beardsley, Monroe C., *Aesthetics*, New York, 1958, Chs. 1-2, 10-12.

Blackmur, R. P., and others, *Lectures in Criticism*, New York, 1949.

Boas, George, *A Primer for Critics*, Baltimore, 1937.

—— *Wingless Pegasus*, Baltimore, 1950.

Brooks, Cleanth, *The Well Wrought Urn*, New York, 1947.

Brunius, Teddy, *David Hume on Criticism*, Stockholm, 1952.

Buchler, Justus, *Nature and Judgment*, New York, 1955.

—— *Toward a General Theory of Human Judgment*, New York, 1951.

Child, Arthur, "The Social-Historical Relativity of Esthetic Value," *Philo-*

sophical Review, Vol. 53 (1944), pp. 1-22

Church, Ralph, An Essay on Critical Appreciation, Ithaca, 1938.

Cohen, R., "David Hume's Experimental Method and the Theory of Taste," Journal of English Literary History, Vol. 25 (1958), pp. 270-89.

Dewey, John, Art as Experience, New York, 1934, Ch. 13.

——— Construction and Criticism, New York, 1938.

Ducasse, C. J., Art, the Critics, and You, New York, 1944.

——— The Philosophy of Art, New York, 1929, Ch. 15.

Eliot, T. S., The Classics and the Man of Letters, Oxford, 1942.

——— "The Frontiers of Criticism," Sewanee Review, Vol. 64 (1956), pp. 525-43.

——— The Sacred Wood, London, 1932.

——— Selected Essays, Revised Edition, 1950.

——— The Use of Poetry and the Use of Criticism, Cambridge, Mass., 1933.

Elton, Oliver, The Nature of Literary Criticism, Manchester, 1935.

Forster, E. M., "The Raison D'Etre of Criticism in the Arts," Two Cheers for Democracy, New York, 1951.

French, R. F. (editor), Music and Criticism, Cambridge, Mass., 1948.

Frye, Northrop, Anatomy of Criticism, Princeton, 1957.

Garrod, H. W., Poetry and the Criticism of Life, Cambridge, Mass., 1931.

Gotshalk, D. W., Art and the Social Order, Chicago, 1947, Ch. 8.

——— "A Next Step for Aesthetics," Journal of Aesthetics, Vol. 18 (1959), pp. 46-51 (criticizes relativism).

Grabo, Carl, The Creative Critic, Chicago, 1948.

Greene, Theodore M., The Arts and the Art of Criticism, Princeton, 1940.

Harré, R., "Quasi-Aesthetic Appraisals," Philosophy, Vol. 33 (1958), pp. 132-37.

Heyl, Bernard C., New Bearings in Esthetics and Art Criticism, New Haven, 1943.

——— "Relativism Again," Journal of Aesthetics, Vol. 5 (1946), pp. 54-61.

Hodin, J. P.; Hungerland, Helmut; Michelis, P. A.; Read, Herbert; and Rieser, Max, Articles on Aesthetic Judgment and Criticism, XII Congresso Internazionale di Filosofia, Venice, 1958.

Hungerland, Isabel C., "The Concept of Intention in Art Criticism," Journal of Philosophy, Vol. 52 (1955), pp. 733-42.

Hyman, Stanley E., The Armed Vision, New York, 1948.

Isenberg, Arnold, "Critical Communication," Philosophical Review, Vol. 58 (1949), pp. 330-44.

Kaplan, Abraham, "On the So-Called Crisis in Criticism," Journal of Aesthetics, Vol. 8 (1948), pp. 42-48.

Levin, Harry (editor), Perspectives of Criticism, Cambridge, Mass., 1950.

Lewis, C. I., An Analysis of Knowledge and Valuation, LaSalle, Ill., 1946.

Margolis, Joseph, "Proposals on the Logic of Aesthetic Judgments," Philosophical Quarterly, Vol. 9 (1959), pp. 208-16.

Matthiessen, F. O., The Responsibilities of the Critic, New York, 1952.

More, Paul Elmer, The Demon of the Absolute, Princeton University Press, 1928.

Morris, Bertram, "The Philosophy of Criticism," Philosophical Review, Vol. 55 (1946), pp. 611-33.

Morris, Charles, Varieties of Human Value, Chicago, 1956, Ch. 7.

Nahm, Milton C., The Artist as Creator, Baltimore, 1956, Book II.

Osborne, Harold, Aesthetics and Criticism, New York, 1955.

Pell, Orlie, Value-Theory and Criticism, New York, 1930.

Pepper, Stephen C., The Basis of Criticism in the Arts, Cambridge, Mass., 1945.

––– *The Work of Art,* Bloomington, 1955, Chs. 2-3, 5.

Perry, Ralph Barton, *Realms of Value,* Cambridge, Mass., 1954, Ch. 18.

Pottle, Frederick A., "The New Critics and the Historical Method," *Yale Review,* Vol. 43 (1954-1955), pp. 14-23.

Pratt, Carroll C., "The Stability of Aesthetic Judgments," *Journal of Aesthetics,* Vol. 15 (1956), pp. 1-11.

Ransom, John Crowe (editor), *The Kenyon Critics,* Cleveland, 1951.

––– *The New Criticism,* Norfolk, Conn., 1941.

––– *The World's Body,* New York, 1938.

Read, Herbert, *Coleridge as Critic,* London, 1949.

––– *The Tenth Muse: Essays in Criticism,* New York, 1958.

Redpath, Theodore, "Some Problems of Modern Aesthetics," *British Philosophy in the Mid-Century* (edited by C. A. Mace), London, 1957.

Rice, Philip Blair, *The Knowledge of Good and Evil,* New York, 1955, Ch. 12.

Richards, I. A., *Practical Criticism,* New York, 1929.

––– *Principles of Literary Criticism,* New York, 1926.

Robertson, John M., *New Essays Toward a Critical Method,* London, 1897.

Santayana, George, *Essays in Literary Criticism,* New York, 1956.

––– *Reason in Art,* New York, 1922, Ch. 10.

Seiberling, Frank, *Looking into Art,* New York, 1959, Part Three.

Schorer, Mark *et al.* (editors), *Criticism,* New York, 1948.

Shipley, Joseph T. (editor), *Dictionary of World Literature: Criticism—Forms —Technique,* New York, 1943.

Stauffer, D. A. (editor), *The Intent of the Critic,* Princeton, 1941.

Stevenson, Charles L., "Interpretation and Evaluation in Aesthetics," *Philosophical Analysis* (edited by Max Black), Ithaca, 1950.

––– "On the 'Analysis' of a Work of Art," *Philosophical Review,* Vol. 67 (1958), pp. 31-51.

Sugg, Redding S., "Hume's Search for the Key with the Leathern Thong," *Journal of Aesthetics,* Vol. 16 (1957), pp. 96-102.

Trowbridge, Hoyt, "Aristotle and the New Criticism," *Sewanee Review,* Vol. 52 (1944), pp. 537-55.

Ushenko, A. P., *Dynamics of Art,* Bloomington, 1953, Ch. 5.

Vivas, Eliseo, *Creation and Discovery,* New York, 1955.

Weitz, Morris, *The Philosophy of the Arts,* Cambridge, Mass., 1950, Ch. 9.

Wellek, René, *A History of Modern Criticism: 1750-1950,* New Haven, 1955.

––– and Austin, Warren, *The Theory of Literature,* New York, 1949.

West, Ray B. (editor), *Essays in Modern Literary Criticism,* New York, 1952.

Wilson, Edmund, *Axel's Castle,* New York, 1932.

––– *The Triple Thinkers,* Revised Edition, New York, 1948.

Wimsatt, W. K., *The Verbal Icon,* Lexington, 1954.

––– and Beardsley, Monroe C., "The Intentional Fallacy," *Sewanee Review,* Vol. 45 (1946), pp. 468-88.

––– and Beardsley, Monroe C., "The Affective Fallacy," *Sewanee Review,* Vol. 57 (1948), pp. 31-55.

––– and Brooks, Cleanth, *Literary Criticism: A Short History,* New York, 1957.

Index

[Names or topics mentioned only casually have been omitted.]